Phaidon Encyclopedia of Expressionism

Phaidon Encyclopedia of

Expressionism

Painting and the Graphic Arts – Sculpture – Architecture
Literature – Drama – The Expressionist Stage – Cinema – Music

Lionel Richard

Phaidon

Translated by Stephen Tint

Phaidon Press Limited
Littlegate House, St Ebbe's Street, Oxford

Published in the United States of America by
E. P. Dutton, New York

This edition first published 1978

ISBN 0 7148 1913 1 Hardback
ISBN 0 7148 1914 X Paperback (U.S. Only)
Library of Congress Catalog Card Number: 78–62589

Original French edition *Encyclopédie de l'Expressionnisme*

Filmset by Jolly & Barber Ltd, Rugby, Warwickshire.

Printed in Italy

Contents

The expressionist movement

From the end of the nineteenth century, terms which originally belonged to the plastic arts spread in a curious manner to all art forms and were essential to defining the trends, intellectual movements, and even the spirit of the age. In Germany especially, this applied to impressionism, neo-romanticism, and Art Nouveau. Was painting the predominant art? Since the invention of photography had contributed to allowing it to free itself from conventions, it certainly anticipated the fundamental changes that occurred in the relationship between art and reality. But there is no doubt that another reason exists for the extensive penetration of pictorial concepts into the world of the arts: the fact is that the sudden appearance of a new phenomenon was rarely restricted to a particular art form. The new style was linked in a more general way to a specific age, society, and aspect of civilization. From romanticism to surrealism, it encompassed all forms of artistic expression.

Expressionism was a prime example. The works of art it produced can be described as professions of faith, in which the general feelings of a generation emerged in all their diversity. Yvan Goll has rightly suggested that it was certainly not a school, in the sense that it was not a question of a number of artists forming a group on the basis of a specific programme and devoting themselves to the same techniques. Expressionism represents, he said in 1921, 'a state of mind which, in the intellectual field, has affected everything, in the same way as an epidemic does, not only poetry and painting, but also prose, architecture, the theatre, music, science, university and school reforms.'

The history of a term

The problem before us is how to define the term expressionism, and primarily, to find out how it came into existence. Many writers maintain that it entered Germany via Willhelm Worringer, the author of *Abstraction and Empathy*, who, it is claimed, used it for the first time in 1911. Others, by contrast, grant this honour to Paul Cassirer, who, in 1910, is said to have announced, in front of a picture by Pechstein, in answer to a question as to whether this was still an example of impressionism, that it was an example of expressionism. As a result of this quip, the term is said to have come into vogue in artistic circles, before spreading into the news columns of the journals.

In their concern for accuracy, researchers have sought to go further into its etymology. Armin Arnold has shown, for example, that in July 1850, an English newspaper, *Tait's Edinburgh Magazine*, mentions in an anonymous article an expressionist school of modern painting, and that in 1880, in Manchester, Charles Howley devoted a lecture to modern painters at the heart of whom he identified the expressionists, using the term to describe those whose intention it was to express their emotions and passions. In the United States, still according to Armin Arnold, in 1878, a group of writers calling themselves expressionists appeared in a novel by Charles de Kay, *The Bohemian*.

In fact, this Anglo-Saxon usage is far from corresponding to a description of a clearly defined style or of a specific artistic tendency. The same is true in France, where the mediocre and largely forgotten painter Jules-Auguste Hervé exhibited, under the heading *Expressionnismes*, eight of his paintings at the time of the *Salon des Indépendants* in 1901. Obviously, the word was coined with reference to impressionism and as a reaction against it. But, contrary to what has often been suggested in Germany, it remained just as uncommon in the vocabulary of everyday French as in art criticism. Its use has remained all the more exceptional because Jules-Auguste Hervé has left no memorable mark on the history of French painting. Moreover, the use he made of the plural instead of the singular suggested that he was not thinking of promoting it as an aesthetic movement.

Justifiably, therefore, in 1919, in the journal *Das Kunstblatt*, the famous art dealer Daniel-Henry Kahnweiler attacked the idea which was spreading throughout Germany, that expressionism was of French origin. This notion, he emphasized, was not in use in France and was completely foreign to the fine arts. He knew what he was talking about because, as a passionate promoter of new talent, he was embedded to the hilt in the Parisian art world. This concern for accuracy was dictated to him by the desire to dispel the confusion that was distorting all aesthetic judgement. He was replying in particular to Theodor Däubler, who almost went as far as establishing Matisse as the authentic leader of expressionism, and who claimed, no doubt confusing the term with fauvism, for which he was indeed responsible, that the critic Louis Vauxelles was the originator of this new description of Matisse.

In fact, Theodor Däubler's allusion to Matisse was not totally without foundation. Mentioning the name Matisse as a way of describing the direction that German painting had been taking for some time, is to recognize in it certain traits of which he was indeed the precursor after he had broken away from neo-impressionism: a work does not copy nature; it is a rejection of all constraints; it is irrational and emanates from the temperament of the creator, in opposition to the pretensions of the positivists and the scientists; it embodies a relationship with colours which is aggressive and commanded by an unknown force. Moreover, whereas in Berlin, Matisse had the right during the winter of 1908 to the first important exhibition of his works in Germany, *Kunst und Künstler* published in 1909 his *Painter's Notes*, which had appeared in the *Grande Revue* in December 1908. Here he claimed to be individualistic and subjective, and wrote, 'what I am looking for above all is a means of expression.' It is not impossible that this admission by Matisse, although it is accompanied by other statements which are rather incompatible with the aspirations of German painters usually described as expressionists, led to the formation of the generic term *expressionismus*.

But the arrival of the word on the public scene occurred neither through a borrowing from English-speaking countries nor through a reference to Jules-Auguste Hervé or Matisse. The opportunity arose through an exhibition: the Berlin *Sezession*, which took place from April to September 1911. Under the direction of Luis Corinth, its impressionist tradition was continued, but, unusually, a group of new French painters were invited. Assembled in one room were pictures by Braque, Derain, van Dongen, Dufy, Friesz, Manguin, Marquet, Picasso and Vlaminck. They were introduced in the catalogue as expressionists.

Who was responsible for this description? It is difficult today to discover the answer to this. Nevertheless, it is certain that it did not originate with the painters concerned, as was thought for a long time in Germany. Kurt Hiller, in his memoirs written after 1945, persisted in still believing the legend that the term had been invented by young French painters who were discontented with impressionism. From April 1911 onwards this was indeed what was reported by contemporary art critics in their reviews of the exhibition of the Berlin *Sezession*. Walter Hegmann, often described as the first person to use the word 'expressionism' in Germany, in an article in *Der Sturm* in July 1911, did precisely this. He stated, 'a group of Franco-Belgian painters have decided to call themselves *expressionists*.'

A reaction against impressionism

It is undeniable, however, that as a result of the articles and discussions on the new art, whether French or German, a whole aesthetic movement took shape. Beginning with no more than an imprecise term, expressionism became more clearly defined thanks to skirmishes between two distinct movements, the traditionalists and the modernists. When, in the camp of the former movement, Carl Vinnen raised his voice against the invasion of German galleries by foreigners, Wilhelm Worringer replied in *Der Sturm*, in August 1911, by trying to show that the expressionists (he too was describing the French painters who exhibited at the Berlin *Sezession*) did not begin in a void, but had inherited techniques from Cézanne, van Gogh and Matisse, namely that they were artists who had broken away from the influence of impressionism.

This last distinction soon became crucial and allowed French and German painters who represented the new art to be linked together without discrimination. All those who reacted against the impressionist aesthetic were labelled expressionists. Only those who no longer wished to represent, copy or imitate reality counted. In a book written in 1914, the Austrian writer Hermann Bahr therefore included, as forming part of the expressionist movement, Matisse, Braque, Picasso, the futurists, the fauves, members of the German groups *Die Brücke* and *Der Blaue Reiter*, the Viennese Oskar Kokoschka and Egon Schiele.

With the exception of a few names, this image of expressionism remained valid in Germany. Someone who greatly contributed to propagating this, as director of the journal *Der Sturm*, namely Herwath Walden, wrote a history of expressionism: at the beginning, he says, came Kokoschka, then the futurists, especially Boccioni, then the Russians, Kandinsky and Chagall, the Germans Franz Marc, August Macke, the Swiss Paul Klee, the French Albert Gleizes, Robert Delaunay and Fernand Léger. For him, expressionism was art which gave form to the lived experience that lies deepest within oneself. The nuances of style were not important, as long as all imitation of nature was rejected.

For 'imitation can never be art, whether applied to pictures or nature,' is how Walden sums it up in his preface to the catalogue of the autumn *Salon* that he organized in Berlin in October 1913. And a little further on he describes the creative process as he saw it: 'what the painter paints is what he perceives in his innermost senses, it is the expression of his being; all that is transitory is for him only a symbolic image: his own life is his most important consideration: what the outside world imprints on him, he expresses from within himself. He conveys his visions, his inner landscapes, and is conveyed by them.'

From then on, all artistic creation had to be the projection of the artist's profound self. It is this opposition to impressionism and more generally to naturalism that appears as the keystone of the new aesthetic. That is first and foremost what expressionism means. Herbert Kühn, in an article on the theatre published by the journal *Die neue Schaubühne* in 1919, clearly showed the fundamental principle on which creative activity now rested, whatever its form of expression might be. 'The aim of impressionism was the object it represented: what he could see on the picture was also the meaning of the picture. Nothing more. Nothing less. With the imitation of something external, its universe was restricted to what was concete. With expressionism, the subject to be represented and the object itself, the representation, were fully dissociated from one another. This representation was no longer what was being represented. This representation (the concrete element) was only an invitation to understand what was being represented. To a certain extent, what was being represented began beyond the picture, the drama, or the poem.'

The work no longer took external reality into consideration, but advocated another reality, namely, that of the artist. Already in 1912, Carl Einstein, the author of the novel *Bebuquin*, had insisted on this point in the journal *Die Aktion* by indicating that the role of art was to achieve a liberation from everything that everyday reality imposed (the incidental, psychological and logical) and to accomplish, thanks to individual creative and imaginary impulses, a *reconstruction*. For the expressionist, as Kasimir Edschmid also explained in 1918, the real reality lay inside oneself: 'Nothing can place in doubt the fact that what appears to be external reality cannot be authentic. The reality must be created by us. The meaning of the object is to find out what lies beyond its appearance. One cannot be content with believing in a fact, or imagining or registering it. One must give a pure, unblemished reflection of the image of the world. And this is only found within ourselves.'

Expressionism therefore gained momentum as an anti-naturalist reaction. Whether it be the inner need to create, advocated by Kandinsky, the interiority demanded by Nolde, the visionary power of Barlach, the illogicality that Carl Einstein wanted to make the only law in his *Bebuquin*, the instinctual forces in short stories like Carl Sternheim's *Busekow* or Alfred Döblin's *The Assassination of a Buttercup*, Oskar Kokoschka's violence in *Murderer, the Hope of Women*, a subjectivity posed as an absolute emerged everywhere, as an expressive exteriorization, or a defence of the self. It was less and less a question, as in naturalism, of a preconceived idea to illustrate, or of a subject to convey, a model to reproduce or of an external motivation.

In 1911 Schönberg wrote in his *Manual Of Harmony* that the artist does not try to succeed in rendering what others consider beautiful, but to express what is essential for him. A year later, in the almanach, *Der Blaue Reiter*, he clearly showed what it is that united the *avant-garde* creators in their condemnation of Aristotelian mimesis, the limitation of nature on which naturalism and its offshoot, impressionism, were founded. 'When Karl Kraus says of language that it is the mother of thought, when Wassily Kandinsky and Oskar Kokoschka paint pictures of which the object, in its outer material form, is now almost only a pretext for giving free rein to the imagination through colours and forms, and to expressing itself as until now only composers did. These are the signs which prove that knowledge of the real essence of art is gradually spreading. And it is with great joy that I read Kandinsky's book *On the Spiritual in Art*, a book that shows the path to follow in painting and arouses the hope that those who at present still question the content will soon no longer feel the need to do so.'

After the First World War, this liberation from naturalism even occurred in the cinema. Not only did it free itself from a reproduction of reality, which was considered, as it were, inherent to the technique of the cinema, but a fully cinematic art was born out of another emancipation: it asserted its autonomy by dissociating itself from the methods belonging to the theatre and forging others that were specifically its own. The merit of films like *The Cabinet of Doctor Caligary* (1919) and *From Morn to Midnight* (1920) was precisely that they exploited the cinema as an artistic form of expression. Here, the sets, the lighting, the camera movements and the acting were fused in a synthesis, which exteriorized a subjective vision of the world.

At the time, this cinematic originality scarcely caught on in Germany: *The Cabinet of Doctor Caligary* was mocked for its supposed expressionism by the collaborators of the review *Die neue Schaubühne*, and *From Morn to Midnight* did not even have the right to be shown publicly. In France, on the other hand, they were appreciated for their originality, an originality which, from 1922, was very well commented upon by a film-director like René Clair: 'Here, in opposition to realist dogma which, with a few exceptions, seemed to us invulnerable, we have *Caligary* which came along to prove that the only interesting form of truth was a subjective one,' he wrote in *Films*, and he went on to make this remark, the sign of a specialist: 'We must admit that nature which has been touched up is at least as expressive as everyday nature. The sets, the acting, lighting, the actors' faces, all artificially made up, form a whole, which the intellect enjoys knowing it controls.'

Two anti-naturalist trends

To give preference to the expression of subjectivity by rejecting all intention of fidelity to concrete reality pre-supposed that two essential elements were taken into consideration by the creator: the heart and the intellect, and no longer the senses as with impressionism. This resulted in considerable differences in the means of expression available, but from which two approaches emerged, depending on whether priority was given to one or other of these two elements: an art of intellectual elaboration, sometimes described pejoratively as cerebral, and an art of sentimental effusiveness. This is also why the two extremes fused in expressionism. There was a purifying of the forms to create an expressive symbolic rigour, as if the language had become overburdened with an infinite variety of possibilities. This distinction is indeed only approximate, and cross-fertilization took place between the two approaches. However, they constitute, in the context of all the arts, the particular situation that existed in Germany between 1910 and about 1925.

In the first instance, its ultimate aim was abstraction. This is what was defined by Oswald Herzog in *Der Sturm*, in 1919, as abstract expressionism. 'It is the physical configuration of what is achieved at a spiritual level. It creates objects and does not begin with objects – but with subjects. The object, for material expressionism, contributes to the configuration. It distils the essence of a subject by rejecting everything that is not essential to its purity and intensity.' From this, one can discern an approach that defines Kandinsky's pictorial and theatrical experiments, August Stramm's poetic analysis, Lothar Schreyer's drama, Emil Pirchan's sets, and some of Hindemith's music. In drama, the rejection of psychology led to more or less abstract characters who above all embodied ideas. In every field, to achieve maximum expressive force, forms and lines were purified to excess. This was true even in the case of the novel, as Paul Hatvani demanded, 'that prose be abstract! The important thing is not what it has to say, but the fact that it says it. It has to express itself.'

The legacy of French and Belgian symbolism, as a reaction also against naturalism, needs to be noted here. Pure painting, pure music, pure poetry, as Walden's circle and *Der Sturm* enjoyed insisting, were demands in the symbolist tradition and which led to the elimination of the object in order to concentrate the artistic activity on a particular material. It is through a stylization carried to the extreme that its power of suggestion, which was the fundamental element of the symbolist aesthetic, culminated in abstraction in Kandinsky's ideas for the theatre. He also claimed to have painted his first abstract composition around 1910, and reached a stage where he read the symbolist poets assiduously. Moreover, it was on Maeterlink that he relied in *On the Spiritual in Art*, to explain how, starting out from the pure sound of a word detached from the object, that it was supposed to 'materialize', the listener heard an abstract representation of this word.

The other trend corresponds more to an explosion of suppressed violence. In art, there were convulsive grimacing traits and distorted forms. It consisted of a pathos, an exaggeration, the cry of revolt, the ecstatic enthusiasm of poetry; a theatre of paroxysms and haranguing; a morbid climate, an atmosphere of anguish, a universe of tensions. Yvan Goll, in 1924, only expressed part of this side of expressionism, when he described it as 'an impotent man's fist clenched against the firmament in a fury.' It was not always grotesque and desperate. It was also represented, in a style reminiscent of negro art, by a wood-cut by Conrad Felixmüller, where man, standing upright in all his original purity, brandishes in a Promethean aspiration, the ideal of humanity.

In 1913, the journal *Die Weissen Blätter* tried in fact to encapsulate this aspect of expressionism in the following definition: 'Concentration, economy, massive force, forms solidly assembled, a pathos expressing an intense passion, these are the characteristics that reveal its real nature.' As for the art critic Wilhelm Hausenstein, he regarded it with a touch of irony, but was completely lacking in seriousness, as we shall see: 'In expressionism,' he wrote in 1919, 'there is as it were an overloaded circuit, which is perhaps a diagrammatic representation of it. One could define it approximately in this way: a form created out of distortion. This would be a negative judgement. More positively, one could say, a form created out of the imagination.'

A problem of pictorial style

It is through this art of distortion, deformation, exaltation, exacerbation, and intensive expression that individual styles generally received the mark of expressionism. And as this created a problem of terminology, particularly with regard to the plastic arts, it is possible to maintain, that there is in fact, a universal and timeless expressionist style which is by no means the attribute of a specific historical period in German-speaking countries. Being nothing more than the projection of an inner world through expressive traits, expressionism is clearly discernible even in prehistory, in negro, Indian, and Aztec sculpture, in painters like Grünewald, Greco and Daumier. In this way, a great part of Western music also becomes expressionist, quite simply because it is expressive. But the term expressionism ends up by meaning only a stylization and distortion, and an oppressive simplying of forms. It has just as much conceptual significance as attributing the term to a young painter today, on the pretext that he transmits on to the canvas the reality he perceives according to his impressions. As soon as one tries to define a style without taking into consideration its historical context, the terms of reference become so unclear that it is impossible to be accurate. The differences in the various analyses of expressionism are very often explicable through ignorance of concrete national situations and a desire to reject all historical considerations. Now, as I have previously shown, the word expressionism only really became fully part of the artistic climate in Germany, where it initially meant the discovery of all modern art, before assuming a meaning adapted to the historical situation in Germany. If one only considers the formal aspect, which is a very dubious approach in this particular instance, the same aesthetic innovations were given different names in other countries. This is why, from one country to another, and with reference to the same pictures, certain painters who were either actually German or closely linked to Germany (Hans Arp, Lyonel Feininger, Otto Freundlich, Erich Heckel, to name but a few) are alternately classified as expressionists, cubists, cubo-expressionists, and sometimes as dadaists or surrealists.

In Russia, artists who are normally called futurists have been described as expressionists. The term here seems to refer without discrimination, as in Germany, to all artists representing modernist tendencies. Lunacharsky, the first People's Commissar for Public Education in the Soviet Union and a distinguished authority on German literature, bestowed on Maïakovsky in the twenties the title of the most typically expressionist poet. In the Belgian review *L'Art Libre*, in 1919, an article by David Eliasberg, translated from the Russian, announced that the Soviet Government had wholeheartedly adopted expressionism and all the teachers in the art academies had been replaced by expressionists. A Soviet critic, G. A. Nedochivin, did not hesitate to write, in the sixties, that at last the label of futurists attached to Larionov, Goncharova, the brothers Burliuk and Maiakovsky, in relation to Italian futurism was inadequate, and that they were much closer to the German expressionists than to Severini, Carrá and Marinetti.

As far as France is concerned, as we have already said, the concept of expressionism remained unknown for some time. Imported from Germany in the inter-war period, it had to be adapted to the

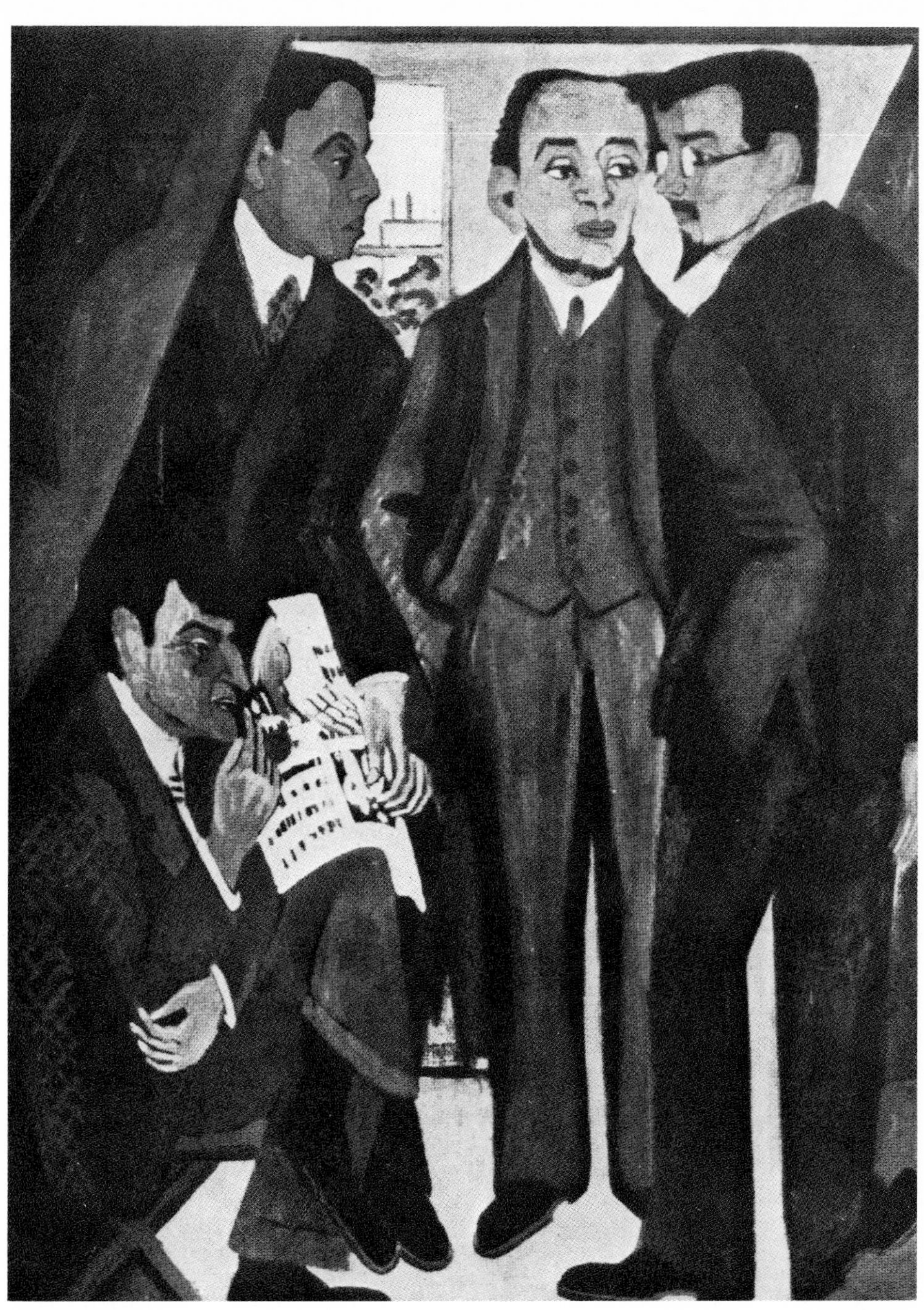

KIRCHNER, ERNST LUDWIG: *The Painters of Die Brücke.* 1926.

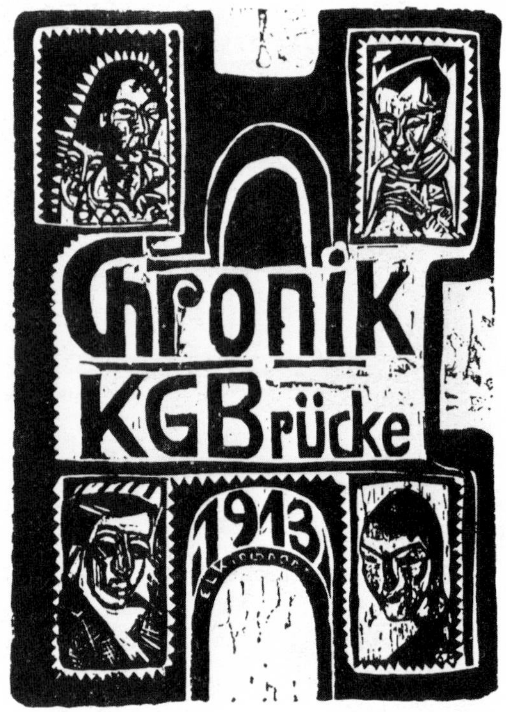

KIRCHNER, ERNST LUDWIG: Poster for *Die Brücke.* 1913.

French situation and be given a pictorial meaning among existing categories. Expressionism could not be either futurism or cubism, nor orphism nor surrealism. Moreover, anti-Germanic feeling was so strong that the cultural output of German-speaking countries was often misunderstood or denigrated, and no acceptable definition of the movement emerged. Klee was exhibited for the first time in Paris in 1926 at Aragon's instigation, and the surrealist was greeted as a German who could not draw!

The use of the word tended to spread in painting to include expressive art, and André Lhote in 1928, in the *Nouvelle Revue française*, spoke up against this practice. One of the first exhibitions where the term was used to describe French painters took place in Paris at the end of 1935, under the aegis of *La Gazette des Beaux-Arts.* Devoted to 'instinctive painters', it had as a sub-title 'birth of expressionism'. Whom did it include? Pictures by Chagall, Marie Laurencin, Modigliani, Pascin, Henri Rousseau, Utrillo and Soutine were gathered together. In the introduction to the catalogue, the influence of German expressionism was dated back to Chagall, thus crediting him with bringing together German and French expressionist styles. 'An important exhibition of his work, mounted in Berlin in March 1914, on Apollinaire's recommendation, had a great impact – and this was the beginning of German expressionism.' As proof of this legendary status as the originator of expressionism, reference was made to his memoirs and to an extract from a letter by Ludwig Rubiner, who wrote to him from Berlin before the declaration of war, saying, 'Do you know that you are famous here? Your pictures have created expressionism. They are selling at a very high price.'

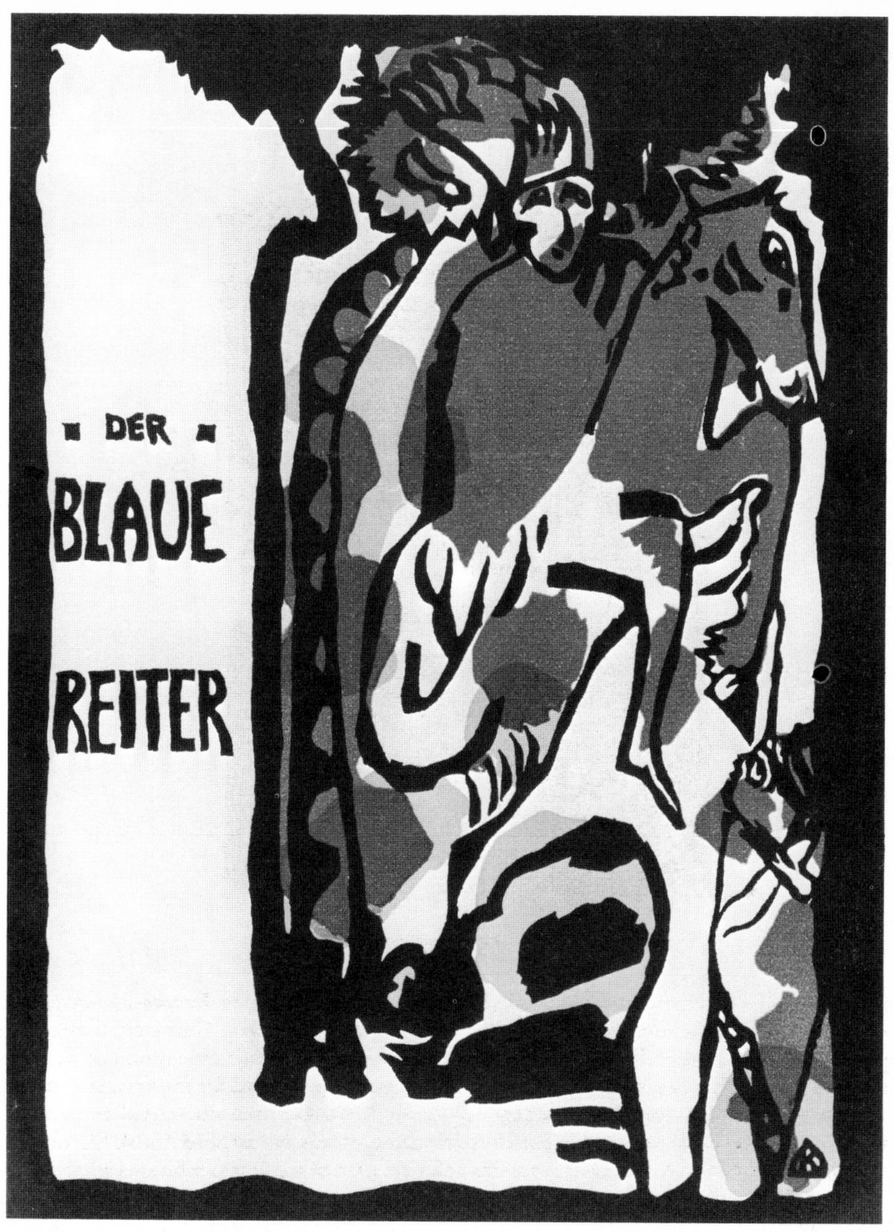

KANDINSKY, WASSILY: Cover for the review *Der Blaue Reiter*. 1911

In spite of its confusion, one aspect of this exhibition should be remembered: the instinctive side that is attributed to the expressionist style. More and more, this style was characterized by the exteriorization of the painter's impulsive reactions to life, and less concerned with the elaboration of pictorial material and forms, than with the expression of his deepest inner feelings; the expressionist painter himself became the creator of an art of anxiety, unease, neurosis, and apocalyptic threats, in short, an art of fantasies which were projected in the form of a creative spontaneity. Whatever the method of painting, external reality was sacrificed to the benefit of its internalized image. This view, which now predominated among French art critics, was not entirely foreign to the doctrine of German expressionism, although it is not an adequate description of it. Above all, because of its general nature it allows one to classify painters who are difficult to include in other categories, and who are only seeking an outlet for their repressed feelings, their emotions and passions. It allows one also to describe as expressionist, artists whom one had not been able to, simply because the word did not exist: the Norwegian: Munch, van Gogh, the Belgian: Ensor at the beginning of the century, and the fauves. In the case of the latter group, the person who coined the term at the autumn *Salon* of 1905, namely Louis Vauxelles, varies his terminology: in 1958 in a work of fauvism, he presents Rouault as 'the leader of French expressionism.'

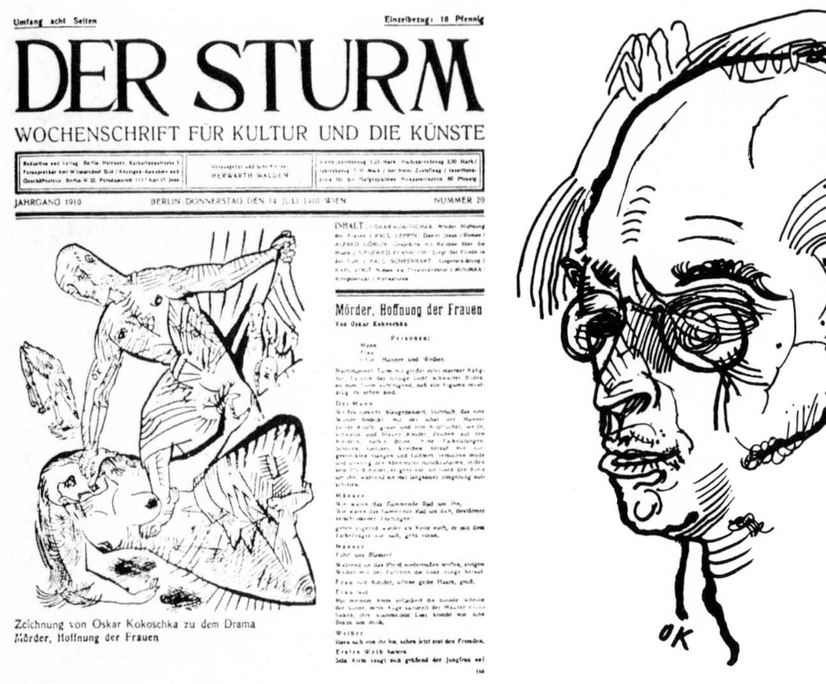

Umfang acht Seiten — Einzelbezug: 10 Pfennig

DER STURM

WOCHENSCHRIFT FÜR KULTUR UND DIE KÜNSTE

HERWARTH WALDEN

JAHRGANG 1910 — BERLIN DONNERSTAG DEN 14. JULI 1910 WIEN — NUMMER 20

INHALT:

Mörder, Hoffnung der Frauen

Von Oskar Kokoschka

Personen:

Mann

Frau

Männer und Weiber.

Der Mann

Zeichnung von Oskar Kokoschka zu dem Drama Mörder, Hoffnung der Frauen

KOKOSCHKA, OSKAR: Drawing for the cover of *Der Sturm*

KOKOSCHKA, OSKAR: *Portrait of Herwarth Walden.* 1910.

For a revival of the arts

This correlation between the terms and the consequences, especially in Germany, and an irrefutable conformity of outlook in Europe, obviously justifies the inclusion of the fauves, in a general book on expressionism such as this.

But when considering the strictly pictorial techniques and profound intentions of expressionism, their presence would necessarily appear rather dubious if a certain amount of interplay between the two movements had not taken place: indeed, as regards the fauves, the difference between their expressionist style and what was really German expressionism is very clear.

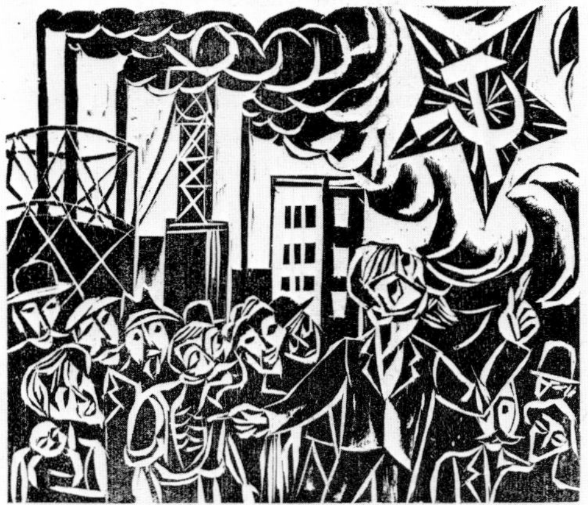
Die Aktion

X. JAHR. HERAUSGEGEBEN VON FRANZ PFEMFERT NR. 51/52

INHALT: Felixmüller: Der Weihnachtsstern leuchtet in die Nacht der Menschheit (Titelblatt) / K. A. Gerlach: Roter Gesang / Heinrich Zernack: Proletarische Madonna (Holzschnitt) / Pol Michels (Paris): Proletarische Weihnachtspredigt / Franz Pfemfert: Die Tagung der Götter / Die Marburger Proletariermörder freigesprochen / KLEINE AKTION / Georg Charasoff: Die Natur des Profits / Theodor Liebknecht: Zum Casseler Freispruch / Max Dortu und Oskar Kanehl: Bürgerliche Revolutionshelden / Erich Mühsam: Gesang der Intellektuellen / Adolf J. Schmidt: Die Bourgeoisknechte / F. W. Seiwert: Zum Aufbau der proletarischen Kultur (mit einem Holzschnitt) / Max Dortu: Arbeiter / Inhaltsverzeichnis des X. Jahrgangs der AKTION / An die Abonnenten der AKTION

VERLAG · DIE AKTION · BERLIN-WILMERSDORF

HEFT 2 MARK

FELIXMÜLLER, CONRAD: Drawing for *Die Aktion*

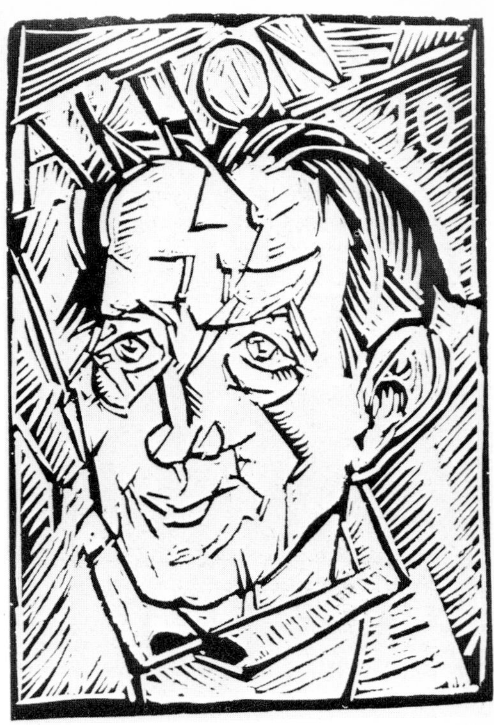

TAPPERT, GEORG: *Portrait of Pfemfert.* 1920.

It is, in fact, natural to regard the foundation in Dresden in 1905 of a group aesthetically very close to fauvism, *Die Brücke* (The Bridge) as marking the decisive change in Germany's cultural life. The initiative came from a student of architecture, Ernst Ludwig Kirchner, who was joined by other young artists: Fritz Bleyl, Erich Heckel, and Karl Schmidt-Rottluff. Though older, Emile Nolde also mixed with them, before abandoning them eighteen months later. Max Pechstein, from 1906 to 1912, and Otto Mueller from 1910, were also of their number. This group broke up in 1912, and officially dissolved in 1913. Now, if, like the fauves, they claimed affinities with van Gogh and Gauguin, they were quick to distance themselves from them in the significance they granted to the pictorial qualities of art. Whereas the fauves inherited from Gauguin the use of vast flat tints of colours, and were interested primarily in decorative art, Kirchner and his friends maintained the importance of the intellect, and were not simply concerned with form. They sought to emphasize the profound presence of nature. Exacerbation and ruggedness were designed to convey above all a sense of original communion.

Certainly, this primitiveness was one of the major phenomena of the beginning of the century. International co-operation between painters was at that time frequent and fruitful, and in Paris, as in Dresden and Munich, primitive art was rediscovered. But *Die Brücke* was based on a philosophical programme, prefiguring the general movement towards a revival in the arts that became German expressionism. This programme expressed the need for a collective ideal, a desire to break with the past, a messianic view of art and exalted intuitive creative powers. Influenced by Nietzsche and Bergson, it appealed to artists to allow themselves to be carried away by the vital sources of the elements. A vague desire to transform the existing order was combined with an individuality that privileged the creative impulse.

This situation, for which Kirchner is responsible, can be seen in the many pictures composed by the

Die Brücke painters. A reality charged with meaning for the community was impregnated with a religiosity or symbolic significance. This is also the distinguishing feature of the fauves. The artist did not simply mirror the age he was living in: beyond the anecdotal subject, there had to be a universal human truth.

At the end of 1911, at a time when already the *Die Brücke* movement was beginning to break up, another group came into being in Munich, centring around Kandinsky and Franz Marc, *Der Blaue Reiter.* The differences in conception from *Die Brücke* are noticeable, if only because of its more artificial organization. However, both reacted against naturalism, against impressionism, and insisted on the instinctive forces of the artist. As for the *Die Brücke* artists, a return to man's origins haunted Kandinsky's circle. There was an anti-materialist and especially anti-positivist reaction, which led to a literary interest in mystical thinkers and which also claimed to include a certain element of primitivism. In 1912, *Der Blaue Reiter* published an almanach in which the illustrations, which were carefully chosen by Kandinsky, alternated between pictures and numerous popular prints from Russia, China, Borneo, Cameroon, Easter Island and New Caledonia.

Are these affinities only of relevance to painters? In fact, a mood shared by practically an entire generation of intellectuals was born in approximately 1890 and developed from 1911 onwards. That year, the new aspirations began to break out. In June, Kurt Hiller opened in Berlin his *Cabaret néo-pathétique.* Jakob van Hoddis suddenly became famous by reading a poem there, called *End of the World*, which was felt to mark a crucial turning-point. Something as yet ill-defined was glimpsed. There was a desire to break with the past. All conventions were overthrown in order to reach out towards a new world which they could already foresee. People gathered around reviews that publicized their revolts and aspirations. In fact, when the word expressionism itself was coined, it provided a focus for their feelings, which had been in gestation for decades and which destroyed everything that was in their way. Previously, when talking about the subjectivity on which the aesthetic common to the expressionists was founded, we have intentionally used examples dating from before 1912: fragments of *Bebuquin* by Carl Einstein were published in 1907. *The Assassination of a Buttercup* is a short story written by Döblin in 1905. Oskar Kokoschka published the first version of *Murderer, The Hope of Women*, in 1910.

It was on 3rd March 1910 that the most famous of the *avant-garde* reviews, *Der Sturm*, brought out its first number. It was founded by Herwarth Walden, who was a critic and a leading artistic figure. From 1903, he represented this new mood, with 1910 marking its real rise to popularity. By bringing together painters and young writers, it tried to achieve a synthesis of the arts. It gave details of existing artistic movements, like futurism and cubism, and provoked general reflection on aesthetic problems: Franz Marc, Hans Arp and Kandinsky all elaborated theories which have greatly added to our understanding of modern art. Among the foreign artists, Walden published Delaunay, Boccioni, Cendrars, David Burliuk, Apollinaire, Fernand Léger, Marinetti. In addition to the review, in March 1912, a picture gallery was opened, and inaugurated by an exhibition of *Der Blaue Reiter.*

A year after the founding of *Der Sturm*, another journal came out which, as a competitor, for ten years successfully reflected the mood of a generation in revolt against its age: *Die Aktion.* Franz Pfemfert, its director, defined it as a politico-literary weekly. His avowed aim was to combat pitilessly and tirelessly what he called 'aculture', or all barbarity. He claimed it was a difficult battle, in so far as the impression one had was of being carried away in a whirlwind of triviality that threatened to swallow one up. 'The absence of a soul is the destructive sign of our age. To be an individual is to have a soul. The age we live in does not recognize individuals.' The soul, the mind, these are the key words that insistently crop up everywhere. It was essential to restore the individual in all his creative power, to destroy the shackles imprisoning his imagination. It was against soulless reality that part of German youth rebelled. What it rejected was the enslavement of the mind. It attacked the machine age, the ruling moral values. It wanted to regenerate the human condition. As Kurt Pinthus wrote in his preface to a famous anthology, in which he grouped together the poets of his generation, *The Twilight of Mankind* 'one saw more and more distinctly the impossibility of a society entirely dependent on its own creation, its science, technology, statistics, commerce and industry, on a fossilized social hierarchy, based on bourgeois conventions.' This demand for an ideal blurred the apparent variety of styles in expressionism. Gottfried Benn provided a definition of this which has the advantage of synthesizing in the same aspirations all the differences, when he sees it as 'revolt erupting, an ecstasy, hatred, and a thirst for a new set of values', using a language that is self-destructive in order to destroy the world as well.' By bringing together all the means and the power of art, the hope was to achieve a renaissance of society. The revival of the arts which was achieved through the destruction of concrete reality, and in favour of the creation of a re-humanized reality, implied a moral reform of society.

Franz Marc, in an introductory article for the second almanach of *Der Blaue Reiter*, which was not published in the end, expressed perfectly this link, that was established by the expressionists, between their artistic endeavours and the social meaning that they attributed to them. The creative adventure lay in a complete break with the world of the past: 'It is by taking this action that we will live up to the great challenge of our time. It is the only activity that makes living and dying worthwhile. An action which implies disrespect to the past. But we want something different; we do not want to live like happy inheritors, living off the past. And even if we wanted to we could not. The legacy is now redundant: continuing the past makes the world vulgar. This is why we are in the process of advancing into new domains and living through a great upheaval where everything has still to be achieved, to be said, organized and explored. The world lies before us in all its purity; our steps falter. If we are prepared to risk walking on our two feet, the umbilical cord that is linking us to our maternal past must be cut. The world is bearing a new age: there is only one question we must ask: has the time come to abandon the world of the past? Are we mature enough for the *vita nuova*? This is the worrying question our age is asking.'

A new Man

Considered from this point of view, German expressionism by far transcended the idea of an expressionist style. Despite the innumerable programmes to which it gave rise, it did not present, moreover, the coherence of a literary and artistic school. If it was a movement, it was because it influenced all aspects of life, and not because it relied on a framework of principles like futurism or surrealism. It is impossible to limit it to an aesthetic movement. The subjective individualism which was its foundation rejects all restrictions and taboos of every kind which might have constrained its initiative. It necessarily increased its means of expression by favouring, on everybody's behalf, the blossoming of man's most inner originality. It is not surprising that many expressionists were tempted ideologically by anarchism, or that they were admirers of Nietzsche. In expressionism, a vision of the world prevailed; it presented necessarily disparate images depending on the groups and even individuals, but it is part of a particular period of history, namely that of Germany from 1910 to approximately 1925.

First of all, expressionism was inseparable from a feeling of crisis. This was lived through and expressed by all the representatives of the generation who were beginning to write, paint and produce plays between 1905 and 1914. What they felt was a disquiet, an impossibility of self-realization, a dissatisfaction with the reality they had before their eyes. They suffered the consequence of the increase in the industrialization of Germany, which found its moral foundations shaken. Fragile human relationships, the frenetic pace of life in the towns, slavery of every kind, were the norm. As proof against the endeavours of the individual, this reality showed itself to be a formidable machine to destroy. It had to be killed off. This was what emerged in their works, through their themes and their forms. There was a real generation gap, a conflict between father and son, that was illustrated in expressionist drama. They defended revolt. They were against the family, teachers, the army, the Emperor, all the henchmen of the established order. Solidarity, on the other hand, with all humiliated souls, those on the fringe of the system, the congregation of the oppressed, the poor, the prostitutes, the madmen, and the young was advocated.

Thrown into the slaughter of the First World War, they had foreseen the horrible cataclysm in striking prophetic visions. The expressionist generation then began to call for the rise of a New Man. From 1916, it inclined in the direction of pacifism (even Hanns Johst, the future paragon of Nazi writers). After the announcement of the end of the world, the Apocalypse, regeneration, reconstruction, were key words. Faced with atrocities, utopian idealism seemed to many to be the basis for a possible solution. Salvation was not seen in the context of a collective social struggle, in an economic and political transformation of society, but in an inner renewal of Man. Each individual had to reach an *ascesis* and believe in ultimate happiness. Some of the expressionists (Ludwig Rubiner, Rudolf Leonard, Ludwig Bäumer, Johannes R. Becher, the activists gathering around Kurt Hiller and his publication *Das Ziel*) also found in various ways the road towards political commitment. The revolutionary events that shook Germany in November 1918 left some of them uncertain what to do (Gottfried Benn, Oskar Kokoschka, Paul Kornfeld), but many actively participated: Ludwig Bäumer was one of those responsible for the Council of Bremen, Ernst Toller was one of the leaders of the independent socialist republic of Bavaria. The painter Conrad Felixmüller and the playwright Friedrich Wolf were at the battle of Dresden. Wieland Herzfelde and Franz Pfemfert were thrown into prison in Berlin when the counter-revolution was winning; Carl Einstein was one of the architects of the soldiers' Council at Brussels in November 1918.

Herbert Kühn, in 1919, saw in this type of commitment, which often had a religious and mystical dimension, a logical extension of expressionism: 'expressionism – as in the case of socialism – raised a great cry against Matter, against intellectual Barbarism, against the Machine, against Centralization, in favour of the Mind, of God, of Man in Man. They had the same spiritual attitude, the same position with regard to the world, only the difference in the field of action explains why they have different names. There is no expressionism without socialism. It is not a coincidence that Art Nouveau was so vigorously open to politics.' Yvan Goll, in 1921, made a statement that went in the same direction: 'Expressionism is the literature of war and revolution, of the intellectual struggling against the powerful, the revolt of the conscience against blind obedience, the cry of the heart against the thunder of massacres and the silence of the oppressed.'

These opinions were uncompromising and not all those who were regarded as expressionists shared them (e.g. Herwath Walden, whose political evolution in the direction of communism dates from the end of the twenties, and who, at that time, was opposed to all politicalization of art). Even among those who shared them a number of ideological varieties existed. But what is certain is that the revolutionary failures only hastened the break-up of the movement. Its failure and its demise began in 1919–20. Some became embittered and succumbed to irrationally, others adapted to the climate of the times. The latter group formed revolutionary political organizations, in particular becoming members of the German Communist Party. The beautiful dream of the new Man had definitely collapsed. In an acid tone which evokes Georg Grosz's caricatures, Yvan Goll made this assessment in 1921: 'The solidarity of the intellectuals. – Marching troops of men of the truth. But the result is, alas, without its being the fault of the expressionists, the German Republic of 1920. A shop sign, interval. Please use the exit on the right.' It was historical conditions, without a doubt, that determined the outcome of German expressionism. Already almost exhausted, another crisis slowly brought about its death: the inflation and the misery of the post-war period. The communion between artists and the masses was over. Germany was hungry and shattered. Actors were on strike because their salary was only worth two pairs of shoes. The same generation, after the collapse of its humanitarian aspirations, also witnessed the collapse of the ability to create, because of economic constraints. Another age was beginning: that of a return to order, marked in literature and painting by what has been called *New Objectivity*, a tendency to which Felix Berteaux, a renowned journalist of the post-war period, very pertinently gave the name of 'rigid order'.

Yet expressionism did not die immediately. Its last sparks continued for a few more years, especially in the theatre with the productions of Leopold Jessner, or in the cinema with Carl Mayer's scenarios. But its fundamental aspirations were a thing of the past. Only its principles and artistic techniques remained, until they became a fashion that no longer corresponded to the famous inner need to create that Kandinsky had spoken of, and which led to an aggressive snobbery. Broken lines and forms, disharmonies, dissonances, aggressive colours, and artificial recourse to primitiveness, all these methods were only used to provoke calculated emotional shocks in the public. Paradoxically, it was precisely those characteristics which were retained to affirm the existence of an expressionist style.

It is obvious, on the other hand, that many writers and artists who had lived in the expressionist climate, whilst moving on to another phase of their creativity, retained in their approach something of their former selves. Schönberg's work, for example, had until *Moses and Aaron*, composed in 1920–32, a pathos about it which was again present in *The Happy Hand*; it was a long time since Becher had used an explosive and ecstatic language despite his having become a Communist. The architects Erich Mendelsohn, Bruno Taut and Hans Scharoun, for their part, tried not to sacrifice their own personal imagination in the field of urbanism and the construction of buildings. Directly in the tradition of expressionist aspirations, Carl Sternheim, when he was an exile in Belgium, was interviewed by a journalist from *Le Soir*, and expressed his desire in 1934 'to uplift humanity to create a new Christ', even stating 'we need strong personalities, men capable of directing their life in a metaphysical direction. For life is not simply physical, it is metaphysical.'

Yesterday and Today

In so far as it was closely linked to the history of Germany and of German society, expressionism in its genuine sense had hardly any following abroad, except in countries which had close relations with Germanic culture. In Hungary, for instance, Lajos Kassak who had contacts with Franz Pfemfert claimed affinities with the expressionist aesthetic, and the journal that he edited from 1917 to 1925, *Ma*, has at first sight a lot in common, if only because of its external appearance, with *Die Aktion*. In 1922, one of its collaborators, Sandor Barta, emphasized that his generation had found the path to social reform and a socialist conception of the world via expressionism. In the Netherlands and in Flemish Belgium too, the intellectual exchanges with Germany likewise made them familiar with expressionist art and reviews, and the Flemish renaissance in woodcuts owed much to German endeavours. Above all, Frans Masereel, when considered beside Joris Minne, Henri von Straeten, Jan Cantré, and Josef Cantré, stands apart, because he collaborated directly with the German expressionists, illustrating works by Becher or Sternheim; moreover, as a result of an idealistic inspiration and a sense of the cosmic, his social commitment and themes such as town and revolt, he shared the aspirations that emerged in the *Die Aktion* circle.

As far as France is concerned, one has to take into consideration the political situation between 1918 and 1925, roughly, the period which saw the emergence of German expressionism. Before 1914 very fruitful relationships existed between painters of all countries, to the extent that Alfred Kubin rightly called it fraternization between young artists. But already, most French intellectuals had lost interest. Faced with Wilhelm II's imperialist policies, anti-Germanic feeling became more virulent. Whereas the new generation in Germany was becoming more open in its attitude towards the outside world, through innumerable international contacts, its French equivalent had fallen under the yoke of nationalism. This is the most important difference of attitude that hindered a possible discovery of expressionism. The war followed, and until 1920 the cultural relations between France and Germany were few and fragile. At the moment when expressionism could have become accessible to the French, it was dying out.

The result is that well-established and popular journals hardly paid any attention to expressionism, neither before nor after 1914. Only more modest publications like *Clarté*, *Action*, *Esprit Nouveau*, *La Revue Européenne*, devoted informative articles to it or published extracts from expressionist literature. The principal mediator was Yvan Goll from Lorraine, who, because he was bilingual, had collaborated in most of the German expressionist journals. Even the surrealists, attracted by the romantics, Novalis and Hoffmann, and published by Walden in *Der Sturm*, remained in ignorance of expressionism. Whereas avant-garde painters and poets were widely appreciated in Germany, only the new German cinema aroused any interest in France.

In French-speaking Belgium, on the other hand, writers and painters openly professed expressionist tendencies, and were supported by journals like *Lumière*, *Résurrection*, *L'Art Libre*, *Sélection*, and *Ça ira*. Whatever their differences, for them expressionism was modern art *par excellence*. Two principal trends existed, corresponding to the division between *Der Sturm* and *Die Aktion*. On the one hand, articles by André de Riddler, and painters like Constant Permeke, or Gustave de Smet, betrayed a humanitarian tendency. On the other, with the critic George Marlier and a painter like Paul Joostens, a predilection for abstraction emerged. These young Belgian journals of the immediate post-war period tried to give a lot of space to German poets. One example deserves to be mentioned: Clement Pansaers, the future dadaist and director of *Résurrection*, analyzed and translated by Carl Einstein and Herwath Walden from 1918 onwards.

Claims of wholehearted expressionism, and no longer simply a bowdlerized form, were made in other countries in the twenties. In Flemish Belgium, Paul van Ostaijen is an example, along with the journal *Het Getij* (1916–24). In Yugoslavia there was the group centring around Stanislav Vinaver, who was the author, in 1911 at Belgrade, of an expressionist manifesto. In 1919, in Russia, Ippolit Sokolov published a book-manifesto, *Bunt-èkspresisionista*, as did the painter Matthis-Teutsch in Romania a little later. In Poland, expressionism was brought to the fore by the *Zdvoj* group, and in Czechoslovakia by the *Osmá* group. Finally, in Latin America, it was the subject of a number of articles and debates, concentrating as much on art (in Mexico with Diego Rivera, José Clemente Orozco, David Alfonso Siqueiros in Peru, with Sabogal and Coresido, in Brazil with Anita Malfatti, who had studied in Dresden and Berlin) as on literature, since it was even claimed that the modernistic movement had had in its first period (1915 to 1930), expressionistic overtones.

After this far too brief summary, the principal question still remains: how relevant is expressionism today? When one restricts oneself to considering it as a style devoted exclusively to the plastic arts, it is clear that it is very much alive: the *Cobra* group in the Netherlands, the American Pollock, the Frenchmen Francis Gruber and Bernard Buffet, the Dane Asger Jorn and many others have to be considered a part of it since 1945. But what about expressionism as a movement? Along with futurism and surrealism, both of which also aimed at being applicable to all the arts, it belongs to what is generally called the historical avant-garde. In this capacity, it only began to be rediscovered in the sixties. And more and more it has been noticed how much still remains to be said about it. For it represents both the genesis of modernism, leading to a social art, verbal experimentation, pictorial abstraction, a synthetic drama, contemporary dissonant music, and the meeting point of all the living tendencies of the age. No other -ism of the century has been so involved in the collective and individual conflicts of its time, none has tried so hard to reach the heart of its contradictions in order to try and overcome them.

Painting and the Graphic Arts

1905 saw the emergence of a new generation of painters. In the Autumn *Salon* in Paris a group mounted an exhibition which had formed around Henri Matisse. The works they exhibited horrified the public by virtue of the stark simplicity of style and the way they were built up from bright contrasts of colour. The bust of a child of the most conventional sort stood amongst these pictures by Matisse, Marquet, Manguin, Camoin, van Dongen, Friesz, Guy, Vlaminck and Derain; it prompted the critic, Louis Vauxelles to remark: 'Donatello chez les fauves'. Thus was the name 'Les Fauves' – The Savages – born, soon to be assumed by other non-French artists. Nevertheless, Kandinsky and Jawlensky for example, were directly involved for they showed their paintings in the same exhibition and aspired toward the same goals as the French painters.

At the same time, a circle of architecture students had formed the group of artists known as *Die Brücke* (The Bridge) which looked to the same models for inspiration as the fauves: Van Gogh, Gauguin, Seurat.

A dissatisfaction with the traditional conception of reality as represented by impressionism was what characterized this new generation. These artists were aware that the depiction of outer appearances comprises only one aspect of reality, and cannot penetrate to the essence of things. They had realized that both the most painstaking analysis of what they observed, and the depiction of mental processes were inadequate to express the complete being.

Matisse formulated it thus: 'What I seek above all to achieve, is expression. Expression does not lie for me in the passion which suddenly animates a face or which manifests itself in a violent movement. It lies rather in the whole organization of any painting. The space which the objects occupy, the emptiness around them, and the proportions, all play a part.' And he went on to add, 'The foremost purpose of colour must be to aid expression as much as possible.' But now expression meant the depiction of a deep, inner experience of reality by means of colour, spontaneously applied. The object, the subject-matter, give rise to feelings which must be incorporated into the picture directly and without distortion as an essential component of the reality. The aim is to imbue external reality, experienced through the senses, with the reality of the artist's inner experience. This is the struggle for artistic synthesis of which Kandinsky also spoke.

Three Pioneers

The premises on which the evolution of expressionist art was based, emerge clearly when we think of Seurat, Gauguin and Van Gogh. Georges Seurat, 1859–1891, had a powerful and logical mind which was not satisfied by the spontaneity of impressionism and its analysis of light based on instinct alone. He sought to extend impressionism through a method of freeing colour from substance, using the pure colours of the spectrum to achieve a 'light-painting in colour'. His systematic investigation of scientific colour theories and light analyses, and the study of simultaneous colour contrasts led him to a surprising

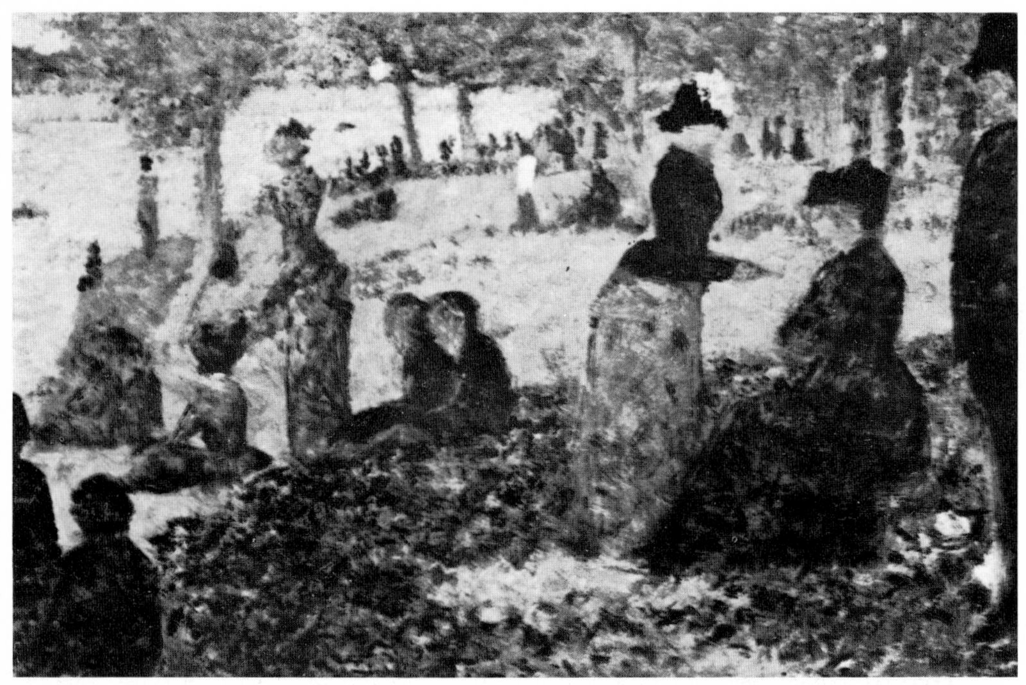

SEURAT, GEORGES: *Small sketch for 'la Grande Jatte'.* 1884–1885.

solution: colours were no longer mixed on the palette; instead this was achieved in the eye of the spectator. The pure colours of the spectrum were therefore painted as small dots next to each other on the canvas. They merge on the retina of the observer who is sufficiently far away from the painting.

In this way, Seurat won the freedom to create a harmony from the unique order of colour which was independent from momentary impression. 'The picture was no longer a copy of nature, but evolved as an autonomous organism out of line, rhythm and colour contrasts. The artist could determine the character of the painting after a free appraisal. By subordinating colour and line to the emotion which possesses him, the painting becomes a poet, a creator . . .' (Signac). The importance for the following generation of the neo-impressionists, as Seurat and his school called themselves, lay in highlighted colour as a means of expression.

Paul Gauguin 1848–1903 had also opened up a new creative route. His starting point, impressionism, remained too close to nature for him. He wrote that the impressionists 'neglect the secret meaning of thought. Art is abstraction; draw it from nature as you dream of it.' Gauguin was attempting to restore a meaning to painting, in his pictures of figures, that could be interpreted as a universal image of human existence. Both in Brittany, where he formed a group of primitives, and later in the South Seas, Gauguin was seeking for the primal experience in order to achieve truthful expression. For this

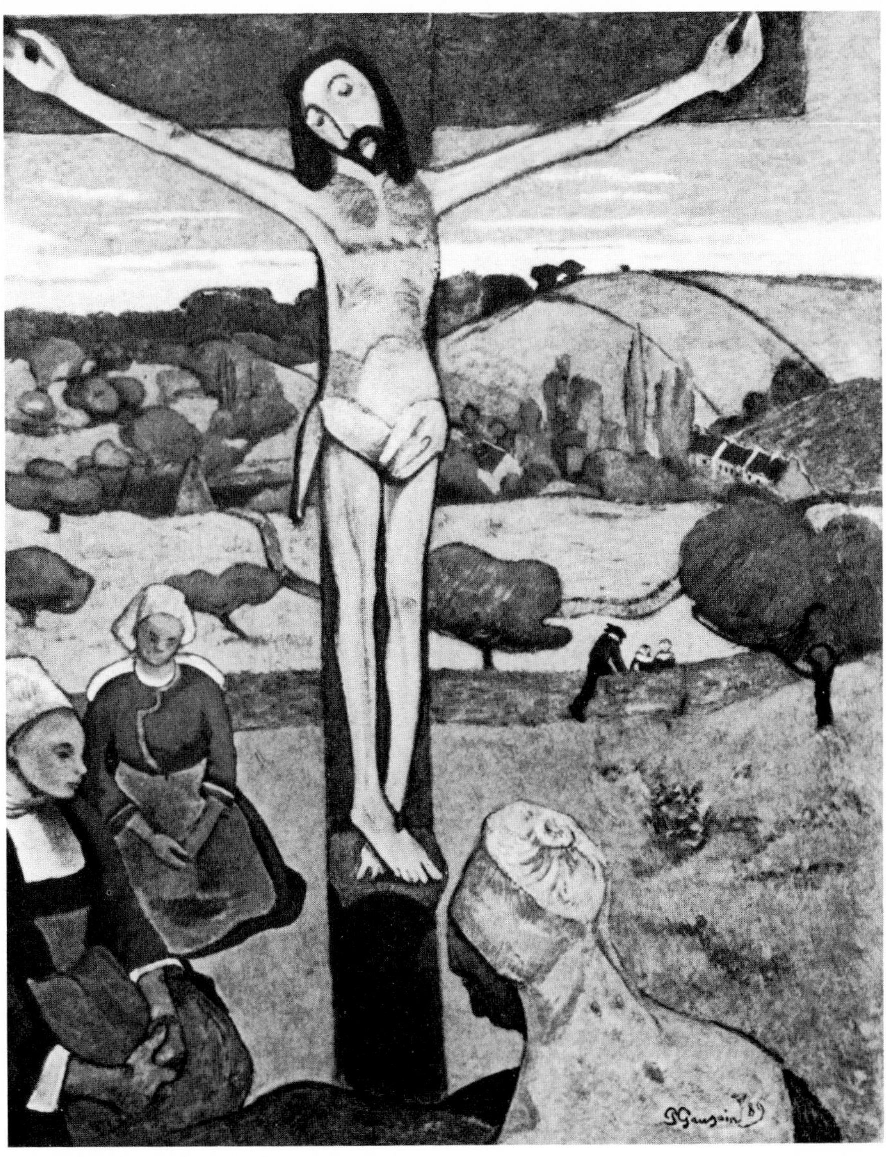

GAUGUIN, PAUL: *The Yellow Christ.* 1889.

reason, he was deeply interested in primitive art and folklore and studied the Japanese woodcuts which were then in fashion.

As a result of such stimulus he evolved a decorative style which for the most part abandoned two-dimensional illusionist techniques in order to portray experience. Colour is applied 'flatly' carefully adhering to the area of the image depicted, and is held together by means of heavily-drawn contours. A flatness and rhythmically decorative drawing style were the active elements, as well as Gauguin's conviction that the colour tone harmonies in painting had their counterpart in the harmonies of music. Hence this regard for the psychological significance of colour which made it possible to hint at a meaning without the need for a 'literary' description.

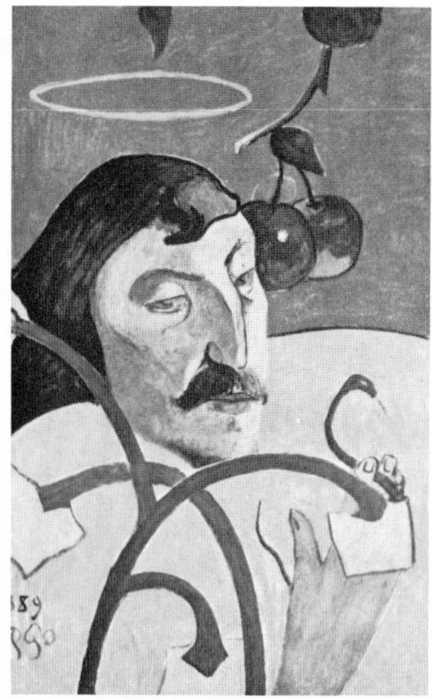

GAUGUIN, PAUL: *Self-portrait.* 1889.

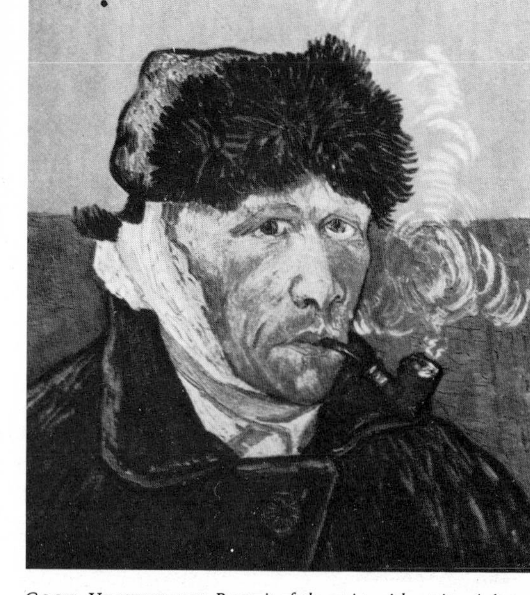

GOGH, VINCENT VAN: *Portrait of the artist with a pipe.* Arles, 1889.

Vincent Van Gogh had met Seurat and Gauguin in 1886 in the Paris art dealer's run by his brother Theo. He owed them much fundamental knowledge about the expressive power of pure colour and line. Nevertheless his point of departure was not one of artistic calculation but of existential need. For Van Gogh, painting proved the only possibile way of expressing his ecstatic love for man and for things. He exposed himself directly to communion with objects, in order to penetrate the dazzle of the external world and the hell of another reality, one discovered in the most intense agitation. This message is conveyed through the heightened tone of his blazing colours and dynamic brush-work like tongues of flame, whose spontaneous strokes are a direct reflection of the artist's mental condition. Van Gogh's compulsion to surrender himself unprotected to the world in order to experience its truth, consumed his strength in a short space of years. The way he chose – to create art as an answer to existential anguish and to sacrifice his life when the tension grew unbearable – became a tragically exemplary fate for those artists who sought to unify life and art in the decade that followed.

The fauves

The conclusions which the fauves advanced in 1905 had evolved slowly. The group round Matisse by no means represented a school and advanced no binding aesthetic programme. On the contrary, it was demanded of each painter that he should express his individuality. Their common goal was to create new forms as a contrast to the mentality of the academy and impressionism. However, while Matisse dreamed of creating an art of 'equilibrium', purity and tranquillity, without ambiguities, one that would 'provide spiritual reassurance' and 'soothe the soul', Vlaminck saw fauvism as a way of living, acting and painting. The former position implies the logical perfection of formal methods, the latter a spontaneous creativity based on instinct. They demonstrate the full range of the various artistic possibilities embraced by the term fauvism. This is even more true of expressionism: it is the sum total of individual personalities bound together by the particular intellectual mood of a generation.

The fauves group had developed out of relations between friends. Matisse and Marquet had met in

1892 during night classes in the School of Arts and Crafts in Paris. Matisse transferred to the School of Fine Arts in 1895, where Marquet later joined him.

Here they met fellow students Roualt, Manguin and Camoin in the studio of Gustave Moreau. After Moreau's death, Matisse had to leave the School of Fine Arts in 1899 and went to the *Académie Carrière* where Derain and Puy were already working. Derain, who lived like his friend Vlaminck at Chatou near Paris, introduced the latter to Matisse at the famous Van Gogh exhibition of 1907. While Matisse and his friends were working together in Manguin's studio, Derain and Vlaminck painted at Chatou in the

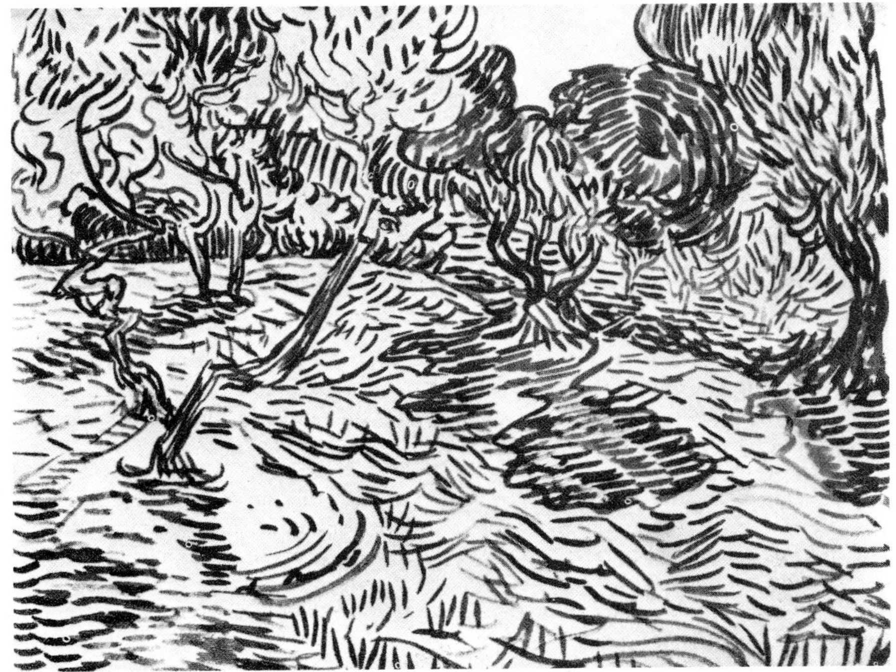

GOGH, VINCENT VAN: *The Olive Trees.* Saint-Rémy. 1889.

same studio. At the same time, the painters from Le Havre – Friesz, Dufy and Braque – were keeping close contact.

In 1901 the circle round Matisse had started to exhibit in the *Salon des Indépendants* and from 1903 in the newly-founded *Salon d'automne*. Van Dongen, Friesz and Dufy showed their paintings at both. They discovered characteristics in common, and in 1905 appeared as a group. Braque was the last to join them in 1906, but barely two years later he had already turned towards new goals.

The sources of inspiration for the fauves' pictures were restricted to landscapes, human beings and objects in their everyday surroundings. The stimulus really was almost a matter of indifference, since the aim was no longer to imitate nature, to deceive the eye, but to provide an interpretation through subjective emotion and perception. Artists could no longer identify with the well-ordered world of beautiful appearances, nor accept it as true; imagination was to take the place of observation.

The means for this transition were already at their disposal: the pure colour of the neo-impressionists, the unbroken surfaces of Gauguin and the heightened expressiveness of Van Gogh. However, Seurat's method was given new meaning. It became a way of lending rhythm and dynamism to the surface of the painting, marked by the spontaneity of the brushstrokes. The contours of objects were reduced in detail, to an ornamental array of lines, which through their stark simplification condense and segment what is expressed. This, however, is determined by the independent power of communication in pure colour now freed from its function as local colour. As a consequence of the introduction of anti-naturalism and of a very great intensity, achieved with the aid of positively aggressive contrasts, colours became the true medium of the new artistic reality. These methods were put into practice with uncontrolled high spirits, sometimes with explosive force – a delirium, an orgy of colour became from then on a recurring characteristic of fauvism.

However, the exaltation which had thus been won from youthful energy only lasted a few years, since, as Braque said, 'you cannot remain in perpetual paroxysm'. By 1908 the need for clarity of construction in focus came to the fore under the influence of Cézanne. Some of the fauves followed his path; others reverted to a type of impressionism.

PICASSO, PABLO: *Les Demoiselles d'Avignon*. 1907.

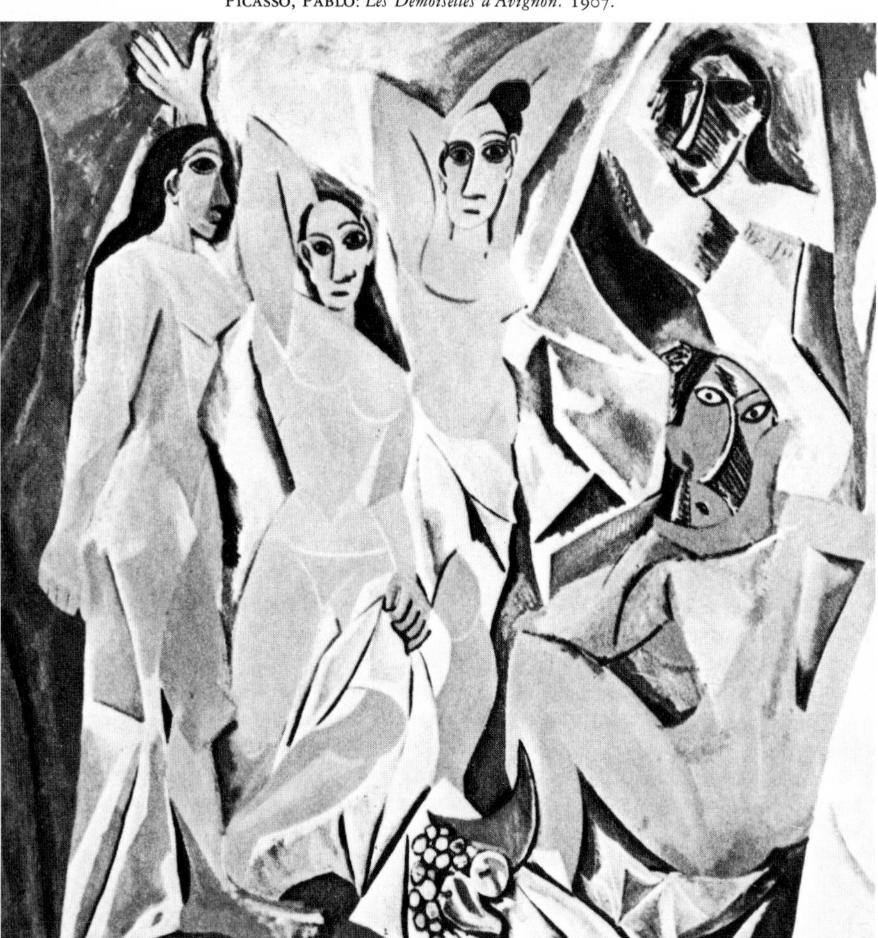

There was another possibility in expressive painting which did not regard ambiguities and the tumult of feeling to obtain artistic truth with suspicion, as did the fauves. Roualt (who counts as the one real French expressionist) followed this direction. He was, admittedly, connected with the Fauves and exhibited with them, but his painting is filled with human problems. It is a reply to existential anguish and an indictment of society. With Christian compassion he revealed the terrible side of reality which can only be conquered by faith. As a result, Roualt, with his impastos and the suppressed passion of his visions, became the most important religious painter of the twentieth century.

The work of Picasso also grew out of compassion and human sympathy, for in his earliest paintings he dramatized misery with powerful colours. Subsequently, he abandoned colour contrast and concentrated this violence of emotion on one colour alone – blue. He achieved the most passionate heightening of expression in the picture *Les Demoiselles d'Avignon* in 1907 through his radical distortion of the object's shape: this painting is simultaneously the greatest achievement of expressionism and the key work of cubism.

In Robert Delaunay, distortion used as a means of dynamic expression together with the agitated rhythm of his colour, combined to produce an expressionist vision, which, due to its splintered effect and plunging lines, came to be the most popular example of expressionist art, extending its influence, on German art in particular, right into the 1920s.

In the same way as Delaunay, Le Fauconnier used the cubist dissection of form in order to analyse the object rather than as a means of heightening expression and he was particularly influential in this in the Netherlands. This gives some indication of the spectrum of expressionist painting in France, which was enriched by important painters, particularly from Eastern Europe, such as Modigliani, Chagall, Soutine, or Kupka.

The Beginnings in Germany

The development in Germany paralleled that in France. Here, 1905 was a critical year, with the founding of the circle, *Die Brücke* in Dresden. However, activities were not concentrated on one spot, as in Paris, but were divided between individuals in different places. They evolved independently of each other and were yet linked with the situation in Europe. This meant adapting native trends such as art nouveau and lyrical naturalism and getting to know of the precepts which had been evolved in France. In addition, the production of Munch and Ensor provided specifically German ingredients.

James Ensor, 1860–1949, portrayed the hideous features of masks and fantastic ghost worlds using quite realistic, even impressionist, methods. An introvert, alienated from men and the world, he was unable to grasp reality. In its place, a world of fear emerged in his hallucinatory fantasies: skeletal, hidden behind masks and disguises, and always threatened by decay and death. Ensor did not paint with the purpose of intensifying his powers of expression, but was driven by inner phantoms which directly reflect the mental condition of the artist. This fateful alienation linked Ensor with Van Gogh, but also with Munch. Edvard Munch, 1863–1944, had received decisive stimuli in the circle of Van Gogh, Gauguin and Toulouse-Lautrec in Paris. He rendered these impressions sensually and intensified his painting into an expressionist art typical of Northern Europe, nourished on hypocrisy and melancholia. He painted landscapes suffused with mysterious forces; men moulded by dark impulses; fear, hatred, jealousy, loneliness and death; paintings which were increasingly pessimistic visions of the artist's own fate.

This revelation of self, the inner scream, which intensifies both clarity and torment, the neurotic and oppressed spirit of Munch's art, was a signpost at the beginning of the century. At the same time, Munch gave an important impetus to the revival of the woodcut, which attained a new significance in German expressionism. At the beginning there were three North German artists who worked in

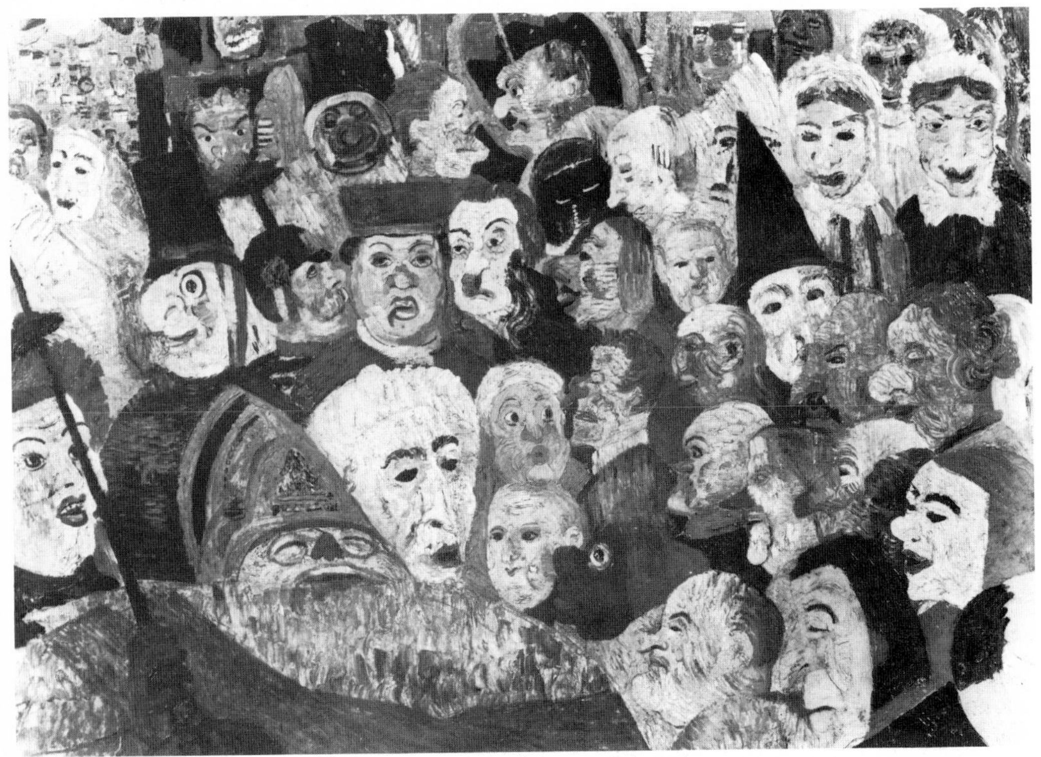

ENSOR, JAMES: *The Entry of Christ into Brussels.* 1888.

different places, drawing their decisive experiences from the native countryside: Paula Modersohn-Becker, Christian Rohlfs and Emil Nolde. Paula Modersohn-Becker had come to the colony of artists in Worpswede as a twenty-two year old in 1898.

This village near Bremen was one of the places where artists had withdrawn in order to re-discover the harmony between man and nature in seclusion. Paula Modersohn-Becker quickly outgrew the lyrical landscape painting which was practised here. She reduced the appearance of objects to their formal essence, a procedure considered mistaken in Worpswede. Several stays in Paris from 1900 onwards confirmed her in her striving after 'a great simplicity of form'. For her, it corresponded with her love for the simple life, for the simple people, whom she painted. She only had six years, from 1901–1907 in which to develop an austere and unsentimental form for the expression of her feelings, which often revolved round love and motherhood. In doing so, she had freed herself from the contingency of nature and created allegorical paintings out of her strength of feeling.

The power of this new direction is clearly exemplified by Christian Rohlfs, born in 1849. For thirty years he had painted landscapes in the most intimate tradition of realism. Now, at almost sixty years of age, he tackled the artistic problems of the age in a burst of development. He finally separated colour

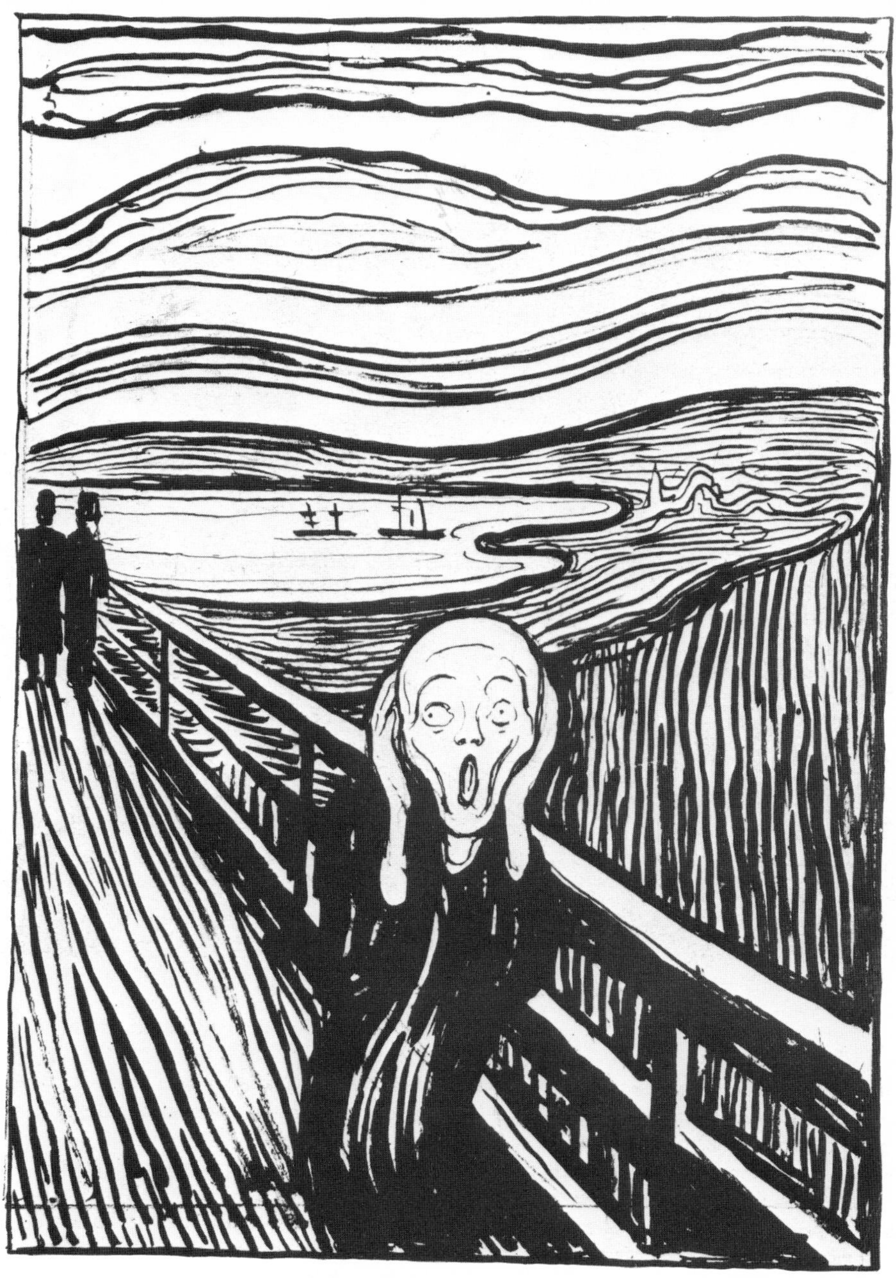

MUNCH, EDVARD: *The Scream.* 1885.

from substance, spread it thinly on the surface – often in water-colour: he gave it rhythm by means of a broken brush line which conveys spiritual agitation and lyrical feeling in expressive arabesques.

The most important of the North German painters was Emil Nolde, in whom the tie with the land is mirrored most strongly. Nolde, like Rohlfs, was the son of a farmer. He grew up in a lonely landscape which was continually threatened by storm and a violent sea. Nature's forms came to life in his imagination often as grotesque ghosts and demons. This experience of nature and a simplicity based on the word of the Bible, determined Nolde's art. Every observation, even the cry of animals, took the form of colour in his imagination, clamouring to be transformed into colour, which was accomplished at a pitch of excitement. In this, Nolde, like Vlaminck, trusted instinct alone. He had learnt by himself that when he began a painting with an exact mental image, he became an involuntary self-plagiarist. He therefore contented himself with a vague idea of the colours, from which the picture could evolve freely in the process of painting. He succeeded in transforming nature by the addition of his own mental and spiritual perceptions into an expressionist vision. These ecstatic storms of colour in which Nolde managed to intensify his personal expression, exercised a strong influence on *Die Brücke.*

Die Brücke

They corresponded exactly to the intention formulated in the 1906 manifesto of the group, *Die Brücke*: every man who reproduces what drives him to create correctly and without distortion is one of us. So in 1906 Nolde became a member of this circle for barely ten years. In the previous year, four architecture students, Ernst Ludwig Kirchner, Erich Heckel and Karl Schmidt-Rottluff and Fritz Bleyl had formed society of artists in Dresden, who – hence the name 'The Bridge' – wished to attract all revolutionary and innovatory elements in order to win the freedom to create, for the new generation.

In 1906 the Swiss Cuno Amiet and the Finn Axel Gallen-Kallela joined the group, but restricted themselves to occasional participation in their exhibitions. Max Pechstein also joined in 1906; he had training at the Dresden Academy behind him and had already won the *Prix de Rome*. In 1910, Otto Mueller, then living in Berlin, was admitted to the circle. Otto, who had studied at the Dresden and Munich academies, and was a skilled lithographer, had already almost completely worked out his personal style, which had little in common with the brilliant colours and flat style of *Die Brücke.* Nevertheless, the sensuous harmony between art and life that he had achieved answered the intentions of the friends so perfectly that a partnership was the obvious conclusion. Finally, the Prague artist, Bohumil Kubista joined the group in 1911, although close contact did not ensue.

They worked together with the assiduity of the possessed in a butcher's shop in a working-class area of Dresden. The subject matter of the paintings was taken from their everyday surroundings: landscapes, street scenes, portraits, scenes in their studio and life models.

The pictures were to be able to be filled directly with life and with experience. They originated in 'the entirely naïve and unadulterated need, to bring art and life into harmony' (Kirchner). Artistic stimuli and models were made available to the young painters through exhibitions in Dresden: 1905 – Van Gogh; 1906– Munch, Nolde, Seurat, Gauguin and Van Gogh; 1908– Van Gogh again, in one hundred paintings, plus sixty of the fauves, including Van Dongen who, on the strength of this, was invited to join exhibitions of *Die Brücke.* What was at first intuitively transformed into art, not as an act of physical strength and revolutionary action, a process in which the spiritual power of colour was still concealed by its substantiality, was refined into a powerfully expressive art composed of a simplified tracery of lines, composition over large surfaces and pure colour. From the outset, woodcuts, as a means of clarifying form, were of great importance in this.

Another source of inspiration was fostered by the fact that normally the friends separated in the summer months in order to perfect what they had learned individually under mutual supervision afterwards. They worked either in the surroundings of Dresden, in Goppeln or by the Moritzberg lakes, at Dangast on the North Sea, on the Baltic Island, Fehmarn, or the Baltic shore at Nidden and so on. Landscape, the nude, and the nude in a landscape as a form of nature, were important themes for *Die Brücke.* The circus and the music halls were also expressions of intensified life.

Naturalness and exaggeration offered possibilities of overcoming traditional bourgeois modes of behaviour. They were roads towards the 'new man' which the expressionists invoked with optimistic fervour. In order to be able to depict the universality and the objectivity they were referring to, colour was made independent, freed from its function of describing the object and used purely as the medium for expression; its effect was heightened by a style of drawing which reduced the object to a cipher.

In 1911 the painters of *Die Brücke* had settled in Berlin where, in the last years before the First World War, the efforts of this modern art were concentrated. Kirchner reacted the most strongly to the change in environment and portrayed the hectic, evil and artificial elements in the modern city in tense and impressive paintings.

In the course of their six years' work together, the individual artist's personalities had become so distinctive that their association no longer corresponded to any inner necessity. Pechstein was the first to leave, and in 1913 *Die Brücke* broke up. Each one continued to work independently. Nevertheless, what remained binding for each one was the ideal of absolute integrity, consistency and responsibility, in art as in human relations, which they had lived together.

Der Blaue Reiter

The avant-garde artists in Munich had organized themselves relatively late into a group. In 1909 a group formed under the name of 'The New Munich Association of Artists'.

The founder members were Jawlensky, Kanoldt, Erbslöh, Kandinsky and Münter. They were able to base themselves on the results achieved in other places when they stated in their programme, 'We start from the idea that the artist is continually collecting experiences in his inner world, separate from the impressions which he receives from nature, the external world. The search for artistic forms that would express the mutual interpretation of all these experiences – for forms which must be freed from anything secondary, in order to throw the existential sharply into relief – in short, the struggle for an artistic synthesis, seems to us to be a banner which currently is again uniting an increasing number of artists.'

The aim of the New Association of Artists was to be international. Their driving force came from the Russians who had been immediately involved with the development in Paris. In 1906 Kandinsky had exhibited in the *Salon d'automne*, and during his year's stay in Paris he had become a member of its jury. Jawlensky had mounted ten pictures with the fauves in the 1905 *Salon d'automne*, and had met Matisse in whose studio he worked in 1907. So it seems logical that Le Fauconnier should also have become a member of the Munich group.

The strong international complexion became evident in the exhibition of the circle in 1910; for Le Fauconnier, the Burliuk brothers, Kandinsky and Redon contributed forewords to its catalogue, while works by Braque, Picasso, Rouault, Derain, Vlaminck and Van Dongen amongst others were to be seen. This exhibition caused Marc and Macke to establish contact with the group.

However, by 1911 there were already rifts in the Association and in December 1911 the renegade members, Kandinsky, Marc and Münter who had left the group, opened the first exhibition by the editors of *Der Blaue Reiter* (The Blue Horseman). This exhibition, which was hastily and rather haphazardly compiled, presented amongst others, works by Rousseau, Delaunay, Campendonck, Macke, the Burliuk brothers and the organizers. In 1912 it was opened in Berlin as the first '*Der Sturm* exhibition' by Herwarth Walden, having been enlarged in the meantime by works by Klee, Kubin and Jawlensky. The second and already the last exhibition, under the name *Der Blaue Reiter* was mounted in March in 1912. It contained only graphic work by the Munich artists, by the Frenchmen who had been exhibited before, from *Die Brücke* and by Arp, Malevitch, Nolde and others. It was clearly evident from this that there was no united group behind these activities – indeed, there was no longer any attempt to form one.

The need for these smaller alliances had already been overtaken by a European movement, now manifest everywhere. When the almanach, *Der Blaue Reiter*, appeared in 1912, it was less the presentation of a programme than a publication describing the positions which had been established.

The new impulse that carried expressionism forward stemmed above all from Kandinsky, but also from those around him – Jawlensky, Marc, and Klee – who aimed at the total liberation of the picture from the object. Hoelzel and Kubin had made experiments in this direction before, and August Endell had already noted in 1898 that they were at the beginning of a completely new art, one 'with forms which signify nothing, and represent nothing and remind us of nothing, which stir souls as deeply and powerfully as only the notes of music can.' Kandinsky's problem, for which he found solutions from 1912 onwards, was to find a way of creating a harmony in colour to parallel that in music.

These unadulterated colour forms were now no longer the expressions of emotion or feelings prompted by some stimulus, but instead corresponded to the inner accord between objects experienced within the soul of the artist; this was transformed and communicated to the observer with a kind of automation. Klee called this process 'psychic improvization'. The content of a painting was from now on the orchestration of colour and the rhythm of forms.

Delaunay in France, had reached similar conclusions. The First World War put an end to this development. Kandinsky returned to Russia, Jawlensky emigrated to Switzerland, Macke and Marc died in France.

In the Rheinland and Berlin

A smaller centre formed in the Rheinland which was important more for the diffusion and recognition of the new art than as a crucial contribution to it – although Macke, Campendonck, Nauen, Rohlfs and Morgner worked here, to name but a few. In 1902, Karl Ernst Osthaus had set up a museum in Hagen out of private means; this very quickly brought together an important collection of expressionist art and the work of precursors, thereby providing an example with lasting effects. In 1909 the Sezession of West German Artists and Art Lovers was founded, whose programme was to mount a joint exhibition of French and German art. This culminated in 1912 in the famous exhibition of the Sezessionists in Cologne which presented post-impressionist European art under the title *Expressionism* in a comprehensive way for the first time.

'Triumphant Expressionism' (Kandinsky), forced the spirit of academicism into retreat; it tried to make itself heard once more in 1911 in the *Protest of German Artists*, signed by numerous professors, which was directed against the supposedly exaggerated value set upon French art by German museum directors and art collectors.

The new art was also successful in the most important German art scene in Berlin. The Berlin *Sezession*, founded in 1898, admitted Barlach, Beckmann, Feininger, Kandinsky, Munch, Nolde and Rohlfs, but also Bonnard, Denis and Matisse as members, and provided opportunities for exhibition to the fauves, the *Die Brücke* group, and the members of the New Association of Artists. After Nolde's exclusion in 1910, a New Sezession formed where young artists gathered.

In the same year, Herwarth Walden had founded the weekly magazine *Der Sturm* (The Storm), a polemical organ of combat for the new literature and painting, which soon reached an astonishing circulation of 30,000 copies. In 1912 a gallery was attached to the newspaper and opened with the first exhibition of *Der Blaue Reiter* and Kokoschka. The Italian futurists contributed to the second exhibition. There followed exhibitions of French graphic art, 'French expressionism', Wouters and Ensor, Delaunay, Kandinsky, Macke, Marc, the Prague artists Filla and Gutfreund, to select but a few displays.

Walden never lost sight of the European sphere and the climax of activity in mounting exhibitions was the first German autumn *salon* of 1913, where he brought together works by eighty-five artists from twelve countries. Walden was an excellent organizer, who despite modest means, allowed numerous exhibitions to go on tour, not only in Germany but also in Scandinavia, London and Tokyo.

The Futurists

Italy's contribution to the revolt of the artistic youth of Europe became known in 1912 through the exhibitions of the futurists, who were to be found amongst other places in Paris, Berlin, Moscow and Madrid. Umberto Boccioni, Carlo Carrà, Luigi Russolo, Giacomo Balla and Gino Severini were the most important painters in this movement.

They had signed the Futurist Manifesto in 1910, which had been proclaimed in a Turin theatre in front of 3,000 people. Under the leadership of the poet Marinetti, an extremely radical art scene grew up which publicized its ideas at mass rallies.

Italian writers and painters felt humiliated that their country had fallen into artistic provincialism in the previous hundred years. Their national awareness, amounting to chauvinism, demanded, in the political sphere, a new empire, a hegemony to which they also laid claim in the field of art. The artistic imperative thus became a national issue which could only be resolved by means of a radical break with all tradition, through a cultural revolution. 'Italy has been a second-hand market long enough': these were Marinetti's words in his first Futurist Manifesto which was published in *Le Figaro* in 1909. 'We want to liberate it from the innumerable museums which cover it like innumerable cemeteries.'

Futurism, the art of the future, which was against tradition that stifled all creativity, was fascinated by the rhythm of modern city life, by the intoxication of speed and the machine.

'A racing car at speed is more beautiful than the Nike of Samothrace,' announced Marinetti, who saw the crucial criterion for artistic expression in the dynamism of modern civilization. Instead of the depiction of a static object, it mattered henceforth that through movement the world around us, the before and the after, should be able to be incorporated into the picture as essential constituents of the object's existence. The appearance of the object was extended by foreknowledge, by emotion and by memories into a complex reality, whose elements were depicted simultaneously. With the help of movement and simultaneity they succeeded in allowing the most disparate levels of reality to interpenetrate and to discover a new creative possibility in art which permitted them to portray the power of the streets and of life; the ambition and fear which one can see in the city; the feeling of apprehension engendered by its noise.

The futurists had begun with neo-impressionism and drawn on what the cubists had learnt for their analysis of the object; they in their turn, however, furnished a concept in the dynamism achieved through their analysis of movement – which continued to have an influence in France and Germany when 'classic' futurism had come to an end with the outbreak of war.

The Russian Contribution

Without the work of the Russian artists the art of *Der Blaue Reiter* would be inconceivable, and that of the Parisian scene the poorer. The evolution of Russian expressionism began in 1906 in Moscow with the founding of the joint association, The Skyblue Rose (Die Himmelblaue Rose), whose leading members were Michael Larionov, Natalia Goncharova and the Burliuk brothers. These artists had made their appearance the same year in the exhibition of Russian art in the Paris *Salon d'automne*. They developed their art in constant contact with Western Europe.

Modern French art in particular had been continuously present in Moscow since the fauve exhibition of 1907, not least through the large Morosov and Shchukin collections. In 1910 the Burliuks were already forming a futurist group. Nevertheless, the Russians did not consider themselves dependent but as kindred spirits, as they clearly stated in the almanach, *Der Blaue Reiter*. Rather, they cited as sources for their expressionist art, folk art, old church frescoes and paintings of the saints, knowledge which Kandinsky had also introduced into the *Der Blaue Reiter* circle. Larionov, especially, appropriated the naïve, lapidary gestures of popular art and formed 'primitivism' from it. The contacts with cubism and futurism led Larionov and Goncharova to Rayonism. In this, objects and figures were split into 'ray' diagrams, into colour bundles out of which purely abstract shapes were eventually formed.

Dissemination Throughout Europe

At the same moment, the Paris-domiciled Czech, František Kupka evolved rapidly, directly from neo-impressionism to pictures built up from colour alone without reference to any object. Czech art, of which the centre was Prague, sought to link itself with France, since France symbolized for these artists their opposition to the Austro-Hungarian monarchy. In 1907 and 1908, the group *Acht*, to which belonged the most important painters of the Czech avant-garde, Emil Filla, Bohumil Kubista and Antonin Prochazka, mounted exhibitions of works which had already absorbed the ideas of the fauves and the expressionists. The Prague artists fostered close contacts. They were part of the European scene; from 1911 onwards, they took part in all important exhibitions in Germany and organized others in which all the French avant-garde and *Die Brücke* painters participated.

Soon various groupings formed in Prague as a result of rifts; they started from very similar principles, but attacked each other violently over problems of theoretical interpretation and the creative evolution of cubism. However, the cubist method was in every case overlaid with expressionist emotiveness and fused with the native baroque tradition; with it a strong predilection for allegorical and visionary scenes created a quite specific cubo-expressionist style.

The Netherlands and Scandinavia who had pointed the way for European expressionism with Van Gogh, Ensor and Munch, were hardly touched inside their boundaries by these artistic developments at the beginning of the century; they did not produce any expressionist works until the 1920s and 1930s, when they are evoked by the names Fritz, Van Den Berghe, Constant Permeke, Albert Servaes, and Gustave de Smet.

In the rest of Europe, artistic goals had undergone a transformation as a result of the devastating consequences of the war. For the generation of artists born around 1880 who were now entering middle life, a youthful and revolutionary attitude was no longer credible. The visions they had derived from their exaltation palled before the horror of reality: the frenziedly intoxicated ego of the artist could not control his overwhelming and dreadful sensations, let alone conceive of form through intensified expression. The change in reality demanded greater tranquillity of form, required an object as a support for expression.

The younger generation in Germany, especially Dix, Grosz and Meidner, for whom expressionism meant revolution and an opening, pursued it as a concept for a short while longer. Nevertheless, the expressionist fervour which was used as a means to political action after the end of the war, had become hollow and exhausted itself in proclamations and exhortations. The expressionist gesture had become empty and degenerated into a mere curiosity.

'Expressionism has nothing to do any longer with the aspirations of active people,' announced the Dada Manifesto of 1918. And at the same time, Ludwig Meidner states: 'What matters for tomorrow, what is necessary for me and for others, is a fanatical and ardent naturalism, a passionately virile and unflinching veracity. We have to create great visions – how else can we do that but with the forms of the visible world?' This led to verisimilitude in the sense of Dix or Grosz.

The return to tangible reality could be achieved in other ways too – in the direction of Picasso's neo-classicism, or in the form of Derain's and the Italians' classical realism. Concern with the world of objects became the new artistic problem for the whole of Europe.

BALLA, Giacomo (Turin, 18.7.1871 – Rome, 1.3.1958). When the fourteen-year-old Balla moved to Rome with his mother, he had already worked on a lithographer's press and followed an art course at night school. In Rome he continued to educate himself. In 1899 he tried in vain to exhibit his work at the Biennale in Venice. In 1900 he went to Paris for several months where he was concerned above all with neo-impressionism. But he only came to grips with painting in Rome, where in 1901 he shared his experiments with Boccioni and Severini.

Divisionism moulded Balla's painting in the years that followed. In 1910 he was one of the signatories of the first Futurist Manifesto. He became one of the most important representatives of futurism, drew up numerous manifestoes and took part in most of the activities of the group. In 1912 he received a commission to execute some murals in the Düsseldorf house of the violinist Loewenstein, which helped him to develop a geometric, flat arrangement in his paintings.

At the same time he was intensively concerned with the analysis of motion, in order to make temporal sequence simultaneously visible by using superimposed images juxtaposed in space. Those lines of movement and energy were concentrated into whirling elliptic shapes, into abstract diagrams of motion, which exer-

BALLA, GIACOMO: *Little Girl Running Along a Balcony*. 1912.

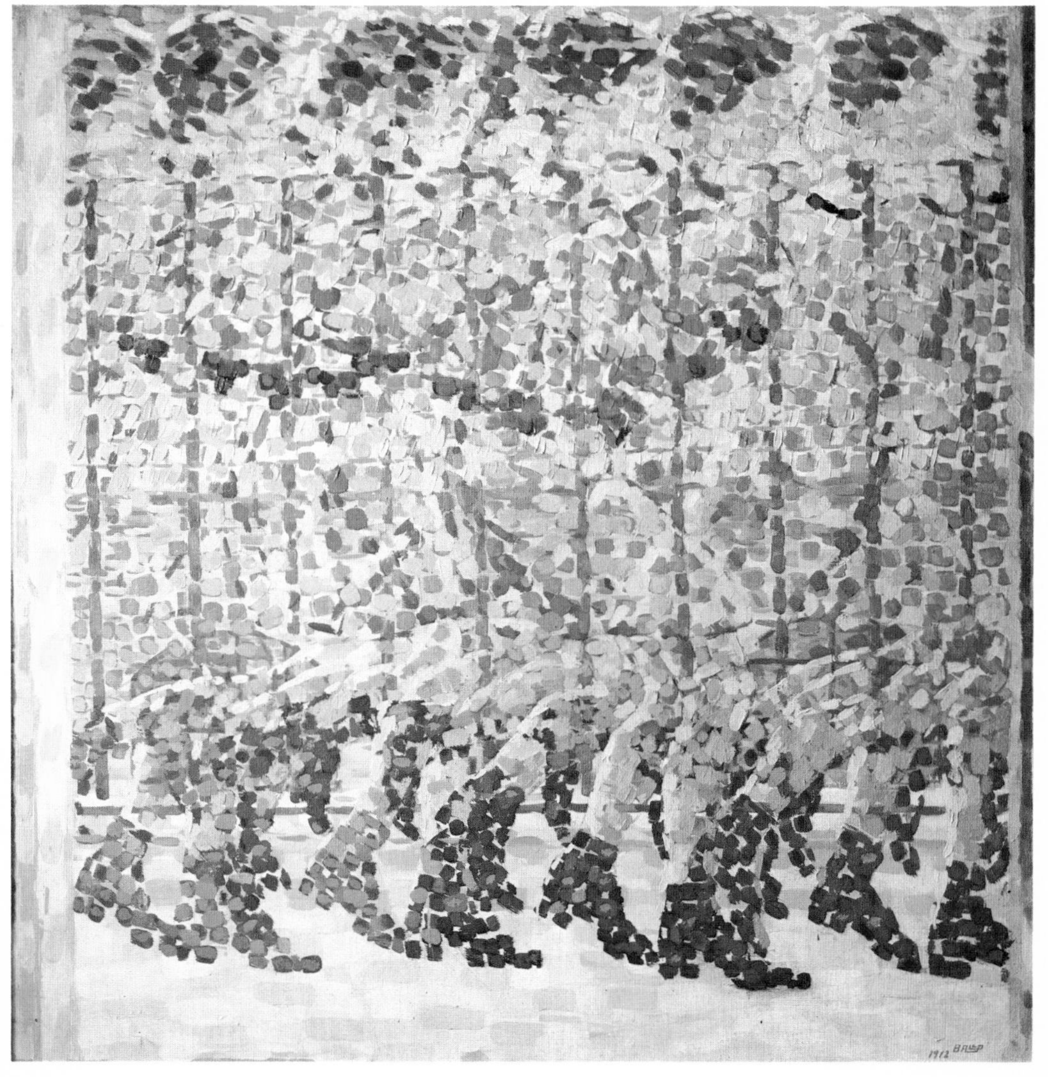

cised a powerful influence on the *Der Blaue Reiter* artists, especially Franz Marc. Balla progressed along this road beyond futurism into a world without objects.

BARLACH, Ernst (Wedel, Holstein, 2.1.1870 – Rostock, 1938). Barlach went to the Arts and Crafts School in Hamburg in 1888; in 1891 to Dresden Academy and pursued his studies in 1895–1896 in the Académie Julian in Paris, to which he returned in 1897. He then lived in Hamburg and Wedel, became a teacher at the technical school for ceramics in Höhr (Westerwald) and settled in Berlin in 1905. The experience which gave

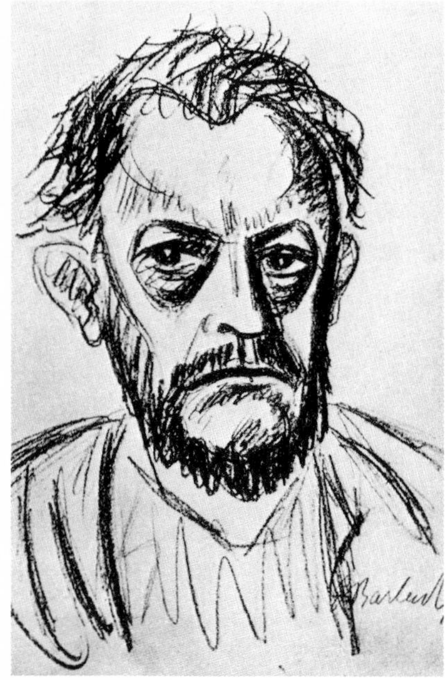

BARLACH, ERNST: *Self-portrait.* 1928.

self-revelation to Barlach, was a journey to Russia in 1906. There he found an opportunity as a sculptor to develop form into self-contained substance which could convey vision and expression. Russian beggars and farmers, whom he saw as symbols of human existence, comprised Barlach's favourite themes after his return. In them Barlach sought, as in his very last works, to embody the realization that the outer clothing of external reality must coincide at one point with the inner expression of its essence. The same motifs were frequently treated in the sculpture and graphic art of this period.

In 1907 Barlach signed a contract with the art dealer Paul Cassirer which relieved him from financial worry. In 1909 he was working in the Villa Romana in Florence. In 1912 Barlach's first play, *Der Tote Tag* (The

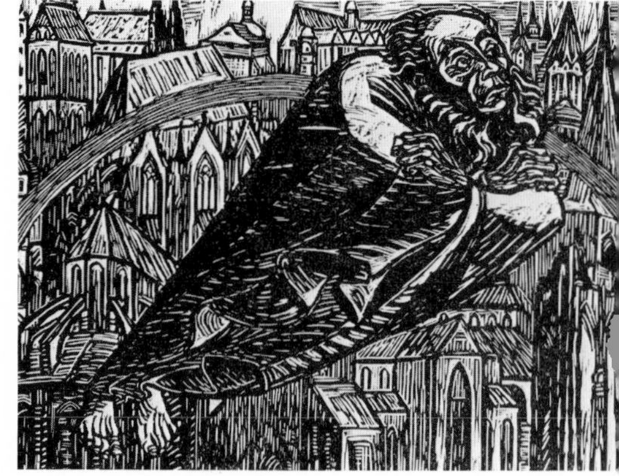

BARLACH, ERNST: *Cathedrals.* 1920.

Dead Day) was published by Bruno Cassirer, together with a series of lithographs. Although Barlach sought for expression and synthesis in his work, he rejected the contemporaneous endeavours of modern art in a similar direction. In 1910 he withdrew to Güstrow in Mecklenburg where in the years that followed, he produced ever more variations on the same themes, both in form and content, until in the end he became a self-plagiarist.

BARLACH, ERNST: *The Dog Catcher.* 1915.

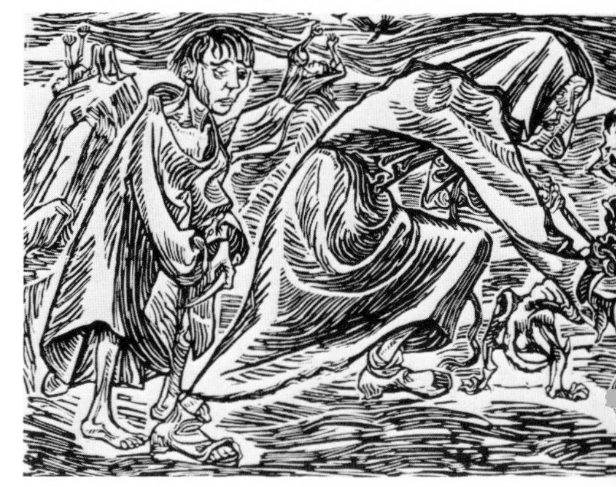

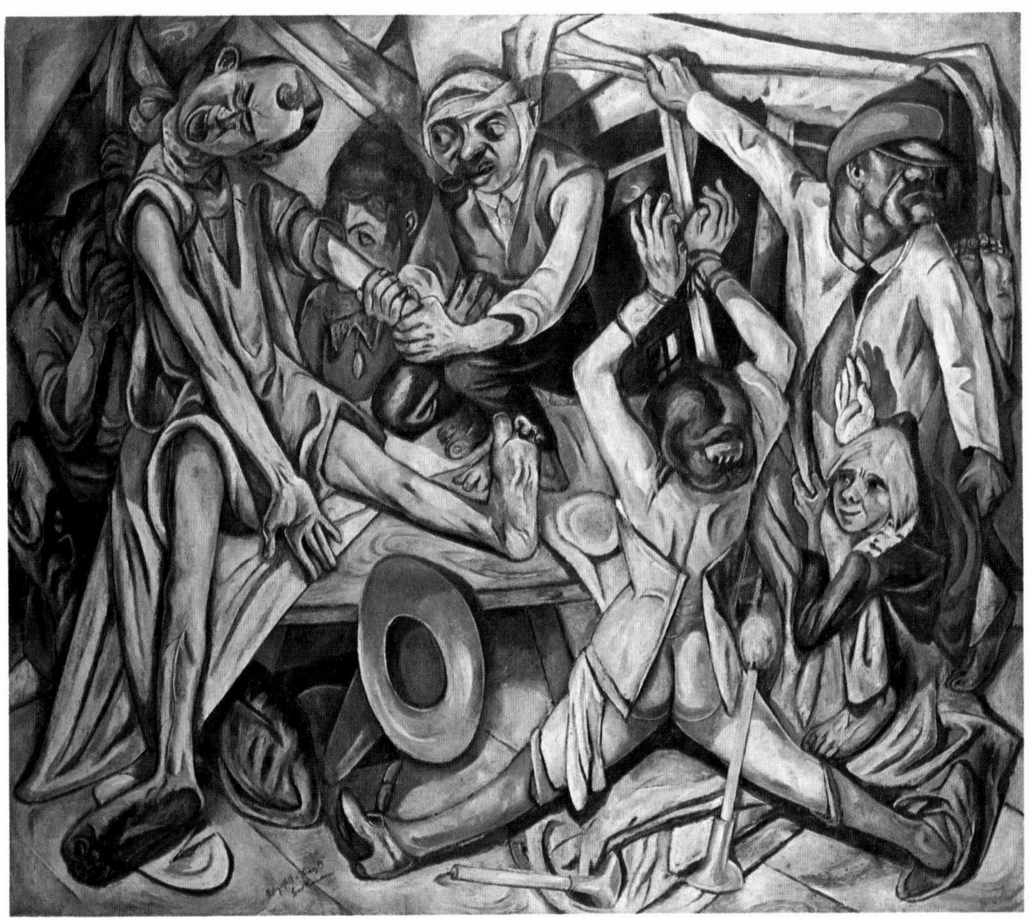

BECKMANN, MAX: *Night.* 1918–1919.

BECKMANN, Max (Leipzig, 12.2.1884– New York 27.12.1950). For a long time, Beckmann remained opposed to the artistic problems of his generation; even in 1912 he carried on a polemic against modern art with Franz Marc in the journal *Pan*. He avoided the radical rejuvenation of form and sought instead to get to 'the root of nature and the soul of things', with a conscious continuation of tradition.

Beckmann went to the Weimar Academy in 1900 where he received a thorough education. In 1903 he left the Academy and went to Paris for six months where he was decisively influenced by Manet and the impressionists, but also discovered Cézanne for himself. From 1904 onwards, he was resident in Berlin. He won the Villa Romana prize, and with it a period of study in Florence, with a large composition of figures shown in 1896 at an exhibition mounted by the artists' union in Weimar. In Berlin Beckmann became a member of the Sezession and in 1910 was elected to their committee.

He sought to express the drama of his time with the methods of history painting and portrayed battles and scenes from the Old and New Testaments on large canvasses, but also drew on current events. He also provided landscapes and portraits in small format. By 1913 he was an artist known far and wide who had already had a monograph, with a catalogue of his works, devoted to him.

But Beckmann himself was well aware that his methods were not suited to 'express the spirit of things.' On the outbreak of war in 1914, he volunteered for the medical service and went to Flanders where he met Heckel. In the proximity to horror and death, Beckmann found himself. In 1915 he suffered a physical and nervous breakdown, was discharged and moved from Berlin to Frankfurt. Beckmann now tried to exorcise fear, torment and loneliness, 'The immeasurable solitude in eternity: to experience the extremities of emotion is already to create form. Form is salvation.'

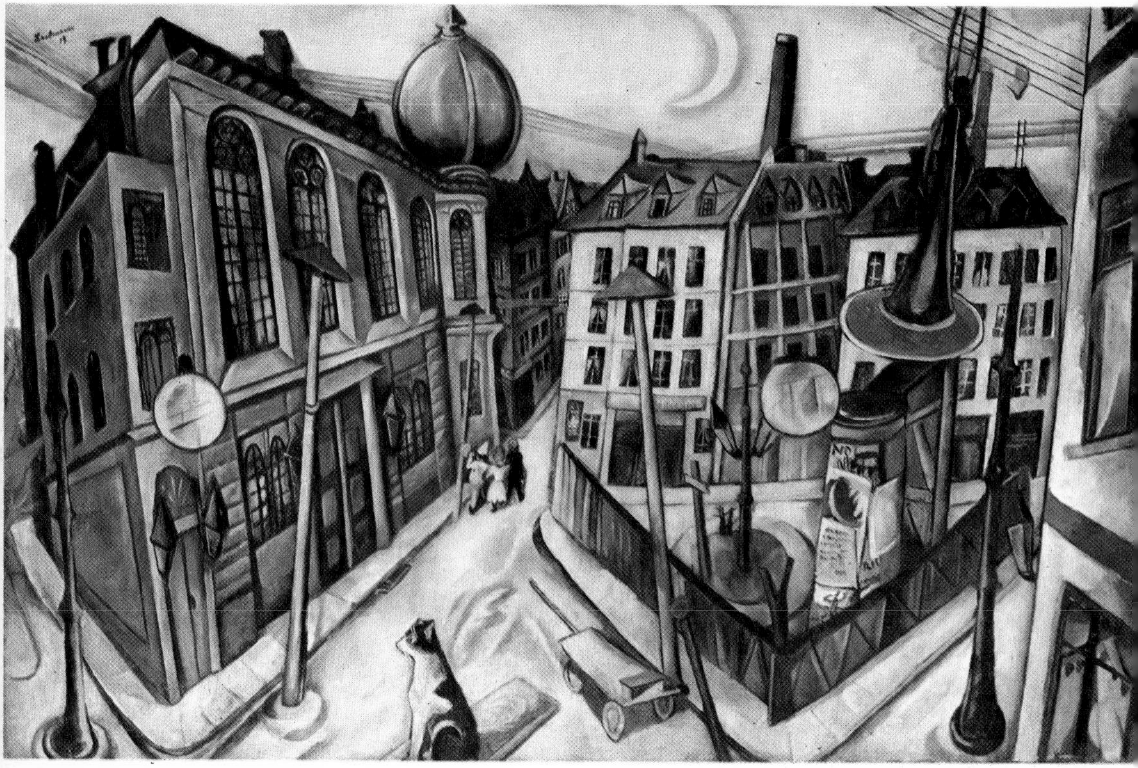

BECKMANN, MAX: *The Synagogue.* 1919.

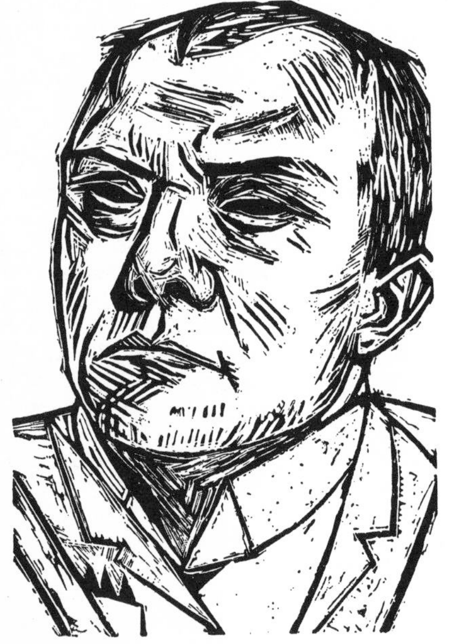

BECKMANN, MAX: *Self-portrait.* 1922.

BECKMANN, MAX: *Tabarin.*

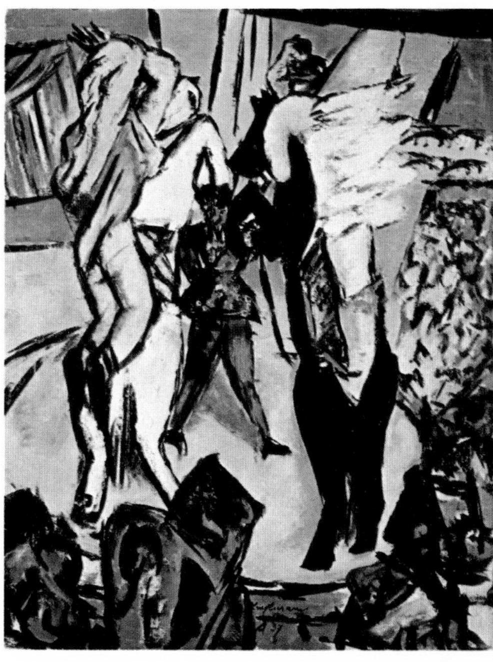

The pictures he now produced were built up from the drawn line into angular shapes which fill the whole field of vision – colour was reduced to local colour. Beckmann could only bear life by conceiving of it as one scene in the theatre of eternity. He gained the objectivity to be able to depict the world as a grotesque, and joyless farce. Distance and a rigid arrangement in his paintings were the means by which Beckmann succeeded in controlling the pressures of emotion from 1922 onwards, in going beyond the phase of his art which had been concerned purely with expression.

BECKMANN, MAX: *Descent from the Cross.* 1917.

BERGHE, Frits Van Den (Ghent, 3.4.1883 – Ghent, 23.9.1939). From 1897 to 1904 Frits van den Berghe attended the Academy in Ghent where Albert Servaes was his fellow pupil and friend. In 1904 he entered the artists' community in Laetham Saint Martin, where he shared a studio with Servaes. Van den Berghe painted in an impressionist manner, like his friends, Servaes, de Smet and Permeke and retained this style until 1916. From 1907 to 1911 he taught painting technique in the Ghent Academy. In 1914 he went to America, was taken unawares by the outbreak of war and went to Holland where he remained until 1922 apart from short intervals. In Holland he often collaborated with de Smet, and later with Permeke. From 1917 onwards he produced expressionist paintings, built up from thick spontaneously applied colour.

Like de Smet and Permeke, he was stimulated by the work of the cubist painter Le Fauconnier, and developed a style of angular surface divisions, and rather matt red and brown tones, with which he achieved an expression of unity.

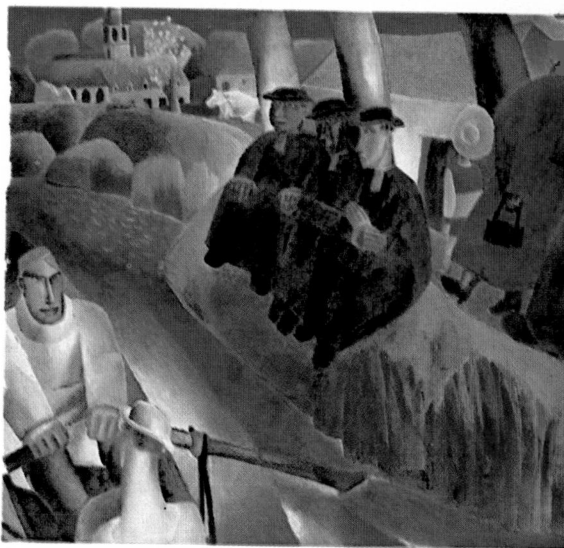

BERGHE, FRITS VAN DEN: *Sunday.* 1923.

BOCCIONI, Umberto (Reggio di Calabria, 19.10.1882 – Verona, 16.8.1916). From 1898 onwards Boccioni lived in Rome where he first worked with a poster painter, and attended life-classes at the Academy. In 1900 he made the acquaintance of Severini with whom he worked in 1907 in Balla's studio and from whom he gained a knowledge of neo-impressionism. In 1902 he went for the first time to Paris, and in 1904 to Russia. He spent 1906–1908 in Padua and Venice before settling in Milan. Here he worked as a commercial artist and illustrator. In 1909 he met Marinetti at whose instigation Boccioni, Carrà and Russolo composed the first Futurist Manifesto, published in 1910. In the same year, Boccioni mounted his first solo exhibition in Venice.

In 1911 he again visited Paris, where Severini introduced him to Picasso, Braque and the cubist circle. Boccioni not only participated in the activities of the futurists, but being the greatest talent of the circle, he was one of its driving forces. Thus he was fundamental in contributing to the theoretical formulation of their goals and to their artistic application. Amongst other

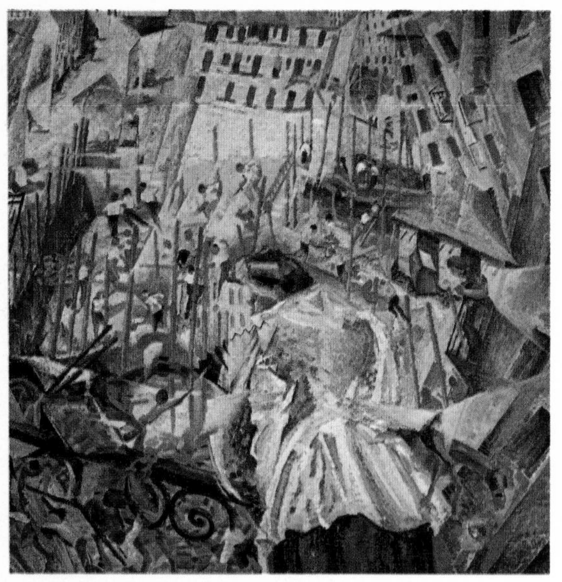

BOCCIONI, UMBERTO: *Street Noise.* 1911.

things, he drew up in 1912, the *Technical Manifesto of Futurist Sculpture*. In 1913 other practical results of these reflections were already being exhibited. In 1915, Boccioni volunteered for military service.

Boccioni, who wished to paint 'the fruits of our industrial age', began in 1909 with depictions of suburban districts, scarred by industry. In 1910 he extended these themes in scenes of moving events and thus realized in painting the futurists' demand for representation of dynamism and motion.

His prismatic dissection of colour also became more intensely expressive. The decomposition of form, gained from cubism was employed as a means of creating vibrancy and lines of energy, through which states of excitement and emotional moods could be conveyed. The reduction of objects, bodies and events to dynamic lines, led Boccioni in 1911 to the brink of abstract painting. However, the power of his imagination in the plastic arts that, as above, had already been realized in sculptures in 1913, required an object as its starting point. His death – he died in 1916 after a riding accident – marked the end of futurism.

BOCCIONI, UMBERTO: *Dynamism: a cyclist.* 1913.

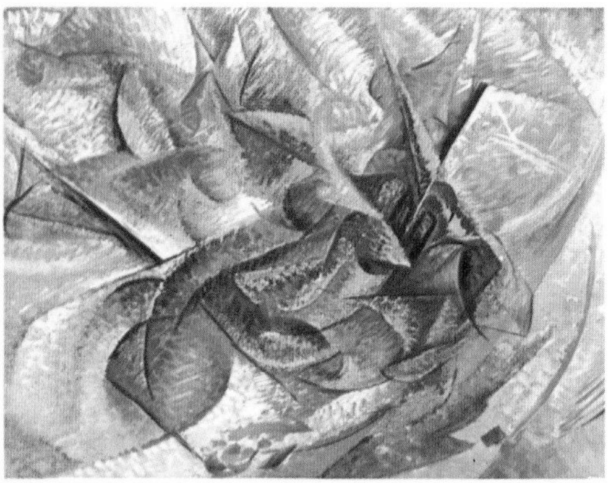

BRAQUE, Georges (Argenteuil, 13.5.1882 – Paris, 31.8.1963). Braque came from a family of interior decorators, who also tried their hand as 'Sunday' painters. In 1890, the family moved to Le Havre. Here the fifteen-year-old Braque attended night classes in the municipal art school and became friendly with Dufy and Friesz. In 1897 he began his training as an interior decorator, which he continued in Paris in 1900. Here too, he attended night classes. After exemption from military service, he entered the Académie Humbert, where he made friends with Marie Laurencin and Francis Picabia. Like the majority of this generation of painters, he learnt through frequent visits to the Louvre. He was especially interested in Egyptian and Greek sculpture, as well as Poussin and Corot. In 1903 he went to the Ecole des Arts, where he again met Dufy and Friesz. However, he returned to the Académie Humbert after only two months. From 1904 onwards he worked by himself. He practised a bland sort of impressionism reminiscent of Corot and early Monet, until the fauve

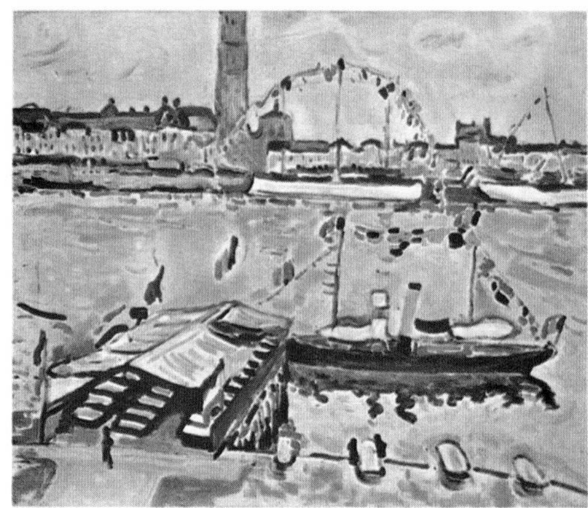

BRAQUE, GEORGES: *Antwerp: Ships with flags.* 1905.

exhibition at the 1905 *Salon d'automne* opened his eyes.

In 1906 he painted fauve landscapes in Antwerp with Friesz. Although he showed Braque the practical possibilities of pure colour, Braque's painting remained cool and less spontaneous. Only the landscape of the South, which he experienced at L'Estaque in 1906, enlivened his palette. When he exhibited six paintings in 1907 in the *Salon des indépendants* with Friesz, every one was sold. Strengthened by this success, he returned with Friesz the same year to La Ciotat and l'Estaque.

The paintings which he now produced, distanced themselves from the subject matter; the lines turned into arabesques which were less important for expression than for structure. Instead of pure colours, he preferred segmented shades. In 1907 the art dealer Kahnweiler signed an agreement with Braque, taking charge of all his work. Braque saw the Cézanne exhibition in the *Salon d'automne*, an experience which gave his own art a new orientation. He met the poet Apollinaire at the exhibition, who introduced him to Picasso. After less than two years, Braque broke away from fauvism, which he had perfected in some twenty paintings. When he painted with Dufy at L'Estaque in 1908 he was already building up his surfaces from geometric forms. The road towards cubism had begun.

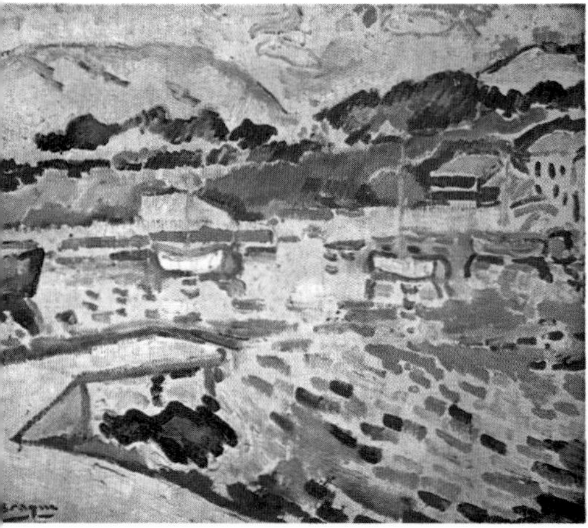

BRAQUE, GEORGES: *The Quay at Estaque.* 1906.

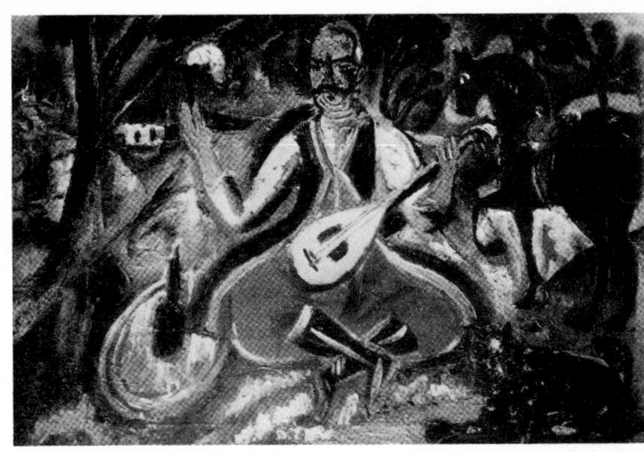

BURLIUK, DAVID: *My ancestor the Cossack.* Circa 1908

BURLIUK, David (Ryabuchky, near Kharkov, 22.8.1882 – Southampton, New York, 15.1.1967). David Burliuk and his younger brother, Vladimir, born on 15th March 1886 at Cherson, killed 1917 near Salonika, were inseparable and were to be found together from their first training at art college in Kazan. In 1903, they went to Munich and became pupils of Azbe. In 1904–1905 they visited Paris and worked in Cormon's studio at the Ecole des Beaux-Arts. In 1907 they organized the first exhibition of the Russian avant-garde in Moscow, together with Larionov and Goncharova. Further exhibitions and the foundation of various circles of artists and writers quickly followed. In 1910 they met Kandinsky in Odessa and from then on they participated in the exhibitions of the New Association of Artists in Munich and *Der Blaue Reiter*, in whose publications they were the spokesmen of modern Russian art. From 1911 on, David was the leader of the futurism movement in Russia, until he left his homeland in 1918 and went to the United States via Japan.

CAMOIN, Charles (Marseilles, 23.9.1879 – Paris, 20.5.1965). Camoin, whose father ran a painting and decorating business, attended commercial school in Marseilles from 1895 on, and at the same time night classes at the Ecole des Beaux Arts in Moreau's studio, where he made friends with Matisse, Marquet and Puy. In 1900 he did his military service at Arles and painted there under the influence of Van Gogh. In 1902 he met Cézanne in Aix-en-Provence, and corresponded until Cézanne's death. In 1903 he visited Monet. The same year he exhibited for the first time in the *Salon des indépendants*. In 1904–1905 he worked with Marquet at Chassis and St Tropez; in 1905 he took part in the exhibition from which the fauves got their name. In 1907 he went to London with Marquet and Friesz; in 1906 he had his first solo exhibition in Kahnweiler's

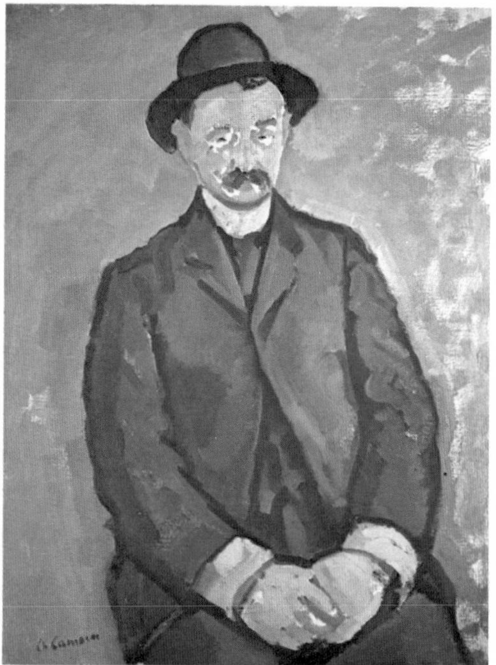

CAMOIN, CHARLES: *Portrait of Albert Marquet.* 1904.

gallery. In 1910 he exhibited in Frankfurt for Scham. In 1912 he went with Matisse and Marquet to Tangiers. Camoin never thought of himself as a fauve. He was a colourist, full of optimism and the joy of living, who remained bound to the external appearance of the world.

CAMPENDONK, Heinrich (Krefeld, 3.11.1889 – Amsterdam, 9.5.1957). In 1905 Campendonk came to Jan Thorn Prikker at the arts and crafts school in Krefeld with the intention of becoming a pattern designer, for the textile industry. He stayed intil 1909, then turned to painting and together with Helmut Macke, the cousin of August, he set up a joint studio in 1910. In 1911 he got to know Franz Marc who invited him to come to Upper Bavaria. Campendonk responded to this request and became closely associated with Marc. He took part in the first *Der Blaue Reiter* exhibition in 1911 and in 1913 exhibited at the German autumn *salon* in Berlin. His membership of *Der Blaue Reiter* was decisive for his artistic development; following Marc, he tried to depict a great chain of being with the art of freely applied expressive colour; but could not get beyond a decorative fairy-tale world, whose story-telling quality was intensified even more by the influence of Chagall, whom Campendonk had met in Berlin in 1914.

CARRÀ, Carlo (Quargnento, Alexandria, 11.2.1881 – Milan, 13.4.1966). Carrà was an interior decorator and had to earn his living thus from twelve years old. In 1895 he went to Milan where he attended night school in Brera, while continuing to ply his trade. In 1889 he went to Paris, attracted by the possibility of finding work in the construction of the World Fair, and at the same time getting to know French art. The impressionists, Cézanne and Gauguin interested him the most. In 1900 he journeyed to London where he discovered Turner and Constable for himself before returning to Milan. In 1903 he abandoned his livelihood and from then on attended the art and craft school in Castello Sforzesco. In 1906 he entered Brera Academy. Here Cesare Tellone became his teacher, who drew him towards neo-impressionism. After Carrà had met Boccioni at an exhibition in 1908, he met Marinetti in 1909. Together with Boccioni and Russolo, Carrà drew up the first Futurist Manifesto, published in 1910. From 1915 he took part in the futurists' exhibitions and activities. In 1911, 1912 and 1914 he again went to Paris where he moved in cubist circles. This contact with French art led him, for his temperament inclined towards heavy austere forms, to an early break with futurism; he was already interested in Giotto and Uccello in 1913; in 1916 during his military service he met de Chirico in Ferrara. Under his influence, Carrà developed towards *pittura metafisica* (metaphysical painting), with which he was to evolve his personal style.

CAMPENDONK, HEINRICH: *The Balcony.* 1913.

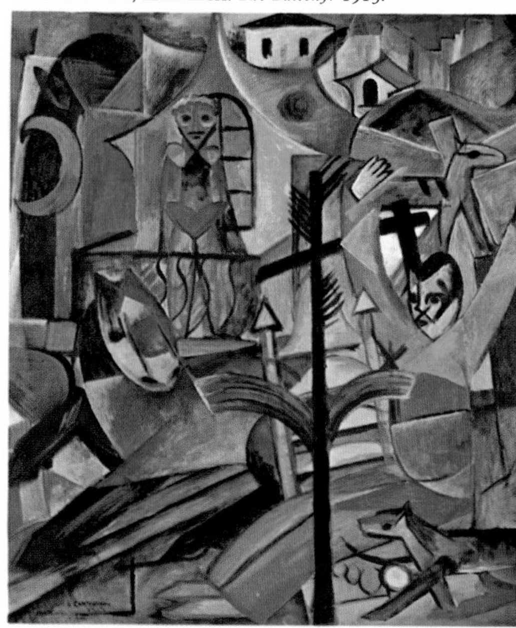

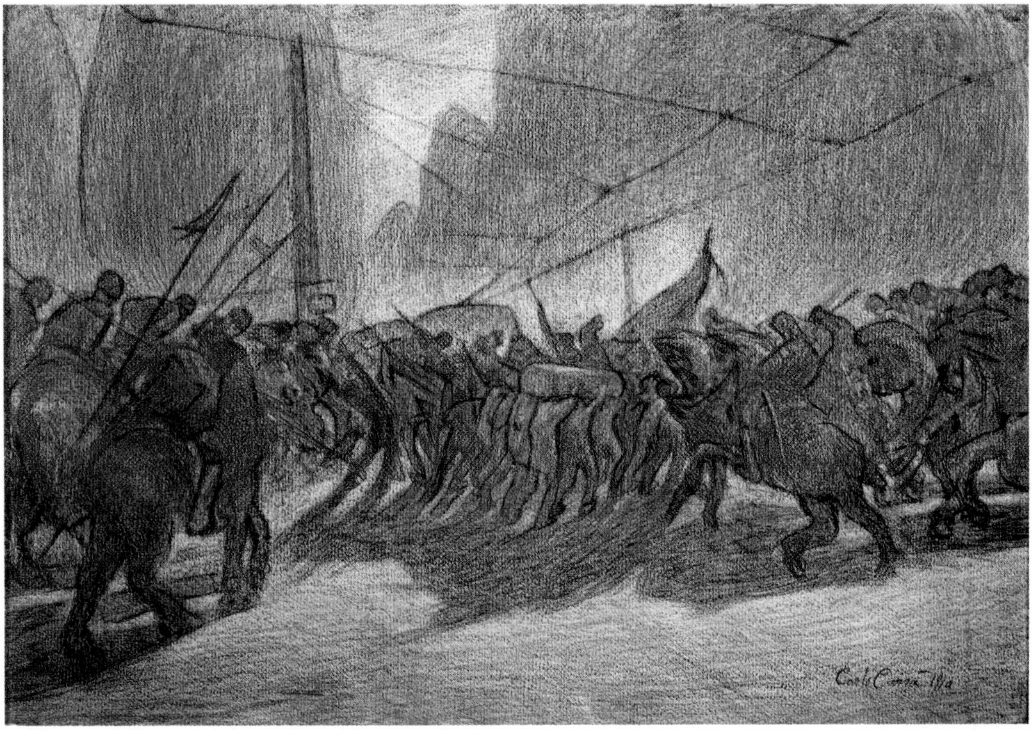

CARRÀ, CARLO: *Study for the funeral of the anarchist Galli.* 1910.

CHAGALL, MARC: *The village and I.* 1911.

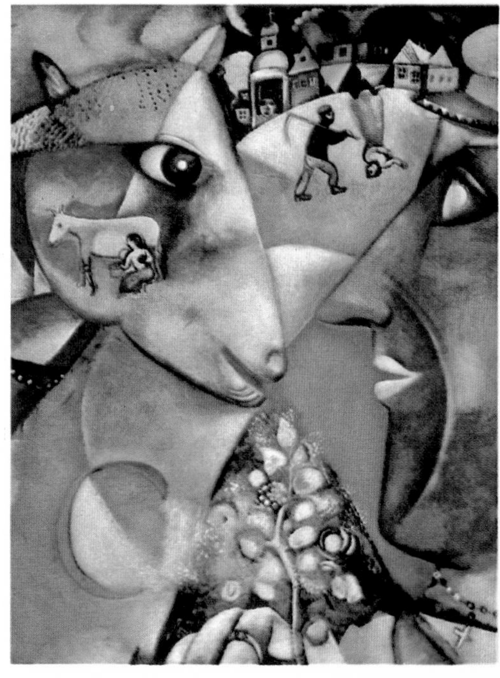

CHAGALL, Marc (Vitebsk, 7.7.1887). Chagall grew up in a poor and numerous family. This single life, in a strict Jewish background provided him with that deeply religious spirit which, together with his memories of village life, was to determine his whole work. In 1906 he began his artistic training in Vitebsk with Jehuda Pen and in 1907 went to the school run by the Imperial Society for the Promotion of the Arts in St Petersburg. In 1908 he changed to the Swansewa School where Leon Bakst became his teacher and acquainted him with the work of Cézanne, Van Gogh and Gauguin.

In 1910 a small grant enabled Chagall to travel to Paris. Under the influence of the fauves he achieved a powerful and expressive colour technique. In 1911 he became associated with Léger, Delaunay, Gleizes, and Modigliani, amongst others, and began to steep himself in cubism. Delaunay's colouring, which aimed at abstraction, and his principle of simultaneity, were particularly helpful to Chagall in how he brought together various inner experiences and memories in a complex picture. In 1911 he exhibited in the *Salon des indépendants* for the first time, and in 1912 in the *Salon d'automne*.

Chagall became friendly with the poet Cendrars who often provided the titles for Chagall's fantastic scenes. In 1913 he met Apollinaire and Walden, who mounted Chagall's first solo exhibition in 1914 in the Berlin Stürm gallery. Chagall's art, which strove less towards form than towards the direct transposition of inner experience, linked him with the efforts of German expressionism.

In 1914 Chagall went to Vitebsk via Berlin. The outbreak of war prevented his return to Paris. He replenished the reservoir of his memories in Russia and painted with a close relationship to reality but without abandoning the cubist division of the picture surface. After the outbreak of the October Revolution in 1917, he was appointed commissar for the arts in the province of Vitebsk and founded an art gallery of which he became director. After disagreements with Malevich he resigned in 1920 and left Russia in 1922 to return to Paris.

CHAGALL, MARC: *Sabbath.* 1909.

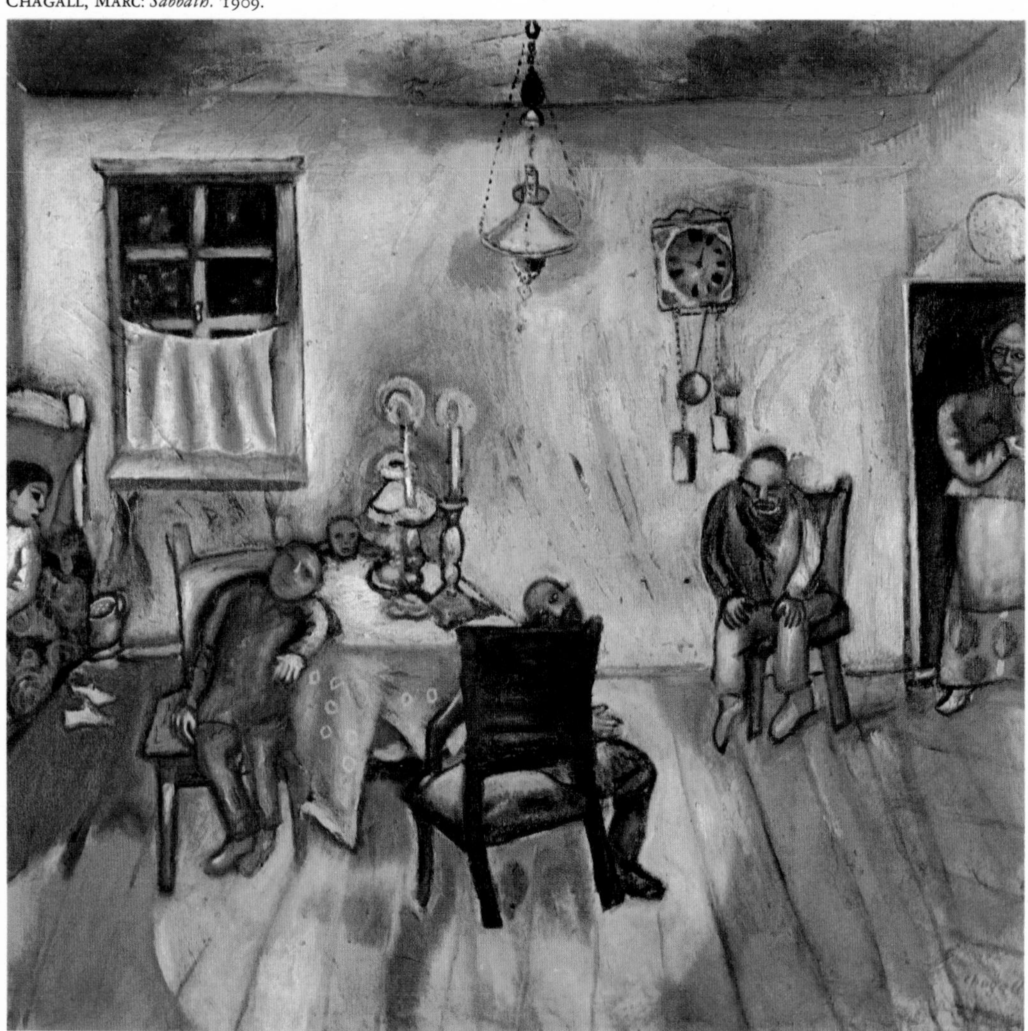

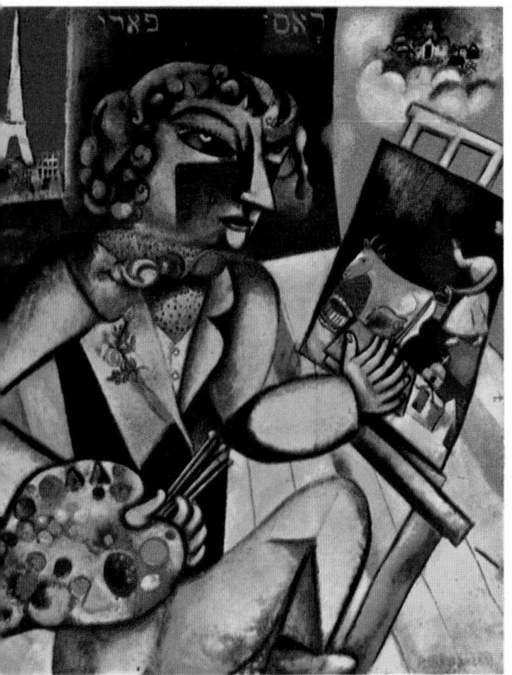

CHAGALL, MARC: *Self-portrait with seven fingers.* 1911.

CORINTH, Lovis (Tapiau, East Prussia, 21.7.1858 – Zandvoort, Holland, 17.7.1925). In the last decade of his life, the world became transparent for Lovis Corinth. In 1911 he had suffered a stroke, the consequences of which were a constant reminder of the proximity of death. Corinth's vigorous, sometimes violent painting had already gone beyond the limits of *plein-air* painting. The man who had taught the expressionist generation – Macke had been one of his pupils – now realized that a picture should reflect not the reality of nature, but the reality of the painter. Admittedly, he still needed the visual experience as the cause and point of departure for his work. However, he intensified colour to express personal feeling, made his application of it more dramatic and created from it expressive visions comparable to those of Nolde, Kokoschka and Beckmann.

CORINTH, LOVIS: *Self-portrait.* 1924.

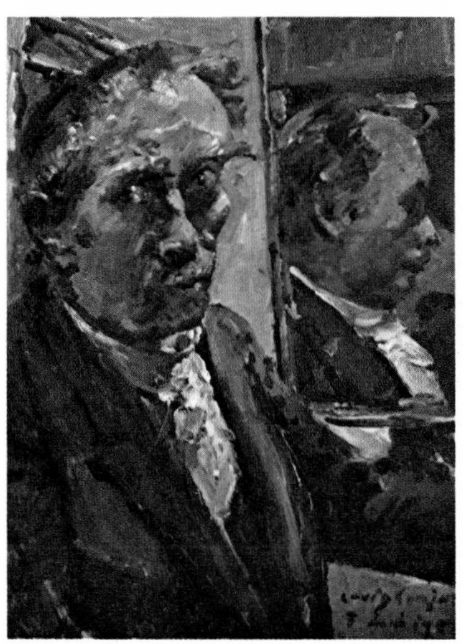

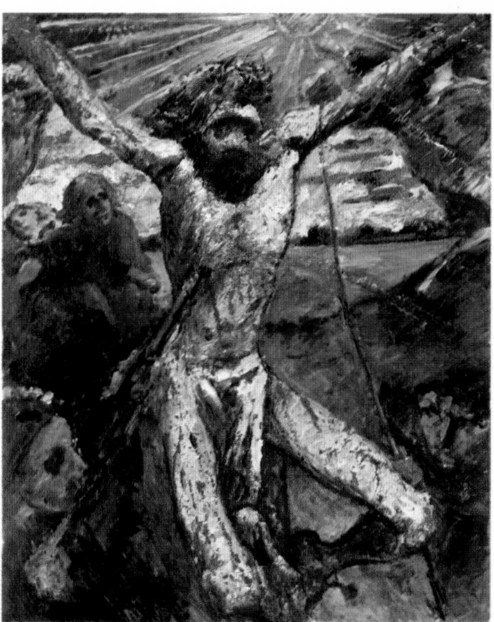

CORINTH, LOVIS: *Red Christ.* 1922.

DELAUNAY, Robert (Paris, 12.4.1885 – Montpellier, 25.8.1941). Delaunay was brought up by an uncle who was a landowner and painter at the Academy. In 1902 his family exempted him from further schooling and he joined a studio which made theatrical scenery in Belleville. In 1904 he went to Brittany and painted his first landscapes in an impressionist style.

His intuitive handling of colour was given full rein in 1905 with his acquaintance with neo-impressionism, which led him to fauvism. In 1906 he made friends with Metzinger, and met Henri Rousseau in 1907. In 1908, under the influence of Cézanne's art, he achieved a

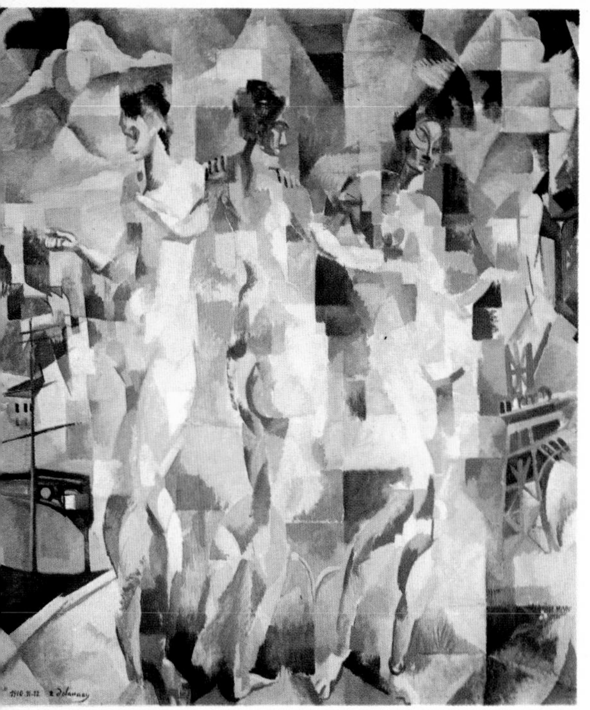

DELAUNAY, ROBERT: *The City of Paris.* 1910–1912. Detail.

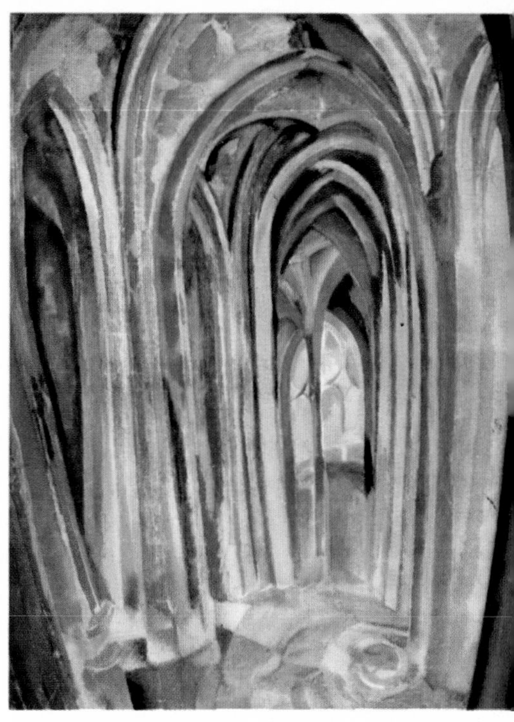

DELAUNAY, ROBERT *Saint-Séverin.* 1908.

geometric simplicity and modelling via colour that brought him close to cubism.

However, Delaunay was interested above all in the problems of rhythm and the dynamic movement of colour. As a result, the first series of paintings on the theme *Saint-Séverin* appeared in 1909, in which dynamism of expression was achieved by means of distortion. It is precisely these pictures, which became known in Germany in 1911, that influenced German expressionism right into the films of the 1920s.

In 1910 Delaunay began the series *The Eiffel Tower*. To emphasize the movement in the colours, the form is splintered and moulded into an expressionist vision. In the same year he married Sonia Terk. In 1911 he took part in the first exhibition of *Der Blaue Reiter* in Munich whose members were personally and artistically close to him in the following years. Delaunay met Apollinaire, Le Fauconnier and Gleizes.

In 1912, Delaunay reduced the forms of objects in order to create rhythm and movement from colour alone. His pictures, whose themes are scarcely recognizable any more, were built up from transparent layers of contrasted colour. Delaunay, who had taken his subject matter from the modern world – airships, aeroplanes, the Eiffel Tower, football – arrived, after 1912, at a purely abstract solution in his 'disc' pictures where contrasting colours are arranged in circles. In 1913 he travelled with Apollinaire to Berlin where two large collective exhibitions were mounted.

DELAUNAY-TERK, Sonia (Ukraine, 14.11.1885). From 1890 Sonia grew up in St Petersburg and began her artistic training there. In 1903 she went to Karlsruhe and completed two years' drawing study, which she continued in Paris in 1905 at the *Académie de la Palette*. Here she met Ozenfant and Dunoyer de Segonzac. Under the influence of Van Gogh and Gauguin she sought her own mode of expression through pure colour, and drew closer to Fauvism. In 1906 and 1907 she painted in Finland. In 1908 she married the German writer and art collector, Wilhelm Uhde, in whose gallery she mounted an exhibition in 1908. In 1907 she had met Delaunay for the first time, and had decided in 1909 to live and work with him. She married him in 1910 and came under his artistic influence. She practised their abstract-geometric style not only in painting but also with great success in the applied arts. She designed tapestries, bookbindings, furniture, interiors and clothes. She was nevertheless esteemed as an artist in her own right from the outset. In the first German autumn *salon* in 1913 in Berlin, she was represented by twenty works.

DERAIN, André (Chatou, 10.6.1880 – Chambourcy, 8.9.1954). Derain's parents wanted him to become an officer or an engineer. He attended the *Lycée Chaptal* in Paris and then the *École des Mines*. As a fifteen-year-old he had already received some artistic training from a painter living in Chatou. He was thus introduced to landscape painting which was later to constitute his favourite field. From 1898–1900 he attended the *Académie Carrière*, where he met Matisse.

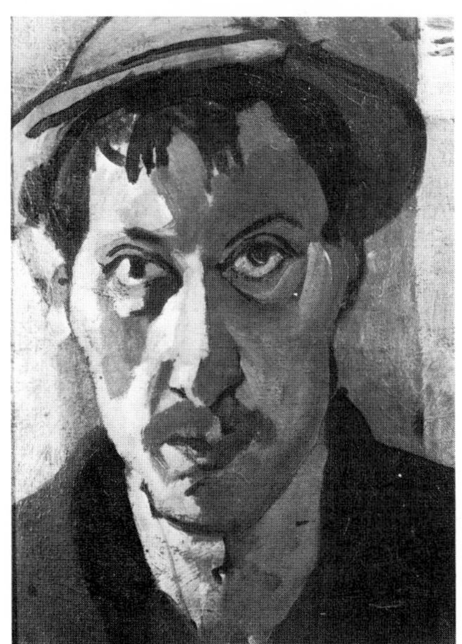

DERAIN, ANDRÉ: *Self-portrait in a Floppy Hat.* 1905.

But his meeting with Vlaminck was more important for him. They set up a studio together in Chatou. Vlaminck's enthusiasm urged Derain to use pure colour as a means of expression. In 1901 the Beckheim-Jeune Gallery mounted a Van Gogh exhibition which made a

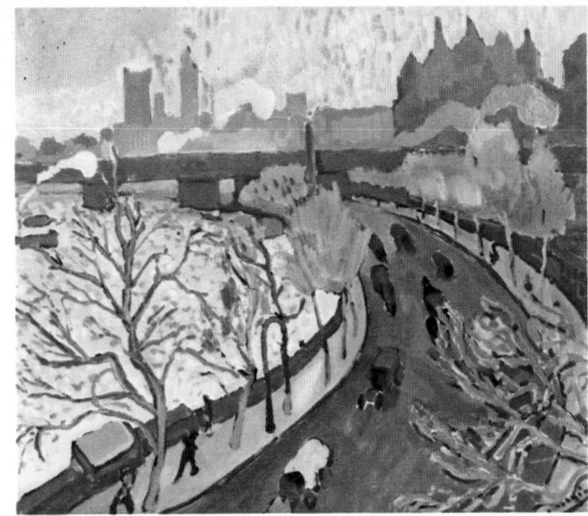

DERAIN, ANDRÉ: *Westminster Bridge.* 1905.

deep impression on Derain. He barely had time, however, to react to these stimuli since he had to do his military service from 1901 to 1904. On his return he

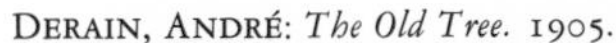

DERAIN, ANDRÉ: *The Old Tree.* 1905.

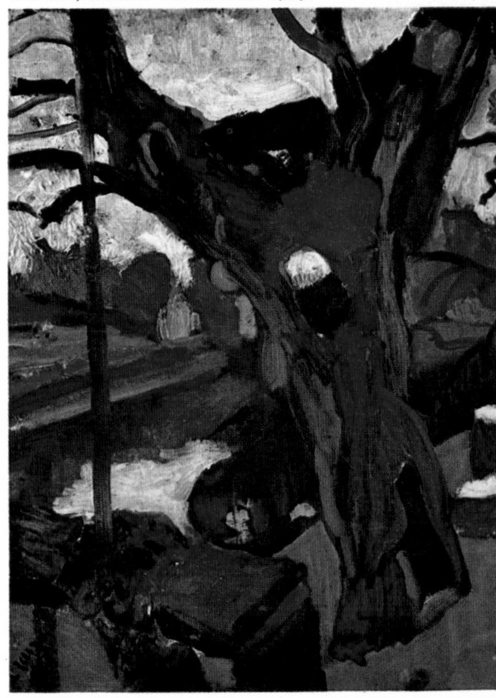

followed the example of Matisse with whom he painted in Collioure in the summer of 1905. Derain was familiar with Van Gogh and neo-impressionism as mentioned previously, and so it only needed a few hints for him to discover intuitively from these precepts a harmonious and decorative mode of expression for his landscape. He showed such pictures in the *Salon d'automne* in 1905. In 1905 and 1906 he went to London; in the summer of 1906 he painted in l'Estaque. His colours were now assembled over large areas and had stronger contours. He was seeking a way from emotion to formal structure. In 1907 he made friends with Picasso and signed a contract with the Kahnweiler Gallery.

In 1909 he painted with Braque in Carrière-Saint-Denis; in 1910 with Picasso in Cadaquès. For Derain this marked his estrangement from fauvism and a turning towards reduced colour. Derain nevertheless followed his friends a little way along the road to cubism admittedly, by carrying the refraction of light, and simplification of volumes beyond Cézanne, but he remained faithful to a continuity of surface.

DIX, OTTO: *Self-portrait as a soldier.* 1914.

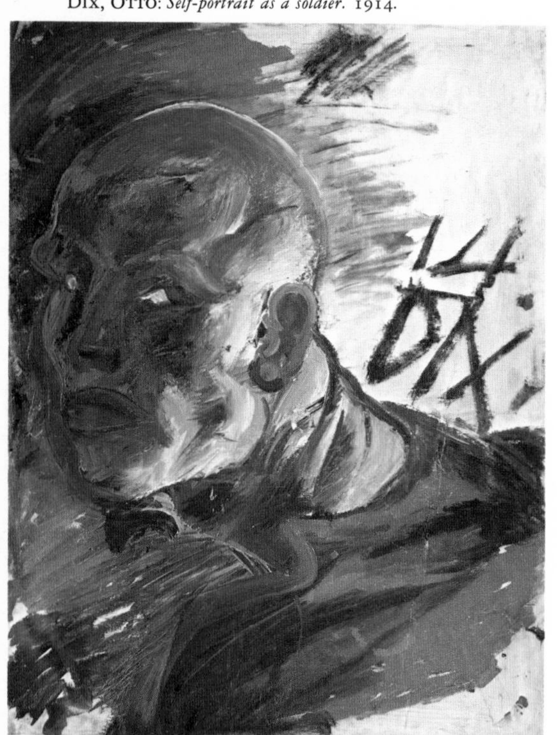

DIX, Otto (Untermhaus, Thuringia, 2.12.1891 – Singen, 25.7.1969). Dix began with an apprenticeship as an interior decorator in Gera from 1905–1909. In 1910 he went to Dresden, the centre of expressionism, to study at the art and craft school. He stayed there until 1914 and gained inspiration from *Die Brücke*, *Der Blaue Reiter* and futurism. In 1913 he was deeply impressed by a Van Gogh exhibition which was directly assimilated into his work.

At the outbreak of war, Dix volunteered for military service. He wanted to witness the end of an epoch and the downfall of bourgeois society, which so many artists hoped from the war. He now painted soldiers in heightened, expressionist colours, and depicted himself as Mars. He captured these apocalyptic events in innumerable drawings and gouaches, not merely recording, but transforming them into ecstatic, expressive visions. These forms, which seem to split asunder of their own accord, and the aggressive rhythms in the lines, are not formulations of an artistic problem, but rather the only possible means of simultaneously portraying these great and earthshattering events that changed the world. It has therefore been rightly said that the aim of the futurists reached its climax in Dix's war paintings.

In 1919 Dix continued his studies at Dresden Academy and became a founder-member of the '19 Group, whose goal was to 'search for a new expression for the new world that surrounds us.' Dix's work continued to revolve around his war experiences. However, heightened emotion evaporated when confronted by the knowledge that only evil and horror had triumphed. This was the new truth which had to be faced objectively and soberly. In order to overcome it, Dix turned to verisimilitude.

DONGEN, Kees van (Delfshaven, near Rotterdam, 26.1.1877 – Monaco, 1968). Van Dongen came to Paris in 1897. He had previously attended a school for the applied arts, in order to become an industrial designer, but his sensuous temperament was more suited to painting. In 1895 he went to America as a ship's steward and worked as an illustrator for the *Rotterdam Nieusblad*. He then earned his living in Paris. He also illustrated several magazines, among others, the *Assiette au Beurre*. He modelled his drawing technique on Steinlen, Forain and Toulouse-Lautrec. In 1905 he set up a studio in the Bateau-Lavoir and became Picasso's neighbour.

Like all the painters who later turned to fauvism, Van Dongen went through an impressionist stage, during which he produced mainly landscapes. These were characterized by lurid colours and free composition, built up from heavy brushstrokes inspired by Van

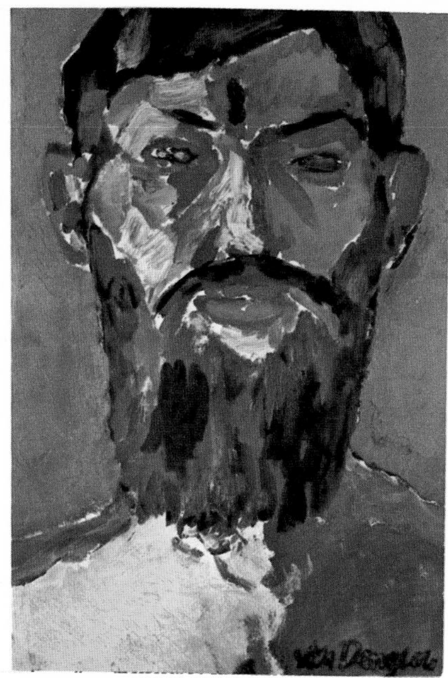

DONGEN, KEES VAN: *Self-portrait.* 1903

Gogh, that solidified into a thick impasto. In 1904 Van Dongen exhibited in the *Salon des indépendants* and mounted a large solo exhibition at Vollard's. He had discovered for himself the colour contrast method, which linked him with Matisse's circle. He exhibited with him in the 1905 *Salon d'automne*. In this year, his application of colour began to cover larger surfaces and was heavily contoured.

Unbroken colour conditions his painting from 1906 and was used by him from 1913 onwards. Van Dongen was one of the first to turn to fauvism, and one of the

DONGEN, KEES VAN: *Riders in the Bois de Boulogne.* Circa 1906.

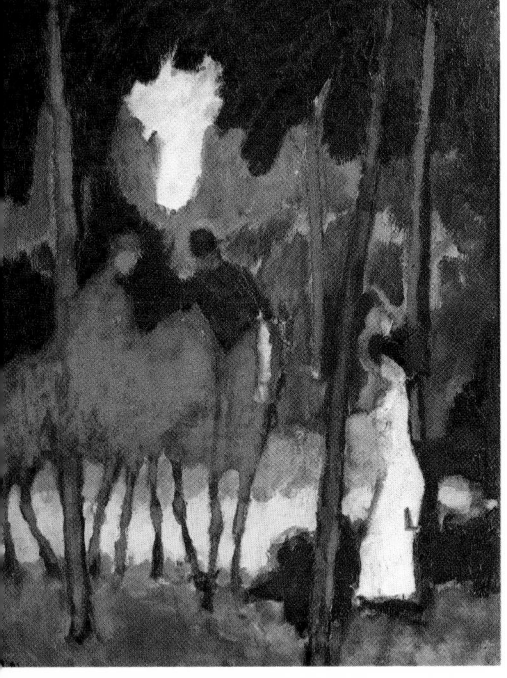

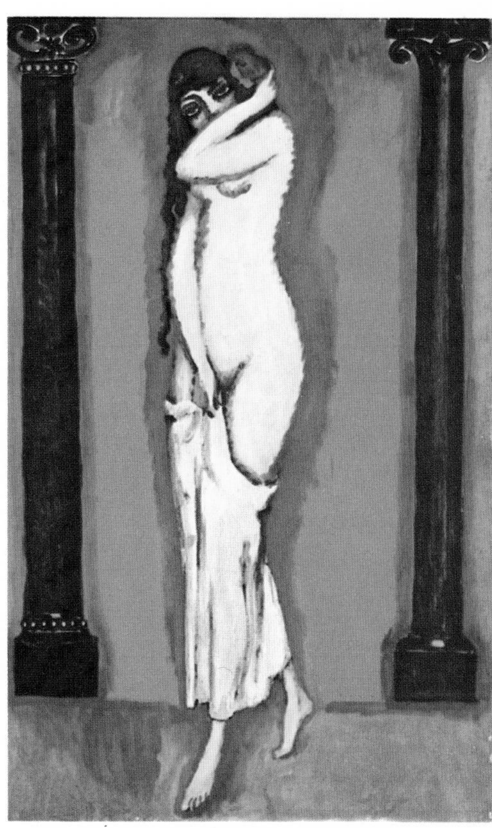

DONGEN, KEES VAN: *Woman and Pillars.* 1908.

longest to adhere to it. For he was most concerned with rendering sense impressions and not primarily with artistic problems. In 1907 he signed an agreement with the Kahnweiler Gallery; in 1908 he became a member of *Die Brücke* in Dresden.

He painted chiefly women – dancers, nudes, portraits. They fascinated him physically, but he was less interested in them psychologically. For this reason, he placed his figures in the foreground, in front of an empty space. However, he soon lost his impetus and inner dynamism. His paintings became so superficial that a nude he sent to the 1913 *Salon d'automne* was removed by the police as indecent. Not long afterwards Van Dongen became the most sought-after painter of fashionable society portraits and female nudes.

DUFY, Raoul (Le Havre, 3.6.1877 – Forcalquier, 23.3.1953). At fourteen Dufy began an apprenticeship with a coffee importing firm; at the same time he attended night classes at the municipal art school from 1892 on, where Charles Lhuillier was his teacher. Here he met Otto Friesz and Georges Braque. In 1900 he received a grant from Le Havre which allowed him to continue his studies at the École des Beaux Arts. Friesz also worked here in Bonnat's studio. Dufy stayed until 1904, not for the teaching, but because the studio models were free. He painted Parisian landscapes under Picasso's influence, and beach scenes which owed something to Boudin. In 1902 he met Matisse and Marquet in Berthe Weill's gallery; in 1903 he exhibited for the first time in the *Salon des indépendants*.

DUFY, RAOUL: *The Fair*. 1906.

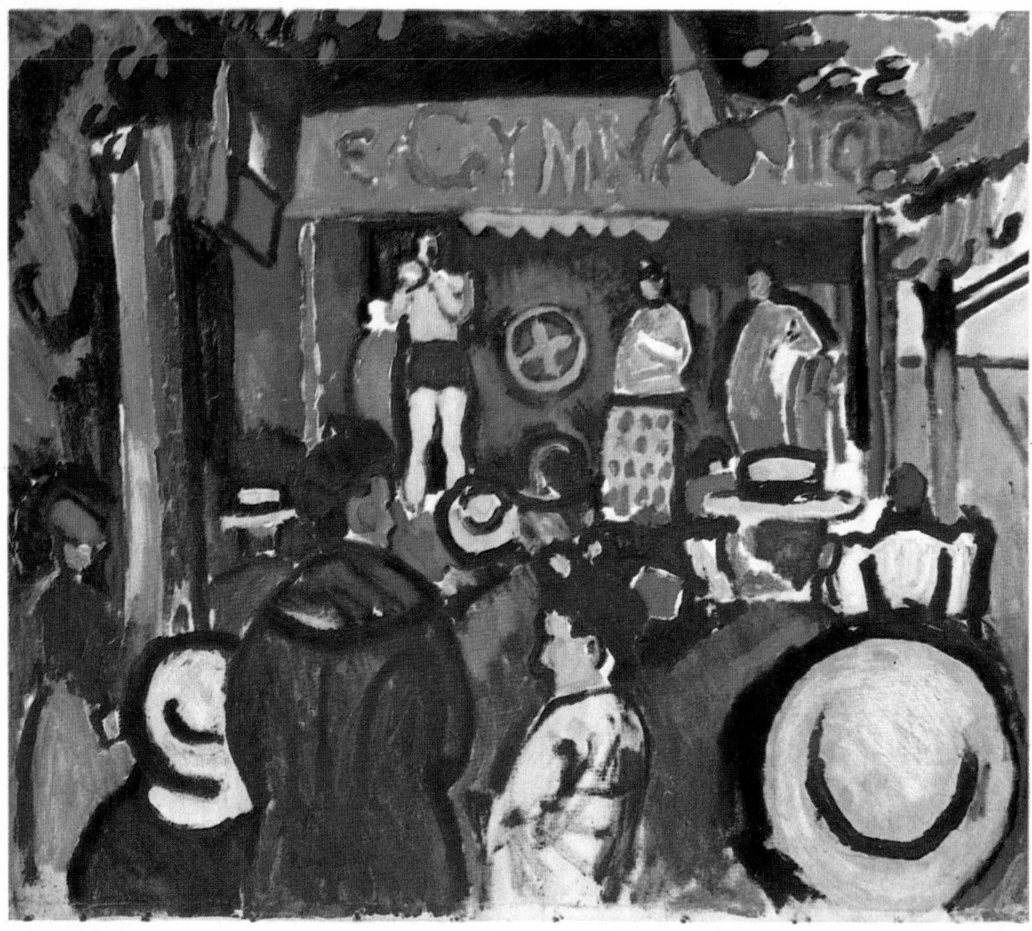

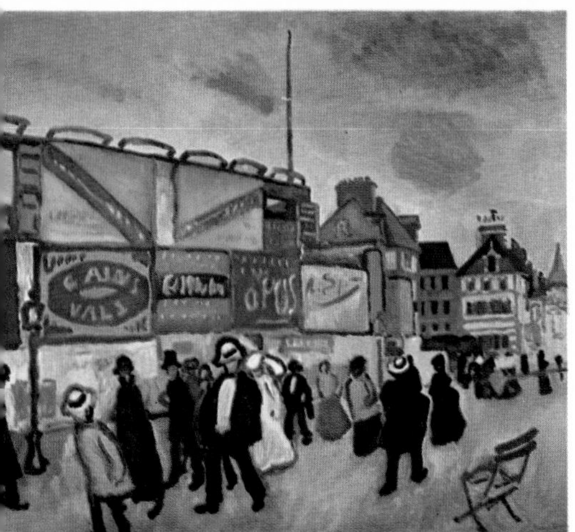

DUFY, RAOUL: *Posters in Trouville.* 1906.

Dufy turned to pure colours after he was directed away from impressionist realism by Matisse, and turned towards the imagination of painters with similar goals; Marquet was the closest, with whom he painted in Fécamp in 1904, and in Trouville in 1906. In 1905–1906, he was with Friesz in Falaise, and also with Braque in Durtal. He intensified colour in order to overcome superficially clarity. He was convinced that 'we need to create a world of objects that we do not see.' To this end, he introduced a drawing technique which simplified not only outline, but also condensed expressive form.

In 1906 he had his first solo exhibition in Berthe Weill's gallery and exhibited for the first time in the *Salon d'automne*. In 1908 he went with Matisse to l'Estaque. Under the influence of Cézanne's painting, Dufy's style also changed completely. He abandoned unalloyed colour and pursued cubist problems of construction. However, the rigours of cubism conflicted with his sunny, lively temperament, so that this stage was also only a passing phase. In 1909 he went to Munich with Friesz; this led to a short contact with the painting of German expressionism.

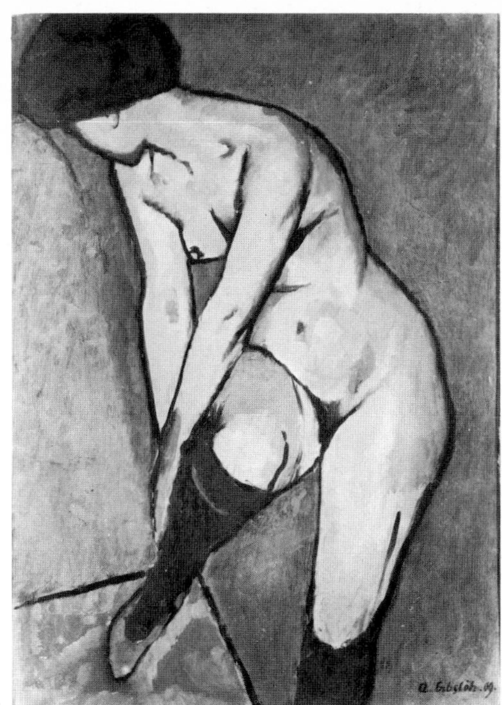

ERBSLÖH, ADOLF: *Nude with garter.* 1919.

In 1904 he moved to Munich and studied at the Academy with Herterich. He also developed through art nouveau, pointillism, Van Gogh and Cézanne. In 1909 he was a founder-member of the New Munich Association of Artists, whose president he became in 1910, after the seccession of Kandinsky and Marc. His friendship with Jawlensky was artistically decisive for Erbslöh. He adopted the latter's palette, which he made somewhat heavier, and also the technique of enclosing the figure in an unbroken outline. The composition of Erbslöh's paintings, always rather constrained in its effect, grew even harder under the influence of cubism into a rigid structure which Erbslöh developed after the war into paintings of the New Objectivity Movement.

ERBSLÖH, Adolf (New York, 27.5.1881 – Irschenhausen, near Munich, 2.5.1947). Erbslöh was born in New York, the son of German parents, and grew up in Wuppertal. In 1910 he went to Karlsruhe Academy with the intention of becoming a portrait painter. Here he made friends with Alexander Kanoldt.

FEININGER, Lionel (New York, 17.7.1871 – New York, 13.1.1956). Feininger was one of the few artists who specifically called himself an expressionist. Painting was for him 'the ultimate goal for heightened expressiveness.' He had come to Europe in 1887 and first studied at the art and craft school in Hamburg, then in

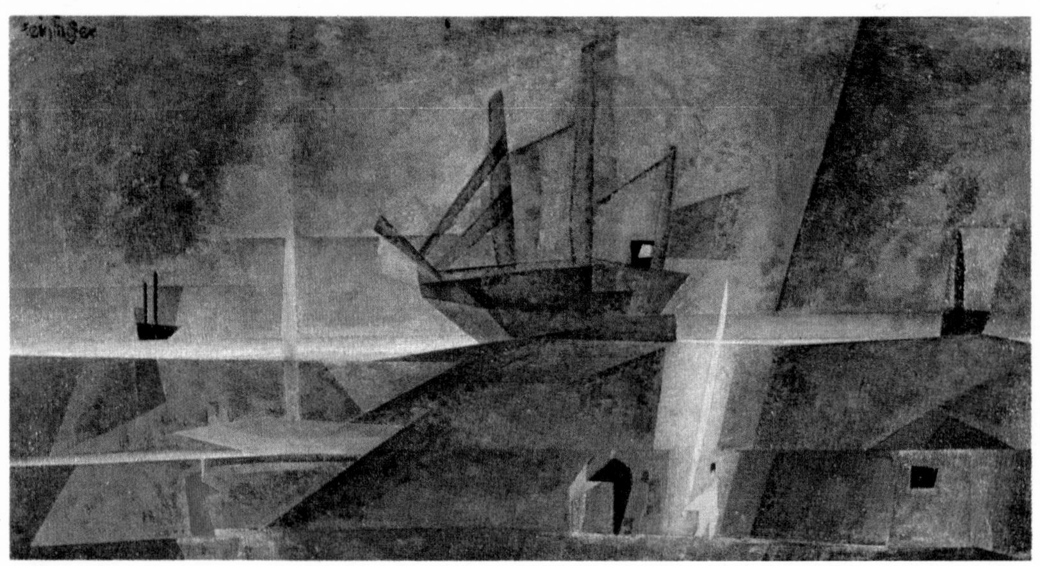

FEININGER, LYONEL: *Dream on the river.* 1937.

FEININGER, LYONEL: *Cyclists.* 1912.

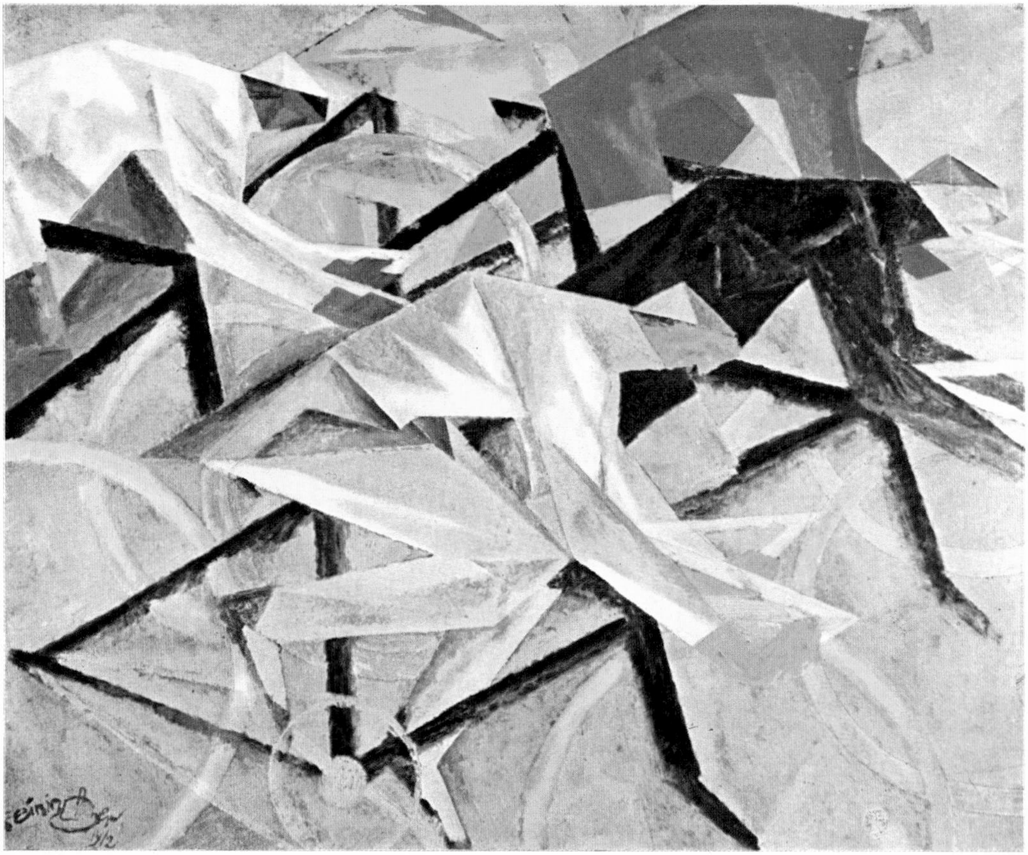

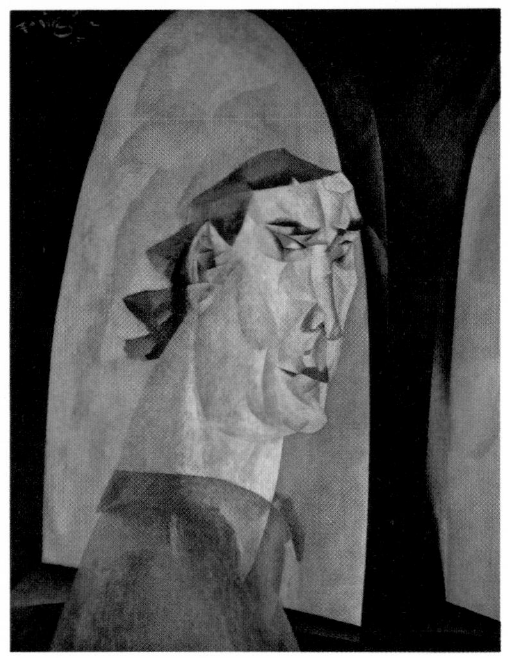

FEININGER, LYONEL: *Self-portrait.* 1915.

the Berlin Academy and in 1892–1893 in Paris at Colarossi's studio. From 1894 onwards he worked as a caricaturist for various satirical journals in Berlin. His success, which also spread to America, was so extraordinary, that he was very soon considered as the best Berlin artist.

From 1905 on, however, this did not satisfy him any more. He began to paint landscapes in Weimar and Thuringia, on which he continually drew later for his themes. In 1906 he returned to Colarossi in Paris and there moved in the circles of Matisse's followers. In 1901 he returned to Berlin, where he now produced pictures of fantastic figures. They reveal his interest in fauvism. In 1911 he again went to Paris and there, with the aid of cubism, discovered a way to explain his artistic idea. But his goal was not dissection, but monumentality and concentration. The crystalline structure of his paintings fostered a synthesis of rhythm, form, perspective and colour. In 1912 Feininger met the artists of *Die Brücke* and made friends with Schmidt-Rottluff, Heckel and Kubin. From 1913 on, he painted again in Thuringia and now resumed his true themes: landscape and architecture. The latter was for him symbolic of an order, an active spiritual force for which an expression must be found. In 1917 Herwarth Walden mounted his first collective exhibition with one hundred and eleven works in *Der Stürm* Gallery which brought Feininger recognition as an artist. In 1919 he was appointed the first director of the Bauhaus in Weimar.

FEININGER, LYONEL: *Gelmeroda IX.* 1926.

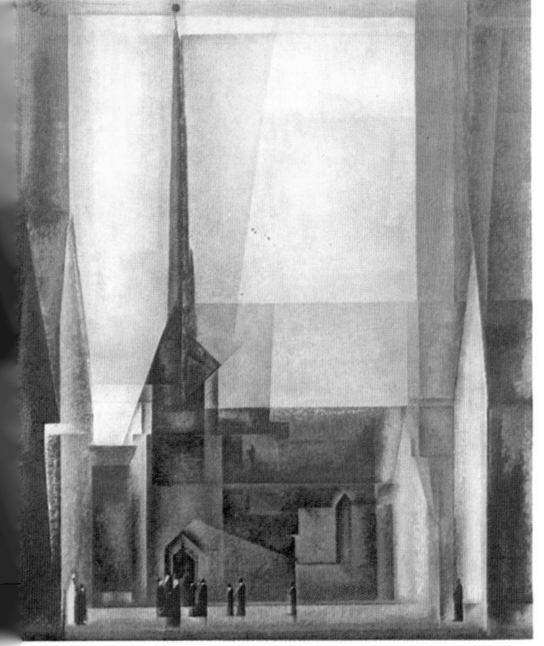

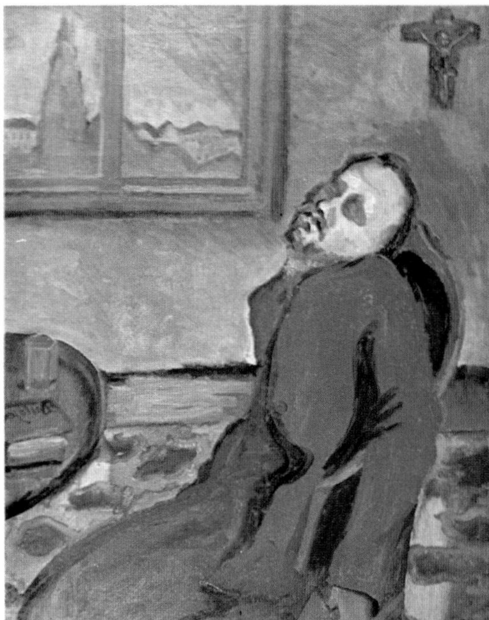

FILLA, EMIL: *Portrait of a man.* 1907.

FILLA, Emil (Chropyné, Moravia, 4.4.1882 – Prague, 7.10.1953). Filla studied from 1903 to 1906 at the Academy in Prague. The impression made on him by the Munich exhibition of 1906 in Prague was decisive. Munich prepared the ground for Filla's endeavours to achieve a passionate, almost elemental power of expression. In 1907 he was a co-founder of the *Acht* group, the first avant-garde artistic centre in Prague. In the years between 1907 and 1914 he travelled on repeated occasions to France, Italy and Germany, and took part in exhibitions such as that of the Sezession in Cologne in 1912. In 1911 he became a member of the Group of Plastic Artists which had formed with the aim of evolving a homogeneous base for their style, founded on cubism. From then on Picasso became the major stimulus in Filla's highly elaborated painting, and Filla followed him through all the phases of cubism.

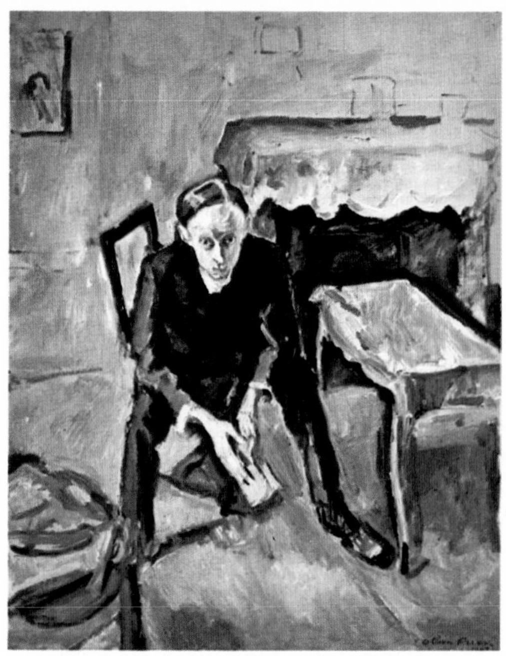

FRIESZ, EMILE-OTHON: *Portrait of Fernand Fleuret.* 1907.

FRIESZ, Emile Othon (Le Havre, 6.2.1879 – Paris, 10.1.1949). When still at secondary school in 1892 Friesz was attending evening classes at the municipal art college in Le Havre, where he met Dufy and Braque. In 1898 he received a grant to study at the École des Beaux Arts in Paris, and there entered Bonnat's studio where he worked until 1904. In 1907 he met Picasso and Guillaumin and under their influence he turned to impressionism. He exhibited his works in the *Salon des indépendants* from 1903 and in the *Salon d'automne* from 1904. In 1904 he fell under Matisse's influence and devoted himself to the study of pure colour. His development towards fauvism was hastened by travels in the South of France. In 1904 he painted in Chassis, in 1905 in La Ciotat, in 1906 he was with Dufy at Falaise and with Braque in Antwerp, and in 1909 with Braque in Le Ciotat again.

FRIESZ, EMILE-OTHON: *The Woman on the green sofa.* 1927.

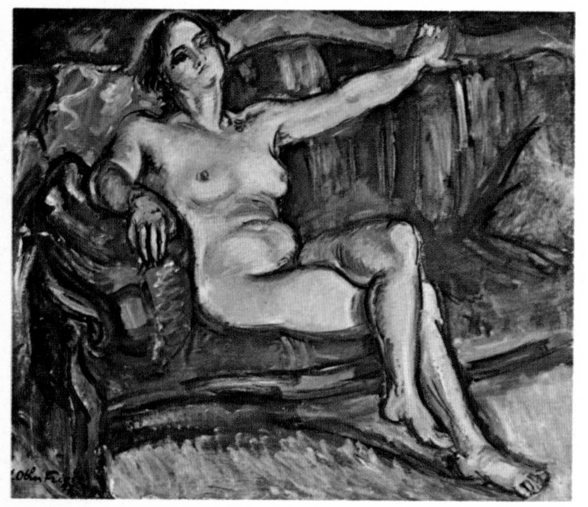

In 1906 he signed a contract with the Druet Gallery, which took charge of all his works. In 1909 he went to Munich with Dufy where he painted rigidly structured urban views which already reveal an estrangement from pure colour. Friesz had never sought after violent contrasts. His colouring always remained relatively discreet, and his forms, circumscribed by curbing outlines, never entirely freed themselves from their connections with tradition. Under Cézanne's influence, his painting was transformed – '1908 marks for me the end of the observation of so-called pure colour which had begun in 1904. Colour ceased to dominate the canvas, form reappeared in light and volume.'

GONCHAROVA, Natalia (Turin, 4.6.1881 – Paris, 17.10.1962). Natalia Goncharova, the daughter of a wealthy architect, went to school in Moscow, and, from 1896 on, studied history, zoology, botany and medicine before going to the Academy, where she entered a sculptor's studio. She was a self-taught artist. About 1900 she met Michael Larionov in the Academy, which she left in 1902. From then on, their artistic paths ran parallel. From 1903 to 1906 Goncharova also painted impressionist and divisionist paintings, which she showed at the exhibition of Russian art in Paris in 1906. She evolved primitivism in company with Larionov until

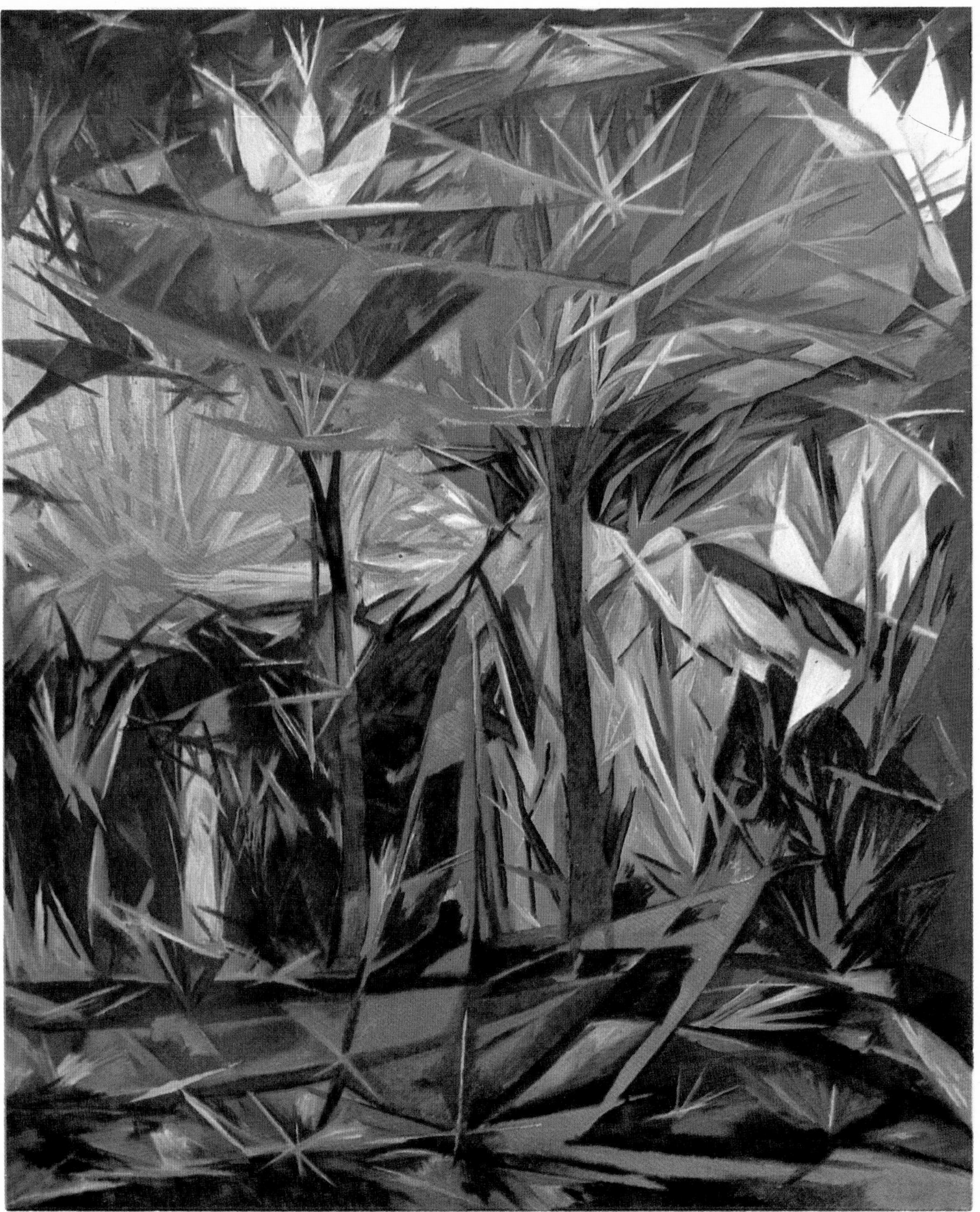

GONCHAROVA, NATALIA: *The Green and Yellow Forest.* 1912.

1911, and took part both in the *Der Blaue Reiter* exhibitions in Munich, and the first German autumn *Salon* in Berlin. In 1913 she also pushed rayonism, the specifically Russian form of cubo-expressionism, into the regions of abstract art. In the same year she began work for the theatre and met Diaghilev, for whom she designed costumes and décor until 1929. In 1914, she moved to Paris with Larionov after she had mounted a retrospective exhibition of two hundred and forty-nine works in Moscow.

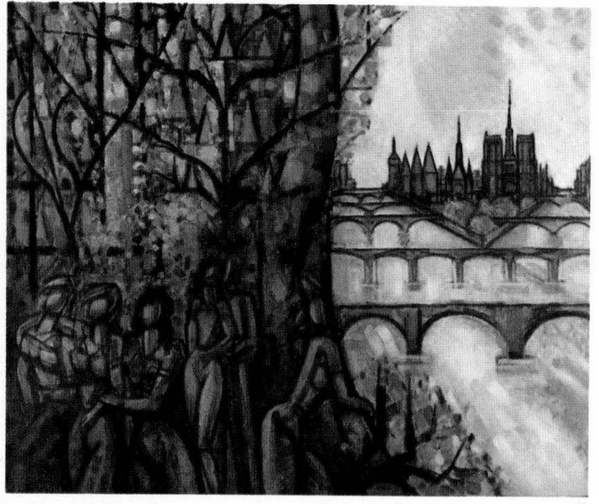

GROMAIRE, MARCEL: *Paris: île de la Cité.*

GROMAIRE, Marcel (Noyelles-sur-Sambre, 24.7.1892 – Paris, 11.4.1971). Gromaire was the son of a French father and Belgian mother. He came to Paris to study law. At the same time he attended various art schools, one of which was the *Académie de la Palette*, run by Le Fauconnier. After two years he devoted himself entirely to painting, continuing to educate himself. He started with Cézanne and the fauves and came into contact with Matisse's circle. In 1911 he exhibited for the first time in the *Salon des indépendants*; from 1914–1916 he took part in the First World War, was wounded at the Somme, and in 1919 returned to Paris. From then on Gromaire assimilated stimuli from Léger and in about 1920, finally evolved from his experiments a monumental, sombre expressionist style, which shows clear Flemish characteristics. Landscapes, workers, peasants, and nudes were his favourite themes, on which he created large paintings, synthesizing them from decorative, figurative and plastic elements.

GROMAIRE, MARCEL: *The lines of the hand.* 1935.

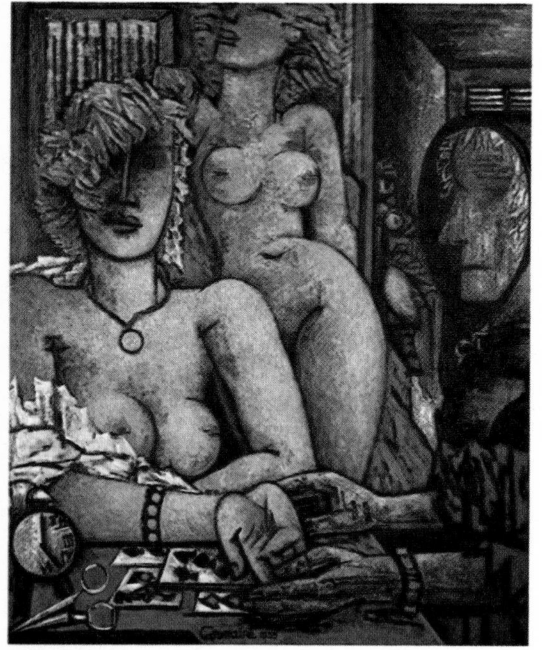

HECKEL, Erich (Döbeln, Saxony, 31.7.1883 – Hemmenhofen on Lake Constance, 27.1.1970). Heckel and Schmidt-Rottluff had become friends in 1901 at secondary school in Chemnitz, and began to draw and paint together. In 1904 Heckel went to Dresden to study architecture. He met Kirchner and Bleyl, and in 1905 founded the *Die Brücke* circle with them and Schmidt-Rottluff. At the same time he abandoned his studies in order to devote himself entirely to painting.

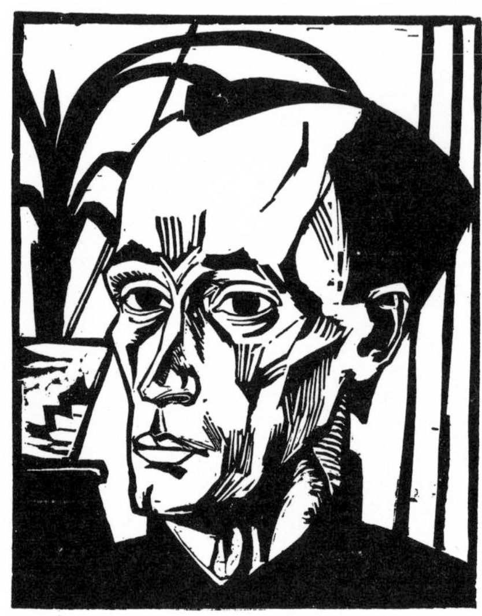

HECKEL, ERICH: *Self-portrait.* 1917.

Heckel, who had an almost fanatical conception of friendship and artistic partnership, became the cohesive element in the group, and as their manager, its practical organizer. This work with his friends, whom Nolde and Pechstein had joined in 1906, also meant, above all, a

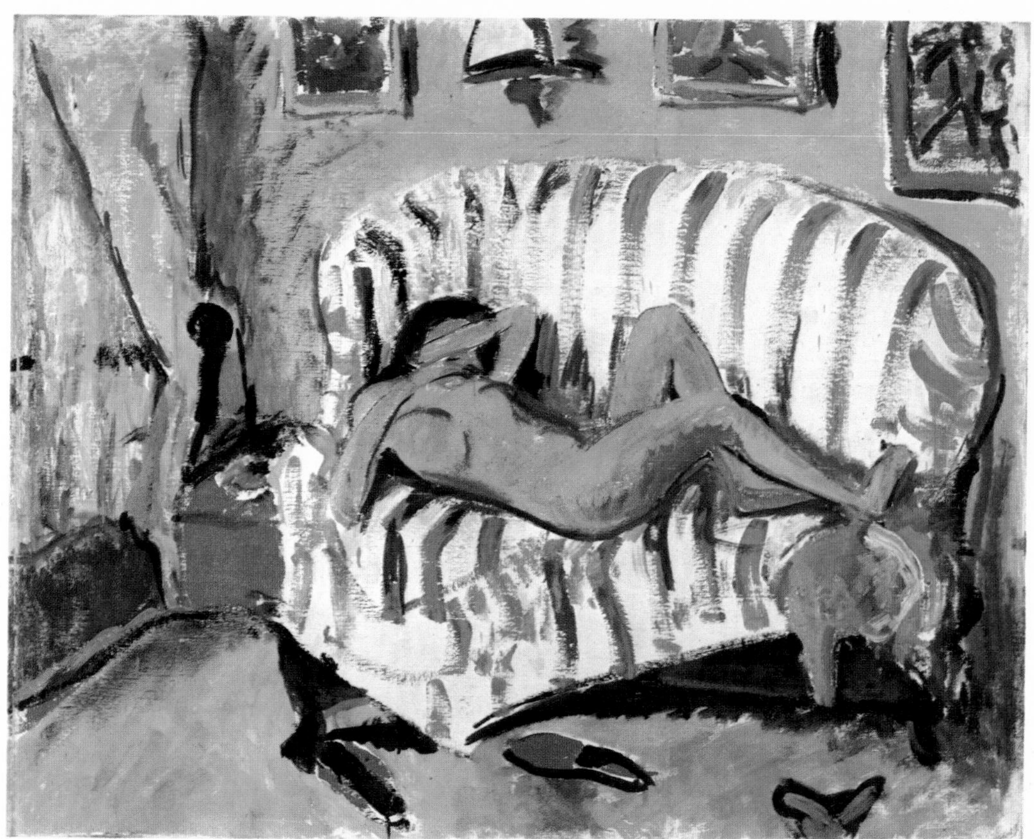

HECKEL, ERICH: *Reclining woman.* 1909.

close examination of Van Gogh, which expressed itself in a vigorous painting style.

However, Heckel very soon realized that for him, painting born from instinct alone could not lead to the discovery of form.

In the summer of 1907 he had gone with Schmidt-Rottluff to Dangast on the North Sea for the first time. The experience of nature in its original state, linked with his own intellectual discipline, led him in 1908 to a grandiose style.

In Spring 1909 he travelled in Italy; he spent the summer with Kirchner at the Moritzburg lakes and in the autumn went to stay with Schmidt-Rottluff. His journey to Italy brought about a clarification of his forms. He was especially impressed by Etruscan art, which confirmed him in his striving after rigour, simplification and increased spirituality. By 1910 the typically flat style of *Die Brücke* had become perfected by Heckel as well. Areas of colour, delineated with jagged, angular contours are intertwined to form a completely compact and immutable composition. Yet Heckel's intensity remained austere, barren and curiously harsh. Landscape followed in close succession at the Moritzburg Lakes and in Dangast, as well as urban views, nudes, bathing figures and music hall scenes. In 1911 Heckel painted at Prerow on the Baltic where Jawlensky was also working.

In the Autumn of that year he moved to Berlin like his friends, where he took over Otto Mueller's studio. This change represents no break in his artistic aims. He was not concerned, as was Kirchner, with the dynamism of the city; from now on he was interested in trends which were not subject to the moment. He directed his attention towards the variety in landscape and the passing of the seasons, and also the behaviour of men in their longings, joys and sufferings. His paintings originated in human compassion.

The year 1912 brought numerous meetings for Heckel, with Macke and Marc, for example and the start of his friendship with Feininger. The high point was the exhibition of the Sezession in Cologne, when Heckel and Kirchner decorated the chapel. In 1913 *Die Brücke*

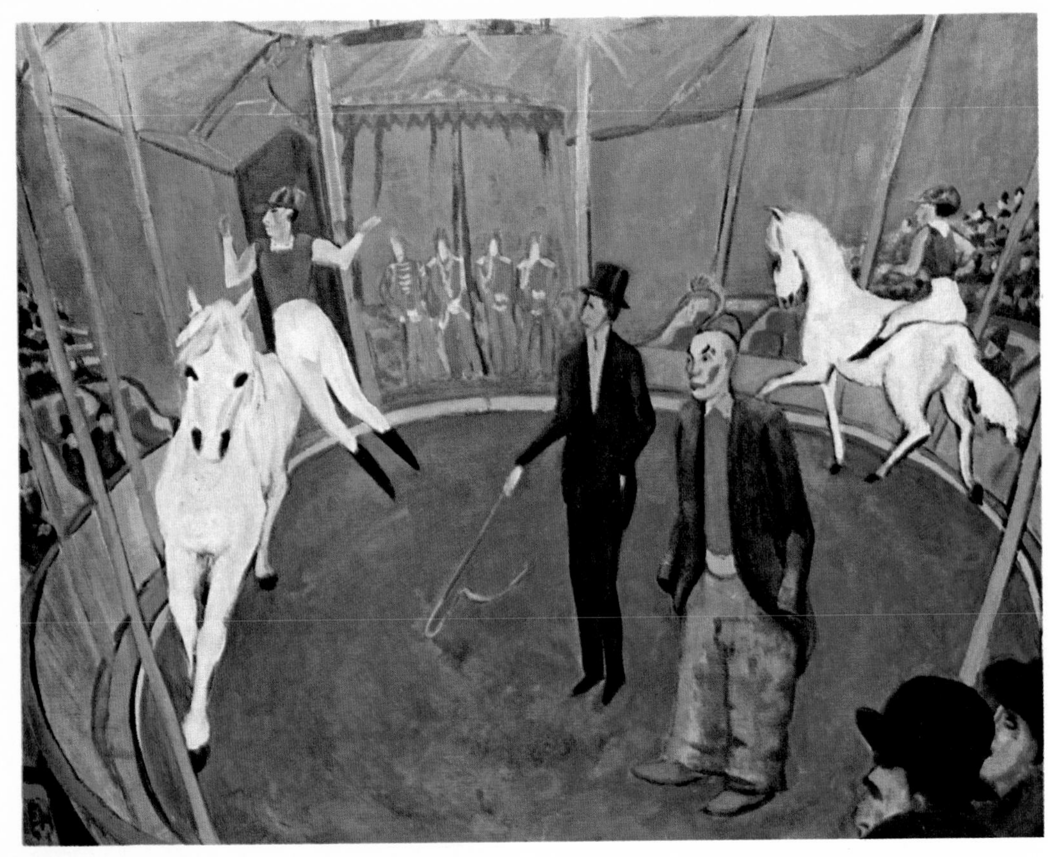

HECKEL, ERICH: *White circus horses.* 1921.

broke up. Heckel mounted his first solo exhibition the same year. He progressed towards ordering objects in his pictures into a stable equilibrium. From now on he transformed his findings from cubism into an angular, as it were, disjointed structure which enabled him to portray light in a characteristic way. He represented reflections as crystalline shapes so that, with the aid of this 'visible' atmosphere, the heavens, the earth, water and man fused into a single mode of expression.

In 1914 Heckel volunteered for military service and in 1915 was appointed to nurse the wounded in Flanders. Here he met Beckmann and made friends with Ensor. Heckel and Beckmann were, with other artists, under the command of the art historian Walter Kaesbach, who so detailed their duties, that every other day was left free for artistic work. In 1918 Heckel returned to Berlin. He evolved his art within the framework of themes he had already elaborated and strove to portray in his pictures what is permanent and universal.

HECKEL, ERICH: *Transparent day.* 1913.

JAWLENSKY, Alexej von (Kuslovo, 13.3.1864 – Wiesbaden, 15.3.1941). Born the son of a Russian colonel, Jawlensky seemed destined automatically for a military career. In 1877 he entered Cadet School in Moscow and in 1882 the Alexander Military Academy. In 1884 he became a lieutenant in a Moscow infantry regiment. He associated with painters and began to copy paintings in the Tretyakov Gallery. In 1887 he applied for acceptance by the Academy in St Petersburg. Since he could not leave the services for financial reasons, he had to be transferred to St Petersburg, which he managed in 1889.

In 1890 he met Ilya Repin, then the most important artist in Russia. He brought Jawlensky and Marianne von Werefkin together. She was his private pupil and already well-known as a painter. In 1896 Jawlensky, now a captain, left the army and moved with Werefkin to Munich. They attended the Azbe School, where they met Kandinsky. It soon became clear to Jawlensky that colour was the only means of expression that suited him; he aimed to achieve harmonic effects in his use of it.

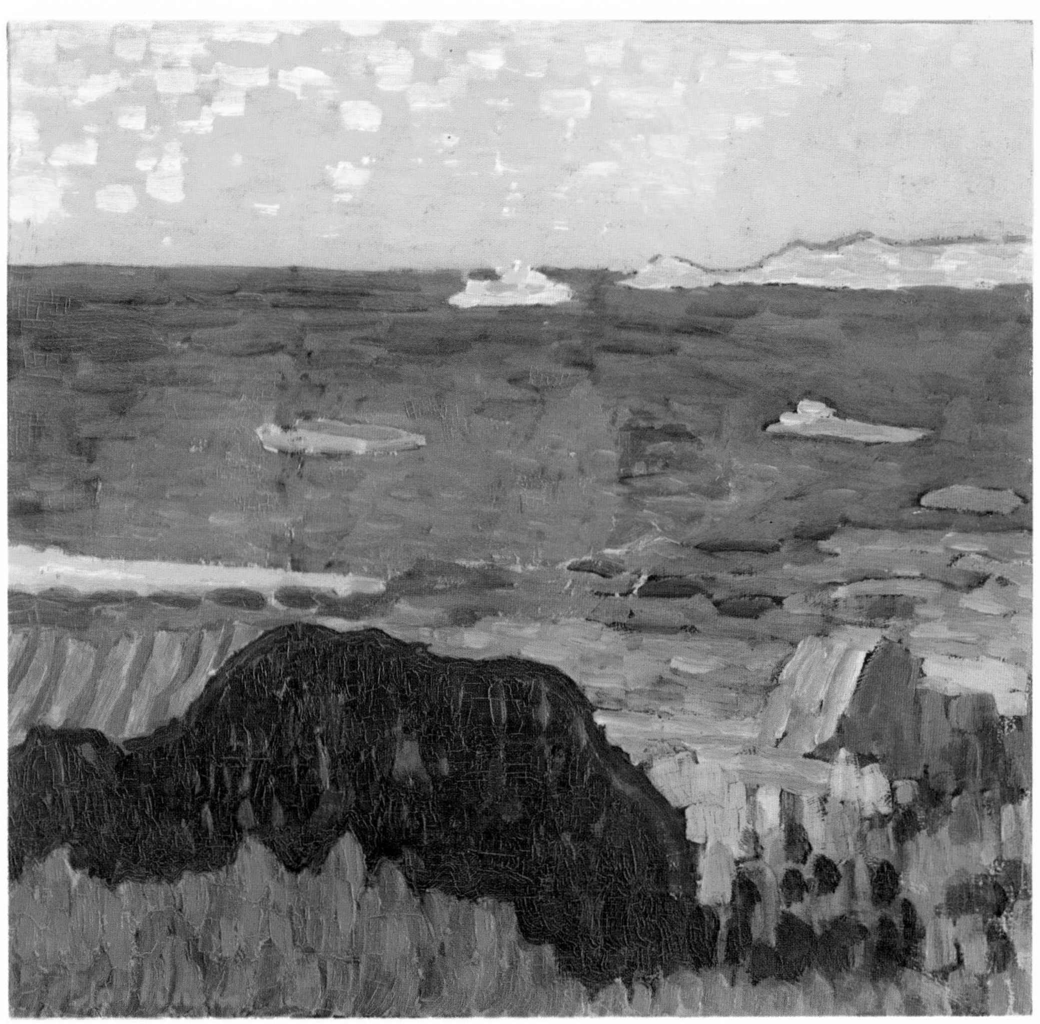

JAWLENSKY, ALEXEJ VON: *The Coast of the Mediterranean.* 1907.

In 1903 he travelled in Normandy and to Paris, and took part in the exhibitions mounted by the Munich and Berlin Sezession. In his work with the medium of colours in motion, Van Gogh was his model and in 1904 he purchased a picture of the Dutchman. In Brittany in

1905 Jawlensky painted brilliantly coloured, crudely pointillist pictures which he exhibited the same year with the fauves in the *Salon d'automne.* He realized that colour was not intended to depict an object, but that the object was the occasion for a structure of colour in which the emotions of the artist and the 'essence of things' was revealed. The colours must unite into a harmony shot through with dissonances 'in order to reproduce the things which exist without being.' (Jawlensky) This conviction corresponded exactly to the aim of the fauves, of whom Jawlensky knew through his meeting with Matisse.

JAWLENSKY, ALEXEJ VON: *Self-portrait.* 1912

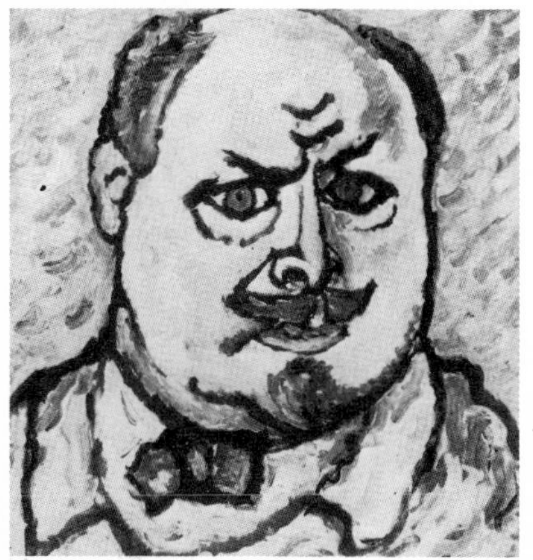

JAWLENSKY, ALEXEJ VON: *Girl with peonies.* 1909.

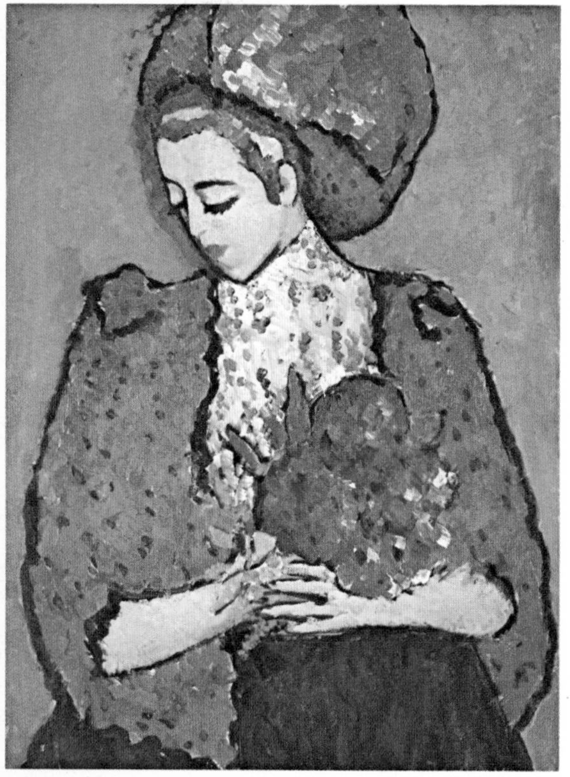

In 1906 Jawlensky exhibited again the *Salon d'automne* and in 1907 returned to Paris, to work in Matisse's studio. In Munich the same year he renewed his friendship with Kandinsky. In the summer of 1908 they went together to paint at Murnau. That summer, Jawlensky created grandiose landscapes out of a rigorous composition. Brilliant areas of colour, darkly outlined produce a two-dimensional structure. These paintings are without dimension and without a story, as are the still-lifes he painted at the same time. The themes are interchangeable and barely have any meaning in themselves any more. Form emerged from a synthesis between impressions of the external world and the experiences of the artist's inner world. Jawlensky required more time for perfecting his portraits, but from 1911 on he succeeded in simplifying the object in his paintings of figures too. Attention was concentrated more and more on the head, where the eyes became the dominant motif. Form was thus made monumental and symbolic.

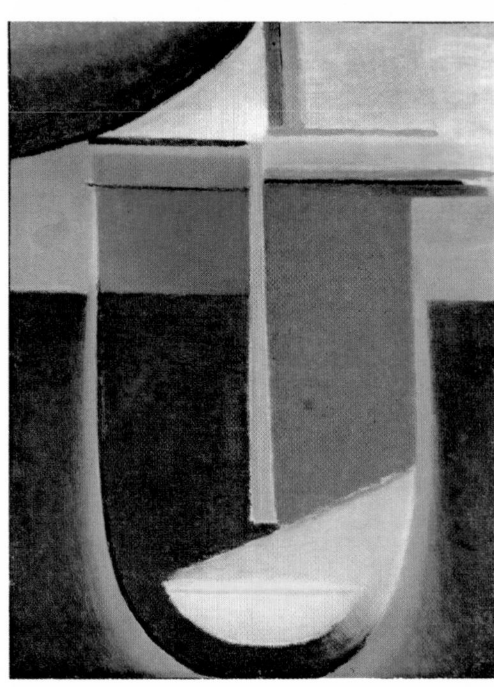

JAWLENSKY, ALEXEJ VON: *The Last Light.* 1918.

In 1909 Jawlensky was one of the founder members

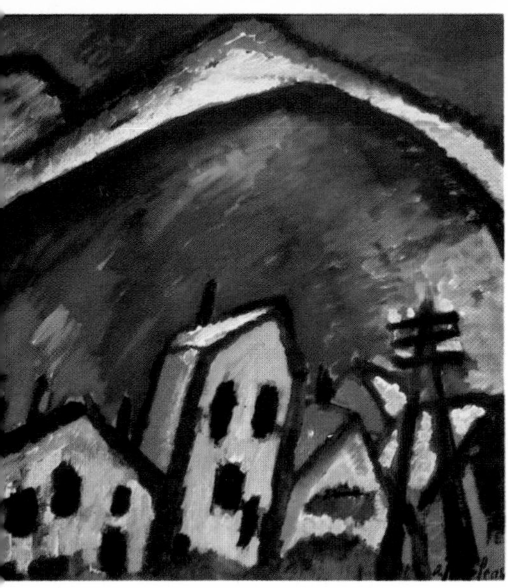

JAWLENSKY, ALEXEJ VON: *Oberstdorf: winter landscape.* 1912.

of the New Artists' Association in Munich and remained a member after the departure of Kandinsky and Marc. He did not therefore take part in the exhibitions of *Der Blaue Reiter* in Munich, although this did not indicate a rupture either on a personal or an artistic level. In 1911 Jawlensky travelled to Paris for the last time and met Matisse and van Dongen. He had spent the summer of that year at Prerow on the Baltic where Heckel was painting. Here he created landscapes from an inner ecstasy that were similar to Nolde's work in expression, something which Jawlensky himself felt. A further heightening of the paintings of the senses was not possible for Jawlensky.

In 1914 he had to leave Germany, when he moved to St Prex on Lake Geneva. Henceforth he painted meditative pictures on a small scale, formal, endless variations on a landscape theme, and the human face, thereby evolving a tranquil expression of religious feeling and intensity.

KANDINSKY, Wassily (Moscow, 4.12.1866 – Neuilly sur Seine, 13.12.1944). Kandinsky had begun studying law and political economy in Moscow in 1886 which he completed in 1892 before entering a university career. As a school-boy he had already painted on the side, and also been deeply interested in art as a student. At an exhibition of French impressionists in 1895 he discovered Monet's *Haystacks* which fascinated him because he could not at first detect any object in them. The problem of an art without objects preoccupied him from then on.

In 1896 therefore he did not take up an appointment to a chair in jurisprudence in Dorpat University, but instead devoted himself entirely to painting and moved to Munich. Munich had become one of the most important places for artistic training in the last decades of the nineteenth century, and particularly attracted young artists from Eastern and Northern Europe. The town was at the same time the centre of art nouveau. In 1895 the journals *Jugend* (Youth) and *Simplicissimus* had been founded. Artists like Herman Obrist, Henry van der Velde, August Endell and Adolf Hoelzel were preparing the ground for an art that was to 'signify nothing, depict nothing and remind us of nothing.'

So Kandinsky found tendencies which coincided with his own vague ideas. He entered Anton Azbe's school and here he met his fellow countrymen Jawlensky and Werefkin. In 1900 he transferred to the Academy and became Stück's pupil.

He had scarcely left the academy when he became a teacher at the college of the artistic circle, *Phalanx* whose president he was from 1902–1904. His first pupil was Gabriele Münter, his companion until 1916. The *Phalanx* group also organized exhibitions, amongst which was one of French neo-impressionists, which was important for Kandinsky since art nouveau and neo-impressionism were the starting point for his work in the years that followed.

Kandinsky painted landscapes in a crude pointillist manner, and scenes containing many figures from a fairy world, drawn from history or folklore. At the same time, he was deeply interested in art nouveau woodcuts. In order to widen his range of vision he went on several journeys. In 1905 he was in Venice, Odessa and Moscow; in 1904–1905 in Tunis for several months. In 1905–1906 he worked for four months in Rapallo; in 1906–1907 at Sèvres near Paris; in 1907–1908 in Berlin. Despite his travels, Kandinsky constantly participated in exhibitions, for example, from 1902 in those of the Berlin *Sezession* from 1904 in the *Salon d'automne*, to whose jury he was elected. He also took part in the second exhibition of *Die Brücke* in Dresden in 1906.

In 1908 he returned to Munich. He spent the summer in Murnau together with Jawlensky, Münter and Werefkin. He now assimilated numerous influences, in particular Cézanne, Matisse and Picasso. The elementary power of colour was released in his many landscapes. His encounter with Bavarian folk art provided additional methods of simplification. Areas of red, blue, green and yellow emerged from hastily applied patches and short strokes; they form stark contrasts, and only serve to a limited extent to describe the subject matter. Kandinsky was on the way towards a synthesis between external reality and the inner world experienced by the artist.

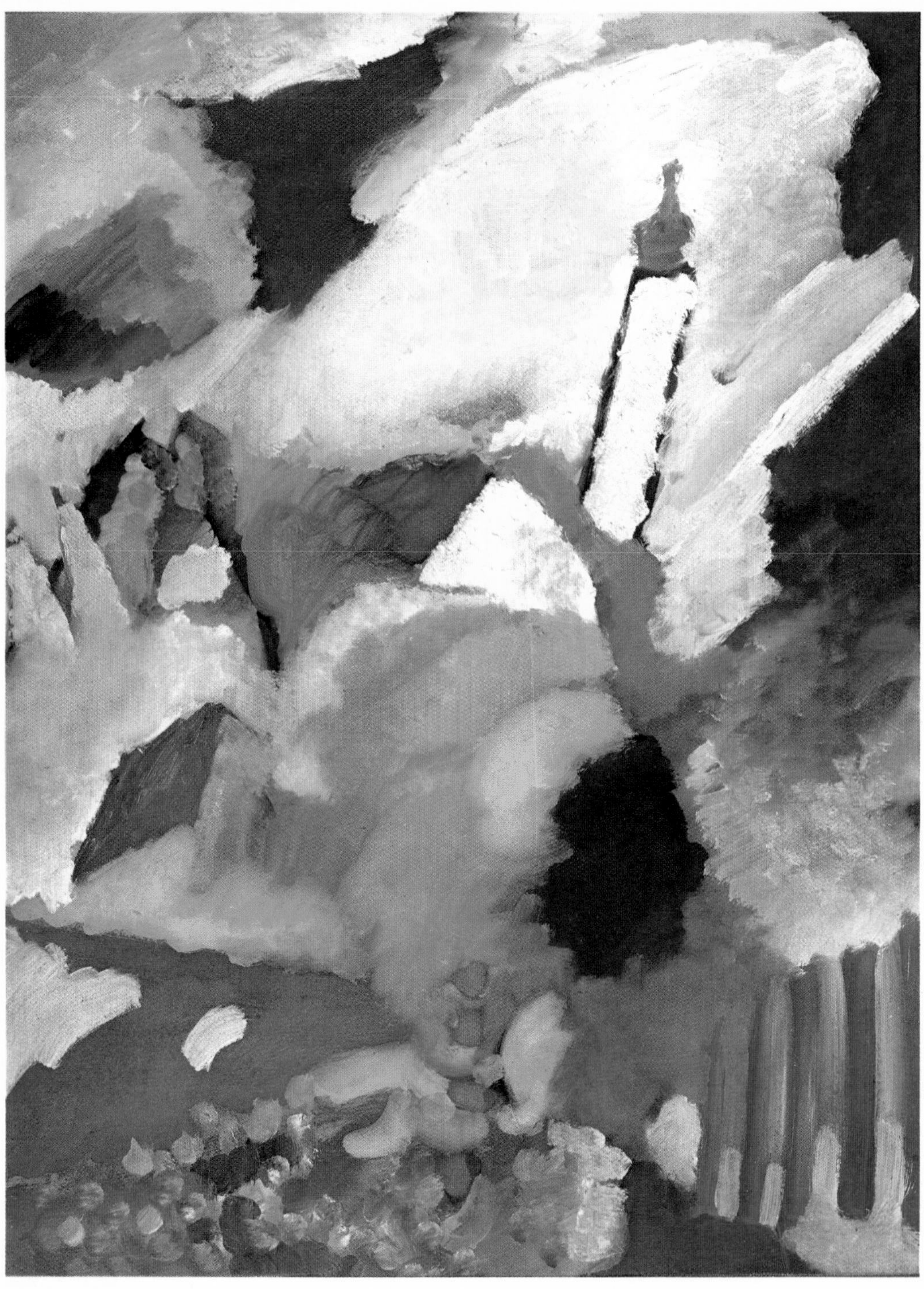

KANDINSKY, WASSILY: *Church in Murnau.* 1910.

In 1909 he was a founder-member of the New Artists' Association in Munich, which elevated this synthesis to the status of a programme. In 1910 he met Franz Marc, and the Burliuk brothers on a journey to Odessa. That year Kandinsky was able to complete his manuscript *On The Spiritual in Art*, which had been written over a period of several years. He now had all he required to take the decisive step. His paintings admittedly still began with a subject, but he subordinated natural shapes to a process of 'rhythmification', so that they now only had the function of building up the picture. These paintings could not longer be understood in terms of an analysis of the object, with the result that it became discordant and superfluous.

Since only Jawlensky and Marc had the power to pursue these developments, a break occurred in the New Artists' Association. Kandinsky and Marc left them and organized the 1911 and 1912 exhibitions of the *Der Blaue Reiter*. In 1912, they, as editors, published the almanach of the same name. Kandinsky had published *On the Spiritual in Art*, followed by *A Retrospective Look* and *Tones* in 1913. Because Kandinsky was seeking a mode of expression for the sensations stored within us, it was not possible for him to move away gradually from the closeness of nature with 'imaginary forms'. He could only use such shapes as formed by themselves in his inner imagination so that he merely needed to copy them down. As a consequence, pictures which referred to some subject were being produced for a time alongside abstract paintings, until Kandinsky succeeded in 1913–1914 in concentrating his imaginative powers in such a way that the last traces of an object could be eliminated. Kandinsky had reached the climax of abstract expressionism.

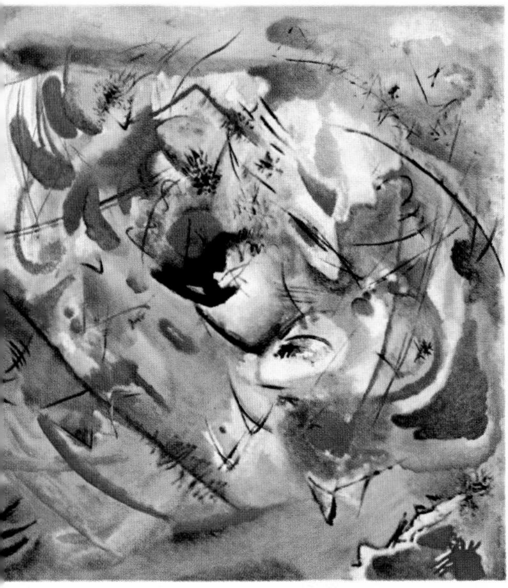

KANDINSKY, WASSILY: *Dreamy Improvisation.* 1913.

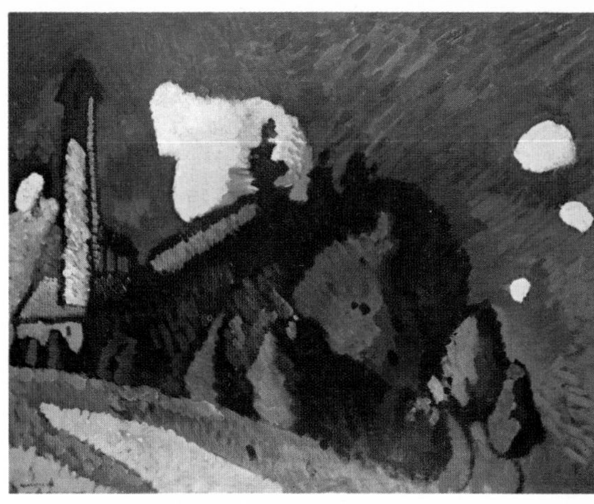

KANDINSKY, WASSILY: *Landscape and tower.* 1909.

The outbreak of war forced him to leave Germany and return to Moscow. When he again became active in Germany in 1922 as a teacher in the Bauhaus, after some years of full cultural and political commitment, his art had also changed and was striving towards new goals.

KIRCHNER, Ernst Ludwig (Aschaffenburg, 6.5.1880 – Frauenkirch, near Davos, 15.6.1938). Kirchner began as an architecture student in 1901 at the technical college in Dresden. After a preliminary examination which he took in 1903 he went to Munich for two semesters at Debschitz and Obrist's studio for the theory and practice of the pure and applied arts. He thus came into contact with the centre of art nouveau in Munich, whose findings were not confined to formal considerations. Obrist's belief in conveying a deepened expressiveness instead of fleeting impressions, and in conceiving of art not as a heightened and intensified form of life, had an effect on Kirchner

His great ideal which took shape in Munich was the desire to rejuvenate German art. He saw that academic studio painting had nothing in common with real life. He set himself the task of grasping life in motion and uniting it with art. Rembrandt's drawings showed a way to him. He began to take notes of what he saw with bold, rapid strokes whenever and wherever possible; a method to which he remained faithful for the rest of his life. In the haste and excitement of work, new forms of expression emerged which were then brought under control, simplified, and preserved, in his studio, in drawings taken from the imagination and in woodcuts. The latter, which has central importance in Kirchner's work, was first used in Munich and evolved under the influence of Valloton and Munch in the years that followed into one of the most fundamental media of German expressionism. Through an exhibition of French

KIRCHNER, ERNST LUDWIG: *Girl with Japanese parasol.* 1909.

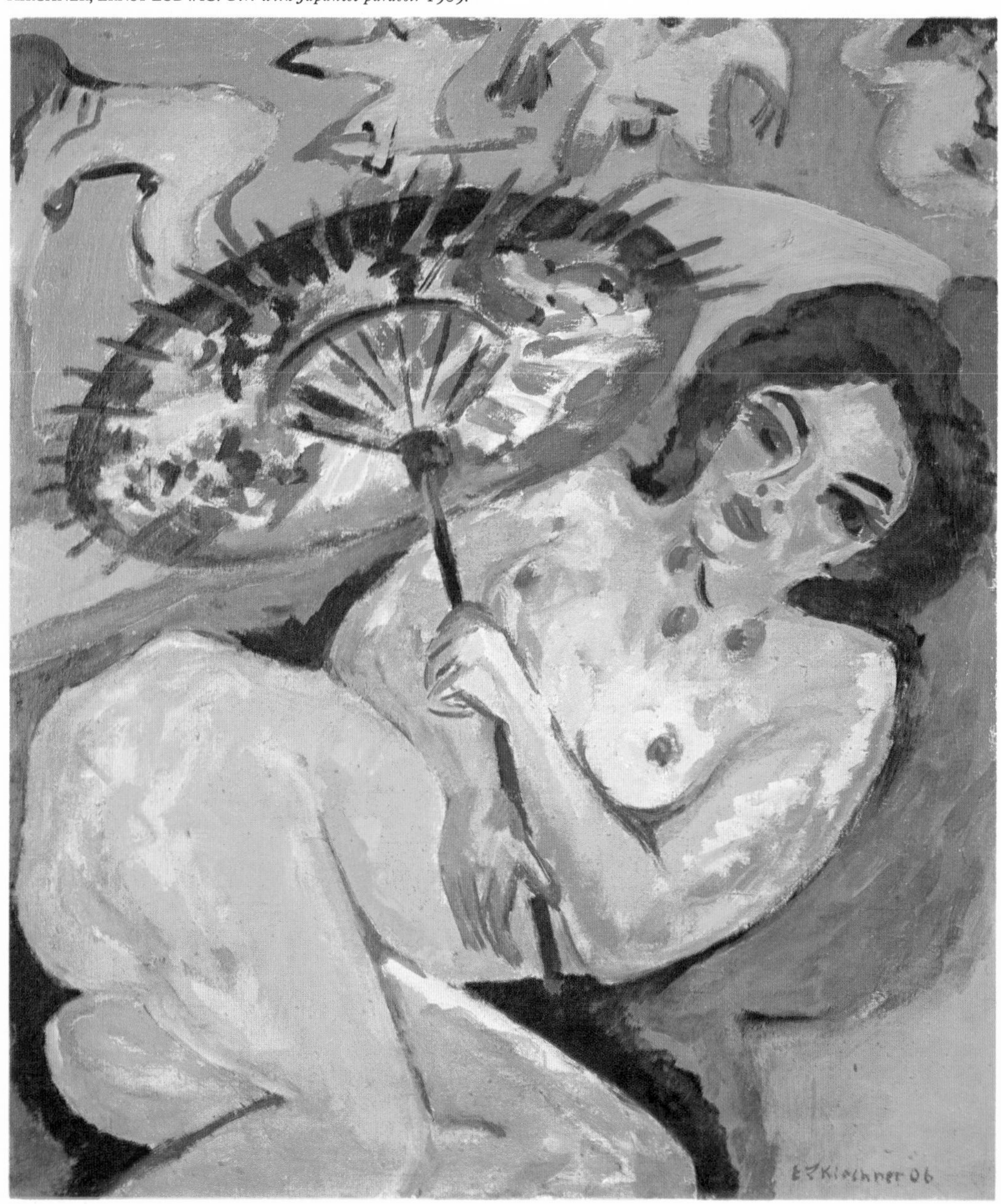

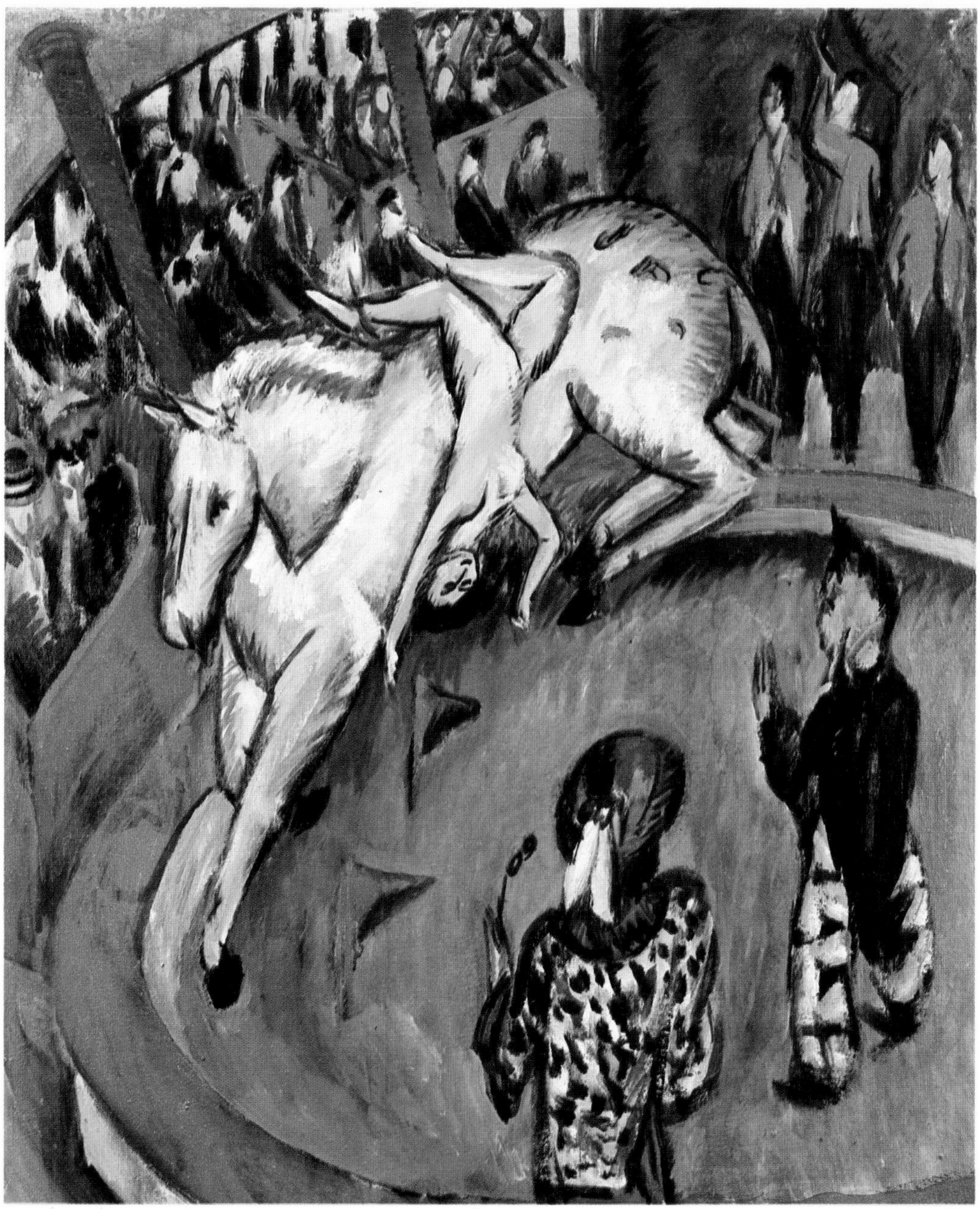

KIRCHNER, ERNST LUDWIG: *The Horsewoman*. 1912.

neo-impressionists organized by the *Phalanx* group, over which Kandinsky presided, Kirchner was made aware of the problems of pure colour. In 1904 he returned to Dresden and got to know Erich Heckel. However, he concentrated at first on his architectural studies, which he completed in 1905 with a diploma.

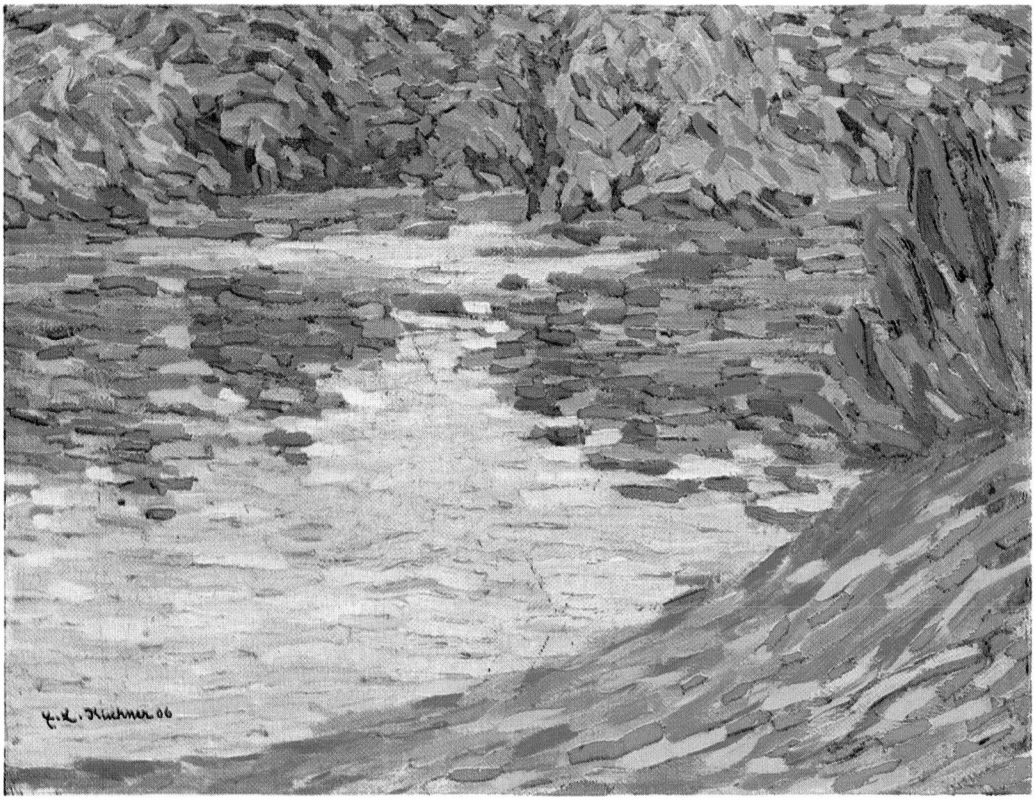

KIRCHNER, ERNST LUDWIG: *Morning beside the lake*, 1906.

KIRCHNER, ERNST LUDWIG: *Small sledge in the snow*. 1926.

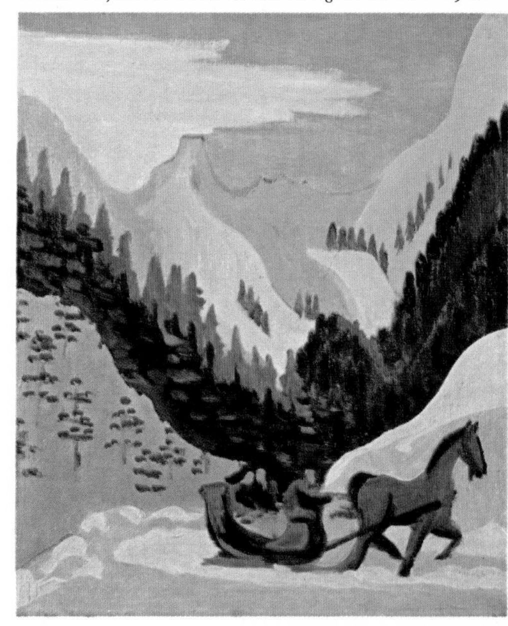

Now he could devote himself entirely to painting and in 1905 he founded *Die Brücke* with Fritz Bleyl, Erich Heckel and Karl Schmidt-Rottluff. In 1906 Pechstein and Nolde joined them. They worked feverishly in joint studies, taking their themes from the environment they saw around them: views of city life, landscapes, portraits of friends and later, also circus and music hall scenes, and, above all, nudes. He learnt from Seurat, Gauguin, Van Gogh and Munch; this is clearly evident in the structure and rhythm of his application of paint in the years up to 1908.

In 1908, he went for the first time to the Baltic island of Fehmarn. From this encounter with nature he evolved his particular drawing style, which he later called hieroglyphic: 'Hieroglyphic in the sense that it reduced the forms of nature to simple, surface forms to suggest their significance to the spectator. Emotion creates even more hieroglyphics which become separated from the mass of lines that seemed so random intially and become almost geometric characters.' Thus, simplified and when necessary distorted, he let shapes emerge from his desire for expression, in order to be able to put across what he thought more forcibly and clearly. In 1910 he evolved a consistently flat picture composition, like the style his friend used, which is known as the *Die Brücke* style; it is created from simple, clear contours and pure colours applied over a large area.

At the same time, Kirchner had discovered sculptures from the South Seas in the Museum of Ethnology in Dresden; these were important to him because of their lapidary form and as expressions of 'primitive state'. In order to portray the simple and primitive elements, Kirchner used to go to the Moritzburg Lakes, accom-

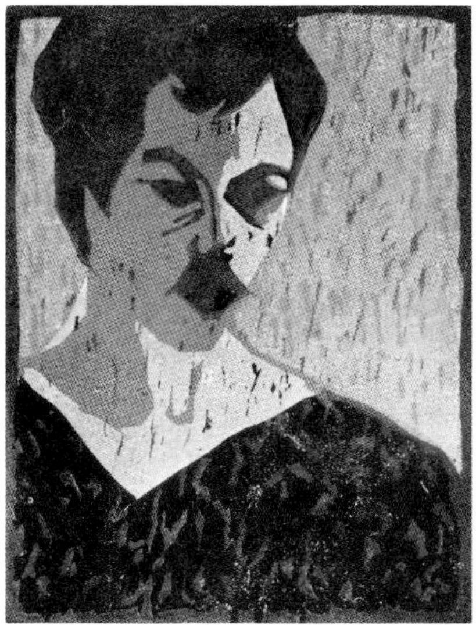

KIRCHNER, ERNST LUDWIG: *Self-portrait*, 1926.

panied by Erich Heckel, during the summer months from 1909 to 1911. There he painted nudes set in the landscape; they were an expression of his longing for the natural harmony between man and nature. Kirchner now developed his particular colouring, which is characterized by the frequent use of pink and violet. In 1910, Kirchner joined the New Sezession in Berlin and made friends with Otto Mueller, with whom he travelled to Bohemia in 1911. In October 1911 he moved to Berlin and founded an art college with Pechstein, which did not, however, meet with success.

In the summers from 1912 to 1914, he again painted at Fehmarn, and pursued the themes of his stays in Moritzburg. In these, he saw man as a part of creation. In sharp contrast to this was his experience of modern city life: on the one hand, a natural liberty and yearning for the 'new man'; on the other, existential constraint, rejection and the loneliness of modern man. Kirchner reacted violently. He drew his mode of expression from the dynamic, bustling, artificial world of the city, to create a hectic, nervous drawing style and fragmented shapes.

He depicted evil and harshness, and laid bare its abnormality with allegorical force in his street scenes of 1914. In this way, he achieved a portrayal of modern life that remains unique in the art world. He fulfilled the task he had set himself, 'to create a picture out of the chaos of the age.'

After his rupture with *Die Brücke* in 1913, Kirchner became dependent on himself alone. The tension which he strove to endure provoked an existential crisis. In 1914 he volunteered for military service. But while still training he suffered a complete mental and physical breakdown. Van Gogh's fate seemed to be coming to pass in Kirchner, who sought in his art to bear witness to his love for men, without inhibiting them. However, friends brought the semi-paralysed artist to Davos in 1917, where he recovered enough to be able to endure life for a while longer, before ending it himself in 1938.

KLEE, Paul (Münchenbuchsee near Berne, 18.12.1879– Muralto-Locarno, 29.6.1940). The son of musicians, Paul Klee grew up in Berne. In 1895 he went to Munich to study painting at Knirr's private art college and from 1900 on in Stück's class at the Academy. In 1901 he travelled in Italy with the sculptor Hermann Haller and returned to Berne in 1902. In 1905 he

KLEE, PAUL: *The Houses of St Germain*. 1916.

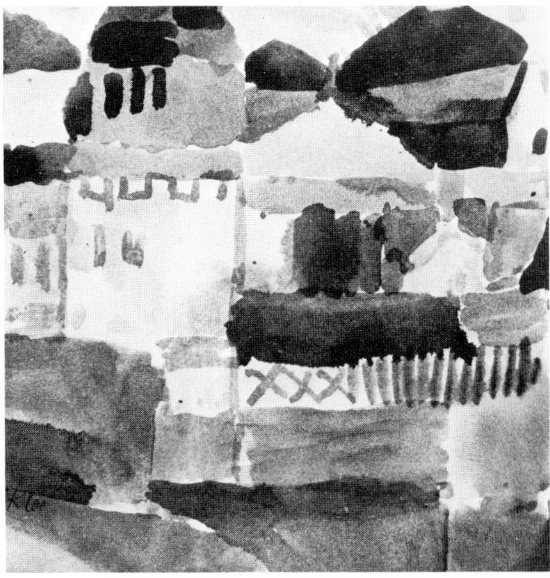

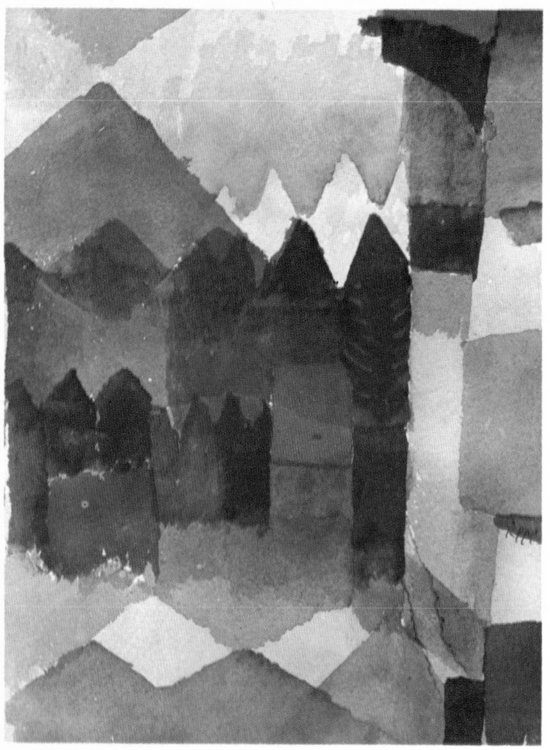

KLEE, PAUL: *Föehn in Mark's garden.* 1915.

group to which Kubin and Schiele, amongst others, belonged. Through Moilliet he established connections with Macke, Marc and Kandinsky. Klee took part in the second exhibition of *Der Blaue Reiter.* His meetings with Kandinsky and Marc were especially important for Klee. His aim of reaching the original via the model was the goal of this group as well.

And Klee was again made aware of the need for a close study of pure colour.

In 1912 he again travelled to Paris, saw mainly cubist paintings there, and visited Delaunay and Le Fauconnier. His meeting with Delaunay, especially, whose essay on light Klee translated for *Der Sturm* magazine, made him alert to the possible use of colour. However, he still could not find a synthesis from these suggestions. The great revelation, the discovery of colour as an independent medium, and as a necessity for him, came in April 1914 through his journey to Tunis which he undertook with Macke and Moilliet. It was here that Klee became a painter. He was now in a position to construct his paintings out of blocks of colour, and to modulate it in such a way as to produce a structure for expression, that was rhythmic in appearance and poetic in conception.

visited Paris with Louis Moilliet; in 1906 he finally moved to Munich. Klee's artistic evolution followed the same course as his contemporaries, though without transposing what he saw into his own works, he used it rather as a form of self-knowledge from which he wished to form his own style. He was aware very early on that he must build a bridge between the inner and the external world. In the course of his search he reduced his means of expression essentially to line, after he had observed its independence as a creative element in Ensor and Van Gogh. 'Freshly strengthened by my naturalist studies, I can then again venture into my original sphere of "psychic improvisation". Now that I am only indirectly linked to nature, I can again attempt to give form to that which burdens the soul. I want to note down experiences that could turn themselves into line pitch darkness.' (Klee, 1908)

As a result, from 1909 onwards he created paintings built up from exceptionally tense, nervous strokes, born of pure imagination; emotions, moods and dream experiences harmonize within them. In 1910 Klee sent an exhibition on tour in Switzerland; this was followed by a similar one in Munich in 1911.

In the same year, he became a member of the *Sema*

KOKOSCHKA, Oskar (Pöchlarn, near Vienna, 1.3.1886). Although Kokoschka was the son of a goldsmith and had tried his hand at painting at a very early stage, he wanted to become a chemist. But since he was entitled to a grant to study at the School of Arts and Crafts in Vienna, he went to study there with the intention of becoming a teacher. Kokoschka learnt a great variety of artistic techniques, but not painting, which he acquired by teaching himself. In 1906 he was deeply impressed by a Van Gogh exhibition. He was interested in Far Eastern Art and studied Klimt.

In 1907 he became a contributor to the *Wiener Werkstätten* (Vienna Workshop) which published his book, *The Dreaming Youth* in 1908. His one act play, *Murderer, The Hope of Women*, was first performed amid tumultuous scenes at the Wiener Kunstschau in 1909. He came to the notice of Adolf Loos, the architect, who introduced him to Karl Kraus. Both of them gave him commissions for their portraits, with the result that Kokoschka left the school of arts and crafts and the Vienna Workshop and hoped to earn his living as a portrait painter. However, his method of projecting his own torments and sufferings on to the his model, in order to be able to express their soul, and his 'distorting' glaze, thwarted any success.

In 1900 he went to Berlin and became a contributor to *Der Sturm*, which admittedly did not relieve his

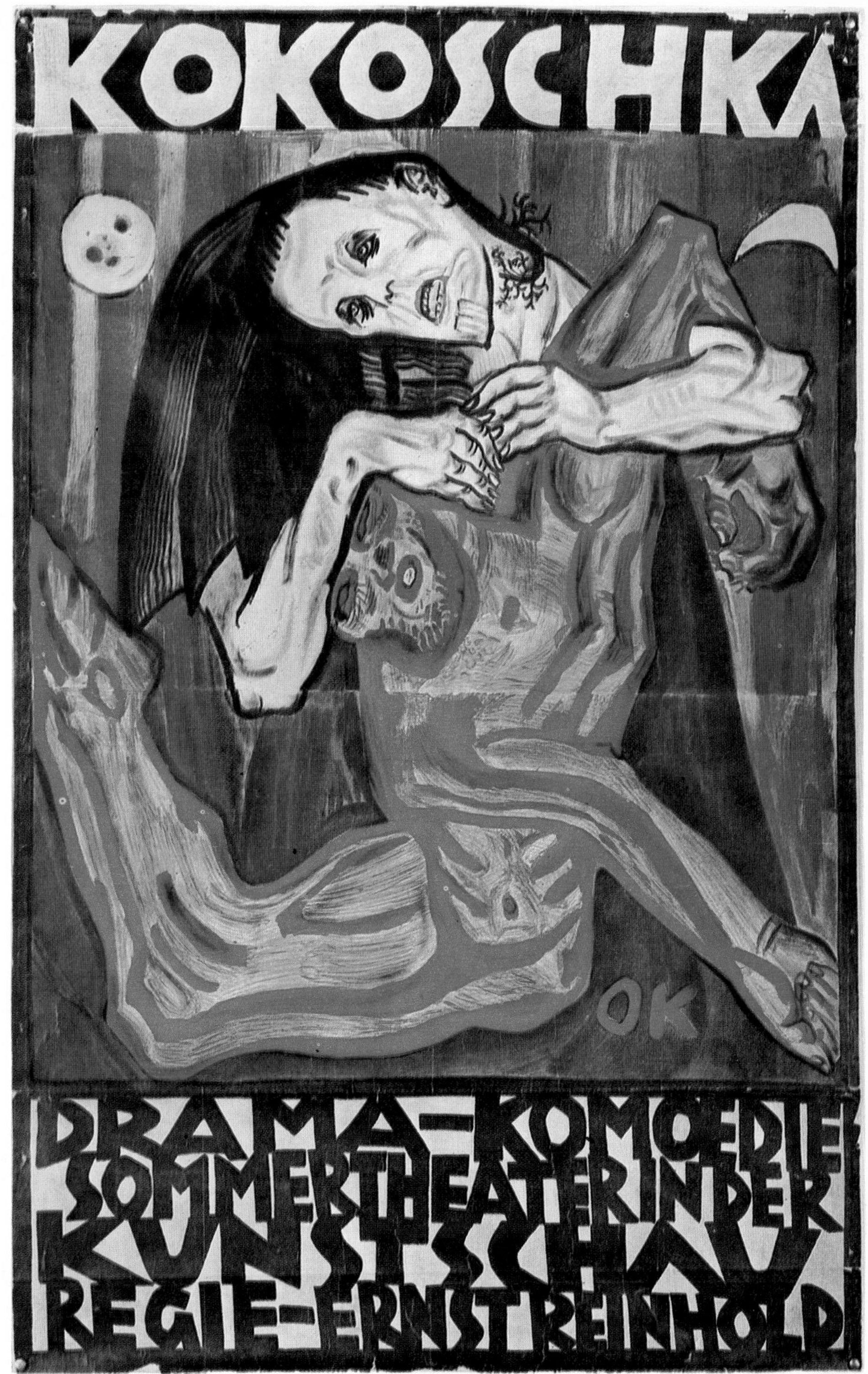

KOKOSCHKA, OSKAR: *The Tragedy of Man.* 1908.

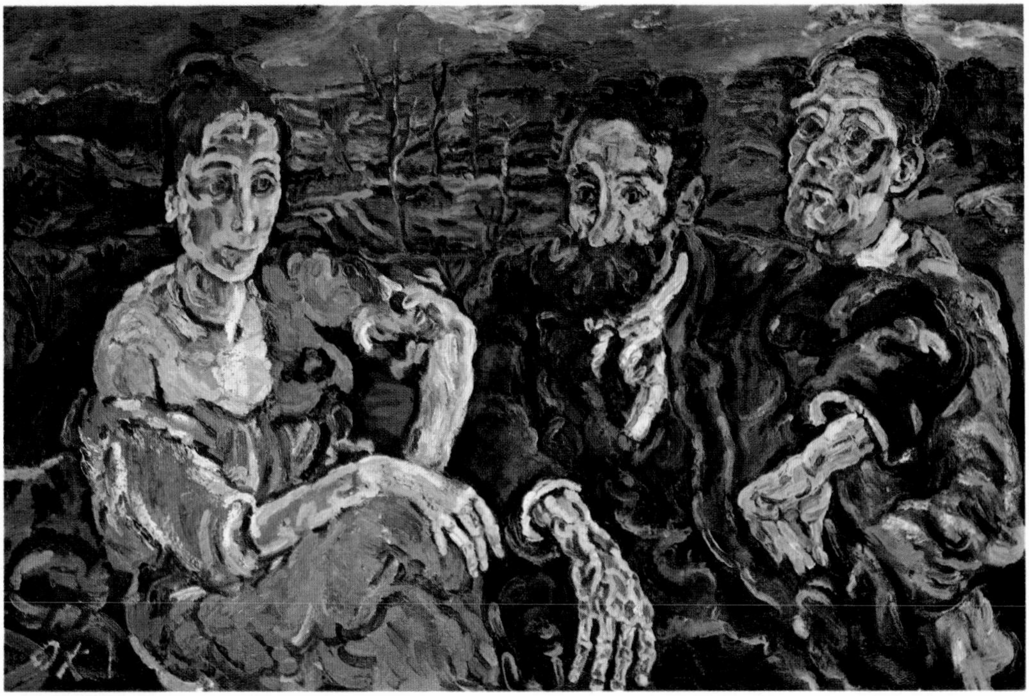

KOKOSCHKA, OSKAR: *The Refugees.* (1916–1917).

financial troubles, but rapidly made him widely known. Paul Cassirer's gallery mounted his first one-man exhibition. In 1911 he returned to Vienna. He continued to exercise his greatest influence in Germany, where he took part in the exhibitions of *Der Sturm* and the

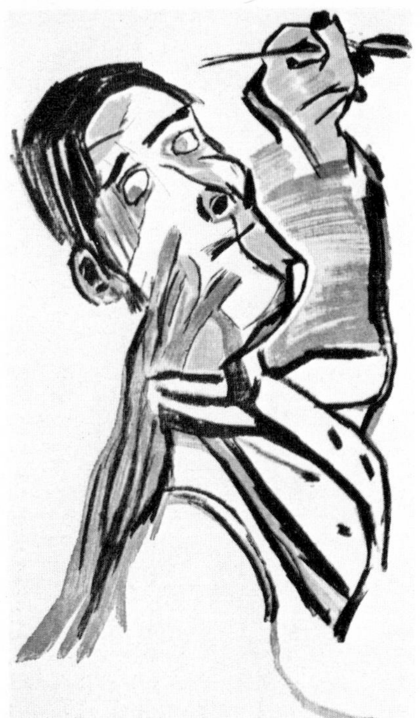

KOKOSCHKA, OSKAR: *Self-portrait.* 1923.

KOKOSCHKA, OSKAR: *Lovers and Cat.* Circa 1917.

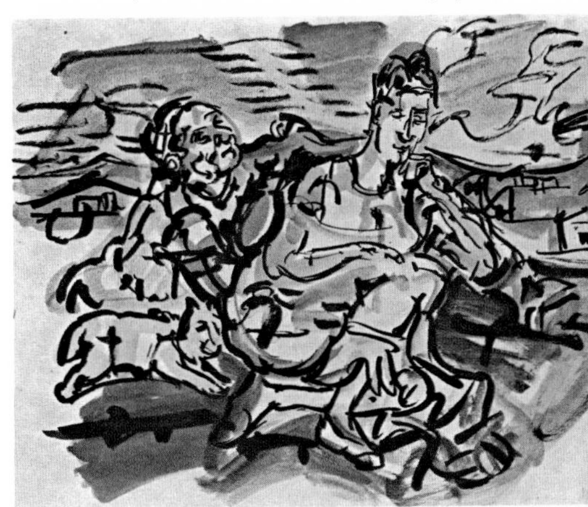

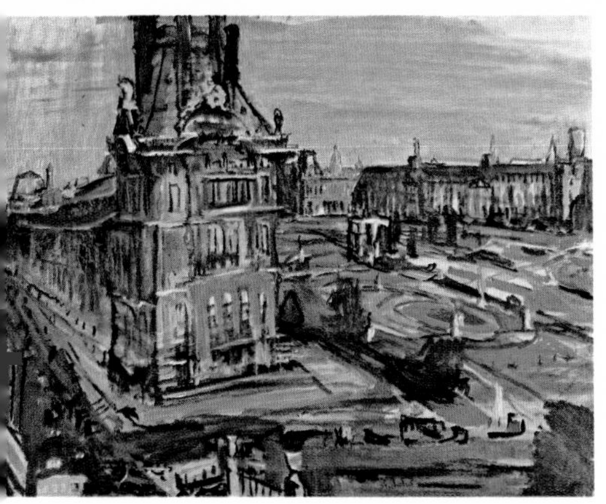

KOKOSCHKA, OSKAR: *Paris: the Louvre.* 1925.

Sezession in Berlin, in Cologne, and the New Sezession in Munich. In 1913 the first monograph appeared in Leipzig; *Oskar Kokoschka – Plays and Paintings.*

From now on he painted predominantly figure compositions, amongst them religious subjects. He overlaid his pictures with a prismatic net of coloured lines, and patches of colour, thus introducing colour as a sensual expressive element. In 1912 he went to Italy, with Alma Mahler-Werfel, and studied principally Venetian painting.

In 1914 he volunteered for military service and was severely wounded in 1915. In 1917 he returned to Dresden to convalesce. His painting now was constructed out of tense, rapid brushstrokes which, combined with softened colouring, reveal how hard Kokoschka had to combat his mental and physical state. In 1919 he was appointed to the Academy in Dresden; and he returned to thickly applied and brilliant colours.

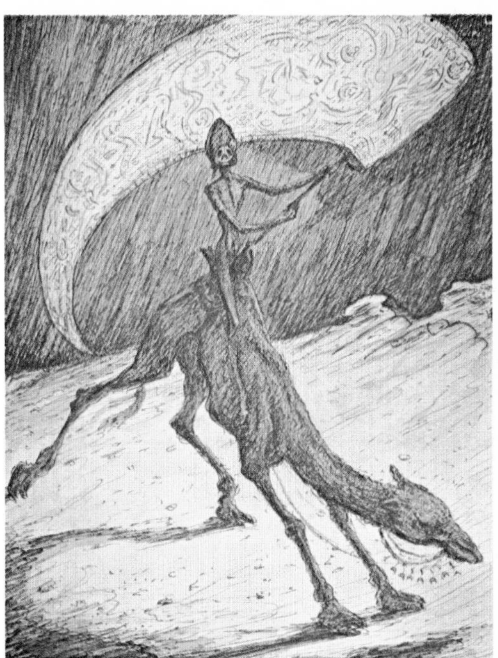

KUBIN, ALFRED: *Death in the desert.*

KUBIN, Alfred (Leitmeritz, Bohemia, 10.4.1877 – Zwickledt, 20.8.1959). Kubin grew up in Salzburg and had attended the arts and crafts school there from 1891–1892 before completing an apprenticeship as a photographer in Klagenfurt from 1892–1896. In 1898 he went to Munich, began art studies at a private college, and transferred to the Academy, where he stayed until 1901.

He was extremely interested in Munch, Ensor and Redon and also Goya and Rops.

He gained fame very quickly as an illustrator and graphic artist and had his first exhibition in 1902 in Berlin. In 1905 and 1906 he travelled in France and Italy. The same year he acquired the small castle of Zwickledt in Upper Austria, where he lived until his death. In 1906, Kubin produced astonishing tempera paintings. Without seeking a point of departure in nature, he created compositions 'out of veils and bundles of light, out of shells or crystalline fragments, out of shreds of skin and flesh, out of leaf ornaments and a thousand other things'. These abstract pictures were produced, without conscious intention, in the process of painting, and were a direct expression of the memories which were oppressing his spirit.

In 1908 he published his novel *The Other Side*, in which he described abstract colour dreams. This corresponded to what Kandinsky believed and felt. As a result he became linked in 1909 with the New Artists' Association in Munich, in whose exhibitions he took part as he did later in the second *Der Blaue Reiter* one. In 1913 Marc developed his plan of illustrating the Bible, in which he himself, Kandinsky, Klee, Heckel, Kokoschka and Kubin were to participate. The outbreak of war prevented this from coming to pass; only Kubin delivered his contribution for the Book of Daniel, which appeared in 1918.

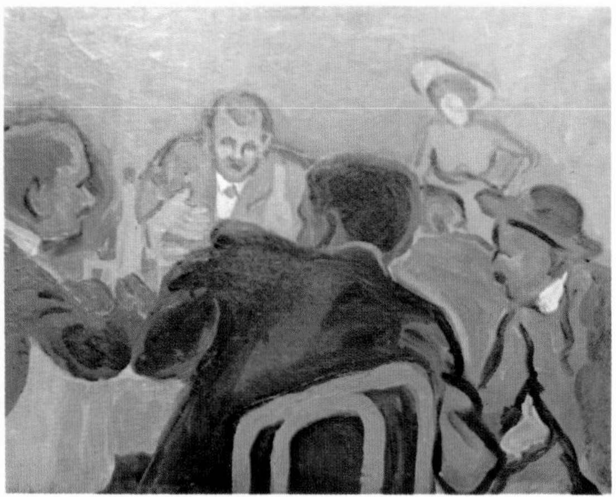

KUBISTA, BOHUMIL: *The Players.* 1909.

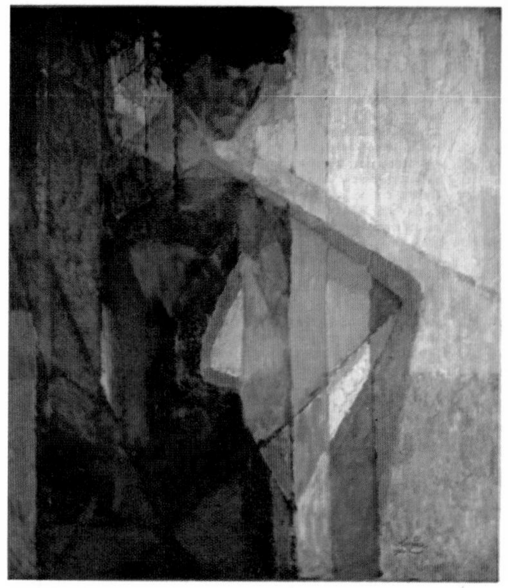

KUPKA, FRANK: *Patterns with colours.* 1910–1911.

KUBISTA, Bohumil (Vlckovice, Bohemia, 21.8.1884 – Prague, 27.11.1918). Kubista began his education at the arts and crafts college in Prague, then went to the academy. In 1907 he was founder-member of the *Acht* group in Prague and was already exhibiting works which had been influenced by the fauves. In 1911 he met E. L. Kirchner and O. Mueller in Prague and on the strength of this, joined *Die Brücke*. From 1911 he exhibited in Germany. Kubista was a severe rationalist who sought to portray the harmony and laws of the new art methodically. From 1910 on, he found an opening into cubism through the stimulus of Cézanne.

Nevertheless, in his paintings he combined an austere construction with symbols expressive of existential unease. Kubista, who was also influential as a theoretician and critic, had to enter active military service in 1913 due to financial distress. Shortly after the end of the war he died of Spanish flu, which also carried off Schiele.

KUPKA, František (Opočno, Bohemia, 23.9.1871 – Puteaux, 21.6.1957). Kupka entered the academy in Prague in 1887 and continued his studies from 1891 on at the Vienna Academy. In 1895 he moved to Paris where he struggled along as a designer, illustrator and commercial artist. His painting was inspired by art nouveau and favoured symbolism in the manner of Redon; he had some success with such pictures. In 1904 he settled in Puteaux. In 1900 he became a member of the *Salon d'automne* and now painted fauve-like works under the influence of Toulouse-Lautrec. This phase lasted until about 1910. Kupka had early been concerned with the problem of portraying motion; his solution was to divide the surface of the picture into vertical strips of colour. Abstract paintings emerged from this colour structure; these were first shown at the 1912 *Salon d'automne*.

LARIONOV, MICHAEL: *The Soldiers.* 1909.

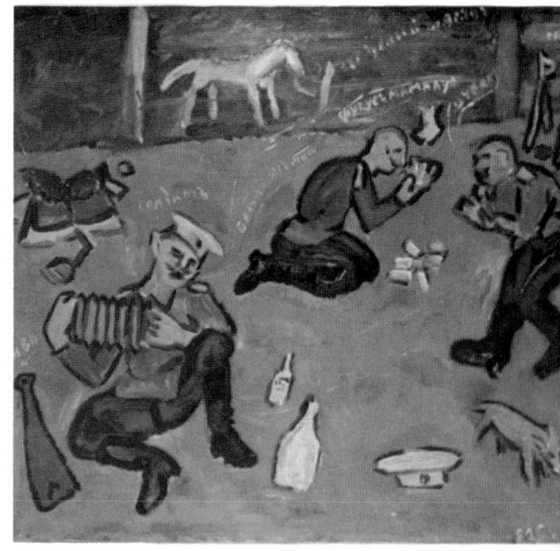

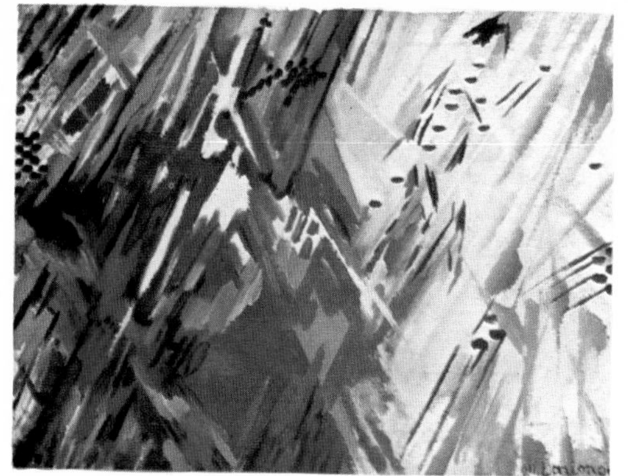

LARIONOV, MICHAEL: *Rayonism.* 1911.

LARIONOV, Michael (Tiraspol, 22.5.1881 – Fontenay-aux-Roses, 10.5.1964). At first Larionov was considered the most gifted Russian impressionist. He had attended the Moscow Academy since 1898; there he met Natalia Goncharova, who from then on remained his personal and artistic companion. In 1903 he discovered Seurat for himself and worked in a pointillist style the following year. In 1906 he took part in the exhibition of Russian art in Paris and travelled to London and Paris. In 1907 he made friends with David Burliuk and organized the first exhibition of The Golden Fleece in Moscow where modern French art was shown. In the years that followed, he freed himself from the influence of the French, and discovered his own means of natural expression in a primitivism based on Russian folk art. In 1912 he turned to futurism which he evolved into rayonism; this he expanded in the *Rayonist and Futurist Manifesto* in 1913. In 1914 he moved with Goncharova to Paris to work on Diaghilev's ballet productions.

LE FAUCONNIER, Henri (Hesdin, 12.12.1881 – Paris, 25.12.1945). Le Fauconnier came to Paris in 1900 and began to study law and political science. In 1901 he changed to painting and entered J. P. Laurens's studio. He painted under the influence of the neo-impressionists and exhibited in the *Salon des indépendants* in 1905. In 1906 he travelled in Brittany and painted in a fauve style similar to Derain and Matisse. Out of this he developed an expressionist simplification of form in 1907. In 1909 he drew close to cubism but in a particular type of 'half-naturalistic cubism based on nature and architecture' (Azenfant).

In 1910 he exhibited with Delaunay and Metzinger amongst others in the *Salon d'automne*; and simultaneously for the New Artists' Association in Munich, to whose catalogue he contributed an article. He maintained contact with *Der Blaue Reiter* in the following years as well. In 1912, he became Director of the *Académie de la Palette*. In the same year he painted with his pupils in Brittany and travelled to Amsterdam. Macke and Marc visited him in Paris.

In 1913 he turned away from cubism more and more, inclining towards a visionary expressionism. He lived in Holland from 1914–1919, met Mondrian and exercised an influence on the Belgian expressionists through de Smet and Van Den Berghe. In 1920 he returned to Paris.

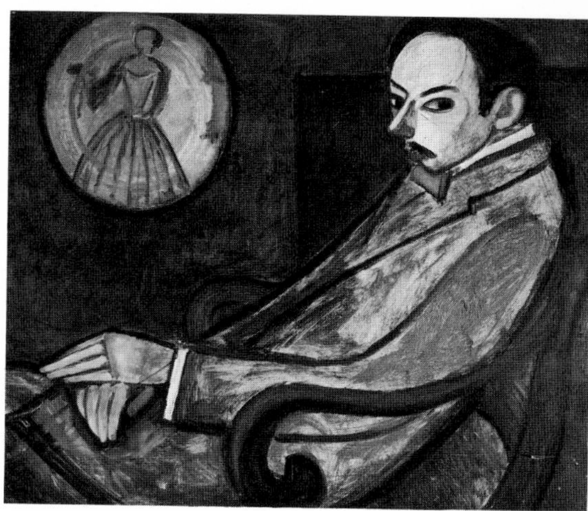

LE FAUCONNIER, HENRI: *Portrait of Pierre-Jean Jouve.* 1909.

MACKE, August (Meschede, 3.1.1887 – Perthes-les-Hurlus, 26.9.1914). August Macke was a close friend of Franz Marc and participated in the activities of *Der Blaue Reiter*. Nevertheless, he was fully aware that his talents placed him in direct opposition to the Munich circle. His was a temperament completely bound up with the temporal world, and far removed from the hereafter. Rather, he considered reflections on metaphysical problems to be a waste of time. The little time that he had was used to satisfy his insatiable curiosity about life.

From 1904 to 1906 he had attended the Academy in Düsseldorf and designed costumes and décor for the theatre there. In 1907 he went to Paris to study the impressionists. Monet and Degas made the strongest impression on him. He experimented with pure colour and seized every opportunity to increase his knowledge and capacities.

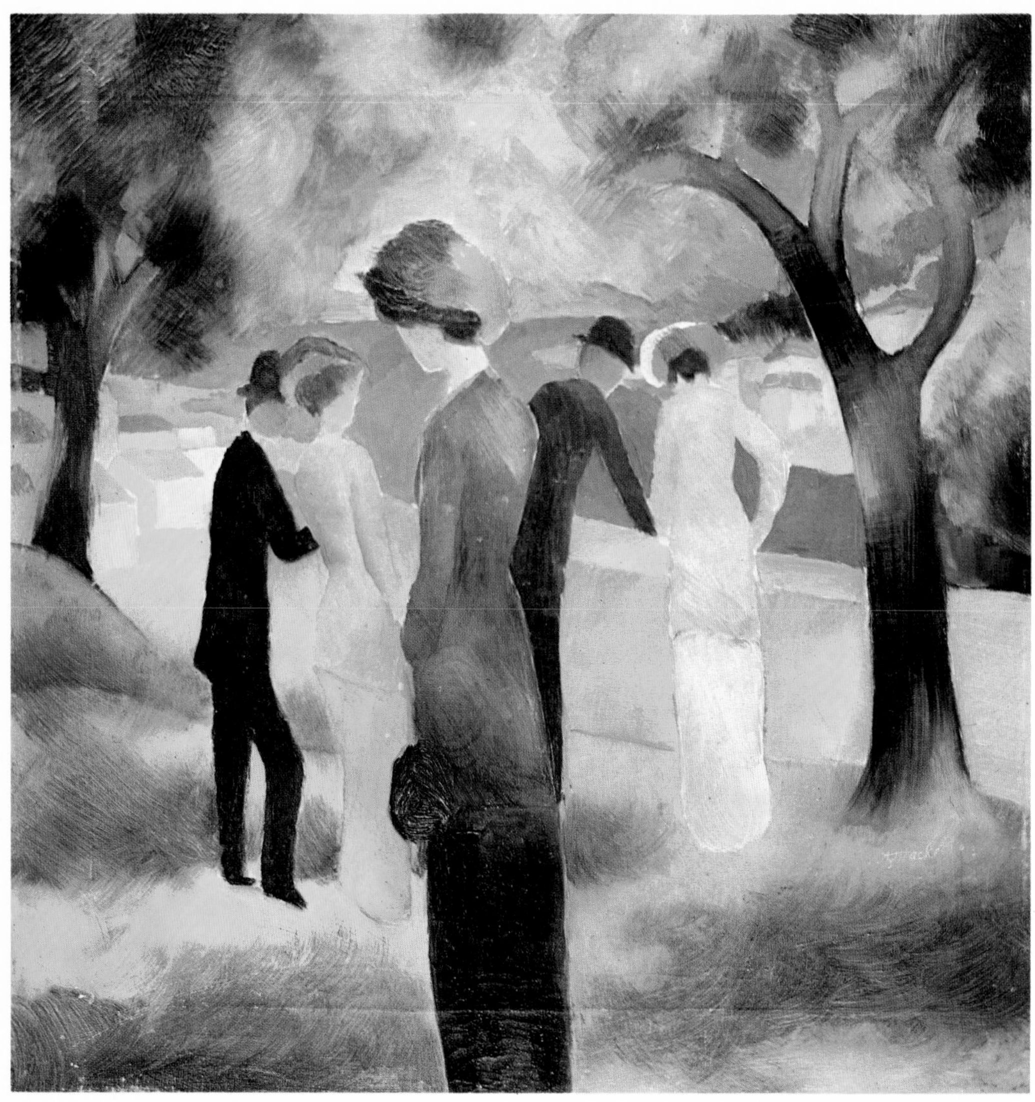

MACKE, AUGUST: *Woman in the green jacket.* 1912.

In 1907 he went to Berlin for six months and was Corinth's pupil. In the summer of 1908 he was again in Paris and studied Seurat, Cézanne and Gauguin in depth. In 1909 he settled for a year at Lake Tegern in Upper Bavaria. During this period he produced about two hundred pictures, and realized what his goal was: 'for me, work is a complete rejoicing in nature'. For Macke, the ordering of his impressions of the visible world included the feelings of the heart, the sense of something mysterious and a wonderment at nature. However much he let himself be influenced by Matisse's 'plastic' use of pure colour, and however much he had adopted views of *Der Blaue Reiter*, and above all of cubism, Picasso, Le Fauconnier and Delaunay regarding formal composition, he was never in danger of being an imitator. His starting point was his experience of reality and whilst painting, he intuitively adapted the formal elements which were useful to him. He thus avoided the danger of which he warned Marc and Kandinsky, that is, that form would become too important and emotion be inadequate to fill it.

In 1910 he had made friends with Marc and established a loose connection with the New Artists' Association in Munich. In 1911 he collaborated in the prepara-

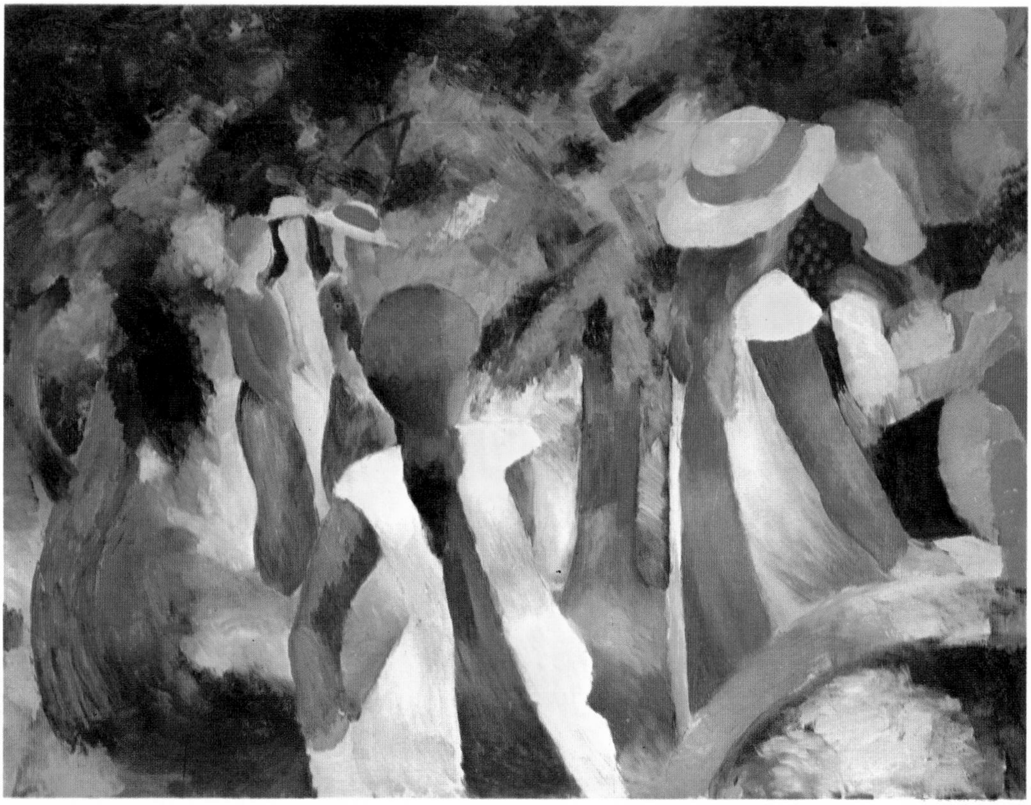

MACKE, AUGUST: *Girls under the trees.* 1914.

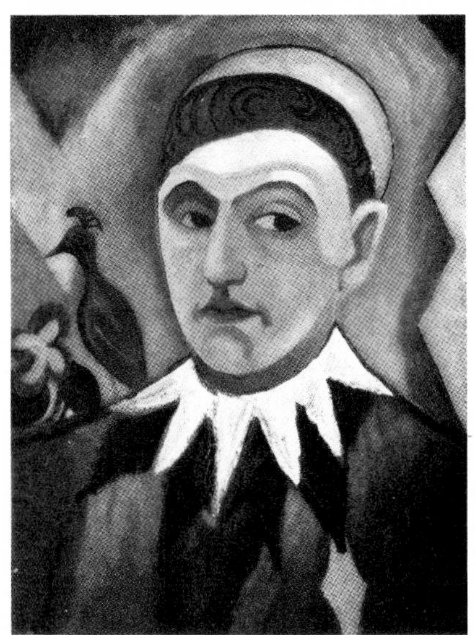

MACKE, AUGUST: *Self-portrait as a clown.* 1913.

MACKE, AUGUST: *Kairouan I.* 1914.

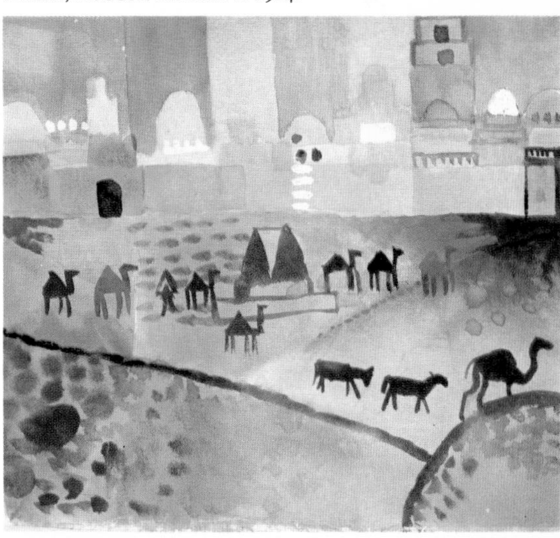

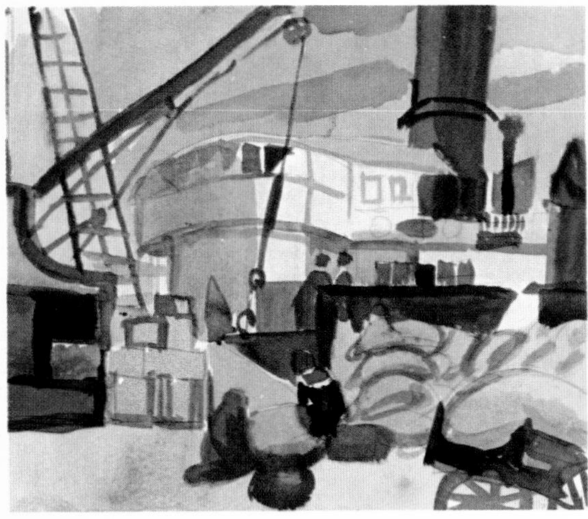

MACKE, AUGUST: *Port in Tunisia.* 1914.

tion of the almanach, *Der Blaue Reiter*, to which he contributed an essay. In 1912 he and Marc visited Delaunay in Paris. A friendship developed – Delaunay and Apollinaire visited Macke in Bonn in 1913 – and Macke gained important insights regarding spatial values and movement in colour.

In the autumn of 1913, he went to Lake Thun in Switzerland for eight months. He now possessed the means to express all the beauty of the world, its joy and the fullness of life, to portray the world as visual poetry. At Lake Thun he conceived the idea of travelling to Tunis with Klee and Moilliet. This famous stay in Tunis in April only lasted two weeks and yielded spontaneous water-colours and hundreds of drawings.

There was no time left to Macke to elaborate this rich material. He was called up for military service on August 8th – six weeks later he was dead.

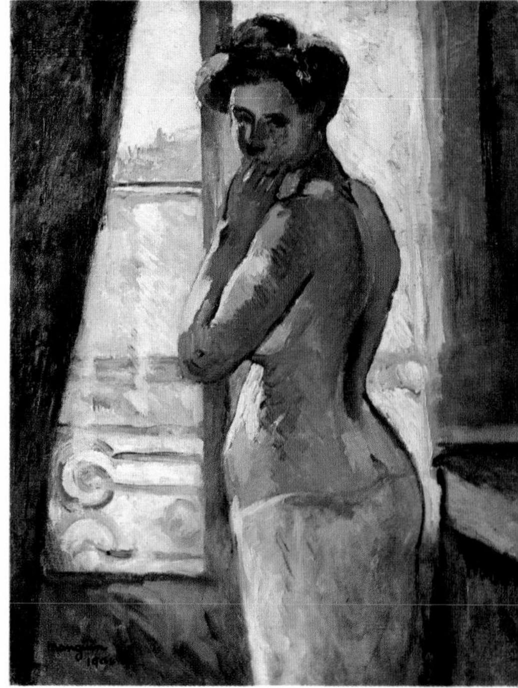

MANGUIN, HENRI: *In front of the window.* 1904.

MANGUIN, Henri (Paris, 23.3.1874 – Saint Tropez, 25.9.1949). In 1894 Manguin entered the École des Beaux Arts and Moreau's studio. Here he made friends with his fellow pupils Matisse, Marquet, Camoin, Puy and Rouault. Since he came from a wealthy bourgeois family, he was able to set up a studio in the rue Boursault in 1899 and employ models. This was why Matisse, Marquet and Puy met at his house to paint. Manguin was far removed from any theory, but was a born colourist who sought, because of his temperament, to create an intense colour in his art. He discovered Cézanne to be his most important influence; he did not admire his construction so much as his manner of introducing light.

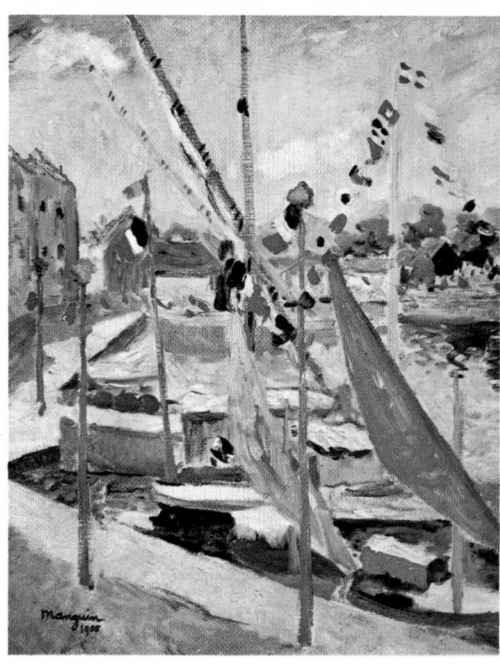

MANGUIN, HENRI: *Saint-Tropez.* 1905.

He exhibited in the *Salon d'automne* from 1904 onwards and had his first one-man exhibition in 1906 in Druet's gallery. In 1905 he had discovered St Tropez, where he later painted regularly in the summer months. In 1905 he met Signac and in the following year, Cross and Van Rysselberghe. In 1909 he went to Naples with Marquet. Manguin always remained close to nature, which he observed with joyful sensuality. He experienced and expressed it as part of himself. 'Manguin took landscape as it really is. He understood it. It was for him magic, a melody, a love song.' (Bonnard).

MARC, Franz (Munich, 8.2.1880 – Verdun, 4.3.1916). Marc began his studies with theology, then philosophy, and suddenly decided in 1900 to follow his father's example and become a painter. He lamented the general loss of religous unity, and chose art as a means of creating a new one. He was convinced that no great art had ever existed, or could exist, without religion. He attended the academy in Munich until 1903 and travelled to Paris for the first time; here he was greatly influenced by impressionism, though this scarcely showed in his paintings. He reacted similarly in 1907. He was enthusiastic about the impressionists, but Van Gogh alone exercised a lasting influence on him, and this was only put into practice in 1909.

Marc already knew that it was necessary to express 'the inner truth of things', and that neither theory nor the study of nature were of use for this. The way could only be found through the imagination. In the years that followed, therefore, he concerned himself with deepening his imaginative powers by learning nature by heart. He studied nature's laws through animal anatomy, in order to be in a position to let new creatures emerge in his imagination, that nevertheless could be genuine because they were constructed according to the laws of nature. He thus hoped to simplify form in order to express the symbolism, the pathos and the mystery of nature. Up until 1910 this problem was only successfully solved as regards structure. Colour which

MARC, FRANZ: *Figures in combat.* 1914.

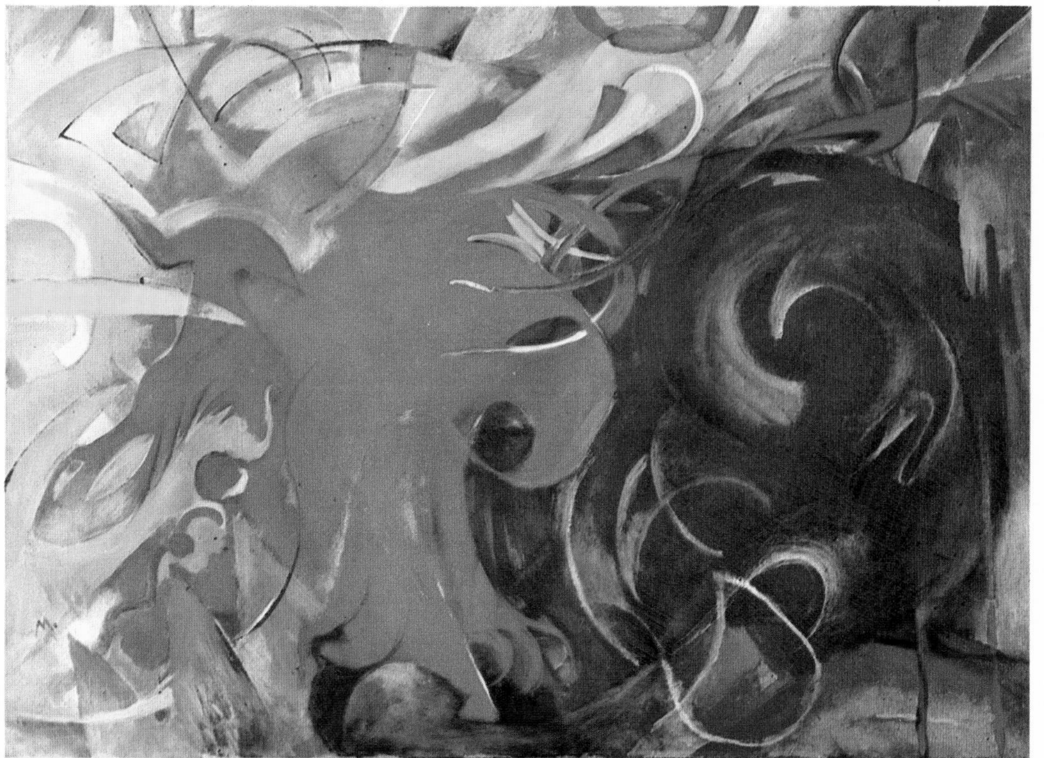

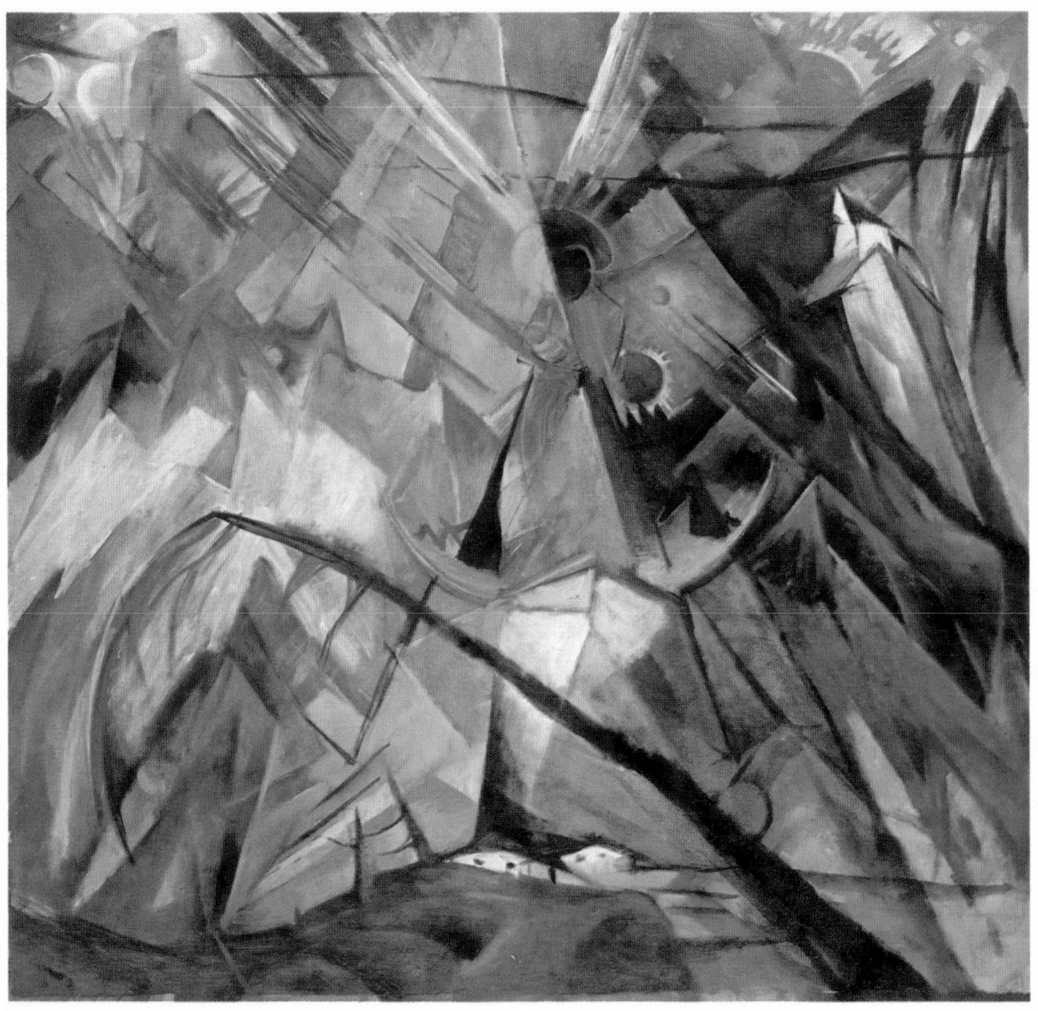

MARC, FRANZ: *Tyrol.* 1913–1914.

remained bound to the object, retained its arbitrary randomness and hindered expression. In 1910 Marc had his first one-man exhibition, bringing favourable reviews, in which he exhibited *plein air*-like pictures still with an overall light base. At the same time, he made the acquaintance of August Macke, who made him aware of the independent power of expression in pure colour. Marc now pursued the problems of colour with the same intensity as he had examined structure before, and developed his own theory about the potential for expressionism in colour. He met Kandinsky in 1911 and joined the New Artists' Association.

The contact with the more advanced endeavours of his friends who were striving in the same direction, enabled Marc to make rapid progress. He concentrated more and more on animal paintings. Admittedly, he did turn his attention to nude portraits, but they did not provide a satisfying solution. 'The ungodly human beings who surrounded me (the men above all) did not arouse my true emotions, whereas the inherent feel for life in animals made all that was good in me come out.' (Marc). He thus defined his goal to be 'an animalization of art', i.e. so to unite the characteristic forms of animals and landscapes into a continuous organic shape, that a cosmic rhythm emerges, held in balance by the pure colour of expression. Marc's experience of cubism was important for fostering the inter-penetration of subject and surroundings. For the process of rhythmification he adapted what he had learnt from futurism. In 1911 Kandinsky and Marc left the New Artists' Association, organized the *Der Blaue Reiter* exhibition and published the almanach of the same name. In 1912 he went with Macke to Paris and visited Delaunay. In 1913 he played a vital part in the selection and hanging of the first German autumn *salon* in Berlin. What he had learnt in Paris and Berlin strengthened his realization that he had

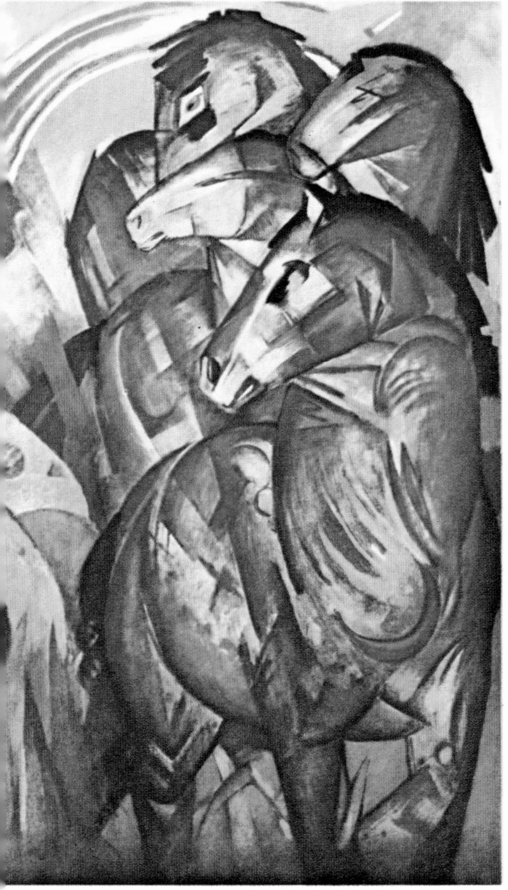

MARC, FRANZ: *Tower of Blue Horses.* 1913.

not yet succeeded in achieving a synthesis of the outer and inner world. Now aware that all forms are memories, he abandoned the object in 1914, and created abstract pictures from his inner imagination alone. In 1914 he was called up; he fell at Verdun in 1916.

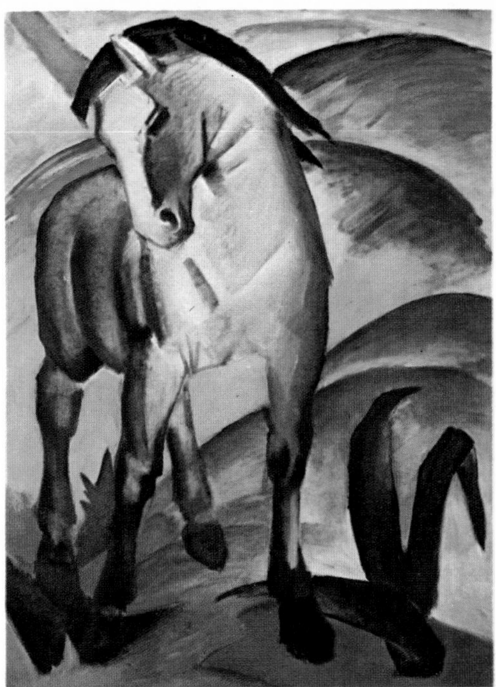

MARC, FRANZ: *Blue Horse I.* 1911.

MARQUET, Albert (Bordeaux, 27.3.1875 – Paris, 14.6.1947). Marquet came to Paris in 1890 and began studying at the School of Arts and Crafts where, in 1892, he made friends with Matisse, a friendship which lasted until his death. In 1895 he transferred to the École des Beaux Arts and learnt under Morot and Cormon. In 1898 he entered Moreau's studio where, in addition to Matisse, Rouault, Camoin and Manguin were working. Marquet too followed the phases of Matisse's thought and turned to pure colour under the influence of neo-impressionism. However, his painting, with its light-dark contrasts, remained more strongly dependent on tradition.

In 1898/1899 he visited the *Académie Carrière* with Matisse and painted street scenes with Camoin. In 1900 he and Matisse painted decorative friezes in the Grand Palais. The exhibited in the *Salon des indépendants* from 1910 on and were co-founders of the *Salon d'automne* in 1903. Marquet travelled whenever possible – 1904–1906 to Normandy with Derain; in 1906 to Southern France, where he met Camoin, Manguin and Cross; in 1907 to London with Camoin and Friesz; in 1910 to Munich with Matisse. But these were only the first steps in a lifetime of travelling.

In 1907 the Druet Gallery organized his first one-man exhibition. It was already evident that Marquet was first

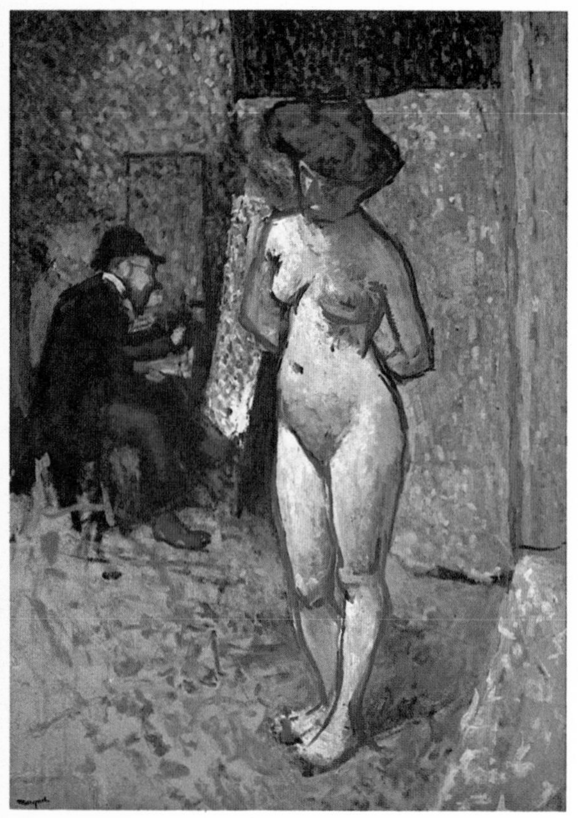

MARQUET, ALBERT: *Matisse painting a model in Manguin's studio.* 1905.

and foremost a landscape painter who was principally attracted by landscapes near water – the Paris *quais*, beaches and ports. His method was to select sections of landscape always viewed from above and with a wide perspective; depth was emphasized by diagonal lines. The draughtsmanship was sketchy, simplified and yet precise.

Even though Marquet used brilliant, strong colours to start with, he often finished his paintings in grey. He did not seek expressivity through an intensification of colour, but sought to make the surface more tranquil, and to give his paintings order through strong outlines. He thus moved rapidly away from typical fauvism and reached a simplified, calm impressionism with softened shades, to which he remained faithful for the rest of his life.

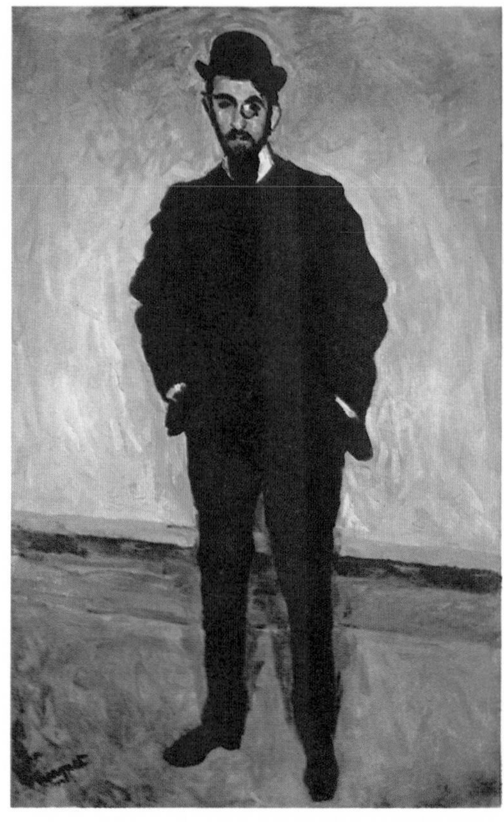

MARQUET, ALBERT: *Portrait of André Rouveyre.* 1904.

MARQUET, ALBERT: *The beach at Fécamp.* 1906.

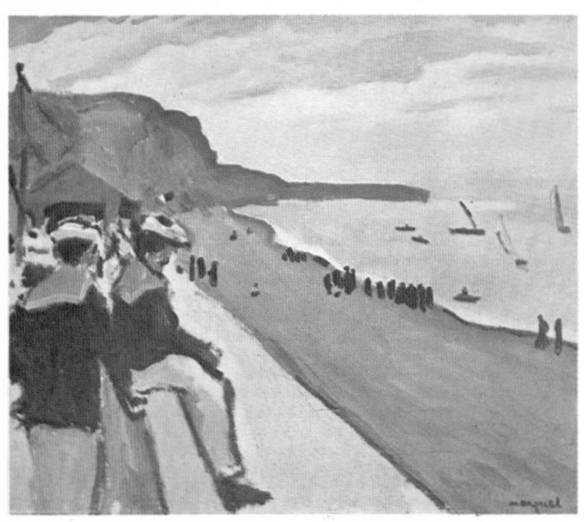

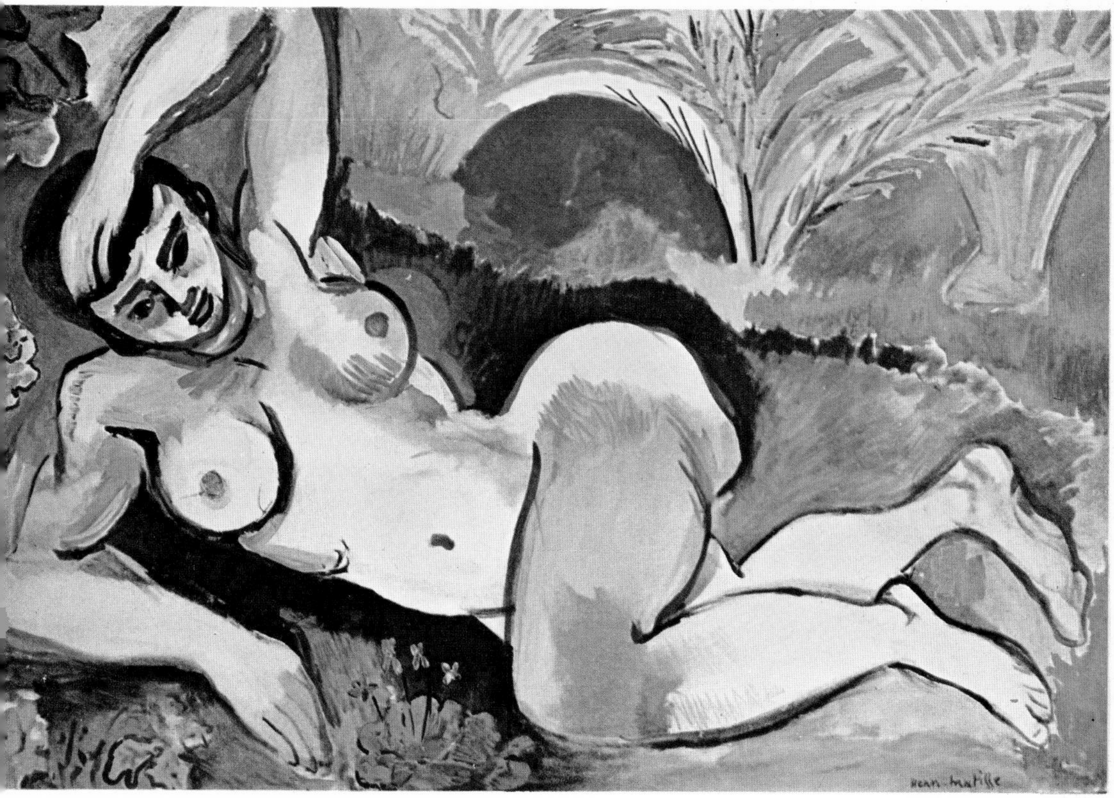

MATISSE, HENRI: *Blue Nude.* 1917.

MATISSE, Henri (Le Cateau-Cambrésis, 31.12.1869 – Cimiez, near Nice, 3.11.1954). Matisse, like Kandinsky, had first studied law before coming, by chance, to painting. In 1891 he went to Paris to the Académie Julian where the preparatory course for the École des Beaux Arts was held. At the same time, he attended evening classes at the School of Arts and Crafts. There he met Albert Marquet, with whom he formed a lifelong friendship. In 1895 he came to the notice of Gustave Moreau who took him on as his pupil.

There were numerous talents gathered together in Moreau's studio – Rouault, Camoin, Manguin and later, Marquet as well. Moreau's teaching method was less concerned with artistic draughtsmanship than with training the eye. His pupils were encouraged to copy paintings in the Louvre and to draw in the streets and in cafés. Matisse remained there until 1899, and quickly established himself as the leader amongst his friends. In 1896 he came under the influence of the impressionists and was made conscious of the possibilities for expression in colour, confirmed by his encounter with Picasso, and Turner's work in London. In 1898, he painted for

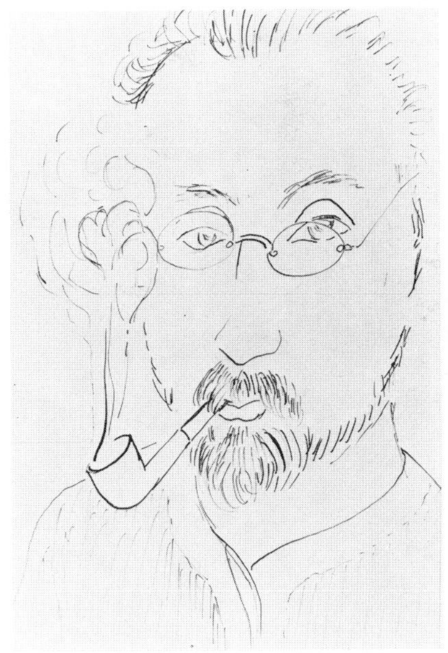

MATISSE, HENRI: *Portrait of the artist with a pipe.* 1919.

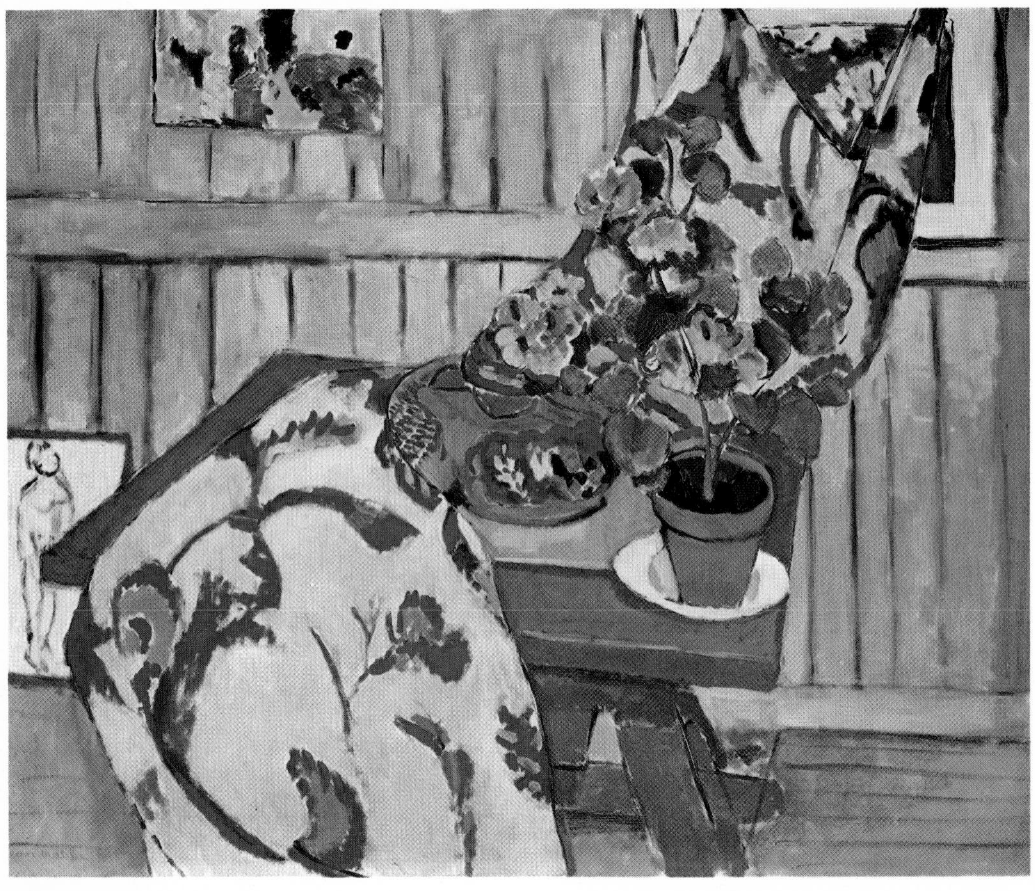

MATISSE, HENRI: *Still life with geranium.* 1910.

several months in Corsica, where the discovery of Mediterranean light led him to pure colour, and the simplification of the picture's subject.

In 1899 he visited the Académie Carrière where he met Derain and Puy. He was principally concerned with the nude figure and produced a series of brightly coloured nudes, outlined in black. At the same time, he learnt how to sculpt. In 1904 he mounted his first one-man exhibition of forty-six works, in Vollard's gallery.

In the same year, he gained new insights and stimuli in the course of a summer stay in Saint Tropez. He painted there together with Signac and Cross. They stimulated him to employ pure colour, as understood by the neo-impressionists, in a methodical and carefully deliberate way. However, it was precisely the constraints of painting pure colour in graduated shades which led Matisse to intensify them for greater expression and heighten them through contrast. Line was not dissolved into light either, but transformed into arabesques of colour. Matisse was supported in this move by the commemorative exhibition for Van Gogh and Seurat in the *Salon des indépendants* of 1905, which he, as Chairman of the Selection Committee, had helped to organize.

He spent the summer of 1905 in Derain's company in Collioure. Here he achieved his breakthrough to fauvism. His pointillist application of colour, now fused into blocks, emphasized by complementary contrasts; but his agitated brushwork was quickly toned down. Colour was applied 'flatly' – disembodied and distanced from all realistic significance – and shapes given rhythm by curving outlines. Simplification and purification led to a decorative, two-dimensional style in which colour and line combined to create the most concise expression. 'We want to attain a serene dignity through the simplification of ideas and the plastic element. A harmonious unity is our only ideal.' (Matisse).

The more Matisse's art strove towards universal and monumental expression, the more it moved away from the currents of his time. Admittedly, the Matisse Academy was founded in 1908 on the request of the

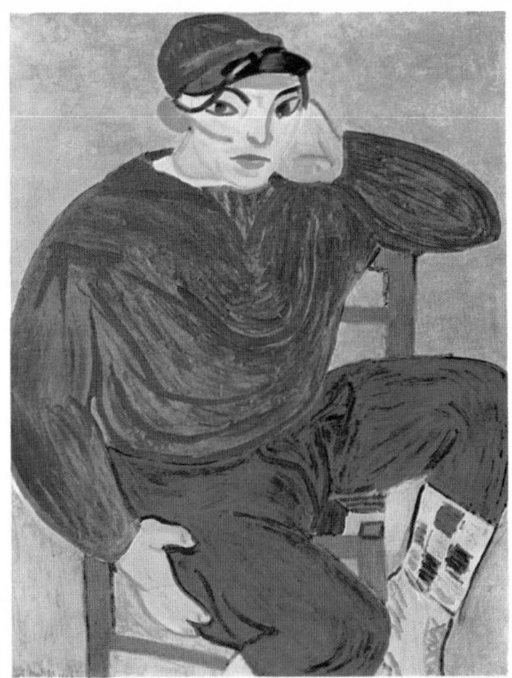

MATISSE, HENRI: *Young Sailor.* 1906.

German painter, Hans Purrmann; this lasted until 1911 and had more than a hundred pupils. Nevertheless, this resulted in external similarities only. Matisse, who had carried a whole generation with him on his way, withdrew into himself.

MEIDNER, Ludwig (Bernstadt, Silesia, 18.4.1884 – Darmstadt, 14.5.1966). In 1912, Herwarth Walden mounted an exhibition in the *Sturm* gallery in Berlin of a short-lived group who called themselves *Die Pathetiker.* Their most gifted member was Ludwig Meidner. He had attended the Imperial Art School in Breslau from 1903 to 1905, In 1906 he lived as a fashion designer in Berlin and went the same year to study at the Académie Julian. Although he made friends with Modigliani, he remained aloof from the concerns of contemporary artists.

MATISSE, HENRI: *The Gypsy Woman.* 1905–1906.

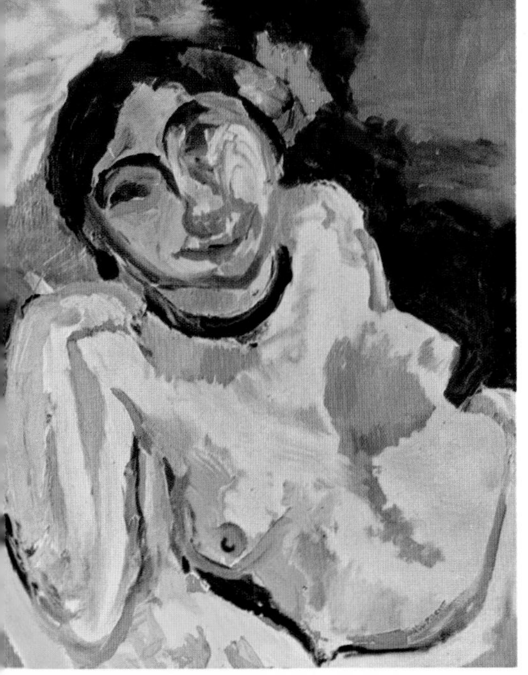

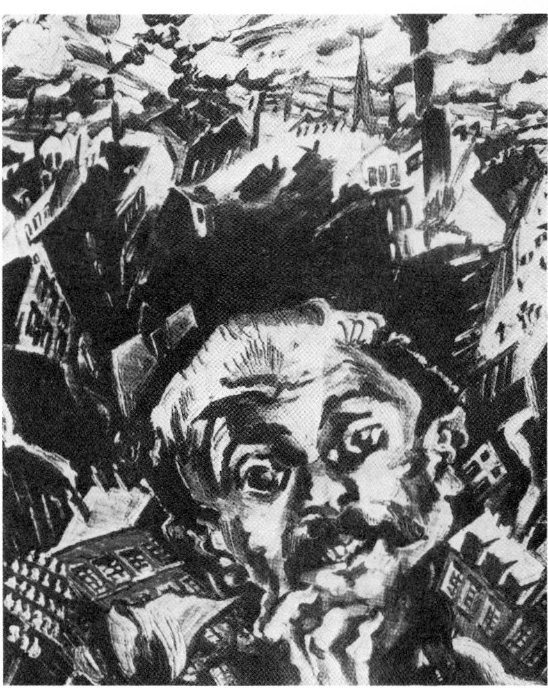

MEIDNER, LUDWIG: *The Town and I.* 1913.

In 1908 he returned to Berlin and lived there in very harsh circumstances. He was encouraged to give free rein to his passionate nature by the exhibitions of the futurists and Delaunay. He now gave utterance to his cries and his ecstacy. Without restraint, nor concern for formal problems, he produced inner visions of apocalyptic landscapes and burning cities using agitated brush- and pencil-work. His distorted portraits were also full of emotion, which appeared in an almost incalculable number of paintings of writers, actors and painters; angry visions full of unease and bitterness; *September Cry: Hymns, Prayers, Blasphemies* for example, is the title of one of Meidner's poems, which he produced alongside his drawings and paintings to describe his inner state. Meidner knew no limits in his endeavour to lay bear his soul.

His visions paled when from 1916 to 1918 he had to do military service and his paintings lost their power of conviction. Confronted with the hideous nature of reality he realized that his previous path had been mistaken and returned to the Jewish faith ten years after his first artistic awakening. In 1923 he disavowed his previous work, which he called an intolerable expression of 'lunacy and indecency'.

MIRÓ, Joan (Barcelona, 20.4.1893). Miró was the son of a goldsmith, who was sympathetic to the artistic leanings of his son. Miró drew constantly as a child and, when fourteen, was allowed to attend the art academy in Barcelona. In 1910 he entered a business house as an office employee under pressure from his parents. In 1912 he again turned to painting and continued his studies in the private art school of Gali, where he remained until 1915. Miró drew on the example of fauvism in a series of landscapes and still lifes, which also reveal contact with cubism. However, his colouring is more melancholy and thicker, segmented by a distorting and turbulent structure, aiming at expressivity. In 1912 he met Picabia. In 1918 he mounted his first one-man exhibition in the Dalmau gallery in Barcelona. This marked the end of his paintings inspired by spontaneous emotion. He turned to a meticulous depiction of landscapes, and an accurate grasp of detail. In 1919 he went to Paris.

MIRÓ, JOAN: *Nude in the mirror.* 1919.

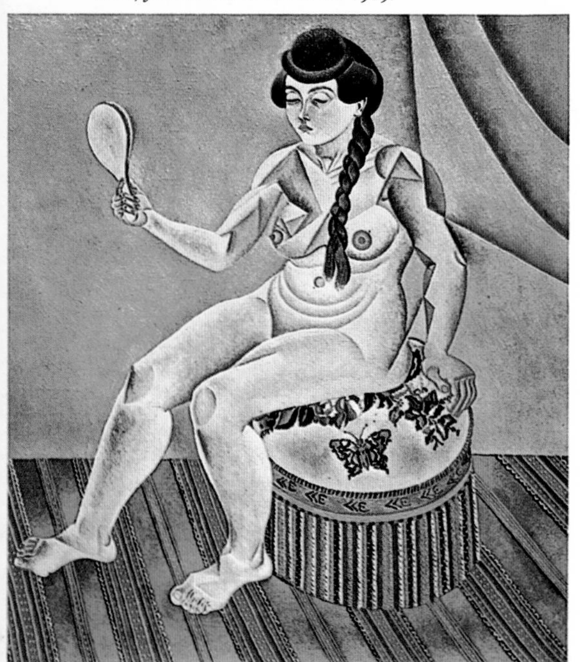

MODERSOHN-BECKER, Paula (Dresden, 8.2.1876 – Worpswede, 20.11.1907). Paula Modersohn-Becker completed her artistic output in only six years. She had first to complete her training as a teacher in Bremen, before she could go to Berlin in 1896 to be able to study at the school for women artists there. In the summer of

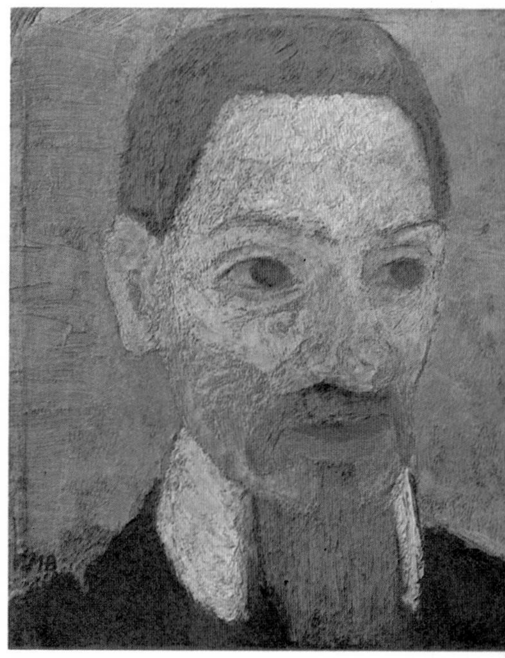

MODERSOHN-BECKER, PAULA: *Portrait of Rainer Maria Rilke.* 1904.

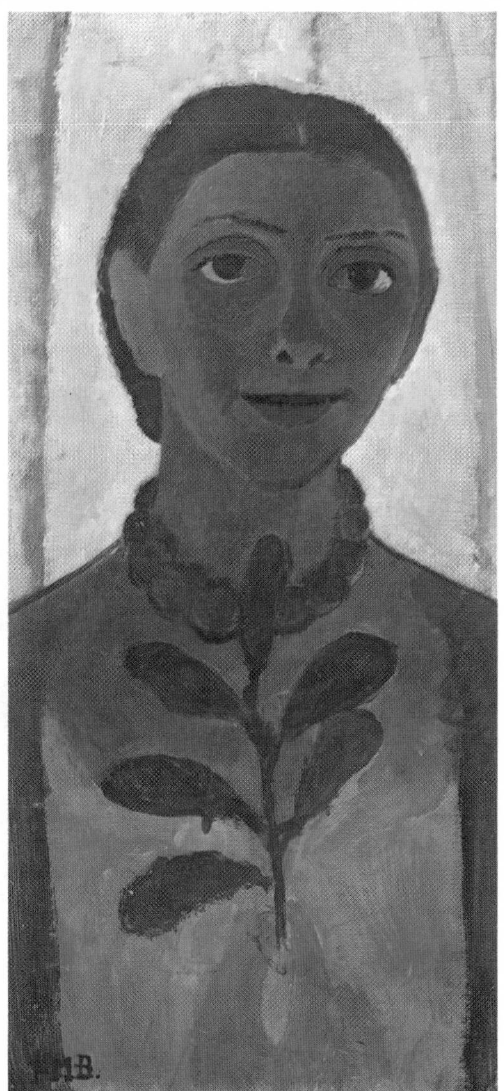

MODERSOHN-BECKER, PAULA: *Self-portrait.* 1907.

1897 she went to Worpswede for the first time, was taught by Mackensen and met her future husband, Otto Modersohn. In 1898 she went on a journey to Scandinavia and moved to Worpswede.

She spent the first half of 1900 as a student in the Colarossi Academy in Paris and set up a studio with Clara Westhoff, later Rilke's wife. In 1903 she returned to Colarossi in Paris, and met Rodin through Rilke. In 1902 she again stayed in Paris and attended the Académie Julian. She returned for the last time in 1906 and stayed for about a year before returning to Worpswede in the spring of 1907 where she gave birth to a daughter on November 2nd and died a short while afterwards.

Paula Modersohn-Becker admittedly started with lyrical naturalism, but quickly progressed beyond it as a result of her experiences in France, giving her painting a restrained radiance, which she fused with a simplification of form learnt from Cézanne. In so doing, she used the expressive potential of colour to give voice to her feelings, and thus pointed out a road which the expressionists in Germany later took.

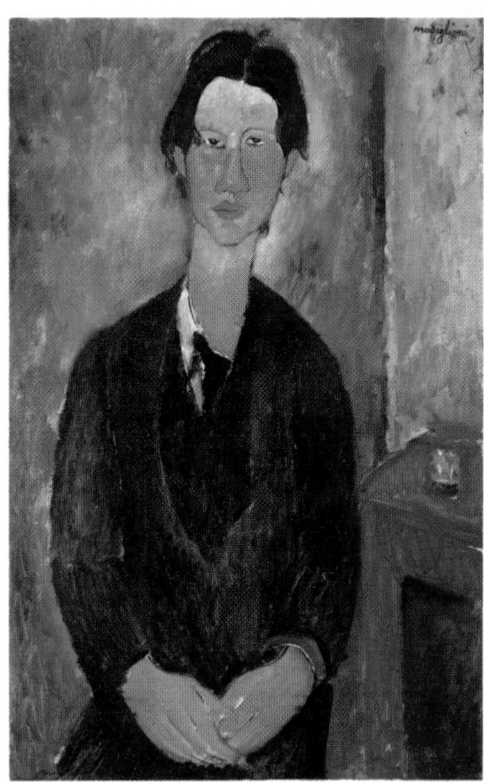

MODIGLIANI, AMEDEO: *Portrait of Soutine.* 1917.

MODIGLIANI, Amedeo (Leghorn, 12.7.1884 – Paris, 25.1.1920). Modigliani came from a family of Jewish businessmen. He began his training in 1898 at the art college in Leghorn. He was forced to interrupt his schooling by illness in 1901. He resumed it again in 1902 in the academy in Florence with Fattori. In 1906 he moved to Paris where he soon came into contact with Max Jacob, Apollinaire and Picasso. In 1908 he exhibited for the first time in the *Salon des indépendants.*

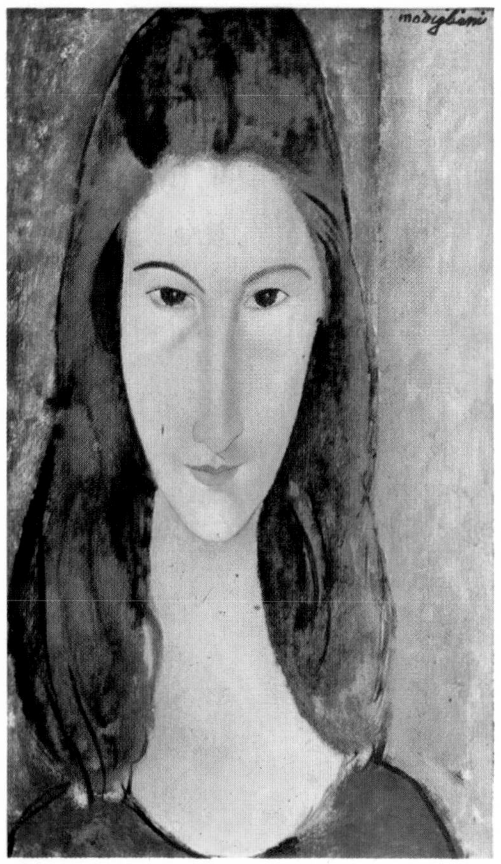

MODIGLIANI, AMEDEO: *Portrait of Jeanne Hébuterne*. 1918.

From the start, he made the portrait genre his own, and later the female nude. His early works are influenced by Toulouse-Lautrec and fauvism. In 1909 he met Brancusi and began, at his instigation, to work as a sculptor. In 1912 he exhibited his first sculptures in the *Salon des indépendants*. The examples of negro sculpture, and Cézanne, showed him a way to give emphatic expression to his feelings via distortion. In 1916 his style was characterized by his elongated and distorted manner. In 1917 the Berthe Weill Gallery showed his first one-man exhibition. In 1918 he travelled to Cannes and Nice where he tried his hand at landscape painting. Nevertheless, he remained bound to lyrical figure painting and subdued colours.

MORGNER, Wilhelm (Soest, 27.1.1891 – Langemark, 12.8.1917). Morgner, of whom it is said that when a schoolboy he watched Christian Rolfs painting in Soest, came to Worpswede in 1908 and became a pupil of Georg Tappert. He began with lyrical naturalism and was strongly influenced by neo-impressionism and Van Gogh. Through the help of his teacher, Morgner was already alble to exhibit with the New Sezession in Berlin in 1911 and to participate in the second exhibition of *Der Blaue Reiter*; and in the Sezession in Cologne in 1912. He transposed his agitated emotions into a rhythmic stylization. Under the influence of Kandinsky and Jawlensky, he sought a way towards abstract art, which he thought was the only means of expressing the emotion in his consciousness of the world.

'My means of expression is colour. I want to communicate the living God in me directly throught the correct use of colour.' However, he barely had time to elaborate this plan. He was called up for military service as early as 1913, took part in the war from its first day and never returned.

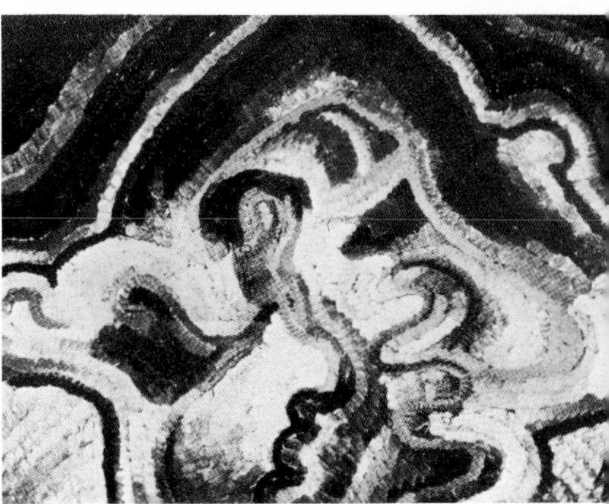

MORGNER, WILHELM: *Astral composition XIV*. 1912.

MUELLER, Otto (Liebau, Silesia, 16.10.1874 – Breslau, 24.9.1930). After four years as an apprentice lithographer in Görlitz, Mueller came to the Dresden Academy where he worked until 1896. In 1896 and 1897 he travelled with the writer, Gerhart Hauptmann, to whom he was related, to Italy and Switzerland. In 1898–1899 he continued his studies with Stück at the Munich Academy. Then he returned to Dresden where the Hauptmanns had furnished a studio for him. Until moving to Berlin in 1908 Mueller withdrew ever more frequently to small villages in the Riesen Gebirge, painted in Bohemia, and the area round Dresden. No paintings exist from this period, for the painter destroyed them.

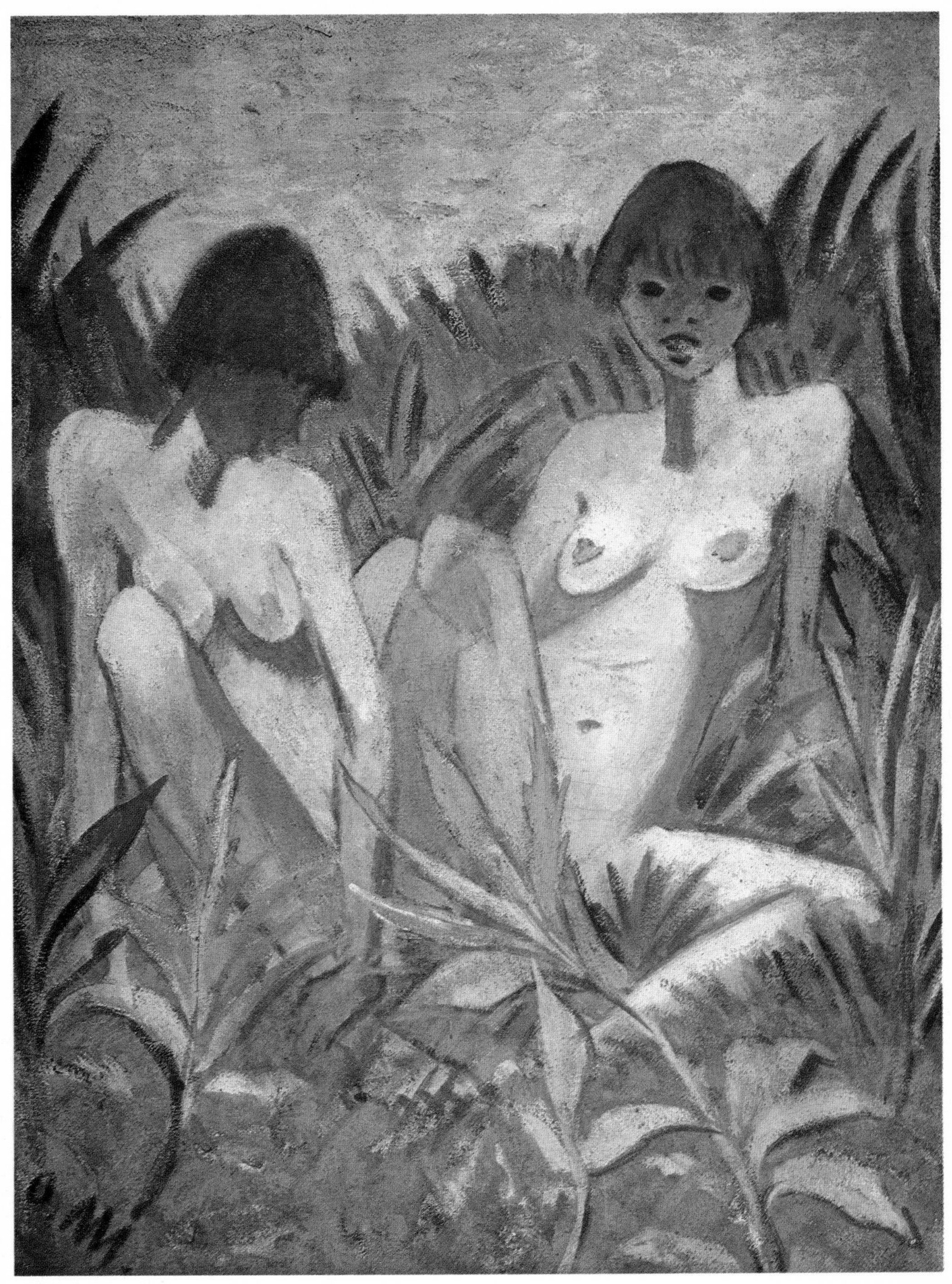

MUELLER, OTTO: *Two women in the reeds.* Circa 1922.

He received a vital impetus from Böcklin whose work gave him important ideas concerning the mythical element in nature and the possibilities of composition from blocks of colour. On the other hand, he remained uninfluenced by all those models which owed their expressivity to intensifying contrasted, pure colour. His use of colour aims rather towards tranquillity, does not go beyond the object and achieves unity within the picture through similarity of colour tone.

What linked him with his contemporaries was his yearning for a simple and natural way of life: 'The chief goal of my endeavour is to express my feelings for landscapes and for men with the greatest possible simplicity.' The essential theme of Mueller's work, which was already decided when he met the *Die Brücke* painters in 1910, was to portray the harmony of man and nature.

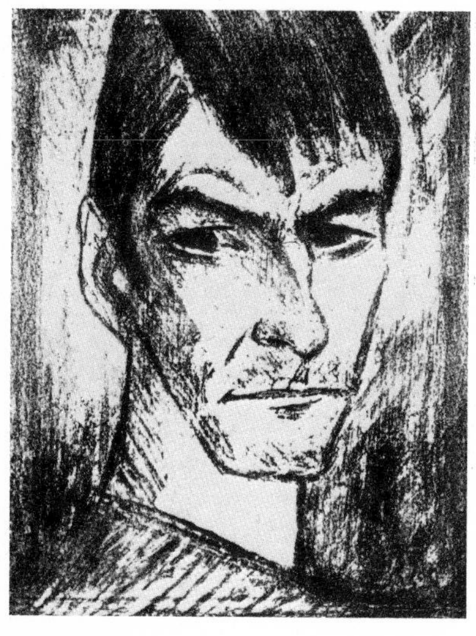

MUELLER, OTTO: *Self-portrait.* 1921.

Kirchner, Heckel and Pechstein were pursuing similar goals so that Mueller became a member of the group as a matter of course. He had already evolved his large-scale two-dimensional nudes, but they were still outlines with rounded, gentle, mellifluous contours. Under the influence of his friends – he went with Kirchner to Bohemia in 1911 – his outlines became more angular and taut and the organization of the surface area clearer. Once he had found the motif of the nude in a landscape, it became decisive for his work. It was followed in the twenties by pure landscape, and a few portraits and paintings of gypsies. Mueller continued to re-work these themes in a self-satisfied manner without any noticeable stylistic change. In 1919 he was appointed to teach at Breslau Academy.

MUNTER, Gabriele (Berlin, 19.2.1877 – Murnau, 19.5.1962). Gabriele Münter came to Munich in 1901 and first attended the school for women painters, for women were not allowed in the academies at that time. In 1902 she transferred to the school of the *Phalanx* group and became Kandinsky's pupil. A close companionship grew out of the teacher/pupil relationship in 1903, lasting till 1916.

Münter accompanied Kandinsky on all his travels in the following years. She was of course Kandinsky's pupil during this time, but since she employed her considerable talent without ambition and almost unconsciously, shenever became overshadowed. On the contrary, the works of Van Gogh, introduced to her by Jawlensky, and of Jawlensky himself, were her models. In the summer of 1908, which she spent with Kandinsky, Jawlensky and Werefkin in Murnau, she found her method. Prepared by the fauves, whom she knew from Paris, she discovered the power of expression in Bavarian folk art in the form of stained-glass work. She saw in Jawlensky, the juxtaposition of heavily outlined, luminous blocks of colour, which also became characteristic of her work. She now gave voice to her emotions principally in landscapes and still lifes, in which melancholy and dream merged.

In 1909 she was a co-founder of the New Artists' Association in Munich. She also belonged to *Der Blaue Reiter* and took part in all important exhibitions in Germany until 1914. In 1914 Kandinsky had to leave Germany. Gabriele Münter met him once more in Stockholm before they finally parted in 1916; Münter became silent as a painter for many years.

MÜNTER, GABRIELE: *Meadow in Murnau.* 1908.

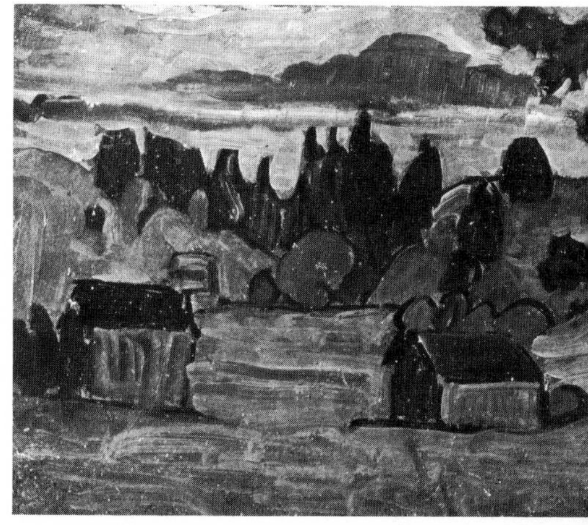

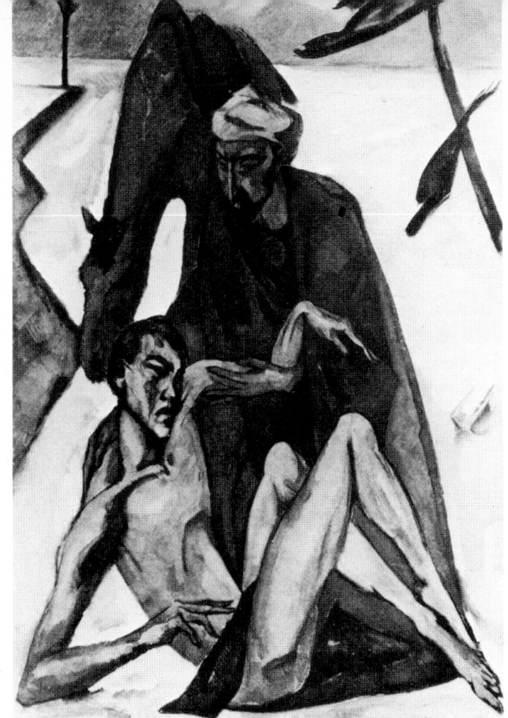

NAUEN, HEINRICH: the *Good Samaritan.* 1914.

NAUEN, Heinrich (Krefeld, 1.6.1880 – Kalkar, 26.11.1940). Heinrich Nauen was a colourist above all. He epitomizes the type of the Rhenish artist, who strove to unite elements of German and French art. Nauen studied at Düsseldorf Academy in 1898, became the prime pupil of Leopold van Kalkreuth in Stuttgart Academy until 1902, before going to Laetham-Saint-Martin. Here he worked in company with the future Belgian expressionists. From 1906 to 1911 he lived in Berlin and maintained contacts with *Die Brücke* and *Der Blaue Reiter.* In 1911 he settled in Dilborn. At first Nauen had sought expressivity after the model of Van Gogh. Then, under the influence of Matisse, he drew close to a form of fauvism. Landscapes, still lifes and modified portraits, with tranquil, harmonious rhythms, emerged from his decorative organization of the picture and its colourful ornamentation.

NOLDE, Emil (Schleswig, 7.8.1867 – Seebüll, 13.4.1956). Emil Hansen, who called himself Nolde from 1901 after his birthplace in Northern Schleswig, was the son of a farmer. After farming, he was allowed to enter a furniture factory in Flensburg as an apprentice wood carver. This lasted four years. In 1888 went to Karlsruhe where he worked as a furniture carver, and attended the School of Arts and Crafts at the same time. In 1890 he moved to Berlin as a furniture designer. He drew a great deal in museums and was especially influenced by Assyrian and Egyptian art.

In 1892 he taught industrial and ornamental design at the industrial museum in St Gallen. Here, Holler and Böcklin came to his attention. Böcklin's allegorical depictions of the soul in nature, in particular, moved him, for they coincided with his own experiences. In 1894 he drew the Swiss mountains personified as grotesque masks, had postcards of them printed and had

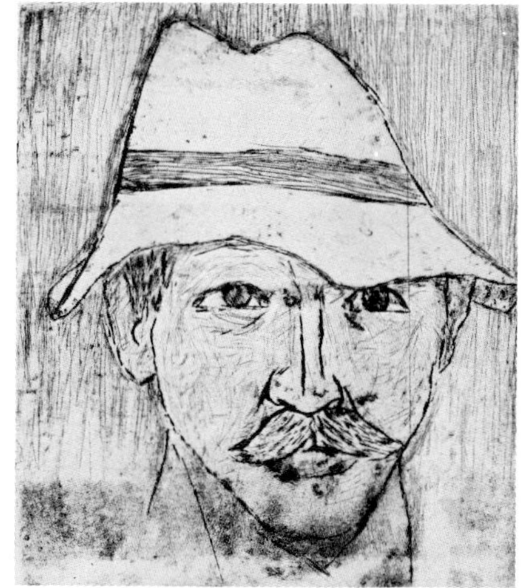

NOLDE, EMIL: *Self-portrait.* 1911.

NOLDE, EMIL: *The Adoration of the Magi.*

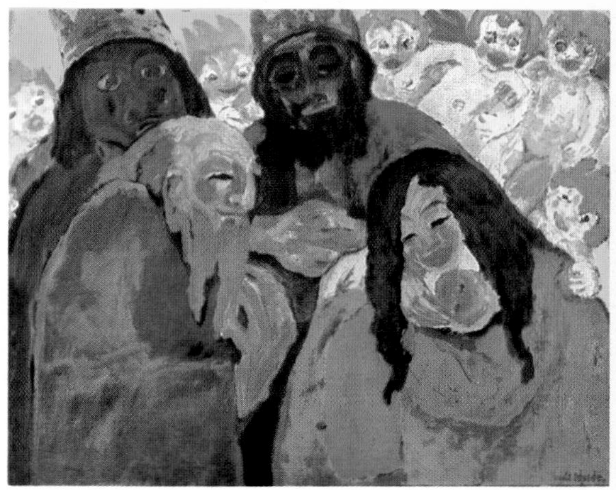

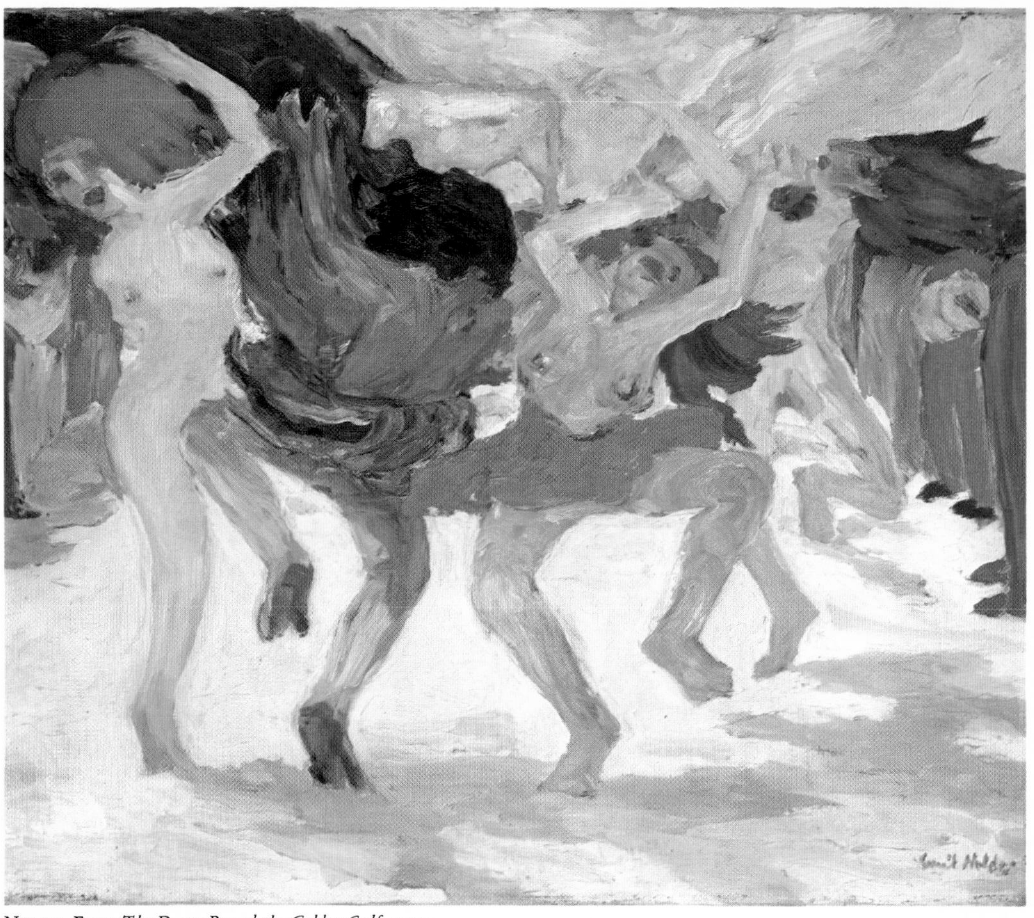

NOLDE, EMIL: *The Dance Round the Golden Calf.* 1910.

such a financial success with them that he was able to become an independent painter.

In 1898 he went to Munich, attended a private art college there and in 1899 painted with Hoelzel in Dachau. A nine-month stay in Paris then followed.

Nolde attended the Académie Julian and steeped himself in impressionism. In the summer of 1900 he returned to his home and spent the next years in various places, amongst others, Copenhagen and Berlin, until he settled in 1903 on Alsen Island.

Painting from instinct, he now transformed the visions that oppressed him into colour. The excitement that seized Nolde when working, expressed itself ecstatically. He applied colour in an impasto with brush, fingers, pieces of car and such like, to give its radiance intensified expression. These storms of colour, which so excited the *Die Brücke* group, have been called dramatic or ecstatic impressionism.

In 1906 Nolde took up the request to become a member of *Die Brücke* and took part in their exhibitions in 1906 and 1907. Close personal contact arose also during a stay in Dresden in 1901. Nolde taught the younger artists his etching technique and took from their style of wood-carving and lithography. Nolde left the group in 1907, but retained friendly links with them and was associated again with them in 1910 in the New Sezession in Berlin.

In the years to 1909, Nolde created portraits, landscapes and garden scenes, taking visible reality as his starting point. He increasingly spread colour over the surface like a carpet. He strove for simplification and concentration, with the aim of 'giving a new value to nature through the addition of the soul and the intellect' (Nolde). He had barely recovered from an illness in 1909 when he was seized by the desire to depict deep religious feeling and ardour. His first religious paintings originated in memory and the inner imagination in which form is so reduced that the vision is drawn entirely from colour and light.

In these years, Nolde painted in Alsen in the summer,

and spent the winter gathering his strength in Berlin. He was also affected by his fascination for the city. In 1910 he recorded his experience of the port of Hamburg in sketches which are filled with life, noise and animation. This is what interested him in the night restaurants, cafés and cabarets of Berlin, and what he transposed into painting.

But religious works were in the foreground from now on. In order to give form to primary emotion, he concentrated colour in large blocks, and abandoned any effect that was still linked to external appearances. These pictures gave rise to violent controversy, with the result that Nolde withdrew from the art world, and from 1913 was scarcely willing to take part in exhibitions. In

NOLDE, EMIL: *Nordermühle.* Circa 1924.

PECHSTEIN, MAX: *Self-portrait.* 1922.

his endeavour to find expression for the primitive state and to make natural emotions visible, Nolde concerned himself with the primitives in 1911–1912. In 1913 he took part in an expedition of the Imperial Colonial Office to the then German colonies in the South Seas, from which he returned shortly before the outbreak of war. In the years that followed, he found the security and the composure to give shape to his work within a thematically and formally circumscribed framework, and to give the impasto of his colours greater tranquillity.

PECHSTEIN, Max (Zwickau, 31.12.1881 – Berlin, 19.6.1955). Pechstein had a versatile talent. After a four-year apprenticeship with an interior decorator in

PECHSTEIN, MAX: *Self-portrait.* 1922.

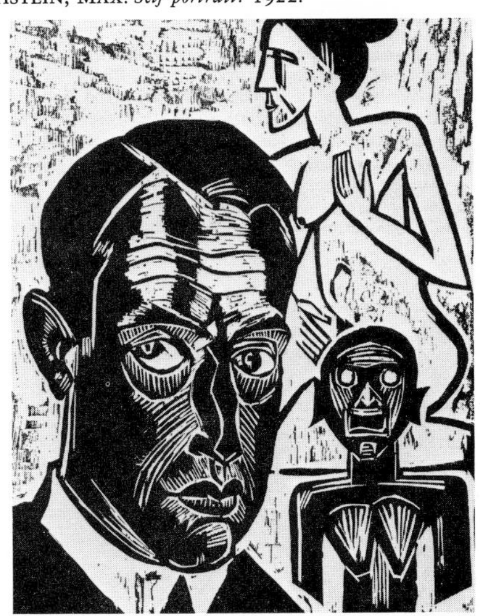

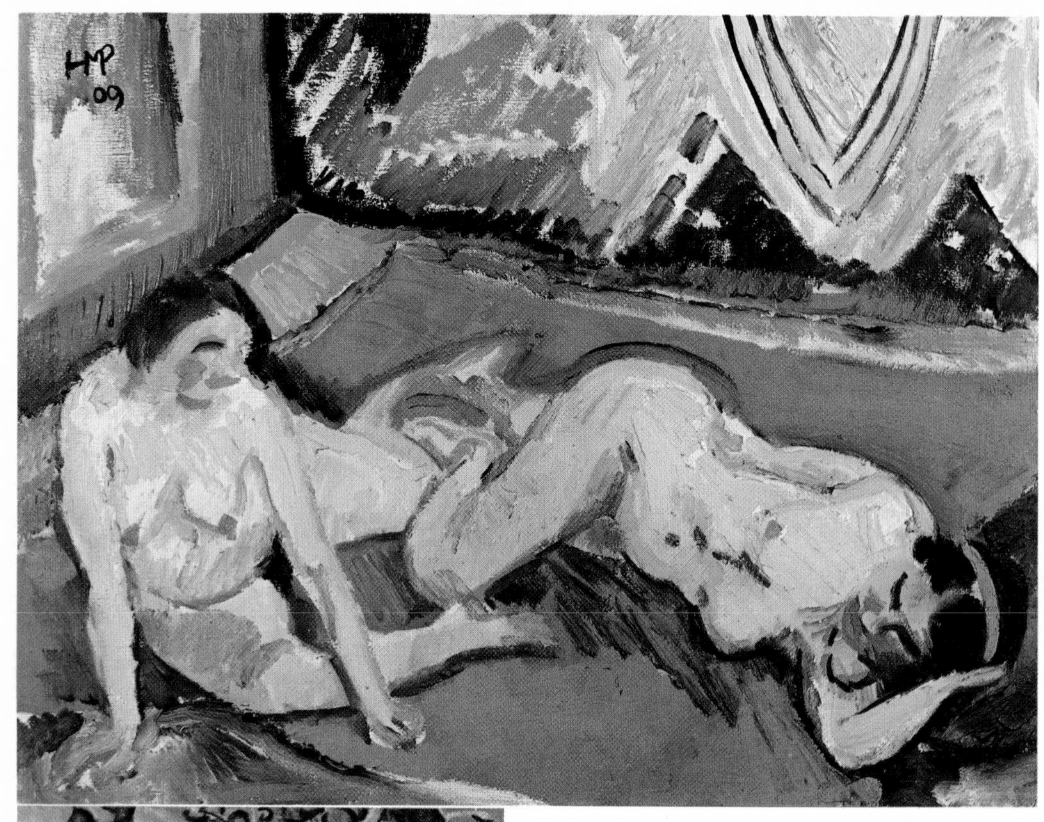

PECHSTEIN, MAX: *Two Nudes.* 1909.

Zwickau he came to Dresden in 1900 to study at the School of Arts and Crafts. As early as 1902 he took part in the school's competition in all six subjects, and won five first prizes and one second. He was immediately asked to become a teacher at the school, but he decided to transfer to the Academy where he remained as star pupil until 1906. The same year he won the State prize in Saxony.

He met Heckel and became a member of *Die Brücke*. In the autumn of 1907 he set out for Italy and returned to Paris in 1908 – where he stayed for six months – settling in Berlin a short while later. His close collaboration with his *Die Brücke* friends thus lasted only a year. He skilfully adapted the discoveries of his friends without having to catch up with their developments in laborious work.

His stay in Paris had resulted in a meeting with van Dongen – who became a member of *Die Brücke* in 1908 – and also a knowledge of Matisse's work, which exercised a direct influence on Pechstein's pictures in 1911–1912. The violent, strong colours which he jux-

PECHSTEIN, MAX: *In the forest.* 1919.

taposed in large areas to emphasize structure are the expression of a powerful and primitive temperament. He intensifies the colourful splendour of the world, without however, wishing to move into symbolism or myth.

His best pictures were produced in the summer of 1910, when he painted with Kirchner and Heckel at the Moritzburg lakes, and then travelled with Heckel to Schmidt-Rottluff in Dangast. The works of the following years, the numerous pictures of bathing figures amongst the dunes, which were created at Nidden in the Baltic, where Pechstein had painted in the summer since 1909, impress principally by their beautifully decorative and rhythmic lines. In 1910 Pechstein was one of the founders of the New Sezession in Berlin, whose Chairman he became; when he returned in 1912 to the old *Sezession*, he was excluded from *Die Brücke*.

In 1914 he went to Palau in the South Seas. He found here the harmony between nature and man which he

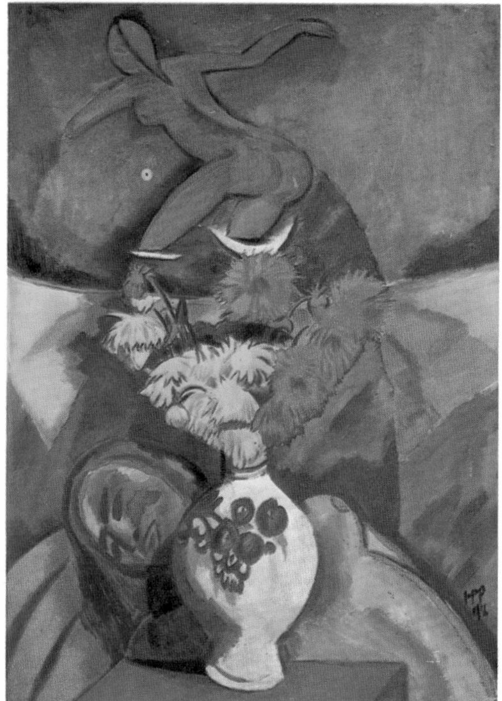

PECHSTEIN, MAX: *Vase of Flowers with Two Nudes.* 1912.

had sought in remote Nidden and in 1913 in a fishing village near Genoa. The outbreak of war soon put an end to his light-hearted way of life, and Pechstein was taken prisoner by the Japanese. In 1915 he succeeded in returning to Germany after many adventures.

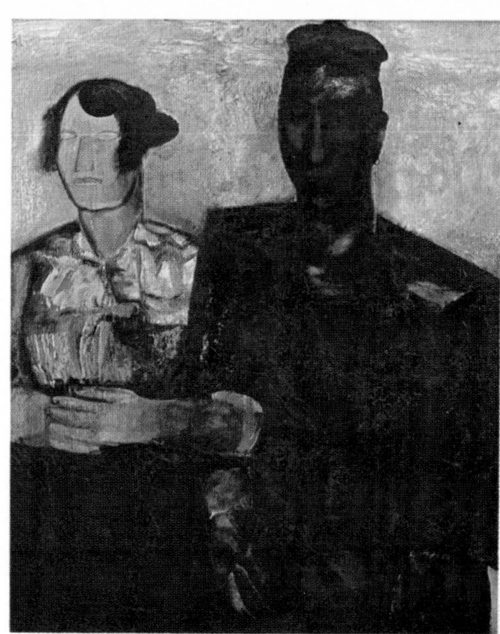

PERMEKE, CONSTANT: *The Fiancés.* 1923.

PERMEKE, Constant (Antwerp, 31.7.1886– Ostend, 4.1.1952). Permeke, whose father was a sea painter, went for a year to the Academy in Bruges and transferred in 1904 to Ghent, where he made friends with Van den Berghe, Servaes and de Smet. After completing his military service he followed his friends to Laethem-Saint-Martin in 1909. An artists' colony had formed there, still concerned with impressionist problems. In 1912 Permeke went to Ostend and turned more and more towards an expressionist style. In 1914 he was called up, wounded and evacuated to England. In 1918 he returned to Ostend. His favourite themes from now on were landscapes and heavy, ponderous figures; peasants and fishermen. Shapes were simplified into angular areas. His palette consists primarily of dark, earthy colours, creating a joyless atmosphere in his pictures, in which a social element is often present.

PICASSO, Pablo (Malaga, 25.10.1881 – Mougins, 8.4.1973). Picasso began his painting at ten years old. When fifteen he was accepted by an art college in Barcelona, where his father taught painting. In 1896 he set up his first studio. In 1897 he passed the entrance examination for the San Fernando Academy, but only

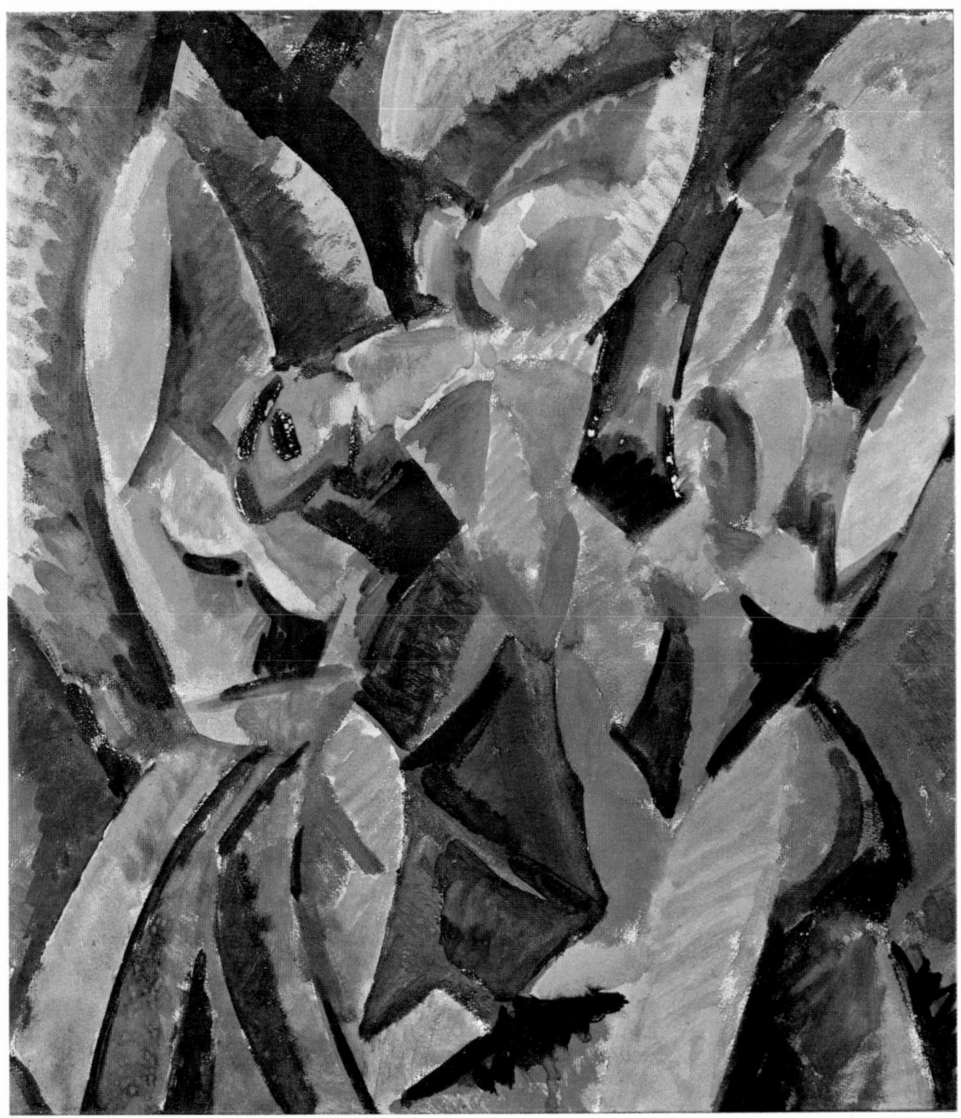

PICASSO, PABLO: *Three women.* 1908.

stayed a short while. In Barcelona he moved in the circles of the artistic and intellectual avant-garde. In 1900 he undertook his first three-month journey to Paris. Under the influence of Toulouse-Lautrec, Steinlen and Munch, whose work he had come to know in Barcelona, he recorded the life of the poor districts, and its wretchedness. In 1901 he returned to Paris after a stay in Madrid. His knowledge of Seurat and Van Gogh helped him towards a powerful use of colour. From now on he juxtaposed bright colours with broad brushstrokes, and worked in a kind of pre-fauvist manner which was separate from the '*vitrail* period'. Large areas of colour applied in a uniform style, indicate the influence of Gauguin. Vollard mounted his first one-man exhibition in Paris.

At the end of 1901 Picasso abandoned colour contrasts and limited himself to one colour: blue. This became the fundamental means of expression for strong emotion and compassion. The themes of his paintings revolve around human suffering, sadness and despair. In 1902–1903 he alternated between Paris and Barcelona, until he finally settled in Paris in 1904 at the *Bateau*

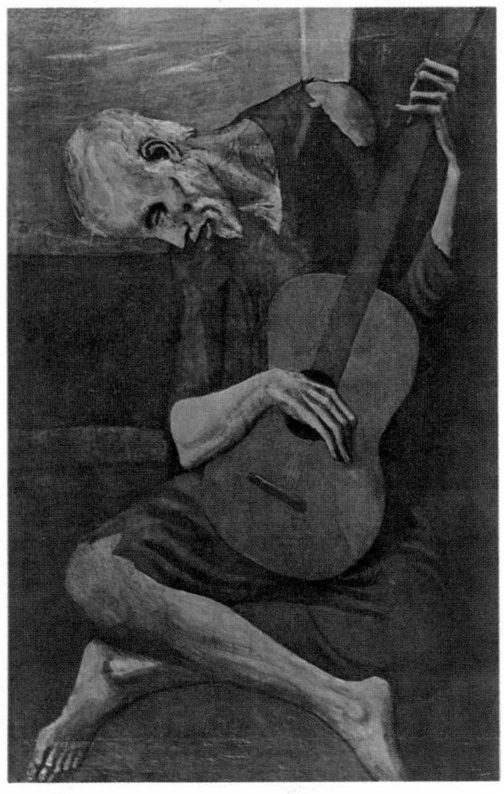

PICASSO, PABLO: *The old guitarist.* Barcelona, 1903.

Lavoir, where he lived till 1909. In 1905 Fernande Olivier became his companion, and he met Apollinaire and the Stein sisters. The same year he travelled to Holland, which resulted in a changed feeling for the human body.

Picasso now began to sculpt. Colour was no longer dominant in his painting, and the so-called 'rose period' began. His type of model changed at the same time. From now on he was interested in the circus: harlequins, jugglers and acrobats. In 1906 he met Matisse and Derain. He spent the summer of that year in Gosol (Andorra). Under the influence of Iberian sculpture and El Greco he arrived at a distortion of bodies and objects as a means of intensifying expression; the monumental nature of *Les Demoiselles d'Avignon* in 1907 represented the climax of this expressionist force. This work is one of Picasso's most important. It calls into question the painting of that era. Indeed the artist's intention was to make the painting 'a summary of Western Art' and confront it with negro art. In this painting Picasso draws the conclusions of a research that took volume of its object. It instigated the period of cubism which came to an end after the 1914–1918 war.

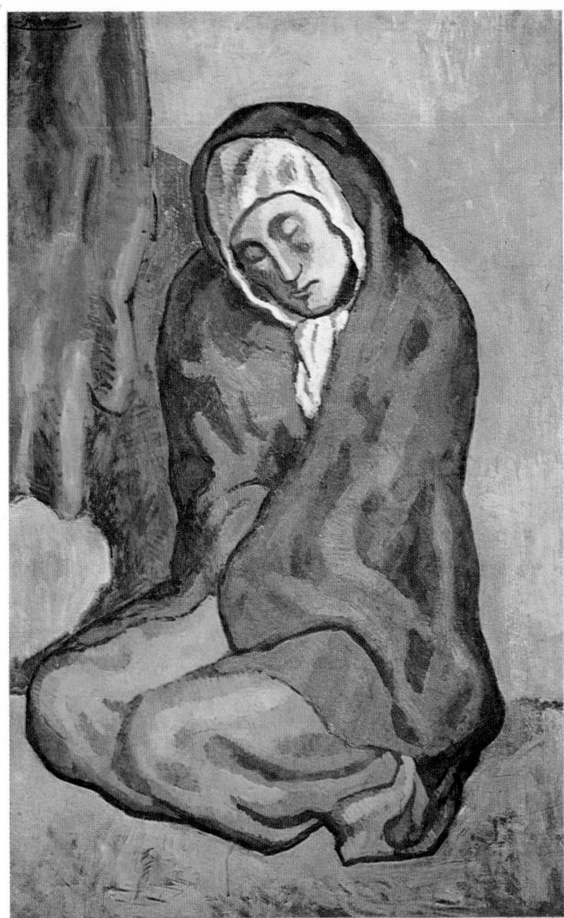

PICASSO, PABLO: *The Crouching Beggar-woman.* Barcelona, 1902.

PROCHAZKA, Antonin (Vázany, Moravia, 5.6.1882 – Brno, 5.6.1945). Prochazka came to Prague in 1902 began his studies at the academy, and finished them in 1906. Travels in Germany, Belgium, France and Italy completed his education. His expressionist figure painting originated in Van Gogh and Munch. Although he had worked in Ostrava as an art teacher since 1910, he was one of the first Czech artists to be influenced by cubism. Prochazka took up the problems intuitively but could not find the strength to elaborate them properly, and thus did not go beyond a superficial style.

PUY, Jean (Roanne, 8.11.1876 – Roanne, 1960). Puy came to Lyon at nineteen to study architecture there at the École des Beaux Arts. In 1896 he transferred to

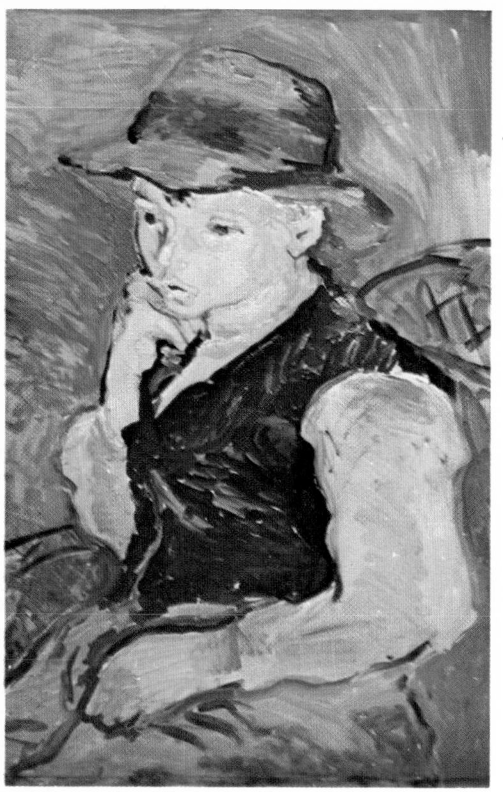

PROCHÁZKA, ANTONIN: *Portrait of a young man.* 1909.

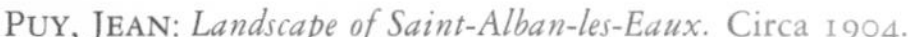

PUY, JEAN: *Landscape of Saint-Alban-les-Eaux.* Circa 1904.

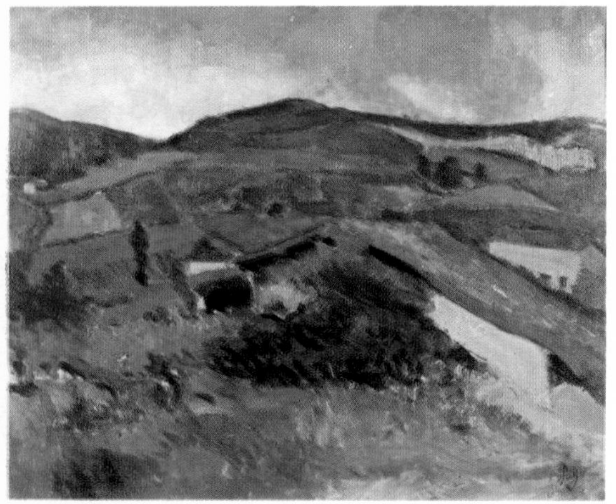

Tollet's studio and turned to painting. In 1890 he continued his studies at the *Académie Julian* and in 1899 at the *Académie Carrière*. Here he met Matisse and Derain. From then on Puy belonged to the circle which met to work together in Manguin's studio. Under Matisse's influence he painted landscapes, nudes, interiors and still lifes in a subdued fauvist style. From 1910 on he exhibited with Matisse, as he did in *The Wild Animal Cage* in the 1905 *Salon d'automne*. Due to his comparatively reserved style he had a strong acclaim from the press. In 1907 he mounted his first solo exhibition in Paris, to which more were added the same year. However, since his art stagnated, people soon lost interest in his painting; his next exhibition was held in 1930.

ROHLFS, Christian (Niendorf, Holstein, 22.12.1849 – Hagen, 8.1.1938). Christian Rohlfs came to Hagen in 1901 to take part in the founding of the first museum of modern art. He was continually forced into new investigations by the collection which was forming in Hagen. He had lived in Weimar for thirty years and painted

ROHLFS, CHRISTIAN: *Ecce Homo.*

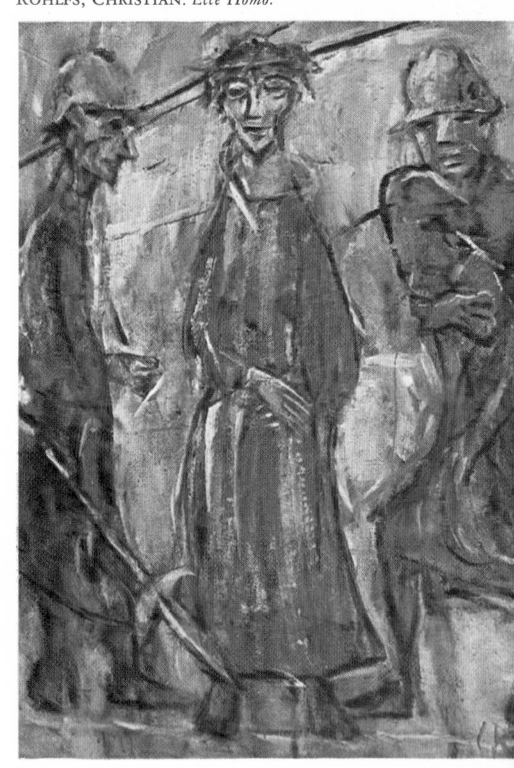

realist landscapes, assimilated Seurat and Van Gogh, but remained bound to the beauty of the physical world. From 1904 he had frequently painted in Soest, where he met Nolde in 1905.

He was inspired by the motifs of the medieval town to create brightly coloured 'flat' paintings. From 1913 on he succeeded in transposing his motifs into flat colour shapes by means of vigorous brush strokes. However, Rohlfs was not seeking to express strong emotions but spiritual agitation. He thus separated colour from the object, and simultaneously subordinated it to the rhythmic line, contour and expressive arabesques of the picture.

ROUAULT, Georges-Henri (Paris, 27.5.1871 – Paris, 13.2.1958). Rouault's work grew out of compassion and his own experiences of suffering.

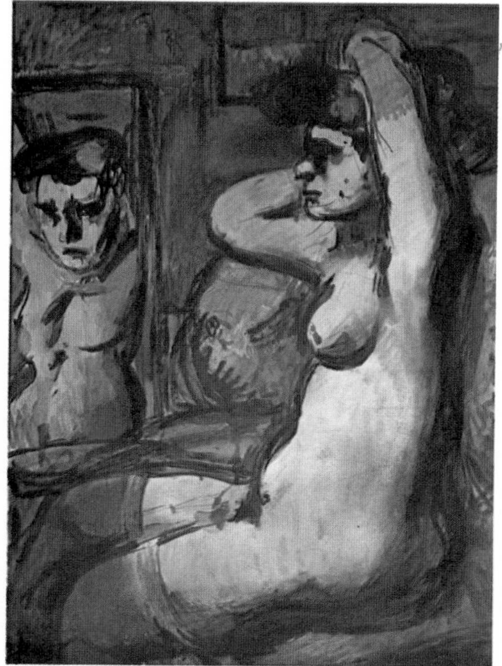

ROUAULT, GEORGES-HENRI: *In the Mirror.*

The son of a carpenter, he began an apprenticeship with a glass painter at fourteen. He stayed there until 1890, collecting impressions and knowledge by restoring medieval church windows. His grandfather had already made him familiar with Manet, Courbet and Daumier, whose reproductions he collected. From 1885 onwards he attended night classes at the Art and

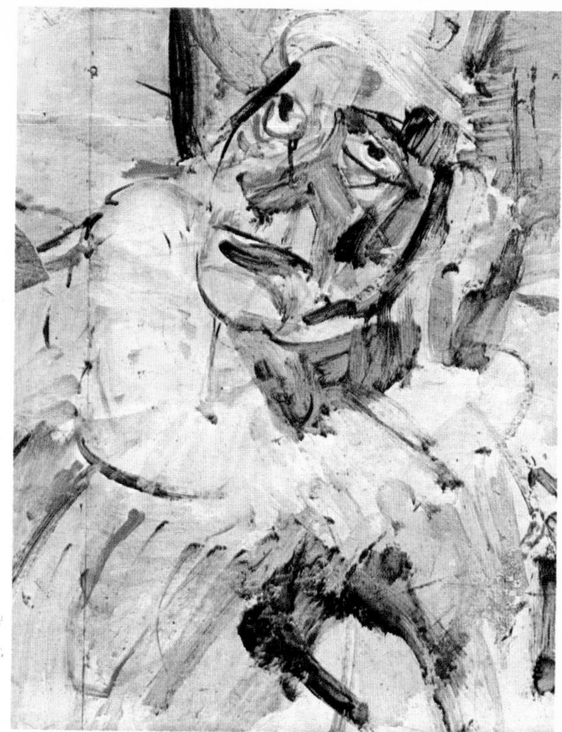

ROUAULT, GEORGES-HENRI: *The Clown.* Circa 1907.

Craft College in Paris. In 1890 he transferred to the *École des Beaux Arts*, to Elise Delaunay's studio. In 1891 Gustave Moreau took over the studio and Rouault became his favourite pupil.

He directed Rouault towards brilliant colour tones and bold effects; Rouault learnt not to start a picture with a preconceived vision. A close friendship soon arose between pupil and teacher. In contrast to his fellow pupils, Matisse and Marquet, Rouault sought his point of departure in Rembrandt.

Moreau died in 1898, and Rouault underwent a profound crisis. He could no longer paint religious subjects, but instead used prostitutes, clowns and acrobats, symbols of a corrupt world, to depict his religious feelings which were intensified by his friendship with the writer, Leon Bloy. Rouault now sought reality in what was hideous and repellent, and formed from it an accusation and homily against society.

He became curator of the *Musée Moreau* in 1903, and founded the *Salon d'automne* with Matisse and others. He exhibited here with Matisse's circle, which gave him the reputation of being a fauve. But this connection was only superficial. His art which he himself described as 'A scream in the night! A stifled sob! A laugh that chokes on itself!', was in direct contrast to fauvism. Until 1910 Rouault primarily worked on light-coloured, translucent water-colours with strong brush strokes. From 1908 he added scenes of judgment to his themes, which recall Daumier. In 1910 he had his first one-man exhibition in the Druet gallery; in 1913 the art dealer Vollard bought the whole of his work to date.

From 1918 on, water-colours and body colour painting became less important and Rouault's preference turned to oils. The surface area of the painting was concentrated into a radiant, opaque texture and he introduced black contours and the lead outline technique from stained-glass windows. His art returned to religious themes, in particular the Passion of Christ. From 1914 onwards, he also produced drawings on which he concentrated almost exclusively between 1911 and 1929. In the decades before his death he re-worked his motifs indefatigably, constantly concerned to give shape to his expression.

RUSSOLO, Luigi (Portogruaro, 30.4.1885 – Cerro de Levano, 4.2.1947). Russolo had at first studied music, but he started teaching himself to paint in 1904–1905. He entered an avant-garde literary circle in Milan and there met Marinetti, who published *Poesia*, to which Russolo contributed. In 1909 he made friends with Boccioni. In 1910 he was one of the five signatories of the first Futurist Manifesto. In the following years although he took part in all the activities of the futurist painters, his own painting, which followed dynamism in a modified form, did not achieve crucial significance. In 1901 he travelled to Paris, where Derain introduced him to his artist friends. In 1913 he became a contributor to the futurist magazine *Lacerba* and published the manifesto, *L'Arte dei Rumori*. After the war, in which he took part as a volunteer, he moved to Paris and turned to realist painting.

SCHIELE, EGON: *Self-portrait.* 1911.

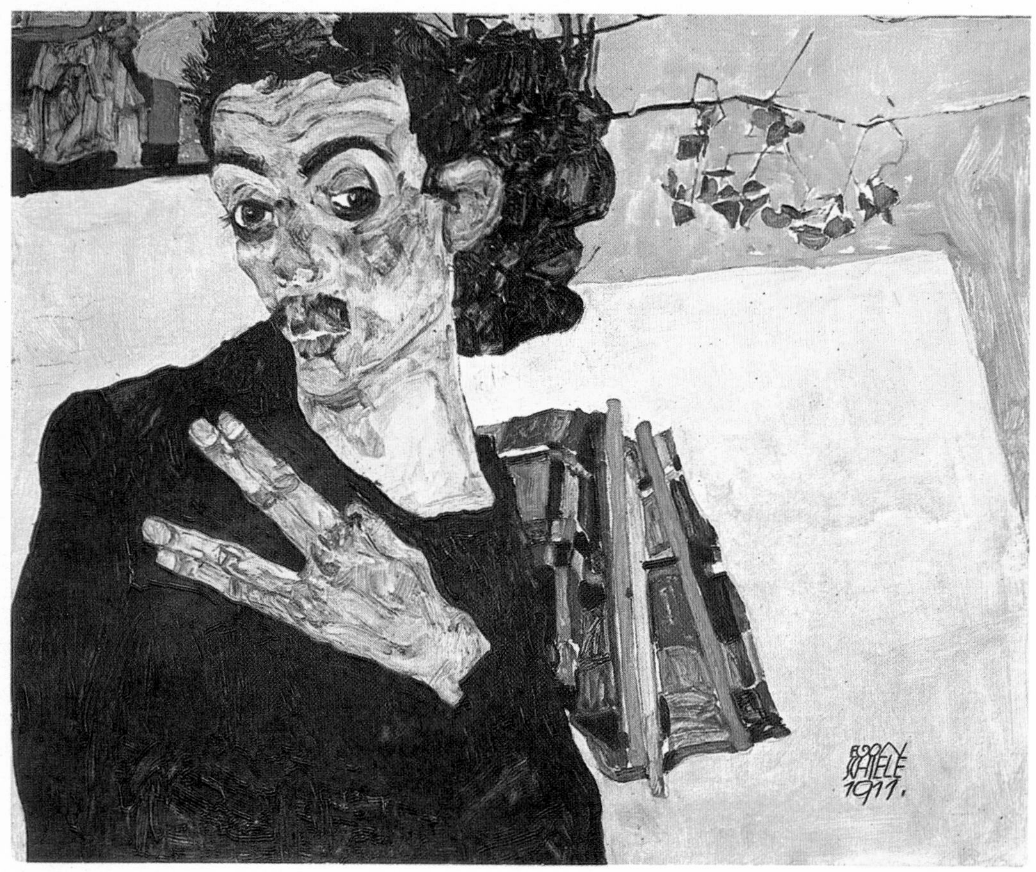

SCHIELE, Egon (Tulln, 12.6.1890 – Vienna, 31.10.1918). Schiele's talent was recognized by his teachers in secondary school, who managed – against his family's wishes – to have him study at the Vienna Academy in 1906. In 1907 he set up his own studio. Schiele met Gustav Klimt and was influenced by him. But it was precisely while studying with Klimt's elegant figures that Schiele evolved his ascetic artistic conception characterized by austere harsh brushstrokes.

In 1909 he left the Academy and founded the New Art Group with Gütersloh, Peschka and Faistauer. In the first exhibition of this group in the same year, Schiele met some art collectors, who soon formed a circle of close friends and buyers. In 1910 came the breakthrough to expressionism via an emotive, uncompromizing and spontaneous distancing from self. Van Gogh and Toulouse-Lautrec, Hodler and Munch were his models. Disquiet, pain and danger were portrayed in tormented, twisted figures. The human figure and the portrait constitute the major themes in Schiele's work, both in his drawings and his paintings. Additional subjects were landscapes – lifeless, deserted cities and villages.

Eroticism which he treats with brutal, concentrated and conscious directness, is entirely confined to watercolours and drawings. It was too direct for the public prosecutor, with the result that Schiele was sentenced to detention for disseminating indecent drawings. In 1911 he had his first one-man exhibition in Vienna, and became a member of the artistic group *Sema* in Munich, to which Klee and Kubin also belonged. After this he took part in numerous exhibitions in Germany and mounted a collective one which started its tour in Munich in 1913. That year he became a contributor to the Berlin review *Action*, the more politically orientated rival of *Der Sturm*, to which he devoted a special edition in 1916.

In 1915 he was called up for military service, which he did mainly in Vienna so that he was nevertheless able to work. In 1918 the Vienna *Sezession* mounted a collective exhibition of Schiele's work which led to real artistic and material success. However, he was not able to profit by it. In October 1918 he and his wife died of Spanish 'flu.

SCHMIDT-ROTTLUFF (Rottluff near Chemnitz, 1.12.1884 – Berlin, 10.8.1976). After finishing secondary school in Chemnitz, Schmidt-Rottluff had at first chosen, like Franz Marc, to study theology, but then followed the example of his friend Heckel and went to study architecture in Dresden. They soon discovered their common love for painting as well as for poetry, and began to paint and draw together.

When Schmidt-Rottluff came to Dresden in 1905 he immediately joined the circle of Kirchner, Bleyl and Heckel and formed the *Die Brücke* group with them. Schmidt-Rottluff suggested the name. This fervent admirer of Nietzsche had been stimulated by the fourth prologue of *Zarathustra*, 'what is noble in man is that he

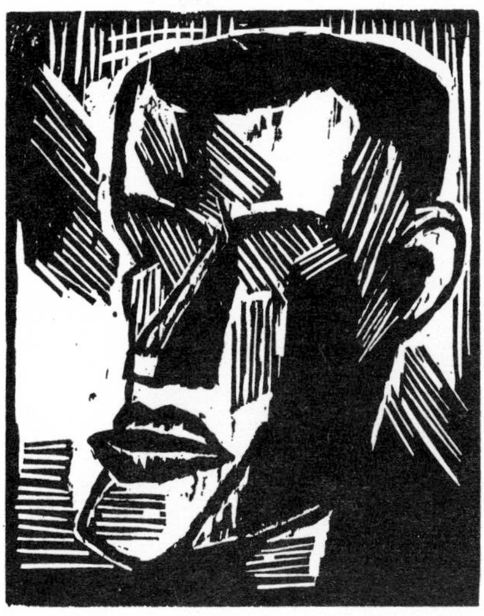

SCHMIDT-ROTTLUFF, KARL: *Self-portrait.* 1914.

is a bridge and not a goal; what can be loved in a man is that he is a crossing over and a going under'. Schmidt-Rottluff persuaded Nolde, whom he had visited in Alsen in 1906, to join the group and corresponded with

SCHMIDT-ROTTLUFF, KARL: *The Pharisees.* 1912.

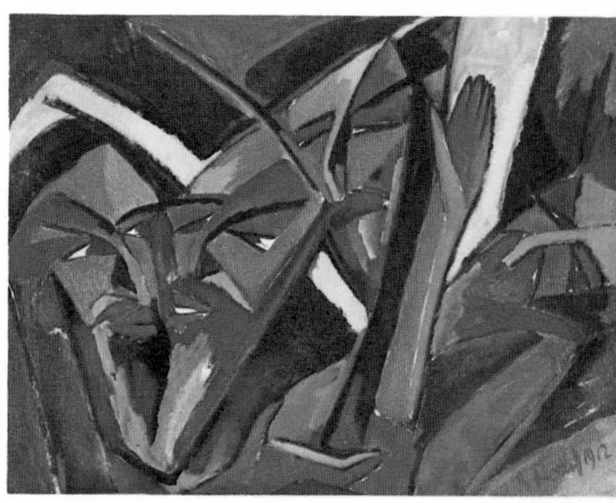

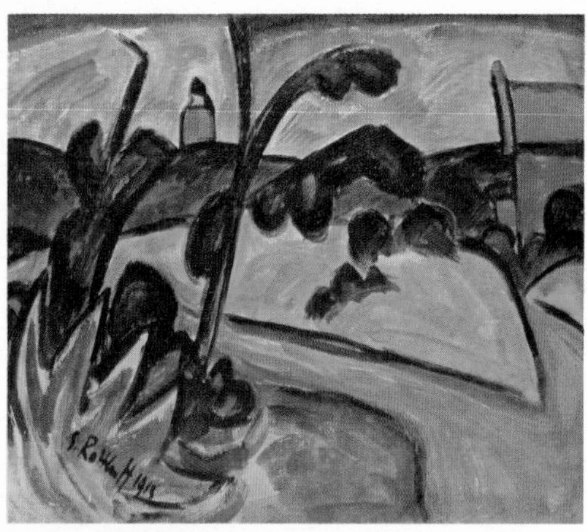

SCHMIDT-ROTTLUFF, KARL: *Lighthouse on the Baltic.* 1913.

Munch concerning his joining *Die Brücke*. It was he who introduced lithography into the group.

Nevertheless, amid all this activity on behalf of the group, he always held himself a little aloof. He visited and shared studios less frequently and also did not take part in the work trips to the Moritzburg lakes near Dresden. Instead, he went to Dangast in Oldenburg during the summer months from 1907 to 1912; Heckel followed him there. He was the only one of the friends to exhibit in Braunschweig in 1907, and in one-man exhibitions in Hamburg in 1910; the rest only appeared as a group until the dissolution of *Die Brücke* in 1913.

Schmidt-Rottluff's temperament was reserved and introverted, but this was necessary to be able to sustain the almost one-sided consistency of his work. Thematically, this meant restricting himself to landscapes, thus avoiding the depiction of city life and, until 1912, he

SCHMIDT-ROTTLUFF, KARL: *Break in a studio.* 1910.

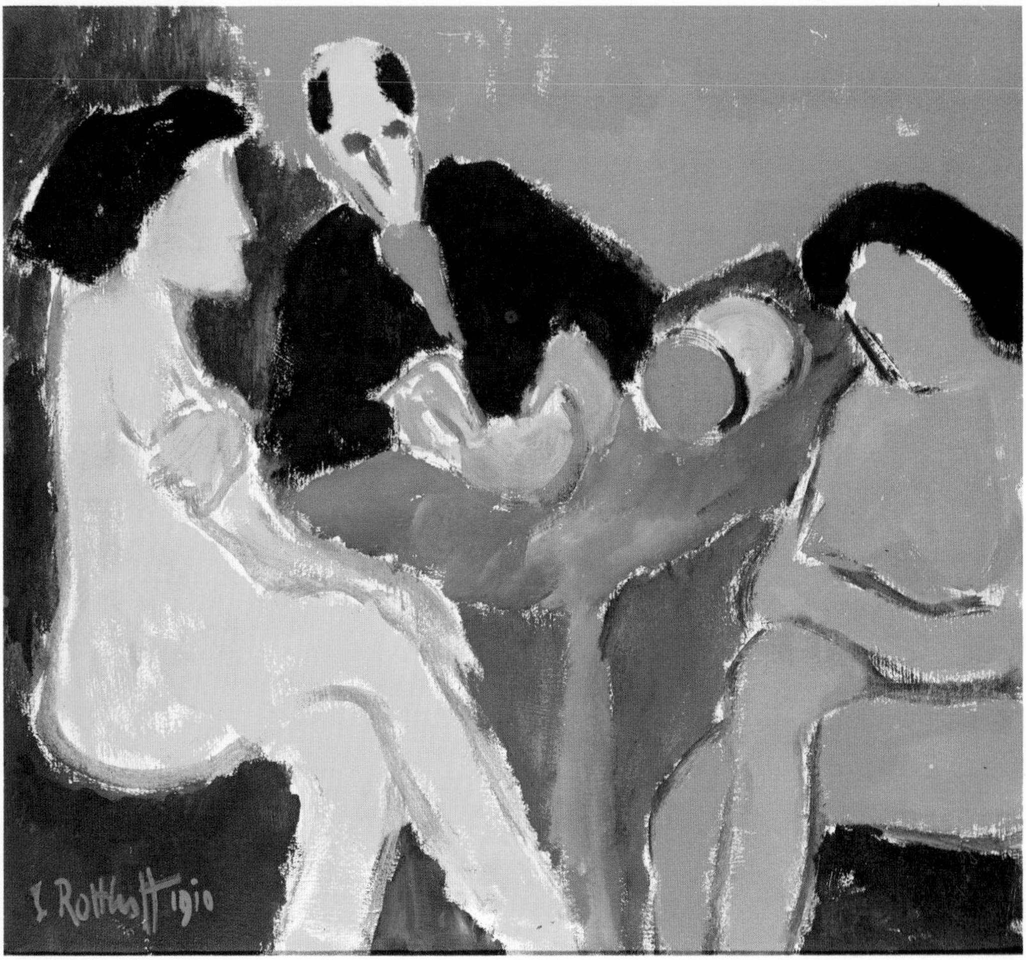

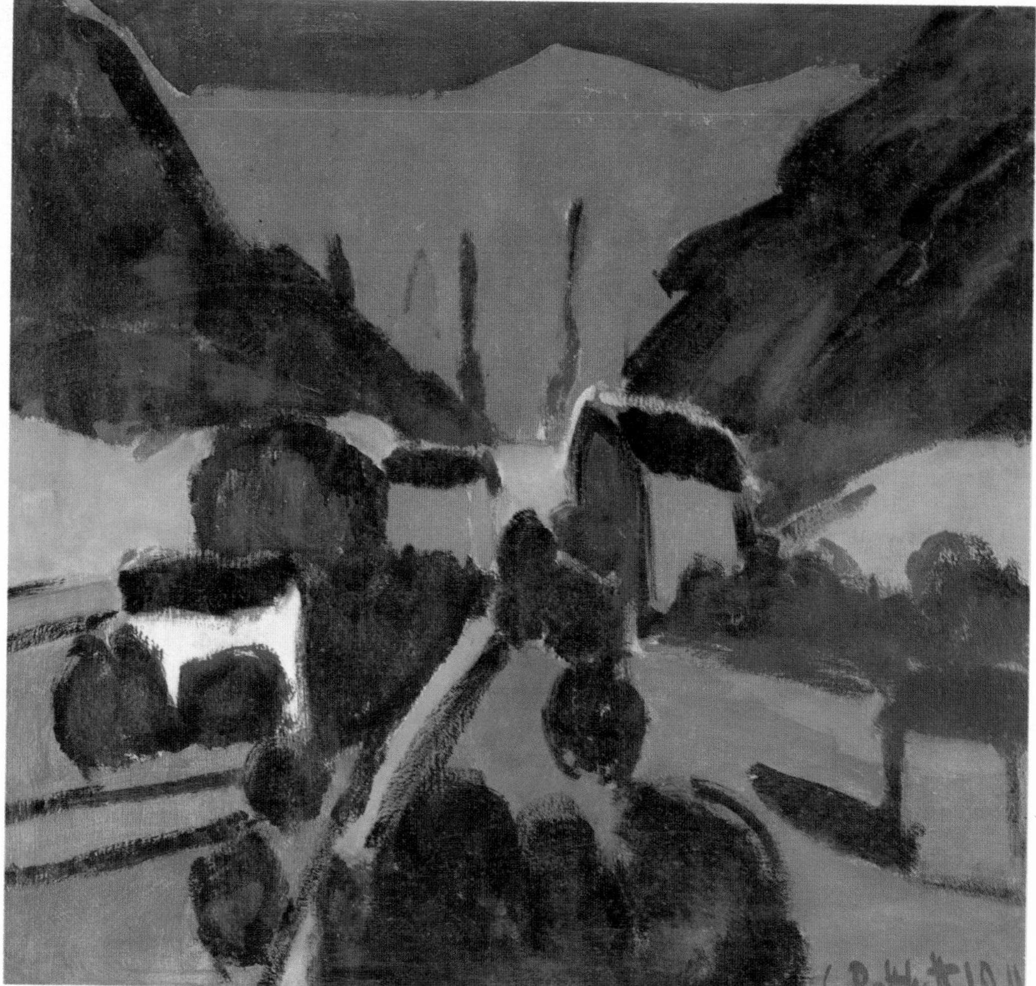

SCHMIDT-ROTTLUFF, KARL: *Norwegian landscape.* 1911.

only occasionally used the human figures, which held the attention of his friends so much.

'The harsh air of the North Sea yielded, particularly in Schmidt-Rottluff, a monumental impressionism', Kirchner wrote in 1913 in the *Die Brücke* chronicle. Thus he described that vigorous brushwork, expressive of great force of will, with which Schmidt-Rottluff produces unity in his paintings. However, the extravagant gesture, still inspired by Van Gogh, gave way in 1910 to a structure of large areas of colour that was also employed as a means of achieving greater monumentality and greater simplification. The paintings that resulted from his journey to Norway in 1911 mark a climax.

In 1911 Schmidt-Rottluff moved (as did his friends at the same time) from Dresden to Berlin, where he lived for the rest of his life. Here he came across diverse artistic stimuli which stirred him to investigate them. However, his approaches to the emphatic expressiveness of abstract art, as well as cubist method, remained experiments limited to a few pictures. He preferred to use figures and still life to find a more exact definition of the object that would encompass space and volume but would not disturb his two-dimensional style.

He found the solution in 1913 in Nidden on the Courland peninsula with what is known as 'a heraldic-symbolic style'. Human figures and the elements of landscape are reduced to images of equal importance in the picture, and promote a symbolic unity.

In 1914 Schmidt-Rottluff again changed his surroundings and went to Hohwacht on the Baltic coast of

Holstein. The paintings that he produced here could not maintain the harmony between man and nature. For the first time the figures show a spiritual opression in his work. From 1915 to 1918 he was called up for military service in Russia. Even though the war left no trace on his work as regards themes – which always reflected the universal and never topical events – nevertheless, the shock could not be hidden. He felt more and more clearly the 'tension between this world and the next,' as he himself wrote. In the years after 1918 he sought to revitalize reality by incorporating the subject into objective existence.

SERVAES, Albert (Ghent, 4.4.1833 – Lucerne, 19.4.1966). Like the other important painters of the expressionist generation in Belgium, Servaes was a pupil at Ghent Academy where he met Frits van den Berghe and Constant Permeke. With them he belonged to the second group in the Laethem-Saint-Martin artists' community from 1904 on. Whereas his friends soon left Laethem again, Servaes remained until moving to Lucerne in 1945. Using symbolism and fifteenth-century art, especially Roger van der Weyden, as his starting point, he attained a monumental and expressive form with which he depicted chiefly religious subjects. He also produced landscapes and pictures with themes from peasant life.

SEVERINI, Gino (Cortona, 7.4.1883 – Paris, 26.2.1966). Severini had lived in Rome since 1899 where he was forced to earn his living in a great variety of jobs – as an errand boy, as an accountant and petty official. In his spare time he attended evening classes in the Villa Medici. In 1901 he met Boccioni, who introduced him to Balla. Balla had been to Paris and taught Severini the divisionist method.

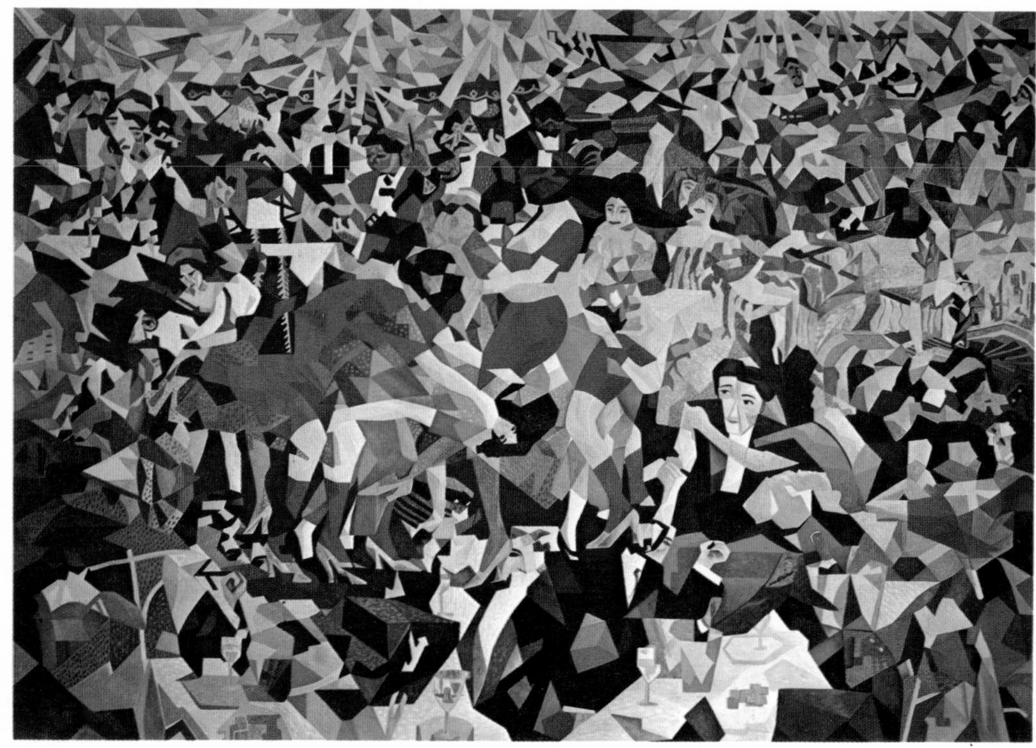

SEVERINI, GINO: *Pam-pam au Monico.* 1913.

In order to study Seurat and neo-impressionism at source, Severini moved to Paris in 1906 where he met Modigliani, Max Jacob and later the cubists. He maintained contacts with Italy and in 1910 was invited to sign the first Futurist Manifesto. In 1911 he went to Milan to familiarize Boccioni and Carrà with the results of cubism. In 1912, he took part in the futurist exhibition, which toured many European cities. Severini lived in Paris during the war and he analysed this event which the futurists dearly longed for in some paintings, before turning completely to Cubism in 1918.

Severini was a talented colourist, who never entirely gave up his links with neo-impressionism. His painting, which became ever more decorative, was admittedly directed towards the typically futurist problems of motion and light – which he studied as a phenomenon of city life in cabarets and revues – yet he treated it, for example, in ball scenes which contain a lyric tone. The influence of cubism early showed itself in the fact that the surface is split up into prism-like areas by applying the colour in dots.

SMET, Gustave de (Ghent, 2.1.1877 – Deurle, 8.10.1943). Gustave de Smet began his education in the Ghent Academy at eleven, and had already been taught by his father who was photographer and scene painter. From 1901 to 1913 he lived in the artists' colony at Laethem-Saint-Martin and there worked with Permeke, van den Berghe and Servaes. In 1914 he went with van den Berghe to Holland, and only returned to Belgium in 1922. De Smet first became aware in Holland of the artistic developments of the previous decade, and in 1916 he turned to expressionism under Le Fauconnier's influence. He now produced mainly landscapes with large, tightly concentrated blocks of colour in subdued browns and ochres. Later, in Belgium, he drew on everyday human activities for his themes and combined his experience of expressionism with the forms of late cubism.

SMET, GUSTAVE DE: *The village fête.* Circa 1930.

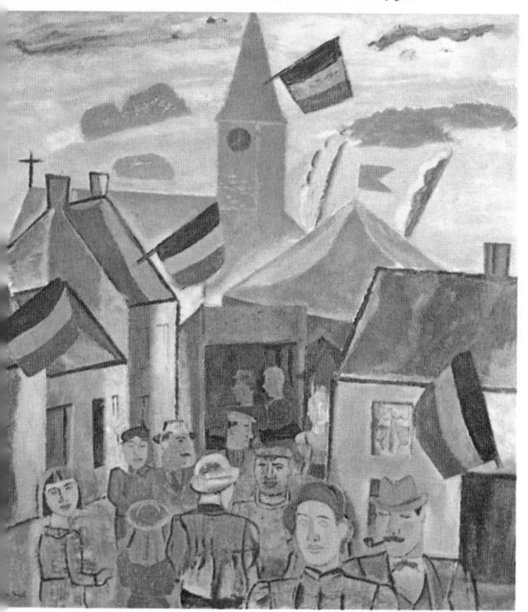

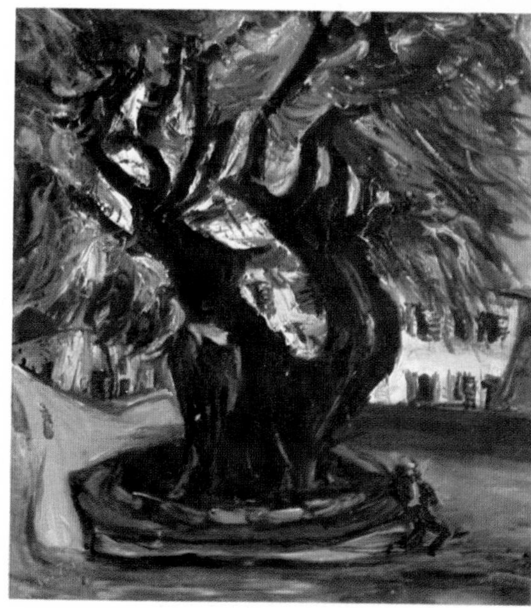

SOUTINE, CHAIM: *The Tree of Vence.* Circa 1926.

SOUTINE, Chaim (Smilovitsch near Minsk, 1893 – Paris, 9.8.1943). Soutine is really the only artist who produced expressionist pictures with extreme intensity for the whole of his life. He was the tenth of eleven children of a Jewish tailor and had the good fortune to be able to attend art college at Wilna in 1910. He stayed there for three years before going to Paris and joining Cormon's studio. At the same time he studied Titian, Tintoretto and Courbet in the Louvre, and later El Greco and Rembrandt as well. But he was most impressed by Cézanne, Van Gogh and Bonnard. Moreover he was influenced by the tendencies most common to expressionism, as represented by his friends Modigliani and Chagall. In 1919 he went for the first time to Céret in the French Pyrenees where he produced about two hundred pictures in the following three years. With the brush strokes of a man possessed, he painted visions of apocalyptic landscapes, pictures of a world deformed by

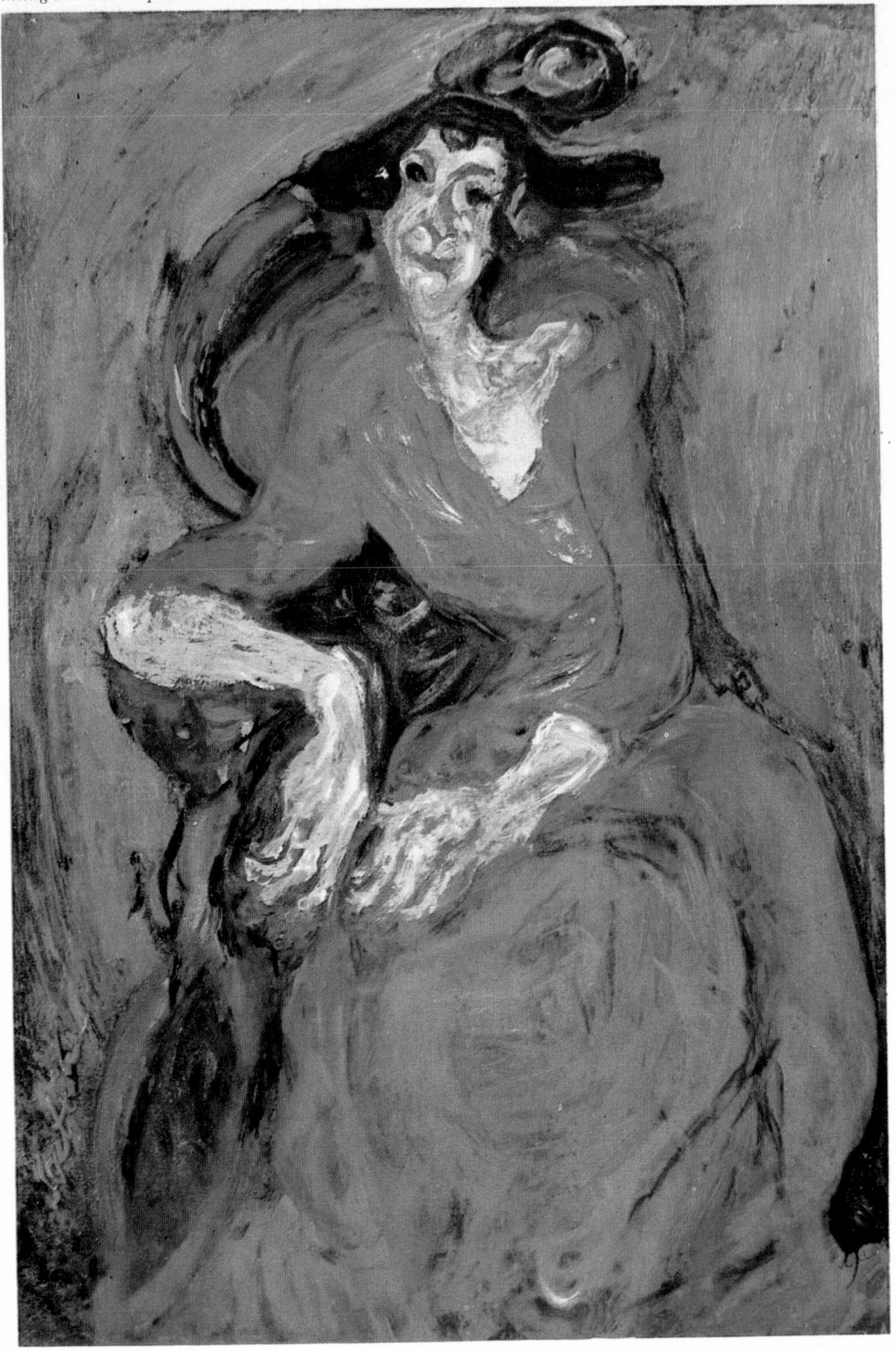

SOUTINE, CHAIM: *The woman in red.* 1922.

suffering. He was thus close to Nolde, Kokoschka and Meidner. There was certainly no imitation in this; their agreement on form originated rather in the similarity of their emotions.

In 1923 the American collector Alfred Barnes bought many of Soutine's paintings, thereby giving him financial security for the first time. In the years 1923 to 1929 he painted in Cagnes sur Mer; in his latter years almost entirely in Paris. In the paintings after 1923 emotion was repressed, the distortions modified and the area of the painting extended. Soutine now sought moderation, drew on Courbet and Rembrandt in some pictures, and renounced his earlier works which he destroyed wherever possible.

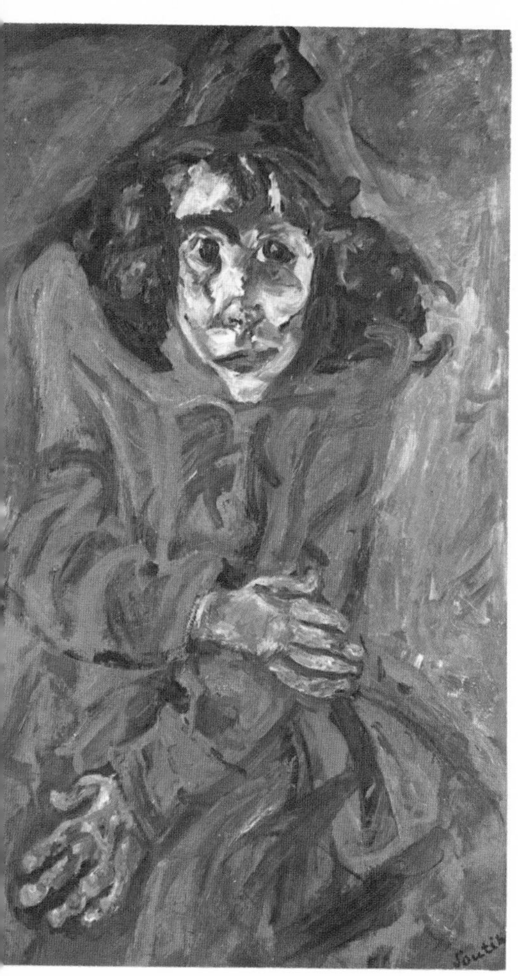

SOUTINE, CHAIM: *The Mad Woman.* Circa 1921.

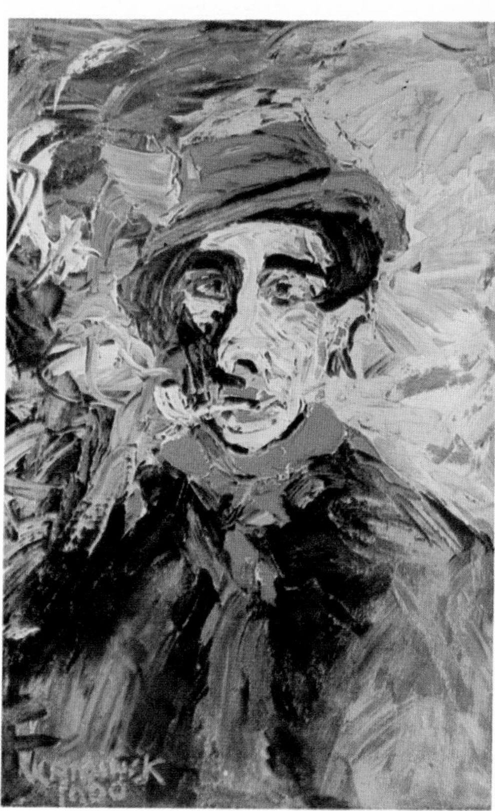

VLAMINCK, MAURICE DE: *Man with a Pipe.* 1900.

VLAMINCK, Maurice de (Paris, 4.4.1876 – Rueil-la-Gadelière, 11.10.1958). If the title fauve applied to any painter, it applied to Vlaminck. He was the son of musical parents, a French mother and a father of Flemish extraction. Vlaminck grew up in Le Vesinet, where he was taught from 1888 to 1891 by the painter Robichon. In 1892 he moved to Chatou. He worked as a cyclist and mechanic until a severe illness in 1896 forced him to abandon this profession and earn his living as a musician. In 1900 he met Derain by chance in a train accident, soon became friends with him and set up a joint studio in Chatou.

To earn money he wrote for newspapers and produced dubious novels, which were published with illus-

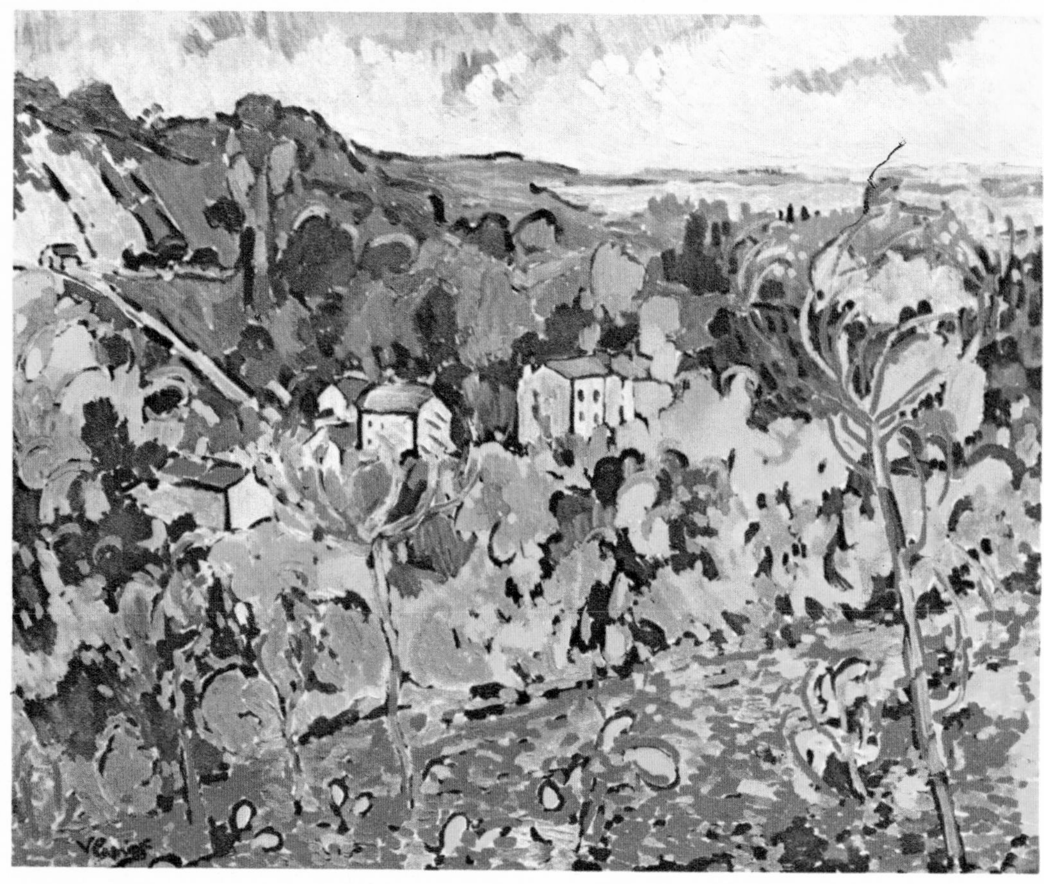

VLAMINCK, MAURICE DE: *Bougival*. 1905.

trations by Derain. In his first paintings Vlaminck applied colour violently and with unrestrained vitality. His encounter with Van Gogh's work in 1901 was decisive. Here he found a passion which encouraged him to express himself as directly and heedlessly as possible. At this Van Gogh exhibition he met Matisse, who visited him in Chatou in 1904 and enabled him to exhibit in the *Salon des indépendants* and the *Salon d'automne*, in *The Wild Animals' Cage* (the fauves). Vlaminck's paintings up to 1907 use unadulterated colour just as it came from the tube, made dynamic by a style of brushwork borrowed from Van Gogh. By painting vigorously, purely from instinct, he achieved the most extreme effects to express a vital and untrammelled world. Fauvism was not an innovation nor an attitude for Vlaminck, but a way of being, behaving, thinking and breathing: 'I am Fauvism'.

In 1906 the art dealer, Vollard bought all his works and organized his first one-man exhibition in 1910. Since 1906, Vlaminck had associated with Picasso and van Dongen, and the *Bateau Lavoir* circle. From 1908 on his palette became more subdued under the influence of Cézanne, and he tried some cubist compositions. But this could only be a short interlude for a temperament so rooted in expressivity. After this, Vlaminck sought another road to expressionist painting in landscapes, made dramatic by contrasts between light and dark.

WEISGERBER, Albert (St Ingbert, 21.4.1878 – Fromelles-Ypres, 10.5.1915). Weisgerber began his education at the School of Civil Architecture in Kaiserslautern in 1891, worked as an interior decorator in Frankfurt and then transferred to the School of Arts and Crafts in Munich.

He was a member of the New Artists' Association in Munich from 1909 and became president of the New Munich Sezession in 1913. He was called up in 1914, and fell six months later in France.

Sculpture

For primarily economic reasons (lack of demand and the high price of materials), sculpture evolved at a much slower pace than painting. The sculptors themselves suffered the direct consequences of this

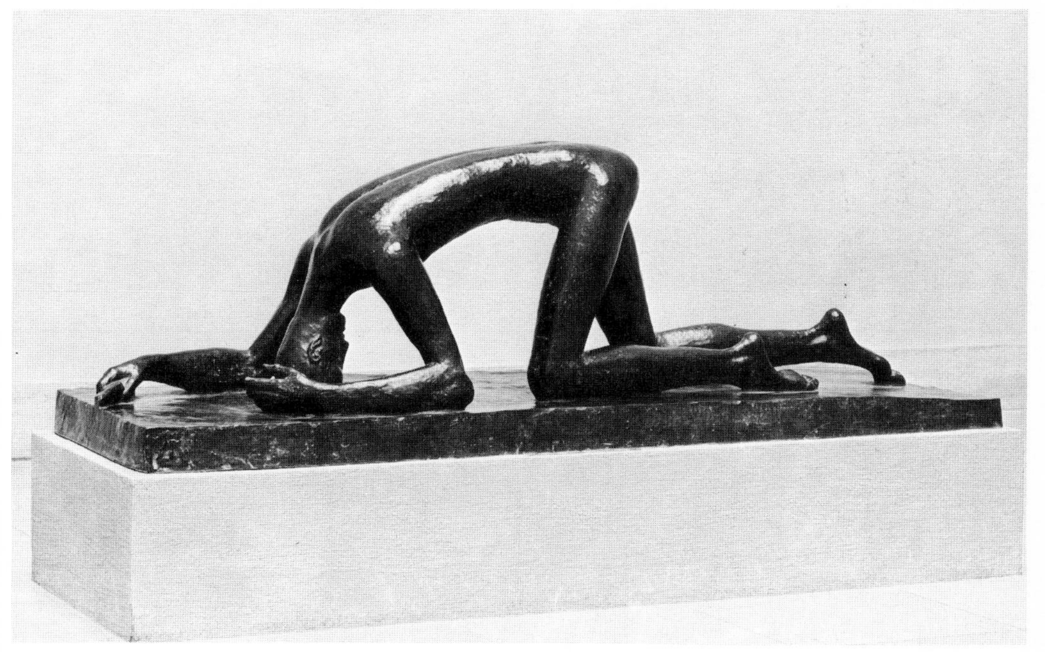

LEHMBRUCK, WILHELM: *Kneeling Woman, leaning on her arms*

situation, not only by having to limit their artistic scope, but also by being compelled, given the length of time needed to complete a work, not to increase their output. It was only with the Russian Revolution, and a year later in Germany, with what has been called the November Revolution of 1918, that the problem of integrating sculpture into society was raised. In fact, it was on this problem that the German sculptors who formed the November Group particularly concentrated: the Group comprised Hoetger, Emy Roeder, Garbe, Max Krause, Milly Steger, Belling, and Mataré.

Must one necessarily see, in this reduced rôle played by sculpture on the art market, the real reason for the lack of impact that expressionism had on sculpture? For it is an objective fact: in Germany as in other countries, sculptors claiming to have affinities with expressionism are few in number, and truly expressionist sculptures are rare. This is a fact that is all the more surprising, given that at the time when expressionism was an influential force in Germany, sculpture was passing through upheavals similar to those that had already occurred in painting: all imitation of nature was rejected. Very great artists were appearing on the scene, but there is no one who can, strictly speaking, be linked with expressionism: Archipenko, Brancusi, Epstein, Nadelmann, Duchamp-Villon. No sculptor of international renown emerged from the groups of artists living at that time in Germany. Only a few individualistic artists like Barlach, Freundlich and Lehmbruck were to acquire a larger audience.

In fact, in sculpture, as in other art forms, expressionism is an imprecise term. Either it can be seen as a product of the general mood of the time, and in that case all modernist movements form part of it, from Archipenko to Picasso, and from Arp to Henry Moore, or as having distinctive traits in relation to other movements. The former tendency is the one that prevailed in Germany: obviously, therefore, this led to sculpture's being very receptive to expressionism, where this term means quite simply the questioning of conventions. The second tendency consists in defining expressionism as an expressive intensity of forms, which become distorted and abstract, but still closely linked to the artist's sense of an inner need to create. This definition, which is accepted today by just about all art critics throughout the world, makes a distinction between a distortion in the interest, both of this inner need to create, and the requirements of sculpture as a plastic art (cubism is an example of this), and a distortion, brought about by an inner *élan*, by impulses which are exteriorized as a spontaneous creative act.

If the confusion existed in Germany, it is because the two tendencies came on the scene side by side. Both of them, moreover, were a reaction against the classicism of Adolf von Hildebrand and his followers, which was predominant at that time. But some only took up, by and large, the form of classical sculpture, stretching them to their extremes, sometimes in a kind of vehement mannerism, or imitating African sculpture (as in the case of the members of *Die Brücke*), whereas others, following the example of Archipenko, sought to endow sculpture with an absolutely autonomous language. In the first category, only Barlach and Lehmbruck are worthy of mention. In the second, along with Oswald Herzog and William Wauer, the name of Belling stands out: in fact he later turned to abstract art.

There is one discovery that is common to both tendencies: sculpture was injected with an inner dynamism. It gained a momentum and rhythm that was exclusively its own. Movement and rhythm predominate from then on in this art form. In the wake of Rodin, who around 1910 also produced numerous figures of dancers, sculptors like Garbe on the one hand, and Archipenko, Belling or Wauer on the other, specifically took up the theme of dancing. For some, sculpture seemed to live off an inner rhythm, whereas for others, this same quest for movement led to a simplifying of the forms until they reached the point of abstraction.

Despite this rather poor showing, one has to recognize that expressionism, in this art form too, allowed Germany to come to terms with modernism. Thanks to expressionism, it acquired its greatest sculptors of the century: Barlach and Lehmbruck. It is without a doubt the climate of expressionism, which they reflect, moreover, in their aspirations, that made their success easier. Thus, in this field too, expressionism was, to however small an extent, a constructive force. In short, no other movement in Germany has been the basis for such an exceptional revival in sculpture.

In general, expressionism as a style, as I have already said, hardly enhanced this art form, outside Germany. However, a few other artists do deserve to be considered as contributors to the expressionist movement. These include, in Belgium, Oscar Jaspers (1887–1970) in particular with his tombstone in honour of the poet van Osayen, worked in granite in Antwerp in 1931; Germaine Richier, whose work is infused with an obsession with death and continuous threats of an apocalyptic nature; Zadkine (1890–1967) around the 1930s who, having freed himself from cubism, strove to express the essence of the movement with a new intensity, and Etienne-Martin and his clusters of roots with their twisted forms. Nor should one omit the Italian Alfio Castelli, the American S. Brandon Kearl nor the Russian, Neizvestny.

ARCHIPENKO, Alexander (Kiev, 30.5.1887 – New York, 25.2.1964). He started out as a pupil at the Art School in his home town from 1902 to 1905. He then went to Moscow, and in 1908 he went to Paris, where he became friends with the avant-garde painters of the period (Léger, Chagall, Modigliani), and where he gave lessons in sculpture. He created his own personal style, consisting of modelling in a mould. From cubism (his *Black Torso* of 1909 is considered his first piece of cubist sculpture), he moved on to a kind of abstract expressionism, replacing the heavy volumes of classical sculpture with an expressive simplifying of the forms. This led him on to abstract art. Rejecting all imitation of nature, he insisted on the creation of an autonomous plastic language. From 1920 till 1923, Archipenko taught in Berlin. He then emigrated to the United States, where he died. His influence on German artists was of crucial importance. Through him, sculpture freed itself from naturalism. Oswald Herzog paid tribute to him in particular for his *Boxing Match* (1913–1914) for the way in which the volumes and the surfaces express the energy, tension and movement of the boxers. In fact, what has been described in Germany as expressionism, in Archipenko is due to his freeing himself from the classical rules of sculpture, and a fusion, in some of his works, of all modernist movements (cubism, futurism, the beginnings of constructivism). But his quest for a means of expression is a result of the needs of sculpture as a purely plastic art, and not a desire to project an inner universe.

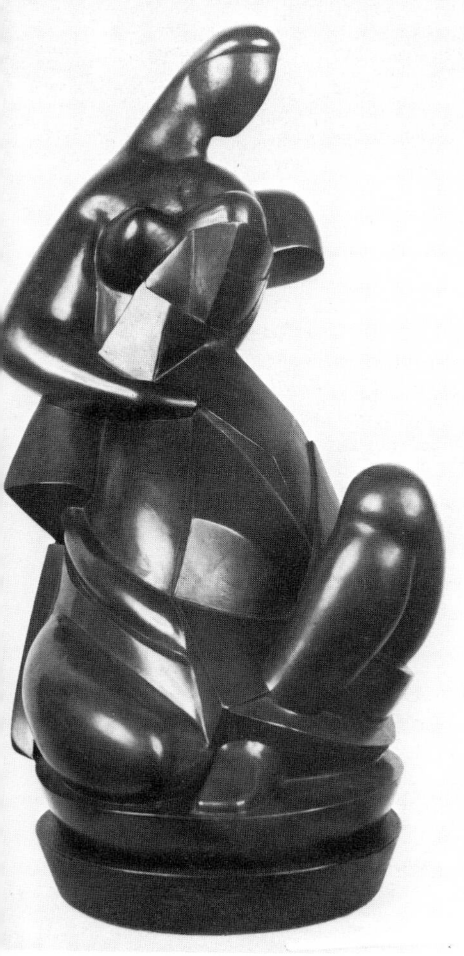

ARCHIPENKO, ALEXANDER: *Draped Woman.* 1911.

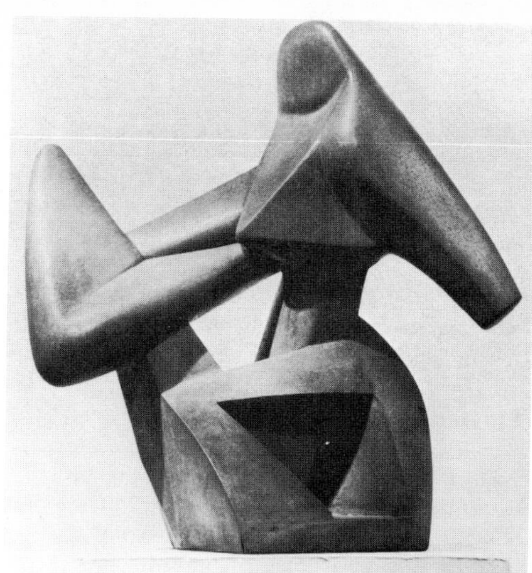

ARCHIPENKO, ALEXANDER: The *Boxing Match.* 1935.

BARLACH, Ernst (see biography p.38). A playwright and novelist as well as a painter and sculptor, he sought above all to achieve self-expression. After a trip to Russia in 1906, he exhibited in 1907 and 1908 at the *Sezession* in Berlin, then in 1908 in Dresden. In 1910, he settled in Gustrow, near Rostock, where he stayed until his death. In 1933, the Nazis labelled his work decadent. Although deeply shaken by this, he continued to produce sculptures. In 1937, under the title of *The Bad Year of 1937* (*Das Schlimme Jahr 1937*), he depicted the silhouette of a woman who, despite her intense suffering, is nevertheless upright, confronting barbarity.

Endowed with an inspiration which is often mystical and religious, Barlach's art conforms to the expressionist aesthetic, through its inner *élan* which is the

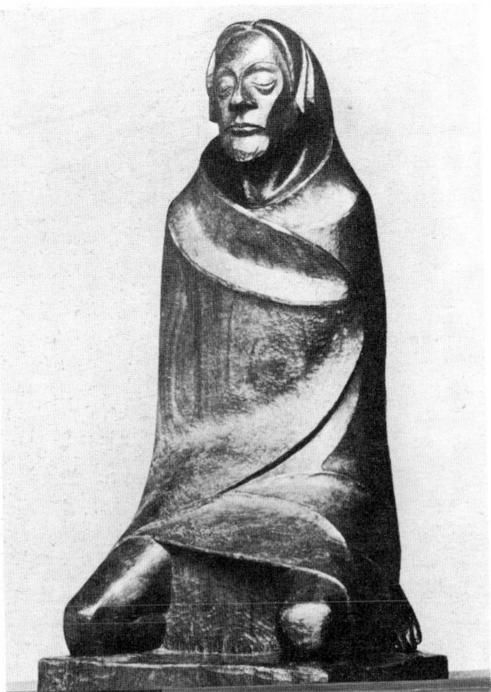

BARLACH, ERNST: *The Ascetic.* 1925.

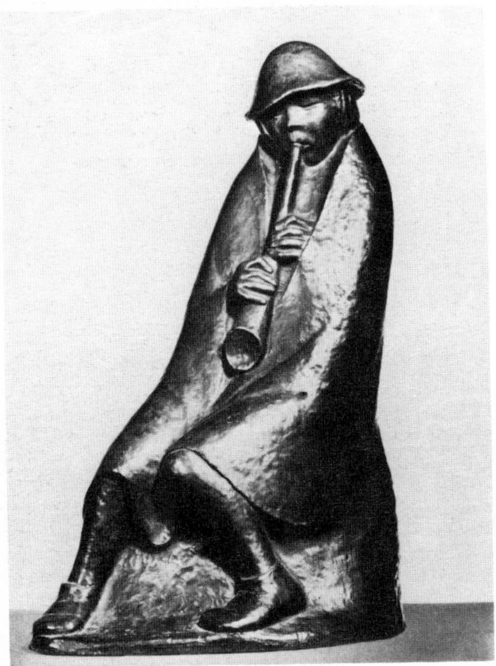

BARLACH, ERNST: *The Flute Player.* 1936

source of the form that he creates. But Barlach himself always remained on the fringe of particular movements. He managed to establish his own personality at the very time when expressionism was emerging. Massive, heavy, his volumes are at the same time compact and concentrated, every detail attaining the most intense degree of expressiveness.

At the time of an exhibition in 1952, Brecht wrote: 'I consider Barlach to be one of the greatest sculptors we Germans have had. The line, the significance of what he is expressing, the technical genius, the beauty without artifice, a grandeur which is not forced, a harmony which is not facile, a vigour without brutality, make his sculptures into masterpieces'.

BELLING, Rudolf (Berlin, 26.8.1886 – Munich, 9.6.1972). He started out as a pupil of Peter Breuer,

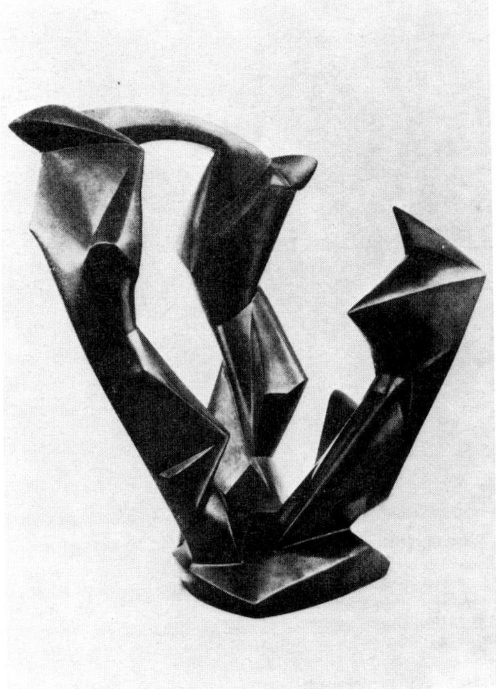

BELLING, RUDOLF: *Triple Accord.* 1919.

then he became associated with Walden's circle, and the review *Der Sturm*. In 1918, he was one of the founders of the November Group. During the Nazi period, he emigrated to Turkey. He taught at the Istanbul Academy of Fine Arts. Through his social aspirations (he was a friend of Bruno Taut), he shared the ideals of the expressionists. As regards the style of his sculptures,

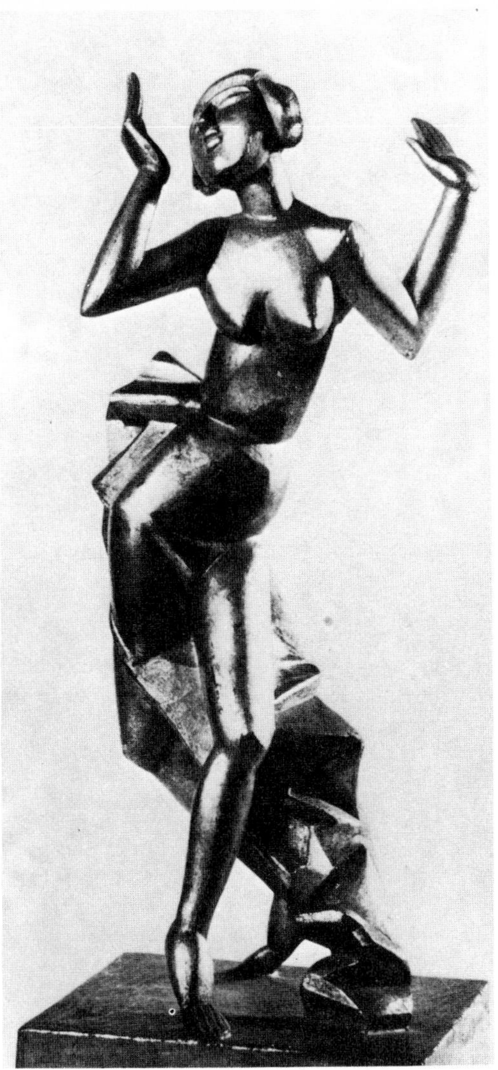

BELLING, RUDOLF: *A Dancer.* 1916.

he at first inclined more towards cubism, and then under the influence of Archipenko, towards abstract art. His originality lies in his desire to convey an inner movement in his forms. Through him, new problems are raised in a radical manner for German sculpture: the interplay between space, movement and matter.

FREUNDLICH, Otto (Stoll, Pomerania, 10.7.1878 – Lublin-Maideneck, Poland, March 1943). A painter and sketch artist, he began to produce sculpture in 1909. He mounted his first exhibition in Paris at the Saguet gallery, when he was living in Montmartre. In 1919, he exhibited in Berlin with the November Group, and in the same year the journal *Genius*, directed by Kurt Pinthus, published a series of reproductions of his works. Arrested in the French Pyrenees, where he had taken up residence, he was deported by the Nazis in 1943 to the Lublin concentration camp, where he died.

Freundlich is generally grouped with the cubists rather than with the expressionists. In fact, he was never either one or the other. But he joined up with the expressionists because of his sympathies with their social aspirations, as his participation in the November Group shows. Moreover, his drawings were published in expressionist journals, especially *Der Sturm*. The relative neglect into which he has fallen is unjustified, and the Catalan painter Antoni Tapiès has paid him tribute in some of his writings.

FREUNDLICH, OTTO: *Architectural sculpture.* 1934.

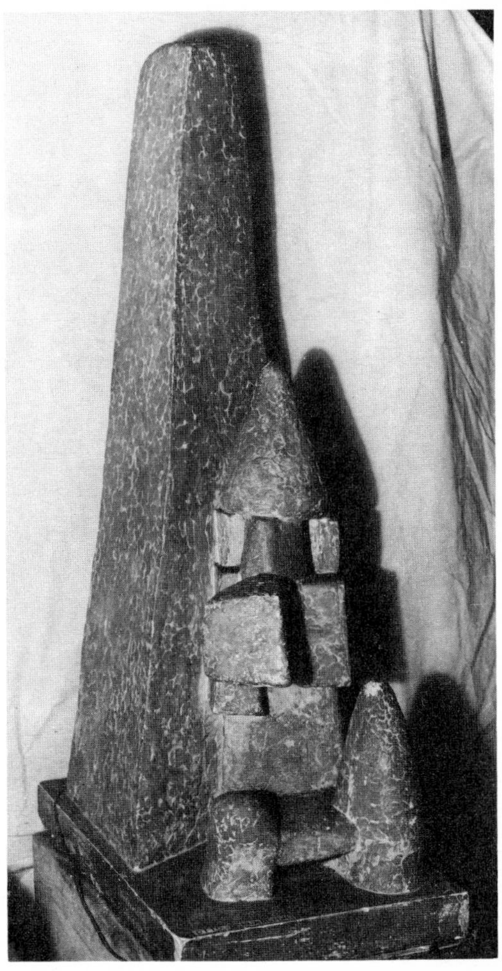

GUTFREUND, Otto (Dvur Kralové, Czechoslovakia, 1889 – Prague, 1927). He studied decorative art in Prague. In 1909, he went to Paris and frequented Bourdelle's studio. He became acquainted too, at the same time, with the first cubist works of Picasso and Braque. On his return to Prague in 1911, he was one of the exponents of cubism via a group of young painters, a group of specialists in plastic art. During the First World War, he lived in Paris, only returning to Prague in 1919. It was Gutfreund who introduced modernism into Czech sculpture. In 1911, his sculptures have affinities with expressionism by the presence in them of a deeply embedded inner tension (for example, *Anguish*, *Job*, *Hamlet*, and *Don Quixote*). In 1912, he abandoned these intensely expressive forms for a cubist approach, with, for instance, *Figures Embracing*. But apart from a style that has sometimes been described as cubo-expressionism, he shared the aspirations of the expressionists as regards the transformation of society and, from 1919, he even returned to the profound expression of his passions and personal feelings through a kind of social art.

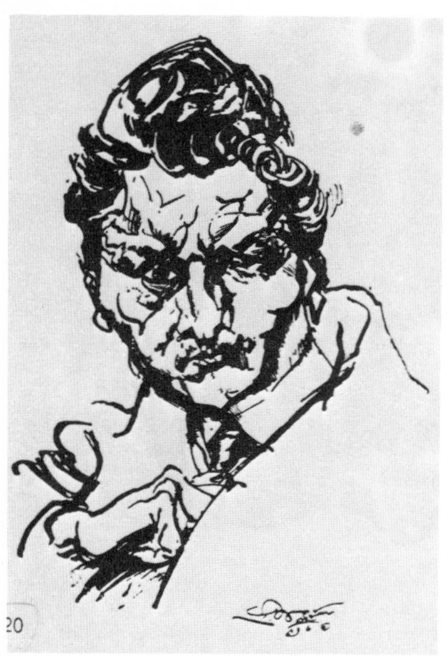

MEIDNER, LUDWIG: *Portrait of Wilhelm Lehmbruck.* 1916.

LEHMBRUCK, Wilhelm (Duisburg-Meiderich, 4.1.1881 – Berlin, 25.3.1919). He studied decorative art at Düsseldorf, from 1895 to 1899. Then, in the same town, he attended the Fine Arts Academy from 1901 to 1907. A stay in Paris, in 1910, led to his meeting Matisse, Brancusi and Archipenko, with whom he became friends. Called up during the First World War, the experience marked him for life. He gassed himself

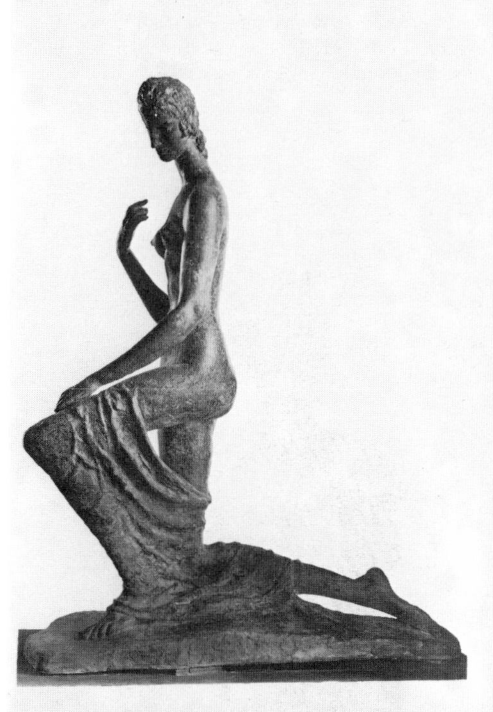

LEHMBRUCK, WILHELM: *Kneeling woman.*

in Berlin, leaving four children. In his sculpture, he was influenced by Rodin and by Gothic art: the forms appear as if rising out of an inner, violent tension, as if enhanced by this very tension. Their movement seems to emanate from their innermost depths. The body is, as it were, cast aside to allow the full radiance of the soul to emerge. This aspect is perceptible in his very first work, *Kneeling Woman* (1919), which is the embodiment of humility and piety. As in the case of Barlach, his art owes so much to the symbolist tradition.

MARCKS, Gerhard (Berlin, 18.2.1889). A sketch artist and sculptor, he studied in Berlin, particularly with Georg Kolbe. In 1918, he became a teacher at the

School of Arts and Crafts and in 1919, at the Bauhaus, where he stayed until 1925. Then he became a teacher at Halle. In 1933, the Nazis barred him from taking any public office, and in 1937, he no longer had the right to exhibit his works. In 1944, a bomb destroyed his studio, and in 1945, a large part of his work was destroyed in the place where it was being temporarily stored. A member of the November Group with Rudolf Belling, Gerhard Marcks shared the aspirations of the expressionists to transform society and to integrate art into society. His expressionism itself was, in his sculpture, very restrained, and in a style tempered by a classical legacy.

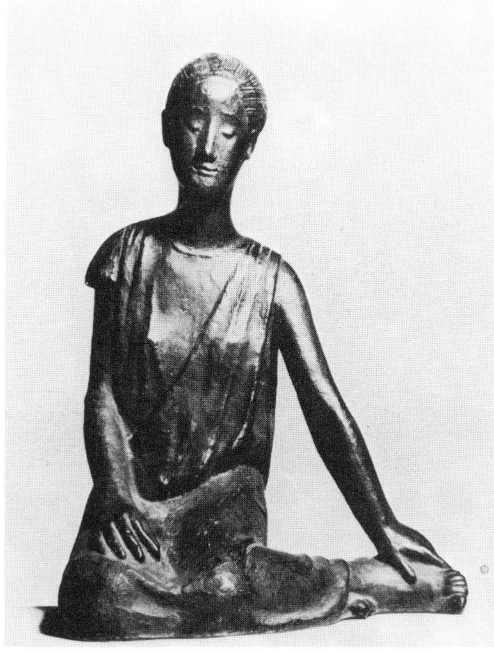

MARCKS, GERHARD: *Cenerentola.* Sculpture. 1941

WAUER, William (Oberwiesenthal 26.10.1866– Berlin, 10.3.1962). He was at the same time a painter, sculptor, art critic and theatre director. A friend of Walden's, he produced one of his plays, *The Four Dead of Famietta* (*Die vier Toten von Famietta*). He studied fine arts in the academies of Berlin, Dresden and Munich. To mark his ninetieth birthday in 1956, two retrospective exhibitions of his works were mounted in Berlin. William Wauer, like Rudolf Belling, sought essentially to express through his forms an inner movement. Concerned to stylize his work as much as possible, in order to attain the maximum intensity of expression, he is one of the representatives of abstract expressionism, as it emerged in the *Der Sturm* circle.

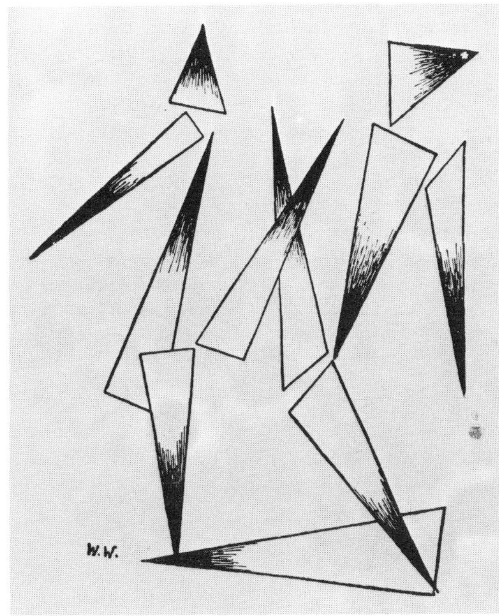

WAUER, WILLIAM: *The Dance.* 1918

WOUTERS, Rik (Mecheln, 2.8.1882 – Amsterdam, 11.7.1916). The son of a sculptor, Wouters began himself to sculpt in his father's studio. He attended drawing classes at the Mecheln Fine Arts Academy and, in 1902, attended the Brussels Academy, attached to the studio of the sculptor Ch. van der Stappen. In 1907, he moved to Boitsfort. He devoted himself simultaneously to sculpture and painting. At first, he worked exclusively under the influence of Ensor. In 1902, Wouters organized the first exhibition of his work in Brussels, and went to Paris. Rodin, the Impressionists and especially Cézanne made a great impression on him. Subsequently, he tried to achieve a synthesis between Ensor and Cézanne. In 1914, Wouters was called up to fight in the war, and, shortly afterwards, made prisoner in Holland. He did, however, have the opportunity to carry on working till 1915, when he was struck down by a serious illness at the very moment he was the great hope of the younger generation of painters in Belgium.

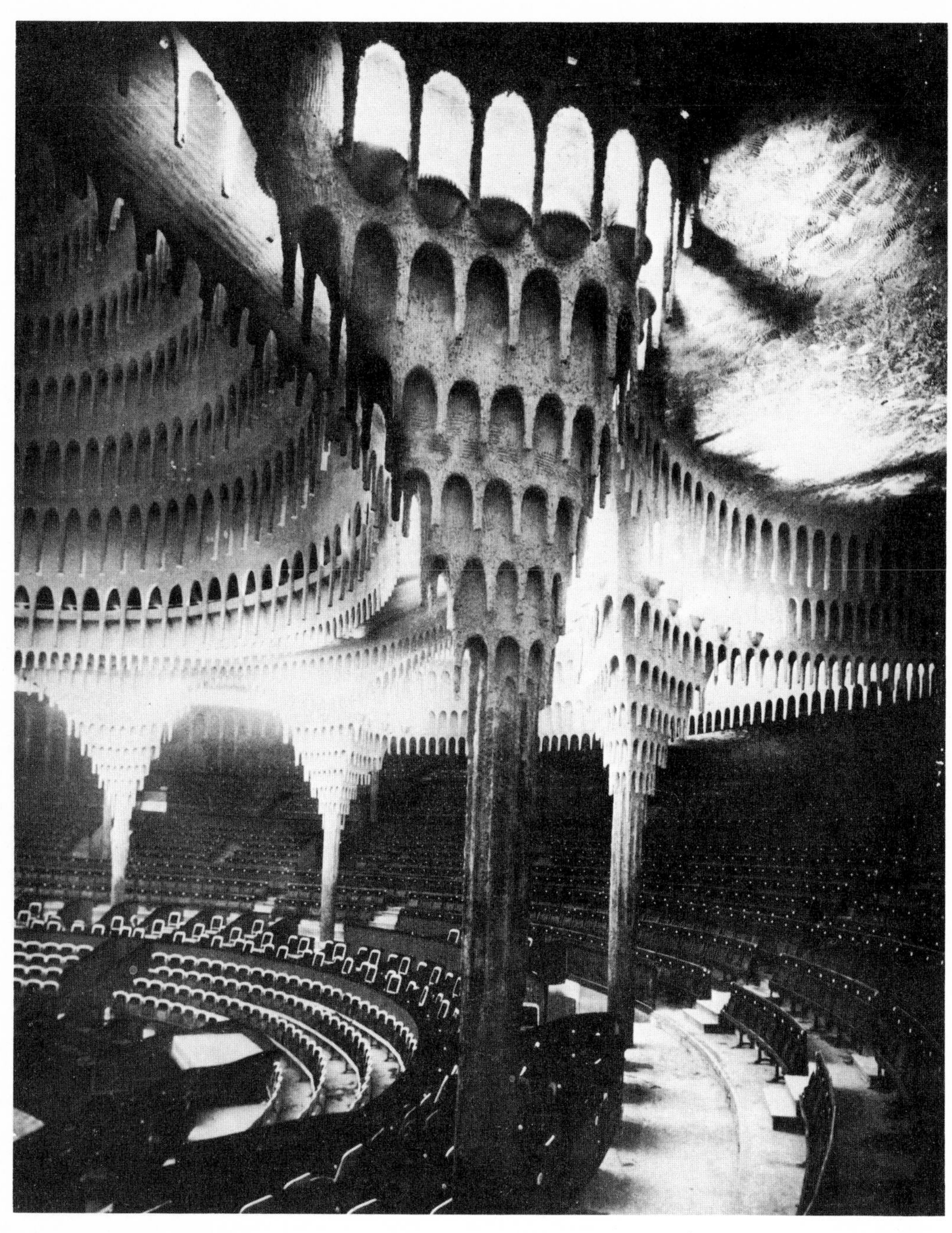

POELZIG, HANS: *Grosses Schauspielhaus.* 1919. Berlin

Architecture

Architecture was also included in the vast movement which began questioning artistic conventions and which affected Europe from 1910. The contrary would be surprising, since the phenomenon which assumed the name of expressionism represented a cultural effervescence that did not simply attack aesthetic forms, but involved society, and a whole vision of the world. In so far as architecture influenced man's day-to-day existence, whether with regards to his family habitat, the collective problems of urbanization, or, more generally, his environment, it was logical that the new 'intellectual' generation should give it extremely serious attention. It was not only the images of towns, roads, and various buildings that haunted the pictures of the painters of the time, even before the First World War, but texts and drawings by architects appeared in journals and publications like *Der Sturm, Die Aktion, Die Erhebung* and *Das hohe Ufer*, which are generally considered representative of literary expressionism.

The Transitional Period

With the increase in the pace of industrialization at the end of the nineteenth century, especially in Germany, the urban phenomenon provoked questions and reflections. Towns were expanding in an anarchic fashion, leading to a congestion of the population, which resulted in bad living conditions and bad hygiene. On the other hand, unknown materials and techniques, until then unused in architecture, made their decisive entry into the building industry, namely, reinforced concrete, metal girders, and glass. Finally overpopulation in the towns necessitated a complete re-thinking of their very organization and their structure.

There were several notable initiatives which confronted the new problems; they are far from forming a unified approach; they rather present a series of contradictory solutions. But they all have in common a desire to escape from the international style which in the twenties was assimilated under various names to *art nouveau*. The latter, in fact, by its rejection of methods born out of the Machine Age and its refuge in a neo-romantic decorative style, bypassed the real problems posed by industrial and urban civilization.

In England, for example, faced with the anarchic expansion of towns, Ebenezer Howard planned, in 1898, city gardens, in an attempt to restore a harmony between man and nature. In Germany, Peter Behrens (Le Corbusier worked in his studio from 1910 to 1914) aimed, through the use of new materials, to create a functional architecture, namely to give a building a form that would essentially be governed by its function. Further still, Walter Gropius, who had also spent a period in Peter Behrens's studio, integrated industrial techniques and the act of building. It was in this spirit that, in conjunction with Adolph Meyer, he had the Fagus factories at Alfeld in Lower Saxony constructed. In Vienna, Adolf Loos also reacted against the *art nouveau* of painters like Gustav Klimt and architects like Fritz Maria Olbrich and Joseph Hoffmann by advocating purer forms.

Now, the new generation of architects, which reached maturity between 1910 and 1915, and was drawn into the whirlwind of the expressionist movement, found itself in a crucial position. It knew about the demise of *art nouveau* and the rise of functionalism. With regard to the former, it liked its imaginative power; it was fascinated by its abundance which appeared to be the blossoming forth of a creative subjectivity. As for the latter, it shared the favourable view it held of the new materials and its desire to take the social context into consideration. It therefore oscillated from one pole to the other, striving to reach a balance between an imprescriptible inner necessity, the right to the expression of the most personal imagination possible and the modern technical demands of an industrial society. Its effective accomplishments until the twenties (those of Erich Mendelsohn, Hans Poelzig, Bruno Taut and his brother Max) mark the period in a very precise way, because they were successful in conciliating these two predominant tendencies.

Rehumanizing man

These young architects did not, strictly speaking, form an organized group, at least not before the war. But their individual experiences and preoccupations were highly personal. They lived together with poets and painters, experiencing a reality they found difficult to bear. They aspired towards something

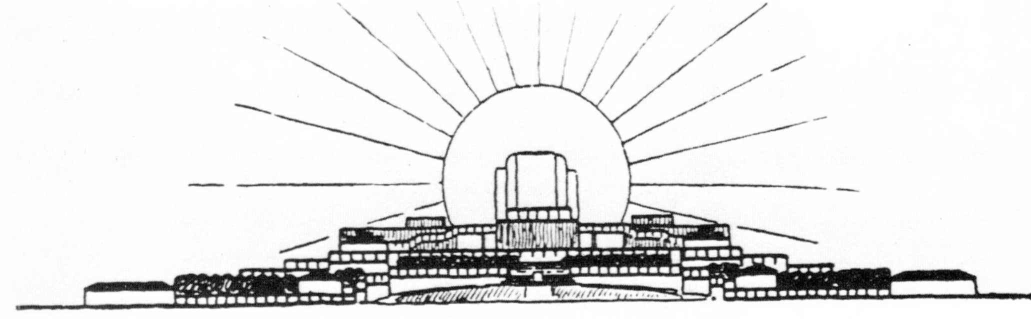

TAUT, BRUNO: *Crown for the town.* View from the east. Detail. Jena 1919

higher. The dream of a new Man, of a transformed society, of a fundamentally revivified existence, was part of their universe. It was no coincidence that several of them (Max Berg, Hans Poelzig, Bruno Taut) were attracted by mystical or Oriental doctrines before 1914. And when the revolution, in November 1918, aroused their hopes for the birth of a new world, they participated in large numbers in the Work Council for Art led by Bruno Taut.

Beyond these common and very strong social concerns, which explain their favourite types of building: factories, hospitals, workers' lodgings, community houses or theatres, their guiding principle was based on a subjective idealism and a creative spontaneity, advocated by all the expressionist journals in German-speaking countries. Through architecture, it was possible for the individual to be entirely creative and to become one with God in his demiurgic function, by subjecting himself only to impulses of his own imagination.

As in the other arts, these tendencies came to an end in the years 1918–20. At the instigation of the Work Council for Art, exhibitions of architectural plans were organized: In April 1919, an exhibition of work by unknown architects was held, and during the winter of 1919–20, there was another one, of workers' districts. Programmes were drawn up. A journal, *Frühlicht*, was published. Letters, the 'utopian letters', were exchanged in 1920–1, in which the great dreams of the architecture of the future were freely revealed. At the heart of this activity was Bruno Taut, organizer and indefatigable theoretician.

In all the texts and plans of this time, one finds the essential themes of expressionism: a synthesis of the arts, which was very easy to achieve in architecture; collaboration with the mass of the people; an impulse given to the whole by a foreman, starting out from his own inner vision. Walter Gropius was at that time himself very close to these ideas; he, moreover, gave the speech inaugurating the exhibition of work by Unknown Architects; and the *Bauhaus*, founded in March 1919 in Weimar, adopted until 1923 a line of approach which was inspired by expressionism.

An ideal material: glass

It is by the pen of Bruno Taut that the essential concerns of these young architects are expounded most systematically. His frequent reference to Paul Scheerbart, a poet endowed with a fertile imagination, is of significance. Regarded as one of the fathers of the modern science-fiction novel in Germany, this inventive genius contributed at the end of the century to two journals in which *art nouveau* was blossoming, *Jugend* and *Ver sacrum*, before being acclaimed and published by Herwarth Walden with the birth of *Der Sturm*. The relationship between the fantasies of *art nouveau* and what was called expressionism can therefore be seen, as far as architecture is concerned, through the personality of Paul Scheerbart.

But this relationship needs to be defined more closely. For it is not as clear as one might think.

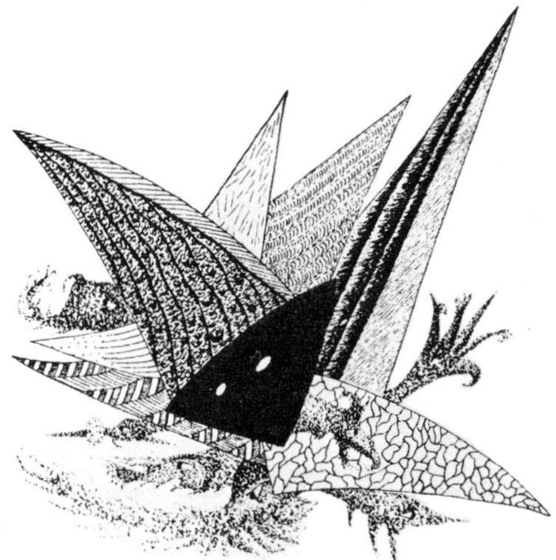

SCHEERBART, PAUL: Vignette for the 'Bibliothèque théâtrale révolutionnaire'. 1904

Scheerbart is definitely not identifiable as one of the typical representatives of *art nouveau*. He only shares their predilection for the imaginary and their tendency to use a decorative style. In place of the artificial vegetable world in which they were accustomed to live, he wanted to create a fantastic reality which would be less ephemeral, but as rich as that of the plants, and which would transform the everyday environment. To this end, glass was an ideal material. For thanks to it, all shapes and forms were possible. Moreover, by virtue of the transparency of crystal, man was compelled to continue relating to his surroundings and was reintegrated into the cosmos.

This enthusiasm for glass is not profoundly original, since Joseph Paxton, in the Great Exhibition of

1851, in London, had already introduced the public to a Crystal Palace. However, Paul Scheerbart had the distinction of advocating the use of glass as the most important material, a coherent system for the renovation of architecture, linked to a general view of man and the world. He did it in a book which he dedicated to Bruno Taut, with whom he had worked in 1913, and which was published by Herwarth Walden in 1914: *Architecture out of Glass.* Its philosophy is expounded on the very first page. 'Most of the time we live in closed rooms. These form the milieu that is a basis for our culture. To a certain extent, our culture is the product of our architecture. If we want to raise our culture to a higher level, we are more or less compelled to change our architecture. And this will only be possible, once we have abandoned the idea of living in an enclosed environment. Now, we can only do this by introducing an architecture of glass which lets in sunlight, the moon and the stars, not simply through a few windows, but through the greatest possible number of walls made entirely out of tinted panes of glass. This is the new milieu that we will create in this way that will bring about a new culture.'

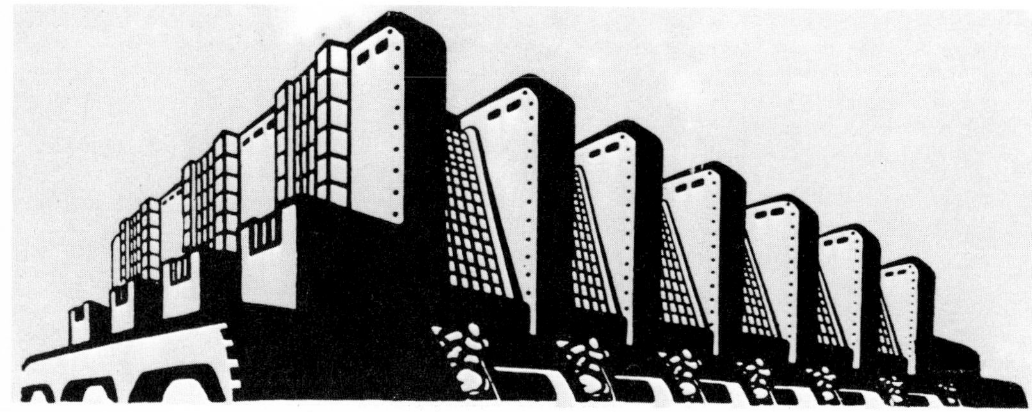

MENDELSOHN, ERICH: *Design for a steel-works.* 1914

Like all the expressionists, Bruno Taut was attracted by Scheerbart's ideas, not only because they broke with the conventions of the time, but also because they pre-supposed a reform of humanity. They gave a glimpse of a new Man. In the review *Das hohe Ufer*, at the beginning of 1919, Bruno Taut paid tribute to Scheerbart when he wrote 'You alone knew what architecture meant,' and he added, 'Architects, here is your world. Enter this world of pure splendour and laugh, far from everything that is intellectual anguish and contrary to construction. Paul Scheerbart removes the bandages from your eyes and you begin to see, what you could not see before, how oppressive the darkness was! Here it is: the marvellous reign of the Imagination.'

Spirituality above all

It was their projection of the architect's inner need to create, grafted on to desire for a collective transformation of the world, in order to restore man's vital dynamism, which had to intervene in the design before any concern about its function. Bruno Taut insisted that all aesthetic production was founded in an individual's inner spiritual life. In his eyes, the impulse to build was something very different from the practical requirement of some utilitarian system: architecture was engendered by the creative imagination which gives life to forms. Sometimes Bruno Taut expressed such a passionate hostility to the *a priori* approach of functional architecture that one could, mistakenly, regard him as an aesthete. Relating his experience to the construction of the glass Pavilion of Industry for the exhibition of the Union for Work *(Deutscher Werkbund)* in 1914, he wrote, 'the public, which at the outset constantly asked what the point of this building was, might eventually manage to understand that architecture is not objective, except by being itself, by having architectural beauty.'

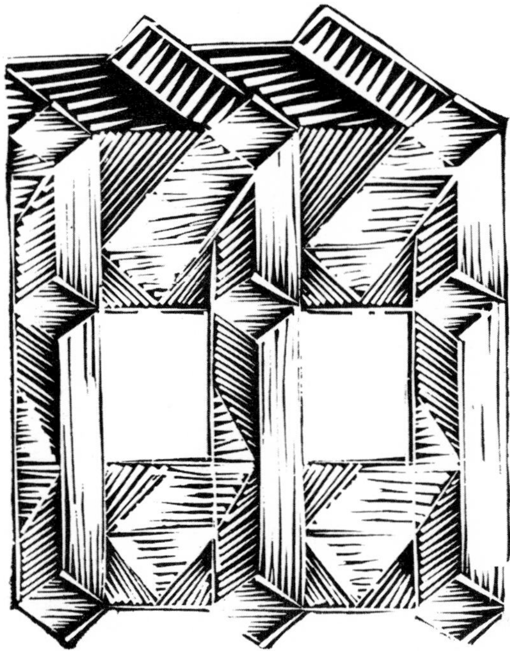

HOFMAN, VLASTISLAV: *Details of a façade: tower.* 1914

In so far as a building was first inspired by a spirituality that it expressed outwardly, Bruno Taut and his companions admired the art of cathedrals. They were also attracted by Oriental (and especially Indian) architecture: 'the Resurrection of Art! We rub our eyes, we who have begun to see again all that is truly real. We are not dreaming, men built these buildings!' Thus Bruno Taut praised the temples or pagodas built from the fourth to the sixteenth centuries in the East. Why? Because their forms fully corresponded to inner aspirations and because a perfect fusion between architecture and sculpture has been achieved.

In opposition to a blind faith in technology

The spirit above all, this is the foundation for the development of the expressionists' artistic experiments. Kandinsky and Franz Marc also strove towards discovering a new spirituality. This aspiration, in opposition to a reality that the expressionists called bourgeois in order to convey their contempt for it, led many of them towards a mysticism or an aspiration of a religious nature. The same was true for the young architects who gathered around Bruno Taut. The drawings that illustrate one of the articles by Bruno Taut in *Die Erhebung*, in 1920, reveal a kind of mystical elevation: Carl Krayl, August W. Kashek, Hans Scharoun, Wilhelm Blückman, Max Taut and he himself had suggestions for towers, churches, domes and temples.

Another tendency, linked to the previous one, consisted in claiming to go beyond the visible and enter into communication with universal forms of life. This 'panvitalism' or 'cosmism', Bruno Taut justified by emphasizing that man cannot be restricted to the perception of his five senses: 'Things in the world are not simply things, but everything lives, and lives in the most complete sense, since all things speak to us in their own manner. What was at stake at that time for art and artists was the capacity to rediscover the world in its creative impulse and to recreate a natural communion between it and the individual. The result, for the architect, was a desire to extend nature, and to find, through the imagination and the construction of buildings a universal and vital impulse.

Thus the expressionist achievements do not really deserve the terms sometimes used to describe them, like 'baroque', 'fantastic' and 'imaginary'. They must be related to a global vision of the world. As Bruno Taut emphasized, a new relationship was being established with matter. 'Mountains shout at us provocatively (Alpine architecture), the surface of the earth offers itself up in all its fecundity, all the earthy matter is alive and what we build is only in obedience to its injunction: to simplicity and ultimate security (my *The Destruction of Towns*).' Is this obscurantism and a flight towards irrationality? It seems more plausible that this attitude emanated from a reaction against a blind faith in technology and science, against the pretentions of positivism to explain everything in nature. Bruno Taut did not question science itself but its abuses: 'Where the rites of the temple ought to exist, is in industry with its avid desire to appropriate, its slavery, misery and crime.'

Towards a modern architecture

All these ideas which indicate the influence expressionism had on architecture held fire, as in other art forms, shortly after the failure of the revolutionary enthusiasm of the years 1918–20. What followed was a return to order, unless they remained completely utopian by devoting themselves exclusively to utopian plans. Expressionist architects were concerned to sacrifice part of their imagination to become integrated in the concrete social situation of the Weimar Republic. Some of them managed this successfully without going back on their convictions, e.g., Erich Mendelsohn, Bruno Taut, Hans Scharoun. Others, like Hermann Finsterlin, who were too enamoured of the absolute, remained visionaries.

Were their dreams futile? It is true to say that the influence they had abroad was slight. In France, they were practically unheard of in the inter-war period. One reads in 1925 in *L'Esprit Nouveau*, Corbusier's journal: 'Neurasthenia. Expressionism! Bruno Taut foresees temples where humanity unveils itself, plunges into purifying lakes and reaches the holy place of another Grail! Expressionism, acute neurasthenia. Madness, the architecture of a tormented soul!' As for the Prague avant-garde, led by Pavel Janák, Josef Chochol, Vlatislav Hofman, while still seeking support from Berlin before freeing itself from Viennese hegemony and being welcomed by *Der Sturm*, it inclined more towards the geometric rigour of cubism. Only the Amsterdam school, centring around Michel de Klerk and the journal *Wendingen*, paid continuous attention to them, but in a difficult opposition to the 'abstract realism' of the *De Stijl* group. The leader of this group, Theo van Doesburg, gave a very good account himself, in 1921, of the change in the architects Oud, Wils, Vant Hoff, and Rietveld, which was at that time making itself felt in the Netherlands, against the ornamentalist tradition inherited from Berlage and continued in the expressionism of Michel de Klerk: 'The aesthetic emotion was subjected to a discipline, art became an organized intuition – all ornamentation, all superficial seduction was sacrificed to construction, to logical structure, to the desire for harmony in installations.'

Is this poor showing evidence of mediocrity? Walter Gropius has admitted that he learnt a lot from associating with Bruno Taut. Not only do the buildings constructed by expressionist architects continue to exist, something which is often forgotten, but they raised the problem of form and the whole validity of modern architecture. Their utopian plans, their illusions, and their confusion are perhaps also indicative of their richness, which they could have further extended, if they had been given the concrete opportunity of doing so.

BERG, Max (Stettin, 17.4.1870 – Baden-Baden, 24.1.1947). He studied in Berlin. Then he became, before the First World War, architect to the town of Breslau. Influenced by the anti-productivist tendencies of the age, he was attracted by the occult and clairvoyance. He was the leading force behind the construction of several buildings in Breslau, including a hydro-electric station, but his most surprising accomplishment was the Centenary Hall. It was inaugurated in 1913 as a tribute to the War of Liberation against Napoleon a hundred years earlier. It was designed for gymnastics, festivals, popular shows and mass meetings. Built in reinforced concrete, its distinguishing features are a huge dome, also cast in concrete, and its dimensions, larger than the Pantheon in Rome. For Max Berg, it was a symbol: its functional character had to be less clear than the historical event it represented. This monument was the incarnation of the ability of an age to last for centuries.

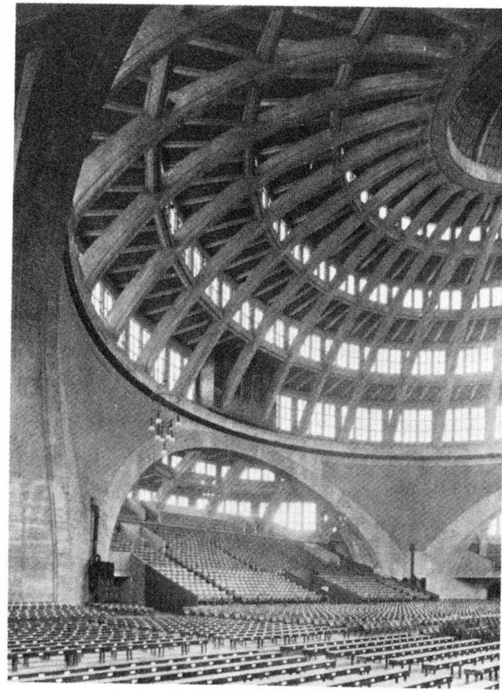

BERG, MAX: *Centenary Hall*, Breslau-Scheitnig. 1911–1913

FINSTERLIN, Hermann (Munich, 18.8.1887). It was after studying natural sciences and philosophy in Munich that he became interested in art. In 1919, he was a member of the Work Council for Art. In touch with Bruno Taut, he contributed to the journal *Frühlicht*. From Schönau, near Berchtesgaden, where he had taken up residence, he also participated in the exchange of 'utopian letters', through which the architects who had formed a group around Bruno Taut tried to express their visions of the future. He has been classified among the expressionist representatives of imaginary architecture. Marked by his education, he wanted to apply to art and its history the laws of evolution, which he thought he had established through his observation of nature. In 1922, he distinguished in this way several phases in the development of architecture: the first, that of the past, had not gone beyond the forms emanating from the combination of a reduced number

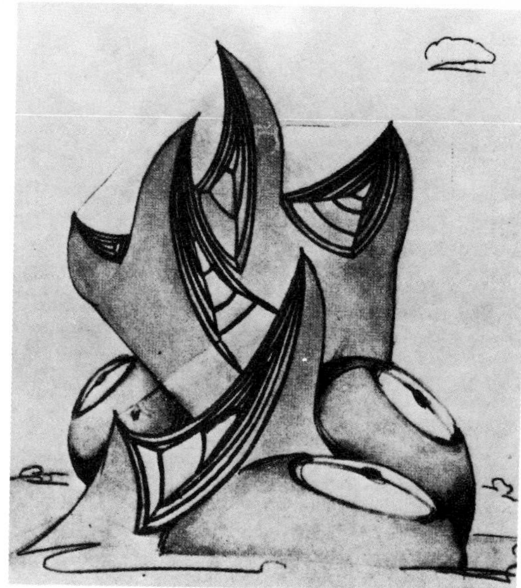

FINSTERLIN, HERMANN: *Atelierbau*. 1917

FINSTERLIN, HERMANN: *Glass house*. 1924

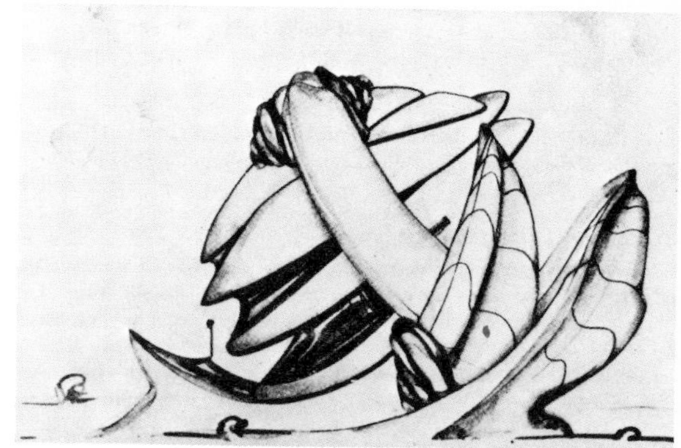

of elements; the second, a contemporary phase, was characterized by a recourse to elaborate geometric forms; the third, and it was this one he was inaugurating, was the architecture of the future. He imagined buildings inscribed in nature and instead of artificially imitating it, being an extension of it. He has left behind, dating from 1916 to 1923, strange drawings, sketches and water-colours. There are forms which escape the grasp of nature just as if they were themselves living beings and react with it by integrating with vegetable, mineral and animal elements. The imagination unfolds freely without taking into consideration any functional constraints, the architect identifying with the demiurgic power of nature to create something never seen before.

In 1933, Finsterlin was called to the Bauhaus. But a few months later, the Nazis were to close what they considered to be the temple of Judaic-Bolshevik art. This meant that Hermann Finsterlin's architectural ideas scarcely got further than the stage of fantasy.

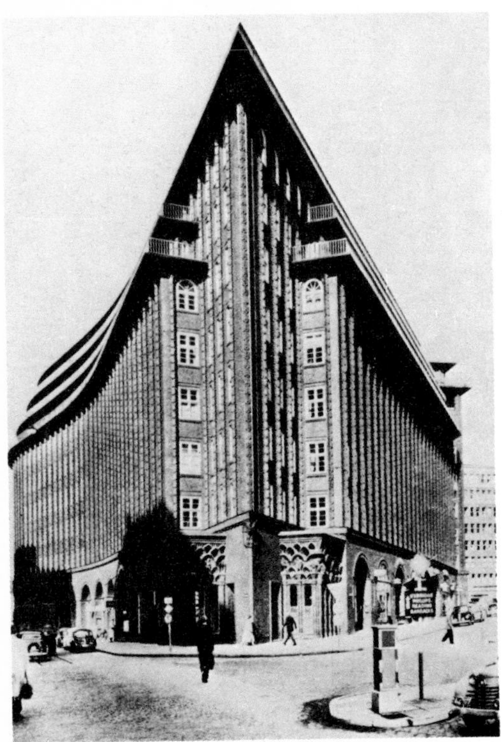

HÖGER, FRITZ: *The Chile House.* 1923. Hamburg

HÖGER, Johannes Friedrich, called Fritz (Beckenreihe, Holstein, 12.6.1887 – Bad Segeberg, 21.6.1949). He represents another branch of expressionist architecture, no longer that of Berlin but of North Germany. His family came from Holstein. He was one of the most important architects from Hamburg; specializing before the First World War in the construction of administrative buildings and offices, he introduced into this type of building, for which he used reinforced concrete, decorative effects by replacing the traditional pebble-dash with a covering of twice-fired brick. His most striking achievement was, in 1922–3, the Chile House in Hamburg.

KLERK, Michel de (Zeichner, 24.12.1884 – Amsterdam 24.11.1923). He was one of the reformers of architecture in the Netherlands. Close to the German expressionists, he was the key figure in what has been called the Amsterdam School. He had the gift of spontaneity, the art of detail and visionary imagination. He dared to shake up the conventions in his use of traditional materials like brick and slate, advocating, for instance, a brick covering over undulating shapes, or the coating of balconies with slate coverings. Rejecting a utilitarianism subjected to strictly rational criteria, he strove to create inhabitable areas which conformed especially to his subjectivity as a remarkable draughtsman and as a painter enamoured of forms. He exerted considerable influence after the First World War, both in his buildings (the groups of houses in Amsterdam-Zuid and in Amsterdam–Westerpark) and as a leading figure in the review *Wendingen*, which, in opposition to the functionalism of *De Stijl*, echoed the expressionist aims in architecture: in 1920, a whole number was devoted to Erich Mendelsohn, and, in 1924, another to Hermann Finsterlin.

MENDELSOHN, Erich (Allenstein, 21.3.1887 – San Francisco, 16.9.1953). After his studies in Berlin and Munich, he acquired the experience of what it was like to be an architect by working in various offices. Then the First World War broke out, with the result that Mendelsohn only really began his career in 1918. He had devoted himself to drawing from 1914, however, and brought back from the Front a number of sketches: plans for the construction of factories and religious buildings, where a tendency to use symbolic forms emerges. Like many of the young architects of his generation, and especially the expressionists, he believed in creative spontaneity and intuition. He also had a social conscience. In 1919 he sat on the leading committee of the November Group. His most striking accomplishment of the time was the Einstein Tower, which was finished in Potsdam in 1921. Financed in part by the Prussian state and in part by private organizations, this building, made out of reinforced concrete, was designed especially to house a telescope and all the equipment of an astrophysics laboratory. It is generally considered to be one of the most impressive testimonies of expressionist architecture. Mendelsohn sought to convey the Promethean liberation that the scientific researches of Albert Einstein made it possible for one to foresee.

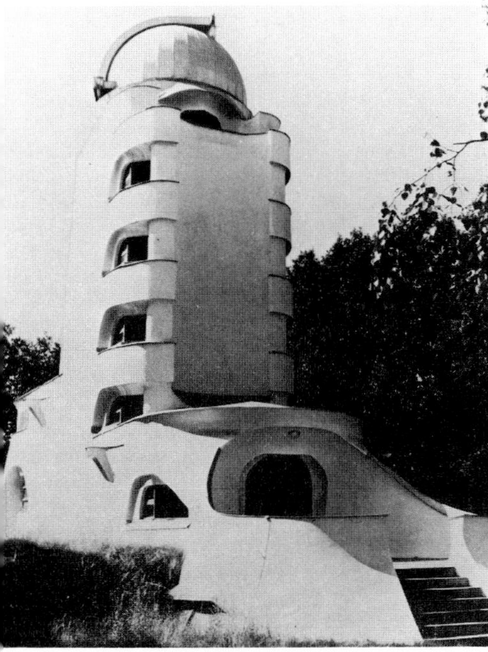

MENDELSOHN, ERICH: *The Einstein Tower: general view.* 1917–1921. Potsdam

While lending itself functionally to a specific use, this tower-observatory was a monument built in honour of a scientist.

From 1923, Mendelsohn turned towards what he called a functional dynamism. Without rejecting emotions, feelings and subjectivity, he wanted to construct buildings so that they would integrate with the rhythm of modern life. He sought in fact to reconcile the imagination of expressionism and the rigour of functionalism.

In 1933, he left Nazi Germany, first of all for Brussels and then for London. For six years he was active both in England and Palestine. He has, moreover, left behind a number of buildings in Haifa and Jerusalem, including hospitals. In 1941, he emigrated to the United States, where he continued to work until his death.

POELZIG, Hans (Berlin, 30.4.1869 – Berlin, 14.6.1936). He has been described as a force of nature which had confidence in a constantly alert spontaneous genius. It was perhaps this that gave him for a short while an active sympathy with expressionist ideas. Tending towards a rigorous style, Hans Poelzig was at the same time attracted by that which stimulated the imagination and by buildings with a social function. In 1911, the water tower he erected at Posen (today Poznan) is an example of this mixture of formal rigour and visionary

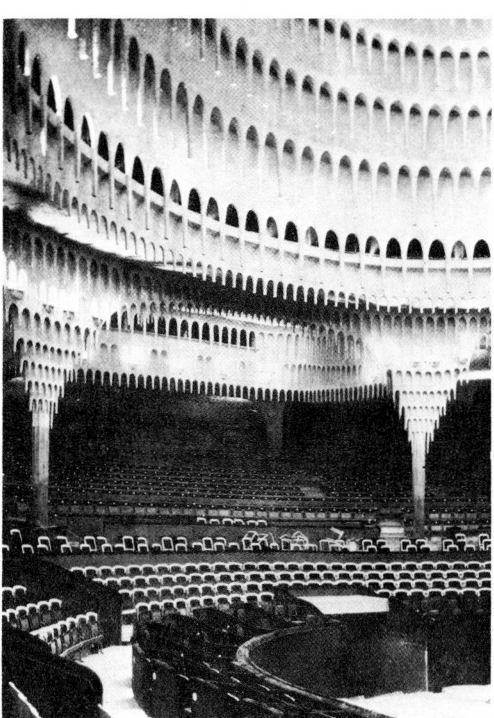

POELZIG, HANS: *Grosses Schauspielhaus.* 1919. Berlin

power: with steel as its primary material, he managed to unite the technical expertise of an engineer and the imaginative vision of an architect. But his most famous achievement, hailed as an example of expressionist architecture, was the Grand Theatre in Berlin, also called the Max Reinhardt Theatre, which opened on November 20th, 1919 with a production of the *Oresteia*, by Aeschylus. It was built quickly, since Poelzig, at that time architect for Dresden, was only engaged at the end of 1918. Two elements used here by Poelzig have become the characteristic signs of expressionist architecture, the mountainous-looking reliefs and the appearance of grottos or caverns, with kinds of stalactites, the function of which was to allow the sound and light to carry more efficiently. It is a characteristic of

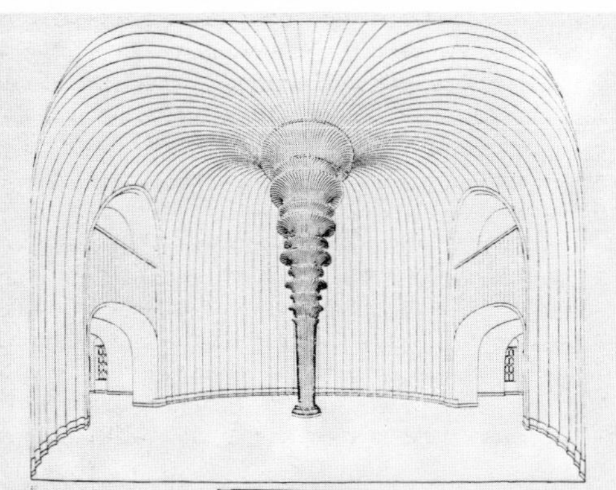

POELZIG, HANS: *Grosses Schauspielhaus*; entrance to foyer. 1919. Berlin

expressionist architecture, as we have already said, to present forms elaborated by man as an extension of nature: in the same way, in 1910, Poelzig's plan for a monument in honour of Bismarck at the Bingerbrück shows that the forms were intended to emerge from the surrounding stone as if they were a continuation of it, like rocks devoured by erosion.

At the end of the twenties, Poelzig definitively abandoned expressionism in favour of a rigorous monumentalism.

SCHAROUN, Hans (Bremen, 20.9.1893 – Berlin, 25.11.1972). After studying in Berlin from 1912 to 1914, he came into contact with Bruno Taut during his military service. He was a member, in 1919, of a circle of young architects who exchanged 'utopian letters'. He especially defended the very expressionist idea that the possibilities of development in architecture were not external, but within the context of the artist's fantasy; one had therefore to abandon oneself to the drunkenness of the *creative act*. The sketches that Hans Scharoun did for a House of the People in 1920 slightly resemble sparks issuing directly from the fire as it were, of the imagination. In this type of building, he also joins the social utopia of the other expressionist architects.

In 1925, he joined the group *Der Ring*, which included Peter Behrens, Walter Gropius, Erich Mendelsohn, M. van der Rohe, Hans Poelzig and the Taut brothers. The age was then dominated by functionalism. But Scharoun, whilst participating through a number of buildings in the renewal of urbanism at the time (in Breslau and Berlin), never abandoned certain expressionist tendencies, such as the affirmation of fantasy, vitalism, and even a kind of irrationality.

Under the Third Reich it was practically impossible for him to work. He only resumed normal activity after 1945. His achievements were then very considerable, since they were closely linked to the rebuilding of German towns (especially Berlin and Stuttgart).

STEINER, Rudolf (Kraljevic, Hungary, 27.2.1861 – Dornach, near Basel, 30.3.1925). He was not himself an architect, but he had designed a building which was to serve as a temple for the spiritual movement that he had founded – the anthroposophical movement, the intention of which was to allow man, through a spiritual life, to discover more ethereal worlds existing beyond physical reality. It was essential to have a building which facilitated this spiritual concentration. Built in Dornach near Basel, beginning in 1913 and ending in 1914, the first Goetheanum (the name given it by allusion to the theory of correspondences, developed by Goethe, between the spirituality of man and the universe) was in the form of two wooden domes supported by an infrastructure of reinforced concrete. It was destroyed by fire in 1922. The inspiration for the building was influenced by expressionism, in so far as the building was above all the materialization of an idea, a symbol. A second Goetheanum, according to plans drawn up during the lifetime of Rudolf Steiner, was finished in 1928. Also built at Dornach, but this time entirely in reinforced concrete, it is considered to be one of the most remarkable achievements of twentieth-century architecture. The work was successfully completed by Ernst Aisenpreis, who had contributed to the first plan, and Olé Falk Ebbel, who completed other buildings for the anthroposophical movement. The general conception is very different from the first Goetheanum. It is a monu-

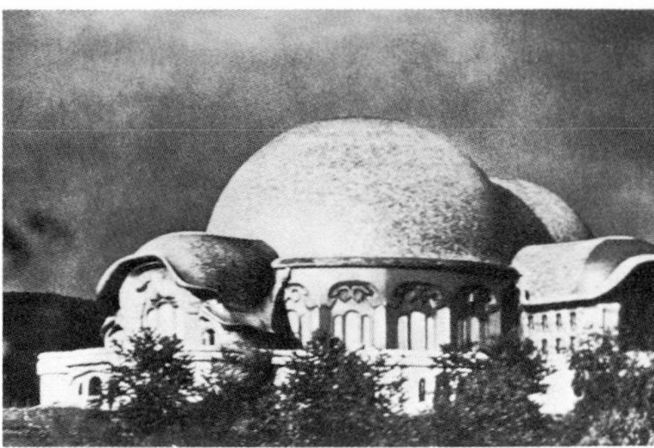

STEINER, RUDOLF: *The First Goetheanum.* Dornach. 1913–1914

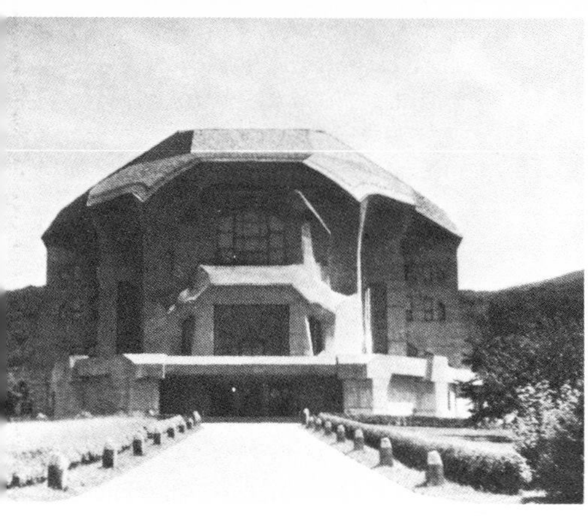

STEINER, RUDOLF: *The Second Goetheanum.* Dornach. 1924–1928. View from the west

mental edifice, as it were moulded out of one mass where all the parts are integrated and link with each other. Beneath the dome, there are lecture halls and editorial offices, a library, an auditorium for a thousand people, and a theatre.

TAUT, Bruno (Königsberg, 4.5.1880 – Ankara, 23.12.1938). An indefatigable organizer and passionate theoretician, he is the one who really managed to bring together the general aspirations of the expressionists and architecture. He recognized not an architect, but the poet Paul Scheerbart, as his mentor. He shared with him the idea that humanity could be reformed by changing its living conditions, and particularly its environment, its habitat. A first phase in the development of his architectural plans is also directly connected with the dreams that Scheerbart had already elaborated, emanating from a material which he reckoned was going to revolutionize human existence: glass. In 1914, whereas the previous year he had presented to the exhibition of the Union for Work (Deutscher Werkbund) the pavilion reserved for the steel industry, Bruno Taut now built, this time in Cologne, a pavilion for the glass industry.

After the First World War, he was active as the leading figure in the Work Council for Art, then in the publication of the journal *Frühlicht* and in the famous exchange of 'utopian letters'. He shared all the social hopes of the expressionists of the time: aspirations towards a radical transformation of society, the communion of the artist and the community, the mystique of a universal human fraternity. He also advocated the use of colour on buildings. In a manifesto in 1919, he wrote, 'These last decades, by emphasizing the purely technical and scientific, have killed all sensory, optic pleasures. Boxes of stone have supplanted with their tones of grey upon grey, the coloured houses, coated in paint. The tradition of painting, cultivated for centuries, has foundered before the concept of "distinction", which is nothing more than insipidity and an inability to use, when building, along with form, the most essential artistic means and especially colour.'

From 1925, Bruno Taut took part in the activities of *Der Ring* and produced urban works as Walter Gropius's associate, or as the faithful foreman to the ideas of the founder of the Bauhaus. From his expressionist period, he nevertheless retained the Promethean desire to transform reality, the idea of an architecture considered as the art above all the other arts, and the meaning of social awareness. In 1932, he went to Moscow, then emigrated to Japan, and finally to Turkey in 1936, where he was asked to do some teaching, shortly before he died there. For a long time he had been regarded as an over-'imaginative' architect, who put forward, particularly in his books *The Alpine Architecture, Crown for the Town*, and *The Destruction of Towns*, impossible ideas. Today, one is in a better position to notice that in all the other areas where architecture was involved (with the material, with the plastic arts, with society) he prefigured in his reflections the great debates that have taken place in Europe on these subjects since the 1950s.

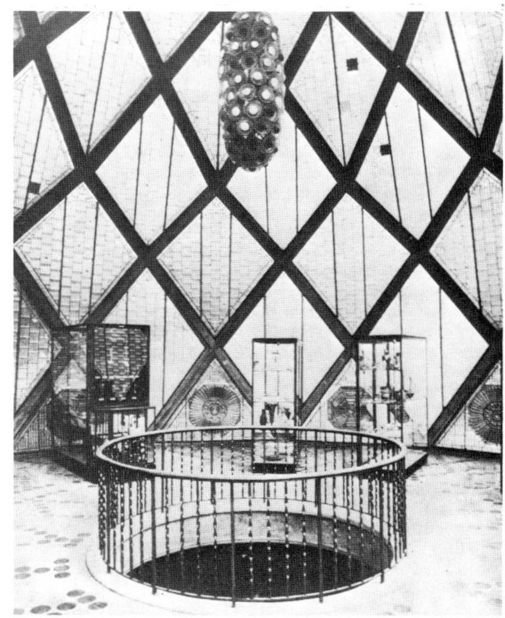

TAUT, BRUNO: *Pavilion for the glass industry.* 1914

Literature

Expressionism is a contrast to naturalism, to neo-Romanticism, to art nouveau: this is how German literature first understood the concept. Kurt Hiller wrote in 1911 that he considered that poets who are capable only of reacting, who are only wax surfaces ready for an impression, and descriptive machines striving for the exact nuance (i.e. impressionists and realists) to be 'inferior'. Hiller continued, 'we are expressionists. We are again concerned with content, desire and ethics.' For Hiller, the expressionist is an activist, an *auteur engagé*, a reformer, a writer with a message. A year later Hiller described Ferdinand Hardekopf as 'The author of the most condensed German prose; the expressionist, the Michelangelo of the 'small format.' Thus Hiller suggests that an expressionist writes in a concentrated, terse style.

Albert Soergel's History of Literature

In 1925 the second volume of Albert Soergel's comprehensive history of literature (*Fiction and the Writers of the Age*) was published with the title, *The Spell of Expressionism*. The volume contained more than nine hundred pages and three hundred and forty illustrations. By 1927, the fifth edition (from 21,000 to 25,000) had already appeared. From then on, Soergel's book was used to decide who was an expressionist and who was not. Neither national socialism nor German literary criticism after the war felt compelled to question Soergel's precepts. It was now accepted that Rilke, Thomas Mann and Gerhart Hauptmann, were not expressionists; neither was Hermann Hesse, who had called himself one for some time. Soergel is principally trustworthy with respect to poetry and drama; he is less reliable as far as prose is concerned. He considers Mynona and Franz Kafka to be similar minds and devotes five pages to each of them. Admittedly, Soergel only knew one of Kafka's novels at that time, *The Trial*. But it is unforgivable that he does not mention the author of the most ecstatic novels, Curt Corrinth, at all. Franz Jung, who had provided a programme for expressionist prose with his *Book of Fools* (1912) is mentioned three times in lists of writers, but Soergel had read nothing by him and did not even know the title (*Trottelbuch*). Nor does Hans Henry Jahnn occur in Soergel. Why were Jung, Corrinth and Jahnn in particular omitted? Was it all because all three had written about sex in what was then a 'repulsive' and 'odious' manner?

Marinetti and Futurism

Soergel devotes nearly three hundred pages of his book to the 'forerunners and vanguard' of expressionism, including non-German writers, such as Strindberg. The chapters on Stanislaus Przybyszewski, Jakob Wassermann, Paul Scheerbart and Peter Hille are particularly informative. But what Soergel could not yet see was that literary expressionism in Germany was part of a cultural revolution in Europe, triggered off by Marinetti's (amongst others) futurism around 1909 and that it left its traces, to a greater or lesser degree, on the literature of every European country. One can date the birth of this revolution to February 20th, 1909 when Marinetti's first futurist manifesto appeared. Before the outbreak of war, Marinetti travelled to London, Berlin and Moscow and gave readings of his manifesto and futurist writings. In April 1912 he went to Berlin where he received enormous acclaim. From then on Herwarth Walden became Marinetti's German herald; he was the editor of *Der Sturm* which, beside *Die Aktion*, was the most important and influential expressionist magazine. Marinetti returned to Berlin in 1913 and read, in the Choralion Hall, the Technical Manifesto of Futurist Literature and its Supplement. The Supplement received the famous description in French in *La Bataille*.

'Midi ¾ flutes glapissement embrasement toumtoumb alarme Gargaresh craquement crépitation marche Cliquetis sacs fusils sabots clous canons crinières roues caissons juifs beignets pains-a-huile cantilènes échoppes bouffées chatoiement chassie puanteur cannelle ...' (and so on for three pages).

The influence of Marinetti's manifesto, which then appeared in *Der Sturm*, cannot be overestimated. August Stramm threw what he had written during the last ten years into the wastepaper basket and began to write his new poems, in which he adhered closely to Marinetti's rules – the greatest possible emphasis on the noun, few adjectives, unconjugated verbs in the infinitive, very concise language, unusual similes. Stramm's poems, recited by Rudolf Blümmer, were considered models by all *Sturm* poets from then on, and still influenced the dada artists Kurt Schwitters and Richard Hülsenbeck. Alfred Döblin criticized Marinetti's theories in *Der Sturm* but was impressed on the other hand by his novel *Mafarka le Futuriste* (1909). In the novels he wrote between 1913 and 1924 Döblin makes increasing use of Marinetti's technique: long series of nouns and verbs not separated by commas.

The Style and Language of the Expressionists

The followers of Marinetti constitute a small but important part of German expressionism; others did not let themselves be influenced by Marinetti. Georg Heym and Georg Trakl restricted themselves to Rimbaud and used new and unusual images and symbols; their poems pointed to new content, but remained conventional grammatically. Ernst Stadler wrote long, unrhymed lines which are sometimes reminiscent of Whitman in the sensuality of their emotions. Gottfried Benn, on the other hand, described crudely and with anatomical accuracy. Johannes R. Becher alternately prayed ecstatically and screamed hysterically. Franz Werfel was moved and inspired to tears, while Alfred Lichtenstein and Jakob von Hoddis wrote poems in the laconic, mocking manner of Heine. Finally the dadaists turned the sense of words into nonsense.

The spectrum of expressionist prose is also well-nigh all-embracing stylistically. Franz Kafka wrote in a precise bureaucratic style, larded with relative clauses, while Alfred Döblin indulged in great word orgies. Hans Henry Jahnn used short, significant sentences, ellipses, and unusual images. Leonhard Frank's prose in *The Robber Band* on the other hand, remained entirely conventional and could have been written by Karl May. Gottfried Benn's prose is scientifically cold; Carl Einstein's cerebral and ironic. Franz Jung gasped and groaned in torment; Curt Corrinth improvised at the height of ecstasy. Carl Sternheim's word order conflicts with normal German syntax: he writes as one translated from Latin into German in secondary school at that time. To sum up, it can be said that the expressionists used a wider spectrum of language than all previous ages put together. The desire for originality and extremes was particularly characteristic. But there are no grounds for crossing Kafka off the list of expressionists merely because his grammar remained rather conventional.

The Five Prophets

The major theme of expressionism is indeed the idea of the new man which, as Soergel shows, had already concerned the 'forerunners and vanguard' (1900–1910). The five philosophical pillars of expressionist literature were: Christ, Darwin, Nietzsche, Marx and Freud. For what else had Christ preached than the new man – the joyful, humble man who loves all other men and does good, who injures no one and does not avenge himself on those who persecute him? Werfel, Becher and Hasenclever spoke enthusiastically of fraternal men of this type. The prostitute as a woman who gives herself to the man without the financial security of marriage, and thus does him good, became an ideal figure for the expressionists. The bourgeois (as a small or big-time capitalist, as a heartless moralist and as a family tyrant) and the soldier, are among the most detestable people of the 'old' era. How could such men be changed?

Marinetti said that they should be sacrificed in the 'hygiene of mankind', war. This was not a Christian sentiment. But many thought that there was nothing to be hoped from Christianity any longer, for in the 1900 years of its existence those who called themselves Christians had not often behaved as such. There were exceptions – Francis of Assisi, for example. At the moment it was the bourgeois and the capitalists who, perversely, considered themselves to be good Christians. Really Marxism and Christianity should have joined forces, for the former was closer to Christ's ideas than those of capitalism. But Marx thought in historical terms, and seen historically the Christian clergy has been mostly on the side of capitalist power; for this reason Marx had rejected Christianity. Some expressionists were not discouraged and managed, until about 1925, to unite Christianity and communism (Johannes R. Becher), or Christianity and socialism. Most expressionists were politically left wing. Only a few later became Nazis: Hanns Johst saw in Hitler the new man.

Nietzsche's *Thus Spake Zarathustra* the epic of the superman also had an effect. Gabriele d'Annunzio and Marinetti had portrayed him in novels, G. B. Shaw on stage. Döblin adopted this superman in his early novels and embodied him in characters like Wang-Lun, Wallenstein and the giants of *Mountains, Seas and Giants*. But most expressionists believed – when they believed in a metamorphosis at all – in an inner transformation in man. Man had learnt from Darwin that he can, and will, change himself. If he does not, he will destroy the world the moment that he possesses the means to do so. Shaw had already said that before 1900. Man will only be able to continue to exist on earth if he changes and renounces his warlike instincts. Most expressionists admittedly were more successful in getting rid of the 'old man' in their works, i.e. murdering fathers, teachers and bourgeois in a literary fashion, than in creating convincing 'new' men. Georg Kaiser put several new men on stage; Döblin and Frank described them in their novels; Hasenclever, Becher and Werfel sang of them in their poems. In the face of the Second World War and the economic depressions of the 1920s, the optimistic utopias of the expressionist writers showed themselves to be unworthy of belief.

One hope still remained: Freud. What were the origins of the perverse lust for power in many people, the hatred, jealousy and greed for possessions which produced war, capitalism and poverty? Perhaps it was only because men had to suppress their sexual instincts and content themselves with one woman only. Freud's disciple, Otto Gross, who was personally known to many expressionists (Franz Jung, Leonhard Frank, Oskar Maria Graf), and seduced their wives and mistresses preached true love as the premise for a healthy mental life. Those not familiar with Otto Gross could find this teaching also in Arcybashev, whose novel *Szanin* became a world best seller around 1909.

Naturally there were all shades of optimism and pessimism. At one end stood the murderers of teachers and fathers (Bronnen, Hasenclever, Frank) at the other the prophets of the new man (Kaiser, Becher, Werfel). In between were those who despaired, who took refuge in absurd or black humour, in the grotesque or the abstract (Lichtenstein, Hoddis, Mynona, Einstein, Kafka, the dadaists).

The Expressionist and the Saviour of the World

In conclusion we can say that a principal theme of expressionist literature was to put and to answer the question: How can man be saved, if at all? Is ideal communism a remedy: the creation of a just, social, fraternal environment for all men; or do we need a dictatorial superman to lead us? Is psychoanalysis the solution? (They were opposed to psychology in literature, since this often tempted the author to want to understand and describe, rather than to preach, to instruct and to depict exemplary models.) Should they perhaps give Christianity one more chance and – for the first time in the history of the world – try to keep to Christ's teachings in politics? Or would unrestrained sexual enjoyment banish all man's evil instincts?

It was not enough for the expressionist author to describe nature, to entertain the reader and to provide him with a pleasurable experience in his armchair. The expressionist felt himself to be a reformer, a Messiah. He wanted to shake mankind out of its lethargy, shock it, make it aware of the dangers of the present and the future. He wanted to save the world for mankind.

Expressionism was taboo from 1935 to 1945 in Germany. Some Nazi patrons of the arts tried in vain to represent it as a particularly 'German' art form. It fell, together with other modern tendencies, under proscription as 'degenerate art'.

After the Second World War, writers such as Günter Grass or Friedrich Dürrenmatt familiarized themselves with expressionist models (Döblin, Kafka). But expressionist visions of a transformation in man and the salvation of the world seem to most people today to be utopian delusions. Of the five expressionist prophets, Christ and Marx have survived; Darwin, Nietzsche and Freud continue to influence literature – but not as potential saviours.

ARP, Hans (Strasbourg, 16.9.1887 – Basel, 7.6.1966). Arp came from Strasbourg where he attended the arts and crafts college. He studied art in Weimar and Paris. In 1909 he went to Weggis near Lake Lucerne, later to Munich where he took part in the *Der Blaue Reiter* exhibition, then to Paris. In 1916 he was in Zurich with the Dadaists. After 1918 he maintained contact also with the Berlin dadaists and Kurt Schwitters. In 1920 he was in the first surrealist exhibition in Paris (with Picasso, Chirico, Klee, and Man Ray). Subsequently Arp became one of the leading sculptors and painters of his age, and worked in the U.S.A., South America, Egypt and elsewhere. During the Second World War and later, he often stayed in Switzerland where he owned studios in Solduno (near Locarno) and Basel. He died in Basel.

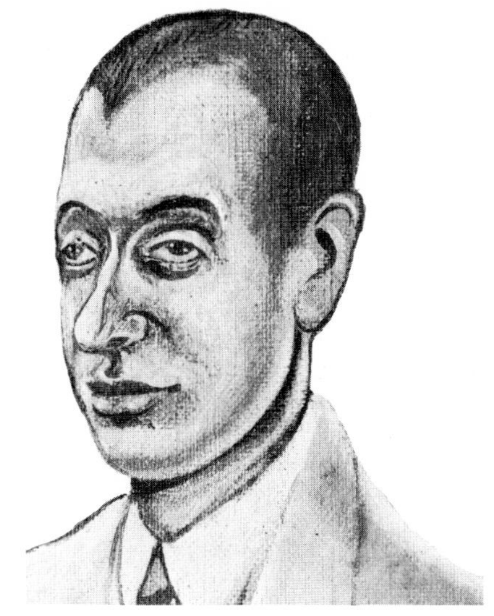

ARP, HANS: *Portrait.* 1922. Detail from a group portrait *A Meeting of friends* by Max Ernst

Arp's fame is based principally on his sculptures. He was also the most productive poet of dadaism. His feel for the linguistic irony hidden in the German language is unsurpassed and can best be compared to Joyce's linguistic acrobatics in *Finnegan's Wake*. Arp mastered everything superlatively – from ballad-like songs in rhymed four-line stanzas to sustained hymns full of pathos. The poems considered to be dadaist appeared in the following volumes: Der Vogel Selbdritt (1920); Die Wolken Pumpe (1920); Der Pyramiden Rock (1924); Weisst Du, Schwarzt Du (1930) and Konfiguration (1930). In the 1930s and 1940s, Arp published mainly in French. After 1951 several volumes of German poems appeared again.

The following is the opening of the Kaspar poem: (in *Der Vogel Selbdritt*). Leonard Forster has interpreted the main figure as being the Alsatian *Wackes cosmique* (Saisons d'Alsace, November 22nd, 1963). It is evidently a parody of a dirge:-

> Alas our good Kaspar is dead.
> Who carries now the fiery banner in his tresses. Who turns the coffee grinder. Who entices the idyllic roe deer. He led the ships astray on the sea with the little word parapluie and he called the winds the father of the bees. Alas alas alas our good Kaspar is dead. Holy Bimbam Kaspar is dead. The hayfish rattle in the bells when we speak his name.
> Therefore I sigh on Kaspar Kaspar Kaspar.

Arp recorded this and other poems; he reads rather slowly and absolutely seriously in a solemn, rather elevated tone. Someone who does not understand German and does not notice the strange associations of sense might think that a national epic was being respectfully recited. In other poems the linguistic humour arises from the fact that Arp tests the elements of individual words with apparent *naïveté*. The interjection cry Herrje (Goodness gracious) to Frau te (Mrs. Te) Klavier (piano) to Klasechs (class-six); Gib acht (Look out) to Gib Neun (give nine), and the combination of Kruzifix (Crucifix) and fix fertig (quite ready) to Kruzifixundfertig. In doing this, Arp naturally awakens associations of another sort as when he writes, for example *The Upstart Guest*:

> I carry tombstones on my head
> And my body is full of water
> I undress the old Adam
> Twelve times a day to pass the time.

BALL, Hugo (Pirmasens, 22.2.1886 – St Abbondio near Lugano, 14.9.1927). Ball was born in Pirmasens, the son of once well-to-do parents. At fifteen he left secondary school and entered a leatherware factory as an apprentice. Four years later he was enabled to return to school, which he left this time after the Abitur. From 1906 to 1910 he worked in Munich and Heidelberg. He spent one year as Max Reinhardt's pupil in Berlin. Then he worked in the theatre in Plauen, and as a producer for the Munich Chamber Theatre from 1913. In 1915 he came with his future wife, Frau Emmy Hennings, to Zurich where, with other émigrés, he founded the Cabaret Voltaire and the Dada movement. In 1917 he abandoned dadaism, withdrew to Ticino and converted to Catholicism. He wrote essays for the Catholic review, *Hochland*, several books on philosophical and theological subjects, a book on his friend, Hermann Hesse who lived nearby (1927) and a highly interesting autobiography, *Flight from Time* (1927). His letters appeared in 1957.

Ball already had a certain reputation as an expressionist poet before coming to Zurich. His first poems appeared from 1913 in the magazines *Die Aktion*, *Revolution* and *Die Neue Kunst*. His sound poems, which he recited in the Cabaret Voltaire, have become particularly famous; for example, *Karavan*:

jolifanto bambla O falli bambla
grossgiga m'pfa habla horem
egiga goramen
higo bloiko russula huju
hollaka hollala
anlogo bung
blago bung blago bung
bosso fataka
ü üü ü
schampa wulla wussa olobo
hej tatta gorem
eschige zunbada
wulubu ssubudu uluwu ssubudu
tumba ba-umf
kusa gauma
ba-umf

Ball wrote two novels. *Fiametti*, or *The Dandyism of the Poor* appeared in 1918. The novel is written in an eloquent, ironic style and contains witty dialogue. It deals with a music hall troupe, whose director is Fiametti. They turn up in the downtown quarter of Zürich where the Cabaret Voltaire was; they fish in the Limmat, become jealous, end up in prison, are hungry and have no money, lie, decline – in short, a wild, strange circus is presented to us, and it is not surprising that Fiametti-Ball was soon finished with it and preferred the tranquil poverty of Ticino to the chaotic poverty of Zurich.

Ball's second novel, *Tenderenda The Fantasist* first appeared in 1967. Biblical language, nonsense in the manner of Jarry and malicious irony combine to create a piece unique in German literature. Poems (for example, *Karavan*), autobiographical and theological material are interpolated into it. Hans Arp, who already knew the novel in 1918, considered it to be one of the most important documents of Dada.

BECHER, Johannes R. (Munich, 22.5.1891 – Berlin, 11.10.1958). Becher was born in Munich, the son of a judge. He studied philosophy and medicine – but without finishing. He contributed to *Die Aktion* from 1912 on. In 1913 he and Heinrich F. S. Bachmair published *The New Art*. He, as well as Werfel, was one of the 'ecstatic' expressionists; he would have preferred to press all men (and the dear Lord) to his heart. He was filled with enthusiasm at the Russian revolution of 1917; here the brotherhood of man seemed to have been accomplished. In 1918 he joined the Spartacus Group and in 1919 the Communist Party. The religious element in his work disappeared during the 1920s. The Communist revolution became the goal of his hopes. When the Nazis came to power they burned his books (on the 10th May, 1933) and took away his citizenship. He spent the War in Moscow. In 1945 he returned to Germany, founded the Aufbau publishing house, the review *Sinn und Form* and became minister for culture in the DDR in 1954.

His autobiographical novel, *Farewell*, and the novel fragment, *Wiederanders* (in the second tribute issue, J. R. Becher, *Sinn und Form*, 1960) give an impressive picture of the expressionist age. The mere titles of his early works express Becher's hymn-like exaltations: *A Hymn to Kleist* (*The Struggling Man*, 1911); *Earth* (1912); *The Grace of Spring* (1912); *De Profundis Domine* (1913); *To Europe* (1916); *The Holy Throng* (1918); *Poems for a Nation* (1919); *Eternal Revolution* (1920); *Sion* (1920); *The Dead Woman* (1921); *About God* (1921); *Workers, Peasants, Soldiers, The Awakening of a People to God* (1921), and so on.

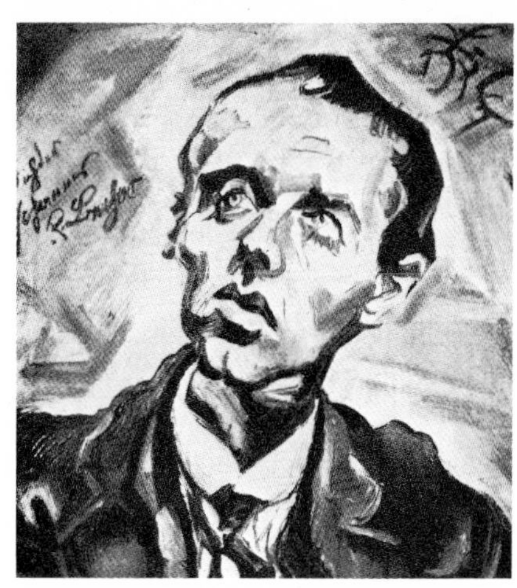

MEIDNER, LUDWIG: *Portrait of Johannes R. Becher*. Circa 1920

In *Um Gott* is the poem 'Man Arises', it consists of about a hundred alliterative lines. Becher begins by describing the situation of contemporary man:

Accursed century! Chaotic! Without song!
You are strung up, a paltry bait
Between torment mist-madness lighting.
Blinded. A Servant. Wrinkled. Raving.
Leprosy and acid
With inflamed eyes. Rabies in your teeth. Blowing the chorus of fever.

So it goes on for a while. Then Becher exhorts the soldiers to pacificism:

When finally
– I ask both in anxiety and full of raging impatience
When finally will you be my brother?

Becher praises the deserters and begs them to destroy their weapons. Then he turns to all other men, demands humility from them and puts a question of conscience to them: whether they wish to be criminals or God's children. Becher demands a decision, a change; he is seeking brothers and ends the poem with the appeal:

Man man man arise arise ! ! !

The real Becher of the expressionist period was a quiet, melancholy man, who took little pleasure in life and suffered from a father who did not understand him. His novel *Earth* gives some idea of this: the young people in it die in every possible way: they love, suffer, marry the wrong partners and in the end commit suicide, with Kleist as a model. In contrast to his ecstatic poetry, Becher's early prose is visionary and gloomy: the basic mood is resignation, a death wish combined with a melancholy worship of nature. The novel is called *Earth* because all the young people who die return to earth.

BENN, Gottfried (Mansfeld, 22.5.1886 – West Berlin, 7.7.1956). He was born in Mansfeld, the son of a Protestant minister and a Romantsch Swiss; he went to secondary school in Frankfurt on the Oder and at first studied theology and philosophy, then medicine. He was a military doctor during the First World War, first on the Western front, then in Brussels. Until 1935 he was a specialist in skin and venereal diseases in Berlin. In 1933 he took a positive stand against the Nazis, condemned those who were emigrating, and on the occasion of a state visit by Marinetti, then Minister of Culture for Mussolini, gave an enthusiastic speech on the former pope of futurism. Most Nazis were not sympathetic to the expressionists and Benn was soon forced into a defensive position. He saved himself by joining the army in 1935 as a medical officer. In 1938 he was excluded from the Chamber of Culture. After the war he opened a practice in Berlin again and began to publish poems and essays. At the time of his death he was the most honoured and respected poet in the new West Germany. Benn's fame as an expressionist is founded on his strange, repellent poems that shocked the bourgeois of his age in *Morgue and Other Poems* (1912). A year later the volume *Sons New Poems* appeared and in 1917 *Flesh. Collected Poems*. The following poem is in *Morgue: Eternal Cycle*:

The single back tooth of a prostitute
who had died in obscurity,
had a gold filling.
The rest, as if tacitly agreed had fallen out.
The undertaker knocked this one out
pawned it and went dancing for, he said,
Only dust should return to dust.

We can understand the situation of the young Benn, who is suddenly confronted with anatomy after the idealistic world of theology: man is a mass of flesh, destined from birth for death and disintegration. Love is the result of certain glands and fluids, a temporary thing. The reality of life is disease, decay, death. Behind the cold, often cynical man who leads us through the cancer ward, hides in reality the medical student shaken to the core by human suffering. Precisely because Benn was aware of the transience of earthly things he led a highly intense sensual life, was married several times and had numerous affairs. Else Lasker-Schüler called him alternately 'Tiger' and 'Barbarian'.

Benn also wrote prose – essay-like, intellectual short stories which he thus called *Brains* (1916) and essays which he published in 1920 under the programmatic title of *The Modern Ego*. The most important part of his extensive mature work is *Static Poems* (1948).

CORRINTH, Curt (Lennep (Rhineland), 20.2.1894 – East Berlin, 27.8.1960). Corrinth was the son of an attorney and was born in Lennep (Rhineland). He studied law in Paris and Marburg, then literature and art history in Bonn. He was a soldier in the First World War and afterwards an editor in Berlin. After 1928 he lived independently as a writer. In his novel *Hellmann the Leader* he allied himself with Nazi ideology. From 1945 to 1955 he ran a bookshop in Leichlingen (Rhineland), and then moved to East Berlin. He re-wrote *Hellmann the Leader* from a socialist viewpoint and published it in the DDR as *The Päker Affair*.

Corrinth began with conventional, mainly rhymed poems which appeared in 1915 under the title *Art-Love-Death. War Poems*, the volume written at Verdun, *Troubadour on Outpost-Duty* (1917) is more advanced and conscious of form.

If Corrinth was still in favour of war in 1915, by 1917 he was begging God for peace. The volume *The Great Prayer, New Poems* (1919) was written in the last year of the war in which Corrinth mentions Becher, Werfel and Hasenclever by name, and enthusiastically mounts the barricades with them – though not against capitalism, but against the narrow morality of the bourgeoisie. Corrinth was an enthusiastic advocate of free love, of everyone sleeping with everyone, of a great sexual orgy of all men, races and nations. Whereas Freud's disciple Otto Gross saw sexual relations in individual cases as a means of salvation for the world, Corrinth preached universal copulation as a world religion: happiness, rapture, love and peace would be the result and war, jealousy and philistinism would come to an end.

Corrinth chose the novel form to spread his message. In 1919, *Potsdam Square* or the *Nights of the New Messiah* appeared, at first in an edition of five thousand copies. The messiah is Hans Termaden from Barmen on the Wupper. He goes to Berlin where he takes a prostitute who is overwhelmed by the sensual activities of the 'youth with the powerful thighs': 'He thrust deeper and deeper into the most secret depths, and achieved such feats of power and inventiveness, that she who had gained him as a pupil soon valued him as a teacher.' Next, Termaden seduces a thin-lipped, closely guarded virgin and changes her into a prodigy of sensuality. Termaden is infectious – the messiah frees men from the nightmares of sexual inhibition.

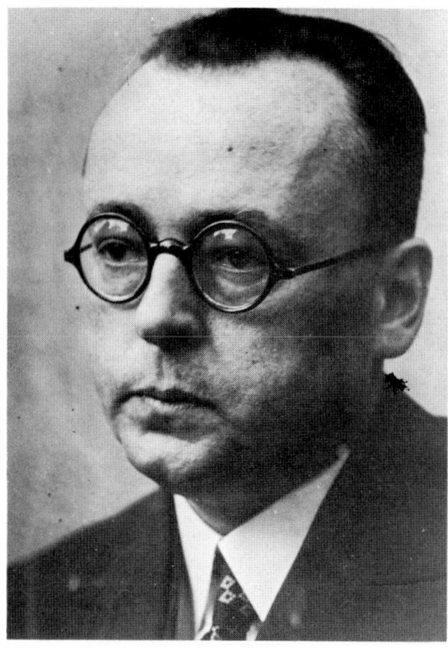

CORRINTH, CURT: *Portrait*

People flock from everywhere to Potsdam Square, the headquarters of the messiah. Soon all buildings round the square are brothels. People from England, France and Mexico now flock to Berlin – the town fills to bursting point. The police and army are called out, but they defect and join in the universal copulation. The 'spring of mankind', the 'world resurrection' has at last come, and at the end, Hans Termaden is carried up to heaven on a white cloud.

Corrinth writes with a good dose of irony which his incensed critics have partly overlooked. *Desire* (1919) is a parody of the German psychological novel ironically transposed into the sexual sphere. *Brothel* (1920) is an experiment with style: Corrinth uses practically only inner monologue. Joachim Pasentrall is an eighteen-year-old barber, extraordinarily attractive and potent, who acts as a gigolo for the women of the town. His consulting hours are booked up for months to come. Gradually he becomes so weary of women and sex that, completely exhausted, he commits suicide by fire.

Corrinth surpassed himself one more time – in the book *Mo Marova* (1920): the heroine is an extremely sadistic woman, who harnesses both herself and her lover to highly sophisticated machines. Soon this is not enough for her: she forms an army of nymphomaniacs who burst upon the streets of the town. The men do their best, but die like flies from the excessive sexual demands made on them. Men continue to arrive from all over the place; when the town is surrounded, they leap from aeroplanes.

After 1920, Corrinth abandoned his ecstatic language but for the moment he remained faithful to his theme. In *Liljol* (1921), mother and son sleep together (while the father looks on) and brother and sister commit incest. *Murder* (1922) is a psychological thriller. *Poison* (1923) is a horror story in which a man – unwittingly – spends a night of love with a corpse. *Horror*(1926) is a spinechiller.

Corrinth is neither the most tasteful nor the most careful stylistically of the expressionist prose writers, but none is so ecstatic, so full of emotion, or so bold stylistically as he. *Brothel*, for example, contains a passage consisting, for seventy-five per cent, of the sounds of Joachim smacking his lips, and twenty-five per cent of the fragmentary thoughts going through his mind as he eats – one might call it naturalism carried to its ultimate conclusion. But the passage is not only there for ironic purposes; it heightens – as a contrast – the ecstatic prose that precedes and follows.

DÄUBLER, Theodor (Trieste, 17.8.1876 – St Blasien (Black Forest), 14.6.1934). He was born and brought up in Trieste and bilingual Venice. In 1898 he went to Vienna. After 1903 he led an unsettled life of travel, came to know the Italian futurists, the modern painters in Paris, and the avant-garde of Berlin. His major work is the epic *Northern Lights*, on which he worked for a large part of his life (first version 1910, the Geneva version 1921). He also published several volumes of poetry and prose which are all forgotten today.

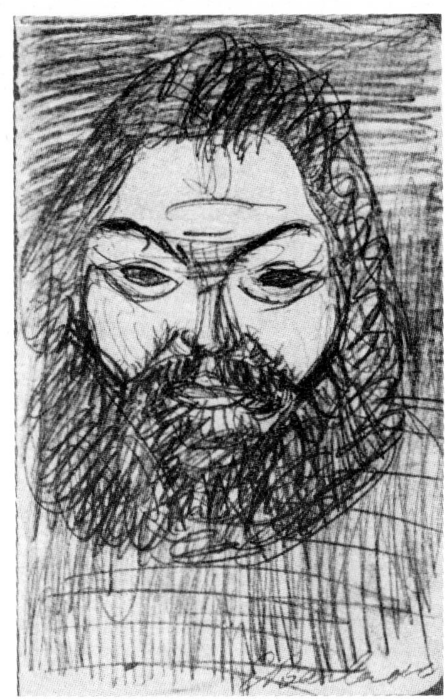

DÄUBLER, THEODOR: *Portrait.* Drawing by Ernst Barlach

DÖBLIN, Alfred (Stettin, 10.8.1878 – Emmendingen in Baden, 28.6.1957). Döblin came from a Jewish business family and was born in Stettin. He studied in Freiburg and Berlin and gained the title Doctor of Medicine in 1905. After 1911 he ran a practice as a nerve specialist and panel doctor in Berlin. He was a friend of Herwarth Walden and contributed to *Der Sturm* from 1910. In 1918 he became a social democrat. In 1933 he fled to France and became a French citizen three years later. In 1940 he fled to the U.S.A. via Portugal and became a Catholic. He returned to Germany in 1945 as a high official in the French occupying forces – which was held against him in his former homeland. He was practically ignored in Germany and it was the Basel Professor, Walter Muschg and the Swiss Walter publishing house that finally organized a new edition of his works.

In the years 1902/3 Döblin wrote the novel *The Black Curtain* which appeared in instalments in Der *Sturm* in 1912. Love and desire awaken in the young Johan. His partner is called Irene. He hovers between hate and love, passion and indifference. He finally bites through her throat, and burns her corpse and himself in the forest. The novel could be called expressionist in content, but the language is still conventional. This changed between spring and summer of 1912, when Döblin came to know futurism, read Marinetti's manifesto and expressionist views on them in *Der Sturm*. He also read Marinetti's novel *Mafarka the Futurist* (1909) and now began – in the summer of 1912 – to write in a completely new style, which Kasimir Edschmid described thus: 'Döblin is a slow bricklayer; he is constantly carrying stones hither and thither, and puts no mortar in between. He merely places one wide square, exactly measured piece on top of another exactly the same. So he arrives at a novel.'

The missing mortar is psychology. Between summer 1912 and spring 1913, Dölbin wrote the novel *The Three Leaps of Wang-Lun*, which is entirely futuristic in the disintegration of commonplace psychology, in its exaggerated content and its free syntax. Whether Hans loves Grete or not, whether Grete loves Hans or Peter, whether her parents are in favour of her marrying Hans, whether Hans or Peter are then unhappy or even both, when Grete rejects them – all these are bourgeois trivialities around which literature has revolved from Richardson to Goethe, Zola and Fontane. These are not problems for Zarathustra, for Mafarka, for Wang-Lun and Döblin's supermen in *Wallenstein* (1918) or *Mountains, Seas and Giants* (1924). Here, thousands of people celebrate orgies, thousands massacre each other; stupendous events occur, glaciers melt, giants walk the earth: the bourgeois world is put in its 'proper' perspective – a flea circus.

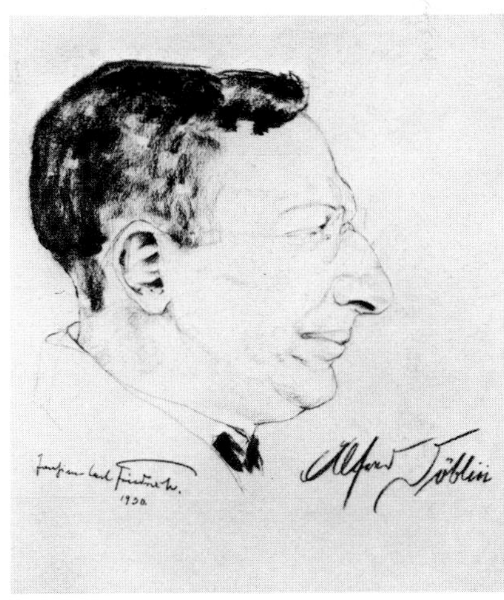

DÖBLIN, ALFRED: *Portrait.* Drawing by J. C. Friedrich. 1936

Here is an example from Wang-Lun – the men who have hitherto been kept separate from the women, rush hungrily for satisfaction up the hill where the women are (note the unusual syntax):

> A thousandfold screaming and shrieking swept over the valley and echoed back from the other side.
> As the horror repeated itself tenfold, a deep rumbling, crackling and roaring became mingled with the shrill voices.
> A vision dreadful enough to make one's eyes stare with horror, tried to escape from the shadows of the Catalpas and was wrenched back. After the moment of frenzy and brightly coloured clothes were strewn over the crest of the hill, settled, sank into the marsh, rolled silently down the slopes. A strange silence settled over the hill, interrupted by long, convulsive cries, as whimpering and piercing as a cat's, the music to a breathless swoon, which bites its own fingers, which shrivels the soul as if in vinegar; music to accompany the madness of desperation which whips bodies into whirlwinds.

Döblin's most famous novel, *Berlin Alexanderplatz* (1929), marks the end of his expressionist phase. Here he juxtaposes all possible styles; the hero, Franz Biberkopf is no longer an expressionist hero, but an optimistic, suffering and confused man who is taken in by illusion after illusion. However, he always works himself back out of the mire – admittedly beaten and mutilated – and finds the courage to continue living and hoping.

EDSCHMID, Kasimir (Darmstadt, 5.10.1890 – Vulpera, 31.8.1966). Edschmid was called Eduard Schmid and was born in Darmstadt. He studied romance philology, became a journalist and, after the war, lived as an independent writer mainly in Darmstadt, from which he undertook extensive journeys which he described in his books. He was an outstanding organizer – especially of his own fame. His volume of short stories – *The Six Estuaries* (1915) – are supposed – in retrospect – to have initiated expressionist prose. The fact is that Edschmid was not one of the first to leap on to the expressionist bandwagon, but did so therefore with much clamour. His short stories are really penny-dreadfuls that do not work because they are written in a language distorted by artifice. Edschmid had already published some of the stories – written in a conventional manner – in newspapers before; no one had described them as 'expressionist'. He contorted his sentences for publication in book form and used far-fetched eccentric images and similes: suddenly the stories had become 'models of literary expressionism, indeed the first that we have had so far.' (Joachim Benn). Here, as an example of Edschmid's prose, is the beginning of the story *Deadly May* from the small volume, *Frenzied Life* (1915):

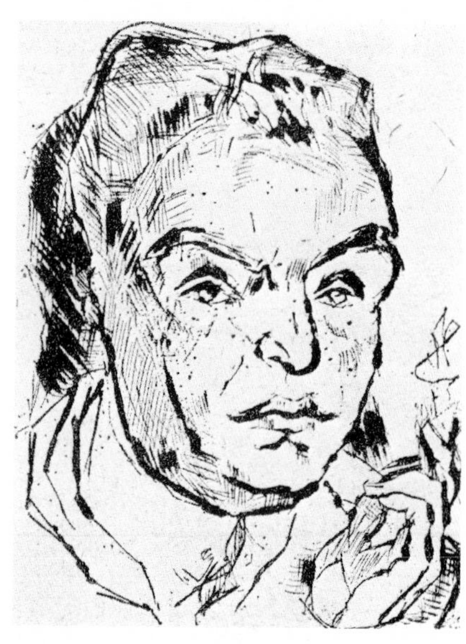

EDSCHMID, KASIMIR: *Portrait.* 1917. Drawing by Max Beckmann

> As the end of the week approached, death tore at his [the painter's and officer's] entrails, and he lay there yelling for two hours; it happened that his nurse was struck by amazement, for his screams turned into silence and exultant shouts, quiet like brightly-coloured balls rose gradually from the suddenly gentle calm of his mouth; they linked themselves together into yodels that waft from mountain to mountain all day long during the summer in Switzerland.

This extract is characterized by false grammar, irrelevant similies and forced syntax. As long as it was fashionable, Edschmid continued with expressionism. He wrote short stories (*Timur*, 1916; *Women*, 1922), critical essays (*On Expressionism in Literature and the New Poetry*, 1919; *The Two-Headed Nymphs*, 1920) and a novel *The Agate Bullets.* He later returned to his earlier, conventional style and wrote travelogues, biographies and novels. In 1941 he was forbidden to write. After the war, Edschmid, who now held the highest post in the PEN Club and the German Academy for Language and Literature, again managed to publish his expressionist stories and get into the limelight.

EHRENSTEIN, Albert (Vienna, 23.12.1886 – New York,8.4.1950). Ehrenstein was born in Vienna, the son of poor Hungarian Jewish parents. He studied history, philosophy and philology and got his doctorate in 1910. He became a journalist, lived in Berlin and wrote for *Der Sturm* and *Die Aktion*, amongst others. In the 1930s he travelled extensively, as far as China. He emigrated from Nazi Germany to Switzerland and then to New York in 1941 where he died, embittered and neglected – in a hospital for the poor.

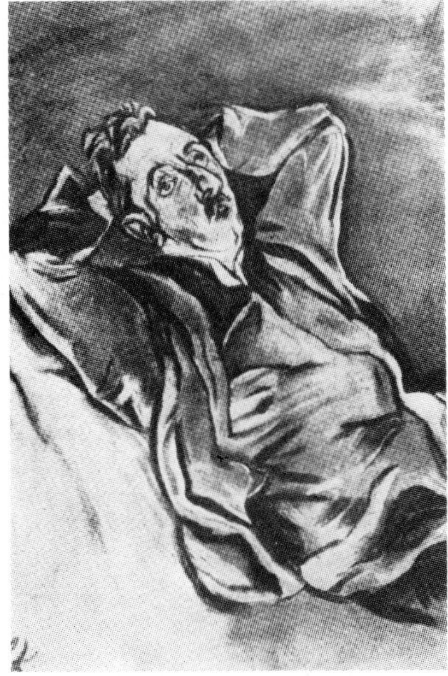

KOKOSCHKA, OSKAR: *Portrait of Albert Ehrenstein*

Ehrenstein was considered an astute critic, a distinguished poet (*The White Age*, 1914; *Man Screams*, 1916), but is known today especially for his early stories: *Tubutsch*, 1911, illustrated by Oskar Kokoschka; and the volume of short stories, *Suicide of a Cat*, 1912. Between 1922 and 1933 he published translations, adaptations and anthologies, especially of Chinese literature.

Tubutsch originated in the decadent movement and the spirit of Andre Gide's *Paludes* (1895). Karl Tubutsch, the first person narrator, has nothing except his name. He is in the situation from which the expressionist ecstatic writers later break out: he is bored to death. The most exciting thing that has ever happened to him, is a broken shoelace. When he ponders over problems, they are questions like 'Why is the cobbler's house called "The Two Lions"?' 'Have the two dead flies in his inkwell committed suicide?' Love, fame, life: all this seems to him to be insipid. 'Life. What a big word. I imagine life as a waitress who asks me what I would like with my sausage – mustard, horseradish or gherkins. She is called Thekla.'

In the short story, *Suicide of a Cat*, an *abitur* candidate, Wodianer, who has been called for a second examination, tells of the fate of a one-year-old tom cat, Keroven, who, threatened with strong competition, is courting the cat Miaulina. Wodianer's own history in love is even sadder than that of Keroven with whom Wodianer identifies. Wodianer removes the cat's competition, but Keroven is not sufficiently appreciative and so is kicked by his master. When the cat steals his sausage, he kills him. Wodianer also kills Miaulina and gives himself up to the police: 'There is blood on my hands. I have murdered my cat.'. The police consider him mad, and it looks as if Wodianer thus escapes his second examination.

Ehrenstein writes a language tinged with Viennese dialect, amuses himself with wordplay and witty associations. His grotesque tales are less offensive and more elegant than those of Döblin (*The Murder of a Buttercup and Other Stories*, 1913) or of Mynona.

EINSTEIN, Carl (Neuwied, 26.4.1885 – Southern France, 5.7.1940). He was born in Neuwied on the Rhine and attended secondary school in Karlsruhe. He studied aesthetics and in 1915 wrote a book on Negro sculpture which influenced dada and cubism. He was a friend of Benn, Sternheim, and Ludwig Rubiner. In 1919 he published the short-lived review *Der Blutige Ernst* with George Grosz. He wrote a lot for *Die Aktion* which, in 1912, published his important novel, *Bebuquir* or *The Dilettantes of Miracles* in instalments. He was a soldier for four years during the war, and afterwards a member of the Spartacus group. He fought for the left in the Spanish Civil War. He fled from the Nazis to Paris. In 1940 he was interned in Southern France. His French guards freed him before the German troops arrived. But because he had fought against Franco, he could not escape through Spain to Lisbon and the U.S.A., so he committed suicide.

Bebuquin is a philosophical novel – little happens, but, on the other hand, there is much thinking throughout. Traditional logic is as outmoded for Einstein as is traditional psychology for Döblin. Straightforwardly normal ways of thinking have become a cliché for him, as they were for dada:

> Too few people have the courage to talk complete nonsense. Nonsense which is frequently repeated becomes an integrating force in our thought; at a certain level of intelligence we are not at all interested in what is correct or rational any more.

> The commonplace rationality of the average man is also abhorrent:
>
> Until now man has used reason to coarsen the senses, to reduce and to simplify consciousness. On the whole, reason impoverished; reason impoverished God into indifference; let us kill reason; reason has created this shapeless death where nothing can be seen any more.

The critics had a hard time with his novel. Many did not know what it was about and thought Einstein mad. Kurt Hiller realised that Einstein had written a novel without events, causality, background or psychology; he suspected that he had written 'a succession of fantastic *aperçus*, clothed in an epic style for a joke. Those who are envious, may diagnose Herr Einstein to be a university lecturer run amok; but I believe that here somebody has written the Jewish Faust.'

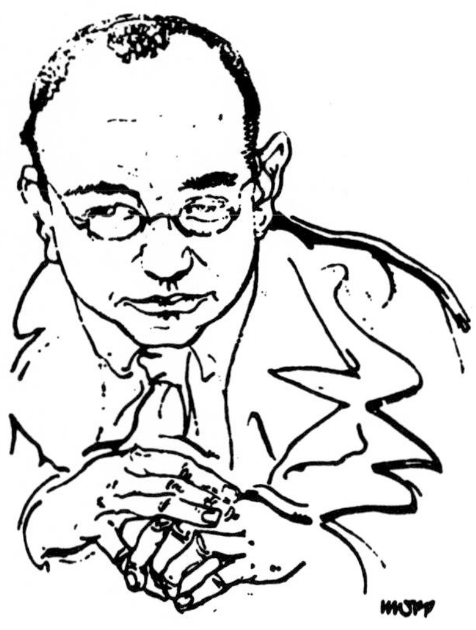

OPPENHEIMER, MAX: *Portrait of Carl Einstein*

Döblin, Jung, Einstein (and Dada, influenced by Einstein) are fundamentally artists who were extraordinarily aware of cliché: they wanted to offer something new at any price, for anything old seemed lost and stale to them. Hence the new tendency towards exaggeration, new syntax, new vocabulary: rather nonsense than a continuation of bourgeois logic; rather the improbable than a continuation of well-founded psychological reactions.

FRANK, Leonhard (Würzburg, 4.9.1882 – Munich, 18.8.1961). Frank was the son of a carpenter's mate and was born in Würzburg. He worked first in a factory and in a hospital, and in 1904 moved to Munich. He was self-taught; politically left wing. In 1910 he was in Berlin. He won the Fontane Prize for his first work, *The Robber Band* (1914). There are echoes of Karl May and Mark Twain in the work – it is a rapturous, but melancholy novel about a group of youths who want to do good, who know what solidarity is, who want to build a better world. We meet these people again in *The Quartet of Ochsenfurt* (1927), and *The Disciples of Jesus* (1949). In 1915, the short story *The Cause* appeared, one of the best achievements on parricide in expressionist literature. The thirty year old poet Anton Seiler is visiting his home town. He knows that something is oppressing his soul – a childhood experience linked with a school outing. Now he remembers: during the outing all the children were allowed to go into an inn and have a glass of milk for ten pfennigs – only he was not, for he did not have ten pfennigs. At the order of the teacher he had to stand at the fence outside. This experience as an eight-

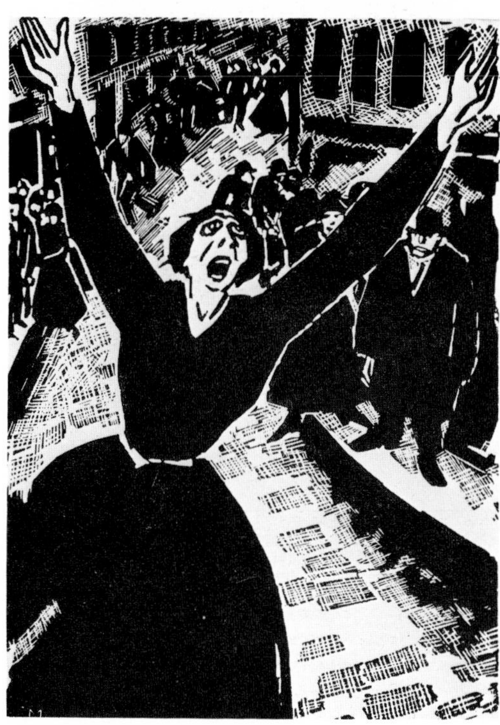

MASEREEL, FRANS: Wood-cut for *The Mother* (Die Mutter) by L. Frank, 1919

year-old has oppressed Anton Seiler for twenty-two years. He now thinks that the teacher should at least apologize. When he visits the sixty-five year old teacher, Mager, he witnesses a scene which proves that Mager still gives his pupils complexes: he mistreats a weak pupil, he gives an apple to a strong one. Anton Seiler subsequently murders the teacher. Only one juryman, his mother and the public prosecutor realize what has happened: that Mager's death is his own fault. Anton is condemned for murder and robbery and executed. In 1915 Frank fled to Zürich where his volume of short stories, *Man is Good* appeared in 1918. He calls, in ecstatic prose, for peace, fraternity and socialism. The book ran into innumerable editions. Frank later returned to his conventional, realistic language and produced more best sellers, until 1939 when he again had to flee to Zürich. In 1940 he escaped to the U.S.A. via Lisbon, and returned in 1950 to Munich. *On the Left, Where the Heart Is* (1952) is his autobiography.

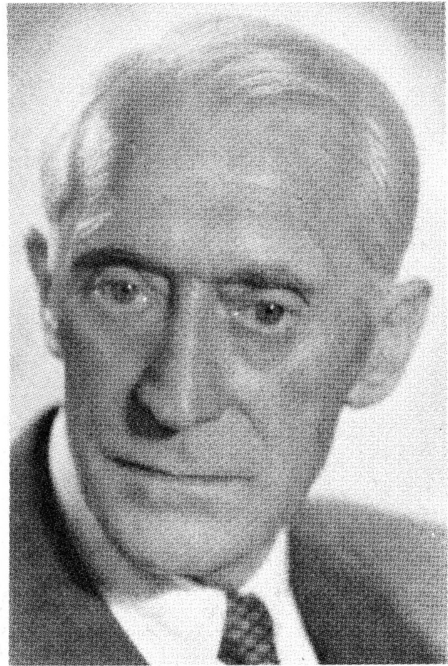

FRANK, LEONHARD: *Portrait*

GOLL, Yvan St Dié, France, 29.3.1891 – Paris, 27.2.1950). Goll's real name was Isaac Lang and he was born in St Dié. He spoke French in his Jewish home, and German in School. When his father died in 1898, he moved to Metz with his mother, where he attended secondary school. He studied philosophy and law in Strasbourg and Lausanne, and finished with a doctorate in both subjects. He spent the First World War in Switzerland, where he got to know the poet Claire Studer (born in Nuremburg in 1891 as Claire Aischmann), who had made a name for herself in 1918 with the volume of short stories, *The Women Awaken*. Her most well-known works are her hate-filled memories of childhood: *The Lost Paradise* (written in the 1930s, published in 1962). The Golls moved to Paris after the war. Yvan Goll had always published in French as well as in German. After 1933 he was forced to write mainly in French. The Golls were in New York from 1939 to1947. He died in Paris of leukaemia.

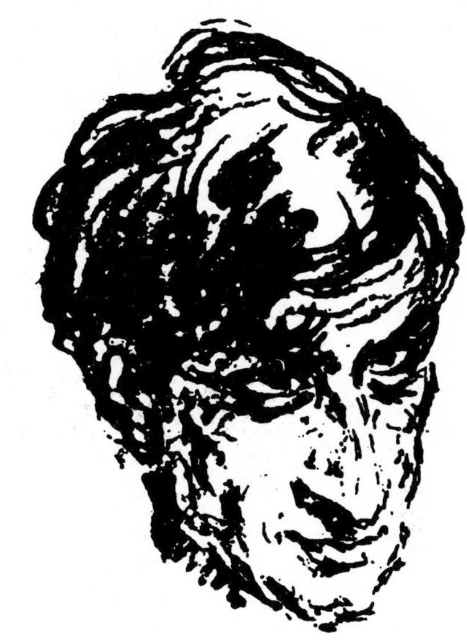

GOLL, YVAN: *Portrait.* Wood-cut

He began as an expressionist – the volume of poetry, *The Panama Canal* (1912, under the pseudonym of Ivan Lessang) is reminiscent of Becher, Werfel and Döblin in style and its feeling of enthusiasm for life. A monumental work is being accomplished in Panama through the collaboration of men of all races and classes: engineers, capitalists, workers. And their goal is the linking of two oceans. The best lines of the poem run thus:

Iron sluices grow with every push and pull

Every inch nailed in with the tiniest of hammers
Huge wings carried by small steel structures
As if by Prometheus into the deep
And when these soon finally do open
when two enemy oceans embrace
O, then will weep
All the nations on earth.

Goll re-worked his most famous poem several times. The 1918 version which appeared in *The Twilight of Mankind*, consists of long lines, a kind of elevated prose, so to speak. Goll has become aware, in the intervening period, that the workers have not accomplished their work in a mood of ecstasy at all:

They however, knew nothing of the Panama canal. Nothing of eternal brotherhood. Nothing of the great gateway of love.
They knew nothing of the freeing of the oceans and of mankind. Nothing of the radiant exultation of the soul
Each one saw the swamp being drained. A wood burning, A sea suddenly seethes, Mountains kneel into dust.
But none could believe in the greatness of what man had achieved! He did not notice, how the cradle of a new sea was born.

After 1919, Goll's poetry became in parts increasingly sophisticated, and begins to recall Rilke and Trakl. On the other hand, one can trace the connection with the surrealists whom he joined. Guillaume Apollinaire and André Breton. His comic surrealist anti-bourgeois play, *Methusalem*, or *The Eternal Bourgeois*, which appeared in 1924 is a somewhat late, but highly original achievement. In France and especially in Quebec, Goll is principally known for his poem, 'Le Mythe de la Roche Percée' (1947); and secondarily for his volumes of poetry on *Jean sans Terre* (1936, 1938 and 1939).

HEYM, Georg (Hirschberg, Silesia, 30.10.1887 – Berlin, 16.1.1912). He was born in Hirschberg, Lower Silesia. His father was a lawyer and transferred to Berlin in 1900. He was expelled from the Joachimstaler secondary school in 1905 and passed his *abitur* in 1907 in the Lateinschule. He studied law in Würzburg, Jena and Berlin. Before he could enter officers' training school, he drowned on the 16th January 1912, while skating on the Havel.

Heym's father was one of those narrow-minded family tyrants against whom many expressionists also preached revolution in their literary works. Heym kept a diary from 1904 in which one can read under the entry for 3rd November, 1911 'I would have been one of the greatest poets if I had not had such a swine for a father. At a time when I needed care and understanding, I had to use all my strength to keep this villain away from me.' Heym was a man of vitality and enterprise. His father tried to tie him down by stopping his pocket money and confiscating the key to the house. Heym wrote on the 15th September 1911, 'My God – I am still suffocating in my enthusiasm that lies fallow in this banal world. For I need strong outer emotions to be happy, in my day-dreams I always see myself as a Danton, or a man on the barricades; I cannot really imagine myself at all without my Jacobin bonnet. I hope now at least for a war!'

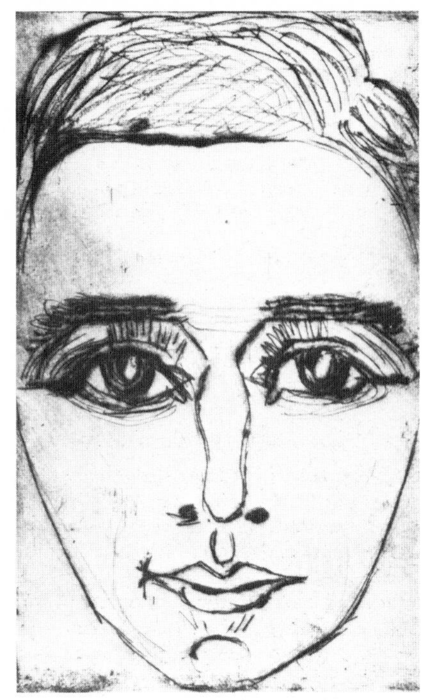

KIRCHNER, ERNST LUDWIG: *Portrait of Georg Heym*

Heym wrote an unusually large amount in the years from 1909 to 1912: hundreds of pages of poems, as well as stories, plays and diaries. He had already prepared his volume of poetry, *The Everlasting Day* (1911).

Heym was a friend of Jakob von Hoddis and recited his poems like him in the *Neopathetisches Cabaret*. Heym's themes range from satirical, anti-bourgeois poems to horrifying visions. He wrote about the demonic city, the wretchedness of suburbs, bodies fished out of rivers, and distress in the hospitals. In his visionary poems he imagined the grandeur and the violence which he so missed in his age and his life – war, for example: the following stanzas come from the poem *War*, composed in September 1911 and consisting of eleven four-line verses:

He who slept so long has arisen
He has arisen from deep vaults down below.
He stands in the half-light, huge and unknown
And crushes the moon in his black hand.

He sends fire across the fields into night
A red dog baying from savage jaws
The black world of night leaps from the darkness
And fearful volcanoes light up its brink.

A great city sank in yellow smoke
Threw itself silently into the belly of the abyss
But he who waves his torch three times in the wild heavens
Stands colossal over red hot ruins.

Spread reflection stirs storm torn clouds
into the cold deserts of the lifeless dark
So that with his flame he withers wide the night
over Gomorrah pitch and fire.

By comparison with his poetry his drama and prose carry less weight. The most readable are the twenty or so short stories he wrote in 1911, seven of which were published under the title, *The Thief*. The Fifth October depicts the awakening sense of solidarity amongst the citizens of Paris at the time of the revolution: 'They had all become an innumerable brotherhood; this rapturous hour had welded them together.' This was the dream of many expressionists: fraternity and solidarity between men. We encounter this central *leitmotif* of expressionist literature again and again – in plays, poems and stories.

HODDIS, Jakob van (Berlin, 16.5.1887 – after 30.4.1942 place unknown). He was born Hans Davidsohn in Berlin and attended the municipal Friedrich secondary school where he obtained his *abitur* in 1906. After he had attended lectures on architecture at the Munich University for a year, he began to study Greek, first in Jena, then in Munich. In 1909 he was in Berlin and recited his poems in the New Club and the Neopathetisches Cabaret, publishing them in *Die Aktion* and *Der Sturm*. In 1912 he abandoned his studies. In November 1912 he was put into the custody of the lunatic asylum Nicolassee against his will; he escaped in December by jumping out of a window. First he stayed in Heidelberg, then in Paris. From June 1913 he was again in Berlin. In autumn 1914 he could no longer deceive himself: he was schizophrenic. At first he lived in private care, from 1933 in an institution in Coblenz. On 30th April 1942 he was taken away by the Nazis as a Jew.

Hoddis's poems appeared from 1910 to 1914 in expressionist reviews. In 1918 the publishing house *Die Aktion* published a small booklet with sixteen of his poems *The End of the World*, number 19 in the *Red Cock* series. When Kurt Pinthus published his famous anthology of expressionist poetry, *The Twilight of Mankind* in 1920, *The End of the World* was placed first, so that his name was never forgotten. But his poems were not collected and published – with some biographical documents – until 1958 by Paul Pörtner. In Hoddis – and other 'neopathetic' poets, an echo of Heinrich Heine's frivolous and amusing poems in the *Book of Songs* is still visible. Except that they have become even more impudent, even more brazen. Heine still felt a genuine, romantic suffering in love, of which, as apparently enlightened man of the world, he was ashamed. Hoddis, Lichtenstein and most other 'neopathetic' poets prefer to give themselves an air of blasé world weariness. They present their poems with boredom and an eccentric manner, with an elephant's

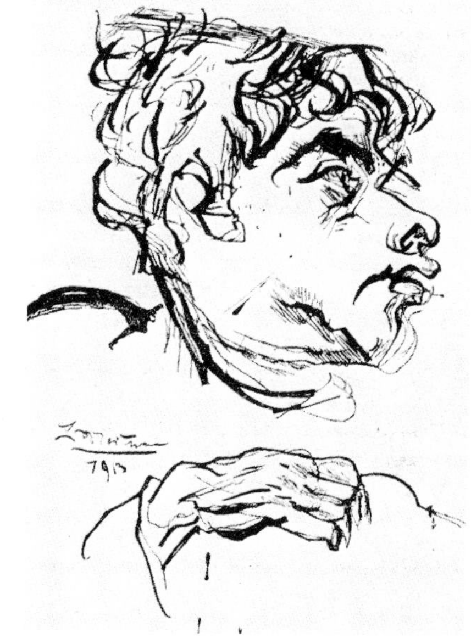

MEIDNER, LUDWIG: *Portrait of Jakob van Hoddis.* 1913

hide surrounding a heart of rubber, and derision on their lips. Thus they annoyed the middle classes who did not notice that behind the apparent arrogance hid youths who were in reality sensitive and whose hearts were as soft as ripe tomatoes.

The cycle *Variété* which consists of nine poems, belongs among his best poems – next to *The End of the World*, *Tristitia ante* and *Aurora*. The last poem of the cycle describes an early film-showing, in the typically insolent style of a culturally sated Berliner no longer capable of being impressed by anything. Short strips on various subjects are shown. As Hoddis describes them in sixteen lines, an impression of the 'simultaneity' of what is happening arises – a technique often used by the so-called expressionist 'Neutoner' (New Sounds) (Hoddis, Lichtenstein, Heym, Ernst Blass). The cycle *Variété* first appeared in *Sturm* in 1911 and poem number nine is called *End, Cinematograph*.

The room goes dark and we see the currents of
The Ganges, palms, temples too of Brahma
A silent frenzied family drama
And then men of the world and masked balls.

Someone pulls a revolver. Jealousy arises
Herr Piefke duels now without a head.
Then we see the Alpine dairy girl
with pick and rucksack on a steeply winding path.

Her way now leads through woods of larches
Now doubles back; the steep cliff face
Looms threatening above. Cows and potato fields
Give life to the view far down below.

And in the darkened room, before my eyes
They flicker on, Oh hideous, each one in turn
the arc lamp hisses at the end for light
We push into fresh air, voluptuous and yawning.

HÜLSENBECK, Richard (Frankenau (Hessen), 23.4.1892 – Minusio (Ticino), 20.4.1974). He was the son of a pharmacist and was born in Frankenau (Hessen). He studied medicine and German language and literature, and went to Zurich in 1916 where he joined Dada. In 1918 he took part with Raoul Hausman, Walter Mehring, and Franz Jung among others in the Berlin Dada movement. Hülsenbeck was a doctor, writer and journalist. In 1936 he went to New York where he had a practice as a psychiatrist. He later returned to Europe and lived in Ticino. Hülsenbeck's Dada poems (*Fantastic Prayers*, 1916) and his three novels are forgotten today; his autobiographical writings, on the other hand – especially his reminiscences of the Dada movement – will be read for a long time to come.

JUNG, Franz (Neisse, Silesia, 26.11.1888 – Stuttgart, 23.1.1963). Jung was born in Neisse, the son of a watchmaker. As late as his autobiography (*The Way Down*, 1967), he still speaks with bitterness about his parents who disapproved of everything about him and even tried legally to deprive him of his child. Not entirely without grounds – Jung studied law in Leipzig, Jena and Breslau – but he gambled away the money sent to him from home; his parents were constantly having to pay off his debts. In his fifth or sixth term, Jung travelled to St Petersburg in pursuit of a dancer and married her. Their marriage was dreadful, for Margot could keep no promise, was apparently unfaithful to him right, left and centre and had no conscience whatsoever. Jung, who loved her and was jealous, suffered very badly, something which Margot – who lived on quite a different wavelength – could not grasp at all. This situation – that is, of two human beings who cannot understand each other at all and, therefore, shout and yell at each other like animals, isolated by wretchedness and frustration – is at the root of all Jung's work till 1918. In 1911 they moved to Munich, in 1913 to Berlin. Jung was published in *Der Sturm*, but above all in *Die Aktion*. The publishing house of *Die Aktion* produced his books during the war. In 1914 – after a quarrel with his wife – Jung volunteered for military service but soon deserted and was put in gaol. His mother must have prayed daily that her good-for-nothing son would fall in battle. She wrote to the prison authorities asking that he should not be freed. But Jung was declared unsuitable for service, owing to manic depression, and set free.

Jung now made the acquaintance of Claire Öhring (born 1892) whom he later married. She was an active communist, wrote for *Die Aktion* and now lives in East Berlin. Jung joined the Berlin Dada movement, was a member of *Spartacus* and in the 1920s wrote novels about the working classes, propaganda for communist publishing houses and plays for Piscator's proletarian theatre. After the Easter uprising in 1921, in which Jung was involved, he had to flee to Holland, was arrested and handed over to the Russians. Two years later he was again in Germany where he thenceforth lived under a false name. The Nazis imprisoned him twice. He was freed by Americans from a labour camp in Bozen in 1945. After a short stay in Italy he spent ten years in America, after which he returned to Germany and died in Stuttgart in 1963.

In December 1912 Jung's *Book of Fools* appeared in Leipzig, which was either received by cries of horror, or, on the other hand, hailed as a pioneer work in modern prose writing. While Benn's *Morgue* tells the sad truth about the physical man, Jung is horrified by the so-called relationship of love between man and woman. What is love? Two human beings exhaust each other, torment each other sadistically, want to bring each other under a yoke, and kill the individuality of each other – love is something terrible, an illness bordering on insanity. Jung's books, until 1918 are long drawn out cries of despair.

The *Book of Fools* consists of four parts. The first called *Idiocy. A Programmatic Introduction.* Who is a fool? The man who loves a woman; the man who wants to live; the earth which jogs along in the universe; and God who created this piece of idiocy. The rest of the book comprises desperate acts of revenge by Jung on Margot, on his prejudiced mother-in-law and on his parents. Characters hate and curse each other, beat and insult each other, 'they chase each other like animals through rooms and streets' (Kurt Hiller). It never occurs to anyone – least of all a woman – to think logically or to reflect first and act later. Their actions are also unmotivated psychologically, not comprehensible; in this respect Jung is close to Marinetti and Döblin.'

The major figure of all Jung's expressionist works is Margot: incomprehensible to him, gypsy-like and not bound by any laws whatsoever. He allows her to live in *The Book of Fools* and the novels, *Sacrifice*, 1916 and *The Leap out of the World*, 1918; he kills her in *Comrades . . . !*, 1913 and *Sophie, the Crossroads of Humility*. Curt Corrinth who was one of her later lovers, confirms how extraordinary she must have been when in *Liljol* (1921) he describes her relationship with Franz Jung from her point of view. One can understand Jung's irritation! Here is an extract from *Sophie* to show his Style. Otto and Sophie are quarrelling:

> Screams. Choking. Hideous torment. Torn Screams poured out, choked, grew, broke out. Choking. He held the woman by the wrist and shook her. He tore his hair, beat his fist against the wall, threw himself across the table, fell on to the floor, thrashed about him and then with a long sigh lay still. Small convulsions still shook his body.
>
> Sophie stood bending forward, with an avaricious gaze. She grew. She filled the room. She arched herself into a prayer. She became a chalice. Its edges darted with flame. Higher. More brilliant.

We are pleased when at the end Otto strangles Sophie and sorry that he then gives himself up to the police.

KAFKA, Franz (Prague, 3.7.1883 – Kierling near Vienna, 3.6.1924). Kafka came from Prague where he studied law at the university and gained his doctorate in 1906. After a year's practice he entered the Assicurazioni Generali as a civil servant. In 1908 he transferred to the Workers' Accident Insurance department where he remained until his premature superannuation (1922). In 1908 his first prose works appeared in the magazine *Hyperion*. His most famous stories, 'Metamorphosis' and 'The Verdict' came out in 1912 as well as the beginning of his first novel, *America* (the title was then still *The Missing Man*). In 1914 he wrote the story *In the Penal Settlement* and began the novel *The Trial*. Kafka's health had never been of the best and in 1917 tuberculosis of the lung was diagnosed. In 1919 he wrote *Letter to My Father* – his revenge on an unfeeling and capricious tyrant whom Kafka also blamed for the fact that he himself always broke off his engagements.

In 1922 he wrote his third novel, *The Castle*. He died in Kierling Sanatorium.

Kafka is the only expressionist prose writer who has achieved outstanding significance in the context of world literature. And yet his works fit into the decade of

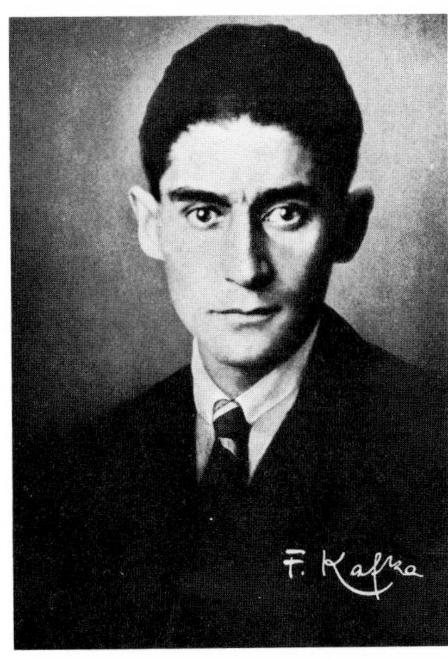

KAFKA, FRANZ: *Portrait*

German expressionism: they appeared in the usual reviews, journals and publishing houses. When he died he had produced six slim volumes of prose: as far as literary prestige was concerned he was one amongst many. This changed when Kafka's friend Max Brod, himself a writer of distinction, published the three novels from the writings left at his death: *The Trial* (1925), *The Castle* (1926) and *America* (1927). Kafka had the gift of being able to personify mental and mythical situations. His father had hoped for a vigorous, hard-working son; Franz, however, had grown into a frail good-for-nothing whom the father despised and was ashamed of. That is the situation portrayed in *Metamorphosis* and *The Verdict*. What many only realize on a second reading is the irony and humour in these pieces. The absolute absurdity of the human situation is the theme of *The Trial, The Castle* and *In The Penal Settlement*. The penal settlement is earth; we are all harnessed to the instrument of torture; only in middle age do we realize what sort of game is being played with us. Wrinkles are engraved on us and at the twelfth hour we are thrown into the ditch. *The Trial* is concerned with man's destiny. We are guilty from birth and condemned to death. Why? Kafka seeks desperately to find out – a helpless detective in a twisted thriller. Dürrenmatt, whose early readings of Kafka played a part in his own work, has expressed it more clearly; God is a sadist who enjoys tormenting us and executing the innocent. Finally *The Castle* is the abode of God, God whom we cannot reach nor call to account.

KLABUND, really Alfred Henschke (Crossen-Oder, 1.11.1890 – Davos, 14.8.1928). Klabund suffered from tuberculosis from sixteen. He published ecstatic novels and brilliant songs, that inspired Brecht. In his nature he belongs near Wedekind: eroticism was also his favourite theme but he had more humour than Wedekind. Klabund wrote too quickly; he was too little concerned with form and so his once famous novels (*Moreau*, 1916, *Refuse*, 1928, *Franciscus*, 1921) are forgotten today. His play, *The Chalk Circle*, 1925, some songs and some adaptations from the Chinese have survived. Like Wedekind and Brecht he stands at the edge of expressionism.

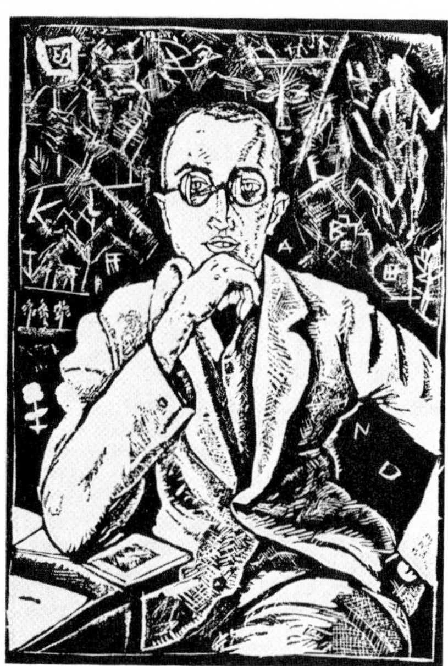

KLABUND, *Portrait.* Wood-cut by Erich Büttner

LASKER-SCHÜLER, Else (Elberfeld, 11.2.1869 – Jerusálem, 11.1.1945). She was born in Wuppertal – Elberfeld. He grandfather was a rabbi, her father an architect. She first married the doctor Berthold Lasker, then Herwarth Walden, the editor of *Der Sturm.* She later had affairs with Gottfried Benn and other expressionists. She was a literary gypsy, always full of longings and hopes; first depressed then again in raptures. She lived mainly in Berlin – in shabby, small rooms, without any means. In her imagination however, she lived in a fairytale world, gave herself and her friends oriental names, and, as she grew older, shifted her birthday to the 11th February 1876.

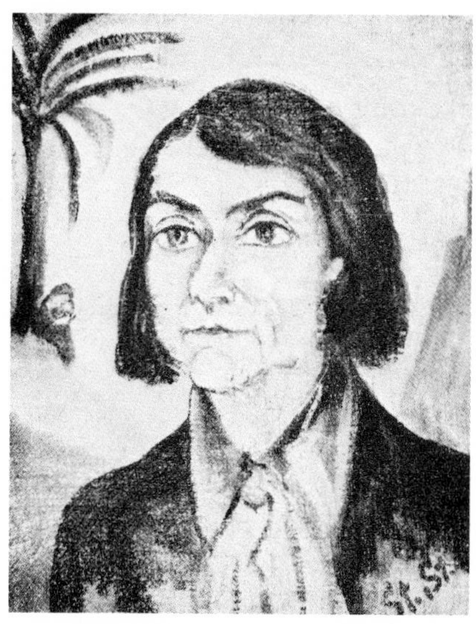

LASKER-SCHÜLER, ELSE: *Portrait.* Canvas by Stanislaus Stückgold. 1916

In 1932 she won the Kleist prize. The next year she emigrated to Switzerland and in 1937 to Jerusalem where she died in 1945.

Her first volume of poetry appeared in 1902 under the title *Styx.* Already a large part of these poems could be called completely expressionist. Her most famous poems are contained in the volumes *Miracle* (1911) and *Hebrew Ballads* (1913). Her last volume of poetry appeared in 1943: *My Blue Piano.* She invented a private language and world of images, which are only understood by initiates but which we can nevertheless enjoy because of the originality of her language and images. Her statements about herself are characteristic: 'I was born in Egypt even though I first saw day in Elberfeld in the Rhineland. I went to school until I was eleven, became a Robinson, lived for five years in the Orient and since then I have been vegetating.' A large part of her poems are love poems. The following is addressed to Gottfried Benn and is called *Listen*:

In the nights I steal
The roses of your mouth
So that no woman drinks there

She who embraces you
Robs me of the trembling
That I painted round my limbs

I am your road's edge
Which caresses you
And falls away

Do you feel my life
Around you
Like a far off bourne?

Else Lasker-Schüler wrote two plays *The Wupper* (1909) and *Arthur Aronymus and his Father* (1932). In both she elaborates in a way peculiar to her scenes from the life and milieu of her youth: the first is a love story set in the early days of industrial weaving, the second the tense relations between Jews and Christians in Westphalia before 1848. Less well-known are her short stories in the volumes *The Nights of Tino of Baghdad* (1908) and *The Prince of Thebes* (1914).

LICHTENSTEIN, Alfred (Berlin, 23.8.1889 – Rheims 25.9.1914). He was born and brought up in Berlin, the son of a manufacturer. He attended the Secondary school in Luisenstadt where he got his *abitur* in 1909. He studied law first in Berlin, then in Erlangen. He gained the title Doctor of Law in January 1914. He published poems from 1910 onwards – first in *Der Sturm*, and from 1912 also in *Die Aktion*. In 1913 a small collection of poems appeared under the title *Twilight, a lyric pamphlet* published by A. R. Meyer (Berlin). Lichtenstein joined up in October 1913, and was mobilized on August 1st, 1914. He fell at the Somme on September 25th.

Lichtenstein first gained his poetic voice from Hoddis and could, if one wished to be malicious, be seen purely as an imitator. After Kurt Hiller, the founder of the Neopathetisches Cabaret, had fallen out with Hoddis, he wrote in his book *The Wisdom of Boredom* (1913), that Hoddis was a 'feeble genius'. On the other hand he praised Lichtenstein and hinted that he had begun writing poetry at the same time as Hoddis. Franz Pfemfert, the editor of *Die Aktion*, opposed this. On October 14th, 1913 he placed a footnote under a new printing of Lichtenstein's poem 'Twilight' in his magazine; in this he drew attention to the fact that Hoddis's poem *The End of the World* had appeared before Lichtenstein's poems, and that Lichtenstein had read this poem before writing anything like it himself. 'I therefore believe that van Hoddis has the credit for having found this style, and Lichtenstein the lesser credit for having perfected and enriched it, for having made it recognized.' Pfemfert is quite right.

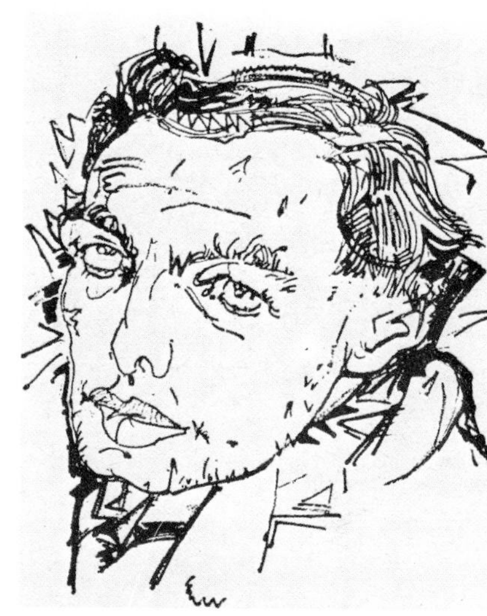

LICHTENSTEIN, ALFRED: *Portrait.* Drawing by Ma Oppenheimer. 1913

The End of the World was recited on June 1st, 1910 in the Neopathetisches Cabaret and first appeared on January 11th, 1911 in *The Democrat.* Lichtenstein's most famous poem 'Twilight', which first came out in *Der Sturm* on March 18th, 1911, is strongly reminiscent of *The End of the World.* The insolent poet looks nonchalantly around him and throws everything he fancies together with apparent indifference, and unconcern.

A fat boy plays with a pond
The wind has caught itself in a tree
The sky looks washed out and wan
As if it had lost its make-up

Bent crookedly on crutches
Two shattering cripples crawl across the field
A fair haired poet will perhaps go mad
A little horse stumbles over a lady

A plump man is glued to a window
A youth wants to visit a soft woman
A grey clown pulls on his boots
A pram cries and dogs curse.

Lichtenstein gave his own interpretation of his poem on October 4th in *Die Aktion.* It is not a 'senseless mixture of odd ideas,' for he is concerned 'to pick up and absorb the objects directly – without superfluous reflection. Of course the poet knows that it is not the pram but the child inside that is crying, but he cannot see the child, he sees only the pram from which the crying emanates.'

Lichtenstein also wrote a number of prose pieces – grotesques, in which he makes fun of himself and some of his acquaintances – after the manner of Alfred Jarry. He himself is the Hunchback Kuno Kohn, Lutz Laus and his dachshund are Karl Kraus and his magazine *Die Fackel* Dr Bryller is Kurt Hiller, Gottschalk Schulz is Georg Heym. Max Mechenmal Jakob van Hoddis and Spinoza Spass is Ernst Blass; Else Lasker-Schüler appears as Maria Mondmilch, Gottfried Benn as Dr Bruno Bibelbauer and the publisher, Alfred Richard Meyer is here called Roland Rufus Miller. Klösschen Café is Lichtenstein's name for the Western Café on the Berlin Kurfürstendamm and the Gnu Cabaret is called the Clou Club. The people he mocks are admittedly known to the initiated but it is not true that Lichtenstein – like Kuno Kuhn – really had a hunchback. The love story between Schulz, Kohn and Lisel Liblichlein for example is entirely fictitious and of course Heym, did not stab himself, as Schulz does, with a salad knife. Lichtenstein was not a militarist, nor a black pessimist who really suffered from life. He was instead parodying such a stance when he has Kuno Kohn say: 'The only consolation is to be sad. When sadness degenerates into despair, love should be grotesque. We should continue to love for the sake of amusement. We should try to find grandeur in the knowledge that existence consists purely of brutal, vulgar jokes!'

MANN, Heinrich (Lübeck, 27.3.1871 – Santa Monica, California, 12.3.1950). Like his more famous younger brother, Thomas, Heinrich Mann was born in Lübeck. He left secondary school before the abitur, and worked in a bookshop and for S. Fischer publishing house. In 1891 after the father's death, the Mann business was sold and the mother moved with her children to Munich. They were now well off; Heinrich travelled in France and Italy and began to write at first for magazines. His first novel, *In a Family* appeared in 1894. Nowadays Mann's most famous books of his pre-expressionist and expressionist days are *Professor Unrat*, or *The Fall of a Tyrant* (1905), the film version of which became famous under the title *The Blue Angel*; *The Little Town* (1909) and *Man of Straw* (1914). The first part appeared in instalments in 1916; the whole novel on a private printing press, and in 1918 in the public book trade. Heinrich Mann was a model for many expressionists: he was truly international and did not allow himself – like Thomas – to be dazzled by false patriotism. Above all he admired Flaubert, particularly *Salammbô*, and D'Annunzio who inspired him to write

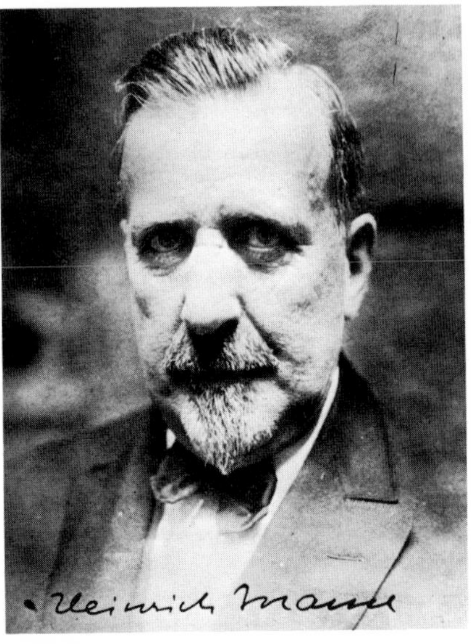

MANN, HEINRICH: *Portrait*

the prodigious book *The Goddesses* or *The Three Novels of the Duchess of Assy* in 1903. This trilogy had a great influence – from Jakob Wassermann's *Alexander in Babylon* (1905) to Kasimir Edschmid's *The Agate Bullets* (1920). We do not know what to make of the three novels *Pallas*, *Minerva* and *Venus* today – just as with d'Annunzio. But at the time W. Fred wrote in *Zukunft* that the book 'at least provides for once an abundance of material, instead of an endless analysis of the artist'. And what material it is! In *Venus* woman is a full-blown, highly sexed animal, who gives herself to everyone and – significantly – dies childless. And the style! A critical reviewer wrote in the Berlin *Lokal Anzeiger* 'His language often infringes all the laws of German grammar. There is really no reason to admire this.' But it was precisely this that the expressionists admired: away from clichés; the expression of enthusiasm and ecstasy by means of a new, spontaneous style.

Some of his short stories can be described as expressionist in a narrower sense – such as the 'Three Minute Novel', 'A Walk by the Gateway' in the volume *Flutes and Daggers* (1905) or some in *Hades* (1911).

In 1933 Mann fled to France; he was deprived of his German citizenship. He now worked at what are perhaps his best works: *The Youth of King Henry IV* (1935), *The Sequel to King Henry IV* (1938). In 1938 he escaped via Portugal to the U.S.A. He intended to settle in the DDR in 1950 where he had been appointed president of the German Academy of Arts. He died in Santa Monica, California.

MYNONA real name **Salomo Friedländer** (Gollantsch, Posen 4.5.1871 – Paris 9.9.1946). He was the son of a doctor and was born in Gollantsch (Posen). He first studied medicine in Munich, Jena and Berlin, and later philosophy. He obtained a D.Phil. in 1902. He wrote several philosophical works – under the name Salomo Friedländer – and grotesque novels and stories (collected in over twelve volumes). Under the pseudonyn Mynona (Anonym written backwards) the most famous collection is *Rosa, The Beautiful Policeman's Wife* (1913). The grotesque range from satires on the bourgeoisie through stories of black humour, parodies, comic science fiction, and fantastic visions to Dada-like absurdity. It is significant that Mynona has been linked with Paul Scheerbart, by whom he was certainly influenced), Franz Kafka (in Soergel's literary history), and Dada.

Let us look for example at Mynona's *The Mockers' Bench*. An anti-novel (1919). Grotesque stories are being told at a party – for example, *The Chaste Cocotte* – the story of a prostitute, where no sexual act is supposed to occur. There are stories about orphans who yet have parents; about horse races without horses and so on. A superb parody of Gustav Meyrink (*The Golem*) and Hanns Heinz Ewers is also there. An orgy follows, when the police have to intervene. A word column poem by Stramm is also parodied, Else Lasker-Schüler, Thomas Mann, and many others.

In *The Grey Magic, a Master Key Novel* (1922), everything with a name in expressionism is ridiculed. Lasker-Schüler is here called Schisskerlaller, Herwarth Walden is the composer Nedlaw. Ludwig Meidner is 'the painter Merdner who forces himself into notorious captures.' The philosopher Georg Simmel as the psychologist Lemmis; Mynona himself is Dr Salomo and Ewers appears under his own name as a sinister second-hand dealer. Contemporary philosophers are also gathered here: Aribert Neinstein (Einstein) announces 'the theory of relativity of our conception of time, that impairs good sense; he is ridiculed however, by the Kantian Sucram (Marcus). Martin Buber and Rabindranath Tagore appear together as Martindranat Buborore. The novel is also a satire on the immense power of film producers who are even permitted to kill people in the interests of a film. Mynona is one of the few great German humourists, but today his work is practically forgotten.

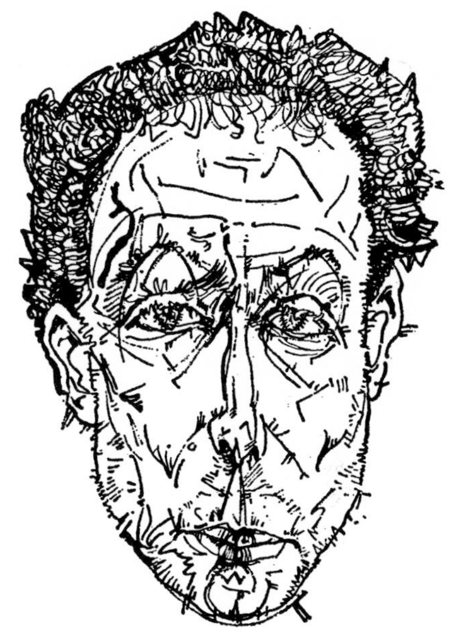

MYNONA: *Portrait.* Drawing by Max Oppenheimer

SACK, Gustav (Schermbeck near Wesel, 28.10.1885 – near Bucharest, 6.12.1916). Sack came from a family of teachers and was born in Schermbeck (Lower Rhine). From 1906 to 1914 he studied German language and literature at several universities, and did military service in between. When war broke out, he first fled to Switzerland in order not to have to enlist. In September 1914 he returned to Germany, was promptly called up and seriously wounded when a lieutenant in France. He fell on the Eastern front near Bucharest. His wife, Paula Sack did for him what Max Brod did for Kafka: she published his works (Sack himself had only published a few poems in journals), built up a Sack archive and wrote a book on him in 1971.

Both novels by Sack, *A Wastrel Student* (written in 1910–1913, published 1917) and *A Man without a Name* (written 1912–1913, published in 1919) are heavily autobiographical. They were successful - 20,000 copies of the first were sold. In 1920 his collected works were published in two volumes. In 1926 – on the tenth anniversary of his death – apparently more than forty appreciations of his work appeared. His novels are in many ways immature, but very promising works. Sack still has no uniform style, but is therefore always vital and animated. He is one whose reading of Nietzsche made it impossible for him to have a naïve Christian faith. Full of energy he searches for the new man, would like to become one himself but is too clever and too sceptical really to believe in the advent of man's happiness. His likenesses in the novels end by committing suicide. The following lines are from the close of the novel *A Man without a Name*.

> On the day before Easter, he returned to his former garrison. But he did not see her whom he had been looking for: she had shot herself and her lover, after she had been unfaithful to him as well, a few weeks before. So he wandered about the streets for the day and hanged himself towards sunset in a thicket outside the town. Here they found him. His pockets were full of bonds and these papers lay at his feet, strewn by the night wind over the grass on whose blades the dew hung in bright drops.
>
> Then the sun rose and the barrel organ played the same old tune.

Sack had hardly any connections with other expressionists. Apart from the novels he also wrote a play to be read, *The Refractory*, two cycles of stories: *The Ruby*, *From the Diary of a Refractory Man*; a fairly large novel fragment (*Paralysis*), essays, poems, a war diary and very readable letters.

SCHICKELE, René (Oberehnheim, Alsace , 4.8.1883 – Vence, near Nice, 31.1.1940). Schickele came from Alsace and was a friend of Ernst Stadler and Otto Flake. He worked as an editor and proof-reader and from 1915 to 1919 he published, in Zurich, *Die Weissen Blätter*, which was important for expressionism. After the war he was an independent writer and lived in Badenweiler. In 1932 he emigrated to France where he settled on the Riviera. He died in Vence.

Schickele began as an expressionist (the early novels – *The Stranger*, 1909 and *Comforter of Women*, 1914). While his poetry of this time is as good as forgotten, his play *Hans in the Schnakenloch*, 1913 is still remembered; in it Schickele describes the situation of the Alsatians who stand between two nations. Schickele's later novels – his major works – are realistic and barely show any traces of expressionism. (The trilogy, *Heritage by the Rhine*: *Maria Capponi*, 1925, *View Over the Vosges*, 1927, *The Wolf in the Pen*, 1927).

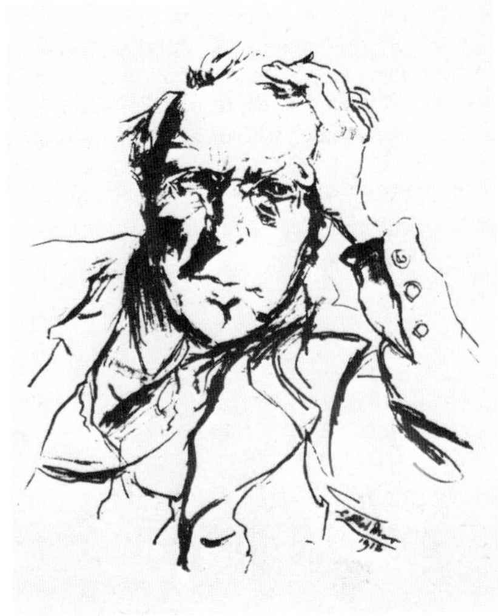

MEIDNER, LUDWIG: *Portrait of René Schickele.* 1918

SCHWITTERS, Kurt (Hanover, 20.6.1887 – Ambleside, England, 8.1.1948). Schwitters was born in Hanover. After passing his *abitur* (1908) he attended the school of arts and crafts in Hanover and the Academy of Art in Dresden. Since the Berlin dadaists did not want to know about him, he founded his own art movement, which he called 'Merz'. In 1919 he joined Herwarth Walden's circle. *Der Sturm* published his poems and its gallery exhibited his paintings and collages. From 1923 to 1932 Schwitters published his own review *Merz* at irregular intervals. From 1923 on he worked on a huge collage in his house in Hanover, the first Merzbau construction, that was destroyed by bombs in 1943. In 1937 he emigrated to Norway, from which he fled to England in 1940. The Merzbau he had begun in Norway was destroyed in 1951, the unfinished English one is now in Newcastle University. Schwitters died in England.

Schwitters indeed wrote very original German poetry. He began in the style of Stramm, but then took increasing delight in Dada-like jokes and word play. He wrote a *First Draft of a Sonata* in capitals, that is twenty-eight pages long. The first motif of the first part runs as follows:

Fumms bö wö tää zää Uu,
pögiff,
kwii Ee

He wrote graphic poetry, poems composed of numbers, concrete poetry, funny proverbs, Dada nonsense stories and dramatic scenes, manifestos and others. His poem 'To Anna Blume', which can be found in almost all Dada anthologies, became famous. In a *Der Sturm* exhibition Schwitters had shown a drawing containing the name Anna Blume. The critics were intensely irritated at the deliberate primitivism of the drawing and asked this poem as a reply; it appeared in *Der Sturm* in August and itself unleashed a scandal.

The poem was translated into French three times, first by Roland Schacht, then by Hans Arp and Alain Gheerbrant and finally by Philip Granville:

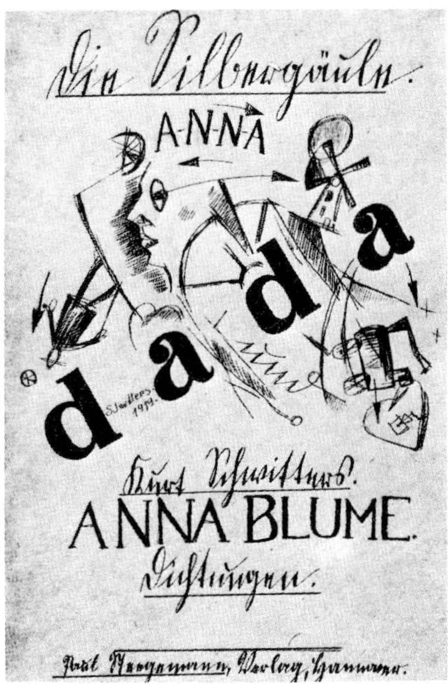

SCHWITTERS, KURT: Poster for 'Anna Blume'. 1919

O you, the dove of my twenty-seven senses
I love you, you, of you, you to you, I to you, you to me, –
We?
That does not (by the way) belong here
Who are you, woman without number? You are –
Are you? People say, you could be –
let them talk, they don't know how the steeple stands
You wear your hat on your feet and walk on your hands,
on your hands you walk.
Hallo your red clothes, saw them into white creases
Red I love Anna Blume, red I you to you.
You of you, you, to you, I to you, you to me, – We?
That belongs (by the way) in the cold embers
Red bloom, red Anna Blume, how do people say it?
Question prize
1) Anna Blume has a bird
2) Anna Blume is red
3) What colour is the bird
Blue is the colour of your yellow hair
And red is the warbling of your green bird
You modest girl in your workaday dress, you sweet green thing
I love you. – You, of you, you to you, I to you, you to me.
– We?
That belongs (by the way) in the ash pan
Anna Blume! Anna A-n-n-a, I drip your name. Your name drips like soft tallow.
Did you know that, Anna, did you know that already?
You can read your name backwards, and you, most splendid of all,
you are the same backwards as you are forwards: a-n-n-a.
Tallow drips caressing across my back.
Anna Blume you simple thing, I love you.

STADLER, Ernst (Colmar, 11.8.1883 – near Zandvoorde, Belgium, 30.9.1914). Stadler was born in 1883 in Colmar. He passed his abitur and studied German language and literature, romance languages and comparative literature in Strasbourg and Munich. He was a friend of Otto Flake and René Schickele. Like them, he wanted to bring France and Germany closer together through cultural activities (reviews, translations). In 1904 his first volume of poetry appeared, *Praeludien*, which is still influenced by Hugo von Hofmannsthal and Stefan George. In 1906 Stadler obtained his doctorate. From 1906 to 1908 he was a Rhodes scholar in Oxford. In 1908 he qualified with a thesis on Wieland's Shakespeare which was published in 1910. From 1909 to 1911 he edited Wieland's translations of Shakespeare (three volumes) in the edition of Wieland's collected works. From October 1910 he was a lecturer in the Université Libre in Brussels. He began a busy life of journalism and wrote poems, articles and reviews for periodicals like *Die Aktion, Das Neue Elsass* and *Cahiers Alsaciens.* He translated Francis Jammes's *Prayers of Humility* into German. Had war not broken out, he would have become visiting professor in Toronto (Canada) in 1914.

He joined up on the September 1st, 1914, received the Iron Cross on the October 9th and was blown up by an English grenade on October 30th.

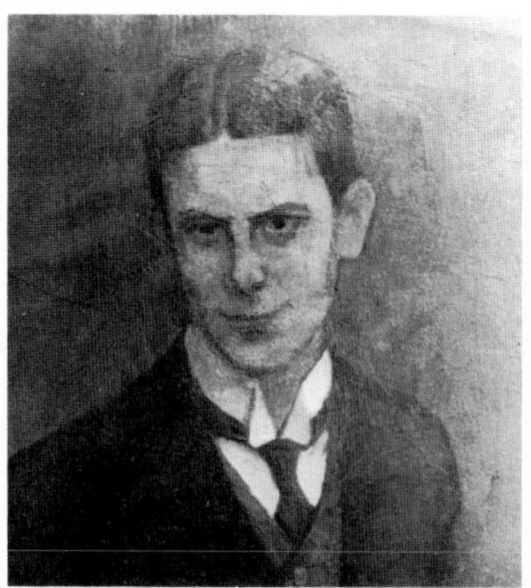

STADLER, ERNST: *Portrait*

After 1910, Stadler preferred to write unrhymed poems with long lines. The feeling behind the poems is one of vitality and enthusiasm. What Curt Corrinth later offered in his novels, is here toned down, discreetly composed. There is no trace of ecstatic utterance. Stadler is a 'world lover' like Werfel. He loves not only the landscape of Alsace, but also city dwellers. The sales girls who can only get a little fresh air in the evenings, and the workers who eat their evening meal in their shabby homes. The following six lines are the beginning of the poem *Evening Closing Time*, which appeared in 1914 in the volume *The Revolt*:

The clocks strike seven. Now all over the town the shops shut
The sales girls stream from halls already darkened, through narrow corner courtyards, from ostentatious halls
Still a little dazzled and as if confused from the long confinement
They emerge, excited, into the summer evening's radiance and soft expansiveness
Rumbling trams come flashing,
suddenly beat a lighter measure
and all the pavements are tightly packed with bright blouses and the laughter of young girls.

Stadler's achievement as a critic deserves mention, alongside his importance as a pioneer in poetry and as a translator of Jammes, Péguy (essays) and Balzac (stories). Admittedly, what he achieved as a literary scholar could have been done by others, but Stadler has the credit of being one of the first 'to write intelligent essays and reviews of René Schickele, Carl Einstein, Georg Heym, Walter Hasenclever, Oskar Loerke, Mynona, Carl Sternheim, Franz Werfel and others. Stadler was one of the most open, tolerant and perspicacious writers of his age.

STRAMM, August (Münster, 29.7.1874 – near Horodec, Russia, 1.9.1915). This upstanding Wilhelminian civil servant, an apparently happily married bourgeois, wrote poems and short plays which in form and occasionally, in their revolutionary content, surpass everything that was considered progressive at the time. He was born in Münster in Westphalia, the son of a sergeant, passed his *abitur* and entered the Imperial

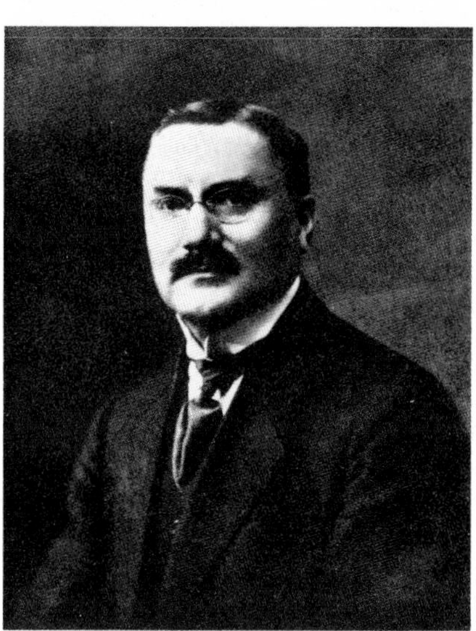

STRAMM, AUGUST: *Portrait*

Post Office as an apprentice in 1893. He reached the rank of officer during his military service. He married in 1902. Three years later he was transferred to Berlin where he had the opportunity to study in his spare time. In 1909 he took his doctorate. On the outbreak of war he joined up and fell on September 1st, 1915 on the Eastern Front.

Stramm wrote poems and plays from 1902 on. In November 1913 the leader of the futurists, Filippo Tommaso Marinetti gave a lecture in Berlin and there is every reason to suppose that Stramm heard it. He destroyed everything he had written hitherto, and made friends with Herwarth Walden, the editor of the review *Der Sturm* who published Marinetti's manifesto. Everything that Stramm published was written in the years 1914 to 1915, and almost everything was printed either in *Der Sturm*, or, in the case of the short plays, in its publishing house.

Stramm is concerned to say what he wanted: 1) in the smallest possible number of words; 2) to say it as concisely as possible; 3) to avoid all cliché. Here for example, is 'In the Fire', which he wrote in 1915; it consists of six lines and eight words:

Death drags
Dying rattles
Lonely
Immures
World-deep
Loneliness

In 'A Shell Attack', there is 'death' and 'dying' – the result of weapons that we can hear 'whining' and 'rattling' – what does a man feel in such combat by fire? The words 'Lonely', 'Loneliness'. 'Immures' 'World deep' occur to Stramm. His syntax can absorb these words without additional vocabulary: the first two lines are two sentences of two words each. The other four form a sentence with 'Lonely' as the subject, or else 'Dying' is also the subject for 'Immures' (World deep Loneliness); 'Lonely' would then be an adverb for 'rattles'.

Walter Muschg and others have mocked this postal employee 'run wild'. There is no doubt that Stramm was in deadly earnest in his art, and that he had the full respect and sympathy of Walden. Stramm is not a dadaist, for he was not given to irony in his poetry. He twice sent letters to Walden in which he explained in detail why in his poem 'Unfaithful' true to expression, 'leafwilted' must be thus, and not 'wilted leaves'; and why in the poem 'Disorderly House', the correct word is 'wild with shame' and not 'devastated by shame'. We know that Rudolf Blümner recited Stramm's poems for many years to a deeply moved and enthusiastic public, and that the young Kurt Schwitters and other poets of the *Der Sturm* school revered Stramm as a master.

TRAKL, Georg (Salzburg, 3.2.1887 – Kracow, 4.11.1914). Trakl is at the same time the most inspired and the most inaccessible of all the expressionist poets. He was born in Salzburg, attended secondary school there, but left it before the final examination and became a pharmaceutical laboratory assistant. From 1908 to 1910 he studied pharmacology in Vienna. He became an army pharmacist in Innsbruck where he got to know Ludwig von Ficker the editor of the review *Der Brenner* in which many of Trakl's poems later appeared. Trakl met Else Lasker-Schüler during a visit to Berlin. On the outbreak of war he took part in the battle of Grodek as a medical lieutenant. Its horror disturbed him so deeply that he had to be taken to the garrison hospital in Kracow for an examination of his mental state. Here he committed suicide with a drug overdose.

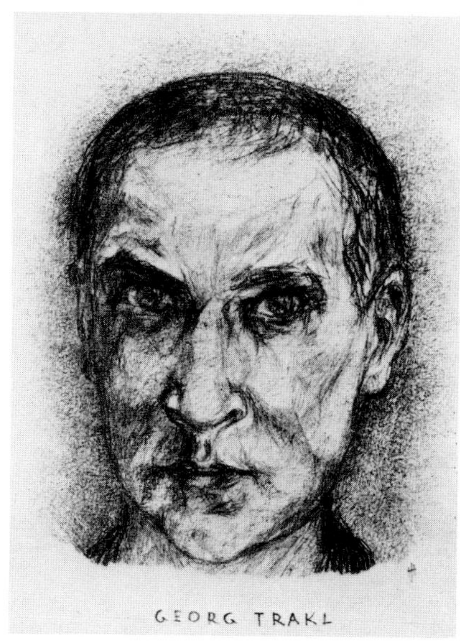

TRAKL, GEORG: *Portrait.* Lithograph by Hildegard Jone

Trakl was shy, melancholy, a drug addict. His early poems are influenced by Rimbaud and Baudelaire. Later, he created his own melancholy language with a world of images that can often only be understood through the emotions. We sense that here dreams a despairing man. He clothes hideous visions in a sad, beautiful and supple language. Trakl is supposed to have had incestuous relations with his sister – hence some of his melancholy enigmatic love poems. His metaphors and symbols often refer to something which is no longer identifiable. Adjectives and adverbs such as colours, for example, can be interchanged – they frequently seem to be there for their sound rather than their meaning. His world is a sick world. But many of his poems are so original and impressive in their hypnotic quality that they are unforgettable.

In the following poem, the sun sets first and the moon rises – then Trakl links together abstract images containing his most private thoughts:

'Peace and silence'

Shepherds bury the sun in the leafless wood
In a net made of hair a fisher drew
the moon from the freezing pond

The pale man
Lives in a blue crystal, his cheek rested against his stars.
Or nods his head in purple sleep

Yet still the black flock of birds
Stir the watcher, holy, of blue flowers
The close stillness thinks of forgotten things, vanished angels

Once more his brow grows sombre in the moonstone
His sister appears
A shining youth in autumn and dark decay.

We can perhaps penetrate this private veil. The pale man is indeed the author thinking of his dead sister: in reality she is a vanished angel, in his dream a shining youth. But the poem gains little by investigating its meaning. The title gives the mood. If it is read slowly and in a half whisper one is struck by its sounds, the melancholy tone, the unusual and rapidly changing images. There are no more clichés here – no word should be lost.

Trakl belongs with the great poets of German literature – Goethe, Hölderlin, Rilke. His influence on German poetry was and is significant. The best of the twentieth century poets have tried, and do try, to use language as carefully as Trakl: scarcely one has succeeded.

WEISS, Ernst (Brno, 28.8.1882 – Paris, 15.6.1940). Weiss was born in Brno, studied in Prague, Vienna and Berne and became a doctor in 1908. He spent the First World War as a regimental doctor. From 1920 to 1933 he had a practice in Berlin. He fled from the Nazis to Prague, and from there to Paris in 1938 where he took his own life as the German troops marched into the city.

Weiss knew Freud, Kafka and Schwitters. The major theme of most of his later works is already present in his first novel, *The Gallery* (1913) which is written in conventional language: man is a slave to his senses – he may indeed wish for good, but when it comes to the crunch, his senses always gain the upper hand. There is also the father-son conflict. In *The Gallery*, it is Dr Erik Gyldendal who spreads unhappiness because of his sensuality and women's conventional nature. A servant girl loves him, but when he becomes passionate, she starts to cry. Enraged, he abandons her. A Russian woman becomes attached to him but becomes stubborn when he tries to get her into bed. When she returns to him later he rejects her. A false friend denounces Erik as a drug addict to his parents – he is thrown out. Helen takes an interest in him, and they go on holiday together. He should remain faithful to her if only out of common decency and gratitude, but he betrays her with her own sister, Edith. She then marries the false friend. Gyldendal is not a drug addict but he has a sore on his hand – cancer from radiation – in six months he will be dead. He gives himself a fatal morphia injection.

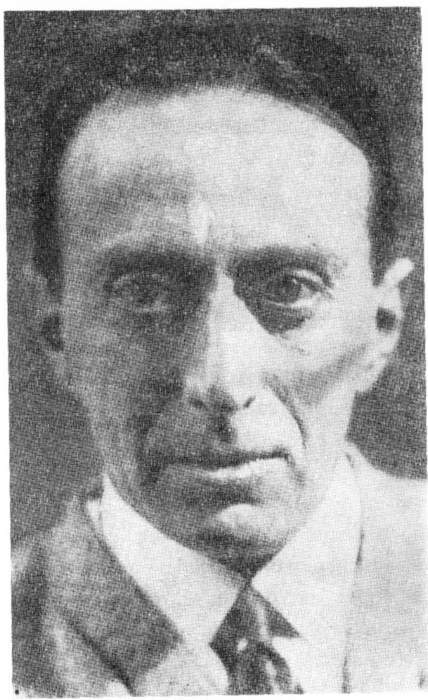

WEISS, ERNST: *Portrait*

In the expressionist works that followed, emotions and language are lifted to an ecstatic level. Man resembles an animal of prey that is at first chained behind bars, but wants to break out and run amok; in so doing, he murders and is himself destroyed, for example, *The Battle* (1916), *Animals in Chains* (1918), *Man Against Man* (1919), and so on. *Nahar* (1922) is the second part of the novel *Animals in Chains.* The hundred pages of the novel are written in an extraordinarily concentrated and taut language. Olga dies in prison. Her soul is reincarnated as tiger. The experiences of this tigress – Nahar – from infancy to capture – run parallel to Olga's fate. The tigress grows up, loves, becomes a mother. As she is helping her offspring from a tray she injures herself. These good impulses betray an inner weakness: her own downfall is the result. Nahar becomes weaker and ugly. Her lover leaves her; she is even betrayed by her father.

Only Nahar's mother behaves as Nahar did to her child: she tries to save her and in so doing is destroyed. Nahar is captured, is faced with buffalo in an arena and trampled to death. She dies as Olga died. Here the world of Kipling's *Jungle Book* is seen through the eyes of Kafka. Nahar is the personified outcry of the author against the senseless evil of life; in this respect the novel belongs with Benn's *Morgue* poems.

After this, Weiss wrote numerous psychological novels, most of which have a medical setting and contain elements of a detective story. Several were published again in the 1960s: *They Eye Witness* (1963) from writings at his death; *The Impoverished Profligate* (1936; 1965); *The Prison Doctor* (1934, 1967); *The Vukobrancovics Case* (1925, 1960). In the 1920s and 1930s he translated works by Balzac, Maupassant, and James M. Cain into German.

WERFEL, Franz (Prague, 10.9.1890 – Beverly Hills, California, 26.8.1945). Werfel was born in Prague the son of a glove manufacturer. After the *abitur* he left Prague and finished a business apprenticeship in Hamburg. In 1912 he was a proof reader in Leipzig. With Walter Hasenclever and Kurt Pinthus he helped the Kurt Wolff publishing house to become the publishing centre of the expressionist movement. From 1915 to 1917 Werfel was an unwilling soldier. After the war he lived mainly in Vienna. He fled from the Nazis first to Italy, then to France, and finally via Portugal to the U.S.A. where he died in 1945.

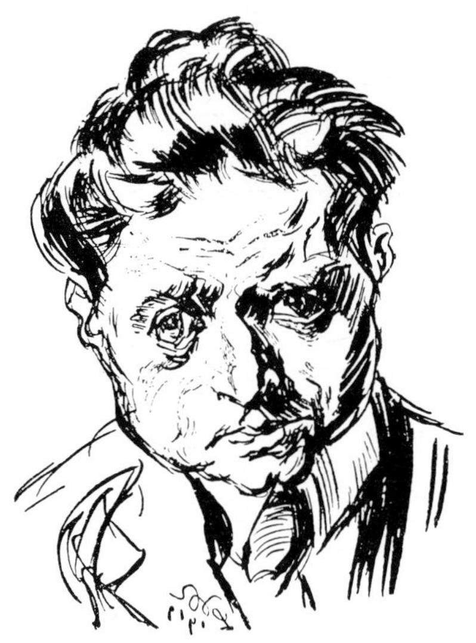

WERFEL, FRANZ: *Portrait.* 1919

When we talk of Werfel today, it is mainly in connection with his late novels: *The Song of Bernadette* (1941), *Star of the Unborn* (1946). Most expressionist elements vanished from Werfel's work at the latest in 1927 (with the publication of the novel *The Day of The Abitur Candidates*) and yet up to 1925 he had been the model for many expressionists. The volumes of poetry, *The World Lover* (1911), *The Arc* (1913) and *Each Other* had set the tone for many, and plays like *Spiegelmensch* (1920) and *Bockegesang* (1921) had been considered to be important expressionist achievements.

What links the early and later works of Werfel is the element of ecstatic religiosity. He was in earnest in his *O Mankind* poetry and his longing for fraternity. His emotion may seem to ring hollow to us today but the youth of 1911–1920 were inspired and swept away by it. The poem 'To The Reader' in *World Lover* is programmatic. It begins thus:

> My sole wish is to be linked with you, O mankind
> whether you are Negro, acrobat, or still lie tranquil in a mother's care
> Whether your girlish song sings across the yard or you lead your flock in the moonlight
> Be you soldier, or airman full of perseverance and courage
> Did you too when a child carry a weapon in a green sling?
> when it fired, another bullet flew from the barrel
> O, man, when I sing of memories
> Be not hard and weep with me.

There are similar sentiments to be found in Whitman. Werfel is not at all afraid of being sentimental. Indeed, this added to his popularity. Male youth before the war was admittedly intellectually progressive; but as regards emotions and the nature of bourgeois society, they had hardly got beyond the Romantic age. Here was a man protesting who was genuinely sentimental and yet cosmopolitan, and who used a form that could not be accused of being old-fashioned. The orthodox religious could not object either, and politically his poems tended to be neutral. His revolutionary modernity lay in the fact that he used a new form and wanted to press to his bosom even such 'human scum' as Negroes and artists. Not all Werfel's poems are ecstatic. Some are noteworthy merely as curious documents of an era and a way of thinking that are no more.

Drama

At first, the concept 'Expressionism' referred only to a new direction in painting. It was thus that artists in France round about 1901 distinguished themselves from the Impressionists and the *'Indépendants'*. They were painters who followed the examples of Gauguin, Van Gogh and Munch. This new style also had an effect in Germany. The towns of Dresden, Berlin and Munich became centres of expressionism for German painting.

From about 1910 on, the term 'expressionism' was also applied to poetry, prose and drama. However, this development had two sides to it in the literary sphere. Walter Sokel, one of the most important scholars of expressionism, has distinguished between 'Expressionism as a form of modern art, whose forerunners are to be found in the "Apocalypse", in Dante's "Inferno", in the pictures of Bosch, Grünewald, Rembrandt and Goya, and in the poetry of Blake, and expressionism as a peculiarly German phenomenon which contains elements – especially in the violent conflict between the generations – that are not found to the same degree in the expressionist literature of other countries.' The significance of the generation gap as a theme of expressionist drama, particularly in Germany, reflects something of the revolution to which this land was especially exposed. For this reason, the direction of dramatic art in that age cannot be seen purely as a problem of form.

The fifteen years of the 'Literary revolution' which Paul Pörtner placed between 1910 and 1925, saw the full cycle of expressionist drama from beginning to end; and the concept 'expressionism' should be extended to cover all post-impressionist art, as far as 'New Objectivity', thus including surrealism, cubism, *'Sturm'* art and Dada, which all leave traces in expressionist drama and have led to its widespread thematic and formal development.

Form and Content

There has been much disagreement whether expressionist drama is characterized by an intellectual unity beneath its stylistic diversity, or whether one should talk of a superstructure of relatively homogeneous forms of expression over a politically and intellectually divided base. Wolfgang Paulsen distinguished between political and 'genuine' expressionists. Sokel contrasts those expressionists 'who contributed to the artistic success of the modern international movement, to which activists like Sternheim also belong,' with others who 'simply copied some of the artistic methods of the moderns, while remaining basically old-fashioned.'

The divisions within the expressionist generation became even more evident when one examines the very disparate aesthetic and social positions of individual authors. They were just as hazy about questions of form as they were impossible to unite politically. Except for Georg Kaiser, there was scarcely any profound programmatic discussion of aesthetic problems, despite a plethora of aesthetic manifestos. Admittedly, expressionist drama exhibits a typical, stylistically uniform language but this uniformity is often interrupted by hymn-like, even aria-like passages. Paul Kornfeld even categorically demanded that such outburts should be an essential part of the drama.

One of its fundamental characteristics, however, is the scream. As a protest it is already more than an aesthetic phenomenon. It is directed against a state of society, and originates in an apocalyptic vision. It demands action when faced with an analysis of the situation against which it is directed. In the scream, an emotion is reduced to its instinctive expression.

Reduction is, above all, typical of the new drama. Authors distance themselves from reality and wrap themselves in a subjectivity already established for two hundred years in Germany's social and cultural development. They were seeking for an autonomous art form, and saw aesthetic progress in abstract art; but they immediately isolated themselves and withdrew, in a kind of 'inner emigration' into an existence on the margins of society.

The 'naïve' or 'rhetorical' expressionists, as Sokel called them, considered that it was particularly sincere to say 'I'. They saw their lack of form, their rejection of logic, and their liking for fragmentation in the same light. But for all that, they achieved the opposite, even rhetorical expression. The 'automatic writing' of many surrealists is the logical conclusion of naïve expressionism. Its attacks on society are more the result of an obsession than a concern for analysis or a remodelling of society's structure. A hysterical tone dominates the depiction of family conflict – the tension between fathers and sons – which is a central theme from Hasenclever's *The Son* to Bronnen's *Parricide.*

Subjectivity is also a characteristic of 'proper' expressionism. It too is indifferent to society both as a theme and as a public. It presents itself without compromise and thus alienates itself. It seeks to separate man from his society and even from his own nature. Only the spirit remains. The ego expresses itself in a rhetorical and radical way via expression alone, and there is a conscious striving for alienation in the search for an autonomous art.

According to Sokel, real expressionism is 'subjective, dream-like, visionary – not so much concerned with the object, not intellectual, nor experimenting with language. It is nevertheless, distinguished from surrealism by its serious approach to existence and logical consistency.' He considers that its modernity arises from making language both musical and functional, as well as from the rejection of external systems and traditional psychology.

The function of the symbol, above all, changed in expressionist drama. This is already evident in Strindberg. The beggar in 'The Road to Damascus', 1898, is nothing other than a symbolic figure. He is completely context-dependent, only an attribute of the main character, a symbolic embodiment of his possibilities and an expression of his unknown potential. *The Road to Damascus* is the first truly expressionist drama, for there are not just elements of the abstract in it: it is entirely abstract. None of the figures can be understood independently; they have a function only in the context of the dramatic idea.

In the first expressionist play, *The Beggar* by Reinhard Sorge (1912), it is clear that abstraction does not entail a rejection of action. Father and son are set against each other, both personified variations of a messianic search; the son's is idealistic, the father's materialistic. This materialism expresses itself in exaggeration, grotesqueness and crude action. But Sorge does not paint a character in the ordinary sense. For him, the father's function is contrapuntal and dependent upon the *leitmotif* of the play.

Strindberg, who, unlike the surrealists, did not yet transpose dreams directly, only adopting their structure, wrote in his preface to *A Dream Play* (1902) that he had tried 'to imitate the disjointed but apparently logical form of the dream. Anything can happen, anything is possible and probable. The laws of space and time no longer apply; reality now only furnished the insignificant basis, on which the imagination elaborates and weaves new patterns.' Here we see a desire for free composition and for the expression of what we cannot see.

Strindberg, who can only be called an expressionist in a part of his work, had an important influence on German expressionist playwrights. They too were always trying to depict 'the inner space' and push external reality to one side. The sphere depicted in the play is no longer the external environment, but the projection of the characters' inner selves. These characters are no longer individuals, but represent

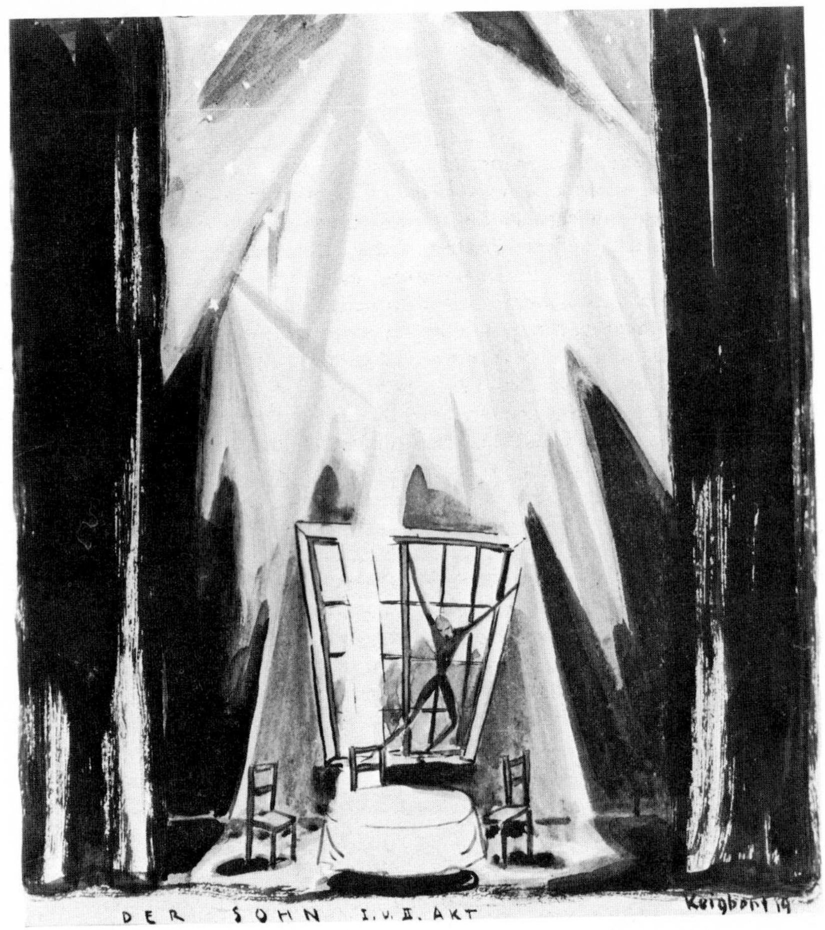

HASENCLEVER, WALTER: *The Son* (Der Sohn). Sketch by Otto Reigbert

psychological forces. Hence one play by August Stramm is simply called *Forces*. They are made flesh and modify the environment around them.

Rapid changes of scene are essential since expressionist drama demonstrates scenically, rather than analysing in dialogue. The visual dominates the intellectual. Space and time become purely functional. Time is either speeded up or reversed. Visual presentation takes the place of analysis. Emotion manifests itself as action. Expressionist diction does not describe, it is not adapted to suit different characters, but tends to be functional. It changes when the mood changes.

Art as Philosophy of Life

The style of expressionist drama is not only a problem of form. Walter Rheiner discerned a 'philosophy of life in the widest sense of the word i.e. an epistemological, metaphysical and ethnical attitude of mind' amongst his contemporaries. The philosophy of life of the German expressionists is definitely linked with the evolution of German philosophy.

Kant had distinguished between 'aesthetic' ideas, which create a work of art, and 'Rational ideas' or 'Logical thoughts'. According to Sokel, Kant thus expresses not only the division between art and logical discussion, but also that between art and empirical experience on which logic draws for its ideas. This division lies at the base of modern art, is the cause of its disconcerting features.

'The nature of modern art' means that it is in a position to express the inner life. So many and such opposing currents flow in as we undergo experience that it contradicts the outer experience and can no longer be communicated 'logically'. For this reason, aesthetics can no longer be seen as the idea of beauty. This merely re-arranges associations and stimuli.

Arthur Schopenhauer was more deeply horrified by nature than Kant, for he saw it as a mask covering a destructive and terrible 'Will'. In an attempt to redeem this, he opposed the 'Imagination' to the driving force of the 'Will'. He went beyond Kant in accusing every art form except music of being an imitation. This philosophy forces certain decisions concerning society's relationship to aesthetics. This ends by destroying its links with, and its transmission to, society. According to this, we would not have a genuine mental existence unless we always felt an aesthetic solution to be 'real'. Surrealism discovered this by abandoning both the natural and the social world and replacing it with an artificial and artistic one.

Just as Schopenhauer had done with Kant, so Nietzsche thought Schopenhauer to 'his logical conclusion'. He wanted to redeem the individual by surrendering the self to the will. In this ecstatic fusion he believed himself to be Dionysos. Nietzsche was a contemporary of Rimbaud, who called for murderers and the destruction of the social order. Rimbaud's super-realism (Surrealism) corresponded to Nietzsche's superman. Both influenced expressionism.

Both were often misunderstood. This explains why the spectre of totalitarianism appears in expressionist drama, even though on the surface it generally seems to be pacifist and socialist. This is the

STRINDBERG, AUGUST: *The Road to Damascus.* Sketch by Knut Ström. 1922

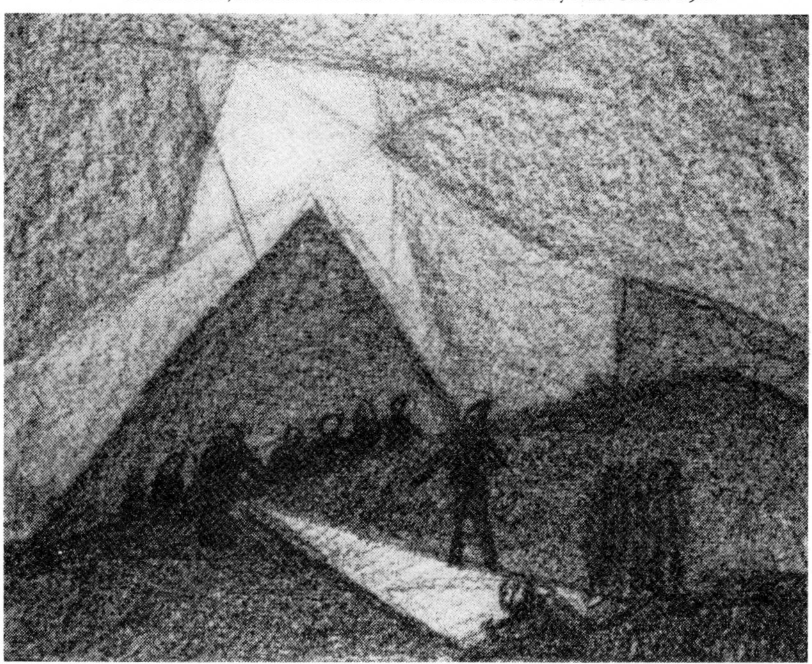

consequence of such expressionist tendencies as we find in the Futurist manifesto. Of the expressionist playwrights, Bronnen and Johst went directly over to German fascism.

The Nazis waged a campaign against intellect that recalls only too well the hostility towards intellect of many expressionist authors. Ludwig Klages propounded this ideology in *The Intellect as Enemy of the Soul.* The intellectual Gottfried Benn wrote in *A Double Life*, 'City, industrialization, intellectualism, all the shadows that the age has cast across my thoughts, all the forces of this century that I presented in my work – there are moments when all this tortured life is swallowed up, and nothing remains but plains and expanses, seasons, simple words; the people.'

In Johst, who relied entirely on his dramatic talent, 'Soul' was soon changed to 'Blood'. There had already been signs in Wedekind and Sorge of a weariness with the spirit and a flight into the physical and the sensual; other authors had gone as far as 'blood and earth'. In the name of 'life' they abandoned themselves to emotional irrationality. The death wish became a cult and suicide a central theme. Johst's *The Adolescent* is an 'ecstatic scenario' and dedicated to a young friend who had committed suicide. In *The Birth of Youth*, Bronnen wrote the sequel to his play *Parricide.* It contains sadistic and criminal elements and clearly reveals a fascist ideology.

Intellectualism and a hatred for intellect stand side by side in expressionist drama; voluptuous thoughts and forms next to bare structures, ecstasy next to analysis, idealism next to ideology. This begs the question whether the term 'Expressionism', as the concept of an era and style, is fitting in the normal sense.

The connection between individual expressionist artists is to be seen less in a uniform intention concerning style than a common denial of a naturalist conception of reality. This failure in the face of reality must be considered the fundamental reason for the ultimate collapse of expressionist drama.

For expressionist playwrights did not want merely to write differently, but also to live differently from ever before. But their claim that they would change reality was not fulfilled. Because of their tendency to ecstasy and their subjectivity they were not able to formulate any social programme. The utopias remained imaginary.

They demanded a 'new man'. But, in this message of salvation, they had overlooked all historical facts and the political potential of their age. In their rapturous and abstract hope for the 'new man', they may well have reacted with great sensitivity and in a spirit of rebellion to the destruction of civilization by war. But they did not produce a revolutionary, only an illusory blueprint for society.

Art in Revolt

That man's conceptions of 'I' and 'The World' had begun to waver since the turn of the century, that the First World War corresponded politically to a universal revolution – this all stemmed from developments which had already been evident throughout the nineteenth century and which were based on even earlier phenomena in their turn. But now, for the first time, this change was seen to be a radical revolution. Expressionist drama is part of this revolution. Thus far, it is relatively uniform, despite all its contradictions.

The representatives of all expressionist trends rejected the nineteenth century with its bourgeois attitudes, its positivistic view of the world, its scientific empiricism, philosophical materialism and empirical psychology. They rejected capitalism, the industrial revolution and bourgeois morality. Thus their attitude was to negate their age.

They fled into illusions or abstract ideals. The work of Georg Kaiser, in particular, appears as an attempt to rejuvenate idealism. Brecht realized and appreciated this. In his own work he probed the question of idealism for an answer. Here we do not find a 'moral condemnation of reality' which Günther Rühle has called 'a particular idealistic sport of the German mind.' For a hundred years, this

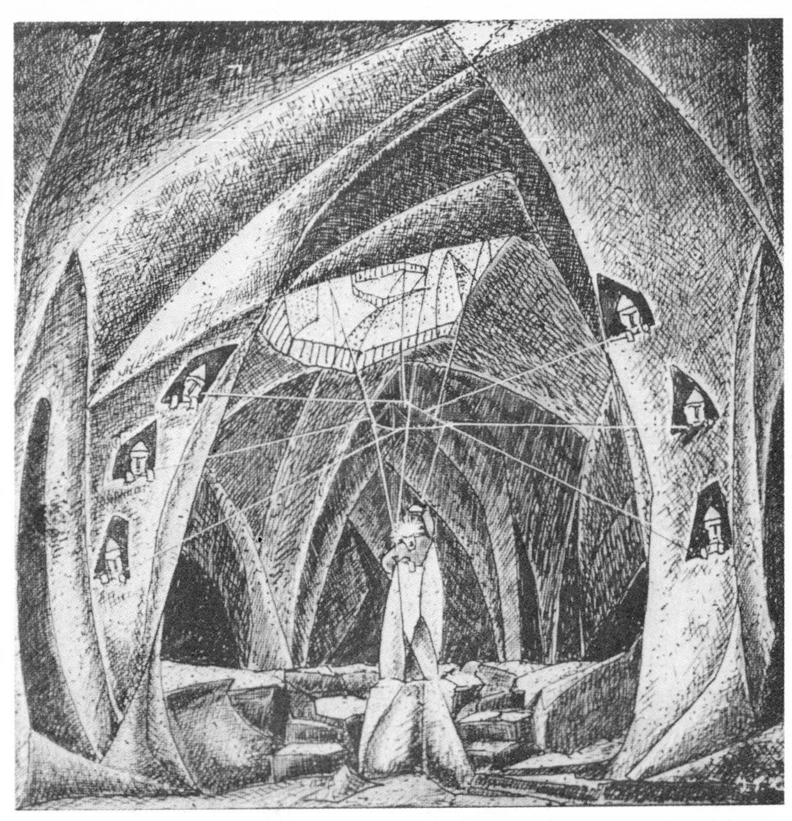

KAISER, GEORG: *Gas I.* Production by Leopold Jessner, sets by Karl Gröning (Stadttheater, Altona 1928)

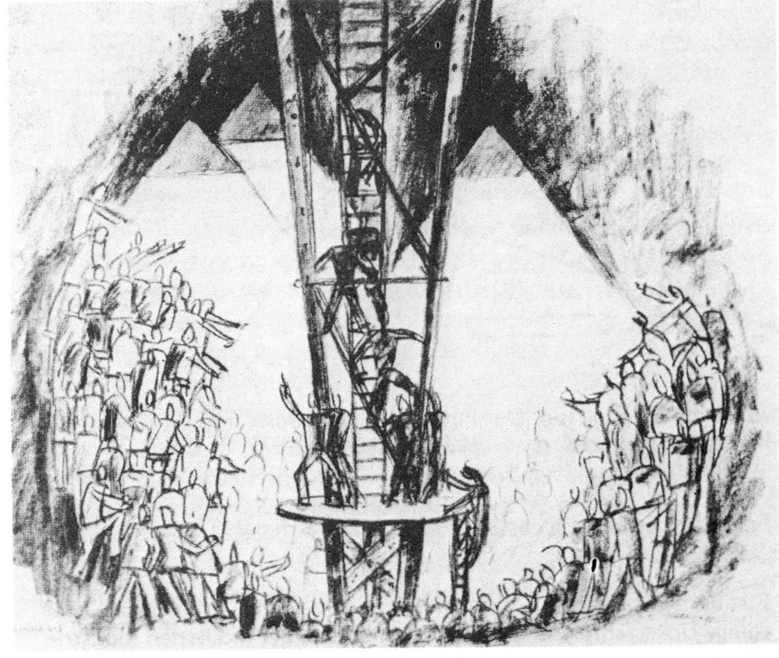

KAISER, GEORG: *Gas I.* Production by Erich Engel, sets by Johannes Schröder (Kammerspiele, Hamburg 1920)

spirit had refused to acknowledge materialism and Marxism, hence the dangerously irrational and mystic traits in their work.

Their liking for abstraction as a renunciation of reality originates in the position of the author in society; here too, historical developments peculiar to Germany are reflected. The writer nearly always lived in isolation. His social status was *petit bourgeois*, but as an intellectual he had no clear social rank or identity. He was painfully aware of this lack and in order to remove it, he withdrew into himself. Thus the artist's sufferings from social pressures have often, in the history of the German mind, led to an art that is an end in itself. The sphere of art seemed the only way of attaining freedom, and art was seen as redemption. The cult of aesthetics took on a religious character.

The Literary Tradition

The representatives of German literature in the late eighteenth century had striven for social unity in the formation of a German nation, and thus had tried to attract a public. This was the case with classicism, which evolved from the 'Storm and Stress' movement. But it found only one centre amongst the German petty states: Weimar. Here their cultural programme was drawn up. But it remained a utopia; it was too abstract, and Weimar itself too isolated. But the classicism after the 'Storm and Stress' was also a kind of resignation. The radical aesthetic tendencies in the 'Storm and Stress' may be called a non-intellectual anticipation of expressionism. But Schiller had already thwarted this tendency with classicism, by adding a moral theory to his revolutionary aesthetics. He is to blame for the moralizing tone of German literature.

This tradition affected German expressionism, and is reflected most clearly in Fritz von Unruh in whose work the formal desire for abstraction is encumbered by his concrete formulation of content and demands. Schiller still understood how to offset the load contained in his theoretical ideas by breathing life into his abstractions. He had grasped the antithetical functions of a play in a practical sense. He counterbalances the lack of the concrete – of realism – by the intellectual nature of dialogue instead of, as in expressionist drama – by emotive monologues. Nevertheless, qualities similar to Schiller's are to be found in the best expressionist playwrights – in the forerunner Wedekind, in Carl Sternheim and, above all, in Georg Kaiser.

End and Consequences of Expressionist Drama

Unlike most expressionist playwrights, who have long belonged to the past in the active Theatre, Wedekind, Sternheim and Kaiser are still put on frequently. But they are hardly discussed as expressionists. This is particularly true of Georg Kaiser who, more than anyone, explored expression as an element of the modern world, and who strove for a long time not to abandon the social theme.

We can also gather how removed from social reality expressionist drama was by the fact that it produced no comedies. It is society which is reflected most in comedy. As a result of the special evolution of society, Germany had always tended towards biting satire and vicious parodies with grotesque exaggeration and distortion, than towards realistic comedy. Grabbe demonstrates the truth of this statement. Wedekind and Sternheim seem to contradict this; but in fact their realistic parts can hardly be ascribed to expressionism. Admittedly Georg Kaiser, Ernst Toller and Walter Hasenclever wrote numerous comedies but they already had expressionism behind them when they turned to this genre.

None of the expressionist authors remained so. Even that part of the movement that seemed most set on a revolution in aesthetics has had no lasting effect. Indeed the problems of the new aesthetic were hardly ever discussed thoroughly. This lack is also due to an absence of a strong awareness of reality. The desire for an aesthetic revolution failed because the expressionists also rejected historical reality.

It is true that expressionist drama cannot be understood purely from an aesthetic viewpoint in the modern world. As a result too many authors between 1910 and 1925 wanted to attack, at least in some of their works, too many concrete, even politically topical trends in society. The activist dramatists, above all, wanted to set up aims for society and combat the lethargy of traditional views on destiny. But their good intentions bore no relation to possible external changes. Realist politics followed in their wake; nihilism became widespread but was only dealt with in art by a few, Benn for example. But Benn was not a playwright.

We are rarely successful either in feeling what we merely know or in shaping what we feel, and this dilemma characterizes nearly all dramatic styles in expressionist theatre. The authors themselves clearly felt this. Hence their hectic striving after communication, their naïve lack of familiarity with the world, the strange mixture of religion and politics. Ernst Toller flatly denied any distinction between religious and political writing.

The expressionist generation was in the end blind to its political causes and consequences in spite of having been moulded by the experience of the First World War. It did not go beyond an emotional pacifism. Many intelligent analyses of the war by expressionists only superficially contradict this thesis, for the progressive conclusions they drew were anarchistic, utopian programmes without any relation to realist politics. The influence of these utopian tendencies lasted from 1917 to 1919, i.e. from the Russian October Revolution to the Bavarian Republic. When they failed, the decay of expressionism began. Rubiner, Frank and Becher became communists; Unruh and Toller turned away from revolt by the people; Johst and Bronnen became National Socialists, while Toller, Kaiser and Hasenclever wrote comedies.

Expressionism, but especially expressionist drama in Germany was, with all its contradictions, its demands, its forms and the progress of its development, the manifestation of a period of radical change. Admittedly its authors did not properly analyse the problems of their age, and they could contribute nothing to a solution. But they expressed them so unanimously and so forcibly that their work is still relevant to us today as the clearest mirror of their age.

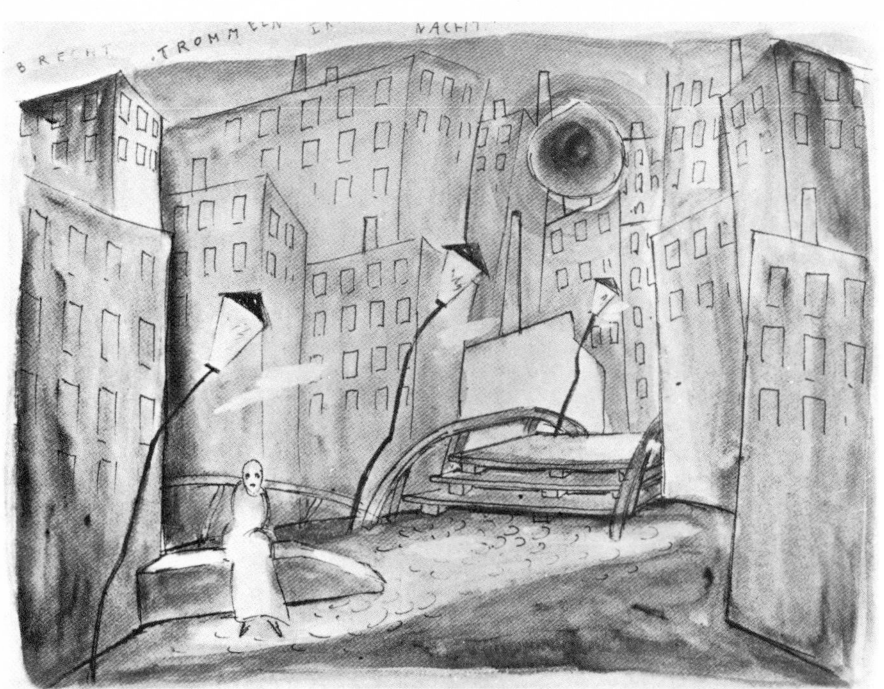

REIGBERT, OTTO: Sets for *Drums in the Night* (Trommeln in der Nacht) by Bertold Brecht, production by Otto Falckenberg (Kammerspiele, Munich 1922)

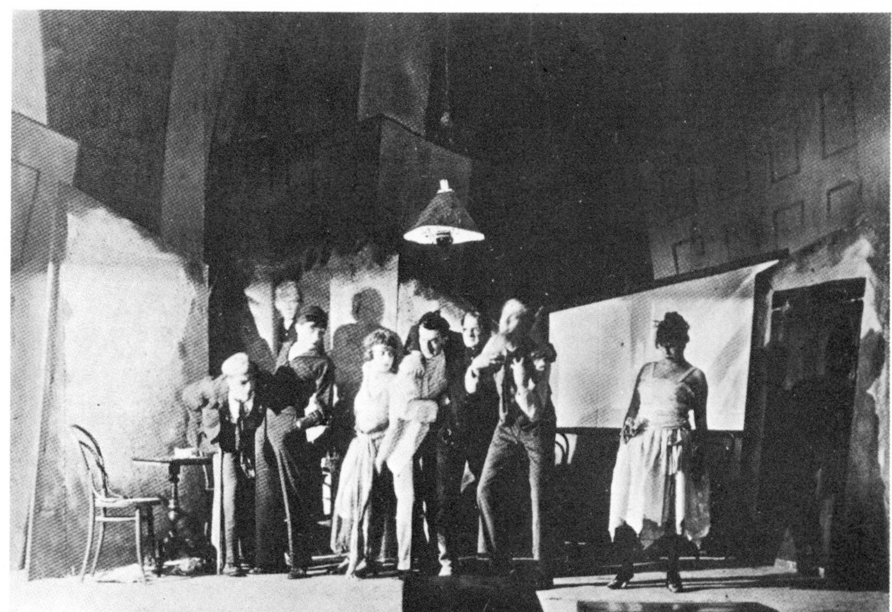

REIGBERT, OTTO: Sketch for *Drums in the Night* (Trommeln in der Nacht) by Bertold Brecht, production by Otto Falckenberg (Kammerspiele, Munich 1922)

BRECHT, Bertold (Augsburg, 10.2.1898 – Berlin, 14.8.1956). His parents were Swabian, his father was the director of a paper factory in Augsburg from 1914. Brecht studied in the secondary school there. Poems by him were published from 1914 on, in an Augsburg newspaper. He reacted patriotically at first to the outbreak of war but soon became a pacifist. He led his own life, away from the bourgeois world of his home, in a circle of friends to which Caspar Neher belonged. He studied medicine in Munich from 1917. In 1918 he organized a private commemoration for Wedekind. He also wrote the first version of *Baal.* He had contacts with literary circles from 1919 on, and only continued his studies formally. Lion Feuchtwanger was now one of his friends. He wrote the play *Spartacus* whose title became *Drums in the Night.* He wrote theatre reviews for the left-wing socialist review *Will of the People*, in Augsburg and appeared with Karl Valentin in Munich. In 1921 he started *In the Swamp.* In 1922 he tried to establish himself in Berlin. He got to know Arnolt Bronnen amongst others. The same year *Drums in the Night* was first performed in Munich. Herbert Ihering awarded him the Kleist prize for it.

New plays followed and were put on stage thick and fast. He moved to Berlin in 1924. He became a playwright at the 'German Theatre' with Zuckmayer. He worked on *A Man's A Man* which still lies within the radius of expressionism; this is not true for all his subsequent works. At the latest, his adherence to revolutionary Marxism is evident in the first production of *A Preventive Measure* (1930) in Berlin. He had his first difficulties with the censor in 1932; and in 1933 came the first prohibition on a performance. After the fire in the Reichstag he left Germany with his family (he married Helene Weigel in 1928). He reached Zürich via Prague and Vienna, and later went to Denmark. He now used his works for a long time to combat Fascism. He stayed in England, travelled to Russia, and spoke in 1935 at the International Writers' Congress in Paris. He also spent time in the U.S.A. before he moved to Sweden from Denmark because of the danger from the war; from there he went to Finland and, in 1941, to New York. He did not leave the U.S.A. until 1947. That year he flew to Zürich.

Since he was refused entry to West Germany, he went to East Berlin via Prague with a Czech passport. He worked producing his own plays first in the German Theatre, but founded the 'Berlin Ensemble' in 1949 (at first within the German Theatre). Brecht also sought Austrian citizenship which he later got. He led the Berlin ensemble (the Theatre on the Schiffbauerdamm) to world fame (until his death, in 1956) as producer, theoretician, playwright and 'teacher'.

Brecht was one of the very few authors who followed the changes in politics and society precisely and attentively; and who became committed in an intelligent and concrete way without losing perspective and involving himself in day-to-day politics. This is not the place to outline his whole oeuvre. Of his plays, *Baal* is influenced in one way by expressionism in its structure and speech, but on the other hand exposes the idealistic weaknesses of expressionist drama to criticism and even parody.

He wrote it in 1918. Its content betrays nothing of the significance of this year. It deals instead with the experiences, debauches and adventures of a young poet and his friends. Nature, as the setting but also the countersetting, is heightened lyrically and emotionally. Everything that is anti-bourgeois and anti-social is suffused with romantic melancholy. The difficulties that this play faced in every performance hitherto, are precisely the difficulties of intensity interpreted purely as a taste for life. Here seems to lie its connection with expressionist drama, 'seems' because in reality this connection, if there ever actually was one, is already past. *Baal* is, in fact, if we look at one of the reasons for the play being written, none other than Johst's *Lonely Man*, admittedly parodied. *Baal*, which is Brecht's first contact with expressionism, has already gone beyond it in a way which is as yet quite non-political. Drinking, love affairs, infidelity, homosexuality, anti-social acts of violence, beauty, savagery, and finally, futility combine to create an early play which the author later claimed lacked wisdom – but from which he only wished to detach himself 'with respect'.

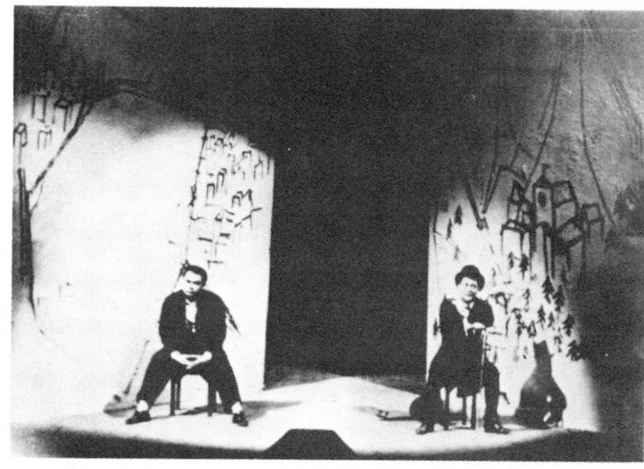

BRECHT, BERTOLD: *Baal.* Production by Brecht and Homolka, sets by Caspar Neher (Deutsches Theater, Berlin 1926).

BRONNEN, Arnolt (Vienna, 19.8.1895 – Berlin, 12.10.1959). Bronnen was born in 1895 in Berlin, an illegitimate son in a bourgeois household; he was later legally acknowledged by the secondary school teacher and dramatist Ferdinand Bronnen as his son. He was influenced by Wedekind and Gustav Wyneken's review *The Beginning.* He found his subject in the theme of an independent youth. His first writings were naturalistic and contained Viennese local colour. The attention of Franz Pfemfert *(Die Aktion)* brought Bronnen into close contact with expressionism. As a schoolboy he wrote the play *The Right to Youth* in 1912. This was the origin of *Parricide* followed by *The Birth of Youth.*

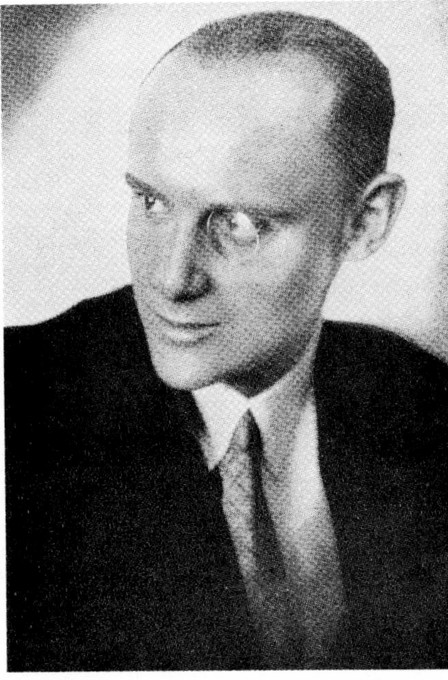

BRONNEN, ARNOLT: *Portrait*

In 1918, while an Italian prisoner, he wrote the one act play *Attack on God* which he later burnt. The attack on God was the anarchy of the soldier, amid the chaos of world war massacre, who begs for a vision of Christ; war interpreted through expressionist eyes. When he rewrote it for Sturm-Patrull, the religious element was removed. His abandonment of expressionism is here hinted at. This became evident in *Excesses* (also begun in captivity, finished in 1921). It involved Bronnen in scandal. From now on he wrote books of worldly naturalism – the world of racketeers, the post-war age, sexual and revolutionary anarchy.

He came into contact with Brecht who began rehearsing *Parricide* in 1922. Brecht abandoned it because he could not agree stylistically with Agnes Strauß and Heinrich George. Up till then Bronnen had been a business employee for Wertheim in Berlin. *Excesses* gave him independence. In 1923 he rewrote an old play *Betrayal* as *Anarchy in Sillan.* In 1924 he wrote *The Battle of the Catalauni*, a war play. Alexander is the hero of the one-man play *Journey to the East Pole*; sometimes he is king, sometimes explorer. In their final search for identity, they fight with death, which cannot be avoided but which grants immortality to Alexander's ambitions. *The Rhine Rebels* (1924), and the comedy, *Reparation* (1926) are topical plays; they defend a policy of national resistance, that remained Bronnen's theme in both stories and novels. Bronnen had become a right-wing radical and became a National Socialist (Tucholsky: 'a failed left-winger, disguised as a fascist').

While a playwright for the radio he had troubles with the Reich's broadcasting service which finally led to his dismissal (1935). In *N* (1935), a play about Napoleon, Bronnen criticized the regime of terror. He was excluded from the Reich Ministry of Culture because he could not produce proof of Aryan descent. He was aryanized 'from above' and survived the war. He changed his politics yet again – became a communist, was a mayor in Austria and then went to the D.D.R. In 1954 he published his autobiography in the form of a court case against himself. *Arnolt Bronnen: for the record, a contribution to the History of the Modern Writer.*

Apart from the plays cited above *Michael Kohlhaas* (1929), *Gloriana* and *The Last Judgement* should also be mentioned. *Parricide* was first performed on 24.2.1922 in the Frankfurt Theatre.

Bronnen wrote this play in 1913. It is more radical than Sorge's and Hasenclever's father–son dramas written at the same time. This applies to the form as well, so that it was said of him that the crime of the schoolboy Walter Fessel has neither social nor structural motives, but is purely an attempt to glorify himself in myth. This is only partially true, as Bronnen's work is not so clearly autobiographical as those of the other two authors. The strength of the form has overshadowed the most important part of the content. In this sense the play is indeed 'structural' just as it is socially motivated in another sense. We are confronted with a family that does not have enough room to live. In the house of the writer Ignaz Fessel they cannot move, stand, breathe or lie down, let alone be creative. Walter Fessel shares his desk with his father, his mother earns money sewing, the younger son is aggressive and spoiled. Walter constantly witnesses his parents' sex life. This makes him homosexually inclined towards a friend, and he rejects his mother's lustful advances towards him. Walter reacts to his crudely drunken father with all his petty bourgeois ambitions by murdering him. The mother lusts after him even more than before. Walter takes his leave of her in a brusque outburst, a hymn-like escape into a freedom, the nature of which remains unknown. But before this, we have seen a drama that seems new and powerful in its rejection of egotistic monologue and rapturous utopias.

GOERING, Reinhard (Schloss Biberstein, near Fulda, 23.6.1887 – Jena, 14.11.1936). Reinhard Goering was born in 1887 near Fulda. His family circumstances were distressing: both his parents committed suicide. Goering had psychopathic tendencies. He became a doctor (after studying in Jena, Berlin, Munich, Paris and Bonn). He contracted tuberculosis when a military doctor and had to go to Davos for several years shortly after the outbreak of war. There he wrote *Sea Battle* his first play, which won him the Kleist prize. In 1919 he wrote *Scapa Flow*; the play takes place on the German and English flagships. Lament and the suffering of war on one, the exultation of victory on the other. This is a dramatic picture, not expressionist drama any more. The play *The First Man* (1917) contains symbolic traits which go beyond expressionism; an egocentric and anarchic medieval priest is defeated by the socially and morally tight-knit forces of society. *The Second* is a conjugal tragedy between two couples. *The Deliverers* depicts two old and dying men who realize, when they witness the love of a couple, that a conscious surrender to the moment is the meaning of life. Karl Otten sees an anticipation of Samuel Beckett in this surrealist play. The austerity of the language is indeed no longer expressionist, but the declaration of a new awareness of existence, tinged with Buddhism. It also expresses Goering's tragically divided self (because of this he could never settle as a doctor for long in one place).

In *Captain Scott's Expedition to the South Pole* (1929), the race to the pole between Scott and Amundsen is depicted by the tragic chorus with the action (for which Goering received the Kleist prize). But the play is more like dramatic reportage and stylistically belongs to 'New Objectivity'. Goering's depressions worsened after illness and serious operations until there was no way out: he committed suicide in 1936.

The first performance of *Sea Battle* took place on 10.2.1918 in the Royal Theatre in Dresden. Scandal ensued; Max Reinhardt's production in Berlin (the same year) brought success.

Since most expressionist playwrights wanted to avoid too close a contact with events in case the art form was endangered by taking a wrong turning towards historicism, Goering's play *Sea Battle* has been considered by many authors to be one of the revolutionary plays of expressionism. This is mainly due to the fact that there is a mutineer in the play. But there is no rebellion, nor is a revolutionary programme evolved. The play has no one direction. The subject matter is turned into tragedy.

The sea battle took place on May 31st, 1916 at Skagerrak. Goering's drama dates from 1917. Seven sailors are going into battle in the gun turret of a cruiser. The audience witnesses their conversations, memories and visions, also battle and death. There is no real 'action', hence the dramatic unity of an extreme situation. The dramatic force is prepared by being enclosed in the gun turret which creates a sense of existential isolation. The sailors feel themselves to be mere cogs in a huge machine. There is something ineluctable and tragic in the sense of the ancients, about them.

Goering takes this into account in his use of language, in an antique, stylized speech with wailing and cries of anguish; the 'classical' repetition of the lament is their response to an external fate. The sailors are powerless to do anything, they can only question the sense of their sacrifice. One, the 'mutineer' can no longer convey his opinions convincingly, faced with the senselessness of war. Before he can be called to account, the battle has begun: 'He still hasn't done anything and it's already upon him.'

Goering has not manufactured a heroic play about individuals out of the theme of war, but written an expressionist play, the characters as functions of the dramatic idea are linked to it musically and by abstraction. And the idea behind the play is to portray the war in one inescapable situation. This already tragic situation reaches a pitch of starkness and terror when all the sailors lose their human features behind gas masks in their fight to the death. But the situation is not really developed.

The evolution – and here we find a political statement by Goering – lies not in the battle, but in the construction of armoured cruisers.

HASENCLEVER, Walter (Aachen, 8.7.1890 – Les Milles (France), 21.6.1940). He was born in Aachen, in 1890, the son of a doctor.

His childhood and adolescence were moulded by early conflicts with his strict, arch-conservative father and an early interest in modern literature and ideas. He studied law in Oxford and Lausanne, but occupied himself, as in his later studies, almost entirely with literature, philosophy and history. In 1909 he wrote *Nirvana*, a critique of life in play form.

He continued his studies in Leipzig. He made friends with Kurt Pinthus, Ernst Rowohlt, Kurt Wolff, and Franz Werfel. He became a member of the literary circle in Leipzig which was the germ of expressionism. In 1913 he wrote the play *The Eternal Conversation*, in 1914 *The Son* (which won the Kleist prize in 1917). In 1915 he was called up, first as interpreter in the postal censorship department in Ghent, then as staff orderly for the army group under Mackensen on the East Front, in Galicia and Macedonia he finished *The Deliverer* and the anti-war tragedy, *Antigone* 1916–7 in a military sanatorium in Dresden. He won the Kleist prize for *Antigone.*

After his stay in the sanatorium he lived mainly in Berlin from 1917 to 1924. His play *Mankind* ends his expressionist phase. He then had a mystic period when he studied Swedenborg. He wrote the plays *The Hereafter, Gobseck* and the film *The Plague.* In 1924 he went to Paris as a correspondent for the Berlin *8.00 p.m. Evening News.* This marked his turn to comedy. The play *Murder* is transitional. He now wrote the comedies: *A Better*

Master and *There are Marriages in Heaven*. In 1929 he set up house in Berlin and travelled in Europe and Morocco. His next comedy is *Napoleon's Attack*. He

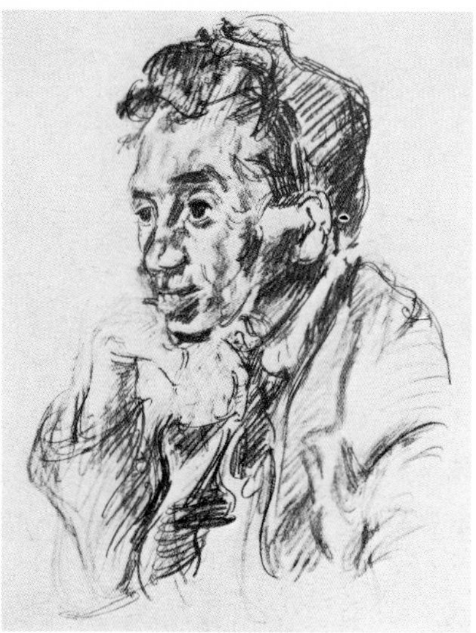

KOKOSCHKA, OSKAR: *Portrait of Walter Hasenclever*. 1918

went to Hollywood in the summer of 1930. He lived in exile from 1933 to 1940, first mainly on the French Riviera and on several occasions in London. He wrote the play *Munchhausen*, and *Conjugal Comedies*.

He lived on his own estate near Florence from 1937 on, was arrested in 1938, fled to London and returned to the Riviera. He wrote the comedy *Conflict in Assyria*. In 1939 he was twice arrested in Antibes, and in May interned in Les Milles camp. He took poison on June 20th, and died on the 21st.

He wrote more for the stage than is indicated here; only the plays which mark turning points artistically and biographically have been mentioned. He has himself described his metamorphoses in several autobiographical sketches and the autobiographical novel *Error and Passion*. The first performance of *The Son*, took place on 30.9.1916 in the German Provincial Theatre in Prague, the first (complete) German production of *Mankind* was on 15.5.1920 in the Small Theatre of the same house. *The Son* was performed before Sorge's *The Beggar*; it was therefore considered for a long time to be the first German expressionist drama. This is incorrect but it is indeed a drama, whereas Sorge already anticipated the end of expressionist drama in his first play.

Hasenclever's hero – *The Son* – is twenty and held prisoner by his father. He has a governess. Literature has to take the place of judgement and experience for him, but also protects him from suicide. In the character of his friend we encounter Strindberg's 'stranger' and Wedekind's 'masked man' again. His friend symbolizes 'life'. The son makes ecstatic 'vitalist' demands to his father. He wants freedom, but this amounts to freedom from exams and private teachers, to life instead of school, to actresses and champagne. His father replies with a box on the ears. This friend smuggles him to a 'Banquet for the Enjoyment of Pleasure' where he meets the temptress 'the great *cocotte*'. His father reappears and the son reacts to his whip with a revolver. His father meets his death accidentally when he is hit; the son, who has grown up without a mother, recognizes the true love of a girl too late. His parting from her is the end of the play.

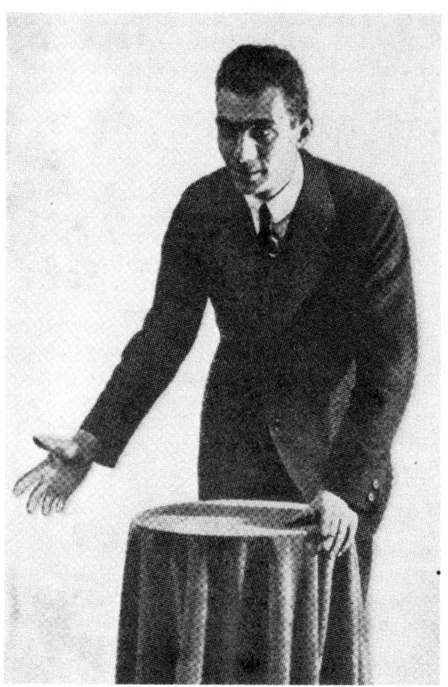

HASENCLEVER, WALTER: *Portrait*

This work also rejects realistic psychology. It sets 'forces' against each other, so that the father has no clear social outline, even though we learn that he is a committed doctor and is genuinely concerned about his son's future. His fault is not exactly sadism but the error of the bourgeois who shows a perverted narrow mindedness. The son's revolt is spectacular. This play is better drama than Sorge's *The Beggar* but encumbered with the same ideas.

JOHST, Hanns (Seerhausen, Saxony, 8.7.1890). He was born in Saxony in 1890. The long, aimless road of the melancholy young Johst is described in several autobiographical sketches and the novel *The Beginnings* 1917. When seventeen he was a nurse at Bodelschwingh's, wanted to become a missionary, then a doctor. He went to Vienna, Munich, Leipzig and Berlin; studied medicine, philosophy, aesthetics, and became an actor. He volunteered in 1914. In the Third Reich he became president of the Chamber of Culture, and for a short time also director of the Berlin State Theatre. Until 1935 he flooded the literary market; and then wrote nothing until 1955 (a novel). After the Second World War he went to Bavaria. His transition from naturalism to expressionism had the same roots as his path to national socialism (which he also supported in theoretical writings): the search to raise the material world to irrational dimensions.

Johst was one of the most successful playwrights, both in and after expressionism. Apart from his narrow, and not entirely 'genuine' expressionism, his work is moulded by religious and national beliefs.

The first performance of *The Adolescent* took place on 13.3.1919 in the Hamburg Thalia Theatre. This work is an 'ecastic scenario' (the subtitle) in prose. A good half dozen, loosely connected scenes show the development of an adolescent, who is pure and wants to change mankind. This programme is described as a 'rebellion of the spirit'. Parents and teachers have failed with him. He is chased out of school, gets into prison, and again out into 'the world'. But he does not find any 'men'. Student lodgings, a brothel, a station, a clinic for nervous diseases, a hotel and the hospital are the stages before the longed-for grave. The dead youth now a man – *The Awakening of Spring* here provided inspiration – finally leaps over the cemetery wall towards freedom and a new life. 'The spirit rebels in the individual personality, but as soon as he sees his personal actions, for which he needs the masses as a witness, sanctioned, he will always be the sorcerer's apprentice who does not know how to exorcise the powers he has called up.' Johst wrote this in 1928, the play in 1916. Had he written that sentence in 1916, he would have been a prophet. But in reality his (undoubted) dramatic talent always followed trends. *The Adolescent* the first part of a trilogy with the Grabbe play *The Lonely Man – The Downfall of a Man* (1917) and *The King* (1920) is thus only really superficially connected with expressionism. Johst was already only a satellite of expressionism at the beginning of the movement, a satellite who was to become a supporter of the Third Reich.

KAISER, Georg (Magdeburg, 25.11.1878 – Ascona, 4.5.1945). He was born in Magdeburg. His father was an insurance broker and came, like his mother from a peasant family. In 1894 Kaiser left secondary school in revolt. He became active in anti-bourgeois cultural societies, began to write and for a few weeks was an apprentice in a bookshop. Then he changed to the import and export business, read Plato and Nietzsche,

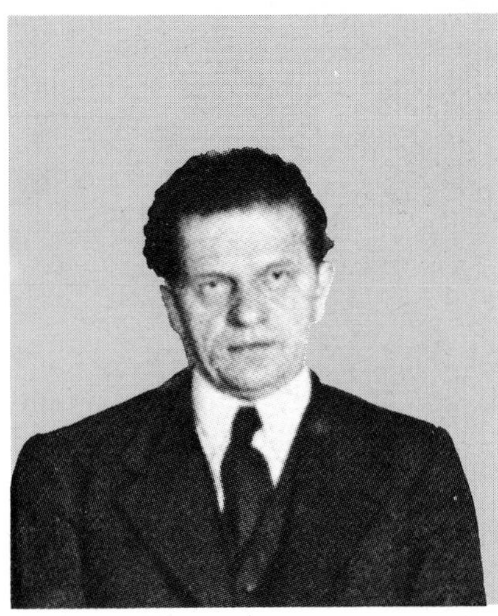

JOHST, HANNS: *Portrait*

played the 'cello and football. 1898 he went to South America as a coal trimmer, then was employed by A.E.G. in Buenos Aires. He read Schopenhauer, Dostoievsky, was enthusiastic about Wagner, got to know the country on long rides, caught malaria, and returned via Africa, Spain and Italy to Germany in 1901. He found it difficult to re-adjust to Europe; his constant changes of abode testify to this.

His first important writing period begins after his encounter with the beginnings of expressionism. Between 1908 and 1918 he lived alternately in Seeheim and Weimar. He did not become a soldier. His military service was deferred on health grounds, but he worked occasionally for the Red Cross. He gained experience of Concert and Theatre in the cities of Hesse. His first publications were on a private press; from 1911 S. Fischer Verlag became interested in him and in 1915 he had his first performance (*The Case of the Schoolboy Vehgesack*, New Stage, Vienna). In 1916 he got to know Gustav Landauer in Italy; he obtained the producer and theatrical director Arthur Hellmer for Kaiser. He produced Kaiser's first big success *The Burghers of Calais* in Frankfurt in 1917.

In 1918 Kaiser was in financial difficulties. In a lawsuit that has become famous he defended the way of life of the 'genius' which conflicts with bourgeois norms. When the verdict went against him, his family was ruined. Nevertheless, he achieved his second great period of work between 1921 and 1923.

From 1915 on he saw forty first productions, and his plays were put on all over the world, far beyond Europe. He knew numerous writers and important theatrical figures. He travelled much and reacted to the political evolution of the Weimar republic towards Nazism by an anti-fascist and socialist commitment.

A political campaign against him began in 1933. He was excluded from the Prussian Academy of Art, and his books were burnt. He wrote anti-fascist pamphlets, which were distributed by workers in Berlin-Siemensstadt. Kaiser fled from the Gestapo to Amsterdam and later to Switzerland.

But life was made dificult for him there. He constantly changed his place of abode, and tried in vain to get an entry permit into the U.S.A. He wrote poetry, film scripts and novels as well as plays. From 1941 on he turned to the Bible and Greek drama for material. His life became even more restless after 1942, and in 1945 he died in Ascona.

This Socialist and opponent of Hitler was not a Marxist, but rather a disciple of Schopenhauer. In the conflict between his humanist-socialist commitment and his extreme subjectivity he was a typical representative of the attitude of mind of German expressionism. But his importance goes beyond expressionism; he also outlived its short era (1910–1925). Between 1917 and 1933 he was a 'playwright of the day' who produced both effect and scandal; as regards the stylization of his biography, he was also fond of hybrid disguises. He was also a writer who distanced himself more and more from reality, came nearer to classical tradition, both in form and content and ended on a note of resignation. He was also a productive writer of comedies in which he continued to exercise an influence. He was separated from Brecht who respected him by the continuation of an idealistic trend in German literature which has not yet, at least theoretically, been completely exhausted.

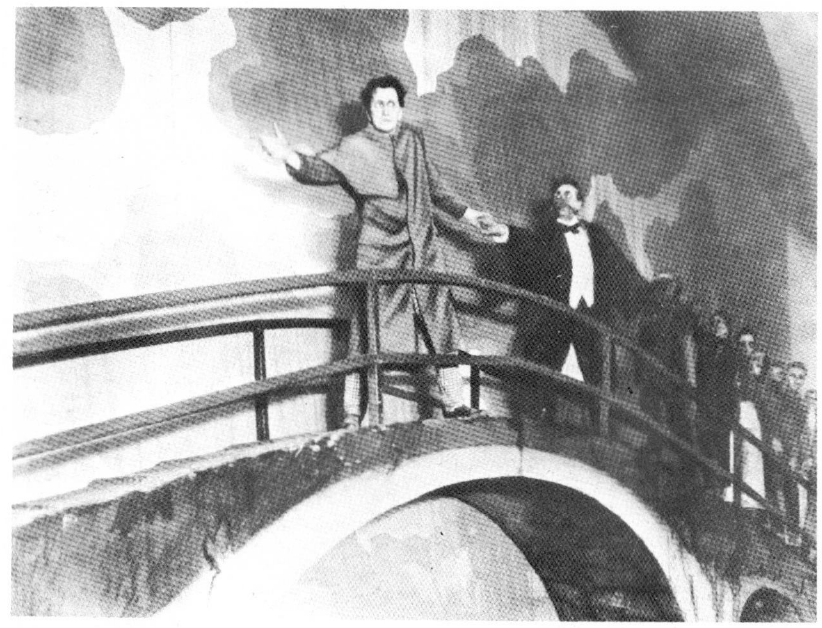

KAISER, GEORG: *Hölle, Weg, Erde.* Production by Viktor Barnowsky, sets by Cesar Klein (Lessing-Theater, Berlin 1920)

Kaiser was not able to portray the absolute nature of his socialist involvement– in which he was also typical of expressionism – in his dramas. The emotion of his *Burghers of Calais* must seem as strange today as the backward-looking utopia of his 'Gas' plays, in which he tried to come to terms with industrial society. We cannot do justice to Kaiser's wide ranging thought and creative powers in a short space. Nevertheless, *From Morn to Midnight* typifies his theatre.

In *The Burghers of Calais*, a concept of self-sacrifice, which we can no longer accept without argument, had triumphed. In *From Morn to Midnight* the attempt at rejuvenation fails. A bank cashier revolts; he hates the real world and rushes through it from one stage to the next (a typical dramatic effect of expressionist theatre). He searches ecstatically for an absolute, he embezzles money to break out of his narrow situation, is disillusioned but cannot turn back because of his crime. He flees into a (symbolic) field of snow to cover his tracks, meets Death, carries on a conversation with him in vain, plunges on and offers high prizes in the six-day cycle race, in which he is only concerned with universal 'movement', the vital and the extraordinary. The frenzied audience is subdued by the entrance of 'His Highness'. The cashier withdraws his offer, disgusted by the bourgeois tameness of the audience. He seeks his brothers in the Salvation Army Hall. Here people confess, are reborn and purified – so the cashier thinks. He confesses too, throws his money into the crowd, and then sees how they fight over it. Everything collapses beneath him. The only person he still trusts is the girl who brought him into contact with these people. But she calls the police; she wants the reward offered for the capture of the embezzler. The cashier shoots himself.

This play is very different from other expressionist plays about the quest for salvation; the religious symbolism is no longer merely a characteristic but a vehicle for a dynamic succession of scenes which is closer to the 1920s and the fascination with 'Americanism' than to the confessions of the 'O mankind' poets.

MARTIN, KARL HEINZ: Extract from the film *From Morn to Midnight* (Von Morgens bis Mitternachts). From Georg Kaiser

KORNFELD, Paul (Prague, 11.12.1889 – Lodz (Poland), 10.1.1942). Paul Kornfeld, born in Prague in 1889 came to Frankfurt in 1916 to join the circle of authors and producers at the theatre there, which was important for expressionism. He was a playwright for a while with Reinhardt, later in Darmstadt. After his expressionist tract *The Genius and the Psychological Man*,

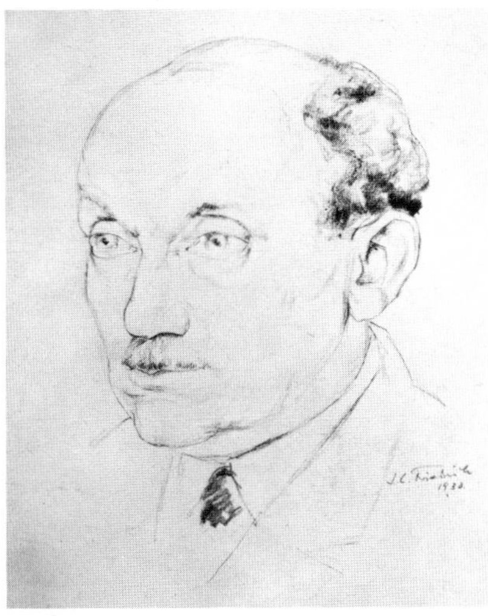

KAISER, GEORG: Portrait by J. C. Friedrich. 1930

and his expressionist plays *The Seduction* and *Heaven and Hell*, his contemporaries expected him to write 'the' expressionist drama. Though with similar outlook, he seemed a more powerful dramatist than Sorge, and more 'intellectual' than Hasenclever, Bronnen or Johst.

But these expectations were not fulfilled and Kornfeld turned to comedy; he parodied his own expressionism in *Kilian or the Yellow Rose.* He left Germany in 1933 and returned to Prague. In 1941 he was arrested, and killed in 1942 in the extermination camp at Lodz.

His drama is more important in the history of the theatre than of literature. *The Seduction* and *Heaven and Hell* were masterpieces of expressionism scenically. The first performance of *The Seduction* was on 8.12.1917 in the Frankfurt Theatre.

The hero is called Hans Ulrich Bitterlich. He is the 'young man' typical of expressionism in the universal nature of his yearnings and his all embracing spirituality. He commits murder though not from conventional motives. His victim is Joseph, fiancé of the old maid Marie Veilchen. This murder, without a concrete motive corresponds to Kornfeld's anti-psychological dramatic theory. The crime is a symbol, only explicable by the mediocrity, the soullessness and the materialism of the victim. Bitterlich's 'spirituality' is in contrast to this; it has a profound effect on the public prosecutor and judge. Both want to acquit the young man. Bitterlich's mother tries to persuade her son to use this chance. But only the young girl Ruth Vogelfrei succeeds in 'abducting' him from prison. Bitterlich now wishes to embrace the whole world, overflow, find his brothers. The place of his mission is a vulgar festival in memory of a battle. There he is laughed at by 'the world'. Ruth's brother Wilhelm wants to bring his sister back into the bourgeois fold. He lures them into his father's house. Bitterlich is poisoned. Ruth and his mother can no longer help him, but as he dies he persuades Wilhelm to commit suicide. Marie Veilchen finds a new fiancé. Ruth dies after Bitterlich.

The plot lends itself to parody, for Kornfeld, in these fourteen scenes, has gone to the extremes of grotesqueness and absurdity. But the abstractions which, in the end, are the only result, prevent Kornfeld from portraying the pandemonium of the bourgeois world of his age. The characters are not concrete enough, and his outline of society too vague. But, above all, Bitterlich is, deep down, an undramatic personality without a fighting spirit. His 'adversaries' are affirmations rather than threats. The figures who support Bitterlich are essentially more concrete but they are more limited and do not have the interest of their author.

RUBINER, Ludwig (Berlin, 12.7.1881 – Berlin, 26.2.1920). Ludwig Rubiner lived mainly in Berlin and belonged to the circle of Pfemfert's *Aktion.* He died on February 26th, 1920 in Berlin. He considered himself a political writer, and he so consistently championed his idea of the individual's merging into society that, instead of giving an autobiographical sketch for Pinthus's anthology *The Twilight of Mankind*, he sent this terse note: 'Rubiner does not want a personal biography.' He believed that the enumeration, not only of deeds, but also of works and dates, originated in an arrogant and outmoded error of the individualistic world of 'dressing-gown' artists. He was convinced that only the anonymous, creative membership of society is of importance for the present and the future. He published several documentary works on the 'World Revolution' and founded the 'First Proletarian Theatre' with Holitscher and Karl-Heinz Martin in 1919.

His revolutionary play *Revolution without Violence* is indeed the most uncompromising one that expressionism produced. He deliberately rejected the 'miserable' viewpoint of the so-called pure artistic work. He was thus speaking as a political activist. His leaning towards abstract art, which was again politically motivated, was a vital link with expressionism: 'The characters of the play represent ideas. A work of ideas helps the age to reach its goal by setting reality itself as its ultimate goal beyond the age.'

KORNFELD, PAUL: *The Seduction* (Die Verführung). 1918. A scene with Fr Brod and H. Feldhauer

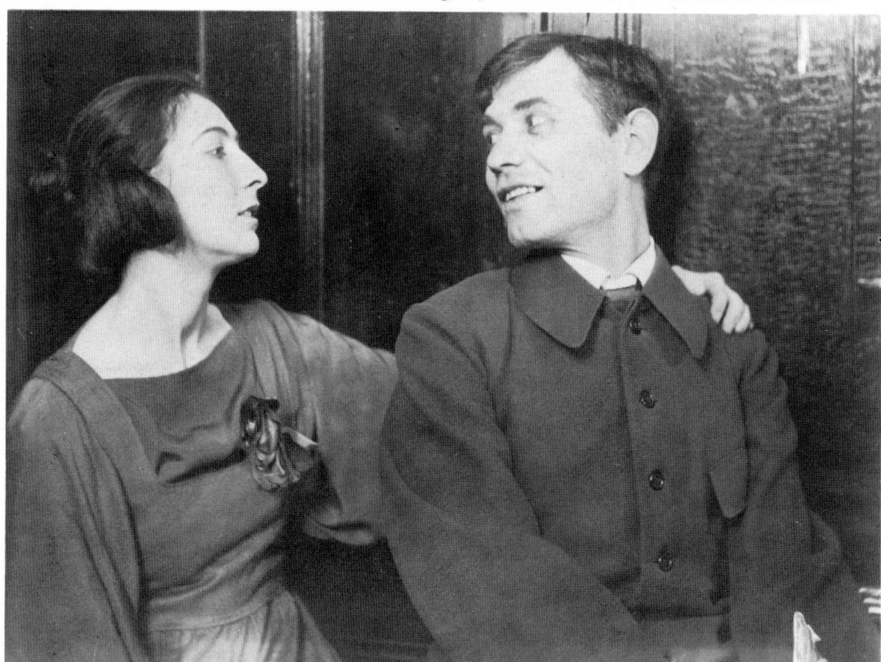

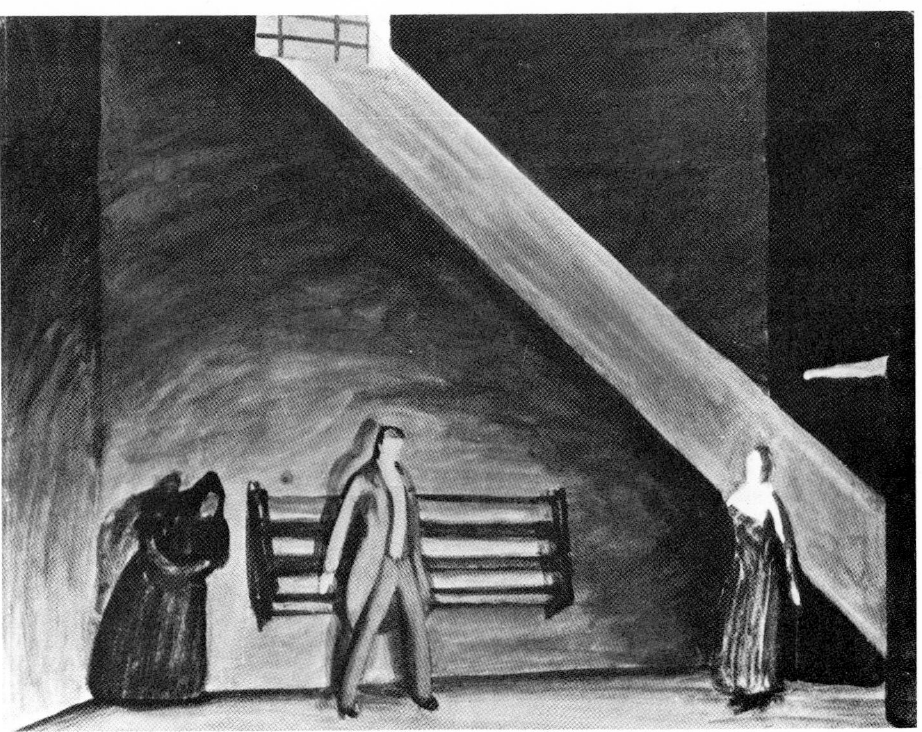

KORNFELD, PAUL: *The Seduction* (Die Verführung). Sketch by F. K. Delavilla, production by Gustav Hartung (Frankfurt-on-the-Main 1917)

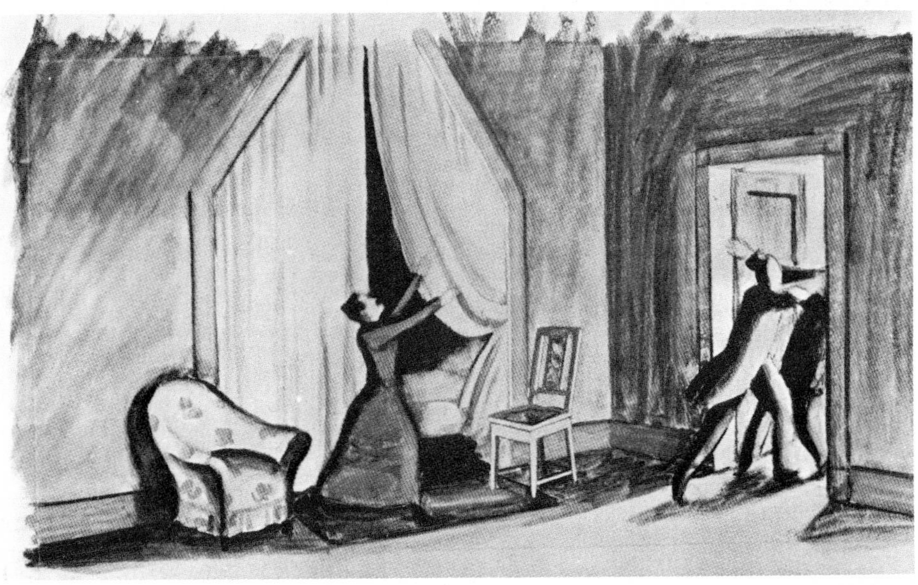

KORNFELD, PAUL: *The Seduction* (Die Verführung). Sketch by F. K. Delavilla, production by Gustav Hartung (Frankfurt-on-the-Main 1917)

Rubiner, who began the work in 1917 and finished it in 1918, depicts a powerless revolution in agitated scenes. The main characters, as so often in expressionist drama, are 'the man', 'the woman', etc. We are shown a society where oppression has provoked a rebellion. The representatives of the new ideas are arrested and terrorized. But the revolt succeeds without using violence. The prisoners win over their warders, the governor, and even avowed sadists.

The new community is now created in a town of light. But soon rifts and flaws appear. Crass materialism appears in the proletariat, and anarchism runs to excess. Persecution and destruction again occur. Rubiner, like Toller, here describes realistic events, but he disposes of reality, sets up a new utopia: the sacrifice of the bloodless revolutionaries is needed to create the true new man: History is outmoded. But the crucial weakness of the whole movement is evident even here in perhaps the purest revolutionary drama of expressionism: The passion for a utopia cannot hide the fact that it lacks concrete alternatives to the historical reality they have rejected.

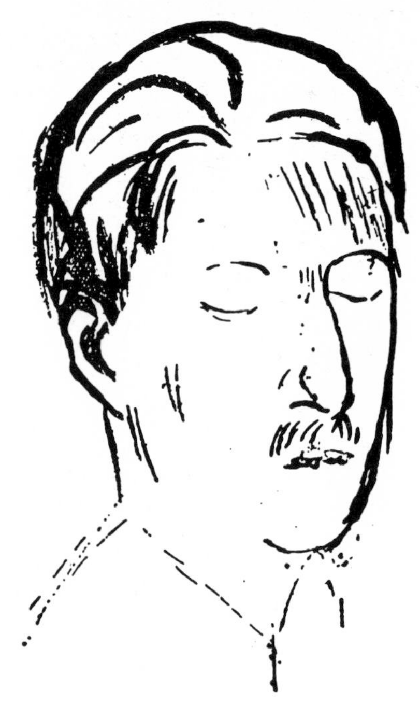

LEHMBRUCK, WILHELM: *Portrait of Rubiner. Die Aktion*, April, 1917.

SORGE, Reinhard Johannes (Berlin-Rixdorf, 29.1.1892–Ablincourt (France), 20.7.1916). Sorge was born in 1892 in Rixdorf near Berlin. His father was a municipal building inspector, who made a rich marriage. He went insane early and was put into an asylum in 1908. Sorge's secondary school education was interrupted by an apprenticeship in an ironware business and a bank. After his father's death his family moved to Jena (1909). In 1910 he left school without his *abitur*; he wanted to become a writer. Dehmel, Nietzsche, and Goethe to counterbalance them, influenced him greatly. *The Beggar* foreshadows his transformation to a religious, lyric dramatist. For Sorge, expressionism was only a prelude.

The Beggar was first performed on 23.12.1917 in the German Theatre in Berlin. Through the organization 'Young Germany' Sorge was awarded the Kleist prize for his symbolic work.

This, one of the earliest dramatic works of expressionism, is also one of the most typical if not *the* most. Awareness of vocation and a mission, and hymn-like, visionary sight prompt the author to hold up 'images of the future' to his corrupt age. Sorge mixed realistic depiction of pre-war Berlin with the emotive language of a Nietzsche.

At first sight the plot is confused, but in fact it has a very sophisticated structure. Typically for expressionism, the characters have no names. We see 'men', 'people in groups', 'secondary characters', 'silent characters' and 'creations of the author'. One might call it an expressionist revue, using the technique of short scenes, and with prologue and epilogue. Sorge does not use psychology, but instead an ecstatic lyricism. This play by an eighteen-year-old is dominated by youthful raptures; this was also typical of the start of a new theatre which considered itself to be the 'art of a new youth', and whose major theme was the generation gap.

The action of the play is lurid, though in fact there is not much to it. It is hastily sketched in prose. As the emotions of the characters become heightened, so the language is elevated by rhythm until finally it turns into verse and the play becomes a song of the song. The title, taken from Sorge's own poem 'Song of the Beggars' itself based on Maeterlinck's 'Treasure of the Poor', is the symbol for a 'great wailing', a 'beseeching and famished entreaty to heaven'. The writer (Sorge himself) wants his friend and patron to give him a theatre which will be a place of healing and sanctity for 'the elect', 'the oppressed' and 'the hungry', but his request is in vain.

This introduces the writer's family drama: we learn of the father's madness, before three crude scenes ensue, images of the dying world, of nothingness, of rumour. But the old world, the world of matter and materialism, is not yet dead. The father, a mad engineer, still wanders about the house beating a child's drum; he wants to exorcize demons and build a new world, having, as he believes, discovered the meaning of the canals on Mars. He calls himself God's master-builder, but writes only nonsense and, as he is dying, kills a bird because he needs its blood, instead of ink, which has run out. The son poisons his parents. The mother was eaten up by her love for her son, as the father was by his madness. But both deaths are not so much 'passion' as 'fulfilment'. Their murder is not a 'crime', it is larded with myth, and given a religious significance. Unconditional love is to banish morality and fear. The son binds himself to a new person. His pregnant mistress symbolizes the vitalist ideal of a new 'biological' life, but also of a metaphysical one: the 'New Man', the Messiah. However, the writer, Sorge, presenting himself at his desk, has reached cosmic and religious proportions which prevent him from formulating a concrete programme for the future. In this play, expressionist drama has destroyed itself 'in exemplary fashion'.

STERNHEIM, Carl (Leipzig, 1.4.1878 – Brussels, 3.11.1942). (William Adolf) Carl Sternheim was born in Leipzig in 1878. His father, who came from Frankfurt, was a banker and owner of the *Hannoverschen Tageblatt.* Sternheim was related to Heinrich Heine through him. His mother came from a Lutheran bourgeois family in Leipzig. He spent his first six years in Hanover. His father reviewed many performances of the Hanover Theatre in his own newspaper, and the young Sternheim gained his first impressions of the theatre at this time. This contact became closer when the family moved to Berlin where an uncle owned a theatre. Sternheim studied law, philosophy, the arts and aesthetics at six German universities. According to Sternheim himself, the Heidelberg philosopher, Heinrich Rickert, was especially important to him.

Since Sternheim was from a wealthy family, he could live independently as a writer. He married in 1900,

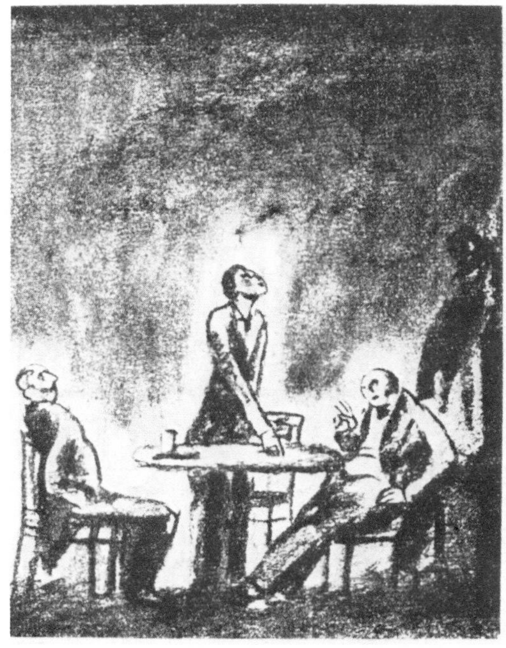

SORGE, REINHARD: *The Beggar* (Der Bettler). Sketch by E. Stern

separated four years later; he lived in Freiburg and Bremen, and occasionally in Italy. He got a divorce in 1906. They had a son who was hanged by the Nazis in 1944 as an opponent of Hitler's fascism.

In 1907 Sternheim married Thea Bauer, the daughter of a Rhine industrialist. He had a castle built near Munich, containing a theatre where his own plays were performed. He was also mayor of Pullach. He published the journal *Hyperion* with Franz Blei, and was friendly with Frank Wedekind, Heinrich Mann, Walter Rathenau and Max Reinhardt.

In 1913 Max Reinhardt's production of *Citizen Schippel* gave a breakthrough to Sternheim as a playwright. In 1911, *A Pair of Drawers* was first performed. Sternheim could not tolerate the criticisms that followed this performance and moved to Belgium. This was to be typical of his whole life: over-sensitive reactions to a public that he neverthless sought and provoked continually. He spent the First World War in Belgium. In 1918 the house he had bought there was commandeered. He went to St Moritz via Holland and later to Uttwil. He was in Dresden for a short time during the period of

Sternheim the dramatist is famous for his 'expressionist telegram style'. Fundamentally he does not belong to expressionism. He adopted and developed their essays in style but never felt himself to be one of the many writers of the 'revolutionary generation'; but rather a writer of critical comedies in imitation of Molière. His major theme was the Wilhelminian era. In his depictions of it he wanted to show that self-affirmation is only possible if the citizen adapts to his society.

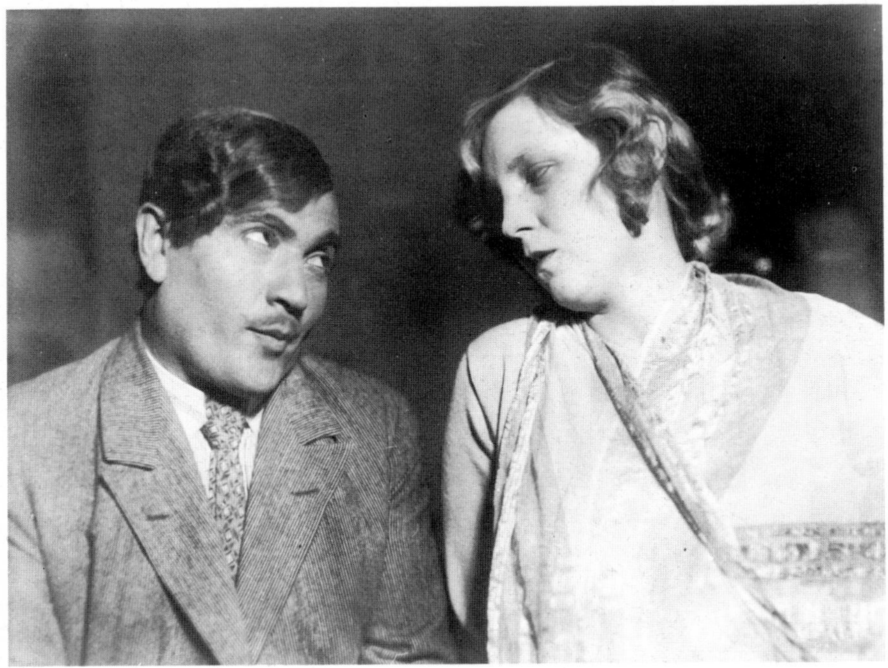

STERNHEIM, CARL: *The Bourgeois Schippel* (Bürger Schippel). A scene with Granach and H. Körber

inflation. In 1927 he was again divorced. Nervous illness prevented him from writing and he had to spend time in a sanatorium.

In 1930 he married Wedekind's daughter Pamela, but this marriage did not last long either. Sternheim lived in Brussels, tended by a nurse, and died there in 1942.

His works had been partially forbidden already before 1938, but after the occupation of Holland and Belgium by the Nazis, they were again proscribed and suppressed. His autobiography, *Pre-War Europe as a Parable of My Life*, was pulped.

In the comedies of 'bourgeois heroism' (a cycle of eleven plays in all) he reveals coolly and analytically how society works. *A Pair of Drawers* and *A Place in the World* portray the rise of the Maske family from *petit-bourgeois* to *parvenu*, and finally to the rank of important citizens and industrial aristocracy. But their heirs are not able to recognize the threat of war and declare their position. *The Fossil* is a 'feudal' epilogue to the Maske trilogy. Sternheim exposed the tenacity of the bourgeoisie as well as its blindness in *Nebbich* which takes place in the Weimar republic; and he depicts the manic desire for possession in *Citizen Schippel*, in which Sternheim perhaps comes closest to his model, Molière.

The complementary character to the hero of the title, the goldsmith Tilman Hicketier, is quite convinced of his bourgeois integrity. He conducts a prize-winning

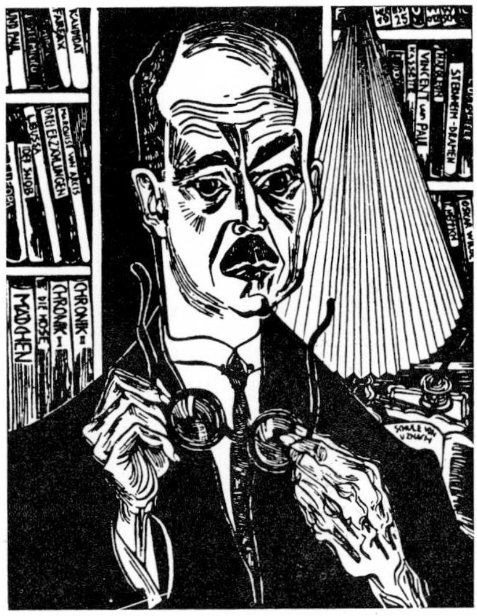

STERNHEIM, CARL: Portrait

singing quartet for which he needs a new tenor, since the fiancé of his sister Thekla has died. There is only one man in the reckoning – the working class Schippel. Hicketier is opposed to Schippel but has to take him on because the prince is interested in the quartet. The singing competition forces Hicketier to employ Schippel; but he does not know that the prince's main interest is Thekla. She, on the other hand, is keen on the robust Schippel, even though she gives the prince a rendezvous. Schippel too is interested in Thekla and joins the quartet with the promise that he will behave 'in a bourgeois way'. When they win the competition, Hicketier has to be prepared for Thekla to marry Schippel. He tries to prevent this with an allusion to her rendezvous with the prince. Schippel reacts with 'proletarian' pride and calls out a rival bourgeois lover, whom he slightly wounds in a duel. He is now 'allowed' to become a 'bourgeois' and remarks on it with pride. This biting satire on the class concept of Wilhelminian Society is not close to expressionist drama dramatically, but is in its language.

STRINDBERG, August (Stockholm, 22.1.1849 – Stockholm, 14.5.1912). Admittedly the Swede, August Strindberg (1849–1912) cannot be called an expressionist playwright, but he is a vital forerunner, and stimulus of German expressionism.

When a small child, this son of a spice merchant and a maid saw the bankruptcy of his father; later he took his *abitur* in Stockholm and began to study in Uppsala. In 1868 he worked as a private tutor and primary school teacher, also studied medicine and tried his hand unsuccessfully at acting. He tried to commit suicide and began to write. In 1872 he was a journalist in Stockholm. He again had no success in entering the theatre. He next worked in the Royal library. In 1875 he first met his future wife Siri von Essen. In 1883 he went to France, 1884 to Switzerland, 1887 to Germany; in 1892 he was divorced from Siri von Essen, and married again in 1893. He, meanwhile, wrote many plays. In 1898, Strindberg, now divorced for the second time, finished his plays *The Road to Damascus I* and *II*. In 1901 he wrote *The Road to Damascus III*, and *A Dream Play*. Apart from the above-mentioned plays, *The Ghost Sonata* and *The Dance of Death* stand out from his extensive corpus of work, which also contains many historical plays. From 1907 on he produced his 'Chamber plays' in his 'Intimate Theatre' which he ran with August Falck.

A Dream Play is a kind of epilogue to the three great '*Damascus*' plays; it is also his most impressive attempt to find expression for his grief at the incomplete nature of human existence. He takes up the religious theme of *The Road to Damascus* when he provides a prelude to the dream-like distortions of reality; in this the God Indra and his daughter hold a conversation as they travel through the heavens on a cloud and enter the earth's atmospher7. The attention of Indra's daughter is attracted by the lament of mankind. She asks her father to be allowed to set foot on earth and help men. At first she is an active Samaritan, then becomes an actress and marries the unhappiest person she meets, a lawyer.

Strindberg, a deeply divided and unhappy man, especially through his relationship with women, movingly portrayed himself in this figure. The lawyer's marriage with the daughter of a god collapses, as did Strindberg's marriages. Agnes returns to Indra and pleads for mankind; Strindberg ends his drama with a huge vision of Christ. He thereby states that the redemption of mankind cannot be accomplished by man himself.

TOLLER, Ernst (Samotschin, near Bromberg, 1.12.1893 – New York, 22.5.1939). Ernst Toller was born into a rich bourgeois, Jewish family. In 1914 he left his studies in Grenoble to volunteer at the border. The war turned the nationalist Toller into a pacifist and socialist. The chronology of his revolutionary dramas reflect Toller's evolution from utopian revolutionary to

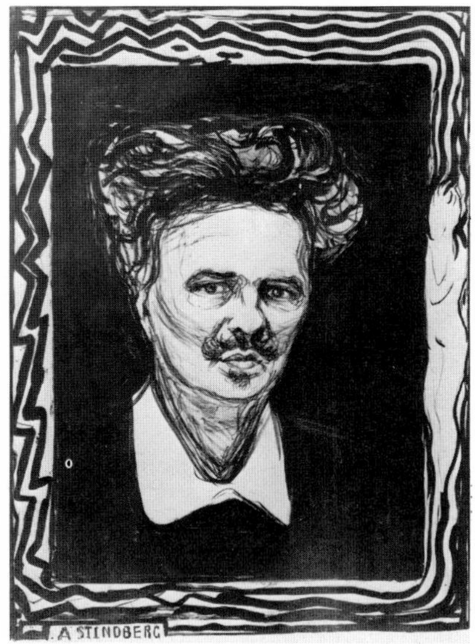

MUNCH, EDVARD: *Portrait of August Strindberg.* 1896

the man disappointed by reality. His development within expressionism is indicated by the depictions in these plays, later Toller wrote the grotesque comedy *Wotan Unbound* (1923), a dramatization of the sailors' revolt in Kiel, *Draw the Fires* (1931), and the dramas *No More Peace* and *Pastor Hall.* His best play dramatically does not belong to expressionism *Hoppla! Such is Life!* It is a play in the 'New Objectivity' school, harshly realistic, with grotesque caricatures.

He fled from Nazism in 1933. He committed suicide shortly before the Second World War in May 1939 in New York.

The first performances: *Transfiguration* 1.11.1919 The Tribune Theatre, Berlin; *Masses and Man* 15.11.1920 in the Nuremberg State Theatre; *The Machine Wreckers* 30.6.1922 Berlin Grosses Schauspielhaus; *Hinkemann* 19.9.1923 The Old Theatre, Berlin.

Transfiguration appears to be a war play, but is revolutionary. This is true historically and politically, as well as aesthetically – it conforms to the affirmation of the ego, the autobiography tendency, the raptures of expressionist youth and the general programme of the early expressionist theatre.

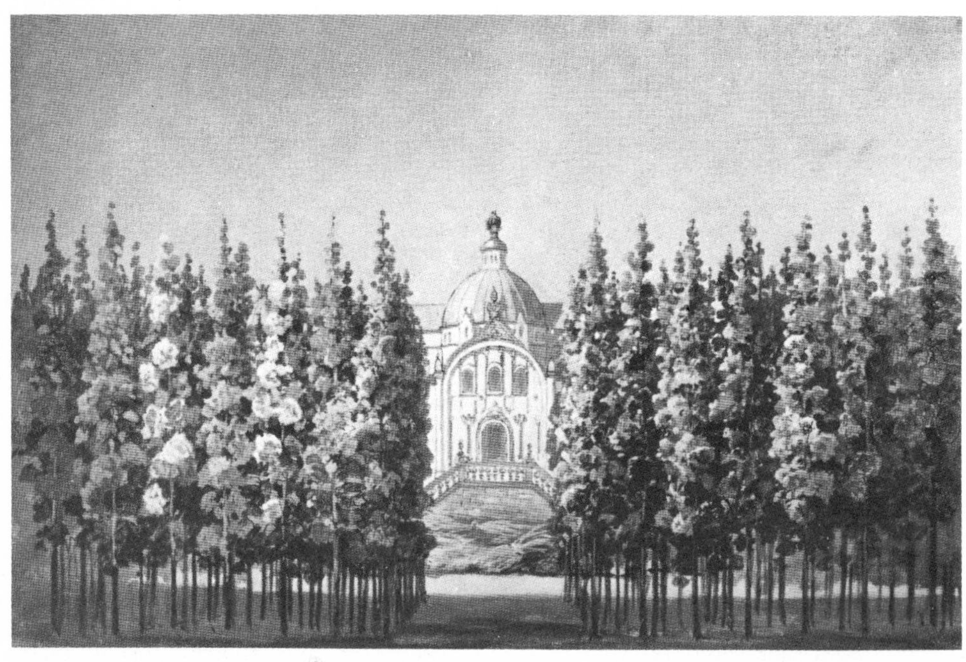

STRINDBERG, AUGUST: *T[illegible] Dream.* Sketch by C. L. Grabow (Svenskateatern, Stockholm 1907)

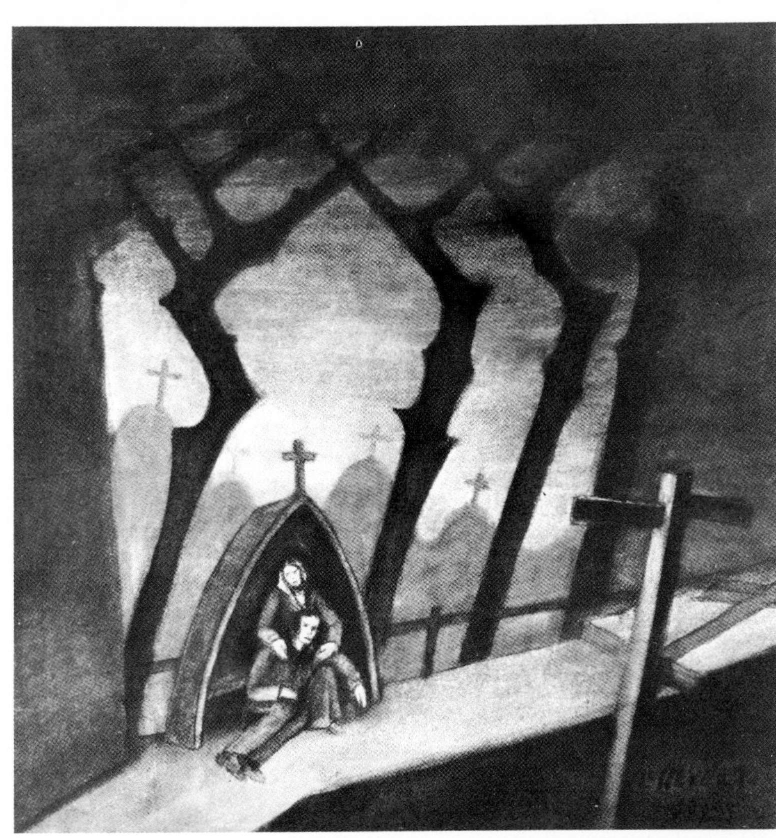

STRINDBERG, AUGUST:
The Road to Damascus.
Sketch by Ludwig Sievert
(Frankfurt-on-the-Main 1922)

STRINDBERG, AUGUST:
The Road to Damascus.
Production by Per Lindberg
(Konserthuset, Stockholm 1926)

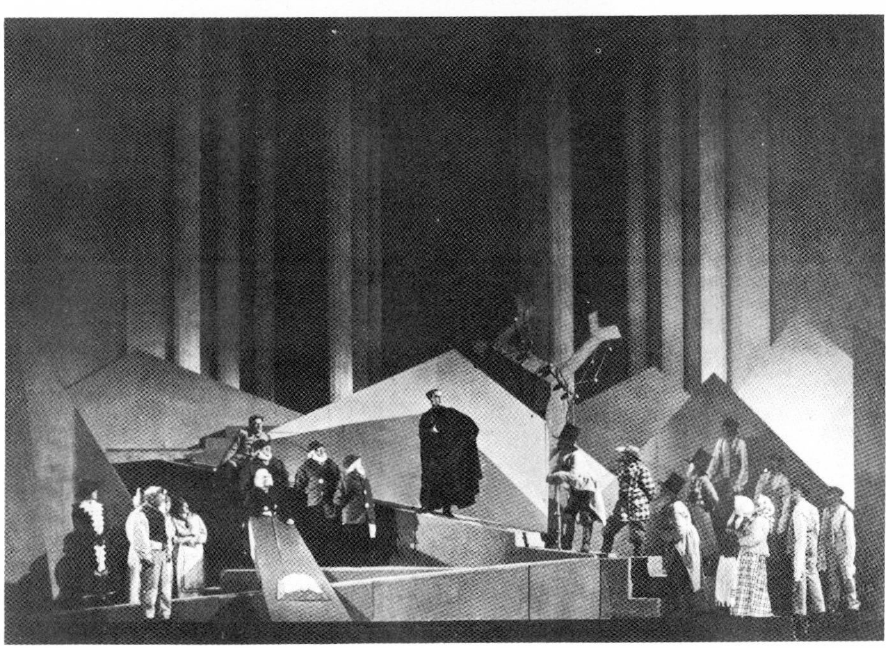

According to his own testimony (*I was a German*, published abroad in 1933), Toller had a 'a racial and capitalist inferiority complex' because he was a Jew and had rich parents. It was because of this that he crossed the border from Grenoble on the outbreak of war and volunteered. He kept quiet about old illnesses at his medical examination, announced his acceptance triumphantly to his family and sought exposed positions in the field. Before the nationalist Toller could become a revolutionary, his quickly growing pacifism had to be reinforced by the realization that the war was a further consequence of capitalist oppression, a more intense form of the exploitation in the factories.

Toller's revolutionary goal – a radical rejuvenation originating in a 'spirit of fraternity' – was related to the spiritual revolt of the early expressionists, but Toller also turned to *'realpolitik'*. After he had been released from the army as unfit, he studied in Heidelberg and Munich, founded a pacifist student club and made contact in Berlin with social democrat leaders. He soon turned from the S.P.D. to the Independent Social Democrats round Kurt Eisner in Munich. He distributed extracts from *Transfiguration* to munitions workers on strike and was imprisoned for a short time for treason.

As president of the Workers and Soldiers' Council, Toller was at the head of the Bavarian revolution. After Eisner's murder he should have become the people's deputy. He refused but accepted the presidency of the Munich Party. When the *Räterepublik* was proclaimed, Toller did not want to sign the manifesto before all the socialist parties were united. He withdrew from the revolutionary committee on humanitarian, not ideological grounds. He saw that all the power lay with the committee since the provincial diet and the government could not act. He wanted to avert disaster.

So Toller was opposed by Levien and Leviné, revolutionaries of Russian stamp and education. His utopia of a brotherly revolution was soon disappointed by reality. Hence his evolution from revolutionary dramatist to dramatist of the revolution. His involvement changed to observation and reflection, even though he retained his militant tone for a long time.

The further he moved away from active politics, the more distanced his medium of expression from expressionism became. Levien and Leviné considered him 'green' because he tore up warrants for arrest, prevented executions and even the planned assassinations of Eisner's murderers. During the second *'Räte'* government he opposed both the arming of the proletariat and the stopping of provisions for the bourgeoisie. He continually strove for discussions with the Bamberg government. He also took over the post of commandant of the Red Guard in Dachau only so that no one else should have it. He wanted a quick end achieved via discussion after the Munich fighting. After the government troops had won, he hid for a short time, was arrested and sentenced in 1919 to five years' fortress confinement. He wrote his expressionist plays during these years.

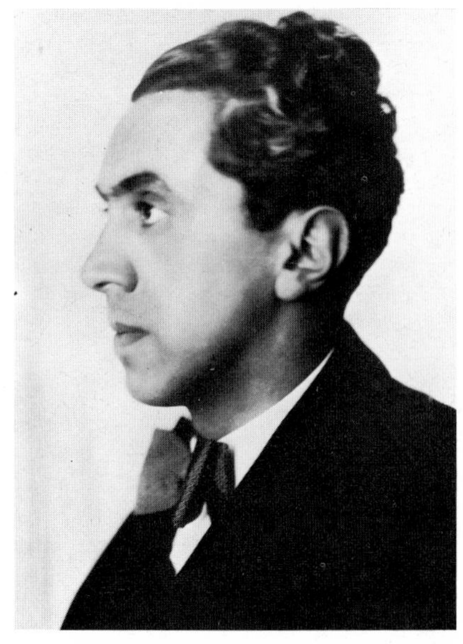

TOLLER, ERNST: *Portrait.* 1930

Toller had however already begun his first play, *Transfiguration* in 1917, and finished it in 1918 in the military prison. It has the subtitle 'The Struggle of a Man'. Youthful expressionism, the revealed self here speaks again after the one war play by Goering. But the motivation is not solely subjective, not in everyday experience; it is nourished by more important, social relationships. 'You are the way' is the play's motto. 'You' are the 'brothers', those who suffer and are ready to sacrifice themselves; the poet's mission is to show them the way.

Toller also often makes his appeal outside the play itself. This scene direction is typical: 'The action takes place in Europe before the rebirth.' The prologue 'The Barracks' is also programmatic. Here Death-in-war leads Death-in-peace into a huge burial ground. The fallen are buried according to rank and regiment. Death-in-war demonstrates a Prussian discipline: he has the skeletons do drill.

The play itself is divided into six stages with thirteen scenes in all. The hero, the sculptor Friedrich, is Toller himself. Friedrich is a Jew, alienated from his country by the feeling that he had been wronged. He thus volunteers for the war in the colonies. On his return he has been transformed. He works on a statue *Victory for the Fatherland* but destroys it when he sees an invalid couple. He thus demonstrates the metamorphosis, the 'transfiguration'. Before he can become a pioneer himself, he has to descend into the depths of suffering, must follow the stations of his cross. Toller shows him in the factory, in prison, everywhere men suffer and bleed. When he is finally reborn, Friedrich is given the role of judge; he delivers his programme for fraternity and inner humanity in front of a church. This brotherhood includes the 'erring capitalist', something which corresponds to Toller's political biography. Friedrich succeeds in conveying his transfiguration to his listeners.

The ethos, the sense of responsibility, which this play contains, stifles the play itself. The emotion and intrusive allegory bring it into the realms of pure spiritual drama with a generally humanist colouring. Though there is more: Toller portrays the consequences of the war very realistically, and in this is more revolutionary than in all his exhortations and programmes.

But there is one defect: his political and dramatic intentions contradict each other, even cancel each other out. The justification of the whole is biographical.

The work *Masses and Man* (1920) is not so heavily autobiographical. The play 'from the social revolution of the twentieth century' is dedicated to 'the proletariat'. The wife of a bourgeois professor has a utopia of no more war. She wants to see this utopia realized in a bloodless general strike. She joins the revolution out of a spirit of idealistic fraternity. This is again an event with an exact parallel in the author's life. A Bolshevik without a name (certainly Levien/Leviné) becomes her adversary. Unlike the woman (and therefore unlike Toller himself) he has known exploitation by society and wishes to combat capitalism with violence. The woman bows to him. In this we see her idealism: an oppressed proletarian is 'sacred' to her. However, the class conflict she accepts leads to excesses which make her change. She now advocates non-violence. The Bolshevik has the masses behind him. He inflames them against the intellectuality of the woman whom he also accuses of hiding hostages. A revolutionary tribunal has her shot.

TOLLER, ERNST: *The Conversion* (Die Wandlung). A scene with Fritz Kortner

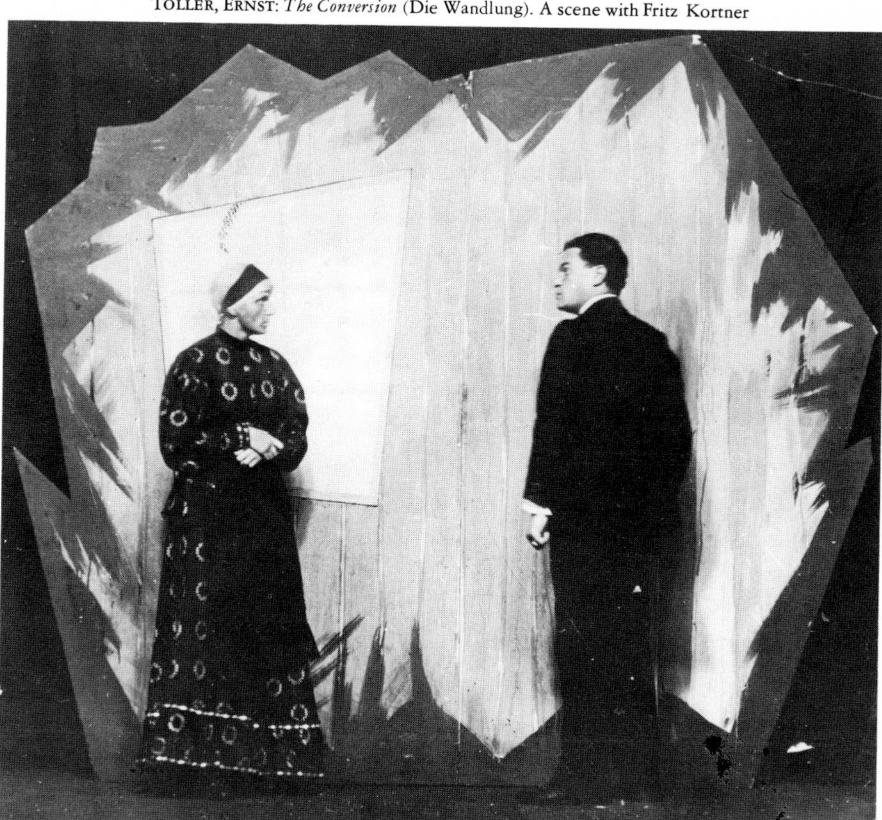

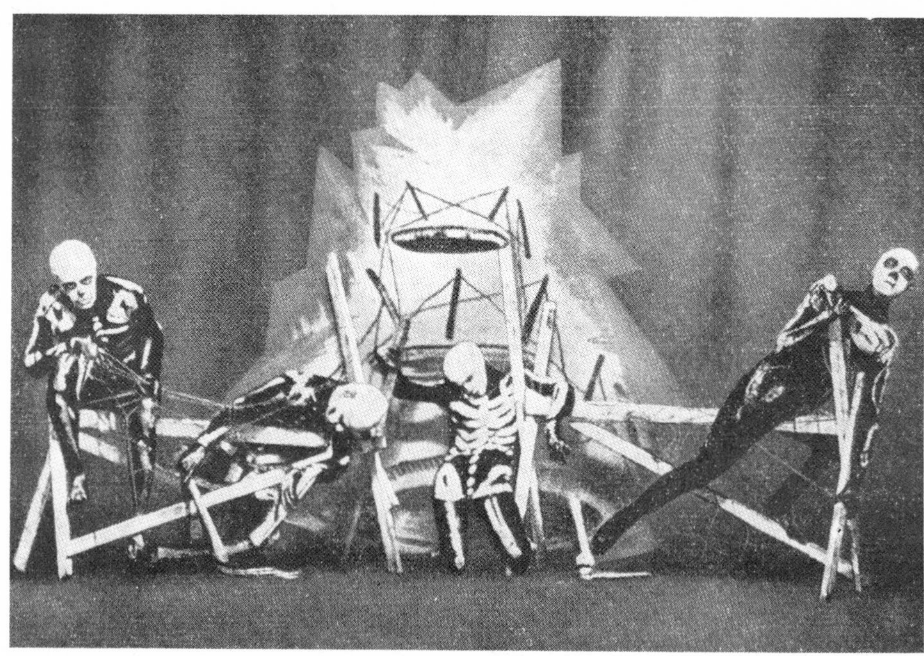

TOLLER, ERNST: *The Conversion* (Die Wandlung)

Toller's understanding of man in revolutionary situations may make him seem counter-revolutionary. This cannot be decided here, but it should be stated that in his fear of reality Toller was a typical expressionist, whose vision of universality remains dubious.

In *The Machine Wreckers* Toller tried to be objective. He used a historical subject to write a *Play in Five Acts and Prologue* from the time of the Luddite movement in England. He also moved further and further away from expressionist forms and language. The *Machine Wreckers* are fighting the economic structure of early capitalism with child labour and other brutal methods of exploitation. The criticism of the new machines by the weavers of Nottingham (1820) is romantic. They become anarchistic machine breakers. They kill the weaver and agitator Cobbett who combines his humanitarian commitment with an awareness of wider relationships and knows that the machines must be integrated, not destroyed.

Hinkemann shows Toller's insight into the impossibility of altering man.

This play (1921–1922) is in no way revolutionary. The woman with her sexual needs can no longer be faithful to Hinkemann, who was castrated in the war and now bites through the throats of rats and mice in a fair stall. Hinkemann's friend is correspondingly interested in his wife. There can be no 'reasonable' solution any more. For it is not the fact of adultery that harms Hinkemann; it is his concept of man that is injured. He is again Toller, who has the woman commit suicide. From now on Toller himself, except in his comedies, worked on the bitter principle that 'man becomes what he is'.

UNRUH, Fritz von (Coblenz 10.5.1885 – Diez 28.11.1970). Fritz von Unruh was the son of a general from a very old Silesian noble family. Family tradition seemed to have mapped out his career: a cadet in Plön, and training as a cavalry officer. But in 1911 his play *Officers* appeared. In 1912 he left the army and became a writer. He lived through the First World War partly in headquarters, partly at the front; and turned to religion and pacifism. After the war he was a republican representative in the Reichstag. He delivered the memorial speech for Rathenau. In 1933 he left Germany, went to Italy, Switzerland and North America. After the war he returned to Germany. In 1948 he gave the official speech on the 1848 revolution in the Paulskirche in Frankfurt. After his expressionist period, he used the technique of dramatic tableaux, of the chronicle, in his plays *Bonaparte* (1927) and *Heinrich von Andernach* (1925). Then he turned to comedy like other former expressionists. *The Race* was first performed on 16.6.1918 in The Frankfurt Theatre; *The Square* on 3.6.1920, also in Frankfurt.

The plays that Fritz von Unruh wrote during his nationalist phase were already in a form that prefigured his later expressionist development. In 1913 he was celebrated as a new Kleist for his patriotic play *Louis Ferdinand, Prince of Prussia*; in 1944 he turned to pacifism, closely connected with his religious experiences. He now hailed in visionary manner the 'new man' of the expressionist generation. He was to be conjured up in the trilogy *The Race*, consisting of *The Race* (1915–1916); *The Square* (1917–1920) and *Dietrich* (1936).

Von Unruh knew well that if a genuinely new drama was to be created, he could not mix day-to-day politics with a vision of universality. So he tried to get away from the concrete historical fact and create a new myth in the first part of his trilogy.

The Race is the prelude to *The Square* and shows the origins of the hero, Dietrich. He, the 'new man', is the vision and the 'will' of his mother. She has four sons and a daughter; she is the bearer of children and the woman who transforms, the new Eve. She controls fates and carries her own. So she stands in the cemetery with her daughter, where the youngest son is digging a grave for his dead brothers. The other two await execution, one because he has committed rape, the other because he was a coward. The youngest son is to perform the execution, in order to redeem his race. He cannot and is taken away. The eldest son and his sister, who free him, lust after each other and want to kill their mother. The eldest son finally commits the deed. Their dying mother hopes for the 'new man' when all classes have been abolished as a result of the war.

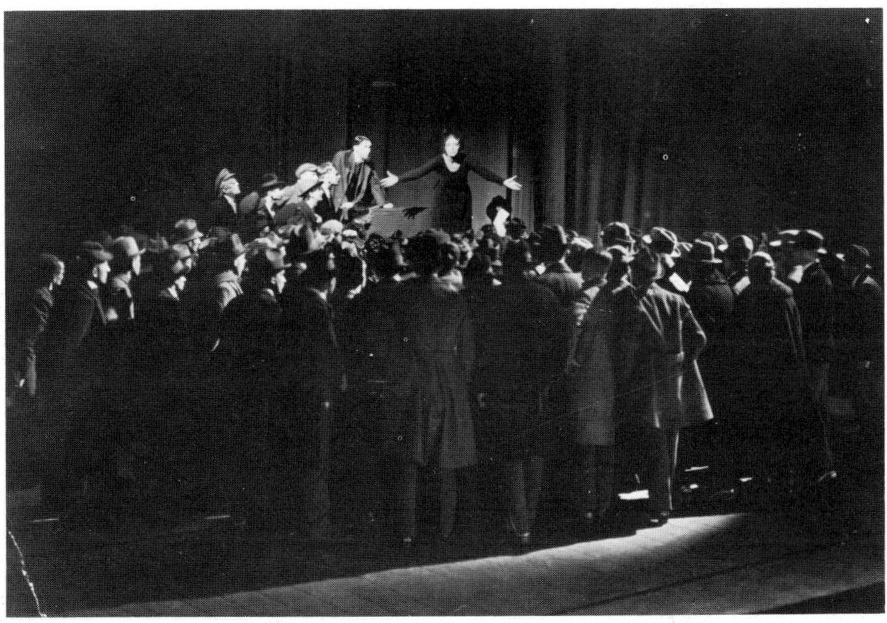

TOLLER, ERNST: *Masses and Man* (Masse-Mensch) Staadtheater, Nuremberg, 1921

In *The Square* Dietrich attacks the old order, which is symbolized by the square. He is soon faced with the concrete problems of revolution. He rejects the use of violence and 'gives himself substance' only in his love for Irene. While others fight in the square and destroy the old world, Dietrich symbolizes a peaceful future in his view of existence and in his life style.

Von Unruh's attempt to write a myth was not a solution to the problem of expressionist drama; his works are merely new disguises for a fundamentally irrational attitude.

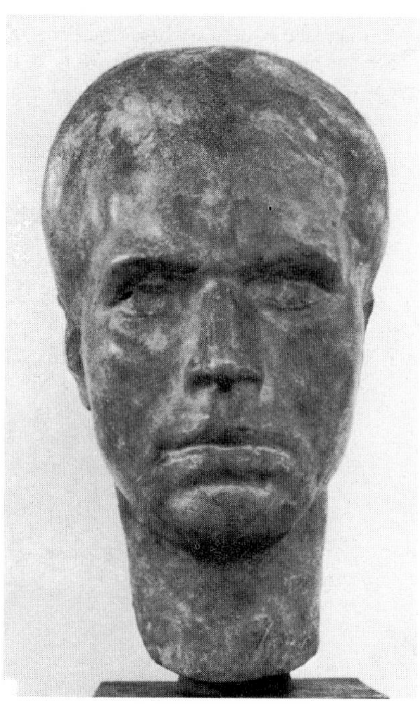

UNRUH, FRITZ VON: Sculpture by Gerald Beck

WEDEKIND, Frank (Hanover, 24.7.1864 – Munich, 9.3.1918). The ancestry and family of this author are of particular importance in his development. His father, a doctor, had travelled in Europe in very varied capacities. In 1848 when a correspondent for the *Reichszeitung* he had witnessed the negotiations at the Paulskirche. In 1849 he had emigrated to America and had a practice in San Francisco. Wedekind's mother was the daughter of an artisan who had fled to Switzerland in 1838 as a political refugee. She herself had gone to the U.S.A. at sixteen, earned her living as a singer and then married Dr Wedekind. They returned to Germany the year Wedekind was born. In 1872 they moved to Switzerland for political reasons: his father was a democrat and determined opponent of Bismarck.

Wedekind began to write in 1877. His Swiss governess blamed his writings for his poor achievements. Love soon became Wedekind's central theme; it also played a great part in the pessimistic discussions so popular in his age. Wedekind was still studying, and had already been published, when he decided, in 1896, to live from his writings alone. He went to Munich, came into contact with naturalism and, politically, with socialism, although he rejected 'Zolaism'. The same year he moved to Zurich where he became advertising manager and press agent for the Maggi firm. He wrote for reviews and was a member of 'Young Germany', a writers' and and scientists' association that was threatened in Germany by Bismarck's 'socialist' laws. Here Wedekind first performed his songs, to the horror of Gerhart Hauptmann.

In the years that followed he was in Berlin and Munich. In 1891 *Spring Awakening* appeared in Zurich. Although he was writing for the theatre, he was more

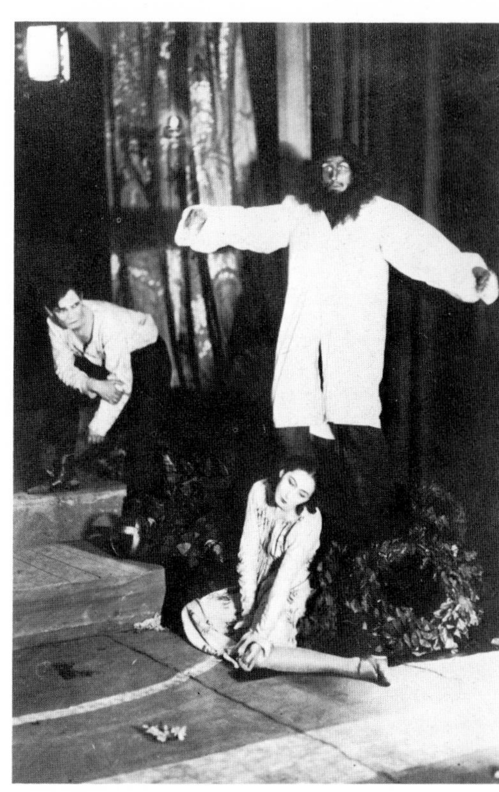

UNRUH, FRITZ VON: *The Square* (Platz). First performance 3.6.1920

interested in the circus and music hall, at least during a visit to Paris in 1892. In 1894 he went to London, and busied himself with the psychology and physiology of love; his play *Lulu* was an event. *Earth Spirit* appeared in 1895, but he was not able, for a while, to put it on because of the domination of naturalism. In 1896 he became a contributor to the satirical magazine

Simplicissimus. In 1897 Strindberg's wife Frieda bore him a son. In 1898 he was secretary, actor and producer for the Ibsen Theatre in Leipzig. He himself played Dr Schon in the first performance of *Earth Spirit*.

He then went to Munich as a playwright, actor and producer. He escaped persecution for his political satires by fleeing, via Zurich, to Paris. In 1899 he wrote *The Marquis of Keith*. The same year he presented himself to the authorities in Leipzig and was condemned to fortress confinement. In 1900 he was freed and went to Munich. There he appeared from 1901 as a singer and entertainer in the cabaret *The Eleven Executioners*.

From 1904 on Wedekind systematically trained himself as an actor since he could find no one to do justice to his plays. Until his death, Wedekind, constantly under attack from political censorship, played in his own

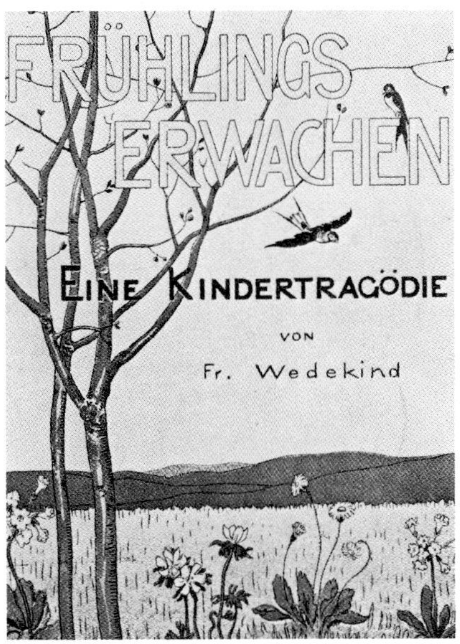

WEDEKIND, FRANK: Poster for *Frühlings Erwachen*

dramas in Germany and abroad. A few are regularly put on; many others still await full recognition. Wedekind's importance for the modern stage has not yet been fully discussed and examined. Apart from this indubitable importance, he had a considerable influence on the expressionist generation which followed him. His work *Spring Awakening* is typical of Wedekind, the 'Scourge of the Bourgeoisie'.

In this play, schoolchildren around 1890 fight against the moral ideas of parochially minded teachers. Their questions are not answered at home or in school. The moral superiority of these fourteen-year-olds has no effect. Melchior Gabor thus becomes a cynic early. He sees knowledge outside the legitimate spheres, while Wendla turns to her mother and receives accordingly no explanation. She becomes pregnant and dies as a result of a clumsy attempt at abortion after her distraught mother has accused her, 'Why have you done this to me?'. The sensitive Moritz Stiefel, like Wendla, is also destroyed by the adult world. Since he receives no answer to his burning questions, his father even denies that he is his son – suicide is the only way out. Melchior, who is blamed for everything, is put into an institution. He escapes and, in a vision, meets the dead Moritz who tries in vain to entice him into the realms of the dead. A 'masked man' (Wedekind himself) offers to be Melchior's guide through life. Unlike many other expressionist plays, Wedekind is here not writing a tragedy or portraying a mystical idea of rebirth. He is instead trying to show a means of reconciliation in a grotesque world and to produce the courage for sensuality and the liberation of the senses.

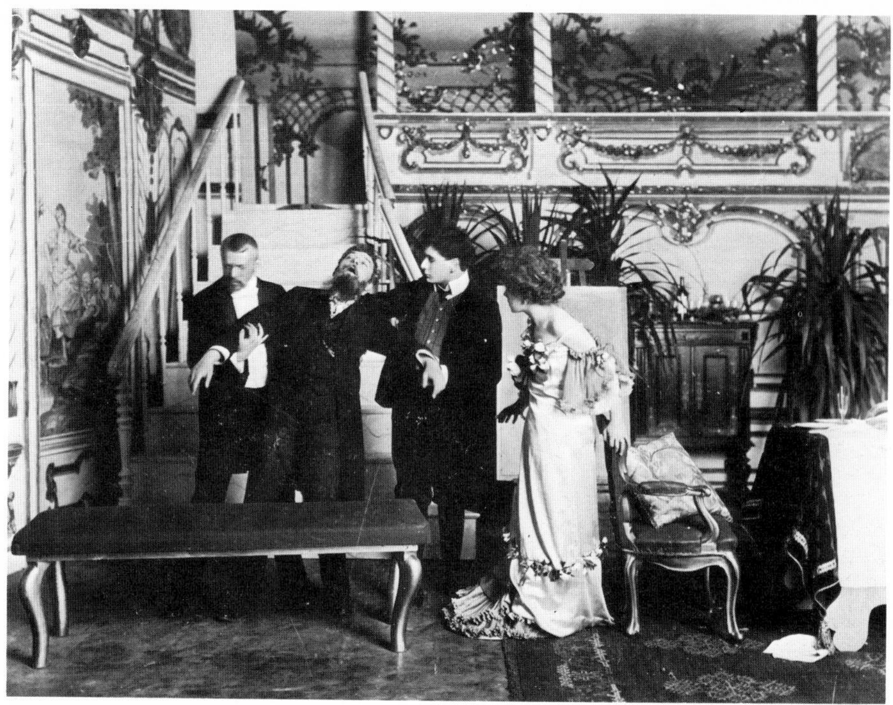

WEDEKIND, FRANK: *Spirit of the Earth* (Erdgeist). A scene from E. Reicher and G. Eysoldt

The Expressionist Stage

Expressionism is not a style. It is even less a set of rules. Before being a means of artistic expression, it is an attitude of the mind, of the soul which can be summarized in two words: anguish and revolt. This attitude led to an artistic movement which, contrary to others (cubism for example) did not restrict itself to the plastic arts, but permeated all the arts (literature and poetry, the plastic arts, music and the theatre), and manifested itself in a number of ways. This movement occurred essentially in Northern Europe (Norway, Sweden) and Central Europe (above all in Germany, Poland and Czechoslovakia). It assumed different forms in other countries, like the USSR, and in general lost its force the further afield it went. The Latin countries remained unaffected by it. No doubt this phenomenon contributes to explaining why it remained unknown for so long.

Born out of anguish and insecurity, expressionism is the manifestation of a revolt. For want of finding the equilibrium to which he aspired in the universe of immediate appearances, the material reality, and the society that surrounded him, man turned away from the external world and tried to dominate it by taking refuge in inner visions, thoughts and dreams. Naturalism, which only offered a reproduction of the external world that he attempted to escape from, was no longer able to satisfy him.

First of all, expressionism fits into the context of the changes in civilization, of a real social crisis experienced as a profound upheaval. The bourgeoisie might have appeared to be at the peak of its economic power, the values it imposed were the very negation of those of the individual which seemed to foreshadow the changes of the First World War and the 1917 Revolution. Hence this idealist revolt, and the anguish that the aftermath of the 1914 war could only reinforce in Germany, one of the most serious crises in its history; the imperialist dreams were shattered, inflation set in, the state was ruined, the government bankrupt, the war had destroyed all illusions. Faced with bourgeois conformity, and its submission to naturalism, expressionism appeared as a sudden explosion of the German soul, as an art of transcending reality and a liberation. 'As an attitude towards the world', declared Bernhard Diebold, 'the new spirit meant an uprising against the redundant formulae of the present age. It was a nostalgic desire for a deeper understanding of life.'

This new spirit had already shown itself in art (Kokoschka, Marc, Kandinsky, Beckmann). In opposition to the passivity of the impressionists' physical eye, the expressionists had already begun to exploit the possibilities of their inner eye with its capacity to discern what is normally invisible, the very essence of existence, and which allows one to discover the innermost depths of oneself, the latent physiognomy of objects beyond the atomical analysis of impressionism. In a number of areas, expressionists sought to convey the world of thought, imagination, the visions of the dream, and to show things not as they are, but as they could be, or, rather than the things themselves, their real meaning. Born out of man's anguish, their art tended towards the abstract and symbolic. It rejected classical methods, perspective, the rules of anatomy, symmetry, description and illusion: 'the world is out there', declared Edschmid, 'it would be absurd to reproduce it: to seek out its real substance, to create in a new way, this is the fundamental task of art.'

It has often been said that the revolution in painting preceded that on the stage. Close analysis proves that this claim is not always valid and that the problems are often more complex, and that there is a real reciprocity between the theatre and the other arts. But it does seem perfectly true in the case of expressionism.

What was the first expressionist production? One must not expect to find it in the theatre, but in art. It is the work by one of the greatest precursors of expressionism, the Norwegian painter Edvard Munch. In *The Scream*, a picture dating from 1893, and from which he made an engraving in 1895, the artist offers us the principal characteristics of expressionism in drama and on the stage. At the centre of the canvas, there is the silhouette of a man, out of joint, who is holding his haggard head in his hands, his mouth wide open, uttering a cry that echoes in concentric waves, throughout nature, the fjord and its banks and the sky with its waves of fire. In the distance, as if indifferent, two characters are walking away. Munch wrote concerning *The Scream* 'I was walking with two friends. The sun was setting. Suddenly the sky became red and I felt a breath of sadness. I stopped and leant on the parapet. Above the dark blue front and above the town the sky was spread out like blood, and flames of fire. My friends carried on and I remained alone, trembling with anxiety. For me it was as if a powerful endless cry was passing through nature.'

The juxtaposition of Munch's canvas and his commentary is sufficient to show, to what extent the work is a symbol of expressionism (anguish, a scream) to what extent too it foreshadows expressionist theatre. Is it not reminiscent of *Traumbühne* (the scene with the dream), of *Ichdramatik*, a play based on the life of a central character through whose eyes we are supposed to perceive the world?

One might just conceivably think that this character passes through one of those 'stations' that constitute the expressionist *Stationendrama*, where often, as here, one does not know the exact identity of people who have been made over-abstract.

Thus expressionist painting preceded expressionist drama, and its constituent parts and structures were to determine in part the nature of expressionist productions. But expressionist drama is not only linked to the evolution of painting and drama but also to the art of producing itself. All the arts are linked, and the techniques involved are bound to influence the evolution of these arts in themselves, and in their mutual links.

In the same way that Munch and Van Gogh prefigured pictorial expressionism, and Strindberg prefigured expressionist drama, so Appia, Craig and Reinhardt were the precursors of expressionist stage directors. Appia, in so far as he wanted to make the stage a rhythmic space contributing to the understanding of the play, and lighting a means of expression, which the effects of stage-lighting and especially the discovery and the improvements in projectors allowed. Edward Gordon Craig was, by his refusal of realism, his concern to discover the major theme of a play, to promote the symbol, also by his condemnation of the naturalist actor and its ideal of the *surmarionnette*, and finally by *his* desire to unite all the scenic means of expression so as to confer on the play the maximum expressive intensity: 'The art of the theatre, he wrote in 1905, is not the acting, the play, the production, or the ballet; it is formed out of the elements of which it is composed: the language of gesture that is the soul of the acting: the words that are the body of the play, the lines and colours which are the very essence of the décor, the pace which is the essence of the ballet'. Max Reinhardt finally, while Jessner, Martin and Weichert were revolting against impressionism and its eclecticism, appeared to be the precursor of expressionism on the stage, and this in spite of his *décorativisme* in using formal methods which were relevant to the use of light and the organization of the stage space. Half-way between impressionism and expressionism, his production of *The Beggar* (*Der Bettler*) by Sorge in 1917 is the image of his contradictions, and to this extent it constitutes a crucial turning-point.

The Art of Producing

One knows how much men like André Antoine, Adolphe Appia, Edward Gordon Craig and Constantine Stanislavsky contributed to ensuring that the rôle of the director was included in the history of the theatre. The expressionists made the rôle of the director even more important. They affirmed their

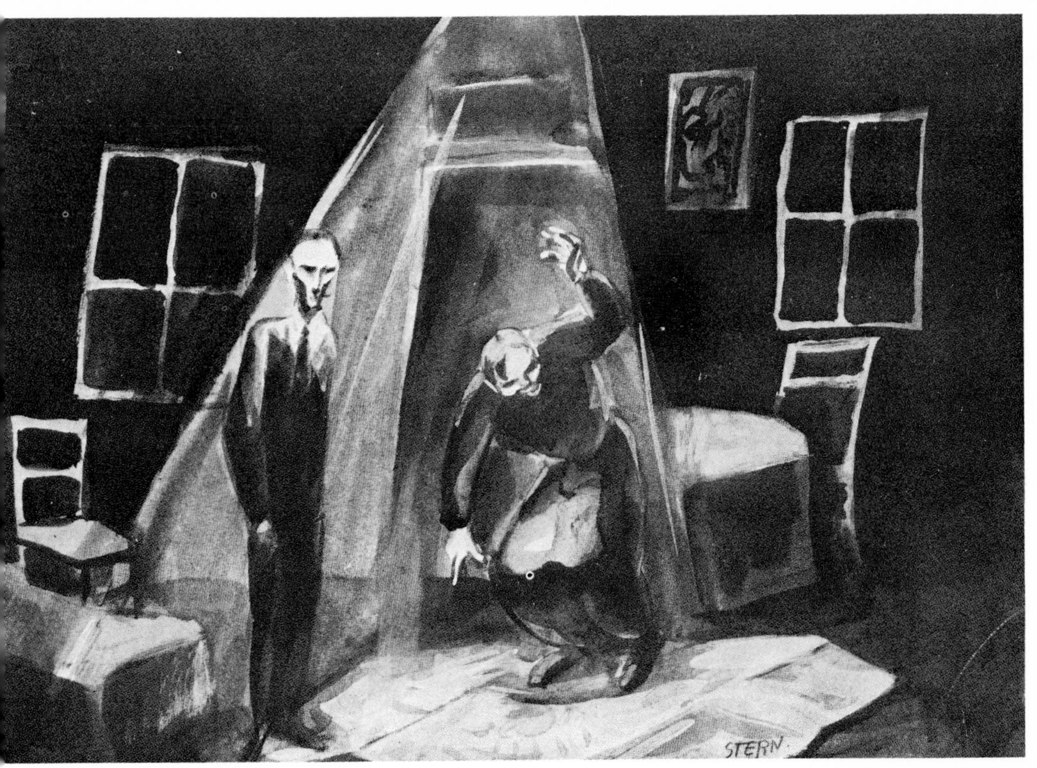

STERN, ERNST: Sketch for *The Beggar* (Der Bettler) by Reinhard Sorge, production by Max Reinhardt (Deutsches Theater, Berlin 1917)

inalienable right to interpret and be creative. They wanted to be independent creators, free directors of the stage production. Richard Weichert wrote, 'The director is from now on the person who puts the author's intentions into practice, and who reveals his visions, is to a certain extent, his spokesman, or, at least, his defence counsel. Henceforth, he is the one who directs and harmonizes the production, because he has grasped the author's most subtle and intimate aims, he is the mediator between the author and the actor; no longer the routine supervisor, but an artist endowed with the greatest sensibility and a most fertile imagination, who transforms the spiritual into the visual, and who conveys an imaginary world on the stage, and who is an independent demiurge. In the theatre, the author is conjecture, the acting is the execution, between the two as both master and servant, comes the director.' And Weichert adds, 'The producer must arrive at the first rehearsal with only a summary idea of the way in which the play is to be produced. What he contributes, and has to contribute with a conscious clarity from the very beginning, is the general style of the words and the acting, the homogeneous rhythm of the whole to which everybody will have to adapt (the art of the director is thus conceived as an art of style).'

The attitude of the producer will be the same whatever the work performed, whether it belongs to the repertoire of the past or is uncompromisingly modern. According to Leopold Jessner: 'In fact there are neither classical nor modern authors. From the point of view of the theatre, the poet does not really belong to any particular generation,' and according to Richard Weichert: 'To look at a classical work in a new and individual manner, is the right and duty of each generation'.

Given this perspective, what was the producer's aim? Not, to be sure, to allow himself to present in a naturalist and illusionist manner, the various vicissitudes of the play, the life and psychological relationships of the different characters, but to reveal the profound essence, by relying on what constitutes the *Grundmotiv* of the work, the key theme, to emphasize, instead of the story, the idea behind the story. Thus Weichert produced *The Son* (*Der Sohn*) by Hasenclever, according to the

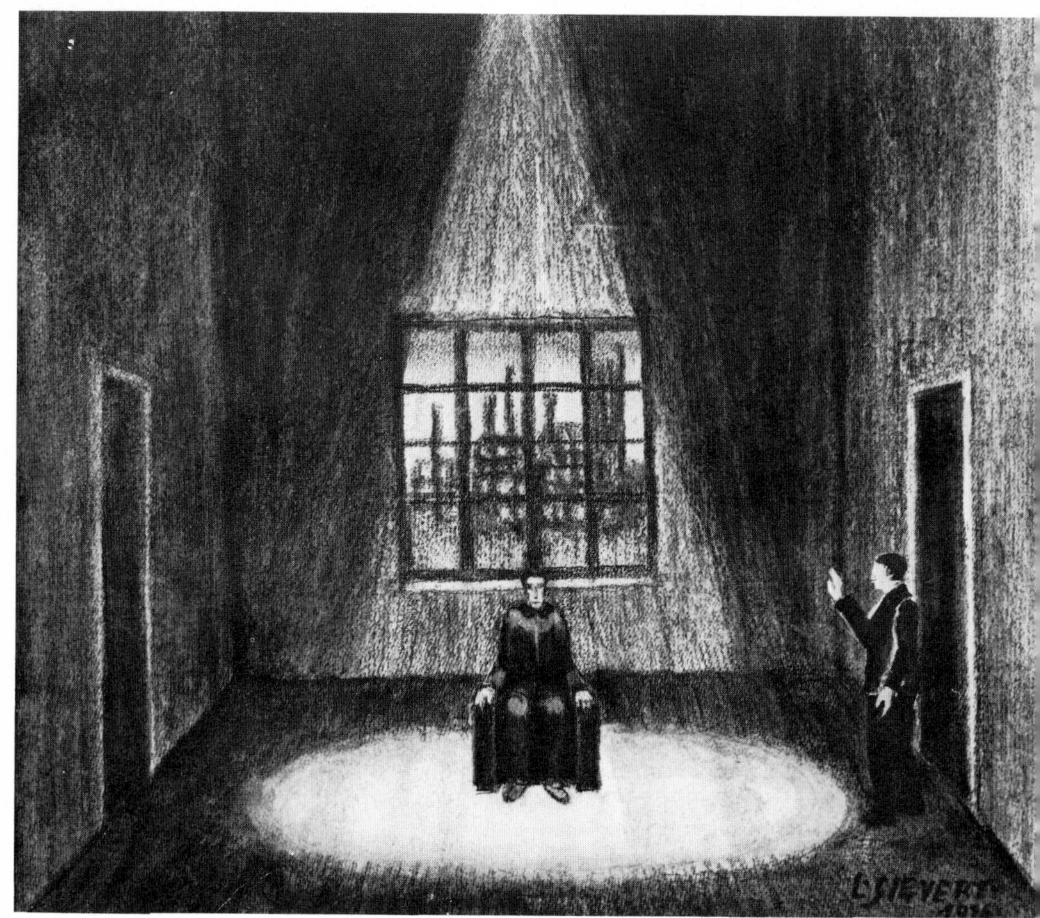

SIEVERT, LUDWIG: Sketch for *The Son* (Der Sohn) by Walter Hasenclever, production by Richard Weichert (National Theater, Mannheim 1918)

following idea: 'All the characters that the son struggles with lack objective reality, are only the extensions of his own inner being.' Whereas the essential idea behind Leopold Jessner's production of *William Tell* was that the play concentrates entirely on the cry for freedom, and in the case of *Richard III*, that Shakespeare's play is based on a double theme: terror in the face of despotism, and the rise and fall of tyrants.

It is clear that this conception of producing led to a significant use of symbolism, and even to a certain abstraction: 'the stage production will not lead', writes Karl Heinz Martin, the producer of *The*

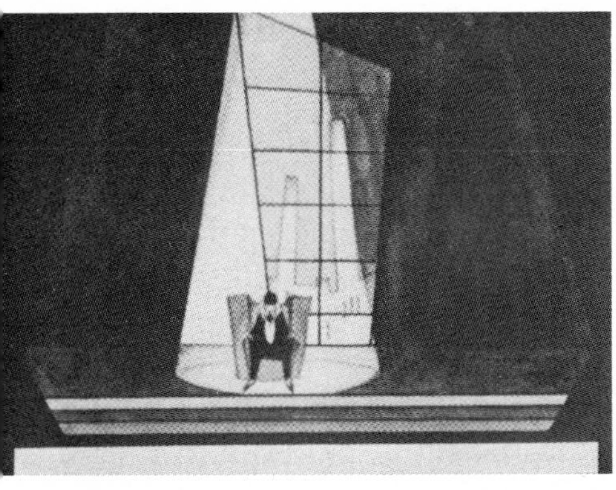

The son's bedroom in the family flat;

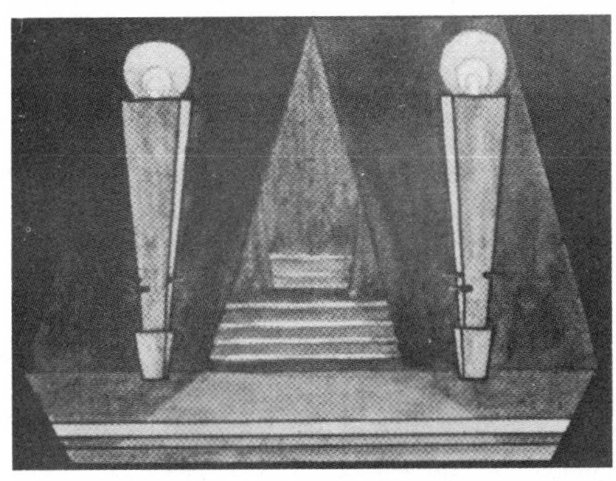

ante chamber of the family flat;

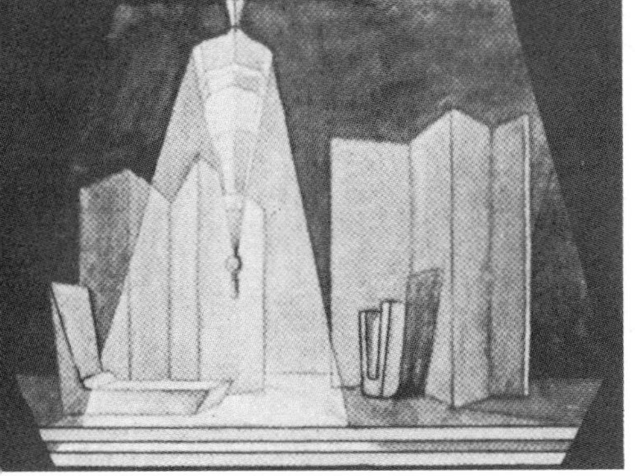

hotel bedroom;

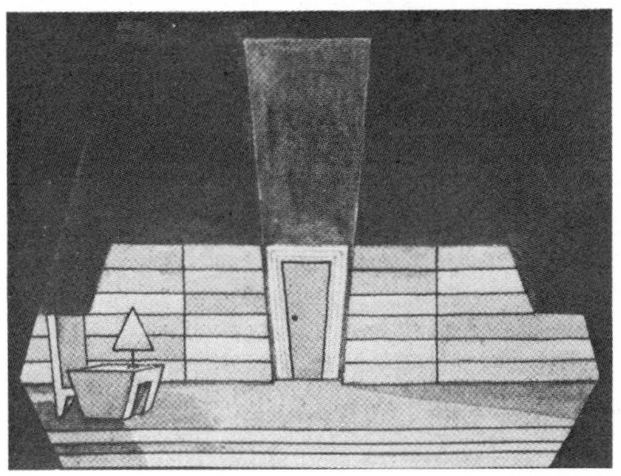

father's study

HASENCLEVER, WALTER: *The Son* (Der Sohn). Sets by Karl Kröning (Stadttheater, Nuremberg 1924).

Conversion (*Die Wandlung*) by Toller, 'towards a real image of reality, but it will strive to express its ideal nature in a highly artistic abstraction': and Jessner stated: 'We are conquering external impressionism, we are replacing it with an expressive situation that one has to present by a concentration of effect. This conception also gives the work a unity based on a vigorous concentration of the various means of stage expression considered as being *mitspielend* "everything actively playing a part"'. Whether he was producing a Kaiser or a Shakespeare, the aim of the producer was to render the play fully effective, to assure it the maximum power of expression, to move the public, to make each scenic element express the core of the soul or the idea. In their brutal revolt against naturalism and impressionism, the expressionist directors mobilized the various means that their art provided and all the modern technical equipment so as to denaturalize the stage. Each producer had his own technique, but the aim remained common to them all: it was a question of removing from the stage all descriptive elements, all realist imitation, in order to express 'the essence of the play' by the antinaturalist acting of the actor, the symbolism of the object, the line, the colour and the stage lighting.

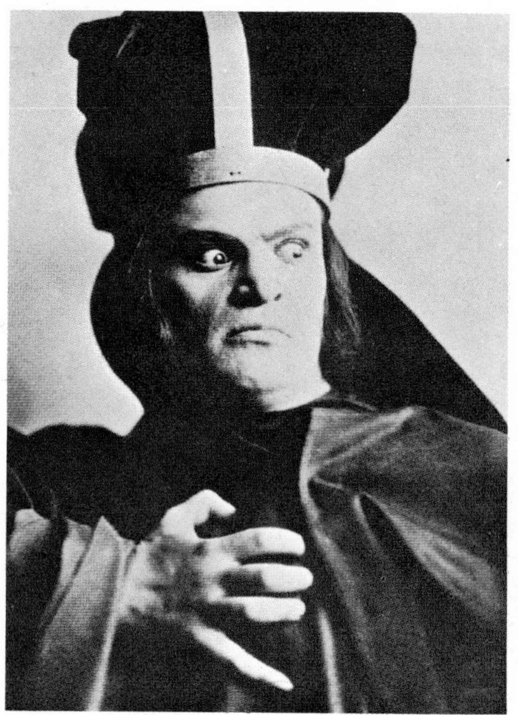
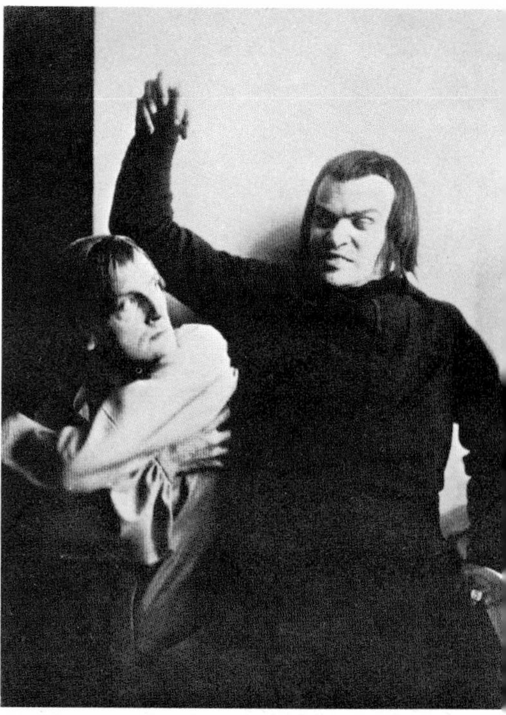

KORTNER, FRITZ: In *Richard III* by Shakespeare. Production by Leopold Jessner (Staatliches Schauspielhaus, Berlin 1920)

The Actor, the Word and the Language of Gesture

All the elements of the theatre had in vain existed side by side. The expressionists established a hierarchy amongst them: the actor was the most important element.

In expressionist productions, the actor was no longer so important for his ability to play particular rôles, but as a bearer of ideas. That is to say, he was not any actor, but a special task was required of him. In a text dating from 1918 *Der beseelte und der psychologische Mensch*, the expressionist author Paul Kornfeld explained what he expected: 'The actor should free himself from reality, render abstract all the attributes of reality in order to be simply the representative of an idea, a feeling, a destiny! If he has to die on stage, he should not go to hospital beforehand to learn how to die, or to the cabaret to find out how one behaves when drunk. Let him dare to open his arms wide and speak as he would never speak in real life, when he reaches an emotive passage; he should not be an imitator and seek his examples from a world alien to actors, in short, he should not be ashamed to act, and should not disavow the theatre'.

At a time when some directors were concentrating on returning to the deep tradition of the art of acting, expressionist theatre was transforming the rôle of the actor. The metamorphosis of the actor into a tragic hero was rejected. At the moment when Stanislavsky was researching into incarnation and the various elements of his system, the expressionists were implicitly opposed to him: it was not a question of incarnating such and such a character, but of conveying states of mind and actions by a symbolic transposition, of underlining the characters' fundamental characteristics, the essential moments of the action, hence a phenomenon of a willed exaggeration.

The expressionist essentially had two modes of expression: the word and the language of gesture. In theory the spoken word, the word expressing profound thoughts and given a rhythmic quality had priority. Weichert claimed to have created a new music of the word, a new pathos 'an unparalleled intensity alongside a clear and transparent spirituality'. Martin thought that when used mimically, the word constitutes 'the bridge leading from the spiritual to the metaphysical'. Fritz Kortner is without doubt the actor who at the time, united all the qualities required.

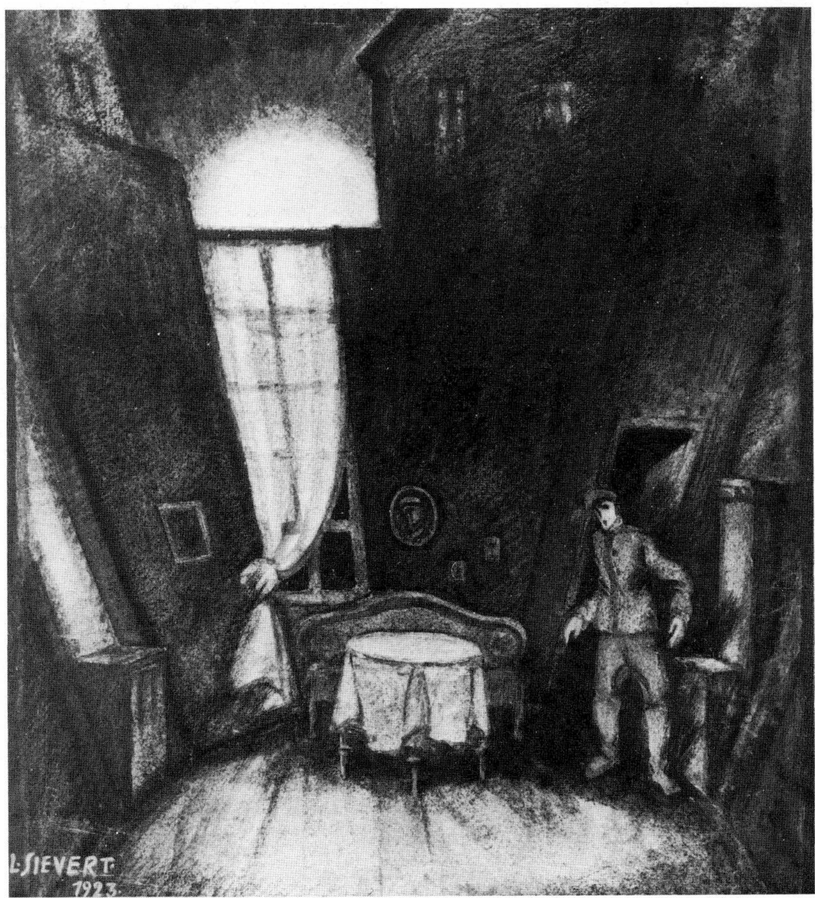

SIEVERT, LUDWIG: Sketch for *Drums in the Night* (Trommeln in der Nacht) by Bertold Brecht, production by Richard Weichert (Städtische Bühnen, Frankfurt-on-the-Main 1923)

But the actor does not only use his voice to act. Walter von Holländer tells us: 'Expressionism is the soul which unashamedly unveils itself through the body'; the actor acted physically. Movement was again given a value it had lost: jerky movements tending towards abstraction, which conveyed the crucial points of the play and the tension of the character: movements which could even be incomplete; beginning them was enough to give an indication of their meaning. The stylization of the movement conformed to the distorted forms of the décor and the sudden changes in the lighting. The human body in its shape and size adapted to the state of the soul expressed in plastic terms and it was through the abstract movement outside the context of all naturalist notions of *vraisemblance*, that it recreated the tension of the soul. Here too, Kortner's acting played a significant rôle.

The Stage Set and the Use of Space

As with the producer, the stage designer did not try to give the play a precise historical setting, to create a real social milieu, not even an atmosphere however approximately realistic. It rejected all superfluous décor in the same way that it rejected reproducing reality. Its art was an art of a direct vision of the dramatic work. It also wanted to decentralize the stage, and leave room for the sheer force of the play to emerge. But the means used differed, according to whether it materialized this vision, whether it represented a pictorial décor, or whether it constructed architectural stage space, allowing a few elements, the development in the acting, the stage lighting, to evoke it in the minds of the audience.

In this first instance, the décor was generally dramatized, false perspectives, truncated elements, the substitution of oblique lines for vertical lines, a taste for the so-called expressive line, calculated dissymmetries, in a word, distortions which in the cinema led to the celebrity of *The Cabinet of Doctor Caligary*. Without a doubt, these distortions harmed expressionism in its reputation, for those with rational minds often saw in it excessiveness and artificiality. But they were by no means gratuitous for sincere expressionists. The stage designer grasped the play as a whole and the vision he had of it, as well as the emotion it created in him; and through his décor, he projected this into the soul of the audience.

This is the case in Ludwig Sievert's vision for Bertolt Brecht's *Drums in the Night*. 'Throughout the play the walls are symbols of chaos and revolution. In other scenes, the walls are the madness of a night during the revolution, a fiery vision of reds and yellows, and constantly towering over everything else the moon like a blood-shot eye. Real events re-inserted in a real world, stylized in the lyrical irreality of that ballad and the dream'. Despite their being very different from those of Sievert, Otto Reigbert's décors for the same play are nevertheless conceived in a similar frame of mind – there too the forms are distorted, but he adds in the background, the vision of a cold mechanized capital, of a chaotic town (a theme dear to the expressionists) dominated here too by a moon, stained with blood, the symbolic image of Berlin and the Revolution.

Wanting to convey the emotion he felt, the stage designer inscribed it in the recreated form of a window, of a door, of a wall, that he brings to life. On the other hand, the properties were often placed in such a way that they revealed the spirit of the principal character. If one wants to understand these distortions one must take into consideration certain tendencies of the expressionist mystique.

But this tendency only represents one of the aspects of stage expressionism and a number of theoreticians, including Felix Emmel (*Das Ekstatische Theater*, 1924), condemned all stage sets that restricted the 'dynamic unfolding' of the play. Emmel considered it was necessary to restore to the inner eye of the spectator his imagination, all its strength, all the means of seeing: hence the need to reduce the decor to the essential, to model the stage space, 'to throw out' all decorative embellishment. The scene often became a void charged with latent powers, the black curtains being used with a view to creating a specific amount of space, which left the spectator's imagination scope for being creative. The young expressionist movement *The Tribune*, founded in Berlin in 1919, also declared in its manifesto that 'the revolution essential in the theatre must begin with a transformation of the use of the stage and the introduction of a new relationship between the stage and the audience. It was on a bare podium of *The Tribune* that Karl Heinz Martin in October 1919 put on *The Conversion* (*Die Wandlung*) by Toller. The sets by Robert Neppach, were very simple, consisting of central painted elements with broken shapes: they locate the action and create an atmosphere, the words are left to the actor.

It was a sort of empty space that Sievert imagined for *The Son* (*Der Sohn*). A luminous cone surrounds the major character. The décor without a ceiling is reduced to three walls of black velvet, which define, beyond the confines of the stage, a cubic space both conventional, charged with mystery, and as it were full of tension. At each side there are two doors, or rather their linear outline. At the back and in the

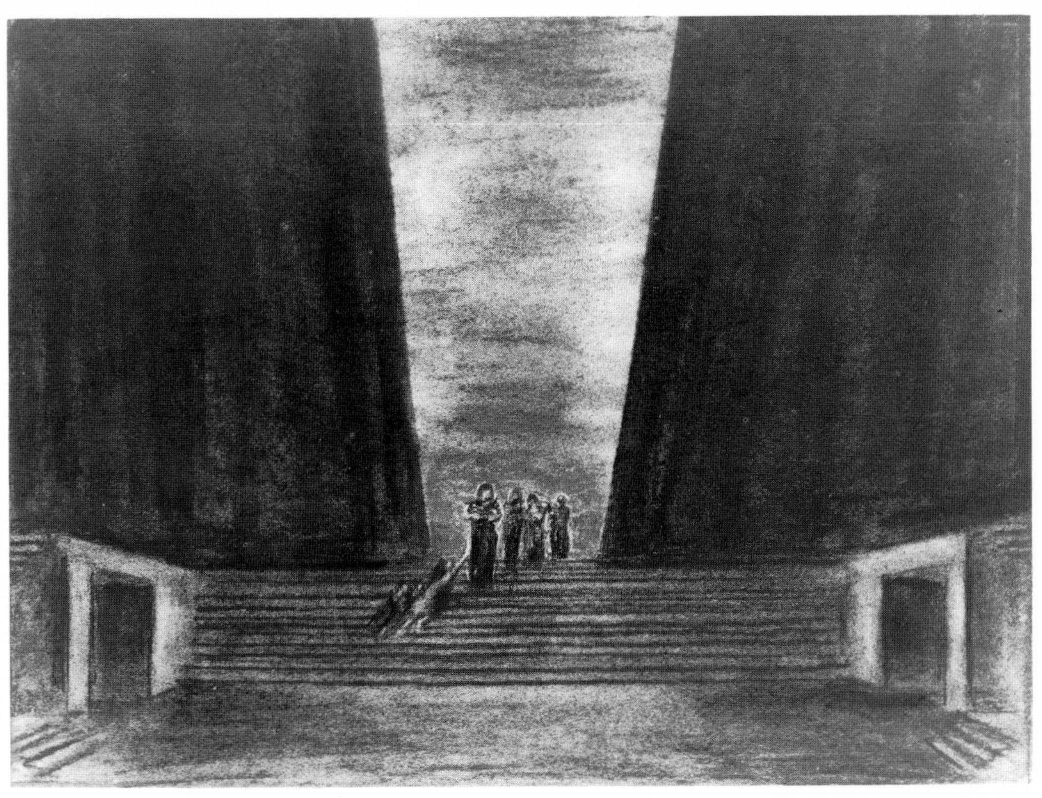

PIRCHAN, EMIL: Sketch for *William Tell* by Friedrich Schiller, production by Leopold Jessner (Staatliches Schauspielhaus, Berlin 1919)

centre there is a motif for each act, a wide window, for example, which looks out to a vista, without any distinctive style, of a threatening town, and which evokes the bars of a prison. There is the bare minimum of embellishment. In this partial and discontinuous décor, space plays a greater part through what it implies, than through what it states explicitly.

This approach is even clearer in the work of the producer, Leopold Jessner who, at the time of the production of *The Conversion* (*Die Wandlung*), took over the direction of the Berliner Staatstheater where in particular he put on *William Tell*, *Richard III*, *Othello*, and *Napoleon* by Grabbe.

The traditional use of the stage just did not suit Jessner: 'Away with the pictorial naturalism of the Swiss landscapes that no civilized spectator can possibly believe to be real', he writes about his production of *William Tell*. Away with all the theatrical lumber of perspective, of the wings. That belongs to an outdated age, we are living in a new period which relies on different suppositions and which must be shown in a meaningful way in the theatre.

Jessner and his stage designers (Pirchan for *Richard III* and *Othello*, Klein for *Napoleon*), refused the slightest appeal to the naturalism or impressionism of a Reinhardt. A lot has been said about dynamic space and rhythmic space, a notion dear to Adolphe Appia and Emile Jaques-Dalcroze. Jessner's achievements are, so to speak, the concrete manifestation of this. Rejecting all illusionism, Jessner and his stage designer constructed for each play an architecture that adapted to the rhythm of the action and where the fundamental lines reveal its validity. Movable platforms, podiums, slopes, staircases allow a three-dimensional production, clarify the action and reinforce it, as it were, make the stage breathe and render it expressive, serve the actor, distinguish moreover, the characters and sharpen their tension and contrast them more clearly. Jessner's famous steps do not link, they separate, isolate, create a dramatic distance between one group and another. Think of *Richard III*: blocking the stage, there is a wall,

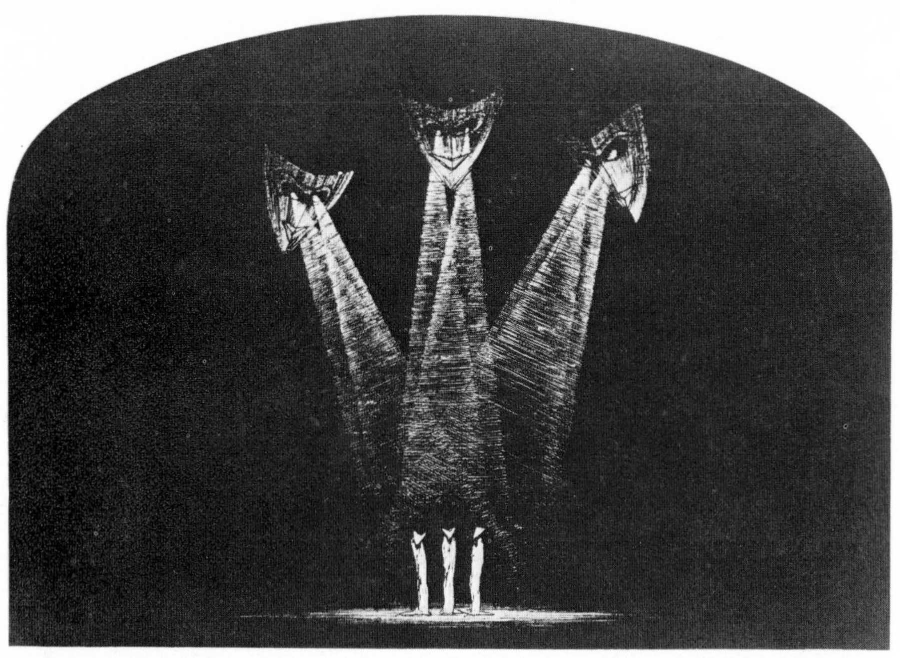

JONES, ROBERT EDMUND: Sketch for *Macbeth* by Shakespeare. Production by Arthur Hopkins (Apollo Theatre, New York 1921)

dominated by a platform, which a staircase with several landings leads to, which will be incorporated in the action, and materialize the rise and fall of Richard. At the end of the play, Richard falls from step to step before finally hacked down at the bottom of the set.

This symbolism which is not without a connection with the ideas of Craig, is found in the choice and use of the stage. There is no longer any question of representing the Tower of London or Desdemona's bedroom, but of giving the idea of their essential distinguishing features. Suggestions of a grey-green wall with a door in it which is sometimes visible, sometimes hidden by a staircase, is sufficient to create the dramatic context for *Richard III*. An element (a bed, a column) which becomes abstract, the corner of a house, sticking out against the conventional background of a cyclorama, a double, elliptical podium, nothing more is necessary to sustain the plot of *Othello*.

But the whiteness of the bed contrasts violently with the Moor's face. It is here that the use of colour symbolism praised by expressionist playwrights appears. Jessner, like the majority of expressionist directors, frequently had recourse to colour as a dramatic element and not only in the coloured lighting of the cyclorama, the tonality of which changes the course of action and adapts to various scenes, but also in the colour of the set (the red staircase in *Richard III*, the red of the royal purple, the red of the blood of the victims), and the symbolism of the costumes which become a sort of psychological and dramatic uniform. *Richard III* begins with a monologue by Richard dressed in black and against a black background, Richmond ends the play dressed in white against a background of white curtains in the battle scenes, Richard's soldiers are in black, whereas Richmond's troops are in white. The symbolism can be primary, but effective, in the associations that it arouses in the spectator.

The difference in certain pictorial décors by Sievert and the plastic masses of a Pirchan are therefore considerable, but beyond the fact that there is between their two modes of expression an entire series of nuanced positions, their opposition lies more in the means they use and their consequences, than in their essential aims. For the expressionists the décor must also participate in the acting along with all the other elements it must 'act with'. In Sievert it succeeds because it parallels the rôle of the actor (does not Sievert say that the atmosphere created is for the actor a 'second self', in Pirchan's work, it succeeds because it dynamically underpins the plot.

Light and Dark

Van Gogh wrote 'instead of seeking to render exactly what I have before my eyes, I use colour more arbitrarily to give strong expression to my feelings.' It is also to express their feelings strongly that producers like Jessner and Weichert use light arbitrarily.

KLEIN, CESAR: Sets for *Hölle, Weg, Erde* by Georg Kaiser, production by Viktor Barnowsky (Lessing Theatre, Berlin 1920)

For them it was no longer a question of limiting nature and of giving the impression that light comes from natural sources; in this area they reflect illusionism. Lighting allowed them to concentrate the spectator's attention, to clarify the plot, to accentuate the tension and achieve this while colouring the public's emotion. Light was also an element that participated in the acting, in the interplay between all the elements of expressionist theatre. If they used the cyclorama, as in lighting or colouring the stage, it was not to suggest a winter sky or a spring morning, but a neutral background, the colour equivalent of a particular dramatic moment which will stay in the audience's mind and convey the state of the soul of the principal character. If the light of the moon appeared to come in through a window, like in a décor by Sievert for *Drums in the Night* it is not so much to evoke moonlight as to deform objects, to project supernatural shadows and increase the pathetic tension. The darkness allowed stage designing to overthrow the world of objects, to enlarge the shadows until they became gigantic, illuminating the actor from below (one needs only to think in this context of a sketch by Cesar Klein for *Hölle, Weg, Erde)*.

Rather than general lighting, producers preferred clusters or flashes of light which at the crucial moment focus on the actor, remove him brutally from the world that surrounds him, cut his links with the external world, other characters, and isolate him in an ecstatic and luminous moment.

Stage lighting which assumes an even more meaningful, significant value in the plastic achievements of Jessner, appears as an equivalent to the stage set; it creates and breaks links between characters. It follows the actions not only illustrating movements but interpreting the essential. The concern to emphasize the essential corresponds to the dramatic construction of *Stationendrama*. It seems both to direct it and allow itself to be directed.

The stage is sometimes kept half-lit, sometimes divided into clusters of light, sometimes brought to life by violent contrasts, then the colours will change. They are the arbitrary accompaniment of the action, it has been said. Arbitrary if one places oneself in relation to normal reality, but logical from the point of view of expressionist stage technique.

Rather than writing an exhaustive history of the expressionist theatre, we have preferred to concentrate on analysis, its principal facets, and on where it appeared with the greatest coherence and purity, in Germany. But stage expressionism also appeared outside Germany, in other European countries, in the United States and in the Soviet Union. In most of these countries, however, we are dealing with a less profound and less sincere form of expressionism, which is not linked to expressionist drama as it is in Germany.

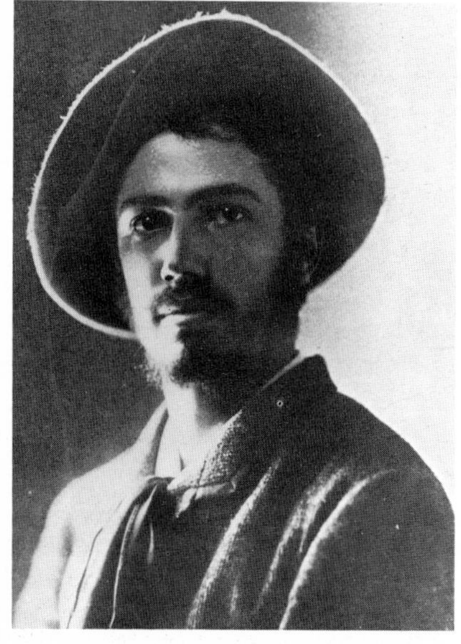

APPIA, ADOLPHE: Portrait

Actors and Producers

APPIA, Adolphe (Geneva, 1862 – Nyon, 1928). Appia was not the founder of any of the great movements of modern theatre, but he often inspired them, in particular with reference to expressionism. He foreshadows it in his writings (*Wagner on the stage*, 1895, *Die Musik und die Inszenierung*, 1899, *A Work of living art*, 1921), in his sketches, particularly those of 'rhythmic spaces' created in 1909, which prefigured certain stage sets imagined by Emil Pirchan for Leopold Jessner, notably for *William Tell* and for *Othello*. To a greater extent than in his own very few achievements, Appia also foreshadows expressionism through his conception of the rôle of the producer, a real orchestra leader, his radical refusal of naturalist realism, the function that he attributes to the lighting as creating and bringing life to the stage.

BARNOWSKY, Viktor (Berlin, 10.9.1875 – Berlin, 9.8.1952). Actor, producer and a director of German theatre. The most important period in his career was between 1913 and 1924, dates that mark the beginning and end of his direction of the Lessing-Theater in Berlin, one of the most important theatres in the capital. The greatest German actors, Bassermann, Dorsch, Jannings, Hörbiger, Kortner, Krauss and Pallenberg acted with him. Amongst the many writers he introduced, figure expressionists and especially Georg Kaiser who he introduced to the stage with sets by Cesar Klein in *Hölle, Weg, Erde* (1920) and *Von Morgens bis Mitternacht* (1920). These sets are among the most typical of German expressionism.

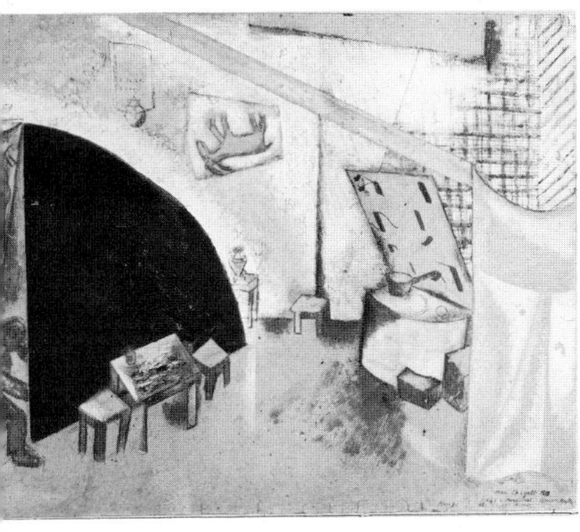

CHAGALL, MARC: Sketch for *Mazeltov* by Scholem Aleichem, production by Alexeï Granovski (Jewish State Theatre, Moscow 1919)

CHAGALL, Marc (Vitebsk, 7.7.1887). Strictly speaking, Marc Chagall does not belong to any specific school. Even if his technique has evolved, even if his themes and his modes of representation have changed, one still perceives in his work his own poetic universe where skies are populated with beings, where the animal and the human are brought very close together. In the U.S.S.R., after the 1917 revolution, on a number of occasions, he found his plans for stage sets rejected, and the Art Theatre in Moscow did not think it right to accept his sketches for *The Playboy of The Western World.* But his plans for various 'miniatures' by Scholem Aleichem put on in 1919 in the Jewish Kamerny Theatre in Moscow can be described as expressionist, notably those for *Mazeltov*, where objects and characters tend to be inserted in the pictorial context, where space is subjected to the pressure of distortions in the expressive opposition between curves and straight lines. Much later Chagall returned to stage sets. But this was for the ballet (*Aleko* by Massine, Mexico 1941) and in a more pictorial and decorative spirit.

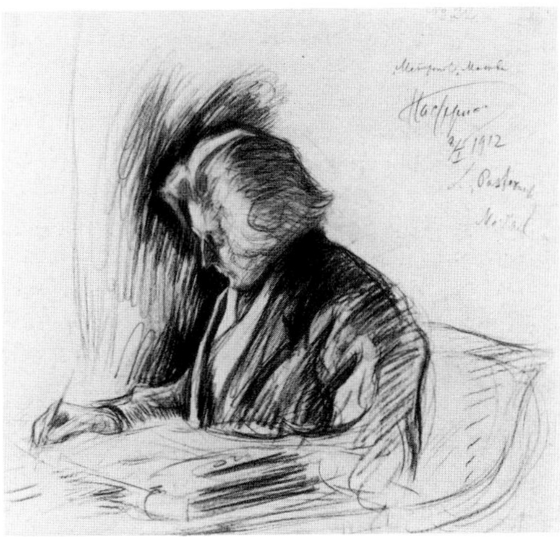

CRAIG, EDWARD GORDON: *Portrait.* Drawing by Leonid Pasternak. 1912

CRAIG, Edward Gordon (Stevenage, 16.1.1872 – Vence, 29.7.1966). In 1905 in his first important theoretical work *The Art of the Theatre*, the British producer, stage designer and theoretician wrote: 'the art of the theatre is neither the acting, the play, the production, nor the dancing: it is formed out of all the elements that compose it: the movement that is the soul of the acting: the words that are the body of the play; the lines and colours which are the very essence of the set: the rhythm which is the essence of the dancing.' This definition is both close to and far from the total work of art, Richard Wagner's *Gesamtkunstwerk* is close to it in so far as it defines a homogeneous work of art, but distant from it in so far as it advocates a union not of artistic forms, of means of expression, acting together, *mitspielend* as the German expressionists called it. In his productions, his sketches for sets exhibited in Germany and his theoretical writings Edward Gordon Craig foreshadowed scenic expressionism; he violently rejected all illusionist realism, all anecdotal naturalism, he was often partisan to an effective use of symbolism. Like Jessner later, he based the art of producing not on psychological depth but on a quest for the fundamental great ideas of the work, the central motif *(Macbeth)*, and when he put on *Hamlet* in the Arts Theatre in Moscow, his view of relationships between the work and its principal character is that of a monodrama. The monodrama is one of the key structures of expressionist theatre.

DEUTSCH, Ernst (Prague, 16.9.1890 – Berlin, 22.3.1969). An Austrian theatre and cinema actor, Ernst Deutsch worked in the Volksbühne in Vienna, in the company notably of Fritz Kortner, and Agnes Straub, but his real career began with the beginnings of stage expressionism. In 1916, in the Albert-Theater of Dresden he created one of the most characteristic

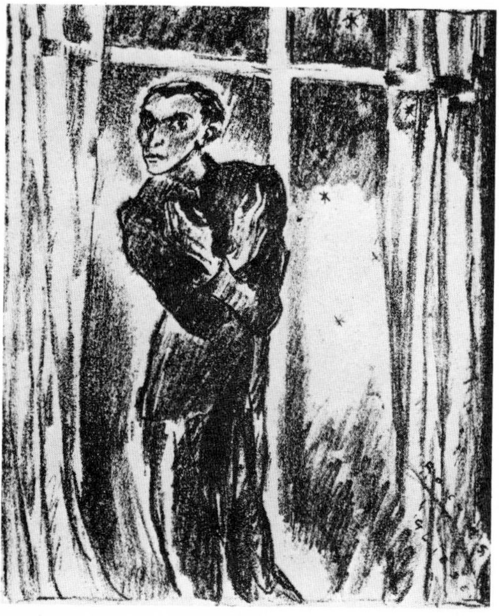

DEUTSCH, ERNST: in *The Son* (Der Sohn) by Walter Hasenclever. Lithograph by Rochus Gliese, 1918

figures of expressionism on the stage, the principal rôle of *The Son* (Der Sohn), the play by Hasenclever. Two years later, he returned to it in the *Junges Deutschland* directed by Max Reinhardt, after having acted in *The Beggar* (Der Bettler) by Sorge. The acting, the attitudes and mimics of Ernst Deutsch are reminiscent of the contorted silhouettes of the painted or graphic characters by Edvard Munch. From 1920 to 1933, Ernst Deutsch played, in different Berlin Theatres, the greatest rôles in the classical and modern repertoire with producers like Reinhardt, Jessner, Engel, Piscator and Fehling. The annexing of Austria by the Nazis compelled him in 1938 to leave Europe for the United States where he continued as an actor, an activity he took up again in Europe after the war. He managed to free himself from the methods of acting that had been his in the past and began so to speak a new career. Of his cinema roles, less important than those he played in the theatre, one recalls in particular his extraordinary acting

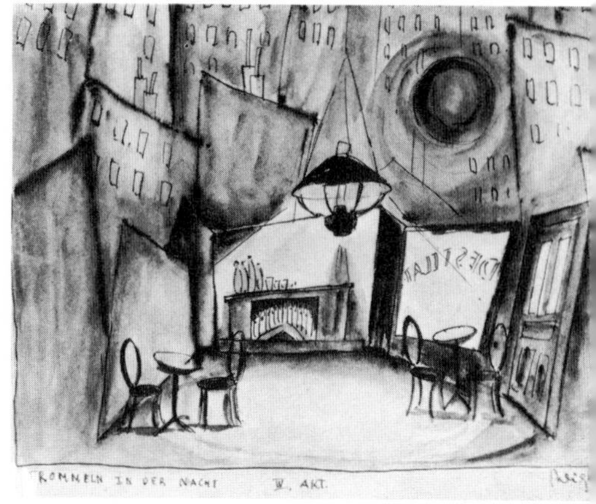

REIGBERT, OTTO: Sets for *Drums in the Night* (Trommeln in der Nacht) by Bertold Brecht, production by Otto Falckenberg (Kammerspiele, Munich 1922)

in the film by Karl Heinz Martin from the play by Georg Kaiser *From Morn to Midnight*, 1920 (Von Morgens bis Mitternacht) and his acting in the successful film after the war, *The Third Man*, 1951.

FALCKENBERG, Otto (Coblenz, 5.10.1873 – Munich, 25.12.1947). Falckenberg was a producer, theatre critic and even a playwright. History will no doubt only remember his activity as a producer, in spite of the success that some of his plays had at the time. Even if this German producer occasionally left Munich, the capital of Bavaria was to remain his main centre of activity. He knew Wedekind there and acted with him in *The Earth Spirit* (Erdgeist) right at the beginning of the century: he became a producer at the Kammerspielhaus (1913) before becoming its director in 1917, a post he kept till his death.

Falckenberg was not a theoretical or dogmatic producer. He attached more importance to the text and to the acting than to the stage presentation, which did not prevent him from working with excellent stage designers like Pasetti or Reigbert. In fact he oscillated between expressionism and impressionism with the sincerity of a man conscious of the needs of individual works. The importance he attached to Strindberg and Wedekind justifies in advance that which he granted to the expressionists, who were to a certain extent their successors: *From Morn to Midnight* (Von Morgens bis Mitternacht) and *Coral* (Die Koralle) by Georg Kaiser (1917) *Louis Ferdinand, Prince of Prussia* (1923) by Fritz von Unruh, *Drums in the Night*, 1922 one of Brecht's first plays and still marked by expressionism in its structure, the conception of the characters and the positions they assume. The staging of this play was the occasion for the stage designer Otto Reigbert to produce one of the more typical series of expressionist sets. (cf. article on O. Reigbert).

GRANOVSKI, Alexei-Azarkh (Moscow, 1890 – Paris, 1937). Granovski studied stage design at the School of Stage Design in Saint Petersburg and did his apprenticeship in Germany, where he was an assistant to Reinhardt in Munich in 1913. After an interruption in his activities because of the war, he returned to Russia, where he put on *Oedipus Rex* and *Macbeth* in the Chinizelli circus in Petrograd (1918). In 1919, Granovski founded a Yiddish Studio which was set up

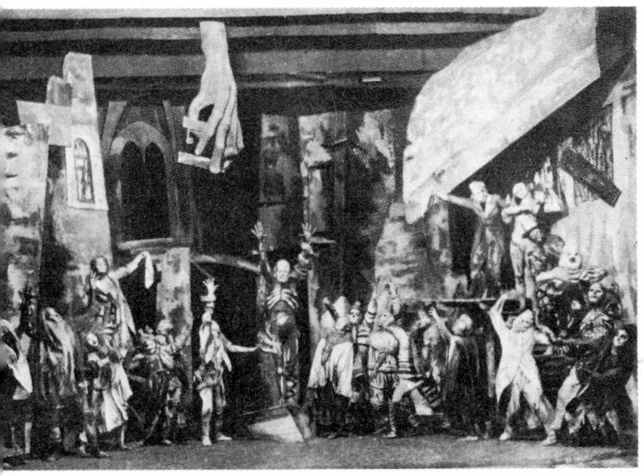

FALK, ROBERT: Sets for *Night in the old market* (Die Nacht auf dem alten Markt) by Peretz, production by Alexei Granovski (The Jewish State Theatre in Moscow. 1924)

in 1920 in Moscow and soon became the Jewish State Chamber Theatre or GOSET (1920). Under Granovski's direction, GOSET developed a number of brilliant ideas. In 1928–1929, he went on an extensive tour of Europe, but Granovski did not return to the U.S.S.R. During his exile in Western Europe, he above all developed his skills as a cinema director he had begun to acquire in Russia.

Even if it was deeply involved in the Soviet revolution in the theatre, GOSET nevertheless retained its own originality. Using the popular sources of the Jewish theatre, it developed as a synthetic theatre based on the concerted use of movement which was rational at the same time as being violently expressive, and on the close co-operation between Granovski and painters like Chagall, Falk or Rabinovitch.

Very important plays like *Soirée Shalom Aleichem* (1921), *The Sorceress* (1922), *200,000* (1923) or *Night in the Old Market* (1925) show all the dimensions of GOSET's stage language, its abstraction, fury and carnival, and, underlying them, this form of critical 'alienation' that constitutes a demystifying irony. Achieving a vital synthesis between two essential currents and which were apparently in opposition to the art of the twenties, it put forward an explosive mixture of rationality and expressivity. In all twentieth-century theatre, it is the most forceful expression of the grotesque.

HILAR, Karel Hugo (Sudomerice, 1885 – Prague, 1935). Czech theatre producer. Hilar, at first influenced

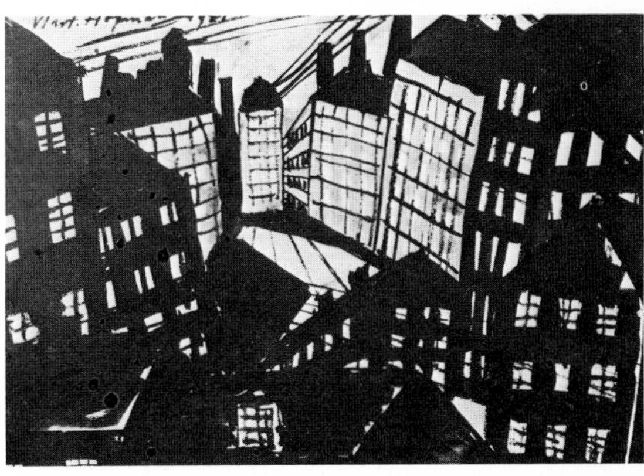

HOFMAN, VLASTISLAV: Sketch for *The Hydra* by Jiri Maranek, production by K. Dostal (municipal theatres, Prague 1921)

by Max Reinhardt's impressionism, began as a producer at the Municipal Theatres in Prague in 1911. He became director of them in 1914. After the war, he turned towards expressionism, an expressionism that is not far from that of Jessner in its interplay between the rhythmical organization of the stage space and the importance of the actors' language of gesture. A producer with absolute power, Hilar soon associated with the scenographer Vlastislav Hofman, and he imposed his style on the National Theatre. Towards 1924–25, his expressionism weakened and he seemed to be turning towards the 'New Objectivity'.

HOFMAN, Vlastislav (Jicin, 1884–?). An excellent Czech theatre director, even if he did not participate in any of the more daring experiments attempted in Prague in the twenties. He achieved his best works by collaborating with the producer Karel Hugo Hilar. Several of his achievements are due to an effective expressionism mingled with elements directly inspired by cubism. This plastic expressionism is reflected both in the representation and the organization of the space, one notices this from 1919 in the stage set for A. Dvorak's *Hussites*. One finds it the following year in Verhaeren's *Dawns*, and in 1928 for Goethe's *Faust*, but it is especially in Maranek's *Hydra* (1921), that he shows his talent effectively, allowing one of the greatest themes of dramaturgy and expressionist scenography to emerge: the omnipresent town, the pictorial distortions and contrasts of night and light enlivened and rendered even more disquieting.

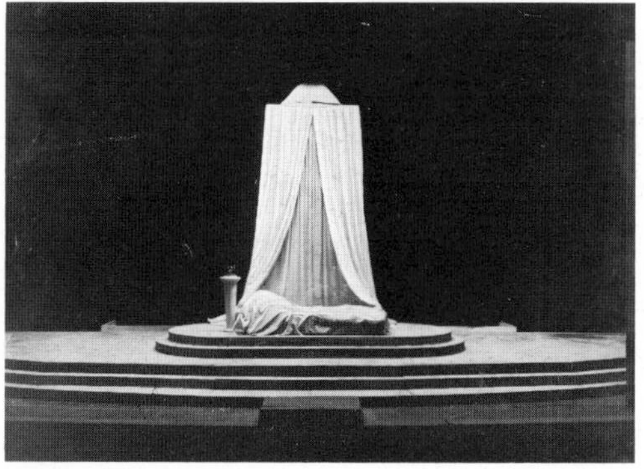

PIRCHAN, EMIL: Sets for *Othello* by Shakespeare, production by Leopold Jessner (Staatliches Schauspielhaus, Berlin 1921)

JESSNER, Leopold (Königsberg, 3.3.1878 – Hollywood, 30.10.1945). Leopold Jessner is without a doubt, along with Richard Weichert, one of the most important German expressionist producers. From 1905 to 1915, he was the *Oberspielleiter* (chief director) at the Thalia-Theatre in Hamburg, where he put on in particular in 1911 *Tartuffe* by Molière which reveals all his qualities. Having directed from 1915 to 1919, the Neue Schauspielhaus of Königsberg, he was appointed director of the Berlin Staatstheater in 1919. Apart from his talent, his political ideas explain his appointment just as they explain his resignation in 1930. Directing the Berlin Staatstheater represents Jessner's most active and original period, dating from his first production, Schiller's *William Tell* in 1919. He appears here as the conscious opponent, on the aesthetic level, both of Reinhardt's psychological-romantic impressionism and the academicism of the court theatres. The production of *William Tell* reveals a few of the major principles behind Jessner's style at this time:

– The production must be based on the discovery and the emphasizing of the fundamental theme of the work, rejecting anecdote and concentrating on the essential points.

– Stage illusionism is violently rejected as is the accumulation of pseudo-realist details. Emphasizing the most essential aspects of a play requires a plastic and symbolic organization of the stage space. Hence the role attributed to the *Stufenbühne*, where the stage is filled with a huge staircase made out of steps and a landing, and thought up by the scenographer Emil Pirchan, then Jessner's associate, which helped the producer by its vigorous conception of space to create 'a style focusing on the essential points, a style of precision.'

– Whatever the use of symbolic means of expression, the producer attached the greatest importance to the force of the word, to the significance of the language of gesture. These characteristics are perfectly epitomized by the actor Fritz Kortner acting the part of Gessler, and he was without doubt the best actor of this part.

After *William Tell*, Jessner put on a series of remarkable productions of classical and modern authors, making no distinction between classical plays, which he regarded as just as modern as the contemporary ones, and the latter. Amongst the works from the past he put on *Richard III* (1920), *Othello* (1921), by Shakespeare, *Marquis von Keith* by Wedekind (1920) and *Napoleon* by Grabbe (1922); among the modern works, *Die echten Sedemunds* by Barlach and *Ostpolzug* by Bronnen.

Having said this, Jessner's personality was not consistent. It evolved, without there being any question of opportunism, but because of political events (the rise of Nazism) and artistic changes, the development of the 'New Objectivity'. His production in 1926 of a political *Hamlet* related to contemporary reality, and in 1929 that of a *King Lear* which is placed in the spirit of the nascent epic theatre, illustrates this. During his career in the Berlin Staatstheater, Jessner produced several films: *The Back Staircase* (Hintertreppe) in 1921, and *Earth Spirit* (Der Erdgeist) in 1922.

In 1933 he had to go into exile. He went to the U.S. and, almost entirely forgotten, he died in Hollywood in 1945.

JOOSS, Kurt (Wasseralfingen, 12.1.1901). Dancer, choreographer and producer. After studying music, Jooss made the acquaintance in Stuttgart of Rudolf von Laban, with whom he studied the theoretical and practical bases of ballet. Turning towards free ballet he became master of ballet and director of 'movement' at the Münster Stadttheater. With Aino Siimola and the stage designer Heinz Heckroth, he founded the *Neue Tanzbühne* and created his first expressionist ballets. He soon entered the Folkwangschule and presented in Paris in 1932 his most famous ballet *The Green Table* (Der grüne Tisch) which won a golden medal in the International choreography competition. This biting satire on war had an immense success throughout the world. At

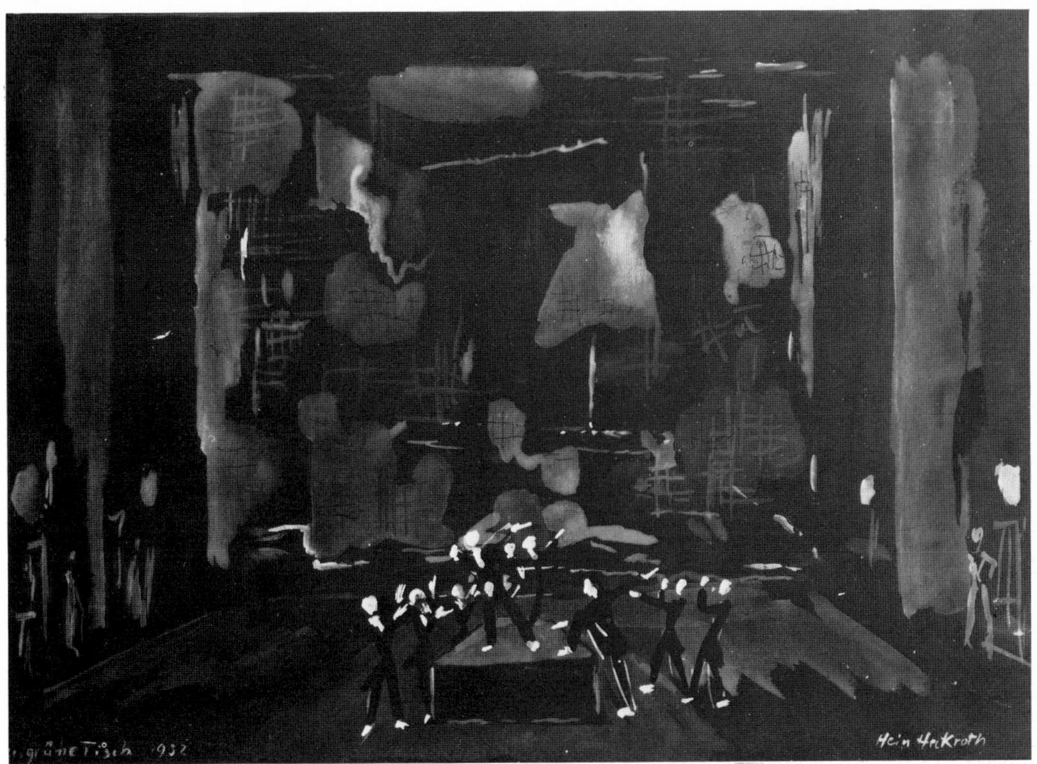

HECKROTH, HEIN: Sketch for *The Green Table* (Der grüne Tisch), ballet, choreography by Kurt Jooss (Théâtre des Champs-Elysées, Paris and Städtische Bühnen, Essen 1932)

the level of the ballet, it mingles traditional elements, free movement, and a kind of purified expressionism. Jooss left Germany for England with most of his collaborators. After the war he resumed his work in Germany.

KLEIN, Cesar (Hamburg, 14.9.1876 – Pansdorf, 13.3.1954). Having studied painting in Hamburg, Düsseldorf and Berlin, he became an important expressionist painter, a member of the *Neue Sezession* (1910) and of the November Group (1910). At the end of his life he tended towards surrealism.

Cesar Klein combined his career as a painter with being a scenographer, he worked for the theatre and even the cinema (*Genuine*, produced by Robert Wiene, 1920). In the theatre, he worked notably with the producer Viktor Barnowsky at the Berlin Lessing-Theater with other stage managers as famous as Leopold Jessner, Jürgen Fehling, Erwin Piscator and participated in a number of productions on stage in Berlin, Hamburg and Vienna.

His most famous productions are without doubt *Hölle, Weg, Erde* by Kaiser (production by Barnowsky, Berlin 1920), *From Morn to Midnight* (Von Morgens bis Mitternacht) by Kaiser (production by Barnowsky, Berlin 1921), *Napoleon* by Grabbe (production by Jessner, Berlin 1922). They illustrate perfectly how Klein used the means of expression of the expressionist stage. In a sketch for *Hölle, Weg, Erde*, what is striking is the transformation of the space in relation to normal reality, its contraction which makes it asphyxiating, it is also the anti-naturalist lighting which illuminates the main character from underneath (monodrama) and projects a very large shadow against the backcloth, and which contrasts violently with purely functional lighting. In *From Morn to Midnight*, Klein still makes the distortion form the image of a central tree, distortions that render it spectral, at the same time as they tend towards anthropomorphism, to animating the inanimate: branches are transformed into a skeleton whose hands stretch out or hang in a threatening way. Expressionism is not afraid of using 'primary' symbolism. For *Napoleon*, Cesar Klein's expressionist stage image veers towards the monumental. Without being equivalent to them or parallel, the sets are linked in their inspiration to Pirchan's in the symbolic organization of space, 'concentrated signs'.

This expressionism is of the early twenties. Subsequently, Klein evolved towards surrealism.

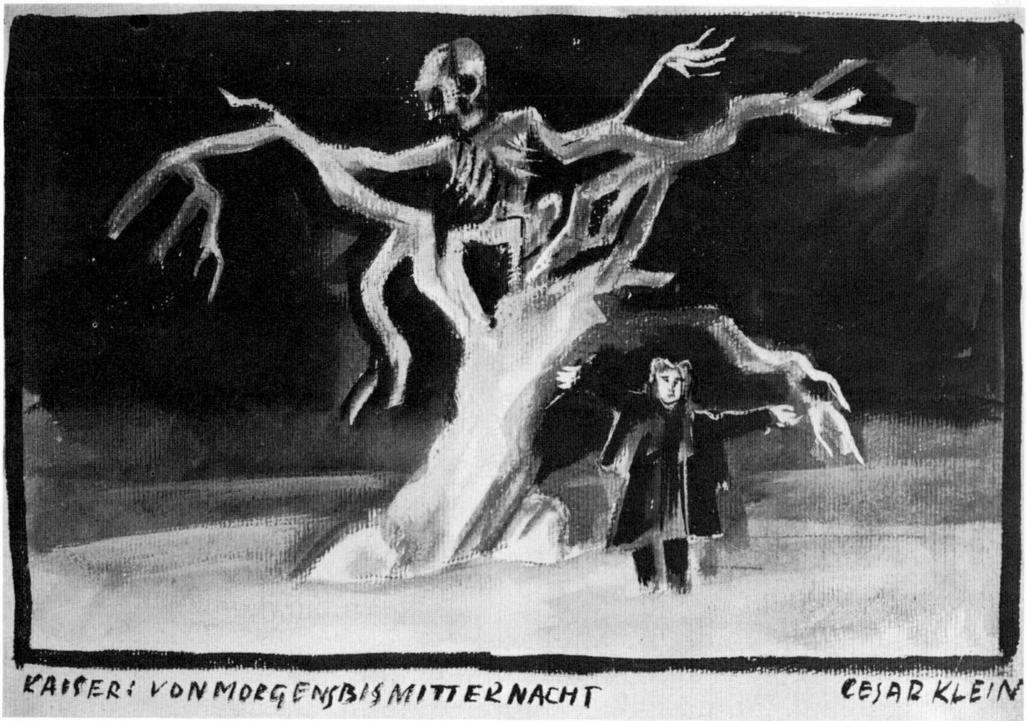

KLEIN, CESAR: Sketch for *From Morn to Midnight* (Von Morgens bis Mitternacht) by Georg Kaiser, production by Viktor Barnowsky (Lessing-Theater, Berlin 1921)

KORTNER, Fritz (Vienna, 12.5.1892 – Vienna, 22.7.1974). Austrian stage and film actor Fritz Kortner made his debut in 1910 in the National Theater of Mannheim. He went on to the Deutsches Theater in Berlin, the Volksbühne in Vienna and the Lessing-Theater in Berlin. It was at the Vienna Volksbühne in 1917 that his real qualities as an actor emerged in *Herod and Mariamne.* But his name was soon associated with the most remarkable expressionist producers, in *The Conversion* (Die Wandlung) by Toller, production by Karl Heinz Martin at the Berlin Staatstheater where in 1917 Jessner, its manager and producer, took him on. He stayed there from 1919–23 and 1926–30. Amongst his major roles on this stage, we might mention Gessler in the famous 1919 *William Tell*, where he revealed an extraordinary power of concentration in his movements and even more in his expressive use of the rhythmical and controlled word; then in *Richard III*, which led to his being called the 'architect of language', where he achieved an astonishing balance between the power of mimicry and expressiveness in the voice, Sedemund in the play by Barlach, Othello and many other roles. Two years after having played the leading role in Jessner's political version of *Hamlet*, when, under the influence of the 'New Objectivity', his acting had further gained in precision, Kurt Pinthus could write: 'Kortner has renounced almost any element emanating from Nature, everything that before appeared as a condition of the actor's art. Neither his physiognomy, facial expression nor his voice is beautiful in any respect, or rich in expres-

KORTNER, FRITZ: In *Richard III*

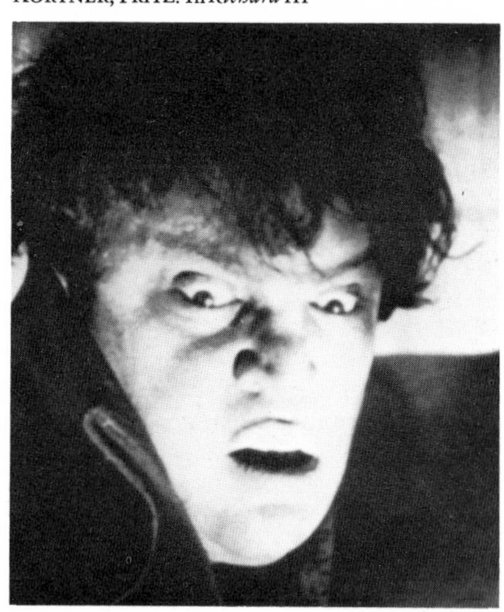

sion. He does not build himself up from the imagination, but from the heart of the expression. His art is not ambiguous, nor is his acting rich in nuances and the language of gesture. Dogmatic theoreticians ought to say: his style is that of the "New Objectivity", that is to say a concentrated but over-sharpened simplicity.'

In 1933, Fritz Kortner had to leave Nazi Germany. First he took refuge in Austria, then moved to U.S.A. in 1928. There he was active as a film actor and as a playwright. On his return to Germany after the war he resumed an active career as a producer and actor at Düsseldorf, Munich and Berlin.

Kortner's parallel activity as a film actor was rich and varied, even if it did not appear as impressive as his achievement as an actor on stage, beginning with his part in *The Back Staircase* (Hintertreppe) by Leopold Jessner in 1921, his career was marked by an impressive number of films.

KRAUSS, Werner (Coburg, 23.6.1884 – Coburg, 20.10.1959). This German stage and film actor went on stage from a very early age. Without having any academic training, he frequented the theatres of Guben, Detmold and Nuremberg. In 1913, when he was playing *Peer Gynt*, he was noticed by Moissi who recommended him to Max Reinhardt, who took him on at the Deutsches Theater. In 1913 he scored his first triumph in Hebbel's *Nibelungen*. This global interpretation, which refuses to become enmeshed in details, is in contrast to the psychological approach of actors in the Reinhardt school, and is particularly suited to the series of Wedekind's characters that he played, keeping them at a distance like an artist in the process of sculpting a work. One understands why such a temperament is perfectly appropriate for the expressionist repertoire (*Seeschlacht* by Reinhard Goering) and the characters he constantly played: Polonius in *Hamlet* in 1920; Shylock, 1921; Lear 1923. He was associated in succession with the Deutsches Theater in Berlin (1913–1924), the Staatstheater (1924–1926), the Burgtheater in Vienna (1928–1929 and 1933–1944). After the war, he still had a number of successes. His film acting is of the same standard as his stage acting.

MARTIN, Karl Heinz (Freiburg-im-Breisgau, 6.5.1888 – Berlin, 13.1.1948). This German producer, who worked for the theatre and the cinema, proved in his creative activity, better than any other, that the expressionist experiment, however decisive and dramatic it might have been, remained ephemeral. But in fact for Karl Heinz Martin it was crucial and can be summed up perfectly in one play – *The Conversion* – produced in 1919 at the Tribune a theatre founded and run by Leonhard and Martin in Berlin and in a film *From Morn to Midnight* (Von Morgens bis Mitternacht) based on the play by Kaiser with the same title (1920).

Karl Heinz Martin began a brilliant career very early on since from the age of 21, he took over the direction of the Frankfurt Komödienhaus, going to the Schauspielhaus in the same town (1915), then to the Thalia-Theater in Hamburg. The Berlin production of *The Conversion* in 1909 made him appear along with Leopold Jessner as one of the major expressionist producers, amongst the most typical, the most marked, the most effective and most significant. He then worked in the largest Berlin theatres: Großes Schauspielhaus, Deutsches Theater, Volksbühne, Schiller-Theater, etc. After the Second World War, Martin continued his career, put on Gorky's *Night Refuge* which marked the return of Busch on to Berlin stages. The intentions of the Tribune theatre are defined in a manifesto *(Die Tribüne)* in 1919, which clarifies its expressionist and social aspect. The production of *The Conversion* is expressionist on every level, in each of its elements, in

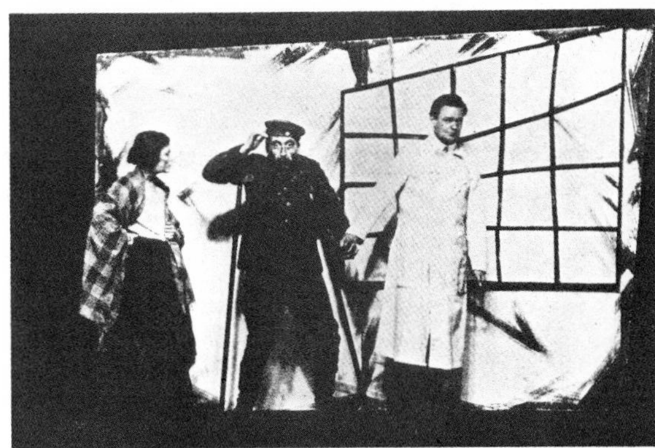

NEPPACH, ROBERT: Sets for *The Conversion* (Die Wandlung) by Ernst Toller, production by Karl Heinz Martin

the very conception of the art of producing, concentrating on major themes and constructed like the drama itself, that is to say as *Stationendrama*, in the acting, and especially that of Fritz Kortner, a real revelation, whose vocal and physical interpretation was built out of tensions, impulses, explosions and restraint that gave a play a decisive presence. The sets were designed by Robert Neppach, who, against an ill-defined and disturbing black backcloth used panels alluding to abstract forms and intentional distortions concerning which, one can use Jessner's term 'concentrated signs'.

It was also Robert Neppach who designed the fantasmagorical universe of the film production by Karl Heinz Martin for *From Morn to Midnight* where Ernst Deutsch showed himself to be the excellent expressionist actor that he had already proved to be on stage.

PIRCHAN, Emil (Brunn, 27.5.1884 – Vienna, 20.12.1957). After studying at the Higher Technical School and the Academy of Plastic Arts in Vienna, where he followed the teaching of the architect Otto Wagner, Emil Pirchan successively did a number of things (teaching, founding a studio for architecture and graphic arts and forming a school for poster art in Munich) before really joining the theatre by becoming the leading stage designer at the Munich Staatstheater. From then on, more than 300 productions span his career, particularly twenty-three in Germany, Austria, Czechoslovakia, and this along with all his responsibilities did not prevent him from also pursuing a career of less importance, but still significant, as an author of novels, short stories, libretti for ballets and operas and monographs on painters (Hans Makart, Gustav Klimt) and also works on his dramatic methods and the history of the theatre. Despite the obvious quality of some of his works, these are not the source of Pirchan's originality. Neither is it the number of his productions that has made him famous with posterity.

In fact, Pirchan's fame and the quality of his work are directly linked to his collaboration with the producer Leopold Jessner. When the latter became the director of the Staatstheater in Berlin, he asked Pirchan to work for him, and he was Jessner's chief designer from 1922 until 1930 when Jessner had to resign. The two men collaborated closely and formed a team. The twentieth century has seen other examples of this kind of collaboration: Brecht-Neher, Vilar-Gischia, Strehler-Damiani. But, in fact it was only during Jessner's expressionist period (1919–25) that this collaboration was fruitful. Pirchan's style was then very concerted, willed, profoundly coherent. After 1925, he tended to lose his sharpness, to become academic, to allow himself to be overwhelmed by curves and decorative embellishment. What, therefore, was Pirchan's style in the great period? An absolute rejection of naturalism that one found in *William Tell* (Staatstheater, 1919) *The Marquis von Keith, Richard III* (1920) or *Othello* (1921). It was no longer a question of copying immediate reality, of keeping to appearances, or not being decorative. It was now a matter of finding expressive elements to convey the *Grundprinzip* (the fundamental principle) the *Grundidee* (the basic idea) of the work, a way of allowing the actors to express it, and all this was to be rendered with the strictest economy and in the most strident manner. The strength of this approach lay first in the organization of the space. Consciously or unconsciously Pirchan showed himself to be the disciple both of Craig and Appia. He had, therefore,

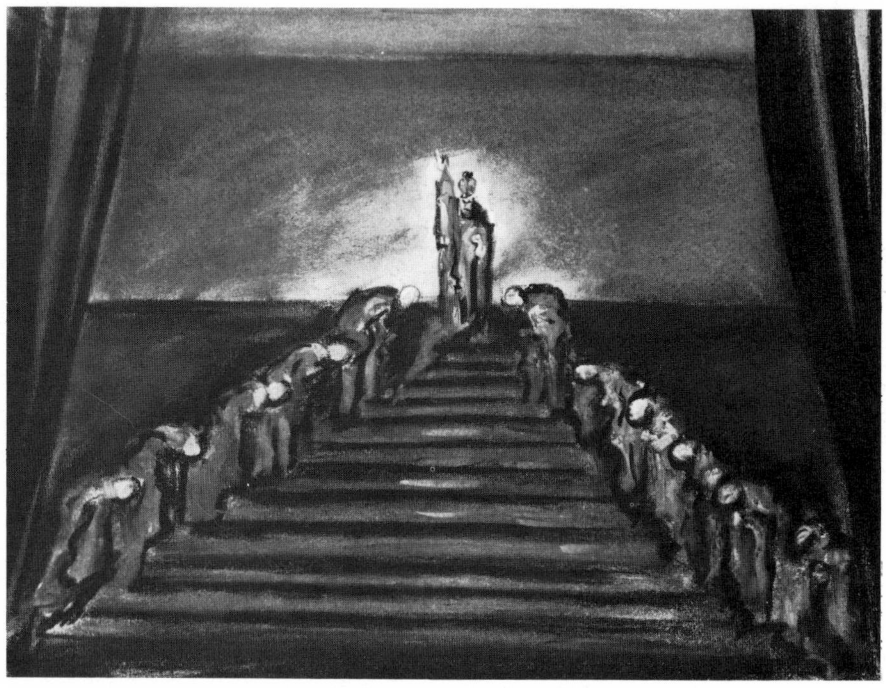

PIRCHAN, EMIL: Drawing for *Richard III* by Shakespeare, production by Leopold Jessner (Staatliches Schauspielhaus, Berlin 1920)

to create zones between which liaisons could be born and very often tensions and breaks which are the image of the profound relationship between the characters. He had to proceed to a *Terrassierung des Terrains*: literally 'dividing the ground up into terraces.' That means the creation of specific areas for acting, levels which are more or less raised and spatially linked. *William Tell, Richard III, Othello* are perfect examples of this approach. In *William Tell*, the basic set consisted of a vast staircase, with overhangings on both sides; the set had two full curtains to add to its suggestive power; there were no longer any Swiss landscapes, only the idea still remained, scarcely evoked in the distance by a white angular form that really has nothing photographic about it. Jessner's production of *Richard III* was based on the same principle. There are two main ideas: on the one hand, the fear of the Tower of London, materialized by a high wall, in the middle of the stage, like a parapet walk, pierced at its base by a central porch that can be both an entrance or a prison cell, on the other hand, the rise and fall of the powerful, rendered in a concrete form by a vast central staircase, the very symbol of development, of the ascent towards power, of the rise of the usurpers and their fall directly materialized by the use the producer makes of them. This is obvious symbolism that some described as 'primary', like the colours that are complementary to it. The play opens with Richard dressed in black against a black background. It ends with the lines that Richmond dressed in white delivers against a white background.

If, in several ways, the stage sets designed by Pirchan might appear old-fashioned and no longer correspond to our conception of the theatre, it is nevertheless true that they are very close to those used at the Theatre National Populaire by Jean Vilar, and which were foreshadowed thirty years beforehand by Pirchan.

REIGBERT, Otto (Kiel, 4.9.1890 – Munich, 3.2.1957). In his youth, this German set-designer was lucky enough to be guided by such experienced designers as Sven Gade, Knut Strom, Rochus Gliese, and Ludwig Sievert. But the event that marked him the most deeply and influenced his creative imagination in a decisive manner, was the First World War with its horrors, the importance of which, in understanding the expressionism of the twenties and its strident tones, will never be fully recognized.

REIGBERT, OTTO: Sketch for *Drums in the Night* (Trommeln in der Nacht) by Bertold Brecht, production by Otto Falckenberg (Kammerspiele, Munich 1922)

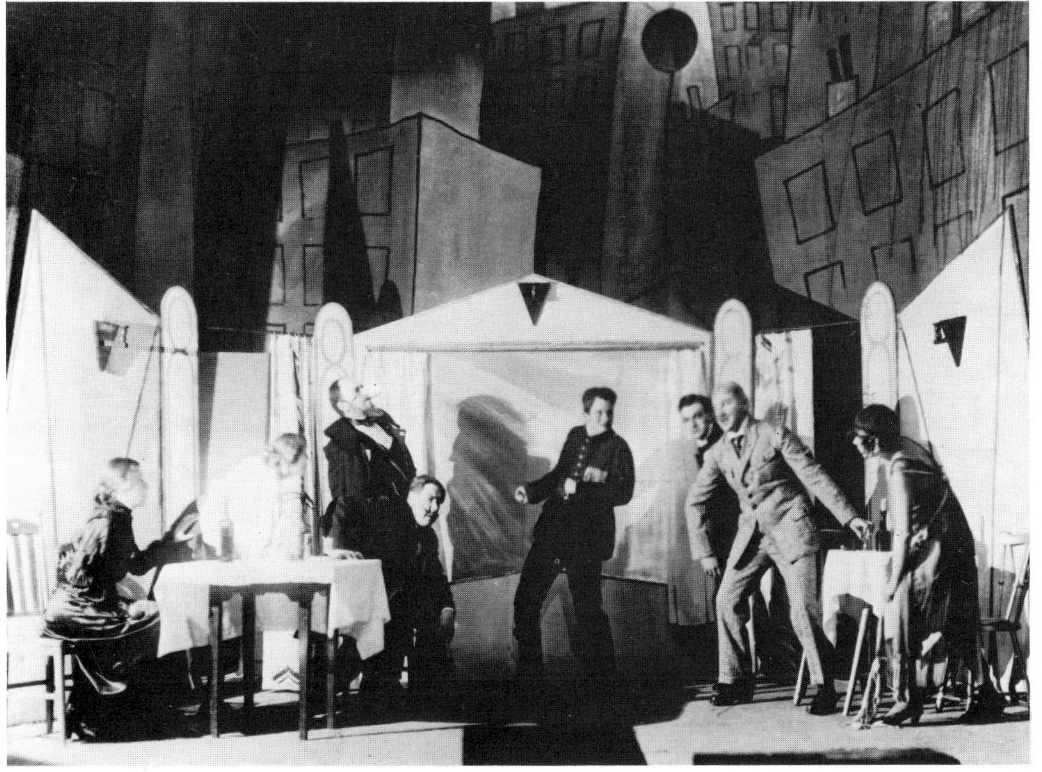

Reigbert's expressionism is not contrived but sincere. Reigbert stayed close to the words and the revolt expressed is also his, and it is translated in his stage design. In 1914, the violence of those he designed for *The Son* (Der Sohn) by Hasenclever (the distortions, the sharp contrasts between light and dark, the chaos of the clusters of light, in a word, the destruction of a universe) led to his being dismissed from the theatre in Kiel. He spent the 1919–20 season at *The Tribunal* Theatre led by the young Piscator in Königsberg, and he too was deeply marked by the war, after which he became the direct associate of Otto Falkenberg. He stayed there till 1932. It was during this period that he designed, out of about 300 productions, his best expressionist sets. For example, *Drums in the Night* by Brecht (1922). The collection of sketches reveal a universe shaken to its foundations, a prey to distortion and symbol of collapse and revolt, sweating with anguish. The stage is often divided in half: in the foreground, the interior, in the background the towns and houses as if brought to life by an omnipresent threat. Suspended as a conventional symbol, a moon injected with blood. Reigbert's solution deserves to be compared with that of Ludwig Sievert for the same play (c.f. article on Sievert). It is a similar solution that Reigbert found for the sets he designed in for example Wedekind's *Lulu* (Munich 1928). But the distortions are then much less obvious. The theatre evolved rapidly, expressionism was superseded and Reigbert's style tempered.

REINHARDT, Max (Baden, near Vienna, 9.9.1873–New York, 30.10.1943). 'I would have great difficulty in saying whether I am a realist, a stylist or fantasist. I reject all systems, all preconceived ideas. I want to be able to commit myself wholeheartedly to all ideas. I like a work passionately. I start from that, I give it life within me, and always when it is the work that excites me, it appears to me to as a spirit, a *Zeitgeist* that I am dying to bring out.' This is what Max Reinhardt declared to Benjamin who interviewed him (in *Je suis partout*, 28.10.1933).

Really one cannot classify Max Reinhardt. He started out with naturalism, but soon freed himself from it. To say that he is an impressionist is to praise the way in which he knows, beyond immediate reality, how to translate impalpable atmospheres, but this is to restrict his talent. To describe him as baroque is to underline his taste for the spectacular and his affinities with an art that inspired him, but this is to emphasize only one facet of his talent. In fact, of all the performers of the theatre at the beginning of the twentieth century (Appia, Craig, Fuchs, Stanislavsky), Max Reinhardt seems the most eclectic. A virtuoso producer, a popularizer of genius, he had feeling for authors and he borrowed from Craig, from Fuchs, principles and visions that he materialized, he was the practician *par excellence.*

Reinhardt's eclecticism lies in his means of expression: black curtains with a very sophisticated décor mounted on a revolving stage; and also in the stages he used, from the small theatre to the theatres for 5,000 built after the war by Hans Poelzig and endowed with a vast buttressed stage (Grosses Schauspielhaus in Berlin), from the Deutsches Theater to the arena of the Schumann Circus and the precincts of Salzburg Cathedral. His desire was to find for each dramatic work the most appropriate way of putting it on the stage, the best relationship between the public and the action on the stage, between the spectator and the actor. Testimony, proof and illustration of a very open mind, ready to exploit everything of use to the theatre, an art form that he considered the most powerful and the most direct. On the other side of the coin, this open-

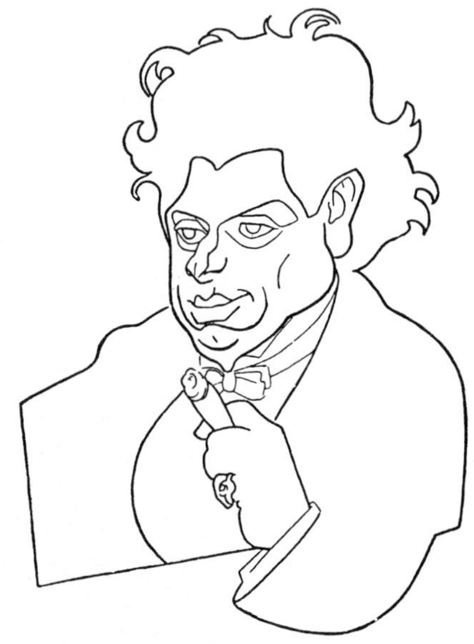

REINHARDT, MAX: Portrait. Drawing by Olaf Gulbranson for *Simplicissimus*

mindedness led him to make errors of judgement; combined with his love for the stage, it did not stop him occasionally being over-elaborate and necessarily arousing the protest of amateurs from poor theatres avid for purity. The consequence of this was that if he was a popularizer, he was also an innovator, but he did not follow any ideological or artistic line.

For several reasons, Max Reinhardt cannot be described as expressionist, even if he prefigured stage expressionism. None of his productions can be called expressionist, because they remain impregnated with a certain emphasis on psychology, with a certain decorativism that detracts from their force and which is only a general cry of revolt. However, he prepared the way for expressionism, prefigured it and brought expressionism to the stage. Firstly, by the means of expression he used, especially that of light and darkness, not naturalist, sometimes violently contrasted, sometimes gentle effects reminiscent of Rembrandt. Then by the plays he included in his repertoire: in the first place Strindberg, whom one cannot easily define as an expressionist, but who has the same relationship to dramatic expressionism as Edvard Munch has to pictorial expressionism. Secondly, and especially, all the young German members of the movement that he welcomed on to the stage of *Das junge Deutschland*, an experimental stage of the Deutches Theater that he founded in 1917. These included Sorge, Goering, Hasenclever, Werfel, Fritz von Unruh, Else Lasker-Schüler, Kokoschka, Paul Kornfeld who produced *The Beggar* (Der Bettler) by Sorge, *The Coral* (Die Koralle) by Kaiser, *Sea Battle* (Die Seeschlacht) by Goering, *The Son* (Der Sohn) by Hasenclever. Parallel to the activity of this experimental studio, Arthur Kahane and Heinz Herald published a monthly review which had the same title of which a number contained the text of the programme by the playwright Paul Kornfeld *Der beseelte und der psychologische Mensch.* He defines in particular the aims of the expressionist actor. The stage and review did not last more than three seasons. But they revealed to the public, however small, and more importantly to a number of practicians of theatre, a new theatre born out of a current of sensibility. This new drama was to be performed on many stages. No doubt the essential nature of the support of Max Reinhardt for the expressionist theatre lies in this latter contribution.

SIEVERT, Ludwig (Hamburg, 17.5.1887 – Munich, 11.12.1966). He was one of the most brilliant figures of twentieth-century German set design, one of the most skilled stage designers of the age, whose virtuosity explains his limits, his change of direction and sometimes his eclecticism. Having received a very open-minded and sound education, Ludwig Sievert began his career at the Stadttheater at Freibourg-im-Breisgau, where he was appointed artistic adviser in 1912. From this year date his sets for Richard Wagner's *Ring* which seem directly inspired by the sketches and principles of Adolphe Appia. From 1914 to 1919, he collaborated with Carl Hegemann, Richard Weichert and Furtwängler (Goethe, Wedekind, Mozart, Strauss). The year 1919 marked the beginning of his collaboration with Weichert in Frankfurt-on-the-Main, the most fertile period in his career, dominated by an expressionist phase which came to an end around 1926. From 1937 to 1943, he worked essentially at the Munich opera. The Nazi era was scarcely a successful one for Sievert; his constant brio could not conceal a real retreat in the direction of illustrative, ornamental embellishment and a tendency towards the monumental, in a word, towards an academicism, a rather official conventional realism. The end of the war led him to attempt greater simplicity, one finds in his new designs for *The Ring* (1955) the same simplicity as in those of 1912, the forms reaching an even greater abstraction. But the shock effect had passed. Already the grandsons of Richard Wagner, Wieland and Wolfgang had gone further in their new Bayreuth.

Sievert's output was considerable. But as is the case with a number of set designers of the first half of the century, the expressionist period was the most original. But of the expressionists, some are distinguished by their systematic use of expressive distortions, others by the provision of a space expertly organized and lit to serve as a springboard to the acting and as a support for the tension of the play. Ludwig Sievert subscribed to those trends, combined them, and moreover managed to incorporate some symbolism. For *Penthesilea* by Kleist (1921) a piece of apparatus like a zigzaging slope, a construction of the space that refuses to be regular like those of Emil Pirchan, but which was given life by an inner dynamism which made Ludwig Wagner say: 'the zigzaging slope of the rocky masses, which rise to culminate in a large arch of a bridge, projects the rhythmic waves of the Kleistian world, through its three stages within the realms of the visible. One is dragged as it were out of oneself into the élan of the rhythmic movement: the actor rises to the ardour of ecstasy.' Sievert's set for *The Son* (Die Sohn) by Hasenclever (1918) is one of the most typical images of expressionism on stage; a cone of light falling from above isolates and detaches the central character. On the boundaries of light and dark, the other characters are only the projection of his obsessions and fantasies. Other elements of this set which

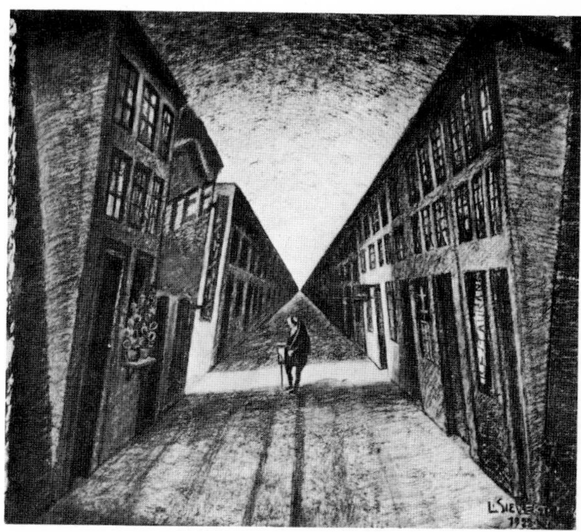

SIEVERT, LUDWIG: Sketch for the *Great Highway* by August Strindberg, production by F. P. Buch (Schauspielhaus, Frankfurt 1923)

is not decorative: the background and the walls of curtains, where doors and windows are reduced to their outline. For Strindberg's *The Great Highway*, Sievert uses perspective to the maximum of its expressive possibilities by combining it with the symmetry which destroys its own classicism, through the sloping sides of the houses, which seem ready to collapse towards the centre. All these are examples of a typical expressionism, even if sometimes rather decorative and if violence is almost totally absent from it.

STERN, Ernst (Bucharest, 1876 – London, 28.8.1954). Of German-Hungarian origin, this painter, illustrator and designer began in 1906 to collaborate regularly with Max Reinhardt and this was to last sixteen years. Of great artistic talent and astonishing technical virtuosity, Ernst Stern was above all an eclectic who sought to adapt himself to the spirit of each work, to the interpretation Max Reinhardt put on it or his collaborators (Holländer, Martin), as well as the various theatres he used, from the traditional Deutsches Theater in Berlin to the Olympia Hall in London which he transformed into a cathedral for Maeterlinck's *The Miracle* (1911). One cannot therefore speak of a style specifically belonging to Stern.

Amongst so many others, Stern also designed sets and costumes that had all the external characteristics of expressionism. In fact it was simply a question for him of carefully using for expressionist dramatic works, modes of expression directly inspired by painting, in the same style. His sketch for *The Beggar* by Sorge (produced by Max Reinhardt in Berlin, 1917) is an example of this, with its black background, its few pieces of furniture, the typical central cone of light absorbing in its cluster two characters one of extreme stiffness, the other completely broken down and as it were out of joint. Or again that of *From Morn to Midnight* (Von Morgens bis Mitternacht) by Kaiser that one can usefully compare with the works of Cesar Klein for the same work; in Stern, the structure of the set is of constructivist inspiration, the expressionist dramatization appears in the lively attitudes of the characters sketched in, and the violent contrasts of the clusters of light. His expressionist style again influenced the sets and costumes that Sievert created for *The Collection of Wax Figures* (Das Wachsfigurenkabinett) by Paul Leni (1924). Stern's expressionism was not so much a stepping-stone in a career, as one of a number of very varied techniques and the testimony of a state of perpetual openmindedness faced with the demands of drama and producers.

TAIROV, Alexander (Romny, 24.6.1885 – Moscow, 25.9.1950). Actor, producer and theoretician of Russian theatre. It would be false to use the epithet expressionist exclusively to describe Taïrov, who was the director of the Kamerny Theatre in Moscow from 1914 to 1949 for if his theatre theory, such as he expressed it in *Le Théatre Libéré* is extremely clear, he is the most aesthetically conscious of all the Soviet producers of the twenties. In his case, expressionism does not emanate from his inner depths. It is more formal on the stage. He often dabbled in cubism or constructivism. In acting, he allied a rather spatial composition with a psychological approach. On the other hand, Taïrov was occasionally inspired by pure 'comédiantesque' traditions, or turned towards the baroque. From the thirties he turned towards neo-realism.

TRÖSTER, František (Vrbicany, 1904–1968). Having received a solid technical and architectural education, Tröster collaborated with a number of Czech theatres as a set designer and notably in the National Theatre in Prague. Without being the representative of any of the movements of modern art, he was not foreign to any of them, hence the multiplicity of his experiments. His inspiration was both constructivist and futurist. Expressionism is present in his work notably at the time of his collaboration with a producer who was himself expressionist, Pujman for Wagner and Berg, and also in certain plays like Gogol's *The Government Inspector* produced by Frejka in the National Theatre in Prague in 1936.

VAKHTANGOV, Yevgeny (Vladikavkaz, 1883 – Moscow, 1922). Russian actor and producer. A great admirer of the Moscow Art Theatre and its producer Constantin Stanislavsky, Vakhtangov put on his first production in an amateur circle in 1904. In 1909, he entered the Adasev Dramatic Art School, where members of the Arts Theatre taught; he was admitted in 1911 as a collaborator at the time when Stanislavsky began to experiment on his system. He was in charge of directing a group of young artists of the Arts Theatre to lead in conjunction with them a parallel experiment and from 1913 he played an eminent role in the Art Studio of the Arts Theatre, notably as an actor and producer. From 1918, he participated as a producer in the works of the Habima Studio. In 1921, he produced Strindberg's *Erik XIV* in the First Studio and in 1922 he put on his two most famous productions *The Dibouk* by An-Ski in the Habima Studio and *Princess Turandot* in the Third Studio. If the term expressionist can be linked to the name of Vakhtangov, that is not, of course, to describe the man or his career as a whole, but to define the style of two of his productions, *Erik XIV* and even more *The Dibouk*. Expressionism, referring not to the play but to the production, to the very stylized acting and the plastic rhythm, particularly in the group scenes, to the link between the lighting and the characters, and especially to the set design of the painter, Nathan Altman, who contributed a lot to the visual success of a production, of which Nina Gourfinkel evokes the constituent parts as follows: 'the poor bare synagogue, the broken lines of Thora's wardrobe, the stupefying foreshortening of the table at the head of which is enthroned the miraculous rabbi, all gentle, all white and who, suddenly, about to hurl anathema at Dibouk takes on the dimensions of a worker of miracles. The whole set is bathed in an uncertain chiaroscuro . . . the striking contrasts the bright white of the bride's long robe amongst the green rags of the poor, the luminous white of the white napkin on the table of the tsadik – and in the corners, the threatening darkness of the sombre forces of the plot.' The stage conceived by Altman is a prey to expressive distortions, which, whilst being reminiscent of German expressionism, is profoundly different from it. The productions are varied, as are the mental and physical presentation of the characters.

WEGENER, Paul (Bischdorf, 11.12.1874 – Berlin, 13.9.1948). German stage and film actor and film producer. After studying dramatic art in Leipzig, Wegener made his debut as an actor in Rostock. Taken on by Reinhardt he made his debut on the Deutsche Theater in 1906 and rapidly became an actor who was open to new movements, while remaining faithful to tradition. He was endowed with a creative temperament and capable of a very refined performance. He adapted remarkably to the expressionist plays that he performed at the Junges Deutschland: *The Coral* (Die Koralle) by Kaiser, *The Beggar* by Sorge. His career continued till his death in 1948, the year during which he again played *Nathan the Wise.* Paul Wegener was at the same time active in an important way in the cinema as an actor in *the Student from Prague* by Stellan Rye (1914) and as a producer. In 1914, he produced, in collaboration with Galeen, *The Golem.* Six years later it was with Carl Böse that he collaborated to put on a new version with sets by Hans Poelzig. Can one really talk of expressionism in his case? His films are the image of his personality; they mingle a genuine expressionism with an equally genuine impressionism that he had probably inherited from his stay with Reinhardt. Granted, these are only two examples, but they are the most significant in relation to the history of expressionist cinema.

WEICHERT, Richard (Berlin, 22.5.1880 – Frankfurt-on-the-Main, 15.11.1961). One of the principal spokesmen of expressionism on the stage Richard Weichert, after being profoundly influenced in Düsseldorf by Louise Dumont, spent most of his career in Mannheim (his main period of production was from 1916 – 1918) and later at Frankfurt-on-the-Main after 1919. It was there that his productions and in his writings (theoretical writings, articles) he affirmed his conception of the role of producer, of stage production, and revealed the nature of his expressionism. In 1919 in the *Deutsche Bühne*, Weichert declared 'The producer is henceforth the creator who puts into practice the author's intentions and who reveals his visions, he is to a certain extent, his spokesman, or at least his defence counsel. Henceforth he is the one who directs and harmonizes the production, because he has grasped the author's most subtle and intimate aims, he is the

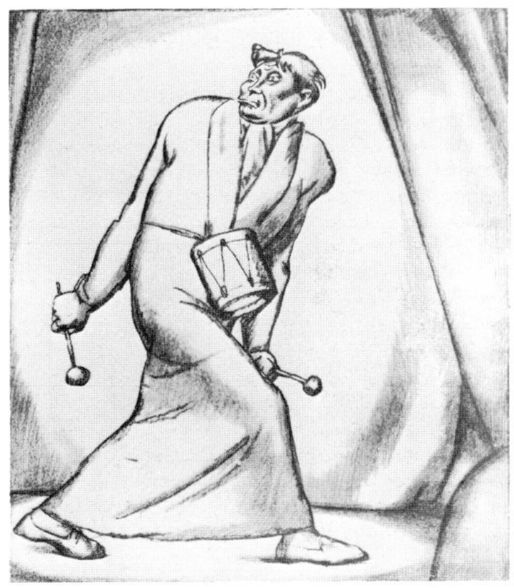

WEGENER, PAUL: in *The Beggar* (Der Bettler) by Reinhard Sorge (Deutsches Theater, Berlin 1917). Drawing by Bruno Paul

mediator between the author and the actor: no longer the routine supervisor, but an artist endowed with the greatest sensibility and a most fertile imagination, who transforms the spiritual into the visual, and who conveys an imaginary world on the stage, is an independent demiurge. In the theatre, the author is conjecture, the acting is the execution, between the two as both master and servant, comes the director.' And Weichert adds 'it is not revolving stages, the pit, the lighting, the technical aspects, the magical effects of the machinery that must prevail, but the words, the text.' This last sentence must not be interpreted as a rejection of all the possibilities of the stage with the exception of the word. On the contrary, Weichert understood the importance of lighting, space, set design, gesture, décor, he used them to elicit the maximum degree of expressivity, as one of his most famous productions shows: *The Son* (Der Sohn) by Hasenclever in Mannheim, which he defines as follows:

'All the characters the son struggles with are lacking in objective reality, they are extensions of his own inner being. The production must be organized around this, for this is the expressionist aspect of the work. Out of this fundamental conception is born any idea of a production which consists in giving the son (illuminated by a cone of light) the centre of the stage, and leaving the other characters in the half-light. My production at Mannheim lives off this fundamental idea that puts the son at the centre of the stage: my collaborator Ludwig Sievert produced the pictorial part with an extraordinary intuition such that some of the pictures are like Munch's visions.' (In *Die Szene*, Berlin, May–June 1918). Was Richard Weichert the 'dionysian producer' the playwright Ludwig Wagner saw in him? In productions as different as *The First Men* by R. Stephan, *Penthesilea* by H. Kleist, and *Drums in the Night* by Brecht he appeared endowed with a volcanic temperament as an artist who has a feeling both musical, rhythmic and plastic for works and their productions, and who found the stage designer Ludwig Sievert the most compatible collaborator.

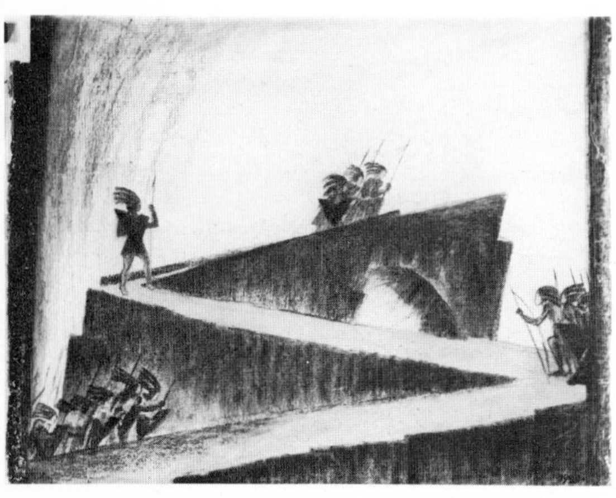

SIEVERT, LUDWIG: Sketch for *Penthesilea* by Heinrich von Kleist, produced by R. Weichert (Schauspielhaus, Frankfurt 1921)

Cinema

Subjected initially to the aesthetic of the theatre, to a simplistic presentation (back drops, the actors always facing the public, entrances and exits on the left or the right), and also to a rudimentary scenography, the cinema, as soon as it wanted to emerge from the rut in which it had become entrenched, could do no better than develop in the shadow of painting.

The first intellectual pursuits in the cinema occurred in Denmark. Outside worldly drama or social drama which it was the first to exploit, Danish cinema considered occasionally, in the form of serials, the themes of anguish and madness, or, more mystical ones, of witchcraft. Film directors focused their attention on achieving a fairly skilful photographic technique, on the search for a simplified décor that would allow the light to play on sharp and clear shapes. Producers like Holger, Madsen, Urban Gad, Robert Dinesen, Wilhelm Glückstadt, Schnedler Sörensen, camera men like Guido Seeber and Axel Graatkjaer, by studying the plastic possibilities of film, tried to apply certain principles emanating from painting and the avant-garde theatres.

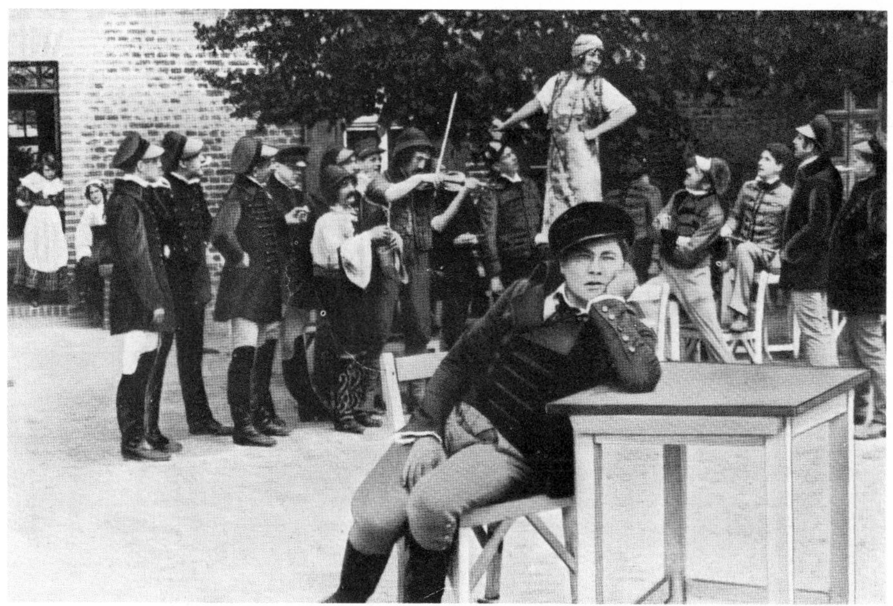

WEGENER, PAUL: Extract from *The Student from Prague* (Der Student von Prag)

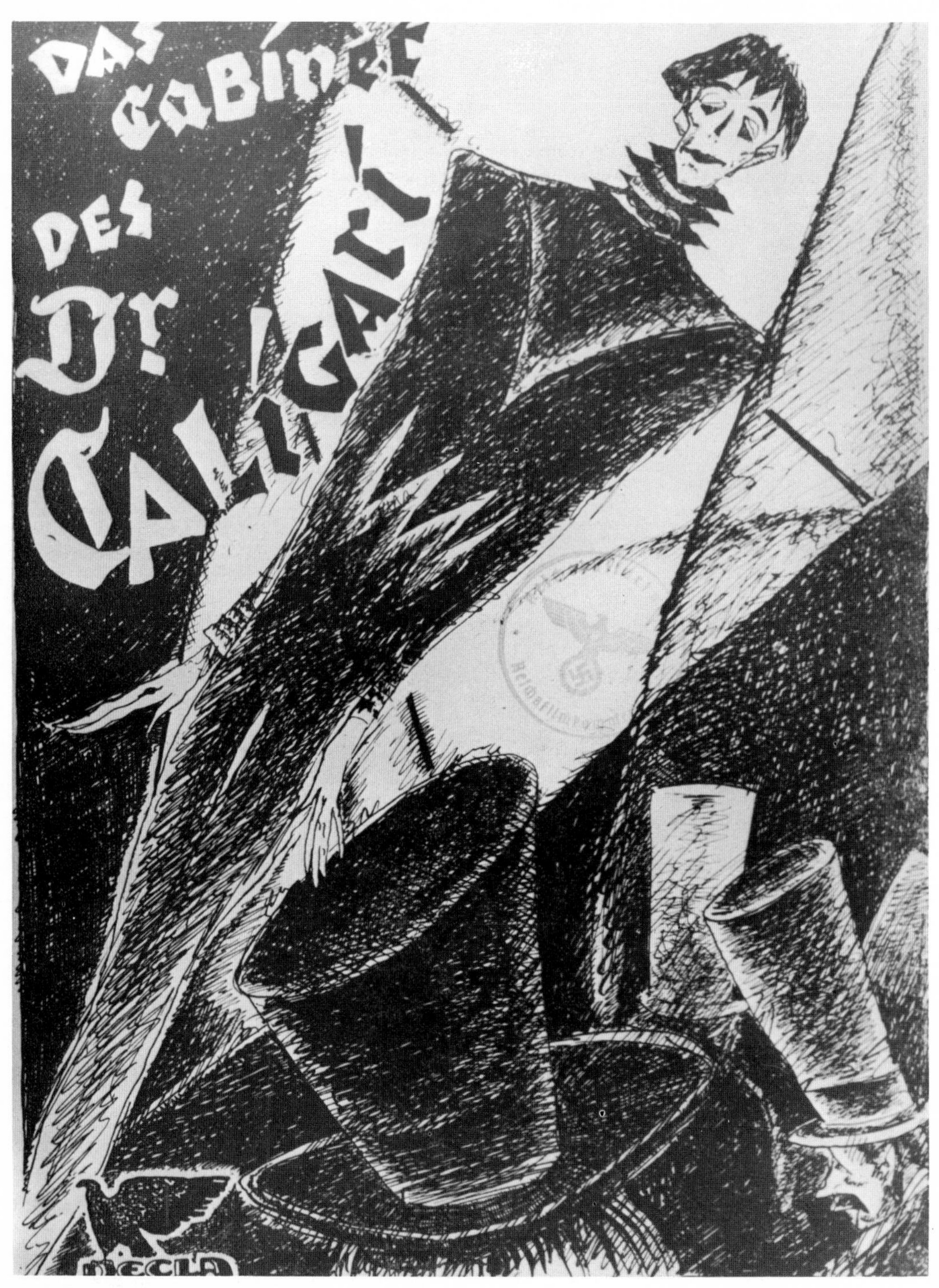

Poster for the *Cabinet of Doctor Caligary*

As early as 1913, Paul Wegener, already a famous actor of the Max Reinhardt company, and who was one of the first famous actors to take an interest in the cinema, had shot the film *The Student from Prague* (*Der Student von Prague*), after being inspired by the aesthetic pursuits of Danish cinema and Reinhardt's theatrical productions. The writer Hanns Heinz Ewers, the writer of imaginary tales, had provided the theme; produced by the Dane, Stellan Rye, this film (the action of which evokes the story of Peter Schlemihl, 'the man who sold his shadow' and that of Erasmus Spikher 'who lost his reflection in the mirror') rediscovers, or attempts to rediscover, the atmosphere of the German imaginary tales, and their romantic anguish, by developing especially the idea of the 'double', the split personality being at that time a fashionable theme in the theatre and literature.

Shot using real-life sets – an old cemetery – the winding roads of a ghetto and in weird countryside – this film emphasizes the very strangeness of nature, which it tries to express more or less symbolically. Some of the sets or the use of light and dark function as in Danish films, creating the appropriate psychic climate by underlining the twilight atmosphere of the drama. This is not yet an example of expressionism in the exact sense of the word, but of the quest for the pictorial and plastic resources of the dynamic image.

The following year, *The Golem* was shot in similar conditions, with even more effort put into it, but with the collaboration this time of Henrik Galeen, a former Czech journalist, and at that time secretary to Hanns Heinz Ewers.

Paul Wegener shot a dozen other 'romantic-fantastic' films such as: *The Daughter of the King of the Alders, the Pied Piper of Hamelin, The Man who has lost his shadow*; but after him and like him, most of those who were to contribute to the rise of German cinema: actors, producers and stage designers, came from various theatrical groups belonging to Max Reinhardt, whose influence, although indirect, was predominant; for even if the expressionist school had the most remarkable influence on the cinema across the Rhine, it was not the only one.

It would normally be necessary, therefore, to say a few words about the theatrical movement at the beginning of the century, for without knowing something about this, the aims of the cinema remain incomprehensible.

This however, is not our role here, and we will restrict ourselves to mentioning the names of Antoine, Copeau, Rouché, Lugné Poe in France; Stanislavsky, Meyerhold, Foregger, Eureïnov, Taïrov, Vakhtangov in Russia; Max Reinhardt, Jessner, Viertel, Weichert, Holländer in Germany, not forgetting the theoreticians Gordon Craig and Adolphe Appia.

As a result of its symbolic and metaphysical pretensions, expressionism was first of all a literary movement, and then an artistic one. But it is possible to hold that theatrical expressionism – or at least its development – was the extreme consequence of the theories of George Fuchs. The founder of the *Artistic Theatre* in Munich in 1913, a critic and theoretician, George Fuchs advocated a return to pure theatricality. All his dramatic work respected the classical unities, had a specific setting. Since Gordon Craig's symbolic 'great machines' were only of use on vast stage floors, it was less important according to him to structure the space than to make it meaningful; less important to organize a series of symbols than to represent them.

If the set was to contribute to the means of expression, this had to be through painting rather than architecture which was cumbersome. However, far from constructing a deceptively real *trompe l'oeil*, it was a question of creating the expressive climate of the play by intentionally accentuating the forms most suited to making it meaningful and achieving this by following in the footsteps of expressionist painting.

Expressionist painting could in fact, better than anything else, translate, express and create this climate as required. The first designer to do this was in fact the expressionist painter Kokoschka who worked with Reinhardt from 1907 to 1912.

The Swiss designer and theoretician Adolphe Appia, and the critic, Fritz Erler, contributed to the

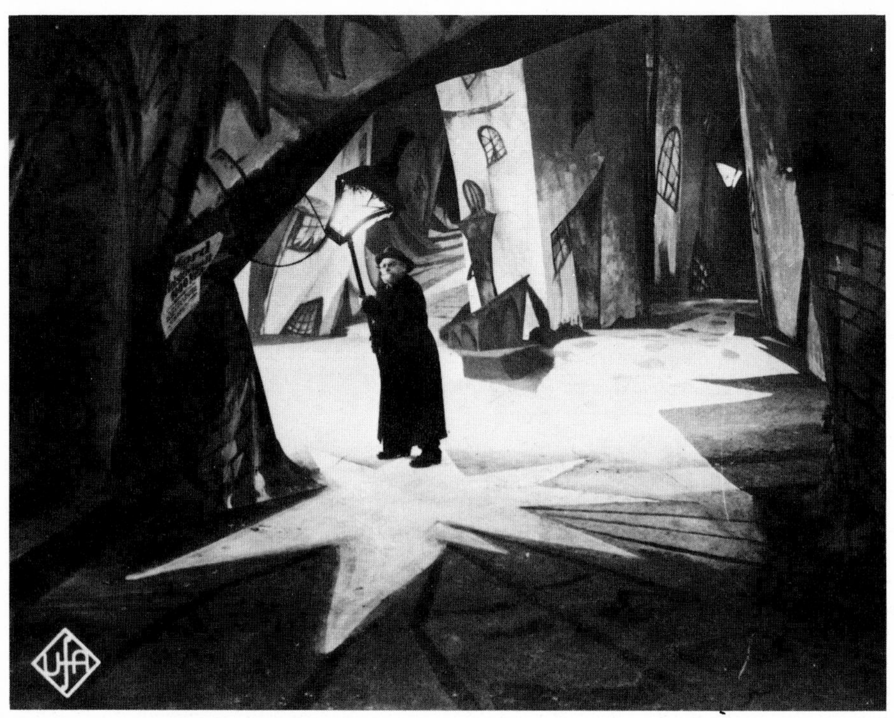

WIENE, ROBERT: Extract from the *Cabinet of Doctor Caligary*

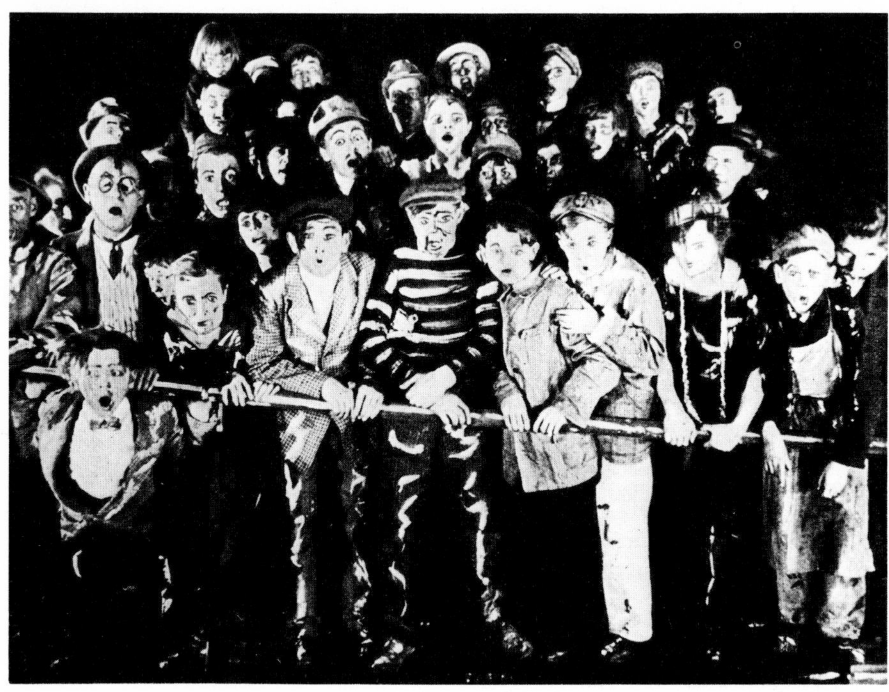

MARTIN, KARL HEINZ: Extract from the film of *From Morn to Midnight* (Von Morgens bis Mitternachts). 1920. From Georg Kaiser success of the movement, and soon, Friedrich Holländer in Berlin, von Gerlach in Vienna, and Leopold Jessner in Munich, put on plays that marked the origin of expressionist theatre, from *The Pair of Drawers* (*Die Hose*) by Carl Sternheim 1911 to *Fire at the Opera* (*Brand in der Oper*) by Georg Kaiser (1919) via *The Beggar* (*Der Bettler*) by Reinhard Sorge (1917).

The cinema followed, but, as regards the sets and formal expression, the subject belonged to German neo-romanticism much more than to the metaphysical symbolism of Trakl or Hasenclever. F. W. Murnau, Fritz Lang and Robert Wiene were the first producers to commit themselves to this path along with the designers Hermann Warm, Walter Riemann, and Walter Röhrig who had persuaded the producer Erich Pommer to make films of this kind.

Caligarism

As the first artistic examples of German cinema, these films began the current that culminated in expressionism. It was with *The Cabinet of Dr Caligary* (*Das Kabinett des Dr Caligari*) that it made its appearance in the cinema in 1919. An appearance that was of shattering importance.

In this story, that a madman is meant to be telling to a mad-woman, the sets are no longer stylized. They create a disordered universe which emphasizes the mental imbalance of the hero; there are mis-shapen roads, crooked houses, shadows, patches of light and dark, that, contrasted in crude black and white paint on the set, add to the number of broken lines and in this way constantly break up the décor. But the means of expression is not simply pictorial. There is a whole network of symbols bringing out the instinctive responses suggested by the verticals, the diagonals, and the other linear elements.

Caesar, the symbol of subconscious aggressiveness, is associated with triangular forms. Played by Conrad Veidt, whose very body is the shape of a triangle, since he has broad shoulders, narrow hips, and is wearing a black skin-tight garment. The eyes, well made up beneath the eye-brows, form white (inverted) triangles inside black triangles. The dagger with which he is armed, constitutes a white triangle which stands out against the black triangle of the jerkin. When Caesar, in his hypnotic slumber, goes to kill the daughter of the burgomaster, he enters the bedroom by breaking the glass of the French window and the bedroom window assumes the form of a triangle etc.

As regards the daughter, she is associated with vertical lines or slender curves. The spacious, almost empty bedroom, where she is lying, looks out onto the garden through French windows, and its frame forms narrow parallel lines facing towards the sky. Behind the bed, a baldachin comprises arches from which long white veils fall languidly; and when Caesar, in a burst of lucidity, grabs hold of the young virgin instead of killing her, her long skirt and the veils that he drags along with him suggest, as they fall to the ground, the idea of a disaster, like the rape of Lucretia.

One sees the aims of expressionism: to convey symbolically, through lines, forms or shapes, the mental state of the characters, the condition of their soul, and also their intentionality, in such a way that the set appears as the plastic translation of their plight. Far from being primary, this network of symbols, which is never explicit, arouses more or less conscious psychic reactions which direct the mind of the spectator towards the idea that it is intended should be suggested to him, just like esoteric symbolism, which proceeds from the same foundations.

But this initial form of expressionism, directly applied to the theatre and painting and called 'caligarism', not without reason, was to culminate in an impasse. As it was impossible to confine oneself to stories about madmen, which alone justified such excessiveness in the distortion of objects, most of the films of this kind were quite simply grotesque. In *Genuine*, the story of a woman vampire who leads her lovers to murder or suicide, Cesar Klein's sets drown the characters in an indecipherable confusion instead of one clarifying the other. In *From Morn to Midnight* (*Von Morgens bis Mitternacht*), produced by Karl Heinz Martin from the play by Georg Kaiser with sets designed by him and carried out by Robert Neppach, the film director is no more successful. The black and white streaks that cover the sets, the objects and even the actor's clothes, suppress the outlines and make everything indistinct in images of which the profundity no longer means anything. Only *Torgus*, by Hans Kobe, and *Raskolnikov* by Robert Wiene escape ridicule. The latter, thanks to Andrei Andreiev's remarkable sets, the entangled and tortured forms of which felicitously convey the happiness of the hero; the former, thanks to Robert Neppach's stylization, which respects the real forms and shapes of things.

The influence of the genre was almost non-existent and, one would not be able to find, in all the history of the cinema, ten expressionist films. But expressionism, which intended to be meaningful, through what the Germans call the *Weltanschauung* (the state of the world that surrounds the plot and circumscribes it, and suggests a transcendental essence), assumes several aspects which only have similarities for being founded on the use of the plastic qualities of the dynamic image. For it must be clearly understood that we are talking here of cinematic expressionism relative to the specific methods available to film, and not to a literary or pictorial aesthetic based on related principles, and that one would restrict oneself to capturing with a camera. Now, one can never over-emphasize that *Caligary*, an exceptional masterpiece based on an exceptional aesthetic, is not a film born out of cinematic expressionism, but out of pictorial expressionism applied to the cinema.

In the direction of a different kind of expressionism

Aware of these formal difficulties, Fritz Lang, Murnau, von Gerlach and Paul Leni, saw the problem in a very different light; having had recourse to a legend that allowed a symbolic interpretation of things and of the world, such as Paul Wegener had already begun to do.

Meanwhile, the cinema in other countries had come up with solutions which were not without influence on German film directors. One must mention above all what was happening in Swedish cinema. Making the countryside the principal character in the plot, or seeking in nature the symbolic expression of their personal tragedies, Victor Sjöström and Mauritz Stiller created images that were less expressionist than expressive; with them, space – the meaning of space – regained its importance. Two films can be considered as the prelude to the new German expressionism: *The Treasure of Herr Arne* (*Herr Arnes Schatz*) by Mauritz Stiller and *Fire on Board* (*Feuer an Bord*) by Victor Sjöström. In the *Treasure of Herr Arne* (1919) where the landscape still has the largest role, the set, which formed a masterly alliance with it, becomes as much as the landscape, the principal character of the plot. The plastic composition surpassing all theatrical convention, subjected to the demands of the action, to the poetic authenticity of the narrative, transfigured the real lyricism of the legend into unforgettable images, such as the flight through the mirrors, the death of Elsalil, and the final procession, which introduces the powerful art of Fritz Lang, even that of Eisenstein (*Ivan the Terrible*), without, nevertheless, confining the plot to a preconceived aesthetic goal.

Following the Scandinavian example, the Germans appealed to an imaginary but abstract world, finding in an art form that was no less visionary a more appropriate expression for the spatial needs of the cinema. Since the evocation of the unreal had the appearance of living reality, it allowed them in fact to stylize, and transpose it, without distorting it. It allowed them above all to play with shapes and no longer only with surfaces or lines on a décor of painted canvas. Architecture replaced painting as the formal condition of expressionism.

If there is a film where, for the first time, light and dark, by playing on the modelling of the shapes and expressive architecture, affected the depths of space, where the mobility of the lighting and forms that had become symbolic definitively, overrode the pictorial values of caligarism, it was the second version of *The Golem* that Paul Wegener shot in 1920 from the scenario by Henrik Galeen, in extraordinary sets designed by Hans Poelzig, constructed by Kurt Richter and photographed by Karl Freund.

Now, in his writings, Paul Wegener claims to have never had expressionist aims, neither in 1913, nor then. In 1925, Lupu Pick said, to whoever wanted to listen, that he had only made films as a reaction

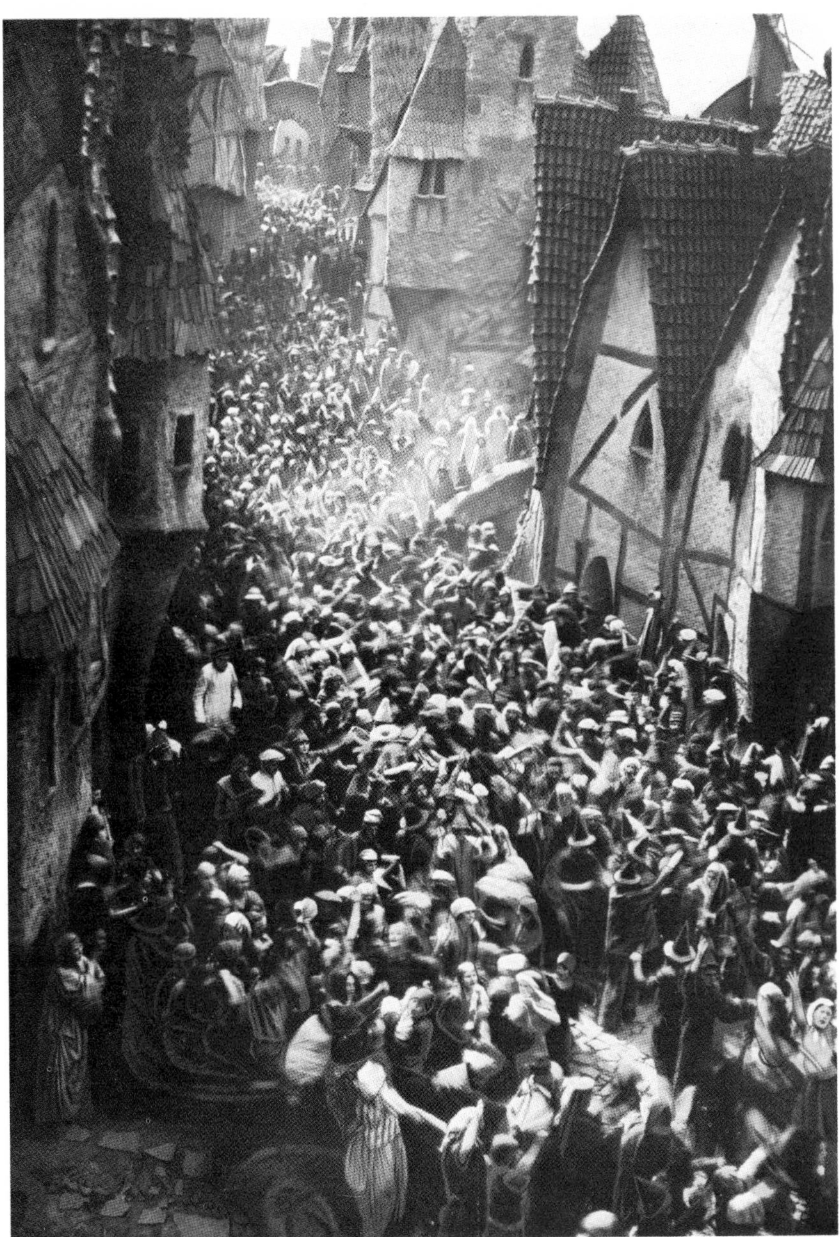

WEGENER, PAUL: Extract from *The Golem*: crowd in a panic

against expressionism, and Fritz Lang confirmed in no uncertain terms that he had never been an expressionist film director.

In all these confirmations and in expressions of faith it is quite clear that they understood expressionism to be what we have intentionally called caligarism so as to distinguish the forms inherited from painting, from forms properly belonging to the cinema. When understood in this way, it is certain that neither they nor Murnau were expressionists any more than Paul Leni, or any of the leading figures of the great period in German cinema.

But if expressionism can, in the cinema, be reduced to caligarism, it is not easy to see why one should make such an issue of it – as critics, historians and cinema theorists do throughout the world; unless, of course, they are concerned with something else.

Whatever the name one gives it, expressionism consists in conveying and making something meaningful through the forms of the world and things: either by gathering these forms into a synthesis which tends towards pure abstraction: or by conceptualizing them (poetry); or by integrating the dramatic events into an 'abstracting' structure (theatre): or, on the contrary, endowing these objective and concrete forms with a symbolic meaning leading less to ideas and concepts than to a climate of anguish and anxiety, to vague aspirations of the collective unconsciousness, or to the assumed 'in itself', of a more or less metaphysical character (cinema).

In pictorial expressionism, the visible world is considered like a prison that prevents one from reaching the essence of things. It is a question of traversing barriers of time and space, of bringing out the most expressive expression of appearances, to grasp – or to make meaningful – the 'in-itself'! But the painters were constantly torn between the object and the form. In this way, the anguish conveyed, by intensive forms further and further removed from the concrete, could only culminate in an 'abstractionism' free from all anguish, the 'objective' absolute, rather than in subjective forms. Reduced to an outline, things found themselves given meaning rather than represented, submerged in a general configuration which encompassed them and absorbed their individuality into the whole.

From theatre sets, one comes to the cinema, to caligarism. But the cinema as a concrete art form, situated in a specific space at a specific time, which it can recreate in its own manner, but not transgress. It can only give meaning to ideas or concepts via things, their perceptible form, the relationship they have between themselves and with a particular whole. Their linear representation could only end in failure. The return to plastic and architectonic structures highlighting the concrete individuality of objects was the step it was necessary to take if the cinema wanted to assert itself as an art form distinct from painting. At first sight, this is the opposite step to that taken by expressionism. But if the cinema could not render abstract things that had to be things and not graphic signs, at least it could have meaning through these things. Anguish, anxiety, obsessions and any other feeling, whether tragic or not, could be born out of a climate, be suggested by the unusual appearance of particular forms that conferred meaning on to a décor, a milieu, a landscape. Instead of being consistent with the relations of different planes (the fixture), the connotations could be consistent with the formalized relationships inside the plane (the context or décor). They could be in the representation, or even in what was being represented, that is to say consistent with the relationships structured in space rather than in time.

It was no longer a matter of conveying things by a sign but of making them part of an organic whole symbolizing by its forms or structures, reduced to their essentials, all possible forms of abstractions: to ensure that the things themselves, without ceasing to be what they are, become a sign or a symbol. In short, the meaningful qualities of cinematic expressionism can be understood as a plastic symbolism, an architectonic symbolism or a realistic symbolism according to the meaning of their appearance.

Carried to this extent, the expressionism of dynamic images was no longer the refusal, the negation of literature or pictorial expressionism, but the attempt to reach, thanks to a contrary step, an identical result – or purpose: to express that which cannot be expressed, to suggest what lies beyond the world and things – the beyond was in fact an *infra*: it comprised latent aspirations, obscure desires, rather disturbed social or moral implications; a whole unconsciousness, individual or collective, of a metaphysical character perhaps, but distinct from the problematic essences and the 'in-itself' with, in legend and in dreams, the expression of the panic-stricken fears of being in the face of the unknown, death playing, in German mythology, the well-known symbolic role, of which there are plenty of examples in literature. Having to express themselves in this way, the films rediscovered the tone and atmosphere of the tales and legends of the banks of the Rhine, even when they were not the source of the plot in their films. At the level of the image, Caspar David Friedrich and Gustave Doré were nearer to them than Nolde and Kokoschka – to such an extent that it was in fanciful romanticism, and its themes and methods, that expressionist cinema was at its best, and not at all by incorporating, even if transposing, the themes and methods of literary or pictorial expressionism, on which it uncompromisingly turned its back.

Once again then, when shooting a new version of *The Golem*, Henrik Galeen and Paul Wegener showed the way. Abandoning the white magic of the Scandinavians and reviving, in this tale, the black magic dear to the Faustian soul, they rediscovered in a dense and sombre Germanic *Valhalla*, just as in the profound myth of messianic judaism, the subterranean currents, the foundation of the social mysticism, the symbol of contemporary collective aspirations.

In this film, the sets, less constructed or given an architectural form, than modelled, appear moulded, shaped in clay, as in the *Golem*. Virtually everything contributes to forming the cave, which symbolizes the maternal womb, the place where the birth of the sacred monster is prepared, which is itself a symbol of the aspirations of an entire people. But, conceived in the mysteries of the darkness, it is a guilty birth, somehow ravished from eternal forces (like the Promethean fire) and which, having withdrawn within itself, isolated from the world, can only turn against its creator. The plot is already inscribed symbolically in the forms of the set: the revolving staircase, in the form of a couch, rolled up like a spiral staircase etc.

This is an example of expressionism in the cinema, at its best: cinematic expressionism, a plastic or architectonic symbolism but with a Freudian character, oniric, esoteric, which rediscovers in very varied influences, the foundations of established liturgical symbolism, also based on the springing forth of vertical lines, the gentleness of the curves, the fullness of the sphere and other virtues of lines – straight, broken, horizontal, diagonal – the shapes and the forms becoming so many appeals to the unconscious and arousing appropriate responses.

In *The Three Lights* (*Der müde Tod*), the shapes, the sharp lines, the gliding surfaces replace, with their precise shadows and their clear delineation, the modelling of *The Golem*. In Fritz Lang, an architect by training, more than in anyone else, the architectonic forms and the light are treated as so many elements forming the space, and things are distorted to the benefit of a worrying or transcendent meaning. An example is the large open staircase in the huge wall that death had constructed around its domain and which is positioned in a very high, narrow vault reminiscent of the form of a candle. The first steps are lost in the halflight whereas those above are bathed in light; this light is identified with the flame of the candles that are the *leitmotiv* of the film; and when death drags the young girl along with her, her silhouette, at the top of the steps, appears like the wick of the supposed flame.

In contrast to the winding stairs, either askew or spiral, which indicate a neurosis, an obscure recess of the heart or a morbid repression, the stairs, here, express the ascent towards an ideal. Wide or narrow, but always rectilinear, they will symbolize in all Fritz Lang's films some form of ascent: an ascent to a triumph, to domination and hope, it will always be an ascent.

Expressionist symbolism

In *The Story of Grieshuus* (*Zur Chronik von Grieshuus*), besides the castle of which the dark nooks, the low vaults, the winding staircases, the walls crushed by age are modelled as in *The Golem*, it is the landscape that is the symbolic frame of reference for the plot. There is a deep link between the infinite sadness of its nostalgic surfaces and the loneliness, the gloomy atmosphere that envelops it, as if their heavy cloaks inflated by the wind, the quiet heroes were torn by anguish and remorse.

Like the Swedish films, the landscape of *Grieshuus* is a state of mind or, using Novalis's expression 'the body idealized by a certain frame of mind'. But more than that, the wind, the gusts of wind, the melancholic ruins buried beneath the undergrowth, the stagnant mists, the water of a dark lake, are all lugubrious appeals, the plaintive image of the chant of fratricidal love, that the wind bears, wailing through leaves, uprooted trees, whole rows of them, to die on the terrible heath, harassing like an expiatory *lied*.

On a certainly much more sombre and desperate level, Scandinavian impressionism here becomes the very form of a strange expressionism. Looked at from an unusual angle, individualized in the extreme, the chosen elements appear as their own essence through an exceptional moment in their existence. The fleeting moment becomes timeless, and the infinitely concrete here becomes a figure of abstraction.

The cinema is, in particular, a language of objects, of things that assume, through the context, a second sense, symbolic or otherwise. Now this sense can be a formalization of the concept which they in some sense guarantee temporarily, to be the symbol of what they represent, the value that is attributed to them. Expressionism is the obvious proof of this. The idea, or the feeling, is always the function of the object (a thing, décor, or natural element) and all the more because it is more concrete and individualized, in contrast to literary or pictorial expressionism, where the abstract is dependent on an elimination of 'things', or an arrangement which generalizes and depersonalizes represented objects. Like von Gerlach in *Grieshuus* – but two years before – it is to real exteriors that Murnau has gone to seek out the sets for *Nosferatu*. However, if he shoots in small medieval villages, on the banks of the Rhine or near the Baltic, it is only to find in the strange façades of the deserted countryside, a sense of the bizarre, the sinister side of things, a universe of loneliness and desolation, and to bring alive the inorganic world, to envelop the bodies in darkness, to express finally the supernatural through nature itself.

The film is like a 'journey to the bottom of unconsciousness'. It is no longer only the fantastic world of a strange milieu, the splitting of the self, the weight of the shadows; it is no longer Hoffmann or Chamisso, but Hölderlin, Novalis, or Jean Paul; it is the night of the soul, metaphysical anguish in all its powerful horror, and it is this feeling of the nocturnal, the inexorable that the film conveys most intensely, and, it seems, in the most obvious and natural way possible.

The symbolism in Murnau is always, in fact, that of things themselves, of the feeling reflected by things. However pictorial it might be, it is a symbolism that addresses itself to the intellect and to the mind far more than to the symbolism of forms arousing intuitive responses as in Fritz Lang for example.

The things are there, they bear witness to what the whole film is leading to. But it is leading to it, only because it has postulated it. It is a work of art and things only reveal what they are supposed to reveal.

In reality, things, without a doubt, have meaning, but they are no more signs than their images. Their meaning is contingent. If there exists an obvious relationship between certain frames of mind, and certain aspects of nature, it is only through human psychology, not through some form of transcendence. A sombre and melancholic landscape expresses sadness, that is to say that we find this in it; it conveys it, reflects it, makes it meaningful, but it is not its ontological expression. The feeling we express on seeing it, is similar to the feeling which envelops us when we are sad. Nothing more.

But it is obvious that if nature can be meaningful to the extent that it manages to provoke metaphysical responses and the feelings that stem from them, these moments are few and difficult to express.

This is why most expressionists, Fritz Lang in particular, found it more convenient to recreate nature in the studio or in similar circumstances. In this way, they could create an ideal nature, by materializing a concept; all the more because the symbolism of Fritz Lang relates to ideas and principles – right, justice, guilt, vengeance – that dominate the whole plot and transcend it, whereas Murnau's symbolism is that of

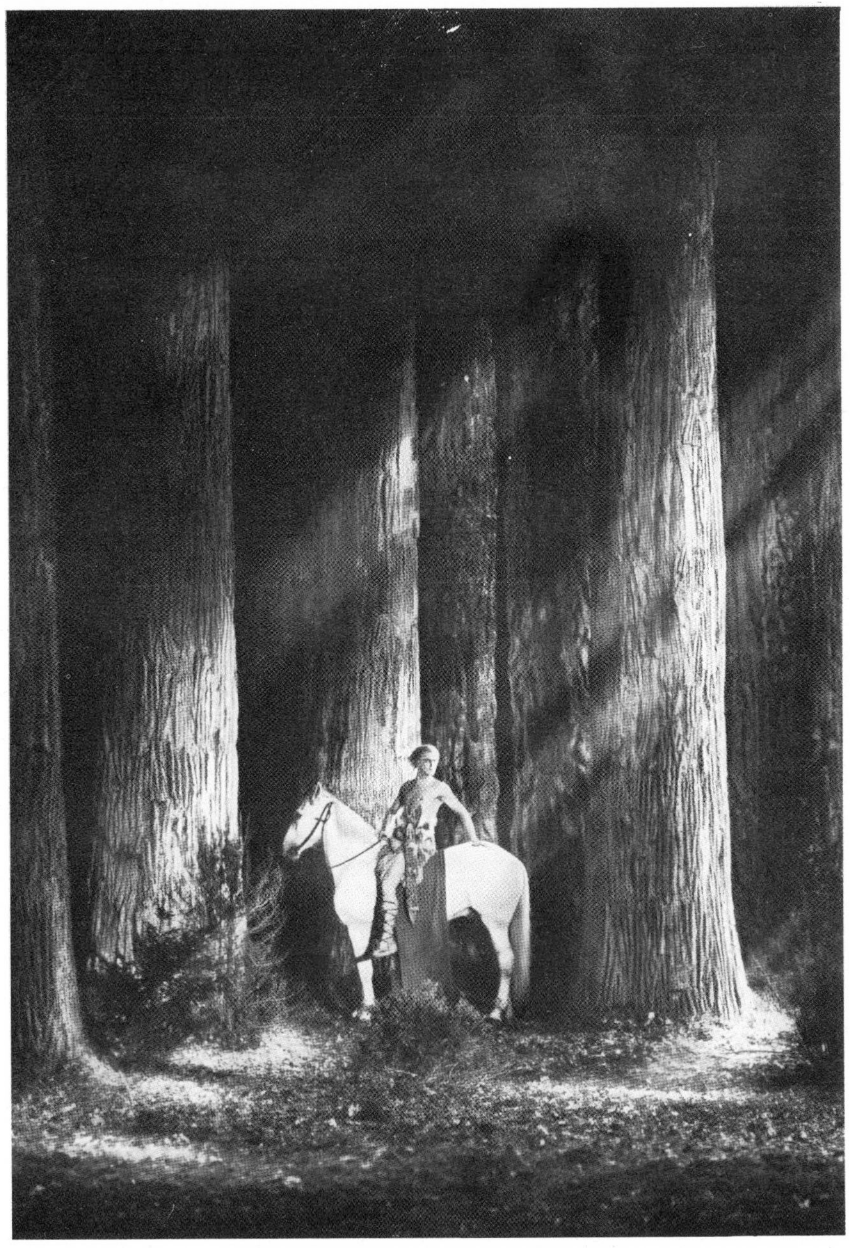

LANG, FRITZ: *Extract from the Nibelungen*: the forest

a climate, a state of mind – anxiety, fright implied by the plot, troubled feelings reflected by fugitive appearances and its transcendent quality is only due to the way one understands it.

Thus, in *Die Nibelungen*, the forest where Siegfried leads his white horse among the huge trees under the oblique rays that pierce the foliage, is no longer a forest, but the forest. All the images that the idea black forest can conjure up in the consciousness, can be found united in one which summarizes them all and exhausts them in an objected abstraction, possible however in the most concrete and natural meaning of the word (although this forest is in reinforced cement).

The spring also which rises from between the rocks, on the moss, in a glade full of flowers, and surrounded with white birches, becomes the very expression, the total image of the idea-spring, which also symbolizes youth, purity, the very mind of Siegfried who comes to refresh himself there.

False when compared to immediate reality which rarely presents such a complex of meanings, the nature artificially created thus becomes more real than reality itself, it attains an essential truth, and becomes the material form of an imaginary world. This art, so full of artifice was, therefore, perfectly sufficient for the representation of a legendary world somewhat transfigured or conceptualized, of which, based on Murnau's *Faust*, the film by Fritz Lang was undoubtedly the masterpiece.

To a greater extent than in natural settings, the sets which represent castles, cathedrals, etc., express at the same time the plot that is being played out. In other words, each image is composed in such a way as to convey the plot symbolically through forms as if the set crystallized them, by materializing the intentions, which in return, are as it were the dramatic expression of its architecture.

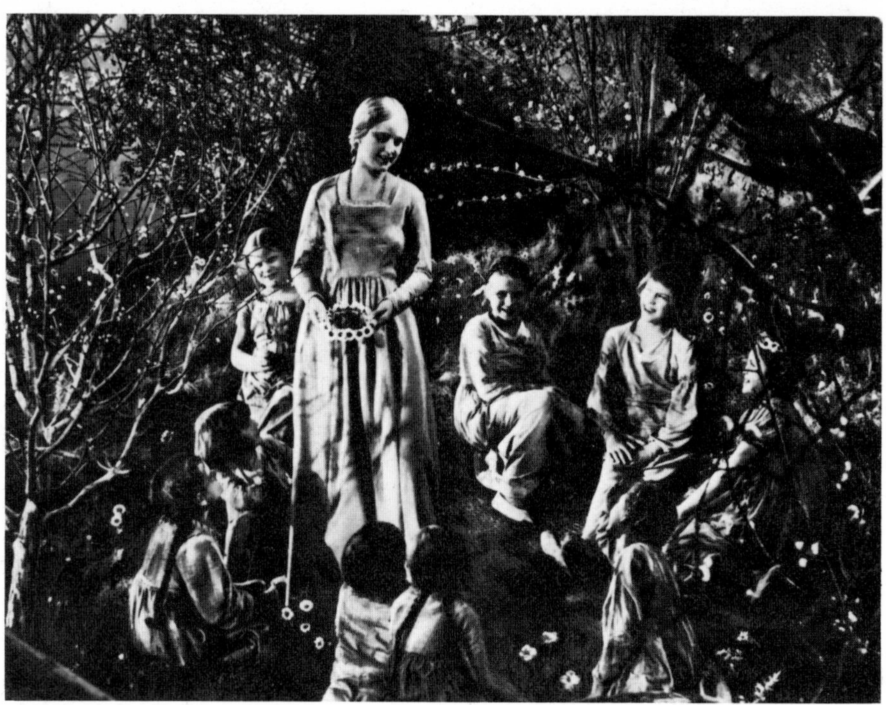

MURNAU, FRIEDRICH WILHELM: Scene from *Faust*: Marguerite's garden

The equilibrium (moral, psychological and dramatic) which runs through the first part is conveyed by symmetrical images (symmetrically composed in relation to their vertical median). The characters evolve like pawns on a chessboard. The effect of their forms, whether black or white, near or far, dominating or dominated, creates constantly differentiated plastic relationships out of this and gives meaning to the entire plot, according to a grandiose structure that circumscribes the movement in a hieratic representation.

In the tragic scene that contrasts Hagen and Kriemhilde (the latter in her white coat, the former, helmeted, clad in iron, leaning on his sword), both of them upright opposite each other on either side of

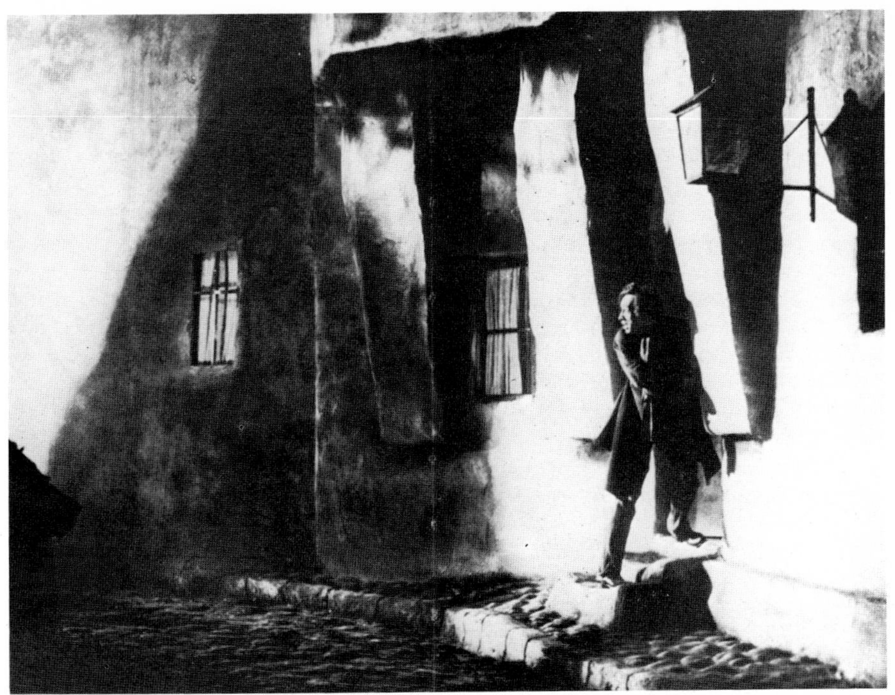

GALEEN, HENRIK: Extract from *The Student from Prague*

the monumental gate of Worms, are nevertheless symbolically united by the trefoil arch of the portal: sworn enemies, they are nevertheless of the same clan, the same race. Kriemhilde's fault and mistake is to fail to accept this. Later, in the chapel where Kriemhilde, surrounded by her mistresses of the robes, watches over Siegfried's tomb, one does not know whether the weepers, bent forward in mourning, assume the shape of the vault or whether, on the contrary, it is not the curves that follow the bent forms of the women, as if a hemicycle was gushing forth from between the folds of their heavy cloaks.

Here and there, soldiers arranged in geometric shapes, are lined up, arched upright like the posts of a hedge dominated by the points of their spears.

After Siegfried's death, the equilibrium is broken. The thirst for vengeance carries the day, the movement is unleashed; a movement conveyed by the inner lack of symmetry of the images far more than by the movement represented, a lack of symmetry that progressively replaces the rigorous symmetry of the first scene.

This arrangement of the story, this skilful organization of the planes, the lines and shapes, is only due to the dramatic movement, because of the functional meaning which is intelligently presented. An art of form in the fullest meaning of the word. It is the culmination of architectonic expressionism, where its meaning is akin to that of a liturgical ceremonial because of its desire to be esoteric and sacred.

Whatever the grandeur and the influence of this masterpiece, it is clear that its aesthetic is only applicable in exceptional circumstances. Despite its acceptable pace, the pictorial composition tends to focus one's attention on the qualities of the image itself. Instead of interpreting the world with the camera's eye, a world is constructed which is interpreted through decorative means; an already established aesthetic fact is reproduced, but not created, and the camera remains a prisoner of the décor. Objects, dominated by a rather overwhelming essence, lose their capacity to exist and disappear behind a representation that renders them static. Living forms are made rigid and stratified.

This manner, which remains cinematic insofar as it expresses the dimensions of reality instead of simply representing them, however, rediscovers the limitations of caligarism. Painting passed caligarism on to architecture, but as long as architecture constructed a legendary world, adequate accuracy was enough. Only the imaginary can hear or support these principles, which is one of the reasons, with a few exceptions, that fantastic expressionism was the only successful genre.

The decorative element was to reach its apogee in *The Collection of Wax Figures* (Wachsfigurenkabinett), a baroque masterpiece, where the dream, the fantastic and the fairylike fuse in the overwhelming ecstasy of a plastic imagination, which although no doubt excessive, borders on pure poetry precisely because of this. In his *Faust*, Murnau too expressed the supernatural through a world created in the studio. No other film has attained this degree of metaphysical meaning simply by using plastic resources. Nevertheless, despite the exceptional beauty of its sets, *Faust* makes the camera men more important for the all-powerful producer than the architects. It was also the swan-song of this form of symbolic expressionism, which was both the mystical and legendary, and which was scarcely ever to be used except in a new version of *The Student from Prague*, shot by Henrik Galeen in 1926.

This ascent, the desperate quest for light in the very heart of darkness, this *élan* symbolized by large, straight staircases, rigid like a sacred or arduous duty, choking and weighed down with anxiety, the desire for grandeur that guided these truly Faustian films, disappeared in a vague need to lose oneself, to abandon oneself to the appeal of the void.

As the influence of Carl Mayer finally became greater than that of Galeen which was predominant at the time, one moves from legend to a 'theoretical' realism closely inspired by Kammerspiel, the *Erdgeist* of Wedekind succeeded the Faustian Lucifer.

With Carl Mayer, who, on the level of construction was the greatest film director of his time (Galeen had contributed ideas, an attitude rather than structure). It was the art of Georg Kaiser and Hasenclever

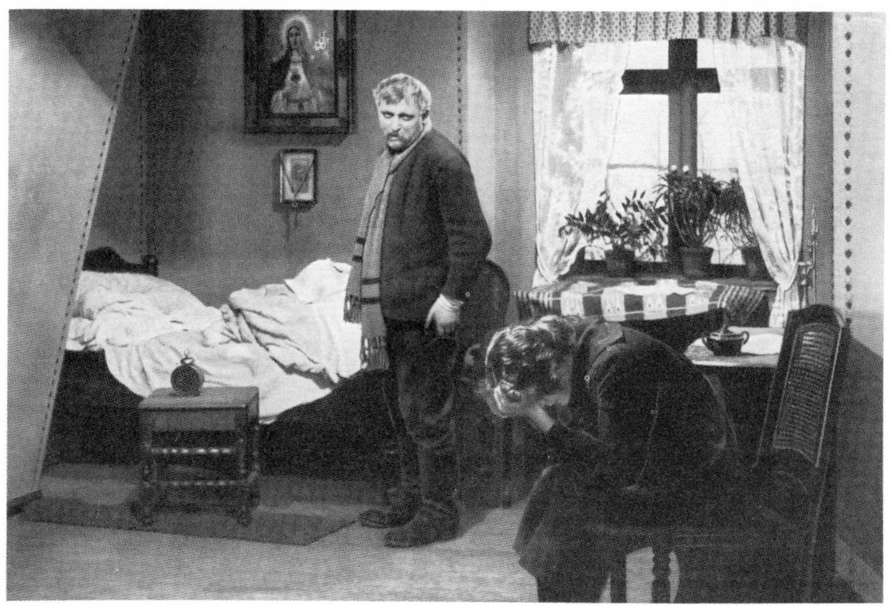

PICK, LUPU: Extract from *The Rail* (Scherben)

– realist in its choice of subject, symbolic in its intentions, expressionist in form – which succeeded that of Schlegel and Eichendorff. Films were now cut instead of the lights being faded out.

The street, that of the night-walker, of course – became the symbol of worrying temptations, of

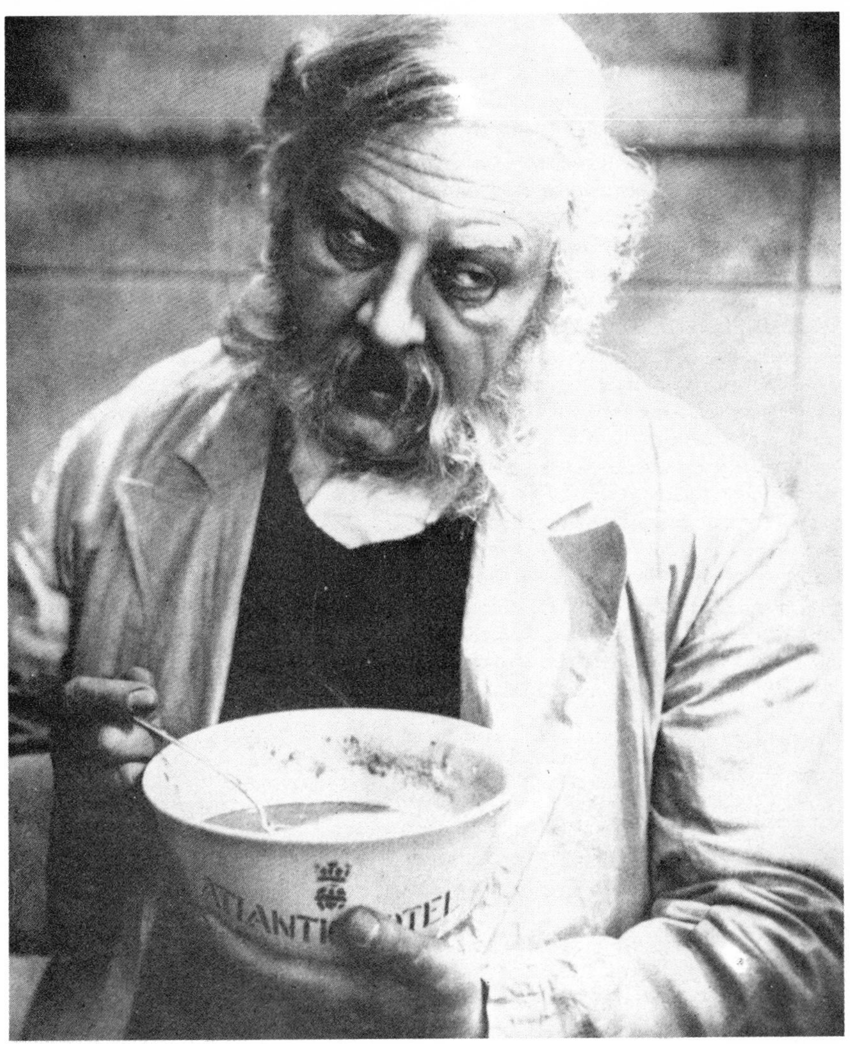

MURNAU, FRIEDRICH WILHELM: Scene from *The Lowest of the Low* (Der letzte Mann) with Emil Jannings

morbid attractions, with its cross-roads flanked by flickering streetlamps and embarrassed prostitutes, with sordid, smokey hovels, with here, there and everywhere, the fascinating obsession with objects – deceptive objects which were treacherous, haunted, diabolic, and which replaced as symbols, Lang and Murnau's architecture. With the hypnosis of spectral glimmers and overwhelming dark shadows, it was the appeal of night, man searching for something other than himself and his mediocre fate, and finally only finding ruin and desolation, that became popular. These are the favourite themes of this realistic expressionism, of which the first significant works were, shortly after *Caligary, The Back Staircase* (Hintertreppe) by Leopold Jessner and Paul Leni, *The Rail* (Scherben) by Lupu Pick and *The Street* (Die Strasse) by Karl Grune.

New Year's Eve revealed an even greater tendency towards a psychological naturalism, claiming to be realist, and which is in its subject matter, but which is conveyed through an elaborate, purely expressionist structure. In this film, where the action lasts a few hours, all that matters is what happens in the plot. For example, it is the life of cabaret revellers in an atmosphere heavy with beer and smoke; it is also the constant use of counterpoint seeking in the surrounding world (Umwelt) symbolic images (a rough sea, a stormy sky, a dark cemetery, a deserted heath). Images which seek to render the eternal side of things which the film is only representing momentarily.

But, seeking to express individual psychology through an exaggerated symbolism only showing obvious actions and reactions, centring on an everyday event, presenting excessively simplified characters in paroxysmal situations, Lupu Pick and the film directors of this school created films that are only realist in name. Their mistake was to want to stylize the plot and the characters by using a psychological realism whose requirements were diametrically opposed.

The expressionism, in fact, of these films, which has often been called *Kammerspiele*, was only possible in poetic realism, namely without any immediate psychological or realist intention, and again it was Murnau who did this.

From a script by Carl Mayer originally intended for Lupu Pick, Murnau created one of the masterpieces of silent cinema. Inseparable and even inconceivable without each other, the form and the content fuse into a whole which was a solidity and harmony rarely achieved on the screen.

Similar in this respect to all the subjects of the *Kammerspielfilm*, the subject of *The Lowest of the Low* is a slice of life restricted in space and time. An everyday event. But this film, which could simply be a sordid and contrived story, has become, in the hands of Murnau, a sort of poem where an imaginary reality allows one to glimpse a network of symbols which never destroys the credibility of situations (except involuntarily at the end, in the episode added on afterwards).

It is not, of course, a question of any old reality interpreted objectively. The real is entirely artificial and is created simply for its relevance to the plot. Nothing is gratuitous. Each gesture, each object is full of meaning, the grand hotel, the square, the roads, faubourgs, are represented by scarcely stylised decors but which are transposed just enough to elicit their maximum degree of expressivity. While necessarily following the narrative development, the action condenses the facts so as to emphasize the most significant. They are never considered as they occur but in a particular order.

The most simple objects such as revolving doors, lifts, mirrors, uniforms, the porter who commands a whole cohort of grooms and presides over the comings and goings of the hotel, are all signs.

In order to be clear, the social realism in this film only appears in a symbolic manner, for the theme of *The Lowest of the Low* does not have to have a specific metaphysical message; it is much more successful at a psychological level than it is in presenting a challenging ideology. The motivation, which comes from the prestige of the uniform, suggests a duality between what one is and what one appears to be. Without his livery, namely what represents him and what it represents, everything that in the eyes of others – and his own – constitutes his status, his respectability, his dignity, the porter is nothing, except what he really is. But who is he really? No longer being compared to anything, he cannot be judged; not even by himself, since his ideal, his patterns of thought and existence have been determined once and for all by his representation which alone gave him an identity, however simple. This is without doubt a social problem, but it is much more of a psychological than a socio-political one, and it is exploited in the film by symbolic means and not by an awareness of an objective reality considered in an authentic context.

How can one conclude? That expressionism, which aimed to be abstract, as it is so often said, collapses if it is only a way of structuring abstract ideas. Abstraction in the cinema is only possible when based on something concrete: on imaginary circumstances modelled on a plausible situation – or a dream – which expressionism endows with a symbolic meaning, but where the heroes, the plot or the world are pre-established symbols. If in *The Lowest of the Low* Murnau managed to escape from the paradoxes that plagued Lupu Pick, it is quite simply because where the latter used as images pre-established symbols, *a priori* ideas, Murnau created a stylized reality which, reduced to its essentials, assumed a symbolic significance only with reference to the context. This is the distinction between them: one proceeds from literature and concepts, the other from the cinema and reality.

FREUND, Karl (Königinhof, Bohemia, 1890 – Hollywood, 1969). Axel Graatkjaer's assistant (1913–1914). From 1915: films by Joe May, Robinson, Dupont, Wegener, Murnau. In the United States from 1930.

GALEEN, Henrik (Czechoslovakia, 1882–). After acting in Switzerland and in Germany and belonging to Max Reinhardt's company, Henrik Galeen opted for journalism and made his debut in the cinema in 1910, by becoming secretary and assistant to Hanns Heinz Ewers, then artistic director of PAGU (Projektions-Aktiengesellschaft-Union), a consortium which united Union Film (Paul Davidson), the Deutsche Bioscop (Jules Greenbaum and Schleussener) and the Vitascope GmbH. (Greenbaum). Supported by Ewers he contributed, as a script writer and producer, as did Paul Wegener, to directing German cinema towards fantastic legends which justified little by little the development of expressionist forms.

He was the script writer of almost all the films by Paul Wegener, Stellan Rye, Rochus Gliese, previously quoted; he was also responsible for others, for example *Nosferatu* (F. W. Murnau, 1922) and *The Collection of Wax Figures* (Das Wachsfigurenkabinett, Paul Leni, 1924). He personally produced above all:

The Golem (co-prod. Paul Wegener, 1914).

Hans Trutz im Scharaffenland (co-prod. Paul Wegener, 1917).

Judith Trachtenberg sc. and prod. Henrik Galeen; act. Erna Morena, Ernst Deutsch, 1919.

The Student from Prague (Der Student von Prague) sc. and prod. Henrik Galeen from Hanns Heinz Ewers; dec. Hermann Warm; op. Gunther Krampf, Erich Nitzschmann; act. Conrad Veidt, Werner Krauss, Agnes Esterhazy, Eliza La Porta, Ferdinand von Alten, Fritz Alberti, Erich Kober, Sylvia Torf, Max Maximilian (Sokal Film, 1926).

GERLACH, Arthur von (Austria, 1879–1925). Producer at the Vienna Opera, director of several experimental theatres, the disciple of Max Reinhardt like Leopold Jessner, Berthold Viertel, Rudolph Weichert and Friedrich Holländer, Arthur von Gerlach is the least well known of the great expressionist producers because of the brevity of his work. He was nevertheless one of the most remarkable. Having come to the cinema late, he produced his first work in 1922, *Vanina*, then in 1924 *The Story of Grieshuus* (Zur Chronik von Grieshuus). He died suddenly in 1925 during the shooting of the *Prince of Homburg*, adapted from Kleist, and which remained unfinished. His disappearance was a great loss to the German cinema and his two films assured him a place similar to that of Lang and Murnau. *The Story of Grieshuus* especially, which was one of the masterpieces of legendary expressionism in the same way as *Faust* and the *Nibelungen* are, of all the films of this genre is the most acutely romantic.

Vanina (Vanina oder die Galgenhochzeit) sc. Carl Mayer, from Stendhal; déc. Walter Reimann; cam. Friedrich Fuglsang; act. Asta Nielsen, Paul Wegener, Paul Hartmann, Bernhard Goetzke, Georg Alexander, Raul Lange (Terra Film, 1922).

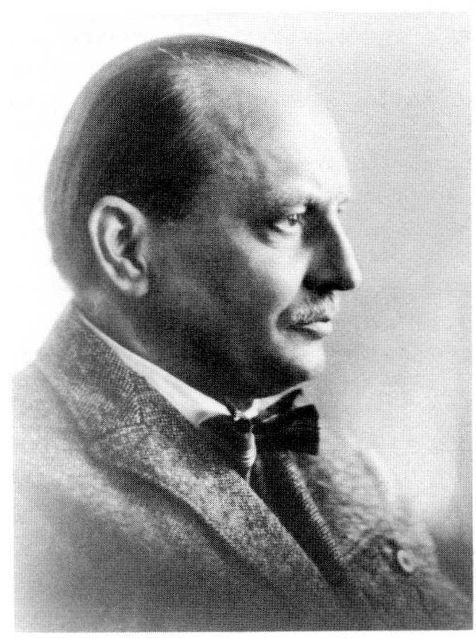

GERLACH, ARTHUR VON: *Portrait*

The Story of Grieshuus (Zur Chronik von Grieshuus) sc. Thea von Harbou and Carl Mayer from Theodor Storm; dëc. Hans Poelzig, Walter Röhrig and Robert Herlth; cam. Fritz Arno Wagner and Carl Drews; act. Paul Hartmann, Lil Dagover, Rudolf Forster, Arthur Kraussneck, Rudolf Rittner, Gertrude Welker, Gertrude Arnold, Joseph Peterhans (UFA, 1925).

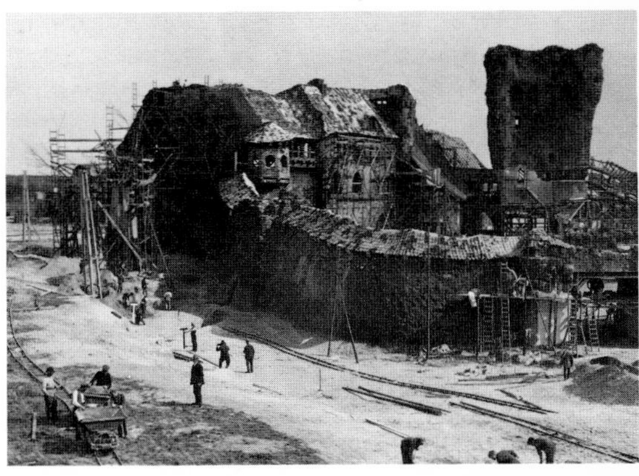

GERLACH, ARTHUR VON: Sets for the *Story of Grieshuus*. 1925

Scenario. The old squire of Grieshuus loves his son Heinrich (P. Hartmann) whereas Detlev, his second son (R. Forster) has gone into exile with an arrogant wife. Heinrich, however, marries

Bärble (Lil Dagover), the daughter of a valet. The father dies and the sons argue over the will. During a duel, Heinrich kills his brother and flees while his wife dies giving birth. A few years later, Heinrich, who feels remorse, returns to save his son from the hands of Detlev's widow and to assure him the inheritance. He dies happy and peaceful with the young inheritor of Grieshuus at his side.

GLIESE, Rochus (Berlin, 1891–?). Designer and producer; designer at the Deutscher Künstler Theater in Berlin (1913–1918); designed the sets and co-produced with Paul Wegener the films mentioned alongside the latter's name (1915–1923). The sets also of *Richard Hutter* (Georg Burkhardt, 1914), *Alexandra* (Theo Bouwmeister, 1922), *Der Kampf ums Ich* (Heinrich Brandt, 1922), *Brüder* (Emile Kuhne, 1923) and some films by Murnau: *Der Brennende Acker, Die Austreibung, Die Finanzen des Grossherzogs.* He accompanied Murnau to the United States in 1927 (1928–1945). He was director of the Landestheater in Potsdam (1945–50). He personally produced several films, including: *Malaria* (s.c. Rochus Gliese; dec. idem; act. Adele Sandrock, Friedrich Kühne, 1919).

GRUNE, Karl (Vienna, 22.1.1890). He was first of all an actor, and then collaborated, through his theatrical activity with Max Reinhardt. It was only in 1920 that he became a producer. He has said that the idea of making films came to him during the war; compelled to live with foreign soldiers, he observed their gestures in an effort to understand them, and his ambition was to find a language for the screen, a visual language which would communicate. His masterpiece dates from 1923: *The Street* (Die Strasse). According to the historian of the cinema, George Sadoul, this film was 'an exception in an undistinguished career.' The film had a great success. It is interesting because of its theme: that of the large town and its fascination, a theme often tackled by expressionists. The production reveals two inspirations: expressionism influencing the acting of the main hero, and realism predominating in the sets.

HOFFMANN, Carl (Neisse, 1881 – Berlin, 1947). The head of a studio of a printing laboratory in Fribourg (1903–1908); in the cinema from 1908; assistant to Guido Seeber (1908–1965). Films by Murnau, Joe May, Otto Rippert, Fritz Lang.

HUNTE, Otto (1883–1946). Painter, stage-designer; Fritz Lang's main designer along with the architects Erich Kettelhut and Karl Vollbrecht: *Die Sjinnen, Die Herrin der Welt, Das Indische Grabmal, Dr Mabuse der Spieler, Die Nibelungen, Die Frau im Mond* (1919–1928); then *Der blaue Engel, Gold.*

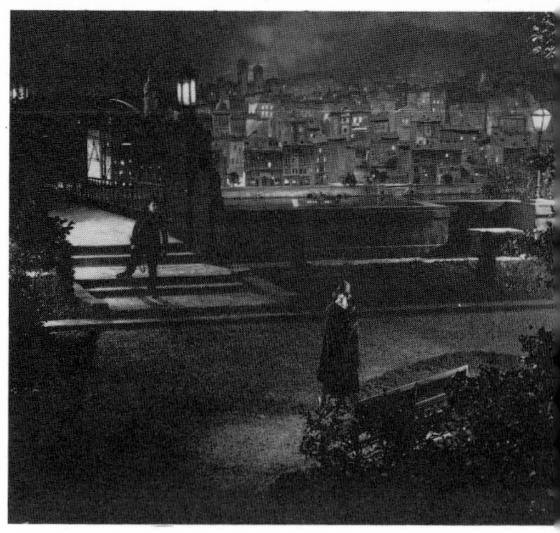

The Street (Die Strasse) sc. Karl Grune; déc. Karl George and Ludwig Meidner; act. Eugen Klöpfer, Aud Egede Nissen, Leonard Haskell, Lucie Höflich.

Scenario. One fine evening a stay-at-home and shy petit bourgeois feels attracted by the street and its mysteries, the lines of moving shadows on the ceiling having sparked off his imagination. The man (E. Klöpfer) therefore escapes from his sad lodging and discovers an unknown world, a nocturnal fascination which carries him away and dazzles him with its mirages. He accosts a prostitute (A. Egede Nissen) and is dragged into a circle of people, where he loses his savings and is incidentally involved in a murder. In the early morning, emerging unharmed from the affair, he returns home sheepishly, and seeks refuge in the cosy mediocrity of his lodgings where his wife (L. Höflich), his slippers and a comforting bowl of soup have been waiting for him since the previous evening.

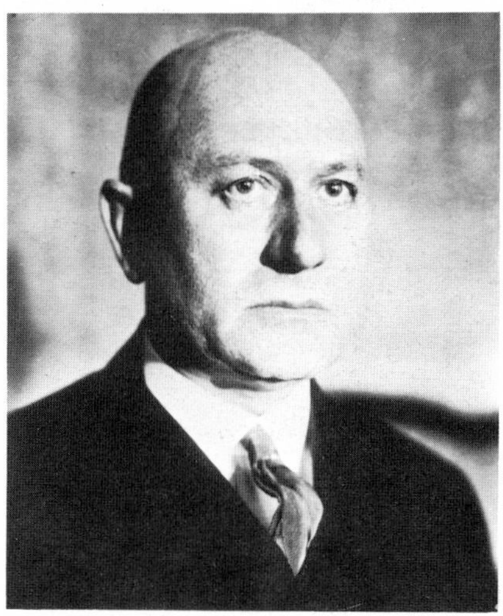

JESSNER, LEOPOLD: Portrait

JESSNER, Leopold (Königsberg, 1878 – Los Angeles, 13.12.1945). Actor and producer, stage director at the theatres in Hamburg and Königsberg, then the general director of the Staatstheater in Berlin, Jessner was, along with Max Reinhardt, Jürgen Fehling, Rudolph Weichert and Berthold Viertel, one of the most famous German producers of the years 1910–1930. A man of the theatre above all, he only directed a few films which were marked by a theatrical aesthetic, but which were a significant contribution to the expressionist movement in the twenties:

Miss Julia (Fräulein Julie) sc. Felix Basch from Strindberg; co-prod. Felix Basch; déc. Robert Herlth and Walter Röhrig; cam. Theodor Sparkuhl; act. Asta Nielsen, Wilhelm Dieterle, Felix Basch, Kate Dörsch (Oswald Film, 1921).

The Back Staircase (Hintertreppe) sc. Carl Mayer; déc. and co-prod. Paul Leni; cam. Carl Hasselmann and Willy Hameister; act. Henny Porten, Fritz Kortner, Wilhelm Dieterle (Gloria Film, 1921).

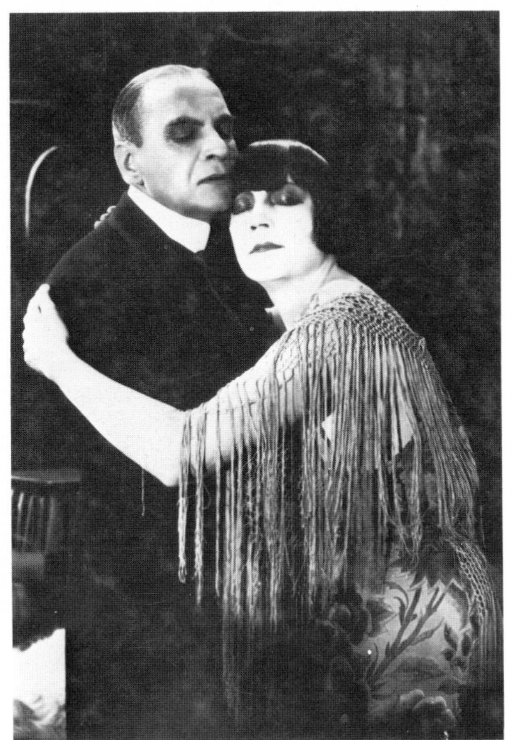

Earth Spirit (Erdgeist) sc. Carl Mayer from Frank Wedekind; déc. Robert Neppach; cam. Axel Graatkjaer; act. Asta Nielsen, Albert Bassermann, Heinrich George, Rudolf Forster, Alexander Granach, Alva Schön, Carl Ebert (Oswald Film, 1923).

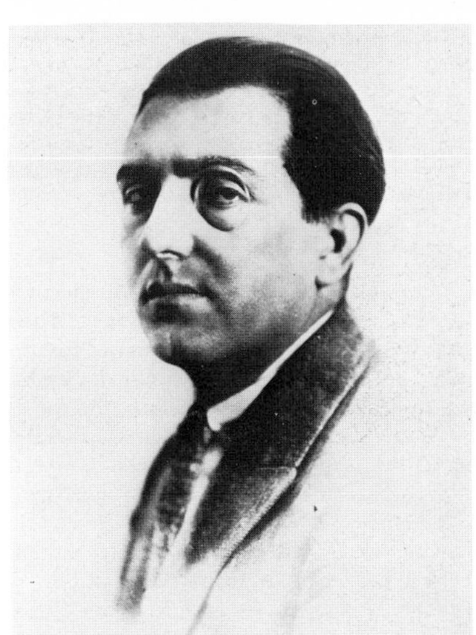

LANG, FRITZ: *Portrait*

LANG, Fritz (Vienna, 5.12.1890 – Los Angeles, 2.8.1976). Since his father was an architect, Fritz Lang also studied architecture at the Polytechnic in Vienna, then in the Fine Arts School in Munich. From 1911 to 1914, he travelled to the East and then settled in Paris, where he painted and earned his keep by drawing for German journals. Arrested by the French on the declaration of war as an Austrian citizen, he escaped, reached Vienna and signed up. Wounded four times and appointed reserve officer, he used his free time while convalescing to design sets, to produce plays for the Army Theatre, to write stories and *novellas.* Invalided out of the army in 1917, he met the novelist Thea von Harbou who introduced him to Erich Pommer, for whom she wrote scenarios. Lang did the same and sold a few to Joe May, to whom he became an assistant. Among others: *Marriage in the Eccentric Club* (Die Hochzeit im Ekzentrik Klub, Joe May, 1917); *The Plague in Florence* (Pest in Florenz, Otto Rippert, 1919); *Woman with Orchids* (Die Frau mit den Orchideen, Otto Rippert, 1920); *The Hindu Tomb* (Das indische Grabmal, Joe May, 1921). In these films, the tragedy of fate and the notions of guilt that were to be found throughout Fritz Lang's career, made their first appearance.

Introduced to producing by Rudolf Meinert, then the artistic director of the Decla, the famous firm run by Erich Pommer, he made his debut in 1919 with *The Seigneur of Love* (Der Herr der Liebe, Carl de Vogt, Gilda Langer, Ressel Orla, Erika Unruh) and *The Rastaquouere* (Halbblut, Carl de Vogt, Ressel, Orla, Gunnar Tolnaes, Gilda Langer). Of the films that followed, these are the most important: In 1933, after Goebbels had

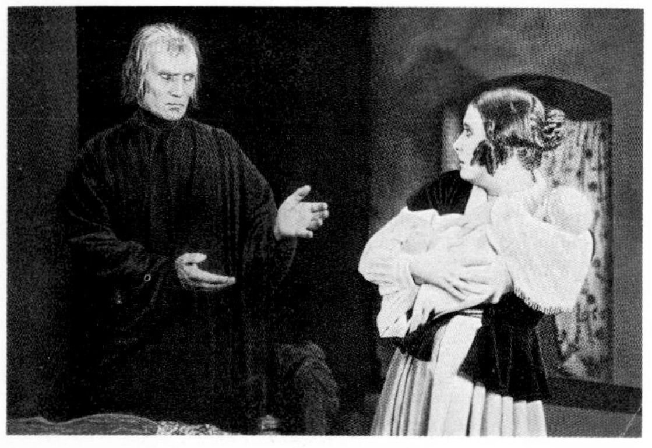

The Three Lights (Der Müde Tod) sc. Thea von Harbou; déc. Hermann Warm, Robert Herlth, Walter Röhrig; cam. Fritz Arno Wagner, Erich Nietzschmann; act. Bernhard Goetzke, Lil Dagover, Walter Janssen, Hans Sternberg, Carl Rückert, Max Adalbert, Karl Platen, Georg John, Herman Picha, Paul Rekhoff (Decla Bioscop, 1921).

In the course of his eternal journey among the living, death (B. Goetzke) snatches from a fiancée (Lil Dagover) her loved one (W. Janssen). The tearful girl begs death to give her back the one she loves. Death then gives her three candles which are on the point. If she can ensure that one of them does not go out, her fiancé will be returned to her. We then see three successive lives lived by the girl from different angles: in the Baghdad of *A Thousand and One Nights*, the Venice of the Borgia, the China at the time of the Ming. But death on each occasion wins. The girl then gives up her own life to retrieve her lover in the world beyond: love is stronger than death.

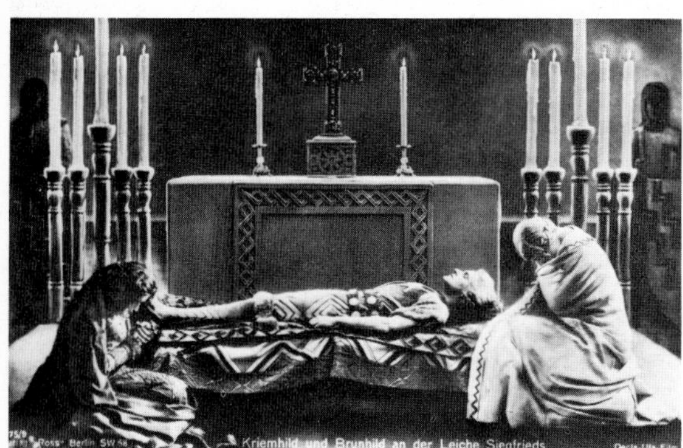

Nibelungen: the Death of Siegfried (Siegfrieds Tod) sc. Fritz Lang and Thea von Harbou from the *Song of the Nibelungen* by Wolfram von Eschenbach, the Scandinavian *Sigurda Saga* and the *Volsunga Saga*; dec. Otto Hunte, Erich Kettelhut and Carl Volbrecht; cam. Carl Hoffmann and Günther Ritten; cost. Gerd Guderian; act. Paul Richter, Margaret Schön, Hanna Ralph, Bernhard Goettzke, Theodor Loos, Hans Adalbert von Schlettow, Georg John, Gertrude Arnold, Erwin Biswanger (UFA, 1923).

Received at the court of the King of the Burgundians (Th. Loos), Siegfried (P. Richter), the conqueror of the dragon, is to marry Kriemhilde (Marg. Schon), the daughter of his host. But he is followed by the jealousy of Brünhilde (H. Ralph), who was hoping to become his wife, and by the hatred of the knight Hagen (H. A. von Schlettow) who is convinced that Siegfried has betrayed the confidence of the king. He makes arrangements to kill him during a hunt.

Nibelungen: Kriemhilde's revenge (Kriemhilds Rache). Ditto. Same actors plus Rudolph Klein-Rogge, and without Paul Richter (UFA, 1924).
To assuage her hatred and her desire for revenge against those she considers responsible for Siegfried's death, Kriemhilde marries Attila (R. Klein-Rogge) and rouses the Huns who in furious hordes destroy the kingdom of the Burgundians.

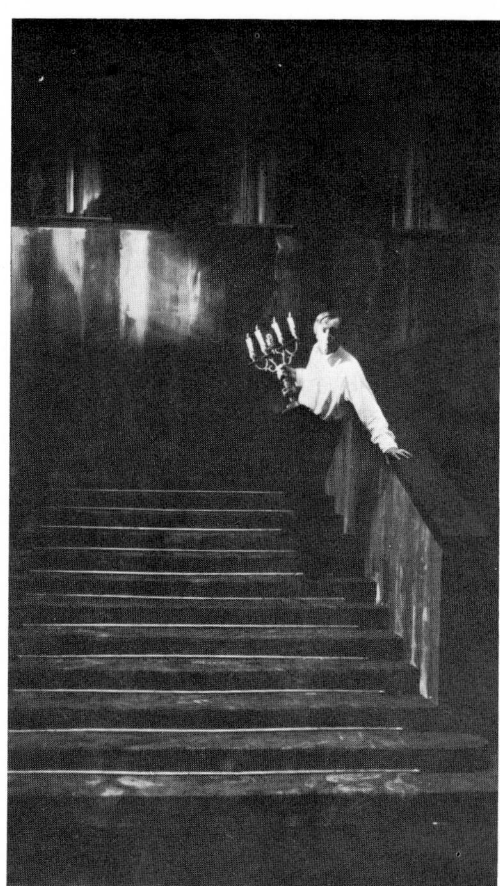

Doctor Mabuse (Dr. Mabuse, der Spieler, I Dr. Mabuse – II Inferno) sc. Thea von Harbou from Norbert Jaques; déc. Otto Hunte; cam. Carl Hoffmann; act. Rudolph Klein-Rogge, Alfred Abel,

Aud Egede Nissen, Gertrude Welcker, Berhard Goetzke, Lil Dagover, Paul Richter, Georg John, Hans Adalbert von Schlettow, Adèle Sandrock (Delca-Ullstein-Ufa, 1922).

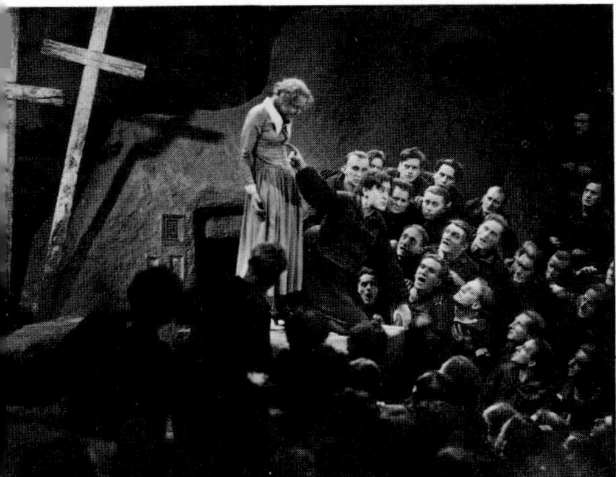

LANG, FRITZ: Extract from *Metropolis*

Scenario. In a gigantic town-factory, workers, who have become slaves want to revolt. A girl Maria (B. Helm), stops them because she knows that if they revolt, they will be massacred. The savant Rotwang (R. Klein-Rogge) a nihilist, makes a robot which looks like Maria, which will persuade the people to revolt. The working class subterranean town defended by the foreman (H. George) will be saved from the massacre and flooding thanks to the intervention of Freder (G. Fröhlich), the son of the boss Fredersen (A. Abel), for Freder is in love with Maria. Finally the disagreements are resolved, the heart serving as a mediator between action and thought.

offered him the post of Director-General of German Films, Fritz Lang fled from Nazism and took refuge in France. In 1934 he divorced Thea von Harbou, a confirmed Nazi, and set off to start a new career in the United States. He was inactive and frequently ill from 1960 onwards. He died in Los Angeles.

LENI, Paul (Stuttgart, 8.7.1885 – Hollywood, 2.9.1929). Paul Leni, who intended to make a career out of painting, frequented the *Der Sturm* group, and was quickly attracted to stage design. He worked in Max Reinhardt's theatre, and then for the cinema and was rapidly considered as one of the best German stage and screen designers in the first part of the twentieth century.

While still continuing with his work as designer till 1927, he took an interest in producing, made his debut in the cinema in 1916, and made his reputation in the years 1921–1929 in some of the most characteristically expressionist films produced; including *The Collection of Wax Figures* (Das Wachsfigurenkabinett) which is certainly one of the most delirious, and where the concentrated onirism constantly invites a formal psychoanalytic interpretation. As a designer, Paul Leni collaborated in many films. Oscillating between the thriller theme and the fantastic, his first films led him progressively towards expressionism. Amongst his output, the following are of note:

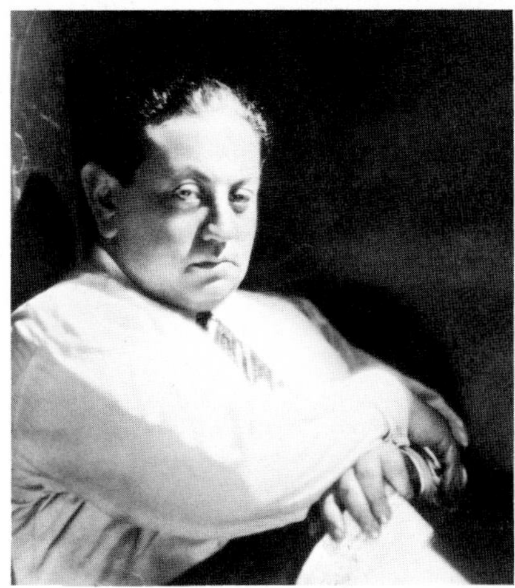

LENI, PAUL: Portrait. 1927

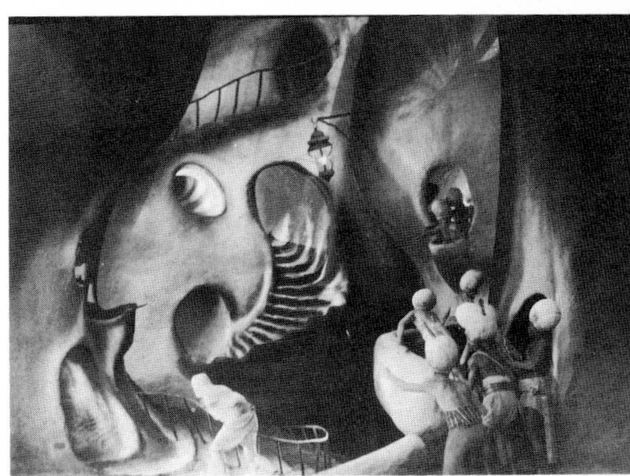

The Collection of Wax Figures (Das Wachsfigurenkabinett) sc. Henrik Galeen; déc. Paul Leni and Ernst Stern; cam. Helmar Lerski; int. Emil Jannings, Conrad Veidt, Werner Krauss, Wilhelm Dieterle, Olga Belaiev, John Gottowt (Neptune Film, 1964).

Scenario. The owner of a mobile hut where wax figures are exhibited (J. Gottowt) takes on a young writer (W. Dieterle) to tell him the life of his most important characters. Thus the young man's imagination gives life – a fantastic life – to Haroun-al-Raschid (Jannings) Ivan the Terrible (C. Veidt) and Jack the Ripper (W. Krauss). Each episode, which it is difficult to summarize, is in a style appropriate to the subject, décors and characters, and creates astonishingly expressive plastic and psychological associations.

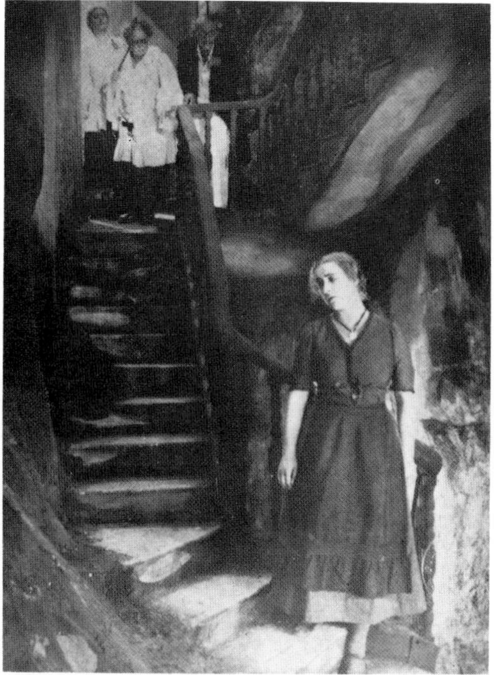

The Back Staircase (Hintertreppe) sc. Carl Mayer; déc. Paul Leni; co-prod. Leopold Jessner; cam. Karl Hasselmann, Willi Hameister; act. Henny Porten, Fritz Kortner, Wilhelm Dieterle (Gloria Film, 1921).

Scenario. A servant is desperately waiting for the man she loves. The postman, who desires her, takes pity on her and writes letters in the name of her real lover. When the girl discovers the subterfuge, she turns towards the postman. But the forgotten lover returns. The exasperated postman (H. Kortner) kills the mason (W. Dieterle). Bertha (H. Porten) climbs the back staircase for the last time, to the roof, and throws herself off.

In 1927 he was invited by Carl Laemmle of Universal Pictures to work in the United States. He continued to work in Hollywood until he died of septicaemia at the age of forty-four.

MAY, Joe (1880–1954). He was first of all the manager of a theatre for operettas. He began to make films in 1911. A popular series of political intrigues, the *Stuart Webbs*, had an enormous success in 1913. He continued this momentum with other films and series. In 1918, he shot a super-production, *Veritas vincit.* Then he became known for his adaptations of scenarios by Fritz Lang, then making his debut in the cinema: *Marriage in the Eccentric Club* (Hochzeit im Excentrik Klub) and in 1921 *The Hindu Tomb* (Das Indische Grabmal). His most famous film at the time was *Asphalt* in 1929. It was one of the many street films that were shot during these years, and which conveys, differing from the films by Karl Grune *(The Street)*, a love of city life. The production is no longer expressionist, but completely realist, at times even in the manner of a documentary film.

In 1934, Joe May emigrated to the United States. He made several films there, including the *Strange death of Adolph Hitler* in 1943.

MAYER, Carl (Graz, Austria, 20.2.1894 – London, 1.7.1944). Actor and painter, art critic and the general manager at the theatre in Graz. Carl Mayer made his debut in the cinema after a meeting with Hans Janowitz, who had a subject for a film, but did not know how to

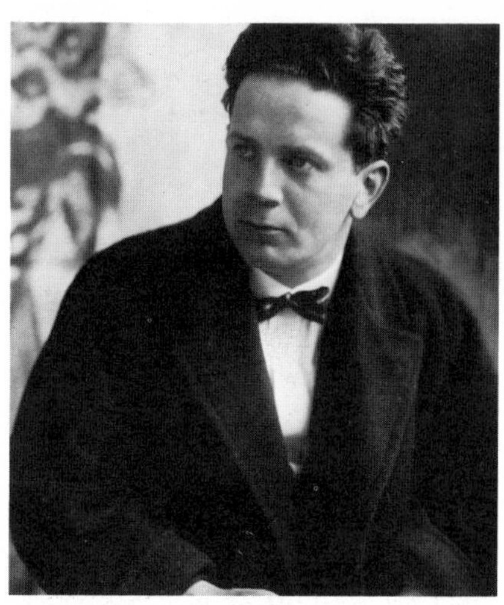

MAYER, CARL: *Portrait*

adapt it for the screen. Mayer who had an idea of how to prepare a script for shooting, gave it a unity and presented it to his friend, the stage designer Hermann Warm, who was enthusiastic about it, and suggested it to Rudolph Meinert, then the director of productions at the Decla GmbH. For a time, there was the idea of entrusting Fritz Lang with its production and asking Alfred Kubin to be the designer. It turned out differently and this way the *Cabinet of Doctor Caligary* was born. After which, Carl Mayer, who was hostile to caligaresque expressionism, devoted part of his output to *Kammerspielfilme* and to a realist expressionism, very different from the legendary climate introduced by Henrik Galeen and Paul Wegener, and of which Lupu Pick was the main representative.

He wrote a great number of scenarios including those of the following films: the *Cabinet of Doctor Caligary* (Robert Wiene, 1919); *The Hunchback and the Dancing*

Girl (Murnau, 1920); *Genuine* (Robert Wiene, 1920); *The Idiot* (Lupu Pick, 1920); *Torgus* (Hans Kobe, 1921); *Das Lachende Grauen* (Lupu Pick, 1920); *The Discovery of a Secret* (Murnau, 1921); *The Rail* (Lupu Pick, 1921); *The Back Staircase* (Leopold Jessner, Paul Leni, 1921). *Phantom* (Murnau, 1921); *Vanina* (von Gerlach, 1922); *The Puppet Maker* (Robert Wiene, 1923); *New Year's Eve* (Lupu Pick, 1923); *The Lowest of the Low* (Murnau, 1924). He emigrated to England in 1933 where he worked with the documentary film maker, Paul Rotha and with the producer Gabriel Pascal. He was director of the scenario department of the Two Cities Film Company.

MURNAU, Friedrich Wilhelm (Bielefeld, 28.9.1888 – California, 11.3.1931). His real name was Friedrich Wilhelm Plumpe, and he was born into a family where his father had made his fortune in textiles. Attracted to the theatre, while continuing his studies in philology at Berlin university, he made his début as an actor in *The Blue Bird* by Maeterlinck, put on by Max Reinhardt at the Deutsches Theater at Christmas 1912. After this, he played various minor parts, in *A Midsummer Night's Dream*, in *Faust* then that of knight in *The Miracle* by Karl Vollmöller and Gerhart Hauptmann. In 1914, he became an assistant to Max Reinhardt and his career as well as his studies were interrupted by the war in which he participated as an officer. After the war, he won the first prize in a competition for the best production, with a play with a regional bias, *Marignano*, and discovered the possibilities of cinema on seeing the *Cabinet of Doctor Caligary*. Fascinated by the art of dynamic images, he formed a society for producers with Max Reinhardt's theatre: Conrad Veidt and Ernst Hoffmann, the *Murnau-Veidt-Film-gesellschaft* and shot several short propaganda films for the German Embassy in Berne. Since Ernst Hoffmann contributed more capital, the society became the *Ernst Hoffmann Filmgesellschaft*, then *Victoria Film GmbH*, and Murnau shot his first full-length film in May 1919; *Der Knabe in blau*, better known under its second title *The Fatal Emerald* (Der Todessmaragd) sc. Hedda Hoffmann; des. Willy Hermann; op. Carl Hoffmann; int. Ernst Hoffmann, Blandine Ebinger, Karl Platten, Georg John, Leonhardt Haskel (Hoffmann Film, 28.6.1919).

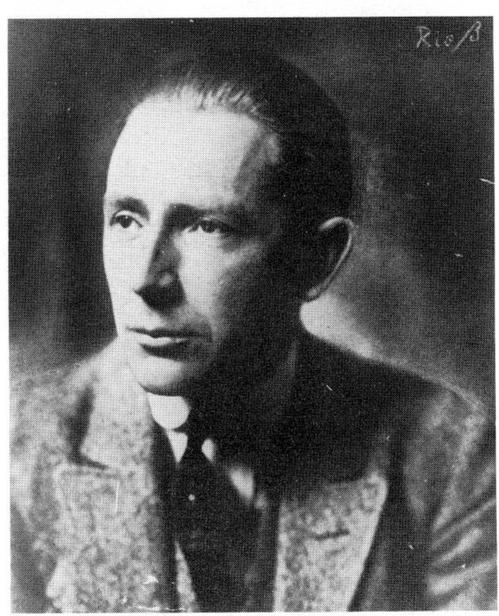

MURNAU, FRIEDRICH WILHELM: Portrait

There followed other films that belong to the period that concerns us:

Satanas sc. Robert Wiene; déc. Ernst Stern; cam. Karl Freund; act. Fritz Kortner, Ernst Hoffman, Margit Barnay, Conrad Veidt, Marija Leiko, Elsa Berna (Victoria Film, 30.1.1920).

The Hunchback and the Dancing Girl (Der Bucklige und die Tänzerin) sc. Carl Mayer; déc. Robert Neppach; cam. Karl Freund; act. Sacha Gura, John Gottowt, Paul Biensfeld, Anna von Pahlen (Helios Film 8.7.1910).

The Discovery of a Secret (Schloss Vogelöd) sc. Carl Mayer and Berthold Viertel adapt. by Rudolph Straz; déc. Hermann Warm; cam. Fritz Arno Wagner; act. Olga Tchekova, Paul Hartmann, Hermann Valentin, Arnold Korff, Paul Bildt, Lulu Keyser Korff (Decla Bioscop, 8.4.1921).

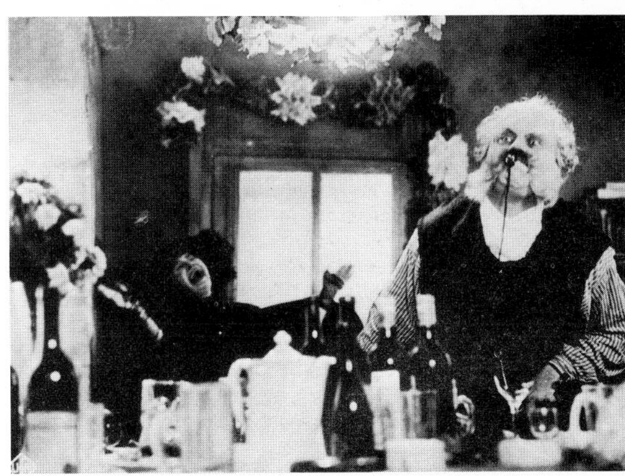

MURNAU, FRIEDRICH WILHELM: Extract from *The Lowest of the Low* (Der letzte Mann)

The Lowest of the Low (Der letzte Mann) sc. Carl Mayer; déc. Robert Herlth and Walter Röhrig; cam. Karl Freund; act. Emil Jannings, Maly Delschaft, Max Hiller, Emilie Kurz, Hermann Valentin, Georg John, Hans Unterkirchen (Union Ufa, 23.12.1924).

Scenario. Having become too old to continue his job, a porter in a luxury hotel is instead made a lavatory attendant, because of his loyal service to the hotel. Otherwise, he would have been pensioned off completely. For the old man, deprived of his uniform, this is a social decline, a degradation. In fact, when he went home in the evening in his gleaming uniform everybody would look out of their windows. He was greeted, and admired. For the people, he was a personality (E. Jannings). Now he is the object for their contempt and of their sarcasms. His sister (Emilie Kurz) who was devoted to him, mocks him with impunity, and even his daughter (M. Delschaft) and his son-in-law (M. Hiller) turn away from him. Only the night watchman (Georg John), who shares his opprobrium is able to help him.

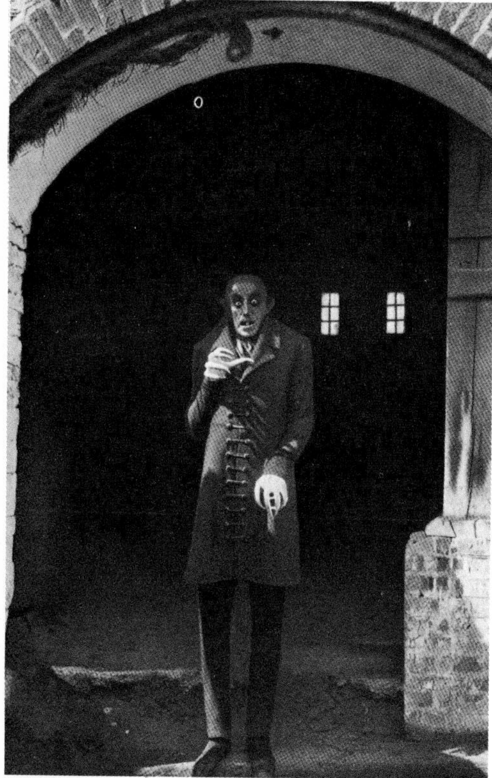

Nosferatu sc. Henrik Galeen, adapt. from *Dracula* by Bram Stoker; déc. Albin Grau; cam. Fritz Arno Wagner; act. Max Schreck, Alexander Granach, Gustav von Wangenheim, Greta Schröder, John Gottowt (Prana Film, 5.3.1922).

Scenario. Hutter (G. von Wangenheim), a clerk for the estate agent Knock (Alex. Granach), is sent by him with a secret message to the Count Orlock (Max Schreck). Knock is a disciple of the count, who, a formidable vampire, sees his death in a Castle of the Carpathians. Hutter, whom no peasant from the area wanted to direct to the castle, is soon a victim of the vampire. Thanks to him, an unaware victim, Orlock Nosferatu returns to Germany with a pestilential cargo. He seems to have to spread death and desolation in the town where Knock had found him a home. Out of love for her husband, Ellen (Greta Schröder) gives herself up to the vampire. She keeps him until dawn (till the cockcrow), and, in so doing, ensures his disappearance for ever.

Phantom sc. Thea von Harbou adapt. from Gerhart Hauptmann; déc. Hermann Warm; cam. Graatkjaer and Ouchakov; act. Alfred Abel, Lya de Putti, Lil Dagover, Aud Egede Nissen, Hans von Twardowski, Anton Edthofer, Frieda Richard, Karl Ettlinger (Decla Bioscop, 29.11.1922).

Faust sc. Hans Kyser adapt. from Goethe, Marlowe and the ancient Germanic legends; déc. Robert Herlth and Walter Röhrig; cam. Carl Hoffmann; act. Gössta Eckmann, Emil Jannings, Camilla Horn, Wilhelm Dieterle, Yvette Guilbert, Erich Barclay, Frieda Richard (UFA, 14.10.1926).

In 1926 Murnau left Germany for the United States. He was taken on by William Fox and made *Sunrise* in 1927. He was the victim of a car accident on the road to Santa Barbara and died of his injuries in Santa Barbara Hospital on March 11, 1931.

PABST, Georg Wilhelm (Raudnitz, Bohemia, 27.8.1885 – Vienna, 30.5.1967). An actor in Zürich and St Gallen (1906), then in the United States (1910–1914), a prisoner in France during the war, artistic director of the *Neue Wiener Bühne* in 1919–1921, then assistant to Carl Froelich and finally a director in 1923, Georg Wilhelm Pabst is too well known for it to be necessary to go into details concerning his

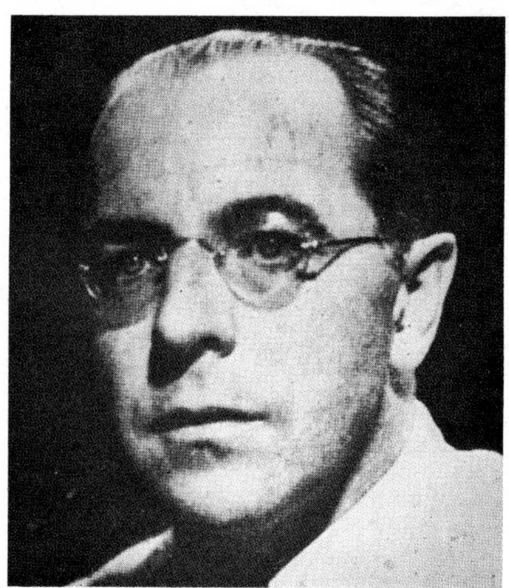

PABST, GEORG WILHELM: *Portrait*

bio-filmography. Although his first films were strongly influenced by expressionism, it would be difficult to describe him as a representative of a movement he moved away from in order to follow in the path of the New Objectivity, which was more concerned with social criticism than aesthetic formalism. Among the forty films that he made, the following are the most visibly influenced by expressionism:

The Treasure (Der Schatz) sc. Willy Hennings from R. H. Bartsch; dëc. Robert Herlth and Walter Röhrig; cam. Otto Tober; act. Werner Krauss, Albert Steinrück, Ilka Grüning, Lucie Mannheim, Hans Brausewetter (Froelich-Deulig, 1925).

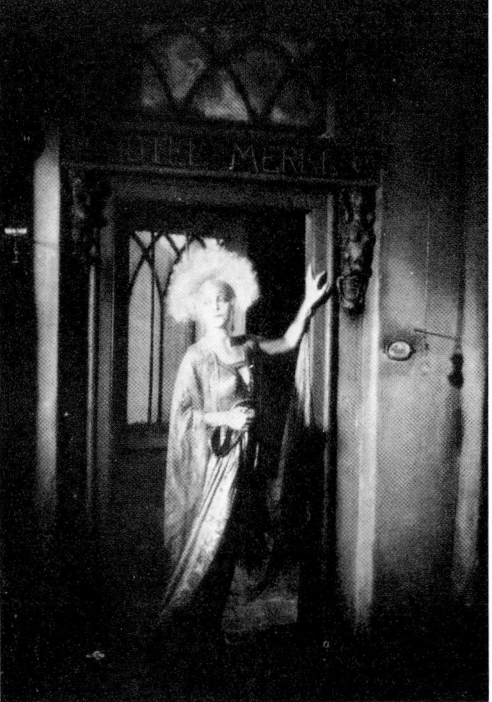

The Joyless Street (Die freudlose Gasse) sc. Willi Haas from Hugo Bettauer; Otto Erdmann and Arthur Söhnle; cam. Guido Seeber and Kurt Oertel; act. Greta Garbo, Werner Krauss, Asta Nielsen, Valeska Gert, Einer Hanson, Agnes Esterhazy, Jaro Furth, Robert Garrison, Ilka Grüning, Tamara Tolstoï (Sofar Film, 1925).

PICK, Lupu (Jassy, Rumania, 2.1.1886 – Berlin, 9.3.1931). He came to Germany around 1908 after having studied dramatic art, and made his début at the Hamburg theatre, and then joined Max Reinhardt's company in the Deutsches Theater in Berlin. Like his friends, he acted in a number of films from 1915. Opting, however, for producing, he formed in 1917 the *Filmgesellschaft* and at first directed films more or less inspired by the *Kammerspielfilme.* His important work

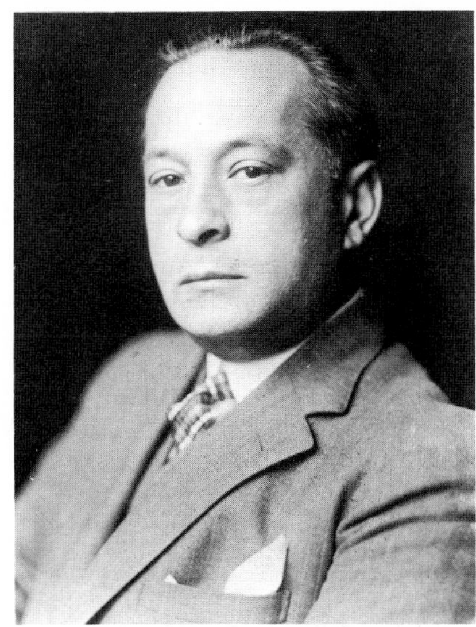

PICK, LUPU: Portrait. Circa 1930

began with the *Idiot* (Der Dummkopf) in 1920. Following the same path, but in a more and more stylized manner, he was the most eminent representative of expressionist realism.

The Idiot (Der Dummkopf) sc. Carl Mayer from Ludwig Fulda; cam. Guido Seeber; act. Paul Heidemann, Ruth von Wedel, Max Adalbert, Rosa Valetti, Lupu Pick, Otto Treptow, Eugen Rex, Else Eckersberg, Hans Fischer, Fritz and Frieda Richard (Rex Film, 1920).

Das Lachende Grauen sc. Carl Mayer; déc. Robert Herlth and Walter Röhrig; cam. Guido Seeber; act. John Gottowt, Edith Posca, Arnold Korff (Decla, 1920).

The Rail (Scherben) sc. Carl Mayer; déc. Klaus Richter and Robert Dietrich; cam. Friedrich Weinmann; act. Werner Krauss, Edith Posca, Paul Otto, Hermine Strassman-Witt, Lupu Pick (Rex Film, 1921).

The Tragic Night (Grausige Nacht) sc. Carl Mayer; déc. Klaus Richter and Robert Dietrich; cam. Theodor Sparkuhl; act. Alfred Abel, Werner Krauss, Edith Posca, Arnold Korff, Adele Sandrock, Paul Walker, Paul Eberty (Rex Film, 1921).

New Year's Eve (Silvester) sc. Carl Mayer; déc. Klaus Richter and Robert Dietrich; cam. Guido Seeber; act. Edith Posca, Eugen Klöpfer, Frieda Richard (Rex Film, 1923).

Scenario. While the rich go and celebrate in the exclusive restaurant on the other side of the road, the poor celebrate in a cabaret, in an atmosphere heavy with beer and cigarette smoke. The boss is busy. However, his wife has decided to celebrate with him in the small room where they live which looks onto the large room on the same level. The mother-in-law (Frieda Richard) turns up unexpectedly. The son (E. Klöpfer) greets her joyfully, but the daughter-in-law (E. Posca) is not pleased. The drama breaks out in the midst of the clients' drunken singing. The two women quarrel over the son or husband. One has a nervous crisis, the other goes mad. Torn between the two, the man, worn out, commits suicide by hanging himself from a noose.

POELZIG, Hans (1869–1936). See the article on page 125. This architect had a great influence on Robert Herlth and Walter Röhrig, for whom he drew up plans of the sets for *The Golem* and *The Story of Grieshuus.*

ROBISON, Arthur (Chicago, 25.6.1888 – Berlin, 1935). Born from German parents, Robison studied at the university of Munich. A doctor, he abandoned medicine for the theatre, acted in and produced several repertory plays in Switzerland and Germany, and made his debut in the cinema in 1914 under the direction of Joe May, for whom he wrote a number of scenarios, notably for the series *Stuart Webbs* and *Joe Deebs.* Produced for the first time in 1916; he was made famous by *Shadows* (Schatten) one of the most remarkable films of the expressionist period. After this, he is only worthy of mention in connection with sound commercial productions. Notably:

The Night of Horror (Nacht des Grauens) sc. Arthur Robison; cam. Fritz Arno Wagner; act. Emil Jannings, Werner Krauss, Ossi Oswalda, Hans Mierendorff, Lupu Pick (May Film, 1916).

Between Night and Morn (Zwischen Abend und Morgen) sc. and déc. Karl Heinz Martin; cam. Fritz Arno Wagner; act. Werner Krauss, Alphons Fryland, Elga Brink, Fritz Rasp (Terra Film, 1922).

Shadows (Schatten) sc. Rudolph Schneider and Arthur Robison based on an idea by Albin Grau; déc. Albin Grau; cam. Fritz Arno Wagner; act. Fritz Kortner, Ruth Weyer, Gustav von Wangenheim, Alexander Granach, Eugen Rex, Fritz Rasp, Ferdinand von Alten, Karl Platten, May Gülstorff, Willi Helder (Pan Film, 1923).

Scenario. In a small town on the Lower Rhine during the Directory, some friends are invited to dinner by a baron (Fritz Kortner). One of them (G. von Wangenheim) seems to be favoured by his wife (Ruth Weyer). The guests and the husband guess everything, while still spying on and being suspicious of each other. An itinerant actor arrives and suggests a session in illusionism. As he projects onto the wall the shadows of the protagonists, these replace the real characters, become flesh and blood, and bring the intrigue to a hasty conclusion. The baroness leads her lover away, the husband discovers them embracing, kills the man in a duel, has his wife tied up and whipped by a lustful valet, and becomes mad with rage. Then, little by little, the fictive beings 'return to their shadows', resume their place on the wall, and disappear beneath the feet of the diners. It is

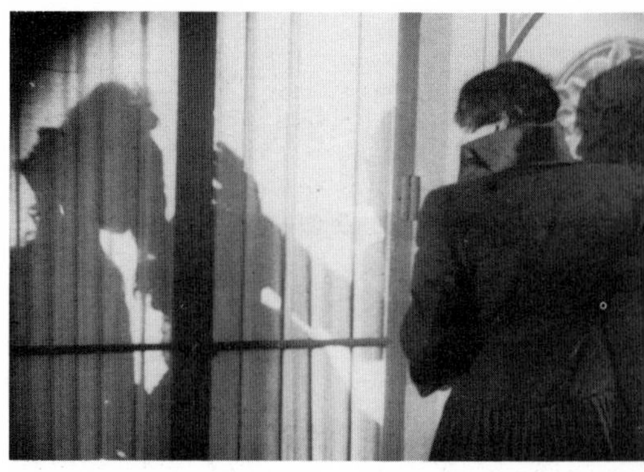

getting late, the guests leave, and the baroness suppresses her disappointment, and the illusionist (A. Granach) on receiving some money from the baron, disappears into the night.

RÖHRIG, Walter (1883–1954). A stage designer in the theatre in Zürich, he met Hermann Warm, in the army. Cinema from 1918: the *Cabinet of Doctor Caligary*, the *Plague in Florence* (co. Warm), in collaboration with Robert Herlth (1893–1962): *Der Müde Tod, Fräulein Julie, The Lowest of the Low, The Story of Grieshuus, Tartüff, Faust.*

RYE, Stellan (Copenhagen, 1880 – France, 14.11.1914). Attracted by the theatre, Stellan Rye left the army where he had a career as an officer to become an author *(The Faces of Treachery, Bellmann* 1909–1910), and a producer in Copenhagen. Having written several scenarios, produced by Wilhelm Glückstadt, he left Denmark for Germany and in Berlin produced several plays, including *A Midsummer Night's Dream*, a fanciful adaptation from Shakespeare by Hanns Heinz Ewers. Ewers, then the artistic director of the Union Film, suggested that he put it on film, which is what he did, after directing one of the first films by Ernst Lubitsch. He then made some of Paul Wegener's first films in collaboration with him. Called up in 1914, wounded at Ypres, he died in a French hospital. Amongst his productions, the following are worthy of mention:

The House without Doors and Windows (Das Haus ohne Fenster und Türen) sc. Henrik Galeen; déc. Robert Dietrich and Laus

Richter; cam. Guido Seeber; act. Theodor Loos, Rose Veldtkirch, Friedrich Kühne (Deutsche Bioscop, 1913).

The Daughters of the King of the Alders (Erlkönigs Töchter) sc. Henrik Galeen; déc. Klaus Richter; cam. Guido Seeber; act. Grete Wiesenthal, Albert Bassermann (Deutsche Bioscop, 1914).

SEEBER, Guido (Chemnitz, 1879– Berlin, 1940). The son of a pioneer in photography, Clemens Seeber, he studied photochemistry. Head of the laboratory in Dr Schleussener's printing and developing workshops in Frankfurt (1908–1912). Cameraman for Urban Gad and Holger Madsen at the Union Film A.G. (1912–1913), technical director of the Deutsche-Bioscop (1914–1918). Films by Paul Wegener, Stellan Rye, and after 1918, Lupu Pick, G. W. Pabst.

WARM, Hermann (1889–1970). A designer at the Schauspielhaus in Düsseldorf (1910–1914). Chronologically the first, along with Robert Dietrich and Klaus Richter, of the great German film set designers. Began in 1912: *Die Blaue Maus, Der Andere, Die Geschichte der stillen Mühle* (1912–1914). In the war, he met Walter Reimann, Robert Herlth, and Walter Röhrig, stage designers like himself for the army theatre, and he introduced them to the cinema in 1918, on the occasion of *Caligary. The Cabinet of Doctor Caligary, The Plague in Florence, Phantom, The Student from Prague, The Trial of Joan of Arc.*

WEGENER, Paul (Bischdorf, Prussia, 11.12.1874 – Berlin, 13.9.1948). Having studied law in Fribourg and Leipzig, Paul Wegener opted for the theatre and made his debut in Rostock. After several seasons in the theatre at Leipzig he was taken on, thanks to his master Rudolph Schildkraut, in Max Reinhardt's company at the Deutsches Theater of Berlin (1906). With Alexander Moissi, Albert Bassermann, and Werner Krauss, he was one of his leading actors for ten years.

Coming to the cinema in 1913, he became not only one of the first film theorists on the cinema in Germany but, following the example of Danish film directors, the real precursor of film expressionism (as distinct from caligarism). After his fifth film, *Die Verführte, The Student from Prague*, marked the beginning of a new era in German cinema. With *Im Schatten des Meers* (Kurt Stark, 1912), *Die Insel der Seligen* (Max Reinhardt, 1913), *Der Schwarze Nisse* (Stellan Rye, 1913), he opened the way to the mystical and legendary fantasy that he was to display in several films he acted in with his wife, Lyda Salmonova, and which he produced in technical collaboration with the script-writer Henrik Galeen and the designer Rochus Gliese during the years 1914–1921, well before Fritz Lang and Murnau made their real debut:

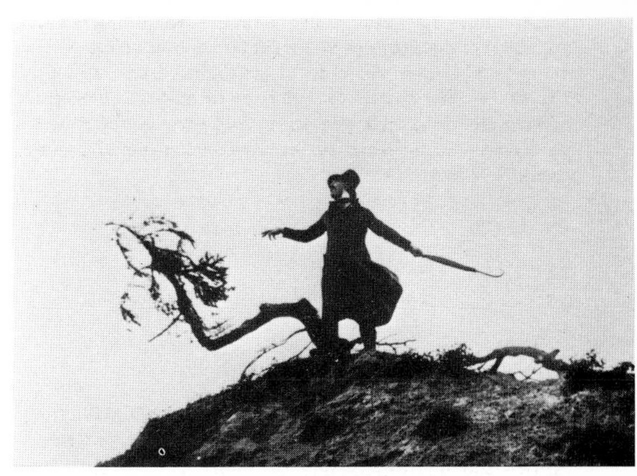

The Student from Prague (Der Student von Prague) sc. Henrik Galeen and Paul Wegener from Hanns Heinz Ewers; prod. Stellan Rye; déc. Robert Dietrich and Klaus Richter; cam. Guido Seeber; act. Paul Wegener, Lyda Salmonova, John Gottowt, Grete Berger, Lothar Körtner, Fritz Weidemann (Deutsche Bioscop, 1913).

WEGENER, PAUL: Extract from *The Golem*

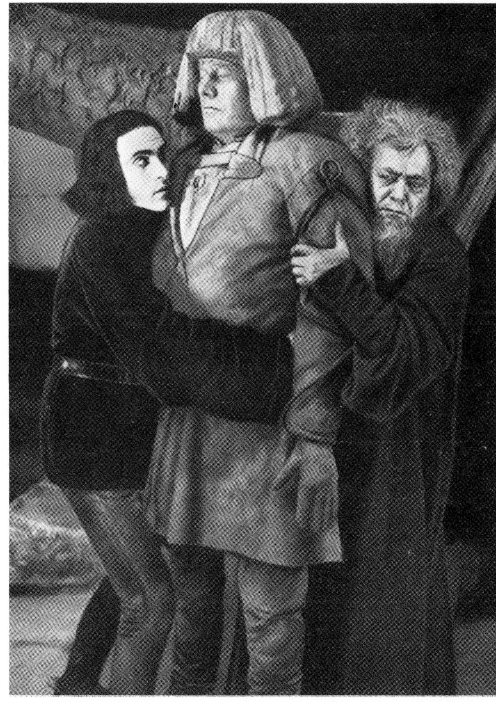

The Golem sc. Henrik Galeen; prod. Henrik Galeen and Paul Wegener; déc. Rochus Gliese and Robert Dietrich; cam. Guido Seeber; int. Paul Wegener, Lyda Salmonova, Albert Steinrück, Carl Ebert, John Gottowt (Deutsche Bioscop, 1914).

Scenario. In the reign of Rudolph II of Habsburg (O. Gebühr), the Rabbi Löw (A. Steinrück), having read in the book of the cabalist that one day a being modelled in clay by the name of Golem, would come to life and deliver the Jewish people from tyranny and oppression, appealed to Astaroth. Only Astaroth, in fact, can inscribe the magic word, enclose it in the Hebrew star and fit it on the chest of the statue and in so doing bring it to life. The Rabbi shows the Golem (P. Wegener) to the emperor to inspire him with fear and magnanimity. But, in his blindness, the Golem turns against his creator, wreaking destruction and death on the ghetto, until the day when his first gesture of kindness destroys him. He takes a girl in his arms, who, while they are playing, removes the star. Immediately the Golem falls backwards and breaks.

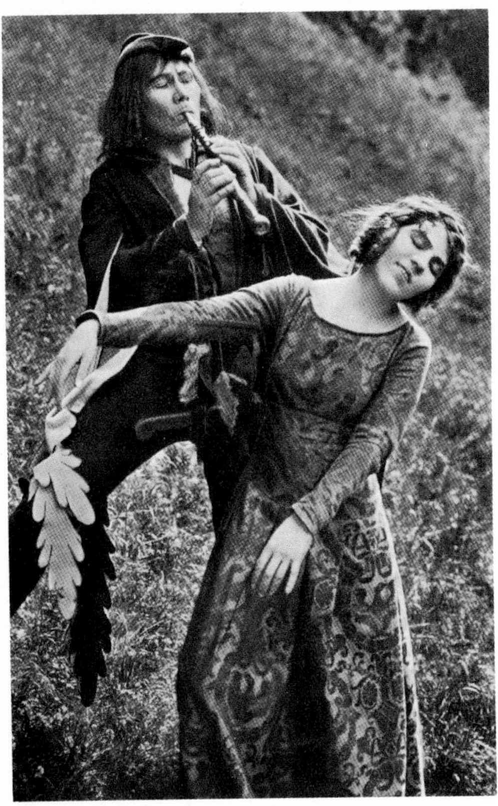

Der Rattenfänger von Hameln sc. Henrik Galeen; prod. Rochus Gliese and Wegener; cam. Guido Seeber and Friedrich Fuglsang; act. Paul Wegener, Lyda Salmonova, Wilhelm Dieterle, Jakob Tiedtke (Union Film, 1916).

The Man who has lost his Shadow (Der Verlorene Schatten) sc. Paul Wegener from Peter Schemihl by Chamisso; prod. Rochus Gliese; déc. Kurt Richter; cam. Karl Freund; act. Paul Wegener, Lyda Salmonova, Hannes Sturm, Greta Schroeder, Werner Shock (Union UFA, 1921).

Der Schwarze Nisse sc. Henrik Galeen; prod. Stellan Rye; cam. Axel Graatkjaer; act. Paul Wegener, Lyda Salmonova, Henrik Galeen, Olaf Fönss (Deutsche Bioscop, 1913).

WIENE, Robert (Sasku, Saxony, 1881 – Paris, 17.7.1938). Born into a family of actors, Robert Wiene made his début in the Theatre in Dresden after studying philosophy, and became stage director at the Lessing-Theater in Berlin in 1908. Having started out in the cinema as an actor and script-writer for the Sascha Film of Vienna in the company of Walter Turszinsky and his brother Conrad Wiene, he wrote between 1914 and 1928, many scenarios, produced by Max Mack, Emil Albes, Carl Froelich, Rudolph Biebrach and Conrad Wiene, most of them acted by Henny Porten. At the same time, he began making films and directed about fifty between 1914 and 1938. Although he owes his fame to the *Cabinet of Doctor Caligary*, the first expressionist film, or, at least, the first film to have brought pictorial expressionism to the cinema, Robert Wiene was only a second-rate producer. There is no doubt he knew how to work effectively with his collaborators, but he never had the chance that might have allowed him to create a masterpiece. Apart from his first important film, in 1915–1916, only his caligaresque films of the period 1919–1923 are remembered:

Poor Eva (Arma Eva) sc. Robert Wiene and Arthur Berger from *Fromont jeune et Risler aîné* (Young Fromont and the older Risler) by Alphonse Daudet; cam. Karl Freund; act. Erna Morena, Emil Jannings, Theodor Loos, Hermann Thimig, Alexander von Anhalfy (Messter Film, 1914 – it came out in 1916 because of the war).

Genuine sc. Carl Mayer; dec. Cesar Klein and Walter Reimann; cam. Willy Hameister; act. Fern Andra, Hans von Twardowski, Lewis Brady, John Gottowt, Albert Bennefeld (Decla Bioscop, 1920).

Die Nacht der Königen Isabeau sc. Robert Wiene; déc. Robert W. Tannenberg; cam. Willy Hameister; act. Fern Andra, Alexander Moissi, Fritz Kortner, John Gottowt, Hans von Twardowski, Harald Paulsen, Lothar Müthel, Elsa Wagner, Albert Lind (Decla Bioscop, 1920).

Die Rache einer Frau (Vera Coraly, Boris Michaïlov, Olga Engl, 1921).

Das Spiel mit dem Feuer (Diana Karenne, Vassili Vronsky, Hans Junkermann, 1921).

Die Höllische Magd (Ossip Routnich, Thea Kasten, 1922).

The Puppet Maker (Der Puppenmacher von Kiang-Ning) sc. Carl Mayer; déc. Cesar Klein; cam. Willy Hameister; act. Werner Krauss, Lia Eibenschütz, Lucie Mannheim, Georg Jurovsky,

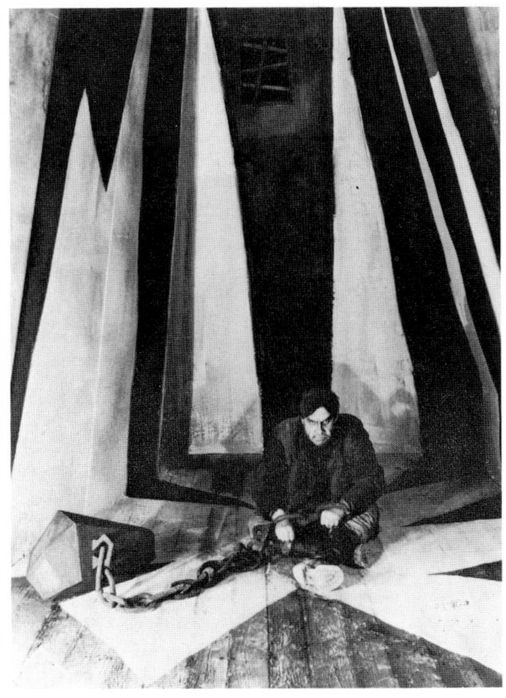

Ossip Routnich, Julius Falkenstein, Eugen Rex, Alexander Alexandrovsky, Hans Schweikart, Fritz Achterberg (Lionardo-Nermann Prod., 1923).

The Cabinet of Doctor Caligary (Das Kabinett des Dr Caligari) sc. Carl Mayer and Hans Janowitz; déc. Hermann Warm, Walter Röhrig and Walter Reimann; cam. Willy Hameister; act. Conrad Veidt, Werner Krauss, Lil Dagover, Friedrich Feher, Hans von Twardowski, Rudolph Klein-Rogge, Rudolph Lettinger (Decla Bioscop, 1919).

Scenario. Having gone mad after the death of a friend in strange circumstances, Francis (F. Feher) can no longer distinguish the real from the unreal. He thinks that the director of the asylum is Dr Caligary, an itinerant actor (Walter Krauss). He tells a mad-woman (Lil Dagover) how he made the acquaintance of this doctor and his somnambulist Cesare (Conrad Veidt); how this somnambulist, when hypnotized, was compelled to kill people by Dr Caligary, and how he killed his friend (von Twardowski) and then his fiancée (Lil Dagover) before Dr Caligary had him put away for insanity. The director of the asylum, having recog-

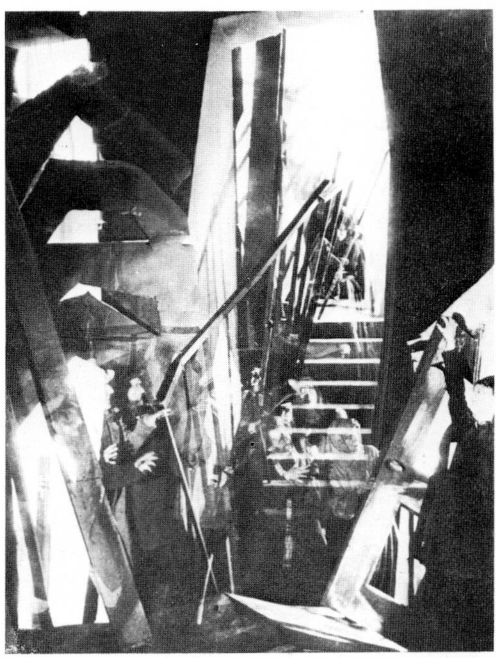

nized the cause of his madness, will try to cure him.

Raskolnikov sc. Robert Wiene from *Crime and Punishment* by Dostoievsky; déc. Andreï Andreïev; cam. Willy Goldberger; act. Gregori Chimara, Alla Tarassova, Elisaveta Skullskäa, Sergeï Kommissarov, Maria Germanova, Vera Orlova, Pavel Pavlov, Ivan Berseniev, Andreïa Schilinsky, Mikhaïl Tarschanov, Maria Kryschanovskaïa, Piotr Scharov (Lionardo-Neumann Prod. 1923).

Having left Nazi Germany for France, Robert Wiene made his last film *Ultimatum.* He died during the shooting of it, and so it was completed by Robert Siodmak, also an emigré.

Music

In music it is more difficult to distinguish between different techniques than in other arts. It does not use a clear language in the way literature does, it does not divide things up in the obvious way painting does. Dependent on an individual interpretation and a concert performance, critical appreciation is necessarily tentative. It is no coincidence that it is rare for normal aesthetic categories to be unreservedly adhered to by musicologists. This is true of terms like baroque, romanticism and impressionism, which were borrowed from the plastic arts.

Expressionism is no exception. The distance is the all more obvious because of the imprecise nature of the term, both in painting and in literature. No musician of 1910–1925 proclaimed himself an expressionist. Only one, Vladimir Vogel, used the word in the title of some piano pieces. Was the movement limited essentially to Germanic countries at a particular moment in time? Or is it a timeless style, that can be found in any country at practically any time? For some, expressionism in music was only an enhanced form of impressionism. For others, it simply referred to a group of composers who were opposed to programme music: Arnold Schönberg, Anton von Webern, Alban Berg, Paul Hindemith, Ernst Krenek. Some, finally, purely and simply rejected the whole idea of a specifically expressionist musical style, on the pretext that in the tradition of western music, music always aims to be expressive, and that, as a consequence, everything is a question of degree.

A historical notion linked to a movement for the revival of the arts

Nevertheless, did music not evolve in a way that links it to the other arts? From the end of the nineteenth century, it could not escape undergoing fundamental changes comparable to those that occurred in literature and painting. The traditional codes and canons were destroyed by Mallarmé, Cézanne and the introduction of free verse, just as much as by Debussy's dissonant chords and Richard Strauss's experiments on the very borders of tonality. Around 1910, another break with the past occurred, and music did not remain outside the general movement overthrowing conventions: Kandinsky destroyed naturalism's system of representation in order to create abstract art, and Schönberg freed himself from the yoke of the tonal system.

When one excludes the historical meaning that expressionism has assumed, beginning in German-speaking countries, namely a reaction against naturalism and impressionism, aspects that one could describe as expressionist are discernible before the twentieth century, and even in the distant past. In the fourteenth century, the *Ars Nova* reacted against the mysticism of the age of Saint Louis through a stylistic freedom, of which the origin lay in the desire to convey the anxiety of the time through an intense expressivity. In the Renaissance, the Franco-Flemish and great European, Roland de Lassus may be considered as already being a genuine expressionist, and especially that haunted genius the

Italian Gesualdo, through his unparalleled harmonies and his resonant ensembles of a totally unforeseen character.

But to be able really to judge the nature of expressionism in music, one has to begin with a historical movement, the emancipation already mentioned. It has been said that it marked the birth of modernism in art. There is, moreover, a deep ideological similarity between Kandinsky and Schönberg. Besides Kandinsky's invitation to Schönberg to participate in the activities of *Der Blaue Reiter*, in the almanach of which, in 1912, there were a number of articles devoted to music (apart from those by Schönberg himself on his art of composing from a poem, an analysis by Sabaneiev on *Prometheus* by Scriabin, a manifesto by Theodor von Hartmann in favour of anarchy in music, and another by N. Koulbine advocating a completely free music), it is interesting that both published their theoretical works, the *Manual of Harmony* and the *On the Spiritual in Art* at almost the same time. They paid tribute to each other.

A romantic inheritance

Between them, one thing that they have in common is of crucial significance: they inherited romanticism and had willingly undergone its influence. Now, does romanticism in music not lead to expressionism? Already in its emotional content, the romantic plaint expressed musically had metamorphosed into a scream. This scream is the voice of Schumann, the revolt of Berlioz. Wagner endowed it with its definitive profundity, one which could still enclose the world of tonality in the solitary wait of the wounded Tristan, where almost each note is an unappeased scream.

Assuming the degree of intensity of the expression to be a sufficient criterion for the appreciation of expressionism in music, the latter movement could certainly be seen as a continuation of romanticism. In German-speaking countries, it is musicians like Gustav Mahler and Max Reger, and later Arnold Schönberg, Anton von Webern and Alban Berg, who were led to extend romanticism by forcing the expressive limits it had reached. These latter composers, who were moving in the direction of expressionism, did not break away from Wagner, but continued to be his enthusiastic disciples.

It would be erroneous to think, however, that this continuity was above all technical: it was aesthetic. The technical evolution was only a consequence of a psychological tension, the result of an inner decision. Schönberg, Webern, Berg, and others like Franz Schreker, Rudi Stephan, Egon Wellesz, sought to convey more effectively the expression of each instant by a consistency of musical time which coincides with an inner necessity. This is the second crucial point in common between Kandinsky and Schönberg; they both believed that a work only obeys one law, that of an inner necessity. It assures the unity of a work of art or a piece of music. Without being descriptive, the work of art must reveal the impulses that led to its birth. It must shout out, bawl the profound truth behind its genesis.

Inner necessity and the Triumph of subjectivity

The originality of the aforementioned composers consisted therefore in the decisive step they took towards the projection of their fantasies and in the power of the deflagration it gave them. They rejected the traditional laws of harmony out of a desire to express their innermost feelings. They rejected all tonal systems which would prejudice, while claiming to convey them, the spontaneous gushing forth of the inner world and the purity of the fantasy. An insistent presence, renewed by fantasies in the same composition destroyed the architecture, and engendered an apparent musical anarchy.

The terms, personal necessity or principle, and anarchy have since then often been used to describe expressionism in music. Theodor von Hartmann did so in the almanach of *Der Blaue Reiter*: 'external laws do not exist. Everything the inner voice rebels against is allowed,' and again 'the correspondence between the means of expression and the artist's inner necessity is the essence of the beauty of a work.' In other words, the semantic values commonly used in music gave way to the expression of the absolute self of the artist.

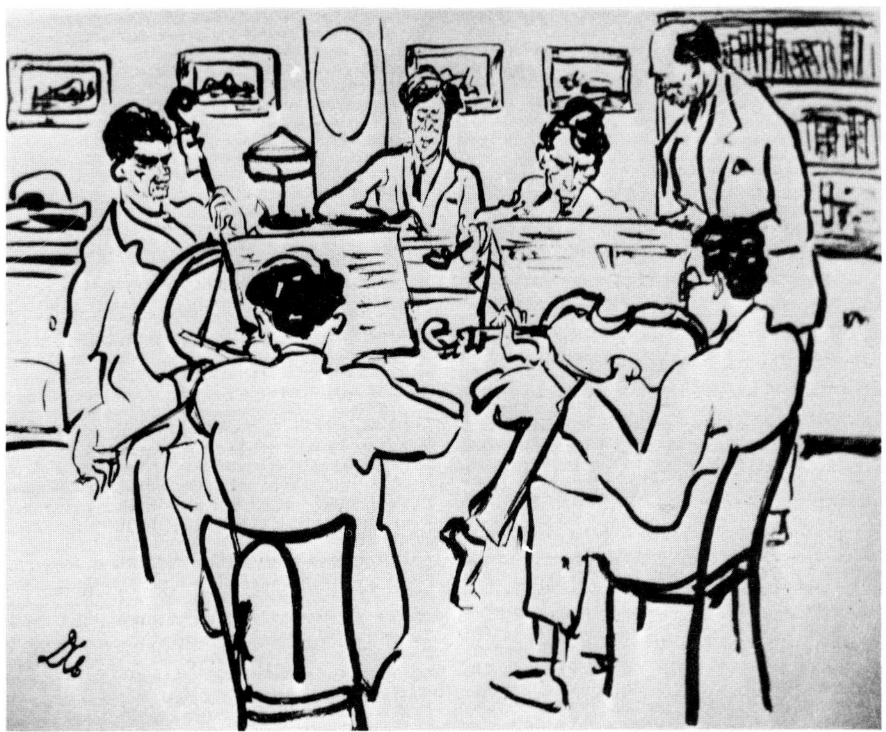

SCHÖNBERG, ARNOLD: Concert led by Arnold Schönberg (Alban Berg in the centre). Drawing

Breaking all links with the aesthetic of the past was the avowed aim of Schönberg in 1910, even at the cost of shocking concert audiences. He was thoroughly familiar with the aesthetic of the past; he reacted to the demands of an inner necessity. In fact, for him it was less a question of radically rejecting traditional forms, as the conventions regarding these forms. Still in his *Manual of Harmony*, he says that each chord is determined by the need for self-expression, but that the harmonic construction also finds a logic, although unconsciously, in the spontaneous gushing forth of one's inspiration.

This is the most important characteristic of expressionism in music: one had to free oneself from the rules in order to achieve a more spontaneous expression of the soul, through an intense and renewed expressivity. The exteriorization of one's innermost feelings was of the greatest importance. Adorno wrote, in reference to this, that the formal law of expressionist music corresponded to the registering of traumatic shocks by a seismographer. And Anton von Webern, rejecting the so-called intellectualism that Schönberg was reproached with, emphasized in 1912, that his compositions were, in contrast, formed from sounds coming directly from the movements of his soul.

The emancipation of dissonance

Just as literature freed itself at the same time from domination by rules of syntax, and painting from line to the advantage of colour, so music freed itself by breaking the regularity of the rhythmic symmetry. This is what Schönberg, during his expressionist period from 1908 to 1918, before returning to strictly formal laws of composition with the twelve-tone scale, accurately and simply called the emancipation of dissonance. It led to an absence of constraint, and was founded on what has generally been called atonality, a term rejected by Schönberg, who preferred those of polytonality and pantonality, for he considered that there are always links between sounds, even if they are obscure and difficult to detect.

This revolutionary innovation was tried for the first time in the history of music in the *Second String Quartet* op. 10 in 1907–08, but the complete destruction of the traditional tonal system was only begun in 1909, in the *Three Piano Pieces* op. 11. To be exact, the suspension of tonality began in the last two movements of the *String Quartet*, when a soprano begins to intone the poem by Stefan George *Litany* (Litaneï), a prayer of a desperate creature invoking the grace of God for her deliverance. But the music which emphasizes all the nuances of pain by a gradual increase in intensity, creates a tension still on the boundaries of the tonal. It is only in the fourth movement, inspired by another poem by Stefan George, *Rapture* (Entrückung), that the tonal scale is daringly suspended. The sounds, from the very first verse: 'I sense an air from another planet,' break all links with the chromatic scale and are totally sacrificed to the unbridled imagination that the rest of the poem inspires. Played in Vienna in December 1908, the *Second Quartet* created a scandal. It is clear that Schönberg was not aware at the time what it was that linked him to expressionism, and it is as it were in spite of him, that his compositions of these years are considered with reference to a musical expressionist style. But he was convinced of one thing, and what it was called was of little importance: that is of having brought about an upheaval in the world of music. Having finished, in 1908, a cycle of *Lieder* based on the *Hanging Gardens* by Stefan George, he stated very clearly that he had at last reached the expressive and formal ideal to which he had aspired, and he knew that in so doing 'he had broken down all the barriers of an obsolete aesthetic.'

Hanns Eisler, who was his pupil, has clearly explained the meaning of the revolution achieved in these years by Schönberg: 'He wanted to express himself, and this desire could not be brooked by any pre-existing form that had been handed down, or any cliché. It is an extremely personal, subjective type of music . . . which is very rare in the history of music. In themselves, the sounds are not new. They are inverted sevenths and ninth chords, triple chords all out of proportion, chords with a full tone and others with mixed forms. His originality lies in the fact that the dissonances are no longer resolved. The history of music is the history of dissonance. The ear had been accustomed for centuries to hearing dissonances which were then resolved, it now demanded unresolved dissonances. Schönberg was the first musician to use unresolved dissonances.'

Common traits with expressionist painting and literature

This upheaval in music makes comparisons with literature and painting all the more essential, since there existed an atmosphere of co-operation between creative artists at this time. Composers shared the desires and rejections of painters, poets and playwrights. More than this; they integrated their interests and works into their own creative activities. For example, Alban Berg was first tempted by literature, and he composed one of his famous operas, *Lulu*, on a text by a precursor of dramatic expressionism: Wedekind. As for Schönberg, being linked to *Der Blaue Reiter*, he devoted himself both to painting and music, and was deeply attracted to the theatre, and even the cinema. Contemporary plays, admittedly few in number, were used by musicians as dramatic sources for operas, even if the music did not always closely correspond to the precise expressionist nature of the text of the play.

This was true in the case of Paul Hindemith, in 1921, with *Murder, the Hope of Women* by Oskar Kokoschka and in 1922 *Sancta Susanna* by August Stramm, and a little later on, in 1924, Kurt Weill with *Royal Palace* by Yvan Goll and in 1926, *the Protagonist* by Georg Kaiser. Another play by Kokoschka, *Orpheus and Eurydice*, was set to music by Ernst Krenek.

In musical compositions, on the other hand, especially those by Schönberg, Webern and Berg, there is a whole atmosphere which is reminiscent of expressionist poetry. The inner being of an individual confronts the outside world. There then break out, with an unbridled violence, as in the famous scream of the poets, outbursts of fear, revolt, anguish and ecstasy. The expression of an absolute self is the result of latent metaphysical aspirations which are exteriorized in the form of a mysticism or prophetic message. With the seer's powers of foreseeing the future similar for example to those belonging to

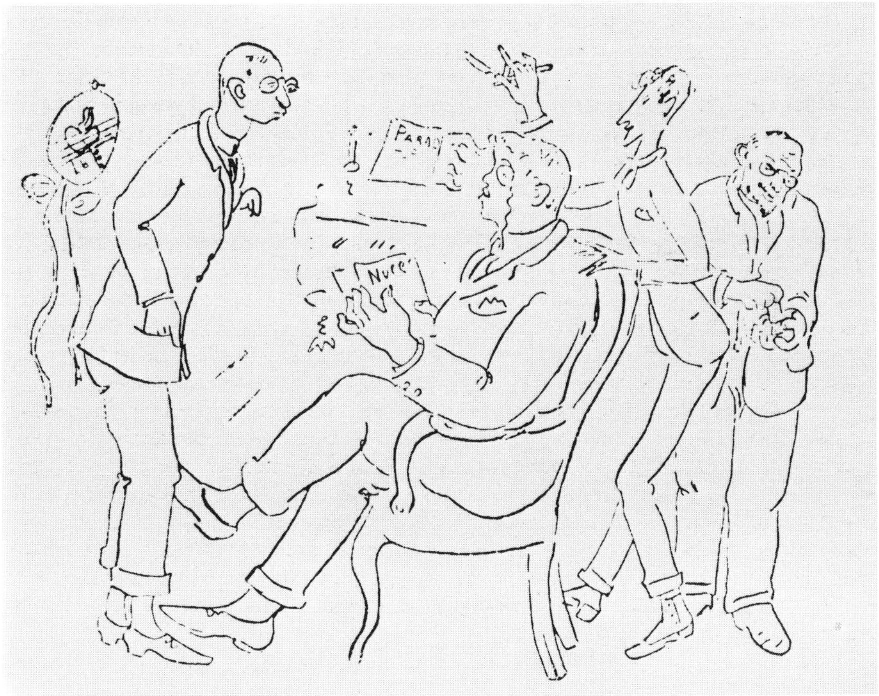

LARIONOV, MICHAEL: *Stravinsky, Diaghilev and Eric Satie.* Drawing

Georg Heym in his poem *War*, of 1911, Webern foresees in his *Funeral March* from the *Six Orchestral Pieces* op. 6, dating from 1907–1908, the forthcoming frightful cataclysm of the First World War.

Schönberg was haunted to an even greater extent by a messianic vision and the desire to use music as a means of conveying a message. In a note in the *Manual of Harmony* on the fourth chords, he stated that one must not simply see this as a technical means, but that a new sound is a symbol of the 'new man' which is being expressed through it.

As regards style, music also has traits in common with expressionist literature. As the written word of the expressionist poet is close to music, as an expression of screams, interjections, exclamations, it is also with regard to this scream that the musical sound is close to the word. The most certain way of identifying music as expressionist appears to be the uttering of this cry, which is only just tonal or which is attacking traditional music. There are many technical points that are linked to this: the extremely tense chords of the new dissonant sounds, the full strength of the orchestral timbres projected beyond the possibilities of recognized instruments, unusual melodic intervals, and rhythmic convulsions.

Apparently there is nothing in common between *Expectation* (Erwartung) by Schönberg, the *Five Pieces for string quartets* by Webern and the *Chamber Concerts* by Alban Berg. Nothing except that the note no longer obeys the conditions of harmonic development. It is isolated like touches of paint at precisely the most expressive moment, or like a poetic image which alone transforms a whole page. The timbres of each instrument are regarded as most important, each timbre becoming the autonomous voice of a musical subject.

This style is born out of aggression, a continual destructuration. The tonal elements constantly contradict every expectation. The judgement that Michel Ragon makes about painting is equally applicable to the new music: 'expressionism is everything that shakes up a pre-established harmony, that which is wild and asymmetrical and that cuts up and screams.' From then on, the melodious aggressiveness of extended intervals was the normal distance: short intervals, the majors or minors of the tonal scale were avoided. The musical scale was broken up, and independent harmonic juxtapositions fragmented.

Opera and Ballet

Although all musical genres were more or less affected, it is understandable that the search for the most intense degree of expressivity was more appropriate to some genres than others. It is obvious that in those genres where there is a real human presence, through the face, the body, the word, either spoken or sung, the scope for expressive intensity is all the greater. This is the case with opera. It is privileged in this way not only because it fuses all the effects of ballet, mime, costumes, libretti, but because, being a total art form since Wagner, it is both a mirror and a focus. A mirror because it is the echo of inner feelings; and a focus because it brings together and concentrates, projecting a more intense message.

It is therefore not surprising that musical expressionism produced some masterpieces in this field. Although they are not operas in the traditional sense of the term, two of Schönberg's dramatic creations perfectly illustrate the nature of the change: *Expectation* (Erwartung) of 1909, reminiscent of Strindberg in its inspiration, is a monodrama concentrating on a character and focusing on his direct expression, with movements of explosive outbursts of feelings and melody using very long intervals; *The Lucky Hand* (Die Glückliche Hand) a work completed in 1913, is even more typical through its mood of anxiety and its very expressionist theme of the experience of deep solitude, and its music freed from all the normative forms of organization. The most famous opera of the time however, was *Wozzek* by Alban Berg, taken from an unfinished play by Büchner and first performed in Berlin in 1925. Its musical style in general is characterized by expressionism, in its recourse to atonality, the tension and the violent contrasts of sounds. Of less importance in comparison to the other works mentioned, and by a composer of a later generation, but also representative of expressionism: *Royal Palace* by Kurt Weill, who had been the pupil of Ferruccio Busoni in Berlin, and based on a text by Yvan Goll.

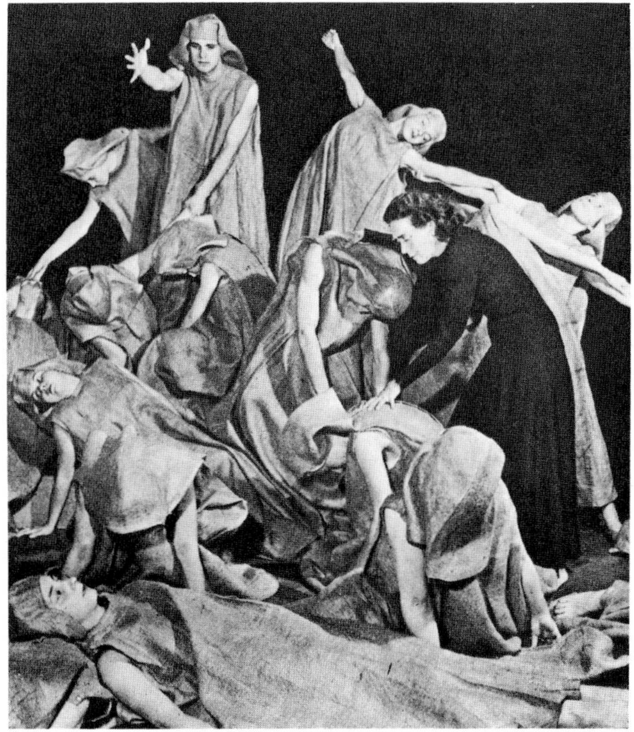

WIGMAN, MARY: *Group correction*

Ballet also has the virtues of concentration and intensity; it borrows from music its qualities of movement and from the plastic arts the expressive rendering of the body. But expressionist ballet tried more to free itself from music and the submission it demanded of the body, so as to become in its turn an autonomous art. Under the impulse of the upheavals sustained in the other art forms, classical conceptions crumbled. This reform, begun by Rudolf von Laban, was essentially achieved by Mary Wigman in Dresden. It was founded on the expressive power of movement through which feelings and emotions had to be conveyed. Here again, it was especially necessary that an absolute self be expressed. Ballet really became creation, and not imitation. In 1921, Alfred Günther explained the appearance of Mary Wigman by the environment of what he called expressionism: 'Mary Wigman's ballet is born in the midst of works by Picasso, Chagall, Stravinsky, and Archipenko', and he clarifies this, 'her ballet does not follow the music in movement and rhythm. Its movement and rhythm transcend the music. Often, it is as if the movement was built up out of the musical themes. But her ballet is not an interpretation of the music, it is an interpretation of existence.'

The Russian ballets of Diaghilev from 1909 to 1929 belong also to the expressionist period. It is no coincidence that he tended to choose works by Stravinsky (*The Fire Bird, The Rite of Spring*, and *Petruchka*), while exploiting the expressionist possibilities of other composers like Richard Strauss's *Salome*, which were sometimes models of expressionism: for example, the erotic violence of the choreography, in the *Prelude to 'The Afternoon of a Faun'* by Debussy.

The example of Diaghilev takes us out of German-speaking countries and we then face a difficult problem; for we may wonder whether or not we are dealing with an international movement. In the German-speaking countries, musical expressionism is part of a vast revival in the arts which was carried along by a social crisis, a collective anxiety, and the feeling that a society was drawing to a close. But what about music in other countries?

When one bases one's interpretation on the distinctions we have made, namely an intensity of expression doing full justice to an inner spontaneity by questioning the traditional tonal system or more generally the musical conventions that obtained, other composers, including only those who made a name for themselves, need to be classified with the representatives of a form of expressionism.

In Russia, besides Scriabin and Stravinsky, Prokofiev deserves to be mentioned for a work as marked by primitivism as the *Scythian Suite* (1914). In Italy, in opposition to the verism that predominated, there were personalities like Alfredo Casella, Gian Francesco Malipiero and Luigi Dallapiccola. In Hungary, one must mention Béla Bartók and Zoltán Kodály, and in Czechoslovakia, Bohuslav Martinů and Alois Haba, and in Poland, Karol Szymanowski.

France, attached to her traditions of equilibrium and clarity, did not respond greatly to the appeals of a commonplace expressionism. But one composer does deserve attention, because of his exceptional originality: Edgar Varèse (1885–1965). Breaking resolutely and aggressively with all the musical styles of his time, and using new ways of making sounds, challenging even the way we listen to music, he ushered in an art that belongs to the contemporary world.

The same must be said of an American who has been unjustly neglected for a number of years: Charles Ives (1874–1954), who does not belong to any movement. His various works make use of polytonality, of techniques not used in Europe, unexpected thematic borrowings and naïve primitivism. They provoke, in their way an expressionism which has no doubt influenced more recent musicians like Edward Burlingame Hill and John Cage.

But mentioning these composers who are already famous invites the question: will the innovating composers of the beginning of the century ever be recognized? It is nevertheless true that a new form of expressionism has become established internationally with composers like Stockhausen, Nono, Berio, Maderna, Penderecki, where this time, since André Jolivet, Olivier Messiaen and Henri Dutilleux and more recently with Jean Barraqué and Pierre Boulez, France has played a leading role. The shock produced by Arnold Schönberg, Anton von Webern, Alban Berg and others by overthrowing the traditional language of music has, therefore, now been accepted. It is perhaps this rejection of conventions that is the source of the inspiration behind all truly modern music.

BARTÓK, Béla (Nagyszentmiklós, Hungary 25.3.1881 – New York, 26.9.1945). His musical education began very early. His mother gave him his first

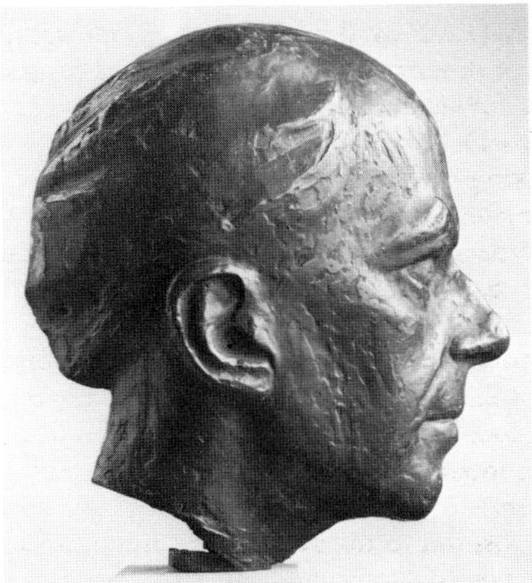

BARTOK, BELA: Sculpture by Andreas Beck

piano lessons, then he became a pupil of Erkel in Bratislava (1894–1899) and finished his studies at Budapest from 1899 to 1903, where he himself was appointed a teacher from 1907. A remarkable pianist, he played Bach, Beethoven and especially Liszt, whose romanticism had a crucial influence on his career as a composer. Tight links exist between Bartók's music and his political, social and national fate. Throughout his life the existence of his nation was threatened, he refused to accept tyranny and he assumed the consequences of exile even to the extent of misery. His work was therefore written as a testimony. Rarely has an artist been affected to such an extent by human anxiety, of which his music is the most striking echo. His work is thus closely related to his personal life.

In 1905, he met Kodály with whom he became friends. Both of them, in 1906, went to Hungary on a working holiday. Bartók discovered Hungarian, Slovak, Bulgarian, Serbo-Croat, and Turkish folk songs, and noted down 10,000 melodies. The popular sounds, their wild violence, but also their poetic serenity are perceptible throughout his work, not only in an imitative form, but in a return to initial sources.

The *Six string quartets* are the most representative of his power of expression. The first, in 1908, is already haunted by a total chromatism of twelve sounds; the second, 1917, by the diminished fifths and the interval of three tones; the third, 1927, and the fourth, 1928, are the very symbol of the artist's expressionist maturity, confirmed by the *Sonata for piano* and the *First piano concerto*, both dating from 1926; the fifth, 1939, sometimes considered less expressive, also has the diminished fifth though, as for the sixth, 1939, it reveals a return to a degree of serenity.

Bartók enhanced the expressionism of tone by limiting the power of the instruments to rare and unusual timbres: already in the works of his youth like *Kossuth* 1903, where he fuses the influence of Strauss and Hungarian folk tunes, he relies on the aggressive nature of the timbres; *Music for strings, percussion and celesta*, composed in 1936 for the Basel Chamber Orchestra. But this expressive tension is especially noticeable in the *Concerto for orchestra* 1943, where the instruments gathered into groups act against each other, in such varied musical domains that they destroy the unity of the whole.

The works written for piano are the most faithful reflection of Bartók's thought. since a whole part of his career was initially devoted to the piano. Among a

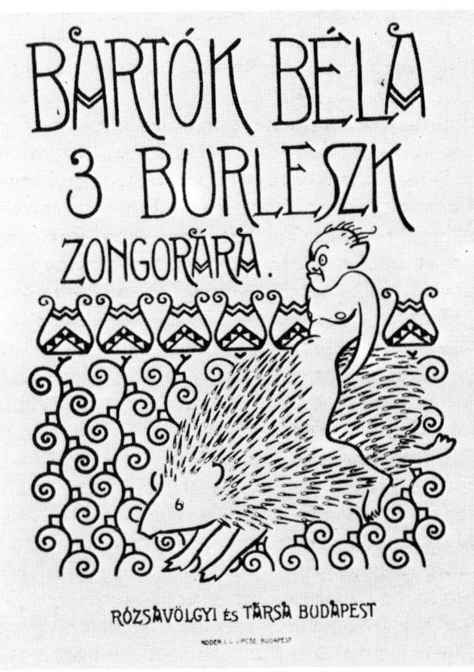

BARTOK, BELA: *Three Burlesque pieces*. Frontispiece of the score

number of folk dances, of note is the *Allegro barbaro*, where the violence foreshadows that of the more aggressive *sonata*. In 1926, the *Three concertos for piano* mark the apogee of the artist's expressionism.

Bartók also composed for the stage. If the ballet *The Wooden Prince*, 1917, is still a happy fairyland, the *Miraculous Mandarin* throws off this mask of a dream world. Composed in 1919, performed in Cologne in 1926, it was only shown in Hungary in 1945. The music for this tense, violent ballet, more sensual than the *Rite of Spring*, transforms into a beast of prey the girl subjected to the harshness of her accomplices. A different expressionist world reigns in *Duke Bluebeard's Castle* an opera written in 1911.

In 1940, the composer left Hungary, then under the reign of the regent Horthy, for the United States. To earn a living, he increased the number of concerts he performed, and he lectured, but he did not achieve the expected success, and died in 1945, badly off.

BERG, Alban (Vienna, 9.2.1885 – Vienna, 24.12.1935). Coming from a family belonging to the Viennese upper bourgeoisie, Alban Berg pursued serious studies of a general nature which directed him more towards literature. Still very young, he hesitated between poetry and music, hence his unwavering desire to unify the expressive text and a pure and rigorous music. It has even been said that, throughout Berg's work, one is listening to an immense opera, an inner lyrical drama, which is both occult and secret and of which *Wozzeck* and *Lulu* are the visible expression.

In 1904, it was as the composer of *Lieder* that he was introduced to Schönberg, and he, docile and confident, remained his pupil till 1910 when he became his devoted disciple. This meeting was crucial for both men, who built up a strong friendship. Schönberg was then going through the most creative period of his evolution: he passed imperceptibly from romanticism to expressionism, from a tonal world to an atonal one. Berg participated in Schönberg's research and all his musical writing was to be marked by the example of the great pedagogue.

The evolution in Berg's style covers three long great periods. From 1904 to 1914, under the direct influence of Schönberg, still not completely freed from the influence of Mahler's style, he progressively eliminated tonality. The string quartet op. 3 (1909–1910) marks the break with romanticism, and ushers in the expressionism of the *Lyric Suite* of the last period. Beyond the scandal of the first performance in 1913, due more to the aggressive eroticism of the texts than to the score, *Peter Altenberg's Postcards* (1911–1912, *five melodies for songs and orchestra*), reveal an incisive concision, a brevity in the cry of provocation rare in a composer. Finally the *Pieces for orchestra* op. 6 (1913–1914) have such a sonorous intensity that they lie beyond the normal conditions of performance.

The second period (from 1914 to 1925) the richest, began with the war. Berg was mobilized, but, being of weak health, was given an administrative post which allowed him to continue his work. *Wozzeck* (1917–1921), the masterpiece of lyrical expressionism, dominated this period. Berg, had discovered the work by Georg Büchner (1813–1837), an aggressive romantic, an expressionist in the wrong century. Fascinated by the play from 1914 onwards, the composer modified the text to give it a dramatic form suitable for musical adaptation: short scenes, a concise expressive style, strong almost brutal feelings. The plot can be summarized as follows: the loves and misfortunes of a poor soldier with a tragic ending: Wozzeck kills his companion Marie and drowns himself. The musical language is that of pure expressionism. The rigorous construction of the whole encloses all of the stage space in a violent tension, controlled by the very classical rigour of the forms used (rhapsody, passacaglia, rondo, the sonata form, fugue). The architecture of the whole, three acts each of five scenes, is balanced around the central act. The refusal of freedom, which would have allowed total atonality, plays the same role here as the twelve-tone constraint that Berg does not yet adhere to. At the heart of this piece, he includes all the exacerbated tones of timbres, rhythms, verbal statements, real harmonic shocks, the defiance of a mass of notes, all the phenomena of the expression of the devil. The opera, performed in Berlin for the first time in 1925, provoked a sarcastic reception from the critics.

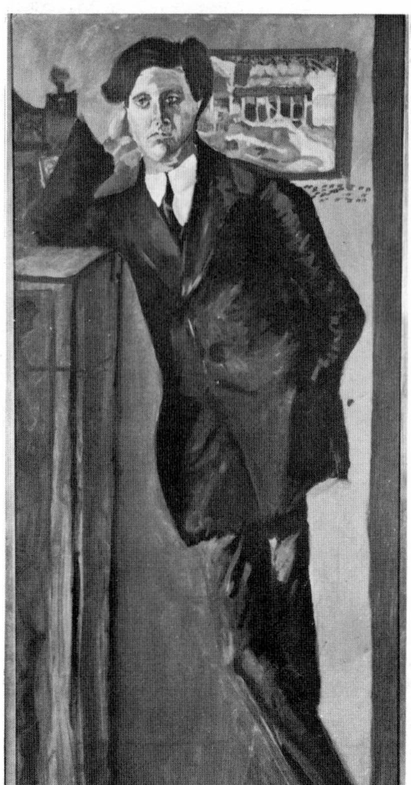

BERG, ALBAN: *Portrait by Arnold Schönberg.* 1910

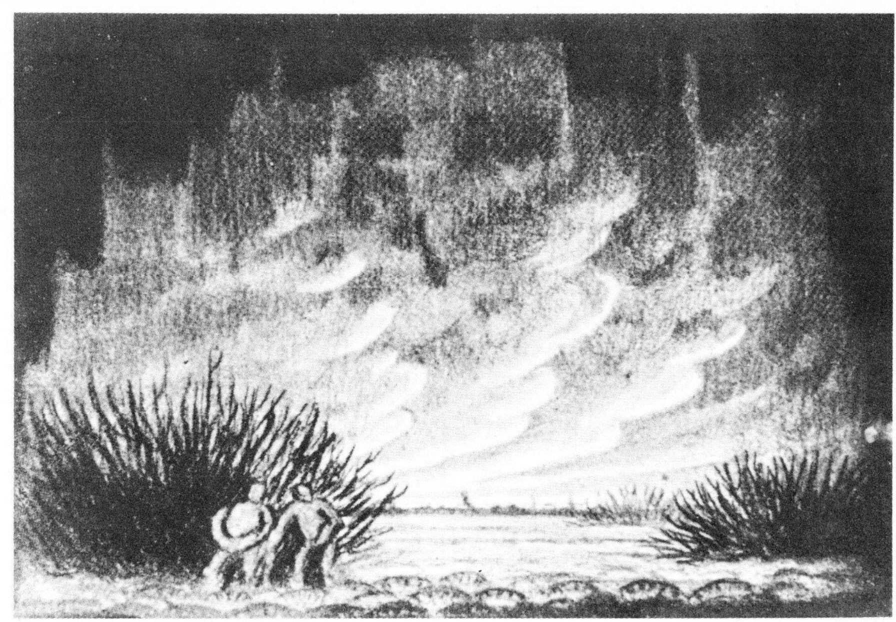

BERG, ALBAN: *Wozzeck.* Sketch by P. Aravantinos. F. L. Horth's production (Staatstheater, Opernhaus Berlin 1925)

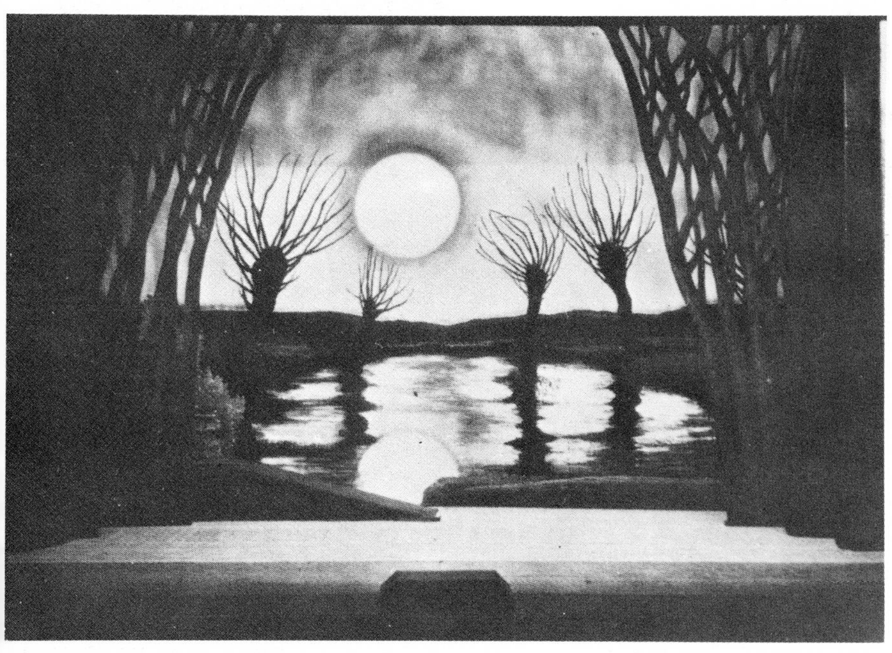

BERG, ALBAN: *Wozzeck.* F. Pujman's production, sets by V. Hofman (National Theatre, Prague 1926)

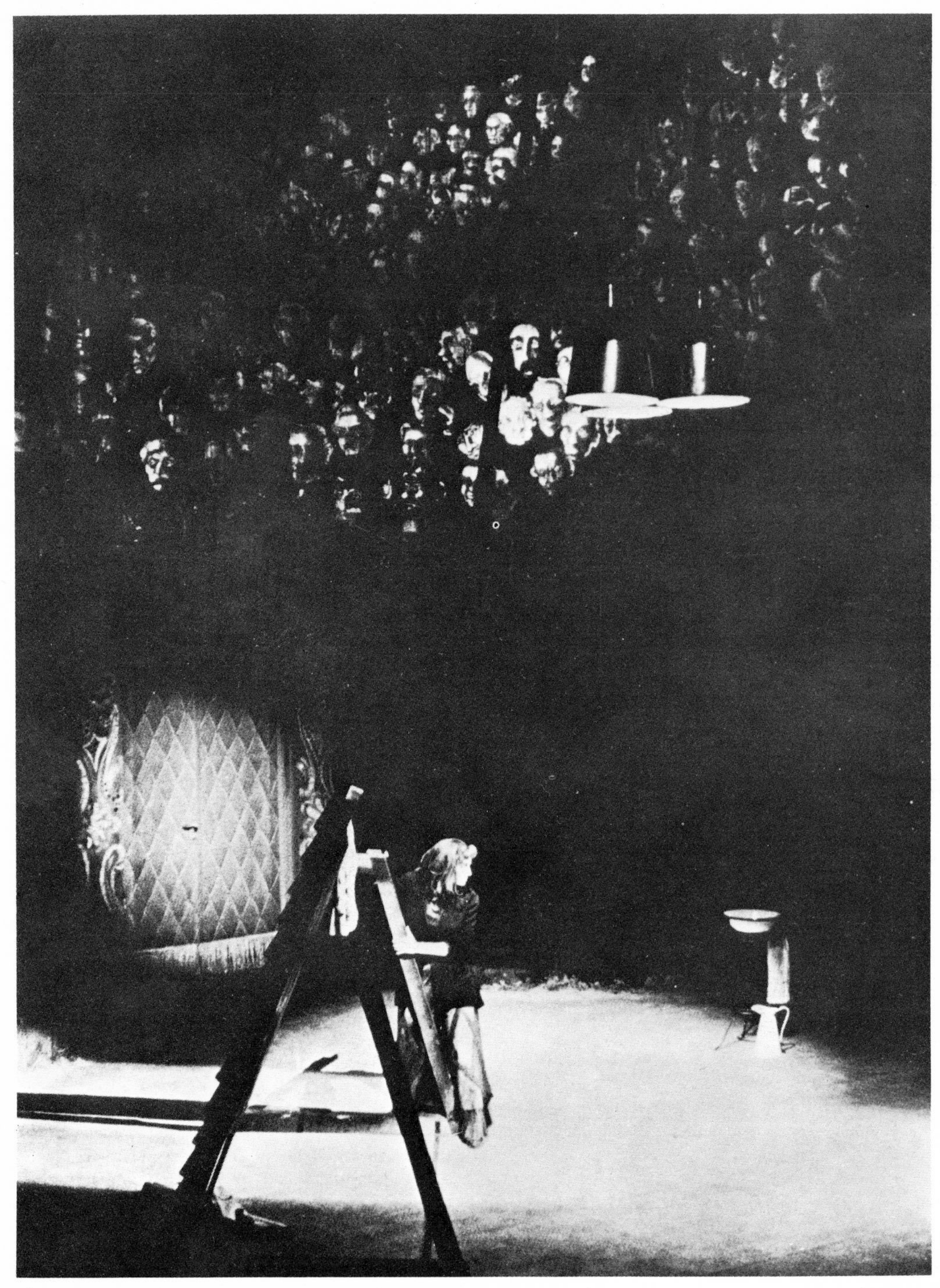

BERG, ALBAN: *Lulu.* Günther Rennert's production, sets by Teo Otto (Städtische Bühnen, Frankfurt, 1960)

The same problems with structure, intentionally restrictive, were imposed in the *chamber concerto* (1923–1925); but the temptation of twelve-tone writing made it even more tense.

The expressionism of the *Lyric Suite* (1925–1926) is due no doubt to the link Berg made between structure and style. The writing is atonal and the technique dodecaphonic. These pages, tightly interwoven and juxtaposed, thus form an expressive alternating effect, a lot of space between free time and a rigorously controlled time, echoing each other like counterparts.

The lyrical drama *Lulu*, the cantata *Wine* (Der Wein) and the *Concerto for Violin* are the key pieces of the artist's last period and do not have the perfection of the previous period.

Berg began working on the composition of *Lulu* in 1928. He wrote the libretto himself, a real satire on the bourgeoisie, a trial of its aesthetic and moral values, from two plays by Wedekind: *Earth Spirit* (Erdgeist) and *Pandora's Box* (Die Büchse der Pandora). The musical style made structural demands that were as intransigent as in *Wozzeck*, but here he uses the twelve-tone system, exploiting its lyrical and dramatic possibilities. It is, however, difficult to judge a work that Berg was not to finish.

HINDEMITH, Paul (Hanau, 16.11.1895 – Frankfurt-on-the-Main, 28.12.1963). Although opposed to all the composers that we have called expressionist, Hindemith has been quoted as such on superficial grounds: his rejection of programme music and the aims of absolute pure music; the contribution of his music to a form of drama recognized as expressionist, revolutionary, and anti-bourgeois, where Brecht and his ideology are important.

From the age of eleven, he left his family, which was opposed to his musical vocation, to study at the Frankfurt conservatoire; at the age of twenty, he became the solo violin player at the Opera in this town. In 1923, he founded the Amar-Hindemith quartet, and went on a number of tours in Germany as well as abroad, with this quartet.

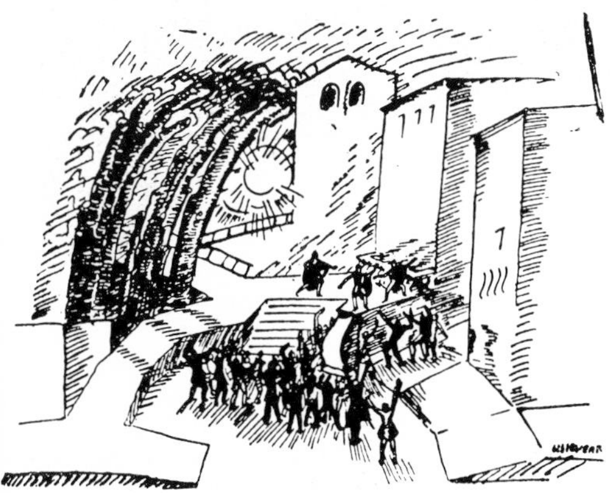

HINDEMITH, PAUL: A scene from *Cardillac*. Drawing published in the Frankfurter Zeitung. 1928

At the time of stage expressionism (1920–1930), he composed musical works with destructive intentions, with regard to the over-bourgeois values of the Germans: *Murderer, the Hope of Women* (Mörder, Hoffnung der Frauen) by Kokoschka, *Nusch-Nuschi* by Frantz Blei, *Saint Susanna* by August Stramm. In three other musical dramas, Hindemith makes an appeal and gives music an expressive function; he delivers a personal message, symbolic of the artistic attitude of the age. The Opera *Cardillac* is a synthesis of his early style, which was spontaneous, and his discovery of ancient German art, in particular Bach and baroque music. He issues another eloquent cry, more persuasive, in his opera *Matthias the painter* (Mathis der Maler), more well known today in its symphonic form. Engaged in a similar struggle between creator and the society of his time, he praised the work of Grünewald, the master of the altarpiece of Isenheim. A third drama insists on the conflict between scientific genius and society: the *Harmony of the World* (Die Harmonie der Welt) which is a portrait of the astronomer Kepler.

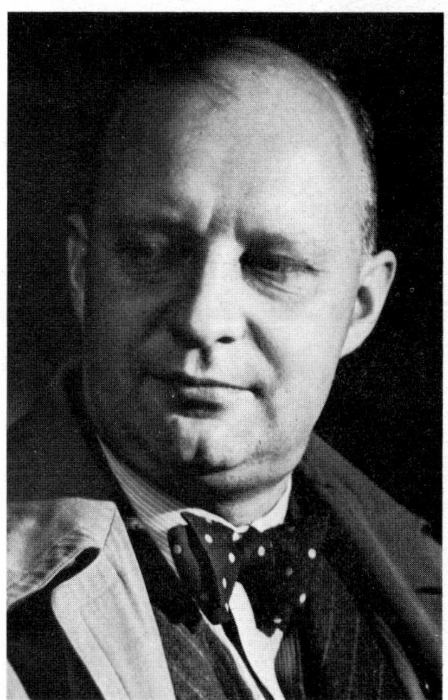

HINDEMITH, PAUL: *Portrait*

Given the political climate that existed in Germany after 1930, Hindemith refused to stay there and went into exile in the United States.

His music uses dissonances which are either spontaneous or on the contrary refined and studied, through counterpoints and slight overlaps; their harmonies are atonal or polytonal, the timbres sharp. One could in fact distinguish three styles: instinctive youthfulness, spontaneous and truly expressionist; a maturity taking into consideration baroque and romantic influences, and all modern techniques; and the last works, trying to reject everything in a style which is still modern and deft. A great composer, Hindemith was also a virtuoso alto and a musical theorist; he published *Introduction to the Musical Phrase, Exercises for the Student of Harmony, J. S. Bach.*

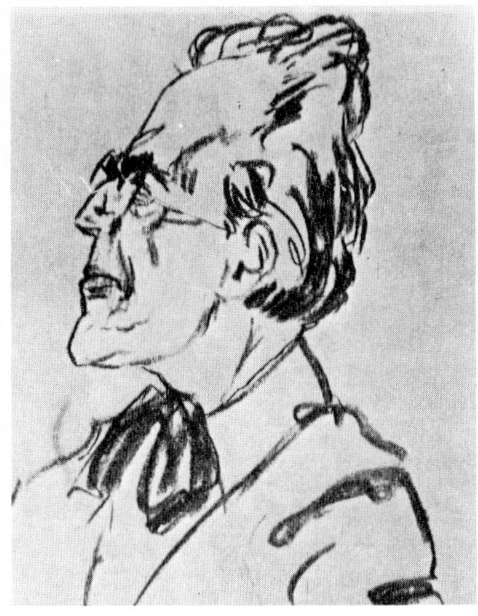

MAHLER, GUSTAV: *Portrait.* Drawing by Döblin

MAHLER, Gustav (Kalischt, Bohemia, 7.7.1860 – Vienna, 18.5.1911). Born into a Jewish family, Mahler suffered very early on from the conflict between his parents, his father's brutality, and their poverty. His future behaviour was to be marked by his difficult childhood.

Admitted at the age of fifteen to the Vienna conservatoire, he studied there for three years and met Bruckner who had a profound influence on the blossoming of his genius. Then he began to study philosophy and the history of music which he did not finish. From 1880, he accepted, in order to earn his living, the post of leader of the orchestra in Ljubljana, Cassel and Prague, then he directed the orchestra at the Opera in Budapest and Hamburg. For ten years (1897–1907), he was the director at the Imperial Opera In Vienna. Henceforth he devoted most of his time to his prestigious career as conductor of the orchestra, spending the summers composing.

As a composer aspiring to convey a personal vision of the world, Mahler was a metaphysician, a thinker who expresses himself musically. Although he precedes expressionism by several years, this attitude links him to the expressionist aesthetic which was founded on the omnipotence of the subjective. His permanent obsession was based on the idea of life and death. When very young, in the heart of his family, he witnessed, powerless, the death of his brother Otto, later it was his daughter that was snatched away from him, and the image of the absurd never left him. He confided in Freud and in his wife Alma, twenty years his junior, whom he had married in 1901. This links him with Bruckner, Hugo Wolf, obsessive musicians, who expressed in their works of an orchestral or vocal expressionism, their aggression against man.

We are going to try and explain briefly in Mahler's music, both his desire to express himself and his reticence to make meaningful a secret solitude that he tried to preserve to the extent of taking refuge in a haughty, hostile, even arrogant attitude.

His work favoured the orchestra, the great richness of timbres, in the dramatization of the symphony, of which each movement was like the act of an opera enhanced by the voice (IInd, IIIrd, IVth, VIIIth symphonies). In the *lieder*, the voice dominated, but the drama is still there: the triptych cantata *The Song of Lament* (Das Klagende Lied, 1880), the cycle of the *Songs of a Wayfarer* (Lieder eines fahrenden Gesellen, 1883–1884), the *Wunderhorn Lieder* (with piano 1882, with orchestra 1905), the *Songs on the Death of Children* (Kindertotenlieder, 1901–1904). The synthesis between the *lied* and the symphony resulted in a supersaturated expressiveness; the *Song of the Earth* (Das Lied von der Erde, 1908) is really a symphony for tenor, contralto and orchestra. On the other hand, certain purely instrumental symphonies borrow themes from the *Lieder*, popular songs, and even the *Dies Irae* (IInd symphony). Finally the influence of the orator in his symphonies (with texts by Nietzsche, from *Veni Creator*, and Goethe's *Faust*) accentuate the union between his metaphysical thought and his means of expression.

One fact is surprising. From 1880, as we have said, he was conductor of an orchestra, was recognized as one of the greatest, and an admirer of the stock pieces (Gluck, Mozart, Weber, Wagner, Richard Strauss), but he never composed for the stage. We also know that his direction, his stage requirements, and his intransigence were inspired by Adolphe Appia's expressionist principles. This contradiction is due no doubt to a reversal in the links between the literary text and music. The alliances between the word and music, his metaphysical thought and the expressionist cry clarify the reasons for the way he combines these, for which he has often been criticized. In the same work, we go from music faithfully expressing everyday life, to that which reflects grandeur, returning from the exceptional to the familiar, even juxtaposing the coarse and the refined. As proof of this one we can take the third movement of the *First Symphony* where the popular song *Frère Jacques* (Bruder Martin) becomes the obsessive theme of the funeral march, where the ironic and the worrying, the demoniac and gaiety confront each other. Mahler's music invites comparison with the painting of some of the precursors of expressionism: one thinks of Van Gogh, Edvard Munch, James Ensor, of their distortions, the effects of exaggerated traits, and the excessively aggressive colours.

In 1910–1911, he went on his last tour in the United States, where he gave sixty-five concerts and directed for the last time one of his works: the *Fourth Symphony*. This superhuman effort exhausted him. In May 1911, accompanied by his wife, his faithful confidante, he returned to Vienna where he died a few days later.

That Mahler did not reach absolute chromatism, the atonal, does not diminish either his creative genius or the expressive power of his works. Perhaps he was aware of being a man whose message was to be understood immediately, and not later, as other composers have no doubt hoped they would be.

REGER, Max (Brand, 19.3.1873 – Leipzig, 11.5.1916). It is rather like placing a bet to mention Reger here, since he passes for a neo-classical German. Even if he remains on the fringes of the expressionism of his time, he does foreshadow it; but he died too early for one to be able to judge the result of his quest for pure expressivity. During his mature period, one recalls his *Fantasies and Fugues* for organ which recall the expressive musical movement in Northern Germany in the seventeenth century and Buxtehude in particular. In his last period, one work stands out: the *Suite*, inspired by Arnold Böcklin, whose morbid very romantic painting strongly appealed to him.

SCHÖNBERG, Arnold (Vienna, 13.9.1874 – Los Angeles, 13.7.1951). Through belonging to *Der Blaue Reiter*, Schönberg belongs to the expressionist movement. Himself a painter, he was friendly with Kandinsky and Franz Marc. Coming from a modest Jewish family, nothing marked him out as a musician. Even before finishing his secondary education, he started teaching himself how to compose, with scarcely any guidance from Alexander von Zemlinsky whose sister he married. From then on he devoted his life to music.

Three creative periods mark his work. Following in the footsteps of Wagner, Brahms and Mahler, Schönberg composed his first pieces in a tense rhythmic language, which already broke with the musical style of his age; as proof, the intense pathetic expression that one recognizes in his first *lieder* and the sextet op. 4. *The Transfigured Night* (Verklärte Nacht, 1899), inspired by a romantic, and at the same time naturalist, poem by Richard Dehmel.

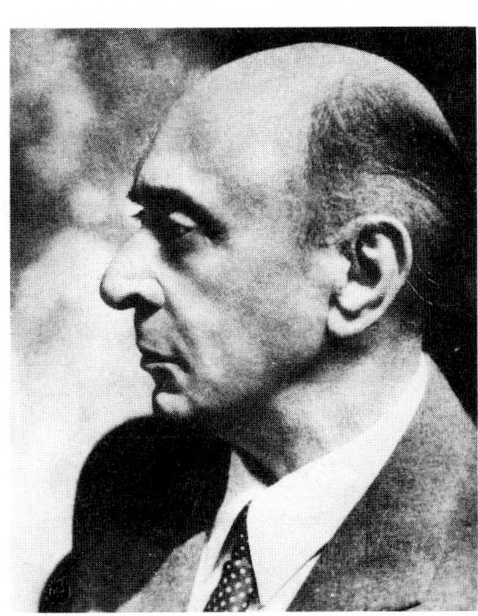

SCHÖNBERG, ARNOLD: Portrait

In 1900, he began to write his first major work: the *Gurre-Lieder* for soloists choirs and orchestra, the style is romantic, but the orchestration, which he continued till 1911, shows a real awareness of the expressive power of rhythm and harmony.

The material difficulty which Schönberg suffered at this time is often offered as an explanation both of his apparent slowness in composition and of his accepting the post of conductor of the orchestra at the Buntes Theater in Berlin, where he directed operettas. But this was not the only reason for the lack of continuity in his work. The composer was also discovering from work to work the richness and expressive density of the orchestra; the expressionism of the production of tones accentuates the chromaticism and the weight of harmonics. Certain pages of his *Gurre-Lieder* are already characteristic of Schönberg's expressionism: they are the cry of a visionary.

In *Pelléas and Mélisande* op. 5 (1903), a symphonic poem inspired by Maeterlinck, the original symbolism is transposed into a hyperlyrical romantic style, all the freer for being an instrumental composition, Schönberg no longer had the constraints imposed by words. After Berlin, Schönberg returned to Vienna where he met Mahler. He then began a long career as a teacher, and his methods have influenced all twentieth-century music. Amongst his first pupils were Alban Berg and von Webern.

We will now consider Schönberg's atonal period. The compositions for this period are amongst his best. They

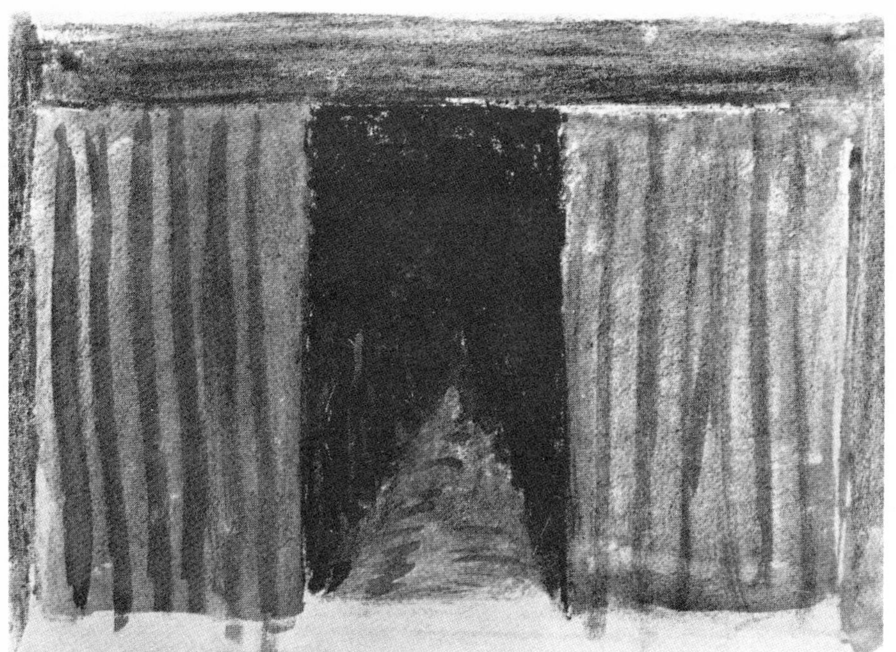

SCHÖNBERG, ARNOLD: Sketch for the production of *Expectation* (Die Erwartung)

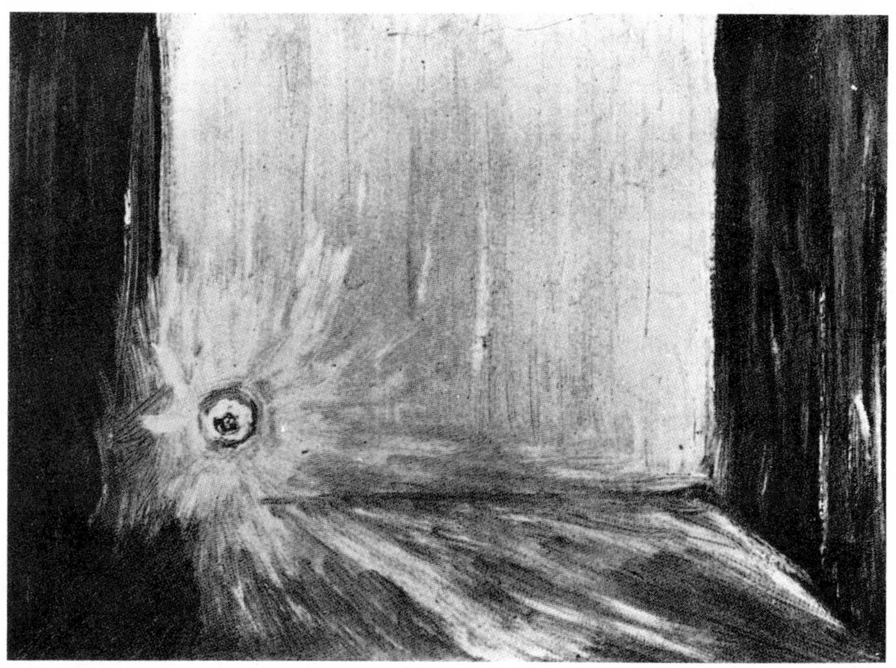

SCHÖNBERG, ARNOLD: Sketch for the production of *The Lucky Hand* (Die Glückliche Hand)

revealed Schönberg to the world, and revealed the world to him, by giving him an unparalleled brilliance. Two pieces illustrate the beginning of this cycle *Hanging Gardens* op. 15, 1908 (Hängende Gärten): fifteen melodies for piano and song, based on poems by Stefan George, the thirteenth passing for the first really atonal piece; three *Piano Pieces* op. 11, 1908. There followed *Five Orchestra Pieces* op. 16, 1909; *Expectation*, 1909 (Erwartung), a monodrama in one act, on a text by Marie Papenheim; the *Lucky Hand* op. 18, 1909–1913 (Die Glückliche Hand), a musical drama also in one act, on a text by Schönberg himself who in addition designed the sets; *Heart-growths*, 1911 (Herzgewächse) for song and three instruments.

In 1912, in Berlin, he had *Pierrot Lunaire* performed for recitative and five instruments op. 21, on poems by Albert Giraud. Vehemently expressionist, this work baffled the public, less perhaps for its actual style than for the introduction of a new form of vocal expression: the *Sprechgesang* (spoken song), halfway between declamation and song, where the voice is instrumentalized, and becomes pure timbre. At the same time, Schönberg revealed his ideas in his *Manual of Harmony*, 1911, modified and completed in 1921, and again in 1948. In 1917, on his return to Vienna, he founded a music school: the famous *Verein für Musikalische Privataufführungen*, where a number of contemporary works were born.

From 1924 to 1953, he was again in Berlin where he was a teacher at the *Akademie der Künste.* This marked the beginning of his third phase with the dodecaphonic scale and the note-row. He formulated his method of composition in terms of twelve equal sounds based on the principle of the 'series' thought of by Josef Hauer, hence the term 'note-row': for some, this period is that of real expressionism, whereas in fact it is almost the negation of it: organization, structure, a restrictive didactism, a renunciation of the spontaneous cry, and the fascination of chaos. *Quartet for Wind* (1924), the *Third String Quartet* (1927), *Variations for Orchestra* (1929), all illustrate this method. An opera, a religious drama of an admirable, expressive force, based on a libretto by Schönberg himself, dominates these years: *Moses and Aaron* (1930–1932).

The year 1933 saw the real beginning of national socialism in Germany. Schönberg then went via Paris, to the United States, where, after having abandoned it in 1921, he became reconverted to Judaism out of a feeling of solidarity towards the persecuted Jews. He assumed American nationality in 1941, and was never again to leave the United States. He successively held the post of teacher in Boston and New York. In 1936 he became head of the musical department at the University of California. During this long period, Schönberg sometimes seemed to be reverting to a more flexible tonal conception, to more romantic considerations, but he never stopped innovating, further extending his researches in order to achieve an exceptional freedom of style. *The Ode to Napoleon* op. 41 (1942), *A Survivor from Warsaw* op. 46 (1947), *De Profundis* op. 50 (1950), according to psalm 130, almost his last work, mark the end of his life.

Although misunderstood in his lifetime, Schönberg is more accepted today. He revolutionized musical notation and thereby exercised an undeniable influence on the development of contemporary music.

SCRIABIN, Alexander (Moscow, 6.1.1872 – Moscow, 27.4.1915). Educated at the Moscow conservatoire by Taneief and Arensky in an atmosphere oriented towards Western humanism, he was influenced by Chopin, Wagner and Liszt. Very early on, haunted by religious and metaphysical problems, he became enthusiastic about oriental philosophers, having discovered them during several visits to India. Most of his compositions bear witness to his philosophical interests. An apostle of a new religion of music, the expressive incantatory and liberating virtues, which are forcefully affirmed in his work, he believed in a correspondence between the arts, not only at the transcendental level of the message, but the musical technique itself, which he tried to enrich by relying on interplay between specific colours and notes. One cannot deny the expressive force of this art, which is a fusion of a certain magic emanating from his Slav soul, his post-romanticism, and Western influences.

We will mention not only the most famous works, but also the most expressive: The *Fifth Sonata* where the technique of *Tristan* still prevails, and which he continued to use while inventing a synthetic chord of six or seven notes; the *Second Symphony* in C minor, the third called the *Divine Poem* and the *Poem of Ecstasy*, which is often considered his most important work. The titles are eloquent and the composition never falls short of the magic incantatory metaphysical intentions: *The Magic Poem, Prometheus or the Poem of Fire* (1911), the Nocturnal Poem, Towards the Flame, the *Satanic Poem.*

Scriabin's innovations, his personality, make him one of the most important composers of the beginning of the century, not only with reference to expressionism, but in the evolution of European music in general.

STRAUSS, Richard (Munich, 11.6.1864 – Garmisch, 8.9.1949). The son of the famous horn player at the Munich Opera, Strauss displayed his musical gifts from a very early age. His musical studies were enhanced by a thorough cultural knowledge acquired at Munich University. His classical German education introduced him very early on to the musical world of the eighteenth

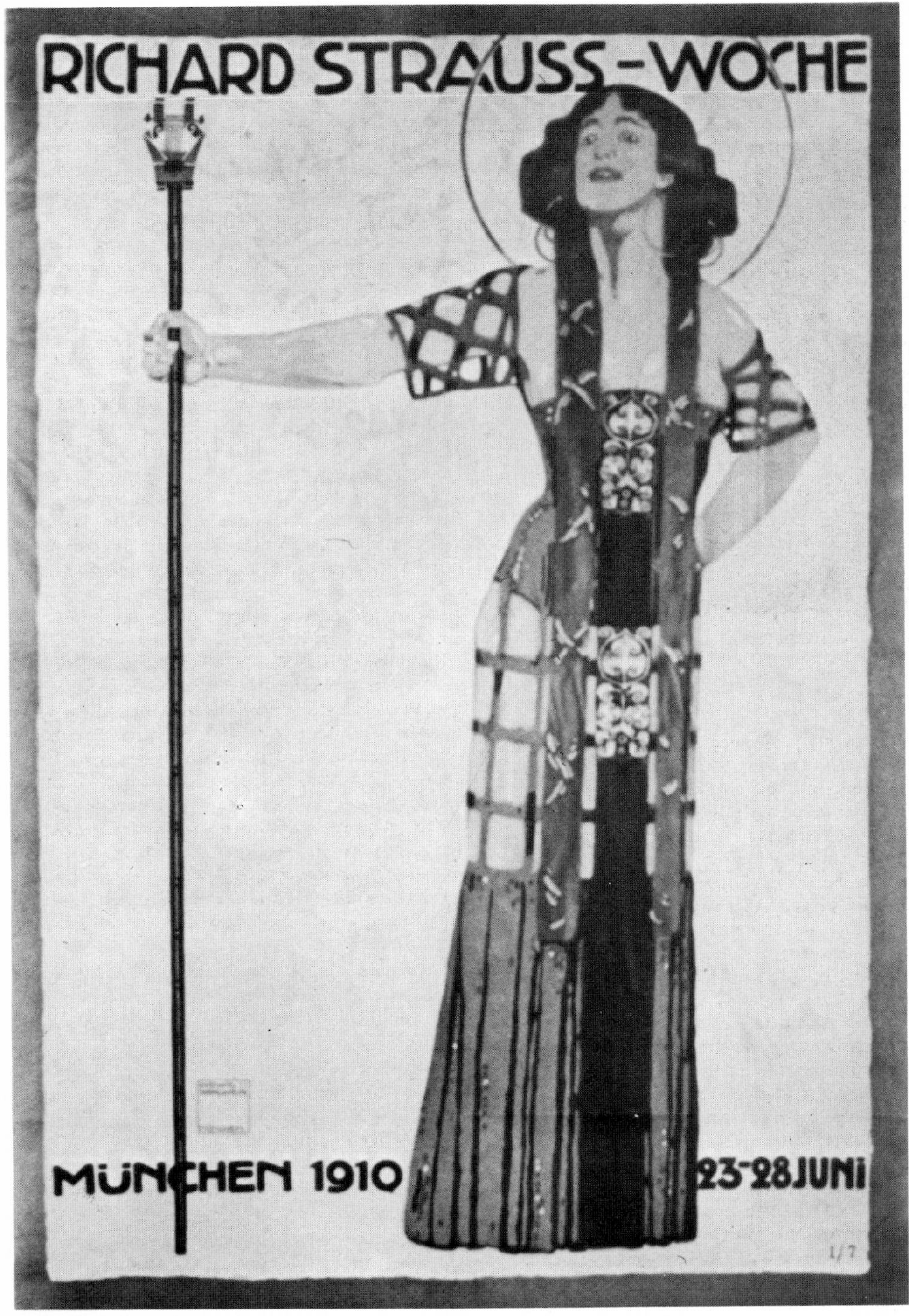

STRAUSS, RICHARD: Poster for *Salome* for Richard Strauss week June 23–28, 1910, by Ludwig Hohlwein century, at its apogee in Vienna, to Mozart in particular and also initiated him to the great romantics. Beethoven, Mendelsohn, Schumann and Brahms, then at the height of their glory. Wagner, whom Strauss's father hated, was initially unknown to him. He only discovered him in Bayreuth in 1882, on the first performance of *Parsifal* and this was a great revelation to him. Hans von Bülow facilitated Strauss's career as conductor of the orchestra and chose him as his successor in 1885, as director of the Meiningen Orchestra. He then directed at the Munich Opera and after that at the Weimar Court, again succeeding von Bürlow as director of the Berlin philharmonic concerts where, in 1898, he was appointed head of the orchestra at the Opera. Very famous in Germany and abroad, he went on a number of European trips. Alongside this public career, which he abandoned almost completely around 1910, he devoted the major part of his time to composition.

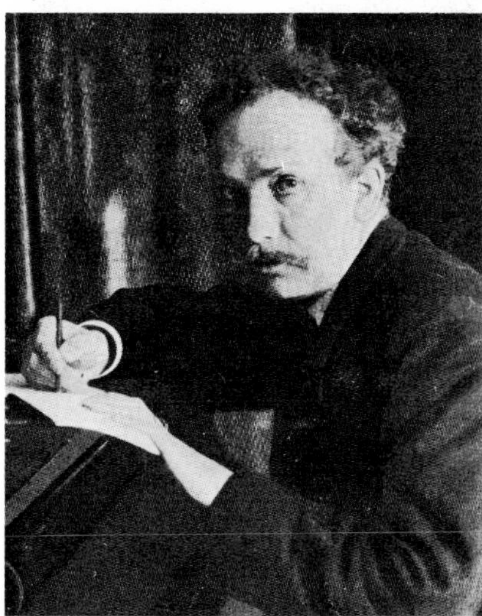

STRAUSS, RICHARD: *Portrait*

Strauss's power of expression is beyond doubt. He shows the links between romanticism and expressionism. He began by composing orchestral music, and was already expressive in his symphonic poems. Here he experimented with the expressive nature of his instrumental rhythmic, melodic techniques that we also find in theatre. *Don Juan, Don Quixote, the Life of a Hero, Zarathustra, Death and Transfiguration*, the audacity of his writing aroused violent controversy at the time.

The expressionist character of some of his works is not recognized by historians. With the blossoming of the expressionist movement he had already found his own style. Aggressive, original, elaborate, he remained consistent. He approached the theatre with works of an opposite nature, all still Wagnerian in nature, *Guntram*, finished in Weimar in 1894, the other amiable, satirical and burlesque *Feuersnot* (1900–1901) which ushered in the twentieth century and his long lyrical period.

Richard Strauss at first produced very intensely dramatic operas in terms of the subject and the themes expressed, in the way violence, death, sexuality and revolt fuse in a musical convulsion: e.g. *Salome* (1905), *Elektra* (1909) and later, in a more nuanced style, *The Woman without a shadow* (1919) and *Egyptian Helen* (1928). Meanwhile, having reached levels of violence and a quasi atonal style never before attained musically, Strauss did not want to go any further. He then formed a neo-classical likeable style, tinged with a certain nostalgic romanticism: the *Der Rosenkavalier* (1910), *Ariadne in Naxos* (1912), *Arabella* (1932), the *Silent Woman* based on a libretto by Stephan Zweig (1934), *Daphne* (1937), *Danaë* (1940), *Capriccio* (1942). However, baroque structures already hover over these dramas or comedies. He freed himself from all constraints and found his path with *Salome* (Oscar Wilde's version 1905): that of a decadent art, mannered to the point of 'turgidity'. Emotion through anguish, the fascination of suffering, death, violence provoke the alliance of baroque and expressionism in the role of Salome. *Capriccio*, the last opera, reflects this struggle. All the expressive heritage of the nineteenth century is in this style which is on the borderline between harmony and auditive capacity: intervals stretched to breaking point, immense vocally, provoking in the same breath two different timbres. And in spite of that, songs, for which each note is written so that the literary text be understood, grasped, and enriched by the musical tension. Although he did not follow them, Richard Strauss, did not ignore the Viennese expressionist composers. He encouraged and approved of Schónberg's rise, he wholeheartedly respected Mahler. The same attitude, the same obsession drew them together: their fidelity to a visionary world.

STRAVINSKY, Igor Fedorovitch (Oranienbaum, near St Petersburg, 5.6.1882 – New York, 6.4.1971). Born into a family where music was their *raison d'être*, Stravinsky devoted himself totally to it right from his early childhood, since, at the age of ten, he was already Rimsky-Korsakov's pupil. During his long career, his style, which was constantly questioned, evolved and culminated in most modern forms of electronic music. He is the absolute paradox of contradiction. Did he recognize, as an essential quality in music, its power to express only itself? He throughout affirmed his desire to create a very resonant form of music. Now, we know that the expressionism of the great Viennese lies in an attitude of revolt, which never seems to have particu-

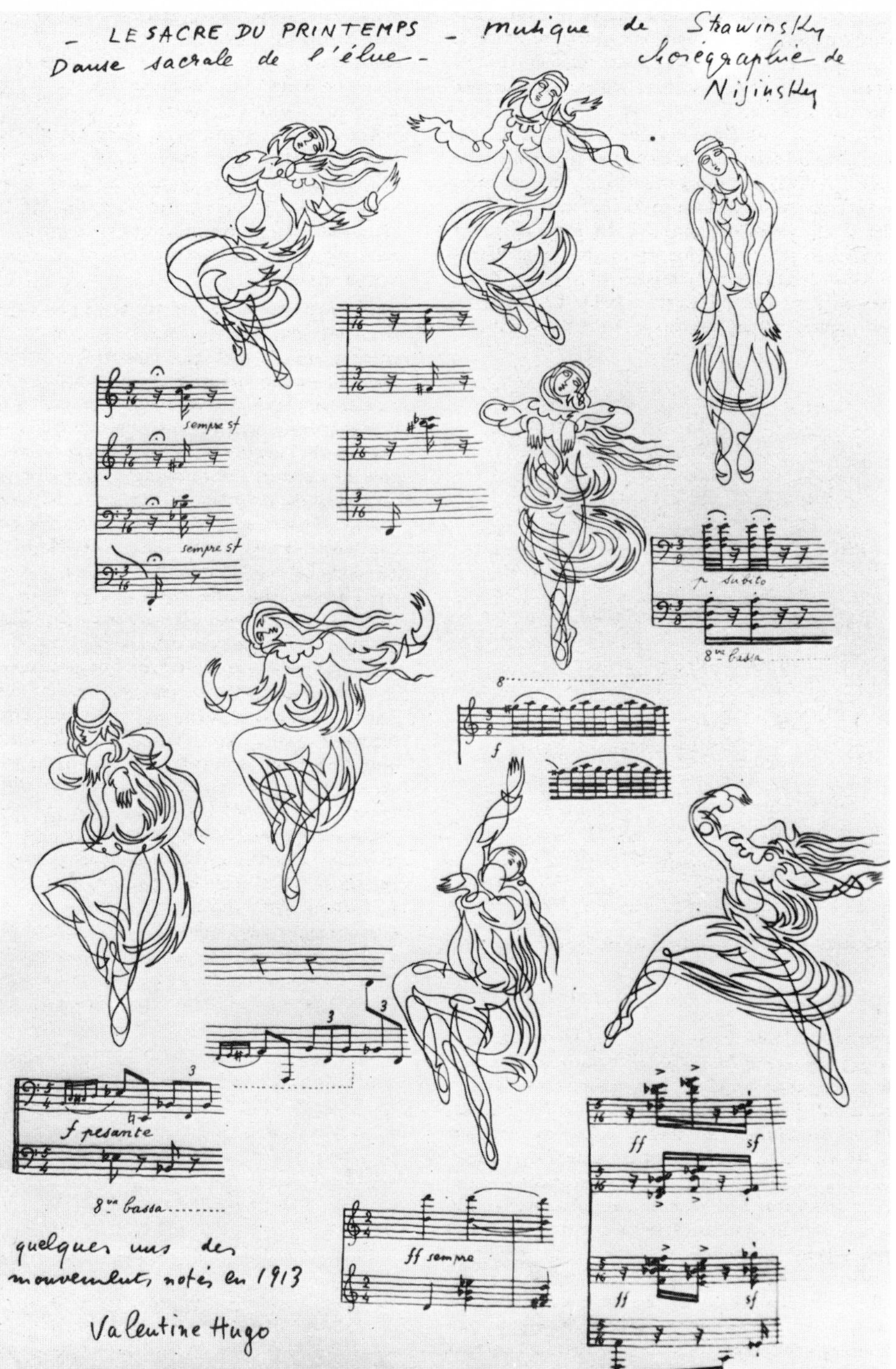

STRAVINSKY, IGOR: *The Rite of Spring.* Choreography by Nijinsky. Some of the movements noted in 1913

larly worried Stravinsky, and a means of expression, enclosed within a strict, imprisoning form, to which he never subscribed. His expressionist tendency can be defined therefore differently: as a violent, resonant and creative affirmation.

His meeting with Diaghilev, the founder of Russian ballets was the event that marked the beginning of his career. Diaghilev also recognized the composer's originality and commissioned him to do *The Fire Bird* (1910), ballet music which accompanies the most obviously expressionist aspects: tension, effort, the carnal offer of the body. In 1911, the creation of another ballet, *Petrouchka*, marked by Russian folklore, where the moods, marionnettes, the shock of the notes are eminently expressionist. Finally, the *Rite of Spring*, in 1913, marks the apogee of this period with its constant aggression of timbres and rhythms. Its première at the Théâtre des Champs-Elysées created a real scandal. Saint-Saens, who was present, left the theatre before the end, but Debussy and Ravel recognized it as the work of a genius.

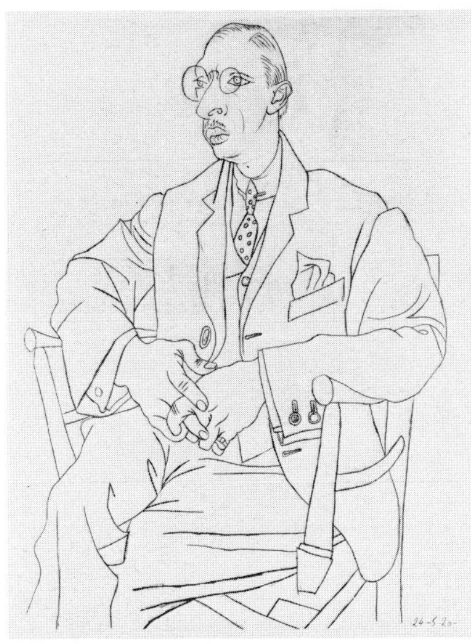

STRAVINSKY, IGOR: *Portrait.* Drawing by Pablo Picasso 1920

We can still detect an element of expressionism in *Rossignol, Renard, Les Noces* and its obsessive choral rhythms, and, in short, in all the music for theatre and choreography preceding the return to the neo-classicism of the twenties with the *Story of a Soldier* (l'Histoire d'un soldat). Then one has to wait till the last period, after 1952, before seeing Stravinsky use Schönberg's dodecaphonic scale in works like *Canticum Sacrum*, which pave the way towards more ambitious pursuits in the direction of avant-garde music.

WEBERN, Anton von (Vienna, 3.12.1883 – Mittersill, Salzburg, 13.9.1945). In Vienna he studied musicology under the direction of Guido Adler, and then presented his doctoral thesis on the late fifteenth-century Franco-Flemish polyphonist, Heinrich Isaac, who spent his working life in Germany. Webern's youth shows Mahler's influence, in the form of romanticism open to expressivity. In 1904, and until 1910, he was Schönberg's pupil, at the same time as Berg and Wellesz. His teaching had an influence on all his work, which, with the exception of op. 1 and 2, was always atonal.

The first works, which are not expressionist, are liberating, the two series of *Lieder* op. 3 and 4 usher in a creative period. Each time that Webern changes his style, the transitional pieces are vocal, apprehending the expressive element of the scream and the body. More than through an alliance with a literary text, his expressionism lies in extreme brevity, or rather in the perfect concision of a style that allows the literary element, the image and the rhythm to remain active. In this concentration, Webern used all the techniques which are all the more trenchant for being assembled together. *The Symphony* op. 20 is its very symbol, opening, with the *Trio for Strings*, the key period of the years 1927 to 1934, when he was at his most austere. The observance of a very rigorous framework remains the main aim behind the style of this period, a concern he shared with the Viennese. The principle of very long, disjointed intervals is used, one of the favourite techniques of musical expressionism. But this division does not only have an expressive force: in fact, the fullness of the Webern interval breaks all possibility of links between over-unified sounds to which the ear might become accustomed, thus encountering the temptation of achieving relations between notes as in the tonal system. Each isolated sound becomes a pure phenomenon. What links the sounds together, in the most expressive manner, is this silence. In the *Symphony* op. 21, they are numerous, immense. They compel our ears to have a real conversation with the sound that preceded it, they detonalize everything, they imprison each timbre, each chord, each melodic cell.

Apart from this pivotal work, the *Symphony* op. 21, it is difficult to choose works which show Webern's different tendencies. Throughout his career, unconsciously, his musical style tends more and more in the direction of concision, ascetic, from 1905 to 1909, as we have already said, the first attempts (the *Pasacaille*), still romantic, already shows a concern for rigour progressively leading to the freedom of the *Lieder* op. 3 and 4.

Between 1909 and 1910, one cannot really talk in terms of expressionism, but stylistic tendencies, both baroque and impressionist are worked out: from op. 5 to op. 7, the *Five pieces for string quartets*, the *Six orchestral pieces*, the *Four piano and violin pieces*. From 1910 to 1914 Webern held several posts as head of orchestra in the North of Germany (Danzig, Stettin and Berlin). He, at that time, composed shorter pieces. Though very short, they present a *resonant* world just on the limits of the audible. These are the op. 9 to 11: *Six Bagatelles for string quartet*, *Five Pieces for chamber orchestra*, *Three Pieces for piano and cello.*

The period preceding *The Symphony* op. 21, covers the period 1914 to 1927. With the war (Webern was exempted from fighting because of bad eye-sight), he soon became musical director at the German Theatre in Prague. After the War, he participated in concerts organized in Vienna by Schönberg, and directed a Worker's Symphonic Association set up by the socialist municipality. He preferred the solitude of his house in Mödling to this public life, and composed a number of vocal pieces, the *Lieder* cycles op. 13 to 19. Influenced by Schönberg, he advocated a constant exchange of new links between the voice and the instruments. Far from being simply accompanied, the voice was predominant, the instrumentation being organized around it, the exchanges and the timbres. This is profound expressionism; the timbres emerge like echoes of the voice and this voice neither sings or recites: but the *Sprechgesang* by Webern is different from that of Schönberg: the voice is restricted to the role of an imaginary instrumental production of the text and rejects all embellishment. Finally, among the *Lieder* of op. 17, the twelve-tone scale is used for the first time. Webern then entered into the phase of his greatest austerity. From 1927 to 1934 the *String Trio* op. 20, the *Symphony* op. 21 that we have quoted as a symbol and the *concerto for nine instruments* op. 24, have a certain value as a testament.

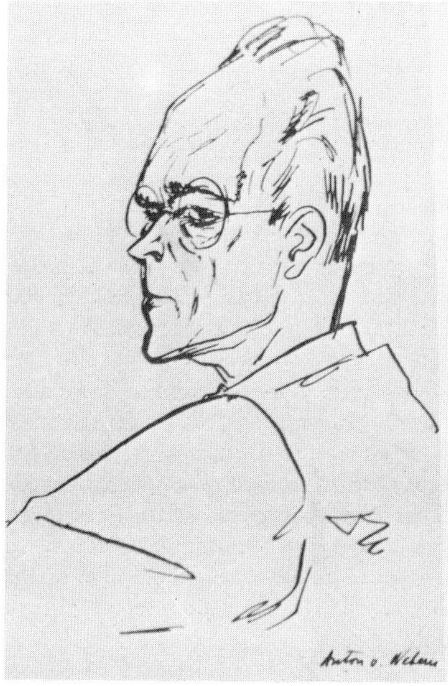

WEBERN, ANTON VON: *Portrait*

After 1934, Webern was more isolated than ever. Schönberg was in exile, Berg was dead. 1938 saw the annexation of Austria by Germany which deprived him of his right to teach and to perform in public. In his solitude, he extended the scope of his research, returning to Vocal Works: in 1935 *Das Augenlicht* op. 26, in 1939 *Cantata* op. 29, in 1943 *Cantata* op. 31, unfinished. In *Variations for piano*, 1936, the *String Quartet*, 1928, and *Variations for Orchestra*, 1940, Webern imposed more constraints on himself as regards counterpoint and twelve-tone writing. He died tragically in 1945, killed through the carelessness of an American sentry. After his death, his influence on the young avant-garde generation was considerable. His last work, the *Cantata* op. 31 goes beyond expressionism and thereby ushers in a musical abstract and lyrical surrealism.

Miscellaneous Aspects of Expressionism

Given the spread of expressionism, and the influence it had, it was difficult to include in the preceding headings (The plastic arts, architecture, theatre, cinema, music) all the artists from throughout the world, who can be related to it. We had to restrict ourselves to the main ones, namely to those who were clearly influenced by the revival in the arts between 1910 and 1925 approximately. But a number of other artists, whether consciously or not are linked to expressionism: either because they, for a certain time, published articles or illustrations in expressionist journals (for example, Walter Benjamin, Frans Masereel, Hans Richter), or because they participated temporarily in events where expressionists were also involved. In fact, an entire period was dominated by expressionism; and when new artistic tendencies appeared from 1919, they were defined in terms of it: neither Piscator, nor Brecht, nor the 'New Objectivity' is fully comprehensible without reference to expressionism. It therefore seems necessary to us to include these short biographies which, without being exhaustive, ought to allow a more comprehensive understanding of the movement and, perhaps, stimulate research into artists simply mentioned in passing in the main body of the book.

ADLER, Paul (1878–1946). Born in Prague, he lived near Dresden from 1912 to 1933. He made his name essentially through his expressionist prose, notably in two novels: *Elohim* (1914) and *Nämlich* (1915). He died near Prague.

BENJAMIN, Walter (1892–1940). He made a reputation not as an expressionist, but as one of the most brilliant essay writers and literary critics of the century. He was even fairly distant from expressionist aims. However, he published two articles on the problems of the young, under the pseudonym of Ardor, in the review *Die Aktion* in 1913 and 1914, articles which state the main issues concerning the expressionist generation, and its revolt against taboos.

BLASS, Ernst (1890–1939). After studying law in Berlin and in Heidelberg, he worked in a bank. From 1924, he was a proof reader at Paul Cassirer's press. A poet, he was the co-founder with Kurt Hiller, of the *New Club* (Der Neue Club) in 1919. He also edited the monthly review *Die Argonauten* (the Argonauts) in 1914–1915.

BLOCH, Ernst (1885–1977). A philosopher he lived at Tübingen. He collaborated with activist journals. With his book, *The Spirit of Utopia* (Geist der Utopie, 1918), he earned himself the reputation of being the most typical representative of expressionist philosophy.

BLÜMMER, Rudolf (1873–1945). It is thanks to this actor, a friend of Herwarth Walden, that a part of expressionist poetry became famous in Berlin: at the time of the cabaret soirées and poetry readings organized by the review *Der Sturm*, he was in fact the most 'expressive reader'. Renowned for the quality of his diction, he also joined in the theatrical activities of the *Sturmbühne*.

BRUST, Alfred (1891–1934). Both a poet, novelist, and author of plays. His plays are typical of expressionism in their mysticism, the freedom of the instincts and their passionate violence. *Eternal Man* (Der ewige Mensch) was performed at the Municipal theatre in Halberstadt in March 1920. Two other plays, not expressionist, were performed by Max Reinhardt and Erwin Piscator.

BUSONI, Ferruccio Benvenuto (1866–1924). An Italian composer, he lived from 1878, in Vienna, then he taught in Finland, at the Conservatoire at Helsinki. He realized the importance of Schönberg from the latter's very first compositions, and he supported him. Kurt Weill, who was his pupil, has paid tribute to him. His *Faust* (performed posthumously in Dresden in 1925) is considered to be an expressionist opera by some musicologists. It is as an expressionist that he performed it in Florence in 1964, as part of the Florentine May, which was devoted to expressionism in general.

CSOKOR, Franz Theodor (1885–1969). He was in Austria one of the most famous representatives of expressionism in the theatre. Having studied history of art at Vienna, he was recruited during the First World War. His plays are pacifist in inspiration and show the influence of Strindberg as regards technique. In 1938, at the time of the annexation of Austria by Hitler, he emigrated. He returned to Austria in 1946.

ESSIG, Hermann (1878–1918). The son of a pastor, he went to technical school in Berlin and became friends with Walden. He collaborated with the review *Der Sturm*, but quickly distanced himself from its aims. He wrote a number of plays where he tried above all to bring out repressed instincts and hidden passions, rather similar to Wedekind.

EYSOLDT, Gertrud (1870–1957). This famous actress from the Max Reinhardt Theatre contributed to the spreading of expressionism, like Rudolf Blümner, through her reciting of poems. Her acting, in expressionist plays, was described by the famous theatre critic Herbert Ihering as quite typical of expressionism.

FELIXMÜLLER, Conrad (1897). An expressionist painter, he was a member of active avant-garde groups and was with Friedrich Wolf, one of the propagators of expressionist activism in Dresden, where he lived for a long time, before settling in West Berlin.

FLAKE, Otto (1880–1963). A novelist and essay writer, he was born in Alsace, where he became friends with Ernst Stadler. He was a member of the Zürich dadaism after the final departure of Hugo Ball.

FREUD, Sigmund (1856–1939). Founder of psychoanalysis, he was never directly interested in expressionism, and the expressionists, unlike the surrealists, never really studied his doctrine on the theoretical level. An interest in psychoanalysis, inspired by Otto Gross, was no substitute. One can perhaps see the influence of psychoanalysis on expressionism in the fact that both pursuits began in the years 1910–1925.

The science of the subconscious presented in fact a knowledge of man that was very different from the psychology current at the time and rejected by the expressionists. With the discovery of the importance of impulses and especially of sexuality, psychoanalysis seemed to be revolting against bourgeois morality just as violently as the expressionist movement. In fact, still today, Freud is often wrongly considered as the defender of total emancipation. This new psychology revealed the struggle between men's different desires, the split personality, a theme that one encounters in most expressionist films.

In his work the *Interpretation of dreams*, 1899, Freud gave symbols a new meaning comparable to what expressionism proposed, even if the link is only obvious to the surrealist. For the first time, Freud evokes the Oedipus Complex, the conflict between father and son, the fundamental idea that was taken up in expressionist plays.

GOLL, Claire (1892–1977). She published under the name of Claire Studer, two anthologies of poetry in Germany during the expressionist period: *Mitwelt* (Der Rote Hahn, Berlin, 1918) and *Lyrische Filme* (Basel-Leipzig, 1922). She married Yvan Goll. She has left memoirs which provide, amongst other things, a panorama of the years 1919–1920: *Following the Wind* (Olivier Orban, Paris, 1976).

GROSS, Otto (1877–1919). Born in Graz and son of the famous crime specialist, he studied medicine and psychiatry. He was the pupil of Freud. Having presented his doctoral thesis in Munich, he joined up with all the expressionist bohemia (Franz Jung, Karl Otten, etc.) and it is through him that the latter discovered psychoanalysis. In 1913, he had dealings with Pfemfert. A military doctor during the First World War, he returned to Berlin in 1918. He became addicted to drugs and died of exhaustion in 1919.

GROSZ, George (1893–1959). Known as a painter, he also wrote poetry and an autobiography. Before the First World War, he can be classed as an expressionist. After it, he became a dadaist. And in the twenties he represents what was called verism, which is linked to the 'New Objectivity'. He was famous at the time for his caricatures of Weimar society. In 1932, he emigrated to the United States. On his return to Germany, he died in Berlin.

GÜTERSLOH, Albert Paris von (1887–1973). Born in Vienna, his real name was Conrad Kiehtreiber. After studying at secondary school, he studied dramatic art, and, with Klimt, painting. From 1911 to 1913, he was the press correspondent in Paris. During the First World War, he met Robert Musil and Franz Blei; he proved himself then as a painter and writer. His first works show his reaction against naturalism. His poems and his novel of 1919, *The Mad Dancer* (Die tanzende Törin), have been described as expressionist, and he himself willingly accepted this description.

HARDEKOPF, Ferdinand (1876–1954). He was part of a group that gathered around Pfemfert and the review *Die Aktion.* A poet from Berlin bohemia, and an excellent translator (especially of Gide), he also had contacts with the Zürich dadaists.

HATVANI, Paul (1892). Born in Vienna, his real name was Paul Hirsch. He published poems and articles while he was still at school in Budapest. He settled in Vienna after leaving school, to study mathematics. He met Albert Ehrenstein, Karl Kraus and Hermann Broch. He collaborated with the reviews *Der Sturm, Die Aktion, Der Brenner*, and with several anthologies, for example *Die Pforte* (Saturn Verlag, Heidelberg 1913). He also published an anthology of aphorisms and essays (Saturn Verlag, 1913). He wrote, after the war, a number of articles, in general on expressionism. In 1939, he emigrated to Australia.

HERRMANN-NEISSE, Max (1886–1941). Born in Silesia, he studied German and the history of art in Munich. In 1924, he was awarded the Eichendorff prize, and in 1927 the Gerhart Hauptmann prize. He emigrated to Switzerland in 1933, and then to London, where he died.

HERZFELDE, Wieland (1896). Son of the German writer living in Switzerland, Franz Held, and the brother of the dadaist 'photomounter' John Heartfield, he collaborated with Pfemfert's review *Die Aktion* and was an expressionist before being a dadaist, in 1919. He was a senior editor on the foundation of Malik Verlag in 1917.

HERZOG, Wilhelm (1884–1960). Author in 1911 of the monumental biography of Kleist, he above all, was significant as a director of several journals. He founded or directed successively, *Pan* (1910–1911), *März* (1913), *Das Forum* (1914–1915, then banned, and appeared again from 1918 to 1929), reviews where the young generation could express itself. He was also the author of several successful plays (*Panama* in 1931), but which are in no way expressionist. He emigrated in 1929, and returned to Munich in 1947, where he died.

HILLER, Kurt (1885–1972). Born in Berlin, he studied law and literature. He represented the activist wing of the expressionist movement. He played a very important role through his articles. It was he who first used the term expressionism to describe a certain type of literature. It was he, too, who founded the expressionist cabarets where poems were recited. He published in addition the almanach *Das Ziel.* After the First World War, he threw himself into politics, advocating a left-wing pacifism. In 1933–1934, he was arrested by the Nazis. Freed, he emigrated. From 1938 to 1946, he lived in London. He finally returned to Germany in 1955.

HOY, Senna (1884–1914). His real name was Johannes Holzmann. An anarchist, he travelled in Russia at the beginning of the century, after having been a primary school teacher. In 1904–1905, he edited the review *Kampf* (Combat). Linked to another anarchist writer Erich Mühlsam, he also created another review *Der Weckruf.* While in Russia, he was arrested and he died there in prison on April 23rd, 1914. Else Lasker-Schüler dedicated a number of poems to him. He has also been mentioned by Wieland Herzfelde. He has left behind some short stories, poems and a number of articles.

KERSTEN, Hugo (1894–1919). Closely linked to Pfemfert, he published a number of articles in *Die Aktion* and also in *Revolution* and *Der Mistral.* A friend of Emil Szittya and of Walter Serner, like them he spent the beginning of the First World War in Switzerland, in Ascona. He returned to Berlin in 1917. He died of poisoning in the course of shooting a film.

KOFFKA, Friedrich (1888–1951). He was known for two expressionist plays: *Cain*, performed at the Das Junge Deutschland Theatre in Berlin, on June 9th, 1918 and *Herr Oluf*, performed in Düsseldorf in 1920. He emigrated in 1939 to England, where he died.

KRAUS, Karl (1874–1936). An Austrian journalist and writer, he is essentially known for his review *Fackel*, which was published from 1899 to 1936. He is also the author of the play which is often considered expressionist *The Last Days of Humanity* (Die letzen Tage der Menschheit).

KURTZ, Rudolf (1884–1960). Born in Berlin, he published his first works at the age of nineteen. From 1913, he was active in the cinema. In 1926, his *Expressionism and Film* appeared. In the thirties he wrote comedies.

LAUTENSACK, Heinrich (1881–1919). After studying at a technical school in Berlin, he went into cabaret. After 1907, he wrote plays for the theatre and film scenarios. He was also the editor of the review *Bücherei Maiandros.* A soldier from 1914–1917, he went mad in 1918. His complete works were assembled in 1966, *The Interrupted Feast* (Das verstörte Fest).

LEONHARD, Rudolf (1889–1953). He studied law. He was called up during the war and was wounded. He shared Karl Liebknecht's views in the face of the horrors he had witnessed. He took part in the Spartacist revolution. In 1927, he emigrated to France, where he was very active from 1933, in anti-fascist movements. He even took part in the Resistance. He returned to Berlin after the war, where he died. He played a very active role in all areas, but especially in the theatre, in the propagating of expressionist activism between 1917 and 1920. Through him, one can see a link between expressionism and the left-wing literature of after the war.

LEYBOLD, Hans (1894–1914). He was born in Hamburg and studied in Munich, where he became friends with Hugo Ball. He edited the review *Revolution*. He was also a poet. He died at the beginning of the First World War.

LOTZ, Ernst Wilhelm (1890–1914). He was born in Kulm, where he published an anthology of poems in 1907. Not very well-known, he is nevertheless one of the most representative expressionist poets, in the tone of his poetry, which is a poetry of revolt, and very rich in original images. He died in Aisne during the First World War.

MARINETTI, Filippo Tommaso (1876–1944). He was born in Egypt, in Alexandria, where his father was a business lawyer. He studied at the *Collège Saint-François-Xavier*, run by French Jesuits. His education was therefore above all in French culture. He even took the second part of the *Baccalauréat* in Paris, in 1894. Then, he studied law at Pavia and Genoa, where he submitted his doctoral thesis in 1899. He founded in 1905 the review *Poesia* and, in 1909, published, notably in the *Figaro*, the manifesto of futurism. From then on, his name was associated with the spread of the movement. He was also noticed for his political affiliations with fascism. In 1929, he entered the Italian Academy created by Mussolini. In 1935, he enrolled as a volunteer and fought in Ethiopia, publishing a manifesto called 'the futurist aesthetic of war'. In 1942, he again enrolled as a volunteer on the Russian front with the rank of colonel of the Italian Army.

MASEREEL, Frans (1889–1972). Born in Western Flanders, at Blakenberg, the Belgian Frans Masereel first lived in Ghent, where he attended the Academy, before going on a number of journeys and settling in Switzerland during the First World War. The war had a crucial impact on his work: his drawings, wood-cuts, published in several pacifist and socially-conscious reviews express his protest against injustice and misery. He also illustrated a number of books which show a social commitment: novels by Barbusse and Andreas Latzko on war, and works by Romain Rolland or Charles Vildrac, for example. After 1918, he settled in Paris, but went on journeys to Russia and Central Europe.

In 1940, with the approach of the German troops, he left Paris on foot, and made a good number of drawings *en route*. They have been published under the title *June 1940*. During the occupation, a studio was placed at his disposal in the Pope's Palace in Avignon. After the war, he taught graphic arts at Saarbrucken, before finally settling in Nice.

It would be difficult to classify Masereel as an expressionist. He is often linked to artists associated with social criticism, like Käthe Kollwitz and George Grosz, but he has been related to German expressionists, sharing their revolt against a society which destroys human aspirations.

MIERENDORFF, Carl (1897–1943). He was active in expressionist circles in Darmstadt, where he was associated with the political-literary review *Das Tribunal*. From 1930, he was a social democratic deputy. Imprisoned in a concentration camp in 1933, he was freed in 1938, and participated in the Resistance against Nazism. He was killed in an air attack.

OEHRING, Richard (1889–1940). Born in Düsseldorf, he was the co-editor of the pre-dadaist review *Die freie Strasse*, and he published poems in *Die Aktion*. In 1933, he emigrated to Holland, where he committed suicide in 1940, in order to escape from the Nazis.

OTTEN, Karl (1889–1963). Born in Aix-la-Chapelle, he studied in Munich, Bonn and Strasbourg. Friendly with Erich Mühsam, Heinrich Mann, Carl Sternheim, he was, like them very hostile to the slaughter of the First World War and active in favour of pacifism. After 1919, he settled in Vienna. From 1924 to 1933, again in Berlin, he published novels and plays. In 1933, he emigrated, first into Spain, then to England. In 1958, he settled in Switzerland where he died. He played a very important part, after the war, in the rediscovery of expressionism: he published several anthologies, including film scenarios, written by expressionist poets.

PFEMFERT, Franz (1879–1954). Born at Lötzen (Eastern Prussia), he spent his childhood in Berlin where he became a journalist in 1904. He edited *Die Aktion*, and brought out its first number on February 20th, 1911. He also founded, by relying on the review, his own publishing house. He was politically active from early on. In 1918–1919, he supported the Spartacists, then the Workers' Communist Party (KAPD), the anarcho-syndicalists, and finally the Trotskyists. In 1933, he emigrated to Czechoslovakia, then to France and finally to the United States. He survived there as a photographer and died in 1954.

PINTHUS, Kurt (1886–1975). He was one of the most perspicacious literary critics of the expressionist generation. A theatre critic, as well as being fascinated by the cinema, he was a proof reader at Rowohlt and Kurt Wolff. He has left behind a work now considered a classic: his anthology of poetry *The Twilight of Mankind* (Menschheitsdämmerung). In 1933, he emigrated to the United States. On his return to Germany after the war, he settled in Marbach am Neckar, where he died.

PISCATOR, Erwin (1893–1966). A man of the theatre, his name is not usually linked to expressionism. However, his first poems were published in *Die Aktion* and his débuts as a producer are difficult to understand outside the context of the expressionism of the time. He belonged to the German Communist Party in 1919, at the same time as Wieland Herzfelde and John Heartfield. In 1934, he emigrated, only to return to Germany in 1951.

RICHTER, Hans (1888–1976). A painter, he collaborated with *Die Aktion* and *Der Sturm* before 1914, then he became a dadaist in 1918–1919. He is important for his experimental films and his writings on the cinema.

RUEST, Anselm (1878–1943). Writer and critic, he was also the author of philosophical works, like his cousin, Mynona. He was an anarchist, in the tradition of Max Stirner and edited the review *Der Einzige.* He emigrated to France in 1933, and died in Carpentras.

SCHEERBART, Paul (1863–1915). This very original and imaginative writer was particularly appreciated by the expressionists. He is considered as one of the precursors of expressionism because of the place he gives to the dream, fantasy, and humour. He was one of the creators in Germany of the science-fiction novel. Ernst Rowohlt founded his printing house with him.

SCHREYER, Lothar (1886–1966). Born in Dresden, he studied law in Heidelberg, Berlin, and Leipzig. He submitted his doctorate in 1910. Then he devoted himself to the theatre. From 1917 to 1920, he directed the *Sturmbühne* in Berlin. In 1921, he was asked to teach at the Bauhaus and he stayed there until 1923. From 1928, he lived in Hamburg as a painter and a writer.

SERNER, Walter (1889–?). Born in Karlsbad, he studied law in Vienna and Greifswald. During the First World War, he emigrated to Switzerland. In 1915–1916, he edited the review *Sirius*, and in 1919, with Tristan Tzara and Otto Flake, the dadaist review *Der Zeltweg.* He has left behind some surprising novels and erotic-detective stories. All trace of him has been lost since 1927.

STEPHAN, Rudi (1887–1915). He studied music at Frankfurt and Munich, from 1905 to 1908. Then he lived as a composer in Munich. In 1914, he was recruited as a soldier. He died at the front. He began by producing symphonic works which aroused considerable interest amongst the music lovers of the time. He wrote an opera *The First Men* (Die ersten Menschen) which is considered expressionist and which indicated great musical talent.

SZITTYA, Emil (1886–1964). Born in Budapest, he settled in Paris in 1906. He became friends with Cendrars from 1909, and edited with him a review with an expressionist title: *New Men*. From 1914 to 1918, he was in Zürich where he frequented all the members of the avant-garde, about whom he has written some very useful portraits and memoirs: *The Curiosity Cabinet* (Das Kuriositäten-Kabinett, 1923). He was the co-editor of the review *Der Mistral.* He has also left behind many novels and several books on art in French: *Notes on Picasso* (1945), *Marquet travels across the World* (1948), *Soutine and his time* (1958).

VOGELER, Heinrich (1872–1942). A famous painter of art nouveau, he became political in 1918. He then sent a letter to William II, calling for peace and was, as a consequence, imprisoned. A member of the Council for workers and soldiers in Bremen in 1919, he founded a community on the land he owned near Bremen, the 'Barkenhof Commune'. In a very typical manner, he went from expressionism to anarchism and communism. In 1931, he emigrated to the Soviet Union, where he died.

WALDEN, Herwarth (1878–1941). Born in 1878 in Berlin, he was really called Georg Levin. He married Else Lasker-Schüler in 1901, and later divorced her. Very early on, he was active as a propagator of the new literature and all modern artistic currents. He founded *Der Sturm* in 1909. He passed for an astute picture dealer, because he deducted a certain percentage from the sale of pictures that he exhibited. But one must recognize that he was a real discoverer of talent and that in Germany, he had a crucial role in this capacity; never would modern art have had such an impact, but for his activity. In 1929, he who had never previously shown any interest in politics, reacted to the rise of fascism and drew closer to the Communist party. In 1932, he decided to emigrate to the Soviet Union. He went and taught at the Institute of Modern Languages in Moscow. After 1933, he collaborated with the reviews of the anti-nazi emigration, notably *Das Wort* and *Die Internationale Literatur*. He disappeared in 1941 in Saratov, probably the victim of deportation in a Soviet camp.

WEBER, Carl Maria (1890–1953). A poet, he was also a teacher. He has left behind an anthology of poems and he collaborated in the publication by Kurt Hiller: *Das Ziel.*

WEILL, Kurt (1900–1950). He studied at the Higher School of Music in Berlin (Musikhochschule) and worked on musical composition from 1921 to 1924, under the direction of Ferruccio Busoni. He first made a name for himself through his works for choir and orchestra, then, after 1925, he turned to opera. In 1928, he produced, based on the libretto by Georg Kaiser, *The Tsar has his photograph taken* (Der Zar lässt sich photographieren) and *The Threepenny Opera*, with words by Brecht. He made music conform to a broad political aim, like Brecht. He declared that he was not seeking in music to fascinate, to entertain, to provoke an illusion, but that he wanted the audience to think. In 1933, he left Germany. He settled in New York in 1935, and died in the United States.

The Threepenny Opera and *Mahagonny*, based on texts by Brecht are rather misleadingly sometimes described as expressionist. On the other hand, one forgets too often that Kurt Weill was also a music critic, and that he tried to promote in his articles modern composers, including expressionists. He notably paid tribute to Schönberg (Der deutsche Rundfunk, 17.6.1926) and to Busoni, whom he considered the 'discreet guide of the new musical life in Europe'.

WOLF, Friedrich (1888–1953). Having studied medicine and having enrolled as a military doctor during the First World War, he participated in the revolutionary events of the years 1918–1919. He was notably one of the members of the Council of Workers and Soldiers in the town of Dresden, where he organized, along with Conrad Felixmüller the activities of the expressionists. Influenced by anarchism and the youth movements, he evolved in the direction of communism. He joined the Communist Party in 1927. His first dramatic works: *That is what you are* (Das bist du, 1919), *The Black Sun* (Die Schwarze Sonne, 1921), belong to expressionism, on which he wrote theoretical programmes. Then, he became the representative of committed realist theatre (*Professor Mamlock*, 1935, the famous play against nazi antisemitism). A refugee from 1933, he settled in East Berlin in 1951.

WOLFENSTEIN, Alfred (1888–1945). Born in Halle, he studied in Berlin, where his parents had settled a short while after his birth. From 1916 to 1922, he lived in Munich. He was, as a poet and critic, and as an editor of the publication *Die Erhebung*, an eminent representative of expressionism. Under the Third Reich, he emigrated. He tried to hide in Paris and in the south of France. After the Liberation, he was found, seriously ill, in a hotel in Paris. Transported to the Rothschild Hospital, profoundly depressed, he committed suicide on January 22nd, 1945.

WOLFF, Kurt (1887–1963). In her memoirs (*Following the Wind*, 1976), Claire Goll describes him as follows: 'In our circle, Kurt Wolff was the leading figure. He was a young man who had married the inheritor of I. G. Farben-Merk, one of the richest fortunes in Germany. Gifted with a rare flair, a constantly alert curiosity, he wanted to become the most important editor of the new generation of expressionists.' Along with the proof readers Kurt Pinthus and Franz Werfel, Kurt Wolff was certainly one of the propagators of expressionist literature. A collection like *The Last Judgement* was especially famous. Kurt Wolff emigrated in 1931 first to France and then to Italy, and finally to the United States, where he founded a new printing house. After the war, on his return to Europe, he settled in Switzerland. He died as a result of an accident, at Ludwigsburg, in October 1963.

ZECH, Paul (1881–1946). Born in Briesen (Western Prussia), he interrupted his studies to work as a miner in the Ruhr, in Belgium and in France. Later, he was a journalist and a librarian in Berlin. He was one of the editors of the expressionist review *Das Neue Pathos*. In 1933, he was imprisoned by the Nazis. Freed, he emigrated to South America in 1937, where he participated in the anti Nazi struggle. He died in Buenos Aires.

Principal Journals and Organizations

AKTION, Die (Action). Franz Pfemfert was the director of this publication, which appeared from 1911 to 1932, but only really exerted an influence on intellectual youth for about ten years. After 1920, it became mainly political and degenerated into being a bulletin of a small group of anarcho-syndicalists and, later, of Trotskyists. Many writers (especially Franz Jung and Erwin Piscator) have recounted the immense role played by *Die Aktion* on their generation, especially for its hostility to the First World War. In 1951, Johannes R. Becher relates how he, who had been under the influence of old-fashioned neo-romantics (he admired Waldemar Bonsels and Richard Dehmel) had in 1911 found the road to modern literature on encountering *Die Aktion*: 'With what a feeling of oppression, I entered, climbed the stairs, held my breath, and rang, until, seated in front of the desk of the all powerful Franz Pfemfert, and waiting for a sentence of life or death, I heard him say that my poem would be published in the next issue. I have never since experienced such tension as when I saw my poem published in *Die Aktion*: it appeared as my confirmation both as a poet and as a revolutionary.'

BLAUE REITER, Der (The Blue Rider). This group assembled in Munich in 1911 around Kandinsky: At first it included, besides Kandinsky, Franz Marc and August Macke. In fact, it was the result of a split in the New Union of artists (Neue Künstlervereinigung), which had been created in Munich by Kandinsky and Jawlensky. The first of these exhibitions opened 18th December in Munich at the Tannhäuser Gallery. The name itself came from a plan for a publication that Kandinsky had had since June 1911, and which, finalized in the autumn, saw the light of day in the form of an almanach in May 1912. The title is explained by the fact that Franz Marc and Kandinsky, according to the latter, both liked the colour blue, and one horses and the other riders. A second exhibition of *Der Blaue Reiter*, devoted more specifically to graphic art, took place in April 1912 at the Goltz Gallery in Munich. Meanwhile, another was opened in Berlin, patronized by Walden and *Der Sturm*, in March 1912. With the death of Franz Marc and August Macke during the First World War, and also with the departure of Kandinsky from Germany in 1914, *Der Blaue Reiter* disappeared, although a second almanach had been planned and Franz Marc had even written the preface.

BRÜCKE, Die (The Bridge). This group was formed in Dresden in 1905. It was an architecture student who took the initiative: Ernst Ludwig Kirchner, with whom Fritz Bleyl, Erich Heckel, Karl Schmidt-Rottluff became associated. In 1906, Emil Nolde joined them, but abandoned them eighteen months later. From 1906 to 1912, Max Pechstein was also part of this group, but then rallied to the *Neue Sezession*. Otto Mueller was the last, in 1910, to join them. After the majority of these artists had left Dresden for Berlin, their community dissolved, this was the case from 1912, and the group was completely dissolved in 1913. For the first time, or nearly, in the history of painting, a real community of spirit and work, had been established: an example for a new humanity, which they later advocated, the expressionists had created new relations between themselves, sharing studios and materials, working together, trying to ensure the financial viability of the works and the sale.

BÜCHEREI MAIANDROS, Die (The Maiandros Library). Appearing every two months, this publication was edited by Alfred Richard Mayer, in Berlin. It lasted two years, from 1912 to 1914. The following people contributed: Apollinaire, Gottfried Benn, Oskar Kanehl, Rudolf Leonhard, Alfred Lichtenstein, Paul Zech, with illustrations by Max Beckmann, Ludwig Meidner, Arthur Segal.

EINZIGE, Der (The Unique). Under the responsibility of Anselm Ruest and Mynona, this review appeared from 1919 to 1921. Expressionists like Arthur Segal, Hugo Kersten, Rudolf Leonhard, Walter Mehring, and Albert Ehrenstein contributed to it. Anarchist in inspiration it combined later with the review of the League of Individualists: *Ich*.

ERDE, Die (The Earth). A political-literary review, like *Die Aktion*, it appeared every fortnight. It was edited by Walther Rillo, first of all at Breslau, and then in Berlin. It did not last very long (1919–1920). Johannes R. Becher, Otto Flake, Otto Freundlich, Yvan Goll, Oskar Marie Graf, Wieland Herzfelde, Kurt Hiller, Klabund contributed to it.

ERHEBUNG, Die (Elevation). An annual publication directed by Alfred Wolfenstein, it brought together what it has been customary to call the activist current. It only appeared for two years (1919 and 1920). All the genres (poems, the theatre, novels and extracts from novels, essays) were represented. Amongst its contributors, one finds: Paul Adler, Johannes R. Becher, Ernst Bloch, Arnolt Bronnen, Alfred Döblin, Kurt Hiller, Paul Kornfeld, Kurt Pinthus, Ernst Toller, Fritz von Unruh, Carl Maria Weber, Franz Werfel.

FORUM, Das (The Forum). A political-literary review edited by Wilhelm Herzog from 1914 to 1929. It was prohibited during the First World War, from 1915, for its pacifist propaganda. It was published again in October 1918 (accompanied by a feature by Wilhelm Herzog on his problems with the censorship). At the outset, in 1919–1920, it supported the positions of Barbusse and the movement *Clarté*. Amongst its contributors were: Paul Adler, Yvan Goll, Georg Kaiser, Heinrich Mann, Franz Werfel, Stefan Zweig.

GEGNER, Der (The Adversary). It was edited by Karl Otten and Julian Gumperz in 1919, and then by the latter and Wieland Herzfelde until 1922. A political-literary review, it published articles by John Dos Passos, Oskar Maria Graf, George Grosz, Raoul Hausmann, Erwin Piscator, Trotsky.

GRUPPE 1919 (The 1919 Group). One of the many groups of painters that flourished in Germany with the November Revolution of 1918. It was founded in Dresden by Conrad Felixmüller, Otto Dix and the architect Hugo Zehder, who subsequently also created the theatre review *Die Neue Schaubühne*.

HOHE UFER, Das (The Upper Bank). A review published in Dresden by Hans Kaiser for two years: 1919 and 1920. With the participation of Kasimir Edschmid, Klabund, Friedich Schnack, Franz Werfel. Amonst the illustrations, some are signed by Lyonel Feininger and Kurt Schwitters.

JUNGE DEUTSCHLAND, Das (Young Germany). It is under this name that Max Reinhardt linked to the Deutsches Theater, in Berlin, an experimental theatre to put on expressionist plays. It was also the title of a monthly theatre bulletin coming from the same circle. It lasted three years, from 1918 to 1920. Max Brod, Alfred Döblin, Leonhard Frank, Reinhard Goering, Yvan Goll, Walter Hasenclever, George Kaiser, Paul Kornfeld, Fritz von Unruh, all contributed to it.

KUNSTBLATT, Das (The Art Sheet). This artistic review, directed by Paul Westheim, reserved the expressionists a place amongst the vast spread of modern painters it offered its readers. In 1921, Yvan Goll introduced in *Esprit Nouveau* (Paris), the new German reviews, and he wrote that *Das Kunstblatt* 'has not many competitors in Europe. Each issue contains a series of reproductions of all the young masters of today, from Picasso to Kokoschka, and thanks to *Das Kunstblatt*, the Germans are very aware of what is going on in Paris'.

MENSCHEN (Men). This monthly review was edited in Dresden by Heinar Schilling. It published especially articles relating to the debates on the Council of Intellectual Workers (RAT der Geistigen Arbeiter). In September 1920, directed henceforth by Heinar Schilling and Walter Hasenclever, it claimed to be unpolitical. Then it supported the movement *Clarté* (Yvan Goll made it into a sister review to Clarté), and it published the appeal by Barbusse in May 1921. It ceased production soon after this.

NEUE KUNST, Die (The New Art). Published every other month, during 1913–1914, it was edited by Heinrich Bachmair, in collaboration with Johannes R. Becher and Karl Otten. Amongst its contributors were Hugo Ball, Adolf Behne, Gottfried Benn, Ernst Blass, Max Brod, Leonhard Frank, Walter Hasenclever, Alfred Wolfenstein, Paul Zech.

NEUE PATHOS, Das (The New Pathos). Under this name, it only appeared in 1913–1914, led especially by Ludwig Meidner and Paul Zech, then its title was *Jahrbuch der Zeitschrift 'Das Neue Pathos'* from 1914 to 1919. It included illustrations, amongst these some are signed by Raoul Hausmann, Erich Heckel, Ludwig Meidner, Karl Schmidt-Rottluff.

NEUE SCHAUBÜHNE, Die (The New Stage). This monthly review devoted to the theatre was founded by Hugo Zehder and Heinar Schilling and appeared in Dresden from 1919 to 1925. In its texts and illustrations (photographs of stage sets, especially), it is an exceptional document on expressionism. One finds in it analyses of productions or theoretical writings by important expressionist writers. (Walter Hasenclever, Carl Hauptmann, Rudolf Leonhard).

NOVEMBERGRUPPE (The November Group). Created in 1918, at the time of the proclamation of the Republic and what has been called the November Revolution. Hence its name. In general, the group of artists from all disciples comprised a majority of expressionists. Its first general assembly was held in December 1918 in Berlin, and included in particular Walter Gropius, Bruno Taut, Heinrich Campendonk, Rudolf Belling. On its initiative, the Work Council for Art was founded in 1919 (Arbeitsrat für Kunst.) A brochure was edited, assembling the replies of a hundred artists to a questionnaire on the place of art in society *Ja! Stimmen des Arbeitsrates für Kunst in Berlin* (Yes! the votes of the Work Council for the art of Berlin). Many exhibitions were also organized. Revolutionary at the outset, the November Group lost little by little its impetuous virulence and ended up by being no more than an amorphous gathering under the Weimar Republic.

REVOLUTION. Edited by Hans Leybold and by Hugo Ball, this bi-monthly review appeared for only one year, in 1913. It was, in its tone, the reservoir for what was later going to be called, by Hugo Ball in Zurich, dadaism.

REVOLUTIONÄR, Der (The Revolutionary). Under the direction of Moritz Lederer, this review appeared from 1919 to 1923. It published notably Hugo Ball, Leonhard Frank, Klabund, Heinrich Mann, Erich Mühsam.

STURM, Der (The Assault, The Tempest). This review, which in Germany, publicized not only expressionism, but all the literary and artistic trends, was founded by Herwarth Walden, in 1910, and was published until 1932. In Berlin, a gallery was linked to it. The most famous exhibitions of modern art were organized there before 1914 (*Der Blaue Reiter* in March 1912, the Italian futurists from 12th April to 31st May 1912). In the autumn 1918, a theatre company and school was created, centring around Lothar Schreyer and Rudolf Blumner; the *Stürmbühne*, which had an annexe in Hamburg, called the *Kampfbühne*.

TRIBUNAL, Das (The Tribunal). Published by Carl Mierendorff in Darmstadt from 1919 and 1921. It was a political-literary review. It launched, for example, a campaign in favour of a reconciliation between France and Germany, advocating meetings between intellectuals. Amongst its contributors were Kasimir Edschmid, Yvan Goll, Kurt Hiller, Wilhem Michel, Paul Zech, Carl Zuckmayer. With illustrations by Max Beckmann, Oskar Kokoschka, Frans Masereel, Ludwig Meidner.

WEISSEN BLÄTTER, Die (The White Pages). A review that appeared from 1913 to 1921, first in Leipzig, and from April 1916, under the direction of René Schickele, in Bern. One of the most important expressionist publications, for the quality of its contributors. It assumed a pacifist stance in the First World War, and Schickele was its apostle of non-violence.

ZEIT-ECHO (Echo of the Time). A review edited first in Munich, then at Bern during the war from 1914 to 1917, it was directed by Ludwig Rubiner, with the collaboration of Johannes R. Becher, Ernst Bloch, Carl Einstein, Walter Hasenclever, Hermann Hesse, Kurt Hiller, Robert Walser, Franz Werfel.

ZIEL, Das. A publication which appeared irregularly, founded by Kurt Hiller, and activist in inclination. The first issue appeared in 1916, published by George Müller Verlag, the second in 1918, at the same publishers, the third by Kurt Wolff, and the fourth and last in 1920 by the same publisher. These issues are very helpful for an understanding of the ideological diversity of expressionism.

Anthologies of the period

Der Kondor (The Condor). Collected poems by Kurt Hiller. Richard Weissbach Verlag, 1912.

Der Mistral. Collected poems by Alfred Richard Meyer. Berlin, 1912.

Arkadia. Annual publication under the responsibility of Max Brod. Kurt Wolff Verlag, 1913.

Brenner-Jahrbuch 1915. Anthology of poems from 1915 published in the review *Der Brenner* by Ludwig von Ficker. Innsbruck, 1915.

1915-1916. Collected poems by Franz Pfemfert in his collection *Die Aktionslyrik.* Berlin 1916.

Vom Jüngsten Tag. A famous anthology edited in 1916. Kurt Wolff Verlag, Leipzig.

Sturm-Abende (The soirées organized by *Der Sturm*). Anthology of poems read at public sessions in Berlin organized by Herwarth Walden. Verlag Der Sturm, Berlin, 1918.

Die Neue Dichtung (The New Literature). Almanach. Kurt Wolff Verlag, Leipzig 1918.

Das Jahrzehnt 1908-1918. Almanach. Erich Reiss Verlag, Berlin, 1919.

Deutsche Dichter aus Prag (German writers from Prague). An anthology by Oskar Wiener. Verlag Eduard Strache, Vienna and Leipzig, 1919.

Kameraden der Menschheit (Friends of Humanity). An anthology edited by Ludwig Rubiner with mainly French poets (Pierre-Jean Jouve, Henri Guilbeaux, Marcel Martinet). Verlag Gustav Kiepenheuer, Potsdam, 1919.

Die Gemeinschaft (The Community). Documents on the worldwide intellectual turning point, an anthology edited by Ludwig Rubiner. Verlag Gustav Kiepenheuer, Potsdam, 1919.

Die Erhebung (Elevation). An annual production (appearing in 1919 and in 1920). Edited by Alfred Wolfenstein. S. Fischer Verlag, Berlin.

Der Anbruch (The Beginning). An anthology under the direction of Otto Schneider and Arthur E. Rutra. Roland Verlag, Munich, 1920.

Menschheitsdämmerung (the Twilight of Mankind). An anthology of poems by Kurt Pinthus Ernst Rowohlt Verlag, Berlin, 1920.

Verkündigung (Proclamation). An anthology of poems edited by Rudolf Kayser in 1921.

Title Glossary

ACTIVISM A movement founded on action. In 1934, a historian of expressionism, Wolfgang Paulsen distinguished between activism and expressionism: the former wanted a new society, whereas the expressionists aspired towards a new fraternity. This distinction today seems arbitrary: the word 'community' (Gemeinschaft) combines both tendencies. The activists did not form a homogeneous group, and were not really distinct from other tendencies of the time. It was essentially marked by the attitude of Kurt Hiller, but it is possible to include the programmes drawn up by Rudolf Leonhard, Alfred Wolfenstein in the years 1917–1918. In the Weimar Republic, the term activism became associated with the extreme right and especially Nazism.

ATONALITY A system of musical composition that rejected the fundamental principles of the tonal system. After Schönberg in 1909, it was called the School of Vienna (Anton von Webern, Alban Berg), and evolved later in the direction of the dodecaphonic scale.

BAUHAUS Literally the word means: the house for building. An establishment for teaching and creating, it was founded at Weimar in March 1919. It was then very much influenced by expressionism. Opened to students in October 1920, it followed a different direction from 1923, with the departure of Johannes Itten and the appointment of Moholy-Nagy as a teacher. A style was evolved, as a result of the various activities, which was later described as the *Bauhaus* style: a rigour devoted to the functional. Dissolved in December 1924, it was reconstituted at Dessau in December 1926. Walter Gropius resigned from his post as director in April 1928, and the direction of it was then continued by the architect Hannes Meyer. Studios for photography and sculpture were created. Little by little, the following sections became the most important: architecture, decoration, publicity, photography and weaving. In 1932, the *Bauhaus* was dissolved by the Municipal Council of Dessau, which had been won by the Nazis in the recent elections. Continued as a private school by Mies van der Rohe in Berlin, it was finally banned by the Nazis in April 1933. The spirit of the *Bauhaus* was then continued in the United States, since its main collaborators emigrated there, including Gropius. Today, the contribution of the Bauhaus remains significant in all fields: furniture, utility objects, advertising, typography.

CONSTRUCTIVISM This word refers to an artistic trend concerned with formal rigour, functionalism, and which developed in Russia after the October Revolution. Two hostile tendencies were at first part of it: on the one hand, that represented by Pevsner and Gabo, on the other the 'productivists' with Tatlin. In 1923, the review *Lef* (The Left wing in art) published the programme of the Soviet constructivists, namely Tatlin and Rodchenko. A large role was played here, particularly in the spreading of constructivism in Germany, by Lissitzky, the Russian architect who lived in Berlin in the twenties, who established links with *De Stijl* and with the Bauhaus, where he found certain elements of his constructivist ideas.

In the main, constructivism advocated the end of individualism in art and production of socially useful constructions. As in the case of *De Stijl* and *The Bauhaus*, the idea was to link technology and art. This is the distinguishing feature of our century wrote Moholy-Nagy in 1922, defining constructivism as technology, machinism and socialism.

DE STIJL At the outset, it was the title of a review which was founded by a group of friends in the Netherlands in October 1917. They included Theo van Doesburg and Piet Mondrian. The first aim consisted in bringing together those who demanded a revival in the plastic arts. Theo van Doesburg's idea had been to achieve a synthesis of the arts. But, little by little, the differences between the various collaborators of the review grew greater, and it became essentially the organ for van Doesburg who led it in the direction of constructivism and functionalism. It was in this way that the theories developed in *De Stijl* went beyond the confines of the review as it had been, and gave birth to an artistic movement which affected architecture above all. Theo van Doesburg died in Davos, in Switzerland, in 1931.

DODECAPHONIC SCALE In modern music, a technique of composition formulated by Schönberg in 1923, and which is founded on the use of a series containing twelve sounds on the chromatic scale. No note is more important than any other, as in the tonal scale, and no sound can recur without the other twelve of the series being audible. There is therefore a functional equivalence between each of the twelve notes in the chromatic scale.

FUNCTIONALISM A trend that developed from the nineteenth century, essentially in architecture. Illustrating the new links between art and industry, it relies on the idea that the forms of an object must first obey the function they are supposed to fulfil.

ICH-DRAMATIK A term describing an aspect of expressionist theatre: that which represents the individual's path. For example *Der Sohn* (The Son) by Hasenclever, *Der Bettler* (the Beggar) by Sorge. These are plays which are entirely constructed around the individual's self. The general problem is that of the central hero and his inner being, contrasted to the world surrounding him.

KAMMERSPIELE A word that describes a type of theatre that does not use traditional stage techniques, that is to say chamber theatre. The idea comes from Strindberg, who defined this new genre of intimate theatre as chamber music transposed to the theatre. He insisted on the importance of diction: 'One can perform a scene in pitch darkness and enjoy it as long as the words are clearly spoken.' Max Reinhardt in 1906, using Strindberg's model created a Kammerspiele in Berlin, an experimental theatre that he linked to the Deutsches Theater bought by him in 1905.

NEW OBJECTIVITY (Neue Sachlichkeit) An artistic and literary tendency that succeeded expressionism and which existed from approximately 1924 to 1932 in Germany. It represents a return to order in painting, a neo-naturalism, and in literature to a predilection for evidence, and documents.

PATHOS In ancient rhetoric, this term referred to characters who were intended to provoke a violent emotion. Then it described, in a pejorative manner, a style expressing feelings which were excessively emotional. The expressionists used the word a lot, talking even of a 'new pathos'. The pejorative nuance was rejected. It was now a matter of a quality of emotion and feeling recognized to be genuine. But the critics of expressionism have often used the word to emphasize the invocatory, grandiloquent style of much of expressionist poetry.

RAYONNISM A movement launched by the Russian painter Larionov in Moscow in 1911–1912. The manifesto he published in 1913, stipulates that the canvas, according to rayonnist technique, must suggest the existence of a fourth dimension and to manage this, the artist must represent the rays of colour.

SPRECHGESANG Spoken chant. A new vocal technique used for the first time by Schönberg in the third part of the *Gurre-Lieder.* According to René Leibowitz, its originality lies in the fact that a dramatic suspense is created without sacrificing the rigour of the musical structure, and this allows the composer to go beyond the traditional opposition between drama and music.

STATIONENDRAMA Literally: drama in stations. This notion of 'stations' belongs to a dramatic construction in successive phases evoking the stations of the Cross of Christ. The technique was used by Strindberg in the *Road to Damascus.* A central character, who evolves in the course of the plot, challenged by protagonists who meet him on his journey.

STURM UND DRANG Literally: storm and *élan.* A literary movement that took its name from a play by Klinger (1777). It represents the German generation of writers dating from about 1750, and who, in a reaction against the philosophy of the Enlightenment, were influenced by Rousseau, substituting emotion for reason. In particular, they exalted 'genius', which they saw as an unbridled force, a power of nature which obeys all instincts. The 'genius' is a rebel, he rejects the laws of society. Besides Klinger (1752–1831) one should mention, as typical representatives of *Sturm und Drang*, Lenz (1751–1792) and the Schiller of *The Brigands* (Die Räuber, 1781). More than with the romantics, it is with these rebels of *Sturm und Drang* that the expressionists present analogies.

List of Illustrations

On the cover, the following pictures are reproduced: Max Beckmann *The Synagogue*, 1919 – Alexei von Jawlensky *Girl with peonies*, 1909 – Ernst Ludwig Kirchner *Girl with the Japanese parasol*, 1909 – Franz Marc *Tower of Blue Horses*, 1913 – Edvard Munch *The Scream*, 1893 – Emil Nolde the *Dance round the Golden Calf*, 1910 – Karl Schmidt-Rottluff *Norwegian Landscape*, 1911 – Chaim Soutine *The Mad Woman*, circa 1921 – Maurice de Vlaminck *Bougival*, 1905.

Index